JANE BRODY'S GOOD FOOD GOURMET

Also by Jane Brody

Secrets of Good Health (with Richard Engquist)
You Can Fight Cancer and Win (with Dr. Arthur I. Holleb)
Jane Brody's Nutrition Book
Jane Brody's The New York Times Guide to Personal Health
Jane Brody's Good Food Book

JANE BRODY'S GOOD FOOD GOURMET

Recipes and Menus for Delicious and Healthful Entertaining

by Jane E. Brody

Illustrations by Ray Skibinski

W·W·NORTON & COMPANY · NEW YORK LONDON

Copyright © 1990 by Jane E. Brody
All rights reserved.
Printed in the United States of America.
The text of this book is composed in 10/12 CRT Garamond,
with the display set in Lucian and Garamond Bold.
Composition and manufacturing by the Haddon Craftsmen, Inc.
Book design by Margaret M. Wagner.

Library of Congress Cataloging-in-Publication Data
Brody, Jane E.
   [Good food gourmet]
   Jane Brody's good food gourmet: recipes and menus for delicious
and healthful entertaining/by Jane E. Brody.
   p. cm.
   1. Cookery. I. Title. II. Title: Good food gourmet.
TX714.B768 1990
641.5—dc20   90–6701

ISBN 0–393–02878–X

W.W. Norton & Company, Inc.,
500 Fifth Avenue, New York, N.Y. 10110
W.W. Norton & Company Ltd.,
10 Coptic Street, London WC1A 1PU

CONTENTS

RECIPES

Soups   *77*

Entrées   *114*

Baked Goods   *390*

MENU SUGGESTIONS

WELCOME TO THE
GOOD FOOD GOURMET

My friend Helen was in a tizzy. She had invited 12 people for dinner a week hence and was trying to devise a menu that would be aesthetically pleasing, culinarily possible, and nutritionally acceptable to all. "One guest doesn't eat meat, another can't eat salt, at least four have to watch their cholesterol, and all the women are watching their weight," she lamented. "What can I possibly serve without having to make three different meals?"

From Helen's consternation this book was born. In it, I present more than 500 wholesome recipes to satisfy a new and growing need in the American kitchen—to serve elegant and nutritious meals to guests and holiday merrymakers. Fewer people these days want to or can "go off their diets" when dining out or celebrating a special occasion. Many have so changed their eating style that they no longer enjoy fatty, salty, or sugary foods. And quite a few have little choice but to avoid such foods if they want to live full and healthy lives. I, for one, am no fanatic (I have been known to indulge in bratwurst on a bun, a choice piece of steak, a rich piece of cake, or a big dish of ice cream). But I no longer crave those foods, and I no longer appreciate being "forced" to eat them if they are served to me. And I am hardly alone. There are millions of other Americans who share my attitude toward food—that it should be enjoyable *and* life-enhancing—and every year, millions more join the fold.

In the four years since the publication of *Jane Brody's Good Food Book,* I have prepared hundreds of meals for company that were more suitable to current nutritional thinking. My family and friends have delighted in guilt-free indulgence at Thanksgiving, where the turkey and stuffing were low in fat yet high in flavor, the sweet potatoes were sweetened with fruit instead of marshmallows, and the "cream" pie had no cream. At a particularly memorable Memorial Day barbecue, 40 friends feasted on shish kebab and salads that were prepared with little or no fat. Five of the guests later confessed to "stealing" my menu plan for their own barbecue parties. A Mexican buffet lunch for 20 was trimmed of three-fourths of the fat normally found in that semitropical cuisine. Still, half the guests requested "people bags" for the leftovers. Worried about guests who don't like fish? At one dinner party for eight, I featured fish in every course except dessert, which I prepared—tongue-in-cheek—in a fish-shaped mold. My only complaint: not a morsel of fish was left for my lunch the next day. Yet another dinner party featured pumpkin—this time even in the dessert. And at the end of the meal, I challenged my guests to name the ingredient common to all courses. To my surprise, no one figured it out.

In the course of these and many other culinary adventures, I have proved beyond any doubt that you can put a "gourmet" meal on the table without killing your guests with nutritional *un*kindness. Try my recipes, and see if you don't agree. These *Good Food Gourmet* recipes are suitable for all occasions— birthday and dinner party, company breakfast and brunch, luncheon and buffet, picnic and barbecue, Thanksgiving and Christmas dinner, Hanukkah and Passover supper, party for 50 or elegant dinner for two. The more-than-500 new recipes included here plus the scores of suitable-for-company recipes previously published in my *Good Food Book* should provide you with a lifetime of options in serving family and guests, whatever the occasion. To assist you in planning, I offer serving suggestions for most entrées and sample menus for special occasions.

In writing this book, I join dozens of cookbook authors who consider themselves "gourmets." There's the natural gourmet and the frugal gourmet, the slim gourmet and the microwave gourmet, the low-salt gourmet and the low-cholesterol gourmet, the 60-minute gourmet and the vegetarian gourmet. Few of the authors come by the term *gourmet* honestly—via years of schooling in classical cooking techniques or apprenticeship under accomplished chefs.

I am no "gourmet" in terms of the word's dictionary definition. I am simply a person who likes to eat and cook but who also likes to live—fully, long, and healthfully. I have learned what I know about cooking largely by trial and error, and by consulting the writings and advice of those who really know what they're doing in the kitchen. I don't even have a particular talent when it comes to cooking. My husband and brother can stand in front of the refrigerator and cupboard and, without consulting a single recipe, can whip up a delicious meal from what's available. I, on the other hand, usually pore over recipes—sometimes as many as half a dozen versions of a dish—before I put together one I can call my own.

I do, however, bring one important quality to this undertaking: *I enjoy good food.* And *good* to me means food that tastes good, looks good, and is good for you. After years of gradually reducing my reliance on "no-no" ingredients, I've reached the point where I no longer enjoy foods dripping with grease, drowning in salt, or saturated with sugar. And I've discovered that an excessive dependence on such ingredients is not essential to preparing wonderful dishes. To be sure, I do not go to extremes. I do not spurn all ingredients that have been deemed less than healthful, like sausage, butter, egg yolks, and cheese. And I have not eliminated red meats from my diet. But I do use such foods in moderation, in amounts no larger than needed to produce a nutritionally balanced and appealing dish. In the case of sausage and cheese, I use these more as flavoring agents than as focal points of a meal. In the case of butter and egg yolks, I use only enough to make the dish work. In the case of red meats, I use only very lean cuts and limit amounts to about 3 ounces per serving, and I use smoked meats mainly as flavoring agents. You'll note, too, that when using chicken, I remove the skin and all visible fat before cooking, and when poultry is roasted with the skin, I urge removal of that fatty layer before the food is served. When it comes to preparing fish—which, in recent years, has emerged as the "health food" your mother may have claimed it to be—I do not undermine its natural, health-promoting properties by drowning it in added fat.

As in *Jane Brody's Good Food Book,* I have included many dishes that do not contain any meat, fish, or poultry. Growing numbers of Americans are learning to enjoy such vegetarian fare, and there is no longer any reason for cooks to fear serving such dishes to company. In fact, these days, when hosting a dinner party, it might be wise to check with prospective guests before planning your menu to be sure no one has strict dietary limitations. Many people now eat no animal flesh or eat only fish. And if you are hosting a buffet or large party, it would be wise to include at least one vegetarian entrée to accommodate nonflesh-eating guests (and be sure to let people know it is there).

As in my previous cookbook, I have tested each recipe myself. The vast majority have been served to discriminating "tasters" who freely rendered opinions about the flavor, appearance, and texture, and, in some cases, gave suggestions for improvements (which I then tested anew). In all cases, I asked my tasters whether they would willingly serve such fare to company, and I included no recipes that were not deemed suitable for guests. The most common complaint from my tasters was: "Do I have to wait for the book to get these recipes?"

The recipes themselves, as you can tell from my notations preceding them, come from a wide variety of sources. Many are derived from favorites published in cookbooks and magazines, especially *Gourmet* magazine, which has been a happy source of ideas and dishes for me since my subscription began in 1970. In all cases, where I know the origin of the recipe, I so state it in the recipe introduction. Many—probably most—of the recipes are of my own devising, some longtime favorites, others created in response to a culinary need, an available ingredient, or simply a whim.

Many others are based on recipes sent to me by devoted readers of the *Good Food Book.* And I will repeat the plea published there: if you have one or more favorite dishes that you think rank with these in nutrient content and suitability for guests and/or family, please take a few moments to send them to Jane Brody, c/o W. W. Norton & Company, Inc., 500 Fifth Avenue, New York, NY 10110.

A Nutrition Message to Remember

For those not already familiar with my nutritional theme, I will provide a brief recap; and for those who have not kept up with revisions in nutritional thinking since the publication of *Jane Brody's Good Food Book,* I will provide up-to-date information. Keep in mind, though, as you read this that sound nutrition information is not written in stone. It is based on scientifically derived evidence and, as such, is subject to modification as new and better scientific findings supplant old. Only quackery stays the same year after year. Good science is in a constant state of flux. I wouldn't be surprised if between the time of this writing and the time of publication still further changes have occurred in the science of nutrition and in ensuing dietary recommendations to promote lasting good health.

Don't be intimidated or discouraged or disgusted by the emergence of new dietary advice. Flexibility is the name of the game. As in the boxing ring, it is best to roll with the punches—as long as those punches come from a reputable source and are rooted in the scientific method. Careful readers will notice a number of changes since my previous writings, although the basic premises remain intact. Here, then, is a brief summary of current thinking on how Americans should eat to promote health.

Protein. This life-sustaining nutrient is needed by the body daily but only in limited amounts. Whether you are a couch potato or an Olympic athlete, your protein requirements can be fulfilled if approximately 12 to 15 percent of your daily calories come from protein. While it is true that athletes need more protein than those who are sedentary, it is also true that almost all Americans eat twice as much protein as their bodies need. And since active people naturally consume more calories, they will get even more protein in the course of normal dining.

Available evidence continues to link a high-protein diet, such as the one most Americans have enjoyed for decades, to an increased risk of heart disease, cancer, obesity, gallstones, osteoporosis, and kidney disease. Not only are there health risks associated with the fats and cholesterol found in the most popular animal-protein foods, but the protein itself can be a health hazard if consumed in excess. Your body can use only the amount of protein it needs each day to build and repair muscle and organ tissues. Beyond that amount, any protein you consume is broken down into nitrogen, which is excreted in urine, and carbohydrate, which is used for energy. Or, if you already consume an adequate number of calories, the extra protein you eat is stored as body fat. You can get just as fat overindulging in steak, chicken, or cottage cheese as from eating too many doughnuts.

On average, protein needs can be met if a meal contains 2 to 3 ounces of an animal-protein food like meat, poultry, fish, or cheese, or if it contains approximately 1 cup of cooked dried beans or peas. Given a choice of protein sources, you'd be best off in terms of health to emphasize the beans and peas and fish. Fish has been shown to contain natural oils called omega-3 fatty acids that may help prevent heart disease, cancer, high blood pressure, arthritis, and other chronic conditions that plague millions of Americans. The fish richest in these fatty acids are the fattier fish caught in cold ocean waters like salmon, mackerel, bluefish, herring, sardines, tuna, and the like. But please note that fish is not a perfect protein. Many fish, especially those from freshwater lakes and rivers, are contaminated with cancer-causing industrial chemicals that pollute our waterways. When shopping, look for those freshwater fish—like catfish and trout—that were raised on fish farms since these farms use unpolluted water. If you have access to fish from potentially contaminated lakes and rivers, limit your consumption of these to once a month. Saltwater fish and shellfish, while coming from less polluted waters, are hard to obtain fresh in many parts of the country and are expensive—two to three times as expensive as meat. While you may be willing to splurge now and again for company, few Americans can afford a high-fish diet day in and day out. My suggestion is to choose fish when you dine out, since a fish entrée is rarely much more expensive than other choices, and to prepare at least one fish meal a week at home. If frozen fish is all you can get, that's okay, too—the food value is the same. As a sushi lover it pains me to say this, but to avoid the risk of acquiring a fish parasite, all fish should be cooked before being eaten. For further information on buying and eating fish and shellfish, see page 151.

Also, many foods not traditionally thought of as high in protein nonetheless supply a substantial amount, such as pasta, potatoes, cereals, grains, milk, and yogurt. Furthermore, additional protein enters most meals in the form of vegetables, bread, and even fruit. So you rarely need to go overboard on animal flesh to fulfill your protein needs. The recipes in this book take this fact into account, and you will find that you'll save quite a bit of money by using less of the costly animal-protein foods.

Fats and cholesterol. One fact remains clear: a high-fat, high-cholesterol diet is hazardous to health. What seems to change from year to year is the amount and kind of fat one should worry about. I have said for years, based on a thorough analysis of available evidence from both international and domestic studies, that Americans eat twice as much fat as good health warrants. I will say it again: a wholesome diet should derive no more than about 20 percent of its calories from fat. This means that if you consume 2,000 calories a day, no more than 400 of those calories should be fat calories. A single tablespoon of oil has 120 fat calories, a 3-ounce porterhouse steak (cooked and trimmed) has 162 fat calories, and ½ cup of "gourmet" vanilla ice cream has 108 fat calories. That adds up to 390 calories from fat. So you see, it doesn't take much to exceed 20 percent of calories from fat.

There are two health-related problems associated with dietary fat. One is that fat is by far our most fattening nutrient. Ounce for ounce, it contains two and a quarter times more calories than sugar, starch, or pure protein. Simply by cutting back on fat, you can painlessly trim unwanted calories from your diet and lose weight without feeling deprived.

The second health problem is that the predominant type of fat in the American diet—so-called saturated fat, the kind that is solid at room temperature—can raise the level of cholesterol in the blood serum of people who consume it. Having learned this years ago, many people switched to the cholesterol-lowering polyunsaturated fats found in most vegetable oils and margarines. But too much polyunsaturated fat may increase cancer risk, according to the findings of a number of studies, and polyunsaturated fat (corn oil, for instance) has no fewer calories that saturated fat (butter, for example).

The latest studies on the health effects of fat have suggested that mono-unsaturated fats—which predominate in canola (rapeseed) oil, olive oil, peanut oil, walnut oil, and other nut oils—are as effective at lowering total cholesterol as the polyunsaturates. But they have one advantage: they do not also lower the desirable form of blood cholesterol, called HDL cholesterol, that acts like Drāno in your arteries, clearing them of fatty deposits. This finding has prompted many people to switch to olive and canola oils for cooking and salad dressings. But here, again, quantity should be considered. Too much olive oil means too much fat and too many calories.

To help you achieve a low-fat goal, I have reduced the fat content of my recipes to what I consider the minimum needed to produce a dish you'd be proud to serve to anyone. Some people may want to cut back even further, and I invite them to experiment with those recipes that lend themselves to even greater fat reduction. In most cases, the fat I use is canola or olive oil. When a recipe "demands" butter, I use a combination of butter and margarine in a 40 percent–60 percent blend. A similar mixture is now available (in stick form) as a "light" spread with a third fewer calories (which means less total fat), and I have used that successfully to prepare many of the recipes in this book.

I have also tried to keep the cholesterol content of my recipes as low as possible. Keep in mind that cholesterol in the diet comes only from foods derived from animals—meat, poultry, fish, dairy products, and eggs. *No plant food has cholesterol,* although certain plant-derived fats, such as the highly saturated coconut oil and palm kernel oil and the less saturated palm oil, can raise your serum-cholesterol level if you eat them. A plant food may be high in fat—avocado or peanut butter, for example—but the kind of fat it contains will not adversely affect your cholesterol level unless you eat too much of it and end up gaining unneeded pounds. In recipes that contain meat, I start with lean cuts and trim away all removable fat; with poultry, I remove the skin; with dairy products, I use nonfat (skim), part-skim, or low-fat versions; and with eggs, I use two egg whites in place of each cholesterol-laden yolk that I omit. If desired, you can also use an egg substitute in nearly all my recipes that call for whole eggs.

Carbohydrates. Those of you who are already familiar with current nutritional thinking know all about the desirability of carbohydrates—the starchy ones, that is. Though long considered foods to avoid (they were mistakenly considered "just starch"—full of calories but devoid of essential nutrients), we now know that starchy foods make up the largest component of a health-promoting diet. They do nothing to undermine health, and they provide stomach-filling satisfaction without overloading the body with fat and calories. Pasta—with low-fat toppings—has thus become a dietary staple among health-conscious Americans, yours truly among them. And, it turns out, starchy foods *are* nutritious, especially when consumed in their unrefined forms—for example, as whole-wheat bread and cereal, brown rice, beans and peas, and potatoes with the skin. They are good sources of protein, vitamins, minerals, and fiber. In fact, starchy foods, fruits, and vegetables are the *only* sources of fiber in the human diet. And fiber, we now know, is a health essential, capable of lowering cholesterol in the blood, washing cancer-causing substances out of the body, keeping the digestive tract in good working order, and maintaining blood sugar on an even keel. Fiber is also a way of filling up your belly without overloading on calories since half or more of the calories in fiber are never assimilated by the body.

Thus, many of my recipes have a strong carbohydrate base, deriving most of their calories from starchy ingredients like rice, potatoes, pasta, bulgur, and couscous. These foods not only are free of health insults, they also provide important fuel for the many demands active people place on their body's muscles.

You'll notice that in extolling the virtues of carbohydrates, I referred only to starchy foods. Sugars are also carbohydrates, but for all their taste appeal, they are less desirable as a source of needed nutrients. Most highly sweetened foods are sorely lacking in essential nutrients at the same time that they are jam-packed with fully absorbable calories. The best source of sweets is fresh fruit, which, in addition to natural sugars, contains vitamins, minerals, and fiber. Accordingly, I use fruit extensively in my desserts (I also happen to like fruit desserts better than almost any other—except, perhaps, ice cream). When sugar is an ingredient—and unless you are diabetic or hypoglycemic, there is no reason to eliminate sugar from the diet—I use as little as possible to produce an appealing food. I am hardly the only one to discover that once you cut back on highly sweetened foods, you begin to lose your taste for them. In effect, your taste buds awaken to the sweet taste and learn to appreciate it more when it doesn't overwhelm the other flavors in the food.

Seasonings. By far, the most popular seasoning in America—and probably in the world—is salt. Unfortunately, salt is one of several factors linked to high blood pressure, or hypertension. A significant proportion of people are sensitive to salt's ability to raise blood pressure, and after years of consuming a diet with as high a salt content as ours, they may develop hypertension. Since it is impossible to predict who is and who is not salt-sensitive, the better part of valor is for everyone to reduce his or her dependence on this much-abused seasoning. As with sugar, I and millions of others have discovered that the amount of salt in the diet is a matter of habit. Once you get used to using less of it, the old amount will taste intolerably salty to you. In most of my recipes, I have steered clear of highly salted ingredients like capers and anchovies. And I have reduced the added salt in recipes to the level I deem desirable, offering you the option to use less (or more) as your taste and dietary needs dictate.

For taste-bud stimulation, I much prefer freshly ground peppercorns, black or white, and hot fresh (or canned or dried) peppers. There are many kinds of black peppercorns, each differing in "hotness," just as there are dozens of hot peppers with varying degrees of fire. I also use a wide variety of herbs, fresh and dried, lots and lots of garlic and onions, and assorted vinegars and mustards as flavor enhancers. I have found that by reducing my dependence on salt, I have actually introduced greater variety to the flavor of my foods. I have also discovered and learned to adore the natural flavors of many foods—especially vegetables—when they are prepared without salt. In my household, foods like asparagus, green beans, broccoli, and carrots most often are eaten right from the steamer *au naturel.*

Why No Nutrition Information?

A large number of readers of the *Good Food Book* have asked me to include nutritional breakdowns for my recipes. I will reiterate my reasons for not doing so.

First, the nutrient data that are in virtually all available computerized analytical programs are, in part, passé. New, more accurate, and more detailed information has been developed by the United States Department of Agriculture, but the published information is not yet complete and thus could not be used to develop most of the analytical programs.

Second, knowing the nutritional breakdown of a single dish does not help you much in calculating the day's nutrient intake. In all likelihood, you have no idea what was in the chef's salad or slice of pizza you had for lunch, the sweet roll you had with your midmorning coffee, or the canned soup you had with dinner.

Third, I have seen too many gross inaccuracies in the nutrition information that accompanies published recipes. A main source of error is the fact that all the ingredients listed in a recipe are not necessarily consumed—for example, the salt and oil in the water in which you cook pasta, the skin of a roasted chicken, the liquid in which fish is marinated, the fat that is cooked out of meat and drained off. I have yet to see an analysis that can accurately take such manipulations into account. Another source of error is the failure to account for flexibility in recipes—for example, "4 to 5 cups whole-wheat flour" or "skim or low-fat milk" or "salt to taste (optional)."

Finally, I do not think people should "eat by number." If you follow a diet that is low in fat, sugar, and salt, you will automatically consume a reasonable balance of nutrients and calories without having to carry around a calculator to add up everything you eat. Besides, all this arithmetic detracts from the pleasure value of food and eating.

So my advice to you is *eat and enjoy good food,* and let the numbers take care of themselves. Ready, set, go. . . .

Jane Brody
October 1989

ACKNOWLEDGMENTS

Acknowledgments are a lot harder to write than most readers realize. Where does an author begin? With her parents, perhaps, who bestowed the genes for stamina and the drive to tackle and complete difficult projects. With her husband and children, who tolerated the author's 18-hour work days, a chaotic household, and the perpetual refrain "I'm sorry, but I have no time to do that now" for 18 months. With her editors at *The New York Times,* who kindly kept work pressures to a minimum so that both jobs could be done simultaneously. With her friends, who always responded quickly and enthusiastically to cries for moral and physical assistance. With her agent, Wendy Weil, who always knows when to lay off and when to push the author to get the job done. Clearly, all played a critical role in the completion of the work you now hold in your hands.

Of course, the readers of *Jane Brody's Good Food Book* were a major source of support and encouragement, especially the many hundreds who took the time and trouble to write letters recounting their successful use of that work and to send along their own favorite healthful recipes, some of which can be found here.

Then there is her publisher. It is the rare author who sings the praises of her publisher and who purposefully returns book after book to the same one. There is good reason for my continuing relationship with W. W. Norton & Company. It is simply a great house, rare among publishers, characterized by extraordinary stability, intelligence, humor, and hard work. In particular, I am grateful for the support and suggestions of my senior editor, Mary E. Cunnane, and my manuscript editor, Carol Flechner, who helped greatly to polish the rough edges of this work and make it shine. Not to mention my appreciation for Norton's technical, sales, and promotion staffs—in particular, production manager Andy Marasia, sales manager Bill Rusin, publicity director Fran Rosencrantz, and subsidiary rights director Jeannie Luciano, whose professionalism, enthusiasm, and plain hard work did so much for the success of the *Good Food Book.*

As before, designer Margaret Wagner and artist Ray Skibinski did a superb job of turning an unwieldy manuscript into a slick, beautiful, and accessible cookbook.

Last but by no means least, I am grateful to my dozens of tasters, many of whom performed their duties at a moment's notice. Especially helpful were my brother and sister-in-law, Jeffrey and Cindy Brody, and my friends Betty Marks, Jo-Ann Friedman, and Jane and Terry Quinn, who not only contributed their taste buds, stomachs, and constructive comments, but offered numerous suggestions for nutritious and delicious recipes *and* cheerfully worked as cleanup crews as well.

Jane E. Brody

JANE BRODY'S GOOD FOOD GOURMET

1 ·
COOKING FOR COMPANY

Even the best cooks can have difficulty putting together a meal for a dinner party, buffet, or holiday celebration. The problem is not how to prepare the individual dishes, but how to organize the preparation so that all the dishes will be ready and at the right temperatures when it is time to eat them. And, of course, the cook—you—wants to be at the party, too, not slaving away in a hot kitchen while the company shares good times and good food *sans* host.

I'm an organized person by nature, which gives me a leg up in these matters. But I also have had to learn by trial and error which dishes can be prepared ahead, how far ahead, how they are best stored (refrigerator, freezer, room temperature), and how they can be reheated (if necessary) and served to their best advantage.

I must also tell you that I do all my parties without professional help or even the cook's equivalent of a mother's helper. I do have some wonderful friends—in particular Jo-Ann Friedman and Jane Quinn—who have often volunteered to come early, help me set up, and do some last-minute preparations such as putting food on serving dishes and making special drinks. They also are a great help when it comes to serving the food and clearing dishes. My husband's jobs are to get the table ready, tend bar (only for large parties do I hire a bartender), and do much of the cleanup when the party is over.

Forewarned is forearmed. It is no help to the cook to have an assistant who is all thumbs in the kitchen, who is totally unfamiliar with your routines and equipment, and who has to ask you every minute where things are and whether she/he is doing it right. Sometimes you have to learn this the hard way, but you can usually predict trouble if the helper-to-be rarely does any cooking or entertaining.

Here, then, are some basic "rules" and tips for a successful party that does not depend on takeout food and a professional army in the kitchen.

- Plan your menu carefully. Start with dishes that can be made in advance and frozen, then go to dishes that can be stored in the refrigerator for one to three days. When making your list, also consider the storage space you have available (and, if feasible, how much space you may be able to borrow from a neighbor or relative). In the dead of winter, I have often used my deck or back yard to keep made-ahead foods cold. (This does not work in raccoon country or where dogs roam unleashed.) If you try this, be sure the food is tightly covered and placed out of the sun, and the air temperature goes no higher than 40° F. Large coolers with good ice packs or packed with loose ice can also be used, but again the temperature in the cooler should not rise above 40° F if you want to keep the food in it for more than a few hours.

- Plan on no more than one or two dishes that require last-minute preparation (except for heating or baking) after the company has arrived. In the recipes throughout this book, I have tried to indicate in the "Preparation tips" whether the dish will withstand advance preparation. For those dishes that cannot be made completely in advance, I have noted how much of the recipe can be done ahead and whether the last step or two can easily be done just before serving.

- In selecting dishes, keep in mind your kitchen's heating capacity—stove-top burners, ovens, toaster ovens, etc. If you have a microwave oven, you can use it to cook vegetables at the last minute or to reheat quickly those dishes that do not have crusts (these tend to get soggy in the microwave).

- Don't attempt more than you can comfortably do. Your social standing and reputation as a host do not depend on serving more dishes or tackling more complicated recipes than your friends and neighbors do. What guests care about is whether the food tastes good and looks good. Besides, these days with so many people worried about their weight, most guests appreciate a host who does not overstuff them. If you choose a limited menu and do it well, people will weep if they have to decline future invitations.

- Once you have established your menu, make a list of all the ingredients you will need along with their amounts. Then make a second list that consolidates the first. For example, if three recipes call for scallions, write down "scallions," how many are needed for each dish, and the total needed for the meal. Then check your larder to see how many of the ingredients on your list you already have. Finally, make your shopping list, remembering to include beverages, ice, and any serving and cooking utensils that you may need.

- Write out a game plan of food preparation and chores, listing when you will shop for which foods, which dishes you will prepare on which days, and how the prepared food will be stored until serving time. Also list tasks such as cleaning up, setting out flowers and candles, preparing the table, etc. Then simply follow your plan, checking off each task as it is done. By party time, all the food will be ready, and you'll be able to join in the fun!

2·
HOW TO DO IT

Food preparation can be greatly simplified if you become familiar with certain basic cooking techniques that appear over and over again in recipes. In *Jane Brody's Good Food Book,* I included a 22-page chapter, "How to Cook Efficiently," which you may want to consult since I cannot repeat all the tips here. However, the following are especially pertinent to the recipes in this book and in many other "gourmet" cookbooks and magazines.

STEAMED RICE
about 6 cups

Although for most purposes boiling rice according to package directions is adequate, this technique produces very fluffy, dry rice (white or brown) that is ideal for rice salads.

- 5 quarts water
- 1 tablespoon salt
- 2 cups long-grain rice, parboiled or unconverted

1. In a large kettle with a tight-fitting lid, bring the water and salt to a rapid boil. Stir in the rice, bring the water back to a boil, stir the rice again, and boil the rice in the *uncovered* pot for 10 minutes (if white rice) or 15 minutes (if brown rice).
2. Drain the rice in a large colander, saving about 2 quarts of the boiling water. Rinse the rice under cold water, and drain it thoroughly.
3. Put the reserved boiling water back into the kettle, and set the colander with the rice over it. Cover the rice with a cloth dishtowel, tucking in the ends of the towel so that they cannot burn. Cover the kettle with the lid, and steam the rice for 15 to 20 minutes or until it is fluffy and dry.

WHIPPED EVAPORATED SKIM MILK

This is an invaluable tool for fat- and calorie-conscious cooks who want to continue to prepare rich-tasting desserts and other dishes but who don't want to pay an unhealthy price for their indulgence. By following these directions, prepared by the New York City Bureau of Nutrition, you should end up with nonfat milk whipped as stiff as cream.

1. Place an *unopened* can of evaporated skim milk in the freezer for about 1 hour. At the same time, chill the whipping bowl and beaters in the refrigerator.
2. Open the can, and pour the milk into the chilled bowl. Whip the milk rapidly with the cold beaters until the milk is very stiff. If the milk does not whip well, it needs to be colder. Just return the bowl of milk to the freezer for a while, take it out, and whip the milk again.

TOASTED NUTS

1. Preheat the oven or toaster oven to 350° F (300° F for pistachio nuts).
2. Spread the nuts in a single layer in a shallow baking pan. Place the pan in the oven or toaster oven, stirring the nuts once or twice, for 10 to 15 minutes or until the nuts are lightly toasted.
3. If you wish to remove the skins, wrap the hot nuts in a dishtowel, and let them steam for 2 minutes. Then rub the nuts with the towel to remove the skins.

NOTE: For toasting pine nuts (pignoli), which burn very easily, use the method for toasting seeds (below).

TOASTED SEEDS

Seeds like sesame, sunflower, cumin, and coriander, and nuts like pine nuts (pignoli) require close attention to keep them from burning. The method I prefer is to heat a nonstick or heavy skillet over medium-low heat, add the seeds, and toast them, stirring them very often, until they are lightly browned.

DRIED BEANS AND PEAS

As people begin to see the nutritional light, they turn more and more to beans as excellent sources of protein and versatile menu ingredients. But few of us grew up knowing how to cook them from scratch. After years of experimentation, I think I have finally arrived at the best overall method for preparing beans that leave the least gaseous legacy. In general, beans should be soaked before they are cooked. In my experience, however, the quick-soak technique of cooking beans in boiling water for 2 minutes and then letting them stand in the water for 1 hour is not adequate for removing the indigestible carbohydrates that result in gas production in the human digestive tract. I prefer the method below.

Preparation tips: One pound (2 cups) of dried beans or peas yields 5 to 6 cups of cooked beans. While you are at it, don't be afraid to make extra beans. Cooked whole and mashed beans freeze well. Place them in recipe-size quantities in freezer bags or in plastic containers with tight-fitting lids. Cooking times will vary with the type of bean, its dryness, and its age—from 20 minutes for soaked lentils to as much as 3 hours for soybeans.

1. Place the beans in a large bowl or saucepan with cold water to cover by at least 4 inches. Let them stand in the water, unrefrigerated, for at least 10 hours. Drain the beans, rinse them, and drain them again.
2. Place the soaked beans in a large saucepan. Add at least 2 quarts of water for each pound (weight before soaking) of beans. Bring the water to a boil, *partially* cover the pan, reduce the heat just enough to keep the water gently bubbling, and cook the beans until they are nearly tender. *Note:* If boiled too rapidly, the beans will lose their skins and may even break apart.
3. When the beans are nearly done, add salt to taste, if desired (I use 1 teaspoon per pound), and continue gently cooking the beans until they are very tender but not mushy. Drain the beans, rinse them under cold water, and drain them again.

ROASTED PEPPERS

Although you can buy these in jars, the flavor is far superior when done at home, if you have the time and inclination. I learned the ice-water method of removing skins from Ellen Brown, author of one of my favorite cookbooks, *The Gourmet Gazelle Cookbook.*

Preparation tips: Using a broiler or grill is the most efficient method of charring peppers because several peppers can be done at once. If you prefer the gas flame of the stove top and do this often, you may wish to purchase a stove-top grill designed for roasting peppers. The following techniques apply to both sweet and hot fresh peppers, but you would be wise to wear thin rubber gloves when removing the skins from hot peppers to avoid burning your fingers on the pepper oil.

1. Stab the stem end of the peppers several times with a fork, or make a few slits through the flesh to keep the peppers from exploding.
2. For stove-top roasting over a gas flame, spear the peppers, one at a time, on a long-handled fork. Place the peppers directly into the flame and sear the skins on all sides. *Or* remove the burner grid, and place a metal rack over the flame. Place the peppers on the rack directly in the flame, turning them as they char.
3. If you are using a broiler or grill, place the peppers on a rack as close to the heat as possible. Keep the oven door open, and turn the peppers often until the skins are charred on all sides.
4. To remove the skins, plunge the hot peppers immediately into a bowl of ice water. When the peppers are cool enough to handle, rub off the charred skins.

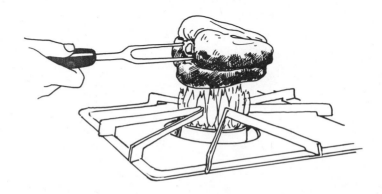

PEELED AND SEEDED TOMATOES

Most people make more of a to-do about peeling tomatoes than is necessary. Unless you are doing a huge number (say, for canning or tomato sauce), it is not necessary to plunge them into boiling water for 30 seconds to loosen the skins. Start with reasonably firm tomatoes, make a U-shaped slit in the skin with a sharp knife at the blossom end opposite the core, and, using a sharp vegetable peeler, remove the skin in a continuous circle or in strips from one end to the other. After the peel is removed, cut out the core with a paring knife.

To seed tomatoes, cut them in half crosswise. Scoop the seeds out with your finger or a tiny spoon.

To slice or dice tomatoes, especially with their skin intact, use a serrated knife, such as a flat-bladed bread knife, or a so-called laser knife.

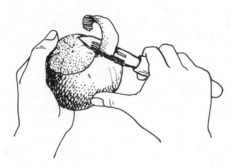

DESALTING FOODS

Many frequently used ingredients in gourmet cooking are too salty for current tastes and health demands. I'm thinking particularly of foods like feta, anchovies, capers, caviar, ham and other smoked meats, and sauerkraut and other pickled vegetables.

You can remove some of the salt before adding such ingredients to recipes by soaking the food in cold water for 15 to 30 minutes, changing the water once or twice if the food is extremely salty.

DEFATTING FOODS

With fat being the major dietary no-no, a main goal of wholesome cooking is to remove as much fat as possible from recipes. My goal is to keep fat content low while still using foods that are traditionally very fatty, such as smoked sausage, ground meat, and cheese. Here are some tricks I use to cut down on fat.

- Start with reduced-fat ingredients, such as low-fat cottage cheese (1 percent or 1½ percent butterfat), skim or low-fat (1 percent) milk, "light" butter-margarine or margarine spreads and sticks, nonfat or low-fat yogurt, light or part-skim ricotta, and part-skim mozzarella. There are also other cheeses, like Cheddar, Swiss, and muenster, that are often available in reduced-fat versions.
- In many recipes, meats can be precooked to remove much of their fat before they are added to the rest of the ingredients. This can be done in a skillet on top of the stove, in a shallow pan in the oven or toaster oven, or on absorbent paper toweling in a microwave oven. Thinly slice sausages and break up ground meat to achieve the best results.
- Prepare soups and stews in advance, and decant the pan juices from roasted foods so that the fat, which rises to the top, can be removed before the food is served. For liquids, a measuring cup in which the spout emerges from the bottom of the cup is ideal; you can pour off the fat-free liquid and leave the fat behind. For dishes that can be chilled, the fat will harden at the top and can easily be removed with a slotted spoon or spatula.

DOUBLING RECIPES

To double most recipes, all you need to do is double the ingredients. However, hot seasonings should not automatically be increased by the same amounts, or you may end up with a dish that is inedible. Try adding half again the original amount, and taste the dish before adding more. Remember, too, that the flavor of peppercorns develops over time, so be judicious in the amount of freshly ground pepper you start with.

When doubling a yeast-leavened recipe, add half again the original amount of yeast. You may also want to divide the dough in half to knead it.

3 ·
WHERE TO BUY IT

A singular source of frustration in preparing recipes from some of the newer cookbooks that rely heavily on fresh and exotic ingredients is where to get these foods, especially if you live in a small city or town far from a major metropolitan area that has specialty food stores and large supermarkets that carry "gourmet" foods. Even in New York City, where I live, I often find it impossible to get some of the ingredients listed in ethnic cookbooks and those that originate in California, the South, or the Southwest. To be sure, somewhere in New York almost everything can be bought, but you have to know just where to go and you have to have a few hours to spare to get there and back. Frankly, there is rarely room in my life for such culinary safaris. Nor do I have time to trek from store to store searching for needed kitchen equipment. So I have taken the efficient way out: I order from catalogues—all kinds of catalogues. My various catalogues feature such items as spices, nuts, pastas, beans, flours, seeds, and dried fruits. I also have a slew of equipment catalogues that sell everything from potato peelers to 20-quart stock pots. The items are delivered by UPS, fully insured and at reasonable shipping costs. And if I am not satisfied with an item, I can always send it back (rarely necessary).

I do almost all my catalogue shopping by phone and pay by credit card, and I can usually be told immediately whether the items I order are available and about when I can expect delivery. Even when buying from stores, I often use the phone first to find out if the item I want is in stock and how much it costs. Many stores will also take credit-card purchases over the phone and ship them UPS. This saves a lot of wear and tear on the shopper and leaves her or him a lot more time to play in the kitchen, which is, after all, the ultimate goal.

Here, then, are the names, addresses, and phone numbers of some companies that carry various ingredients and equipment.

PASTA
> Morisi's Pasta
> John Morisi & Sons, Inc.
> 647 Fifth Avenue
> Brooklyn, NY 11215
> Mail order: (718) 499–0146

More than 200 varieties (shapes and flavors) are available from this family-owned business that has been making pasta on the premises for 50 years. A mail-order catalogue and an order blank are available. To place orders by phone, call between 8:00 A.M. and 5:00 P.M. Eastern time Monday through Friday. Allow 2 to 4 weeks for processing and delivery.

MEATS AND POULTRY

North Country Smokehouse
Box 1415
Claremont, NH 03743
Phone: (603) 542–8323 for credit-card orders

Lean smoked sausages, smoked turkey, chicken, ham, and other items are shipped second-day UPS delivery at no extra charge.

Deer Valley Farm
R.D. 1
Guilford, NY 13780
Phone: (607) 764–8556

A good source of organically raised chicken and veal, very low in fat and high in flavor.

SPICES AND HERBS

The Spice House
P.O. Box 1633
Milwaukee, WI 53203
Phone: (414) 272–0977
33-page catalogue: $1.00

Fresh bulk spices, herbs, seeds, and seasoning mixes—including various no-salt seasonings—are sold in amounts ranging from 1 ounce to 1 pound. Orders can be sent within 48 hours via UPS COD service.

Charles Loeb
Mr. Spiceman
615 Palmer Road
Yonkers, NY 10701
Phone: (914) 961–7776
       (914) 576–1222

From 5:00 P.M. to 9:00 P.M. daily and 9:00 A.M. to 11:00 A.M. on Saturday (Eastern time), call the 961–7776 number for inquiries and credit-card orders. From 8:30 A.M. to 4:00 P.M. on Wednesdays and Fridays, call the 576–1222 number.

Fox Hill Farm
444 West Michigan Avenue
P.O. Box 9
Parma, MI 49269–0009
Phone: (517) 531–3179

Herb plants and freshly cut herbs are shipped UPS. Credit-card orders are taken between 8:00 A.M. and 8:00 P.M. Eastern time. Allow 8 to 10 weeks for delivery of plant material.

Herb Gathering, Inc.
5742 Kenwood
Kansas City, MO 64110
Phone: (816) 523–2653
This seed company also sells fresh herbs by mail.

Old Southwest Trading Company
P.O. Box 7545
Albuquerque, NM 87194
Phone: (505) 831–5144
This company specializes in hard-to-find ingredients used in southwestern and Mexican cooking. Credit-card orders of $15 or more are accepted by phone.

Casdos Farms/Dos Ves, Inc.
Box 1269
San Juan Pueblo, NM 87566

Mexican Connection
142 Lincoln Avenue
Santa Fe, NM 87501

Pecos Valley Spice Company
500 East 77th Street, Suite 2324
New York, NY 10162
Phone: (212) 628–5374
The above three companies sell dried peppers, from mild to ultra-hot, by mail.

VINEGARS AND OILS

Williams-Sonoma
P.O. Box 7456
San Francisco, CA 94120–7456
Phone: (415) 421–4242 for credit-card orders
       (415) 421–4555 for customer service
The order number can be called 7:00 A.M. to 7:00 P.M. Pacific time Monday through Friday, and 8:00 A.M. to 4:00 P.M. Pacific time Saturday and Sunday. Customer service is available Monday through Friday, 8:00 A.M. to 4:30 P.M. Pacific time.

Community Kitchens
P.O. Box 2311
Baton Rouge, LA 70821–2311
Phone: (800) 535–9901
Call the toll-free number Monday through Friday, 7:00 A.M. to 6:00 P.M. Central time. Orders are shipped within 48 hours.

FLOURS AND GRAINS

Nowadays most people can buy whole-grain flours, even the high-quality stone-ground versions, and all kinds of wholesome grains in their local supermarkets or health-food stores. But if you need a mail-order source, try these.

The Vermont Country Store
P.O. Box 3000
Manchester Center, VT 05255–3000
Phone: (802) 362–2400 for credit-card orders
　　　　 (802) 362–4647 for customer service
Credit-card orders are taken 24 hours a day every day.

Walnut Acres Natural Foods
Penns Creek, PA 17862
Phone: (717) 837–0601
Only organically grown products are sold. Credit-card orders are taken 24 hours a day.

DRIED BEANS AND PEAS
Baer's Best
154 Green Street
Reading, MA 01867
Phone: (617) 944–8719
The Baers grow at least 15 different varieties of beans, from commonplace to exotic, on their farm in St. Albans, Maine. All can be ordered by mail or phone, in bulk or 1-pound packages.

Specialty Grain Company
Box 2458
Dearborn, MI 48123
Phone: (313) 561–0421

Walnut Acres Natural Foods
Penns Creek, PA 17862
Phone: (717) 837–0601
This company, which sells only organically grown products, is also a good source of nuts, dried fruits, whole-grain flours, rice, and seeds.

DRIED MUSHROOMS
Gourmet Treasure Hunters
10044 Adams Avenue, Suite 305
Huntington Beach, CA 92646
Phone: (714) 964–3355
This company sells all manner of dried mushrooms, from Chinese to American. It is also a good source of specialty rices (basmati and arborio), Japanese and Vietnamese ingredients, olives and olive oil.

CHINESE INGREDIENTS
China Bowl Trading Company
169 Lackawanna Avenue
Parsippany, NJ 07054
Phone: (201) 335–1000

NUTS

Walnut Acres Natural Foods
Penns Creek, PA 17862
Phone: (717) 837–0601

All manner of organically grown shelled nuts, dry-roasted and raw, can be mail-ordered.

Koinonia Partners
Route 2
Americus, GA 31709

Order pecans and peanuts, shelled, unshelled, or flavored, by mail only (minimum order $10 to each address). Pecans cannot be shipped between late May and late September.

Jane and Harry Willson
Sunnyland Farms, Inc.
P.O. Box 8200
Albany, GA 31706–8200
Phone: (912) 883–3085

Call or write for the Willsons' extensive catalogue of nuts, nut products, and dried fruit. Credit-card orders ($30 minimum) can be placed by phone between 8:30 A.M. and 5:00 P.M. Eastern time Monday through Friday, and on evenings and weekends in November and December.

VIDALIA ONIONS

Bland Farms
P.O. Box 506-G2-S89
Glennville, GA 30427–0506
Phone: (800) 843–2542 (800–VIDALIA)

These succulent, sweet onions are available only in May and June, but the company sells other southern items, too. Call for a free catalogue. Each order of onions (minimum 10 pounds) comes with a free recipe booklet.

SEEDS FOR GROWING HERBS AND VEGETABLES

Burpee Gardens
W. Atlee Burpee & Co.
300 Park Avenue
Warminster, PA 18991–0001
Phone: (215) 674–9633

One of several traditionally reliable sources of vegetable seeds, Burpee accepts credit-card orders by phone Monday through Saturday between 9:00 A.M. and 5:00 P.M. Eastern time.

Shepherd's Garden Seeds
30 Irene Street
Torrington, CT 06790
Mail order: (203) 482–3638 (Connecticut)
        (408) 335–5311 (California)

Shepherd's offers an extraordinary selection of excellent seeds for vegetables and herbs, both common and exotic, along with detailed growing instructions. Credit-card orders are accepted by phone at the Connecticut number between 8:00 A.M. and 9:00 P.M.

Eastern time Monday through Friday, and at the California number between 8:00 A.M. and 5:00 P.M. Pacific time Monday through Friday.

Vermont Bean Seed Company
Garden Lane
Fair Haven, VT 05743–0250
Phone: (802) 265–4212

As specialists in beans, this company has seeds for almost any bean and pea that can be grown in the United States.

Herb Gathering, Inc.
5742 Kenwood
Kansas City, MO 64110
Phone: (816) 523–2653

KITCHEN EQUIPMENT

Saint Paul Bar & Restaurant Equipment Company
655 Payne Avenue
St. Paul, MN 55101
Phone: (612) 774–0361

To me (and many other cooks), the single most important kitchen item is a set of good knives along with a good sharpening steel. I have tried all manner of knives—from the $1 version sold in chain stores to the $50 imported kinds. Without question, the best knives I have ever used (and the ones I now use exclusively and give as gifts) are American-made, stain-free, high-carbon, inexpensive, and have tough, dishwasher-proof *white* synthetic handles. They are called Sani-Safe by Dexter-Russell and are sold through restaurant supply stores in various cities throughout the country. I order them by phone (a salesperson can tell you what kinds and sizes are available and how much they cost) from the Saint Paul Bar & Restaurant Equipment Company, which maintains stock on more than a dozen types.

Colonial Garden Kitchens
P.O. Box 66
Hanover, PA 17333–0066
Phone: (800) 752–5552 for orders
        (717) 633–3333 for customer service

The Wooden Spoon
Route 6
P.O. Box 852
Mahopac, NY 10541
Phone: (800) 431–2207

Call the toll-free number for credit-card orders of $15 or more Monday through Friday, 8:45 A.M. to 4:45 P.M. Eastern time.

Williams-Sonoma
P.O. Box 7456
San Francisco, CA 94120–7456
Phone: (415) 421–4242 for credit-card orders
(415) 421–4555 for customer service
The order number can be called 7:00 A.M. to 7:00 P.M. Pacific time Monday through
Friday, and 8:00 A.M. to 4:00 P.M. Pacific time Saturday and Sunday. Customer service is
available Monday through Friday, 8:00 A.M. to 4:30 P.M. Pacific time.

Brookstone Homewares
5 Vose Farm Road
Petersborough, NH 03458
Phone: (603) 924–9541 for credit-card orders
(603) 924–9511 for customer service
The order number can be reached 24 hours a day every day. Customer service is available Monday through Friday, 8:30 A.M. to 5:00 P.M. Eastern time.

The Chef's Catalog
3215 Commercial Avenue
Northbrook, IL 60062–1920
Phone: (800) 338–3232 for credit-card orders
(312) 480–8305 for customer service
Call 24 hours a day every day for credit-card orders. Customer service is available Monday through Friday, 9:00 A.M. to 5:00 P.M. Central time.

Joan Cook Housewares
P.O. Box 21628
Fort Lauderdale, FL 33335–1628
Phone: (800) 327–3799 anytime
Fax: (305) 522–3424 anytime

Hoffritz
515 West 24th Street
New York, NY 10011–1182
Phone: (800) 962–9699 anytime
Fax: (212) 627–5952, credit-card orders only

Community Kitchens
P.O. Box 2311
Baton Rouge, LA 70821–2311
Phone: (800) 535–9901
Call the toll-free number Monday through Friday, 7:00 A.M. to 6:00 P.M. Central time.
Orders are shipped within 48 hours.

MICROWAVE EQUIPMENT
Microwave and More
779 Mount Read Boulevard
Rochester, NY 14606
Phone: (800) 426–6257
Call the toll-free number Monday through Friday, 8:00 A.M. to 5:00 P.M. Eastern time.

COOKBOOKS
Kitchen Arts and Letters
1435 Lexington Avenue
New York, NY 10128
Phone: (212) 876–5550
Owner Nach Waxman has got to be the most knowledgeable and helpful source on all manner of cookbooks, even those that are not yet published. His store on Lexington Avenue (between 93d and 94th Streets) is a cookbook aficionado's paradise. Mail orders (using MasterCard, Visa, or check) have a minimum shipping cost of $3 east of the Mississippi and $3.50 west of the Mississippi.

Jessica's Biscuit Cookbook Catalog
Box 301
Newtonville, MA 02160
Phone: (800) 225–4264 from outside Massachusetts
        (800) 322–4027 from within Massachusetts
        (617) 965–0530 from metropolitan Boston
A purveyor of all manner of cookbooks.

4·
ABOUT INGREDIENTS
AND EQUIPMENT

The food you prepare and the ease with which you do it are no better than the quality of the ingredients and equipment you use. But this does not mean that you must spend a fortune on kitchenware or spend days searching for particular ingredients to prepare really good food. Here is what I consider most important.

Ingredients I Recommend

In the best of all possible worlds, we would all cook only with fresh foods, organically grown. But for upward of 90 percent of people, this is not possible— at least not for most of the year. In the recipes in this book, when I deem fresh ingredients to be critically important to the quality of the dish, I say so, but where dried or canned or frozen will do, I give you the alternatives. This is what I mean when I use the following ingredients:

PARSLEY Always fresh, unless otherwise stated. When parsley is one ingredient among many that will be cooked together such as in a soup or stew, you could substitute dried parsley flakes—1 tablespoon of dried parsley for every ¼ cup of fresh minced parsley. But you would certainly not want to use dried parsley when parsley is a dominant flavor in the dish, when it is used as a garnish, or when it is added after the food is cooked.

LEMON JUICE Always freshly squeezed *or* fresh frozen (by you). Commercially prepared lemon juice is treated to give it staying power, and this significantly changes the flavor. I avoid it. The same goes for lime juice.

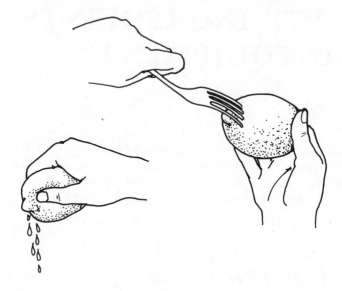

ORANGE JUICE When it is used as a minor ingredient or in a marinade, reconstituted frozen concentrated juice is fine. But try to avoid canned juice; it lacks something in the flavor department.

HERBS It would be wonderful if we could all use fresh herbs, but, alas, most of the time I and most other cooks are stuck with dried leaves. And dried leaves is what I mean when I list herbs like "oregano," "thyme," "basil," etc. If I mean ground leaves, I say so. If fresh herbs are crucial or preferable, I say that, too. If you prefer to use fresh herbs year round and can only get them for a few months of the year, consider freezing them—not ideal, but better than dried—by chopping them, placing them in ice cube trays, adding water, and freezing. Then remove the cubes and seal them in labeled freezer bags. Also, see pages 12 and 13 for how to buy fresh herbs by mail.

SPICES Seeds and berries used for seasoning—like cumin, cloves, cardamom, allspice, and peppercorns—and cinnamon always mean *ground* seasoning, unless the whole berries or seeds are specifically called for. Three seasonings that I use often are far superior if freshly ground: black pepper, white pepper, and nutmeg. If you share my view, I suggest you purchase two pepper mills—one for black peppercorns and one for white—and a nutmeg grinder, the hang-up type shaped like a half-cylinder with a little compartment at the top to hold a whole nutmeg.

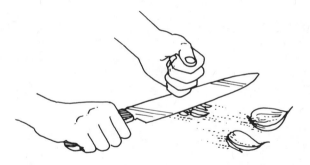

GARLIC Fresh is critical. I use garlic powder in only two recipes, both of them dried seasoning mixes. Otherwise, I mince or grate it fresh as needed. I know that minced garlic packed in olive oil is the rage. But it also has been linked to a risk of botulism poisoning—not a happy event. If you prefer to keep a lot of chopped garlic on hand, do it yourself, cover it with oil, and keep it refrigerated all the time. To keep your efforts to a minimum, look for large bulbs with large cloves (not, however, elephant garlic, which is much milder and considerably more expensive). To simplify peeling, lay the clove on its side, cover it with the flat side of a kitchen knife, then lightly pound your fist against the knife; this loosens the skin.

GINGERROOT Always use fresh ginger when this is called for in a recipe; ground dried ginger has a much different flavor. Gingerroot is now widely available in supermarkets throughout the country. Unless you use enormous amounts of it, it is best stored in the freezer in a sealed plastic bag. To use, peel and grate it frozen; do not thaw the ginger unless you must mince it (in which case, slice off just what you will need from the frozen ginger, replacing the remainder in the freezer—don't, however, thaw the entire piece).

ONIONS I use both yellow and red onions, and when I mean red, I say so. Otherwise use yellow ones. My personal preference is for the large Spanish onions, which yield about 2 cups chopped per onion. They are easy to peel and handy if you do a lot of cooking. Portions of the cut onion, wrapped in plastic, can be stored in the refrigerator for several days.

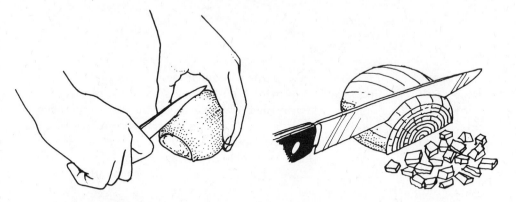

SCALLIONS These have different names in different parts of the country—in the Midwest, they are often called "green onions." But they are the same: small white bulbs with long, slender green leaves.

CILANTRO This, too, has other names: coriander and Chinese parsley. Cilantro is a small leafy herb that closely resembles ordinary parsley but has a very pungent flavor. Some like it, others hate it; I don't know anyone who is neutral about it. Therefore, I nearly always offer regular parsley as an alternative in my recipes or suggest that individual diners add cilantro to taste.

Basic Equipment

If you are serious about cooking from scratch, it is important to have the tools that make it possible to do this quickly and accurately. For a complete list—including illustrations—of useful kitchen equipment that includes a rating system of relative importance, see *Jane Brody's Good Food Book.* For now, I will list the most crucial items to preparing good food that is good for you, too.

KNIVES If you have no other equipment in your kitchen, you could whip up some mighty fine meals if all you have is a good set of knives. Good does not mean expensive or imported from Germany or France. Nor do the knives have to be carbon steel (these rust and are unsuitable for cutting many ingredients like onions and potatoes and apples, which get discolored). My personal preference is for relatively inexpensive, American-made, stainless-steel knives with heavy synthetic handles called Sani-Safe made by Dexter-Russell and available at bar and restaurant supply stores (see page 16 for information on mail-order purchase). My basic set, bought one at a time, now includes two heavy all-purpose kitchen knives—a 10-inch and an 8-inch with wide tapered blades; an 8-inch slim filleting knife; an 8-inch bread knife with a straight serrated blade; a 6-inch serrated knife with a relatively slim tapered blade; and two 4-inch paring knives. In addition, I have a pineapple knife with a 4½-inch curved serrated blade (available from Dole for $2 and a mail-order coupon from fresh pineapple). Also important is a good sharpening steel, which should be used as often as needed to keep those nonserrated knives razor-sharp.

POTS AND PANS You can spend anywhere from $50 for a whole set to $50 for a small saucepan. For the budget-minded and health-conscious, I recommend heavy aluminum pots and pans with Silverstone or comparable nonstick linings (a basic set is under $100 and may be on sale for as little as $50). If you shy away from nonstick linings, the next best is much more expensive: heavy aluminum with stainless-steel linings that require some greasing. Aluminum is very good for distributing heat evenly—the thicker the better. If your pots are lined, you need not be concerned about aluminum getting into the food. If your pots have nonstick linings, be sure to use only plastic or wooden utensils and plastic scrub cloths to avoid scratching them. As for sizes, the bare essentials, in my view, would include 1-quart, 2-quart, and 3-quart saucepans with tight-fitting covers; a 5-quart Dutch oven (great for soups); 8-inch, 10-inch, and 12-inch skillets with tight-fitting covers (often the covers for the saucepans also fit the skillets); and a 10- or 11-inch square griddle. In addition, a pasta pot (with a deep strainer as well as a smaller steaming insert, in stainless steel or aluminum) and a steamer pot (two stacked steaming compartments, Chinese style, made by Taylor and Ng) are among the most used utensils in my kitchen. And a cast-iron skillet is useful for browning and searing.

BLENDER A simple one with five speeds will do, as long as the motor is strong. The best blenders have a heavy glass jar and a lid with a small removable cap that permits addition of ingredients while the machine is running. And some brands (for example, Oster) come with handy mini-jars, ideal for handling small quantities.

FOOD PROCESSOR Although I had promised my publisher that I would not depend on this machine, I found that as I cooked more and more, I used the processor more and more—not for everyday food preparation, but when cooking for parties and when preparing ingredients (like bread crumbs, ground nuts, or large amounts of chopped anything) or dishes (like gefilte fish, relishes, and sorbets) that just work best and fastest in a food processor. You should consider three things before purchasing a processor. First, you do not need a dozen different disks for cutting and shredding. Basically, I use three (in addition to the standard steel blade): a medium slicer, a fine shredder, and a coarse shredder. Second, virtually everything that can be done in a food processor can be done by hand with a far less expensive gadget, if you have the time and energy. Third, if you cannot keep the food processor handy, save your money—you'll almost never use the machine if you have to get it out and set it up each time it is needed.

GRATER The four-sided kind is handiest. I use this much more often than the food processor because it is much easier to clean and to maneuver. It is also useful to have a small one-sided fine shredder for grating garlic and gingerroot.

PEPPER MILL A good one is a must, and preferably two—one for black peppercorns, one for white. I prefer the kind that is filled from the side so that the grind setting is not disrupted each time the mill is filled.

VEGETABLE PEELER I have found that the expensive ones are no better than those you buy in the dime store for 79 cents. If you find a sharp one, buy two and hang on to them. The best have carbon-steel blades and should be washed and dried immediately after use to prevent rusting.

STRAINERS AND COLANDERS At least three in various sizes—a small fine sieve, a larger sieve with medium holes, and a large colander—are essential.

MEASURING CUPS AND SPOONS Here I am profligate. These items don't cost much, and they make cooking so much easier. I work with at least three glass cups for measuring liquids: the 1-cup size, the 2-cup size, and the 4-cup size. If you can handle an even larger one, also try one that measures 8 cups. In addition, I use a set of metal or plastic cups for measuring dry ingredients; they come in graduated sizes, ranging from ⅛ cup to 2 cups. It wouldn't hurt to have several ⅛-cup measures (they are the same as coffee measures); although they are mostly used for dry ingredients, they are especially handy for measuring cooking oil, honey, and other foods used in small quantities. As for spoons, I recommend at least two sets, preferably in sizes ⅛ teaspoon to 1 tablespoon— one set for measuring dry ingredients and the other for wet ingredients.

LEMON REAMER A small metal one (about $2) that fits over a measuring cup and strains out the seeds is perfect.

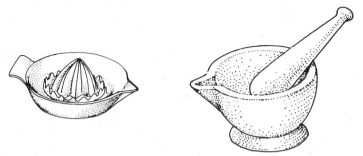

MORTAR AND PESTLE A small, inexpensive one is invaluable for crushing seeds and mashing garlic.

ASSORTED MIXING SPOONS Both wooden and metal, slotted and unslotted, long and short, are "musts" for all cooking purposes.

5·
GARNISHES

People eat as much with their eyes as with their mouths, so preparing and presenting food as attractively as possible can greatly enhance culinary success. You may not worry much about appearances when feeding the immediate family, but for company you certainly want your food to look as good as it will taste. I'll never forget the comment I received from one taster about a ratatouille pita pizza I had made: "It *looks* dreadful, but it tastes good!" Food should never look dreadful. Even dull-looking dishes can be brightened by attractive décor. You don't have to spend hours making fancy garnishes (unless you want to) to make dishes look inviting. The simplest addenda that take but seconds to add can make major improvements. Below are some of my favorite simple garnishing tricks plus a few more complicated ones for ambitious or artistic cooks.

Simple Garnishes

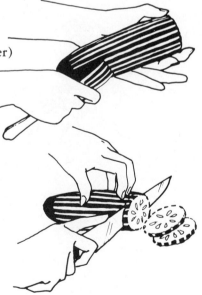

- Sprigs of watercress, parsley, or cilantro (coriander)
- Leaves of basil or mint
- Scallion leaves thinly sliced lengthwise to 1 inch of the base
- Lemon slices or wedges
- Cherry tomatoes, whole or halved crosswise
- Slices of orange or lemon, kiwi, and strawberries
- Alternating slices of tomato and lemon
- Julienne strips of carrot and zucchini (unpeeled)
- Broccoli flowerets with cherry tomatoes or curls of lemon peel
- Mushroom caps with an "X" made from pimiento strips
- Finely shredded red cabbage and broccoli flowerets
- Cucumber (unpeeled) scored with a fork and sliced crosswise

Red cabbage

Edible flowers

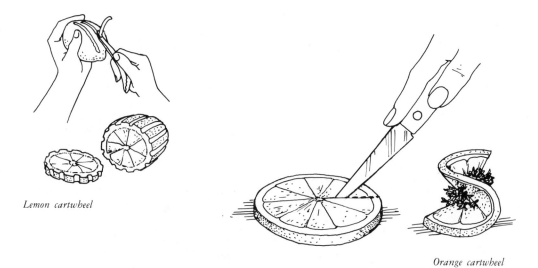

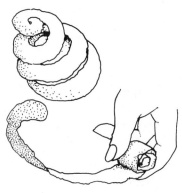

Lemon cartwheel

Orange cartwheel

Radish fan

Orange rose

Watermelon boat

- Edible flowers, including squash blossoms, pansies, nasturtiums, hollyhocks, violets, rose petals, tiger lilies, and day lilies
- Small clusters of grapes (red or green) with mint leaves.

Quick Homemade Garnishes

ORANGE CARTWHEEL Slice an orange crosswise. Make one cut in each slice from the edge of the peel to the center. Twist the cut ends in opposite directions. Decorate the cartwheel, if desired, with a maraschino cherry or short sprig of parsley in its center.

RED-CABBAGE FLOWER With a sharp slim knife, start at the center of the top, and make a lengthwise cut through the cabbage about three-fourths of the way to the base. Continue making cuts evenly around the cabbage, peeling back the layers to resemble the petals of a flower. Use the cabbage as a table center-piece, or scoop out the center and fill it with dip for a vegetable platter.

TOMATO FLOWER Choose firm cherry tomatoes, and with a sharp paring knife make six evenly spaced skin-deep lengthwise cuts from the center of the top of each tomato three-fourths of the way to the bottom. Carefully peel back the skin to resemble the petals of a flower.

RADISH FAN With a sharp paring knife, make closely spaced parallel verti-cal cuts from the top of the radish almost to the bottom. Place the radish in a bowl of ice water until the slats open up to form a fan.

ORANGE ROSE This garnish can also be made with a lemon, lime, grape-fruit, or tomato. With a sharp paring knife or vegetable peeler, start at the stem end, and slice around the orange, cutting a continuous ¾-inch-wide strip of skin from the entire orange. Place the peel in near-boiling water for 1 to 2 minutes to increase its flexibility. From the nonstem end, start rolling the skin inside out into a tight coil. Secure the start of the coil with a toothpick inserted crosswise through the base. Continue rolling the skin, getting looser as you near the end of the strip. Secure the entire rose with a toothpick through its base. Place the flower in ice water to set it, then trim off visible ends of the toothpick.

Miscellaneous Garnishing Tips

- When serving a fresh fruit salad in a watermelon boat, cut the edge of the boat in wedges like the top of a picket fence, and place a pineapple leaf and strawberry on a toothpick in the base of each "V."
- When cutting up fruits and vegetables, use a corrugated slicing tool or a melon baller for a more uniform and attractive look.

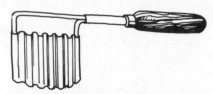

- Soak vegetable garnishes in ice water to make the sections separate and curl.
- To soften rigid vegetables for easier manipulation, soak them in salt water.
- To keep apples, pears, and other fruits and vegetables from discoloring in air, dip them in lemon juice (or brush them with the juice) or a solution of ascorbic acid (crush some tablets of vitamin C).
- To preserve garnishes and make them shiny, coat them with a solution of unflavored gelatin.
- If garnishes must be made days in advance, place them in freezer containers, add water to cover, and freeze.
- When working with brittle vegetables like carrots and turnips, bring them to room temperature before cutting them.
- When using berries, grapes, or cherry tomatoes to decorate a dish or platter, select ones of uniform size before using the rest in food preparation.
- Be inventive about holding garnishes together. Use toothpicks, skewers, florist's tape, pins—whatever will work. But you should warn guests not to eat the garnishes lest the guests encounter a hidden hazard.

For details on more advanced garnishing techniques, consult *How to Garnish* by Harvey Rosen, published by International Culinary Consultants, P.O. Box 2202, Elberon Station, Elberon, NJ 07740. A garnishing set that includes this book and several basic garnishing tools can be purchased by mail order from Joan Cook Housewares, P.O. Box 21628, Fort Lauderdale, FL 33335–1628, or phone (800) 327–3799, or from Colonial Garden Kitchens, P.O. Box 66, Hanover, PA 17333–0066, or phone (800) 752–5552.

6·
YIELDS, EQUIVALENTS, AND MEASUREMENTS

To simplify planning for company meals, I repeat this section from *Jane Brody's Good Food Book.*

One of the greatest frustrations in preparing certain recipes is the inability to determine just how much of a particular ingredient you will need in order to end up with the amount specified. This is especially true for ingredients that are bought by the pound or bunch but are to be cut up and measured by the cup. Adding to this frustration is the fact that how small you cut your pieces, how tightly you pack them, or how moist they happen to be can influence their volume. Even the weather can change the measurement for an ingredient that attracts moisture from the air.

The confusion is compounded by the fact that while some recipes specify amounts in pounds of the whole food, others state measured quantities of the prepared food, such as "½ cup almonds, chopped" or "2 cups diced potatoes." Such designations at least tell you the precise amount you should be cooking and are the kind of instructions I have tried to give throughout this book. My biggest complaint, however, involves the nonspecific instruction like "2 potatoes" or even "2 medium potatoes." What's medium to one person may be large or small to another, depending on how much these people like potatoes or on the size potato that they normally buy. I use such notations only when an exact amount of an ingredient doesn't matter.

Since I have found wide variations in the estimated yields given in different cookbooks, in most cases I have started from scratch and have devised my own. In this section, I have tried to give you a reasonable guide to yields and equivalents as I have measured them.

Yields and Equivalents

BEANS AND PEAS, DRIED

Large beans (e.g., kidney)
1 pound = 2 cups uncooked
        = 5½ cups cooked
1 cup = 2 to 3 cups cooked

Lentils
1 cup = 3 cups cooked

Small beans (e.g., navy)
1 pound = 2⅓ cups uncooked
        = 5½ cups cooked
1 cup = 2 to 3 cups cooked

Split peas
1 pound = 2 cups uncooked
        = 5 cups cooked
1 cup = 2½ cups cooked

BREADS AND CRACKERS

Bread
1 pound = 12 to 16 slices
1 slice fresh = ½ cup fresh crumbs
1 slice dried = ⅓ cup dry crumbs

Graham crackers
12 squares = 1 cup crumbs
1 packet = 1¼ cups crumbs

Soda crackers
22 = 1 cup crumbs

CEREALS AND GRAINS

Barley
1 cup = 3½ cups cooked

Buckwheat groats (kasha)
1 cup = 2½ to 3 cups cooked

Bulgur (cracked wheat)
1 cup = 2½ to 3 cups cooked

Corn meal
1 cup = 4 cups cooked
1 pound = 3 to 3½ cups

Farina
½ cup = 2⅔ cups cooked

Millet
1 cup raw = 3½ cups cooked

Oats (regular or quick)
1 pound rolled oats = 5 cups uncooked
1 cup = 1¾ cups cooked

Pasta
1 pound macaroni = 5 cups uncooked
               = 8 to 10 cups cooked
2 ounces spaghetti = 1 cup cooked
1 cup small pasta = 1¾ cups cooked
1 cup noodles = 1¾ cups cooked

Rice (long-grain), white or brown
1 pound = 2½ cups
1 cup raw = 3 cups cooked

Wheat berries
1 cup = 2⅔ cups cooked

Wild rice
1 cup raw = 4 cups cooked

CHEESES

Cottage cheese
1 pound (16 ounces) = 2 cups

Grating cheese (e.g., Parmesan, Romano)
3 ounces = 1 cup grated

Hard cheese (e.g., Cheddar, Swiss, mozzarella)
4 ounces = 1 to 1⅓ cups shredded

Ricotta
15 ounces = 2 cups

EGGS

White
1 large = 2 tablespoons
Yolk
1 large = 1 tablespoon

FATS AND OILS

Butter or margarine
1 stick = ½ cup or 8 tablespoons or
          4 ounces
1 pound = 2 cups
1 pound whipped = 3 cups

Diet margarine
1 cup = ½ cup butter or stick margarine
        (in cooking)

Vegetable oil
16 ounces = 2 cups

Vegetable shortening
1 pound = 2⅓ cups

FLOURS

Rye (medium)
1 pound = 4½ cups

White, all-purpose
1 pound = 3½ cups unsifted
      = 4 cups sifted
1 cup = ½ cup barley flour
      = 1⅛ cups cake flour
      = 1 cup corn meal
      = ½ cup potato flour
      = ⅞ cup rice flour
      = 1½ cups rye flour
      = 1½ cups oat flour
      = ¾ cup gluten flour

Whole wheat
1 pound = 3⅓ to 3¾ cups

FRUITS

Apples
1 pound = 3 medium
      = 3 cups slices or diced pieces

Apricots
1 pound fresh = about 10 medium
      = 3 cups cooked
1 pound dried = 3 cups dry
      = 4½ cups cooked

Bananas
1 pound = 3 to 4 medium
      = 2 cups slices
      = 1½ cups mashed

Berries (blueberries, strawberries, etc.)
1 pint = 2 cups

Cherries
1 pound = 2 cups pitted

Coconut
3½ ounces flaked = 1⅓ cups

Cranberries
12 ounces = 3 cups raw

Currants (dried)
1 pound = 3 cups

Dates
1 pound = 2½ cups pitted

Grapefruit
1 pound = 2 cups sections (approximately)

Grapes
1 pound seedless = 2½ cups

Lemon
1 whole = 2 to 4 tablespoons juice
      = 2 teaspoons grated rind
1 dozen = about 2½ to 5 cups juice

Lime
1 whole = 1½ to 2 tablespoons juice
      = 1 to 1½ teaspoons grated rind

Oranges
1 medium = about 6 tablespoons juice
      = about 2 tablespoons grated rind

Peaches
1 pound = 4 to 6 peaches
      = 2 cups slices

Pears
1 pound = 3 to 5 pears
      = 2 cups slices

Pineapple
2 pounds fresh = 3 cups cubes

Plums
1 pound fresh = 2 cups cooked

Prunes
1 pound raw = 2¼ cups pitted

Raisins
1 pound = 2¾ to 3 cups

Rhubarb
1 pound fresh = 3½ cups cut raw
      = 2 cups cooked

MILK

Dry
1 to 1⅓ cups = 1 quart reconstituted
¼ to ⅓ cup powder = 1 cup reconstituted

Evaporated
1 13-ounce can = nearly 1⅓ cups

Fresh (whole, low-fat, or skim)
1 quart = 4 cups

NUTS

Almonds
1 cup = 6 ounces whole
　　　 = 5⅓ ounces blanched
1 pound unshelled = 1 to 1½ cups shelled
1 pound shelled = 3¼ cups

Peanuts
1 pound unshelled = 2 cups shelled
1 pound shelled = 4 cups

Pecans
1 pound unshelled = 2¼ cups shelled
1 pound shelled = 3½ cups

Walnuts
1 pound unshelled = 2 cups shelled
1 pound shelled = 3½ cups
NOTE: For most nuts, 1 cup whole (about ¼ pound) approximately equals 1 cup chopped

SWEETENERS

Brown sugar (packed)
1 pound = 2¼ cups
1 cup = 1 cup granulated sugar plus
　　　 ¼ cup molasses

Corn syrup
1½ cups = 1 cup granulated sugar

Granulated (white) sugar
1 pound = 2 cups (approximately)

Honey
1 pound = 1⅓ cups
　　　 = 1⅔ cups sugar

Confectioners' (powdered) sugar
1 pound = 4½ cups unsifted
1¾ cups packed = 1 cup granulated

VEGETABLES

Asparagus
1 pound spears = 3½ to 4 cups cooked

Avocados
1 pound = 2½ cups cubes

Beans, green or wax
1 pound = 2½ to 3 cups cooked

Beets
1 pound = 2 cups cooked, diced or sliced

Broccoli
1 pound head = 2 cups cooked flowerets

Brussels sprouts
1 pound = 3 cups cooked

Cabbage
1 pound = 6 cups shredded (packed)
　　　 = 2 to 3 cups cooked

Carrots
1 pound = 3 cups sliced
　　　 = 2½ cups shredded

Cauliflower
1 pound = 1½ to 2 cups cooked

Celery
1¼-pound bunch = 3 cups diced raw
　　　　　　　 = 2 cups cooked
2 medium ribs = 3 to 4 ounces
　　　　　　 = ¾ to 1 cup sliced

Corn
2 large ears = 1½ cups kernels
4 medium ears = 2 cups kernels
10 ounces frozen kernels = 2 cups

Eggplant
1 pound = 15 ⅓-inch slices
　　　 = 4½ cups raw diced
　　　 = 1¾ cups cooked diced
　　　 = 3 cups raw chopped

Garlic
1 large head = 10 to 15 cloves
1 small clove = ½ teaspoon minced
　　　　　　 = ⅛ teaspoon garlic powder
1 medium clove = ¾ teaspoon minced
1 large clove = 1 teaspoon minced
1 tablespoon minced = 3 large cloves

Mushrooms
1 pound fresh = 5 to 6 cups sliced
6 ounces canned = 1 pound fresh
3 ounces dried = 1 pound fresh

Okra
1 pound fresh = 2¼ cups cooked

Onions
1 pound = 3 large
1 large = 1 cup diced or chopped
1 medium = ⅔ cup chopped
1 small = ⅓ cup chopped

Parsnips
1 pound = 4 medium
= 2½ cups cooked and diced

Peas
1 pound in pods = 1 cup shelled and cooked
10 ounces frozen = 2 cups

Potatoes
1 pound = 3 medium
= 3½ cups raw sliced or diced
= 2 cups cooked and mashed

Rutabagas and turnips
1 pound = 2⅔ cups cooked and diced
= 2 cups mashed

Spinach and similar greens
1 pound fresh = 4 to 8 cups raw leaves
= 1½ to 2 cups cooked
10 ounces frozen = 1½ cups cooked
= 1 cup well drained

Squash, summer (e.g., zucchini)
1 pound = 3 cups raw slices
= 1½ cups cooked
= 2½ cups shredded

Squash, winter (e.g., Hubbard)
1 pound = 1 cup cooked mashed

Tomatoes
1 pound fresh = 2 large or 4 small
= 2 cups diced
1 pound seeded, chopped = 1½ cups pulp

16-ounce can, drained = 1¼ cups
28-ounce can, drained = 2 cups
35-ounce can, drained = 2½ cups

MISCELLANEOUS

Chocolate, baker's
1 square = 1 ounce
= 3 to 4 tablespoons grated

Chocolate chips
6 ounces = 1 cup

Cocoa
8 ounces = 2 cups

Coffee
1 pound = 40 cups brewed (approximately)

Gelatin
1 envelope unflavored = ¼ ounce
= 1 scant tablespoon

Herbs
1 tablespoon fresh = ½ to 1 teaspoon dried

Horseradish
1 tablespoon freshly grated = 2 tablespoons
bottled

Meat
1 pound boneless = 2 cups ground

Tea
1 pound leaves = 125 cups tea (approximately)

Yeast
1 package dry active = 1 scant tablespoon

Basic Measurements

VOLUME MEASURES

Pinch = about 1/16 teaspoon
Dash = 6 drops or about 1/8 teaspoon
3 teaspoons = 1 tablespoon
2 tablespoons = 1/8 cup or 1 fluid ounce
4 tablespoons = 1/4 cup or 2 ounces
5 1/3 tablespoons = 1/3 cup
8 tablespoons = 1/2 cup or 4 ounces
10 2/3 tablespoons = 2/3 cup
12 tablespoons = 3/4 cup or 6 ounces
16 tablespoons = 1 cup or 1/2 pint or 8 ounces
1 pint = 2 cups or 16 ounces
2 pints = 4 cups or 1 quart or 32 ounces
1 liter = 1 quart plus 3 ounces
1 jigger = 1 1/2 ounces

CAPACITIES

Square cake pans
$8 \times 8 \times 2$ inches = 6 cups
$9 \times 9 \times 1 \frac{1}{2}$ inches = 8 cups
$9 \times 9 \times 2$ inches = 10 cups

Round cake pans
$8 \times 1 \frac{1}{2}$ inches = 4 cups
$9 \times 1 \frac{1}{2}$ inches = 6 cups

Pie plates
$8 \times 1 \frac{1}{4}$ inches = 3 level cups
$9 \times 1 \frac{1}{2}$ inches = 4 level cups

Loaf pans
$8 \frac{1}{2} \times 4 \frac{1}{2} \times 2 \frac{1}{2}$ inches = 6 cups
$9 \times 5 \times 3$ inches = 8 cups

WEIGHTS

2 ounces = 1/8 pound
4 ounces = 1/4 pound
8 ounces = 1/2 pound
16 ounces = 1 pound

Recipes

DRINKS

A near-revolution seems to have taken place in people's drinking habits in the last decade or so. Where in years past a typical party ended with half a dozen empty liquor bottles, these days almost no one I know drinks more than one hard-liquor drink an evening. Even wine and beer consumption have dropped off considerably. Now I worry about running out of seltzer and sparkling mineral water, which I buy by the case. A growing awareness of "empty" calories, the anti-drug mentality, concern about the sometimes ugly consequences of drinking and driving, and social acceptance of—even admiration for—the greatly expanded market of alcohol-free drinks have conspired to reduce alcohol consumption, much to the nation's benefit.

Still, there are times when an alcohol-containing drink is desired and desirable, considering that in moderation (one drink a day) alcohol may actually be beneficial to health. Thus, I offer some that I and my tasters found to be delicious as well as reasonably healthful. I also offer some nonalcoholic beverages that are meant to be consumed as substantial between-meal snacks or as part of breakfast, brunch, or lunch.

Skoal!

TWIST OF O.J.

4 servings

A delicious alternative to ordinary orange juice that is minimally sweetened by the grenadine. It is lovely for a breakfast or luncheon or simply as a summer refresher.

Preparation tips: If fresh orange juice is unavailable, you can use reconstituted frozen concentrate. As for the pineapple juice, frozen is preferable to canned.

    4 cups fresh orange juice
 1½ cups unsweetened pineapple juice
 ½ cup fresh lemon juice
    2 tablespoons grenadine

In a 2-quart pitcher, combine the ingredients. Serve the drink over ice cubes.

ORANGE SUNRISE

about 5 cups

The addition of strawberries gives the juice a marvelous color and flavor.

 1 quart freshly squeezed orange juice
 1 cup frozen sliced strawberries (*not* packed in
   syrup)

In a blender, combine the juice and strawberries (they do not have to be thawed), and process the ingredients until they are smooth. If desired, strain the mixture into a pitcher, and chill the beverage until serving time.

GRAPEFRUIT-PINEAPPLE SLUSH

6 servings

This beverage is derived from a refresher (*sans* alcohol) that one of my tennis pals, Eddie Goldman, adores. It can be enjoyed without the tequila, if you prefer.

2½ cups pink grapefruit juice
2½ cups unsweetened pineapple juice
 ½ cup cranberry-juice cocktail
 ⅓ cup tequila (optional)

 1. Combine the ingredients in a pitcher or bowl. Pour all but 1 cup of the mixture into ice-cube trays (preferably metal) fitted with dividers, and freeze it for several hours or up to 2 days. Store the remaining juice mixture in the refrigerator.
 2. At serving time, place the frozen juice cubes in a blender (in batches) or food processor. Add an appropriate amount of the reserved refrigerated juice to each batch, and blend the mixture until it is smooth but still frozen.

SOUTH-OF-THE-BORDER CIDER

8 servings

A tasty but not too deadly drink that can warm you inside out.

Preparation tips: You can use apple juice, if cider is unavailable. And you can set up in advance the first three ingredients in one container and the alcohol in a second to heat just before serving.

 5 cups apple cider
 ¼ cup fresh lemon juice
 ½ teaspoon salt
1⅔ cups tequila

⅓ **cup orange-flavored liqueur**
8 **slices lemon for garnish**

1. In a 3-quart saucepan, combine the cider, lemon juice, and salt. Bring the ingredients to a simmer, and skim the surface, if needed.
2. Add the tequila and orange liqueur, and heat the mixture, stirring it, over medium heat until it is hot.
3. Divide the cider among 8 heated mugs, garnishing each serving with a lemon slice.

MULLED CIDER WITH APPLE BRANDY   *16 servings*

Another lovely cider for a chilly winter night that is not as potent as the South-of-the-Border Cider.

Preparation tip: Simmer the cider in advance of serving time. Then bring the cider back to a simmer before adding the alcohol.

1 **gallon (16 cups) fresh apple cider**
2 **cinnamon sticks**
12 **cloves**
4 **cardamom pods**
1½ **cups apple brandy or applejack**
Slices lemon and orange for garnish (optional)

1. Place the apple cider in a large kettle.
2. Tie together in a cheesecloth bag the cinnamon sticks, cloves, and cardamom pods, and add this to the cider. Simmer the cider for 30 minutes to 3 hours (longer is better). Skim the cider, if necessary.
3. At serving time, return the cider to a simmer, and stir in the apple brandy or applejack. Again, bring the cider to a simmer, and serve the drinks in mugs—heated, if possible, and garnished with lemon and orange slices, if desired.

TROPICAL BREAKFAST TREAT   *2 servings*

A refreshing, nutritious, low-calorie breakfast drink that is ideal for you and your breakfast guests during the hot days of early summer, when succulent mangoes are in season.

- 1 ripe mango, skinned and sliced
- 1 banana, peeled
- 1 cup plain nonfat or low-fat yogurt
- 1 cup skim or low-fat milk
- 2 ice cubes

Place the ingredients in a blender jar, and process them to the consistency of a thick milk shake. Divide the mixture between two tall glasses, adding more ice cubes, if desired.

INDIAN BREAKFAST DRINK   *2 servings*

This popular yogurt-based drink, called lassi in India, is a refreshing change for you or breakfast guests.

Preparation tips: Lassi can be made with any fruit juice, such as apple, pineapple, pear. It is best if the juice is fresh. The more ice you add, the thinner the drink will be.

- 1 cup plain nonfat or low-fat yogurt
- 1 cup fresh fruit juice
- 2 bananas
- 1 to 2 teaspoons honey *or* sugar, to taste
- ¼ teaspoon cinnamon *or* nutmeg
- 2 ice cubes or more, to taste

Combine the ingredients in a blender, and process them at medium-high speed until the mixture is smooth.

HORS D'OEUVRES AND APPETIZERS

No doubt, many of you are accustomed to overindulging in rich hors d'oeuvres—dips and chips, pâtés, stuffed pastry shells, cheese and crackers, etc. After all, you reason, they're so small! But if you're too liberal with the ingredients in hors d'oeuvres, you can do your guests a considerable disservice in terms of fat, cholesterol, and calories before they even start the meal.

I included many tasty and eye-appealing meal openers in *Jane Brody's Good Food Book* that paid more than a passing nod to good nutrition. I have since found many others. I repeat only the Vegetable Platter and Tortilla Chips for those who may have missed them the first time, since they are standard fare at most of my parties.

THE VEGETABLE PLATTER

Nothing has done more to improve the nutritional value of the American cocktail party and to turn it into a feast for the eye as well as the palate than the vegetable platter, known in culinary circles as crudités. Crunchy raw and tender-crisp vegetables are a low-calorie, high-nutrient, and delicious way to curb your hunger and calm your nerves at such affairs. And if served with dips that are low in fat but high in flavor, you can eat as much of these hors d'oeuvres as you please.

Preparation tips: Be sure to include a variety of colors and shapes to maximize the platter's aesthetic appeal. Arrange the platter in an artistic fashion, if that is your bent.

Asparagus, steamed tender-crisp
Beet slices, cooked
Belgian endive leaves
Broccoli, raw or blanched
Brussels sprouts (tiny), steamed or boiled tender-crisp
Carrot sticks
Cauliflower flowerets, raw or blanched
Celery sticks
Cherry tomatoes
Cucumber slices
Green beans, whole and steamed tender-crisp
Kohlrabi strips, raw (if tender) or blanched
Mushrooms, whole raw
Pea pods, sugar snap or snow, raw or steamed tender-crisp
Pepper strips, red, green, and yellow
Radishes, sliced or whole
Scallions, roots trimmed, green leaves slit lengthwise
Turnip sticks
Zucchini strips

TORTILLA CHIPS FOR DIPS

80 chips
(from 10 tortillas)

You need not rely on fatty fried and/or overly salted commercial tortilla chips. It's a snap to make your own low-fat, no-salt-added chips that enhance, not disguise, the flavor of a delicious dip.

Preparation tip: Be sure you don't go too far from the stove while the chips are in the oven, lest they become overbaked.

2 tablespoons oil
1 package flour tortillas *or* corn tortillas

1. Preheat the oven to 350° F.
2. With a pastry brush, paint a very light coating of oil on one side of each tortilla. Stack the tortillas, oiled side up, in an even pile. With a sharp, heavy knife (or serrated-edged knife), cut the stack in half, then in quarters, then in eighths.
3. Separate the pieces, and arrange them, oiled side up, on lightly oiled baking sheets. Toast the chips in the oven for 10 minutes or until the chips are crisp and are beginning to brown lightly.

CHILI DIP

about 1¼ cups

This dip is simple, tangy, and low in salt.

  1 cup plain low-fat yogurt
  ¼ cup bottled chili sauce (*not* the Chinese variety)
  1 small clove garlic, peeled and crushed
Dash Worcestershire sauce
Freshly ground black pepper, to taste
  1 scallion, finely minced

Combine the ingredients in a bowl, and chill the dip well before serving time.

TAHINI DIP

about 1½ cups

This delicious dip, which disappeared fast at my tasting, is a Mollie Katzen recipe from *The Enchanted Broccoli Forest.*

  1 cup tahini (sesame paste)
  ⅓ cup apple juice
  3 tablespoons cider vinegar
  2 medium cloves garlic, peeled and crushed
  ½ teaspoon salt (optional)
  ½ teaspoon ground cumin
  ¼ teaspoon cinnamon
  ¼ teaspoon cayenne

1. In a medium-sized bowl, beat the tahini at high speed with an electric mixer for 5 minutes. Continue beating the tahini, and drizzle in the apple juice and vinegar.
2. Stir in the remaining ingredients. Serve the dip at room temperature.

TOFU-SESAME DIP

about 1 cup

This is another of Mollie Katzen's gems, lower in calories than the Tahini Dip but just as delicious.

  2 tablespoons cider vinegar
  2 tablespoons water
  1 tablespoon tamari *or* imported soy sauce
  1 tablespoon Chinese sesame oil
  1 small clove garlic, peeled and crushed
  1 tablespoon lemon juice
  1 cake (¼ pound) tofu (bean curd)
  ¼ cup tahini (sesame paste)
  1 scallion (including the green top), finely minced
  ¼ cup packed minced fresh parsley
Freshly ground black pepper to taste
Cayenne pepper to taste

1. In a blender or food processor, purée the vinegar, water, tamari or soy sauce, sesame oil, garlic, lemon juice, and tofu.
2. Whisk the tahini in a bowl for a few minutes, and beat it into the purée.
3. Stir into the mixture the scallion, parsley, pepper, and cayenne. Cover the dip, and chill it thoroughly before serving it.

WHITE BEAN DIP

about 1¼ cups

Bean dips definitely needed added pizzazz to make their flavor match their nutritional worth. I think you'll agree that this dip makes it.

Serving suggestion: Serve this dip with various firm crudités like sweet red and green peppers, celery, fennel, and carrots.

  1 16-ounce can cannellini *or* white kidney beans,
      drained and rinsed
  4 large cloves garlic, boiled for 5 minutes, then
      peeled and sliced
  1 tablespoon olive oil
  2 teaspoons fresh lemon juice
  ¼ to ½ teaspoon hot pepper sauce
  1 to 2 teaspoons minced jalapeños (fresh or
      canned), or to taste

Combine the ingredients in a food processor, blending them until they are smooth.

SPINACH DIP

about 1½ cups

This very low-fat dip has a mild Roquefort flavor that really enhances fresh vegetables that have been steamed tender-crisp and then chilled.

Serving suggestion: Serve this dip with carrots, green beans, cauliflower, or broccoli that have been steamed tender-crisp.

 1 large clove garlic, peeled and minced
 1 tablespoon olive oil
 1 10-ounce package frozen chopped spinach,
   thawed and squeezed to remove excess liquid
 ½ cup plain nonfat or low-fat yogurt
 ⅓ cup grated Parmesan
 ¼ teaspoon salt
 ¼ teaspoon pepper

1. In a small skillet over low heat, sauté the garlic in the oil for 1 minute or until the garlic is tender (be careful not to burn the garlic).
2. Combine the garlic and oil with the remaining ingredients in a blender or food processor, processing the ingredients until they are smooth. Cover the dip, and chill it until serving time.

DOUBLY HOT CHEESE DIP

about 2 cups

This dip is high in calcium and flavor, and, although it is more caloric than most, a little goes a long way. It is excellent with unsalted Tortilla Chips (see page 44).

Preparation tips: The ingredients can be mixed together in advance and heated just before serving time. If the prepared dip will be sitting on the table for a long time, serve it in a small chafing dish over boiling water or in a fondue pot to keep the cheese melted.

    1 cup skim or low-fat milk
    4 ounces grated Monterey Jack (about 1 cup)
    4 ounces grated sharp Cheddar (about 1 cup)
    1 cup fresh bread crumbs
    ¼ cup minced fresh parsley
    2 tablespoons minced jalapeños (fresh or canned),
      or to taste
    1 tablespoon Dijon-style mustard
    1 teaspoon Worcestershire sauce
    Cayenne pepper to taste (optional)

1. Bring a few inches of water to boil in the bottom of a double boiler. In the top half of the pot, combine the milk, cheeses, and bread crumbs. Heat the mixture, stirring it often, until the cheese melts.
2. Stir in the parsley, jalapeños, mustard, Worcestershire sauce, and cayenne (if desired). Serve the dip hot.

HUMMUS

about 2½ cups

This dip or spread is a perennial favorite. Whenever I serve it at a party, it's always the one that disappears first, so I often double the recipe. This version is simpler than the one I offered in *Jane Brody's Good Food Book,* but it is equally delicious.

Preparation tips: Although easiest to prepare in a food processor, the hummus can also be made in a blender, in batches, or the chickpeas can be puréed in a food mill. The hummus can be made days—even a week—ahead and refrigerated, covered, until it is needed.

Serving suggestions: Serve the hummus at room temperature in a small bowl with an hors d'oeuvre knife, surrounding it with vegetable "spoons" like carrots and zucchinis sliced diagonally, sections of celery, blanched snow peas, and wedges of green and red peppers. Also offer triangles of pita, crosswise slices of plum tomatoes, and small sprigs of parsley for those who wish to make mini-sandwiches.

1⅔ cups (1 15-ounce can) cooked chickpeas,
    drained and the liquid reserved
 ¼ cup tahini (sesame paste)
 ¼ cup lemon juice
Water, if needed
  3 large cloves garlic, peeled and crushed
 ½ teaspoon ground coriander
 ¼ teaspoon cumin
 ¼ teaspoon paprika
Dash cayenne
 ¼ cup minced scallions
  2 tablespoons minced fresh parsley for garnish

1. In a blender, in batches, or in a food processor, process the chickpeas, tahini, and lemon juice until the mixture reaches the consistency of a coarse paste; use as much of the chickpea liquid and/or water as needed.
2. Add the garlic, coriander, cumin, paprika, and cayenne, and process the ingredients again to combine them thoroughly. Transfer the hummus to a bowl, and stir in the scallions.
3. Cover the hummus, and chill it until 1 hour before serving time, adding the parsley garnish just before serving the dip.

BABA GHANOUSH

about 2 cups

This "baba," which has more texture than most, was devoured at a Memorial Day barbecue. The fat content of traditional recipes was reduced by using non-fat yogurt in place of some of the tahini and the olive oil. Martha Rose Shulman, author of *Mediterranean Light,* devised the dish and gave me the best method I've yet tried for roasting an eggplant.

Preparation tips: To avoid bitterness, seed the eggplant before mashing it, drain off some of the juice after mashing it, and mince rather than crush the garlic. If you want to prepare this a day ahead, add the tomato, green pepper, seasonings, and parsley shortly before serving. To speed preparation, while the eggplant bakes, prepare the rest of the ingredients.

Serving suggestion: Scoop up the dip with tortilla chips (preferably home-made, see page 44) and raw vegetables or triangles of pita.

  2 **pounds eggplant, halved lengthwise**
¼ **cup plain nonfat or low-fat yogurt**
¼ **cup fresh lemon juice**
  2 **tablespoons tahini (sesame paste)**
  1 **or 2 large cloves garlic, peeled and finely
     minced**
  1 **medium tomato, finely diced**
  1 **medium sweet green pepper, cored, seeded, and
     finely diced**
½ **teaspoon salt, or to taste (optional)**
½ **teaspoon sugar (optional)**
Freshly ground black pepper to taste
  2 **tablespoons minced fresh parsley for garnish**

1. Preheat the oven to 450° F.
2. Make three or four slashes in the cut side of the eggplant to, but not through, the skin. Roast the eggplant in the oven, cut sides down, on an oiled baking sheet for 25 minutes or until the skin is charred. Remove the eggplant from the oven, and let it cool.
3. When the eggplant is cool enough to handle, scoop out and discard the seeds, and mash the flesh in a medium-sized bowl.
4. Stir in the yogurt, lemon juice, tahini, garlic, tomato, green pepper, salt (if desired), sugar (if using), and black pepper, and combine the ingredients thoroughly. Transfer the dip to a serving bowl, cover it, and chill it until 30 minutes before serving time. Sprinkle the dip with the parsley.

GUACAMOLE GRANDE

about 2 cups

My tasters, when asked about possible improvements, said: "Don't mess with it. It's terrific as is." I think you'll agree.

Preparation tips: To slow discoloration of the avocado, place the pit in the center of the bowl after preparation of the dip, cover the bowl tightly with plastic wrap, and refrigerate the guacamole. Another trick that allows for advance preparation is to combine all the ingredients *except* the avocado, which you should mash and add to the mixture an hour or two before serving the guacamole. To preserve the crunch of the pumpkinseeds, add them shortly before serving the dip as well. You can use canned jalapeños or chilies in place of fresh ones.

Serving suggestion: Serve the guacamole with tortilla chips, toasted pita triangles, or cut-up vegetables.

    ½ cup onion (preferably red onion), peeled and
         finely chopped
    2 small firm tomatoes (plum tomatoes are best),
         finely diced
    2 small jalapeños (2 tablespoons), seeded and
         minced, or to taste
    2 tablespoons fresh lime juice
    1 large clove garlic, peeled and minced
    2 tablespoons finely chopped Italian parsley *or* 1
         tablespoon cilantro
    ¼ teaspoon salt
Dash or more hot pepper sauce
    2 large ripe avocados, peeled, pitted, and mashed
    3 tablespoons pumpkinseeds (pepitas), toasted
         (optional)

Combine the ingredients in a medium-sized bowl, placing the avocado pit in the center of the dip. Cover the bowl, and chill the guacamole until serving time.

BLACK BEAN AND SALMON SPREAD   *2½ cups*

My good friend Betty Marks included her version of this unusual, colorful, tasty, and nutritious spread in *The High-Calcium Low-Calorie Cookbook.*

Preparation tip: The hotness of the spread can be adjusted by adding more or less pepper flakes and cayenne.

Serving suggestion: Serve this spread as an hors d'oeuvre with toasted tortilla triangles, wedges of firm vegetables, or whole-wheat pita. Or serve the dish on a bed of lettuce as a first course.

  1　7-ounce can pink salmon with bones, drained
1⅔　cups (1 15- or 16-ounce can) black beans,
　　　drained and rinsed
  ½　teaspoon grated lime rind
  ¼　cup fresh lime juice
  2　tablespoons olive oil *or* canola oil
  ¼　cup chopped fresh parsley (preferably Italian)
  1　tablespoon minced onion *or* minced scallion
  1　tablespoons minced celery
  1　teaspoon minced garlic (1 large clove)
  ¾　teaspoon cumin
  ¼　teaspoon hot red pepper flakes
  ¼　teaspoon cayenne

In a medium-sized bowl, flake the salmon with a fork. Add the remaining ingredients, stirring them to combine them well. Chill the spread for 1 hour or more before serving it.

MACKEREL SPREAD   *about 1½ cups*

Easy to prepare and nutritious, a good hors d'oeuvre to serve to health-conscious guests.

  2　4¾-ounce cans water-packed mackerel fillets,
　　　drained
  1　to 2 teaspoons prepared mustard, to taste
  ⅓　to ½ cup plain nonfat or low-fat yogurt
  ¼　cup minced fresh parsley
  ¼　cup minced scallions
  2　tablespoons white wine (optional)

Mash the fillets in a medium-sized bowl. Add the remaining ingredients, and combine them well. Chill the spread before serving it.

SARDINE SPREAD

about 2 cups

Friend and "taster supreme" Betty Marks devised this make-ahead spread for *The High-Calcium Low-Calorie Cookbook.* It has a nice, not-too-fishy flavor and is packed with calcium but is low in fat. See also its kissing cousin, Mackerel Spread, on page 52.

Preparation tips: Be sure to grate the lemon rind before cutting the fruit or squeezing out the juice. To use the spread as a dip, add more yogurt until the desired consistency is reached.

Serving suggestion: Serve the spread with low-salt crackers or crudités.

   1 3¾-ounce can water-packed sardines with
      bones, drained
   2 tablespoons plain nonfat or low-fat yogurt
   2 tablespoons grated Parmesan
   1 tablespoon chopped scallion
1½ teaspoons Dijon-style mustard
   1 teaspoon grated lemon rind
   3 teaspoons fresh lemon juice
Freshly ground black pepper to taste
Dash or more cayenne, to taste
   1 teaspoon toasted sesame seeds

   1. Mash the sardines with a fork, and combine them well with the remaining ingredients *except* the sesame seeds.
   2. Place the spread in a small bowl, and sprinkle the spread with the sesame seeds. Chill the spread for several hours.

SUN-DRIED TOMATO SPREAD

about 1 cup

I originally prepared this recipe from *Health* magazine to use up some sun-dried tomatoes I had received as a gift. But after raves from my tasters, I had to search for a new supply of tomatoes. Jessica Zachs, a caterer from Avon, Connecticut, devised the recipe.

Preparation tips: Note that the tomatoes should marinate for at least 5 days before you make the spread, which can be prepared days before you use it and refrigerated or weeks before you use it and frozen.

¼ pound loose (dry) sun-dried tomatoes
Warm water to cover
2 large cloves garlic, divided
2 tablespoons olive oil
⅛ teaspoon hot pepper flakes
1 bay leaf
¼ cup packed grated Parmesan

1. Up to 2 weeks and at least 5 days in advance, rinse the tomatoes to remove any debris, and place them in a bowl covered with the warm water. Let them soak for 10 minutes, drain them, and soak them again for another 10 minutes. Transfer the drained tomatoes to a steamer rack, and steam them over boiling water for 7 minutes or until they are plumped. Transfer the tomatoes to a clean, quart-sized glass jar with a tight-fitting lid.
2. Peel and mince 1 of the cloves of garlic, and add it with the oil, pepper flakes, and bay leaf to the jar. Cover the jar tightly, and shake it to combine the ingredients thoroughly. Set the tomatoes aside for at least 5 days to marinate, shaking the jar once a day.
3. After 5 or more days, remove the bay leaf, and transfer the contents of the jar to a blender or food processor. Peel and mince the remaining clove of garlic, and add it and the Parmesan to the tomato mixture. Blend the mixture until it is smooth.

TERRIFIC TURKEY SPREAD

about 2 cups

Nancy Cooper, a registered dietitian at the International Diabetes Center in Minneapolis, has come up with many delicious yet healthful recipes, including this simple one, originally published in *Diabetes Self-Management* magazine.

Preparation tips: You can use home-cooked turkey or deli-style turkey. The dish is at its best when the turkey is combined with the onion in a food processor, but the two ingredients can also be chopped together by hand.

6 ounces cooked turkey breast, cut into small
  pieces
⅓ cup finely chopped onion
¼ cup packed grated carrot
¼ cup finely chopped apple
⅓ cup plain nonfat or low-fat yogurt
1 tablespoon mayonnaise (optional)
1 tablespoon lemon juice
¼ teaspoon curry powder

1. Process the turkey and onion together in food processor, or chop them together by hand.
2. To the turkey and onion, add the remaining ingredients, mixing them well. Chill the spread before serving it.

PARTY PÂTÉ
3 to 4 cups

Some may find this spread too sweet, but most of my tasters loved the flavor. The final dish has the color and consistency of liver pâté.

1 teaspoon vegetable oil
1 large clove garlic, peeled and minced
1 pound raw ground turkey meat
½ cup sliced scallions (about 4)
¼ cup sesame seeds, lightly toasted
1 cup cooked chickpeas (about 8 ounces)
½ cup golden raisins
⅓ cup apple juice
¾ teaspoon hot pepper sauce
¾ teaspoon salt (optional)
¼ teaspoon allspice

1. In a large nonstick skillet, heat the oil, and sauté the garlic for about 30 seconds. Add the turkey and scallions, and cook the mixture over medium heat until it is done, frequently turning it with a spatula to break up the pieces.
2. Place the cooked turkey mixture in a food processor or blender. Add the remaining ingredients, and process the spread until it is smooth.
3. Spray a 1-quart mold or loaf pan with vegetable oil, and press the turkey mixture into it. Cover the pâté with plastic wrap, and chill it for 1 hour or longer before unmolding it.

CHRISTMAS PÂTÉ

This is a beautiful hors d'oeuvre in layers of red, white, and green. But since it takes a lot of effort, it is best prepared for someone else's party, when you have but a single dish to make. The recipe is adapted from one originally published in *Family Circle* magazine.

Preparation tips: The tomato layer (the best, in my view) would make a lovely dish on its own with cooked bay scallops, half tomato juice and half V8 juice, and a little more gelatin. The three-layer pâté is tricky to slice if unmolded. I would recommend using a glass pan and slicing the pâté while it is still in the pan.

SPINACH LAYER
- 1 envelope (1 scant tablespoon) unflavored gelatin
- ¼ cup cold water
- 2 10-ounce packages frozen chopped spinach, thawed and well drained
- ½ cup minced scallions
- ½ teaspoon nutmeg
- ¼ teaspoon salt (optional)

CHICKEN LAYER
- 1 envelope (1 scant tablespoon) unflavored gelatin
- ¼ cup cold water
- ½ cup chopped onion (1 medium)
- ¼ pound mushrooms, chopped (1 cup)
- 1 pound boneless, skinless chicken breasts cut into ½-inch cubes
- 1 tablespoon butter *or* margarine
- 2 teaspoons dry sherry
- ½ teaspoon dried basil, crumbled

TOMATO LAYER
- 1½ envelopes (4 teaspoons) unflavored gelatin
- ¼ cup cold water
- 2 cups tomato juice *or* 1 cup each tomato juice and V8
- 1 red bell pepper, cored, seeded, and chopped
- 1 canned green chili *or* jalapeño, seeded and minced
- 3 cloves garlic, peeled and minced
- 2 tablespoons lime juice
- 2 tablespoons red-wine vinegar
- 1 teaspoon drained prepared horseradish
- ¼ teaspoon pepper

TO PREPARE THE SPINACH LAYER
1. In a medium-sized heatproof bowl, sprinkle the gelatin over the cold water, and let the ingredients stand for about 5 minutes. Then heat the gelatin over boiling water, stirring the mixture until the gelatin dissolves. Combine the gelatin mixture with the remaining ingredients for the spinach layer. Pour

this mixture into a 9-inch square pan that has been lined with foil or heavy plastic wrap and then sprayed with vegetable oil. Refrigerate the spinach layer while you prepare the chicken layer.

TO PREPARE THE CHICKEN LAYER

2. In a medium-sized heatproof bowl, sprinkle the gelatin over the water, and let the ingredients stand for about 5 minutes. Then heat the gelatin over boiling water, stirring the mixture until the gelatin dissolves.
3. Meanwhile, in a medium-sized skillet, sauté the onion, mushrooms, and chicken in the butter or margarine until the ingredients are just tender. Add the sherry and basil, and cook the ingredients 5 minutes longer.
4. Add the skillet ingredients to the dissolved gelatin, and mix everything well. When the spinach layer is firm, remove it from the refrigerator, and carefully spread the chicken layer over it. Refrigerate the two layers while you prepare the tomato layer.

TO PREPARE THE TOMATO LAYER

5. In a medium-sized heatproof bowl, sprinkle the gelatin over the water, and let the ingredients stand for about 5 minutes. Then heat the gelatin over boiling water, stirring the mixture until the gelatin dissolves. Add the remaining ingredients to the gelatin, and mix everything well. When the chicken layer is firm enough, remove it from the refrigerator, and pour the tomato-juice mixture over it. Refrigerate the pâté for 4 hours or until the entire dish is very firm.

TO SERVE THE PÂTÉ

6. Either unmold the pâté onto a platter, or leave it in the pan, slice it into 1½ inches cubes, and arrange the pieces attractively on a serving dish.

EGGPLANT SPREAD

about 1½ cups

This quick-to-prepare, rich-tasting spread is remarkably fat-free if made with nonfat yogurt.

Preparation tip: The microwave oven is ideal for cooking the eggplant without oil, but the eggplant can also be prepared in a traditional oven (see page 50). In the latter case, boil the unpeeled garlic in water for 5 minutes.

    1 to 1¼ pounds eggplant, halved lengthwise
    1 large clove garlic, unpeeled
  Pinch plus ⅛ teaspoon salt, or to taste, divided (optional)
    3 tablespoons plain nonfat or low-fat yogurt
  ¼ teaspoon cumin
  Pinch cayenne, or to taste
    2 tablespoons chopped fresh parsley

1. Place the eggplant, cut sides up, and garlic in a microwave-safe plastic bag; tuck the opening under, but do not seal the bag. Cook the vegetables on high for 1 to 2 minutes to soften the garlic slightly. Remove the garlic, setting it aside, and continue to cook the eggplant for another 10 to 12 minutes or until it is soft.
2. Peel the garlic, and either mash it in a medium-sized bowl with the pinch of salt or put it through a garlic press.
3. Remove the eggplant from the microwave. Scrape the pulp from the skin into the bowl, discard the skin, and mash the pulp with a pastry blender or two knives. Stir in the yogurt, cumin, cayenne, parsley, and the remaining ⅛ teaspoon salt (if desired).

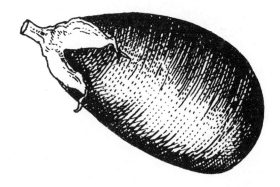

WALNUT SPREAD

about 2 cups

Gwennyth Noroian of Dinuba, California, devised this rich-tasting yet wholesome hors d'oeuvre. I added the coriander.

Preparation tips: This spread can be made days ahead and kept chilled. But allow it to come to room temperature before serving it. If you prefer hot foods, double the cayenne.

Serving suggestion: Serve with lavash (Armenian flat bread), pita, crackers, or firm crudités.

  2 **cups fine fresh bread crumbs (from French or**
     Italian bread)
  2 **cups finely chopped walnuts**
1½ **teaspoons cumin**
1½ **teaspoons paprika**
 ¾ **teaspoon coriander**
 ¼ **teaspoon cayenne, or to taste**
 ¼ **cup fresh lemon juice**
  2 **tablespoons vegetable oil (optional)**
 ½ **teaspoon salt**
  3 **to 4 tablespoons water or more**

1. In a food processor, blend the bread crumbs, walnuts, cumin, paprika, coriander, cayenne, lemon juice, oil (if using), and salt until the mixture is just combined.
2. Add the water, and blend the mixture until it is smooth, adding additional water, if necessary, to achieve a spreadable consistency.

MUSHROOM PÂTÉ

about 1½ cups

Carolynne Knisi of Norwich, Vermont, brought this to a party that I attended in Hanover, New Hampshire, and I pried the recipe out of her. This pâté is so rich-tasting, a little can go a long way.

Preparation tip: The task of chopping is fast and simple if a food processor is used.

Serving suggestion: Stuff cherry tomatoes and mushroom caps with the pâté, or spread it on crackers, party bread, or crisp vegetables.

  1 tablespoon butter *or* oil
  1 medium onion, peeled and very finely chopped
     (about ⅔ cup)
  1 pound mushrooms, very finely chopped
  ¼ cup fresh lemon juice
  2 tablespoons Madeira (optional)
  ½ teaspoon Worcestershire sauce
  ½ teaspoon salt
  ⅛ teaspoon black pepper

1. In a large skillet, heat the butter or oil, add the onion, and sauté the onion until it is soft.
2. Add half the mushrooms to the skillet, and sauté them until their volume is reduced. Then add the rest of the mushrooms and the remaining ingredients. Cook the mixture, stirring it occasionally, over very low heat for 30 minutes or until the consistency of a spread is reached.

LENTIL PÂTÉ

about 2 cups

What can I say? This is truly wonderful. It looks and tastes like chopped liver but has none of liver's artery-clogging drawbacks. And almost no one guesses its true contents. I thank Edith Griffin of Morrisville, Pennsylvania, for this recipe, which has become a party staple for me.

Preparation tip: The secret of this dish's success is to caramelize the onions by long, gradual browning. Do this step while the lentils cook.

  ¾ cup (4 ounces) dried lentils
  3 cups water
  1½ tablespoons vegetable oil
  1 very large onion, peeled, quartered, and sliced (2 cups)
  2 hard-boiled egg whites

5 whole walnuts, shelled and crushed (optional)
½ teaspoon salt (optional)
¼ to ½ teaspoon freshly ground black pepper, to taste

1. In a small saucepan, cook the lentils in the water for 35 minutes or until they are soft. Drain the lentils, and reserve them.
2. While the lentils are cooking, heat the oil in a skillet, and add the onion, browning it very slowly.
3. Place the lentils, browned onion, and remaining ingredients in a wooden bowl, combining them well, and chop the mixture until a pâté-like consistency is reached.

STRING BEAN PÂTÉ

about 3 cups

Monte Rogers, one of the best amateur cooks I know, devised this delicious spread, which, like the lentil pâté, kept tasters guessing but coming back for more.

½ pound string beans, steamed for 12 minutes
3 hard-boiled egg whites
3 large onions, peeled and sliced (3 cups)
1 tablespoon vegetable oil
4 ounces (1 cup) walnut pieces
½ teaspoon salt (optional)
½ teaspoon freshly ground black pepper

1. While the string beans steam and the eggs boil, sauté the onions in a large skillet in the oil until they are well done.
2. Place the string beans, egg whites, onions, and remaining ingredients in a food processor, and process them until a pâté-like consistency is reached.

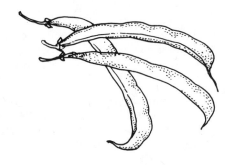

HOT NUTS

about 3 cups

You can prepare this recipe in all gradations of hotness. I offer a mild version that I have used, to great acclaim, at many parties. To make the nuts hotter, just double all the seasonings. These nuts freeze well, so you can prepare a big batch at once. They also make great holiday gifts.

1⅓ cups (about 7 ounces) whole almonds
1¼ cups (about 5 ounces) pecan halves
  1 cup (about 4 ounces) walnut halves
  1 tablespoon vegetable oil
  1 teaspoon cumin
  1 teaspoon curry powder
¼ teaspoon cayenne
⅛ teaspoon white pepper
¼ teaspoon salt (optional)

1. Preheat the oven to 350° F.
2. Toss the nuts with the oil in a large bowl.
3. In a small bowl, combine all the spices *except* the salt. Add the spices to the nuts, tossing the nuts to cover them evenly with the spices.
4. Spread the nuts on a baking tray in a single layer. Bake the nuts for 10 minutes. If desired, sprinkle the nuts lightly with the salt.

CHILIED CHICKPEAS

4 cups

Here is a different twist on the usual chickpea dip or spread.

Preparation tips: These chickpeas can be seasoned hot or mild, according to taste. They can also be made a day ahead.

  2 tablespoons vegetable oil
  4 cups cooked chickpeas (2 20-ounce cans,
    drained, rinsed, and dried)
  2 cloves garlic, peeled, halved, and slightly mashed
  1 teaspoon or more chili powder (use less if it is
    hot chili powder)
Dash or more cayenne, to taste (if mild chili powder is used)

1. Preheat the oven to 350° F.
2. In the oven, heat the oil in a shallow baking pan large enough to hold the chickpeas in a single layer. Add the garlic, baking the cloves on both sides until they are golden brown. Then remove and discard the garlic.
3. Place the chickpeas in the garlic oil in a single layer, and bake them, stirring them a few times, for about 30 minutes or until they are lightly browned.

4. Sprinkle the chickpeas with the chili powder and cayenne (if desired), and bake the chickpeas for another 5 minutes. Transfer the chickpeas to a serving bowl. Serve them at room temperature.

HERBED CAULIFLOWER

about 4 cups

This is one for lovers of oregano, basil, and vinegar. It is a tangy accompaniment to milder dishes or an addition to a salad plate, and it needs no salt or oil. The marinade is one suggested by Marian Morash in *The Victory Garden Cookbook.*

1½ pounds cauliflower, cored and flowerets cut
    into bite-sized pieces
Boiling water (salted, if desired)
¼ cup minced fresh basil leaves
½ to 1 teaspoon dried oregano leaves, crumbled
½ cup white-wine vinegar
1 large clove garlic, peeled and finely minced
½ teaspoon mustard seeds

1. In a large saucepan, blanch the cauliflower flowerets in boiling water (salted, if desired) to cover for 3 minutes. Drain them immediately, and transfer them to a glass bowl.
2. Toss the cauliflower with the basil and oregano.
3. In a small saucepan, heat the vinegar, garlic, and mustard seeds to boiling. Pour this mixture over the cauliflower, tossing the ingredients well. Cover the bowl, and refrigerate the cauliflower for 8 hours or longer, occasionally tossing the ingredients.

TOMATOES STUFFED WITH EGGPLANT

about 30 hors d'oeuvres

Here is an elegant hors d'oeuvre or first course from *Gourmet* magazine, with some reduction in the oil and salt.

Preparation tips: The salt is needed to extract the bitter juices from the eggplant (you can rinse some of it off afterward); and the capers, anchovy paste, and olives add yet more salt (I made the recipe without the capers and was still pleased with the outcome). No matter what you do, however, this will never be a low-sodium recipe. Note that the filling should be chilled overnight.

Serving suggestion: For an exquisite first course, serve 3 tomato halves per person, arranged on the plate like the spokes of a wheel, with a black olive in the center and sprigs of watercress in between each tomato half.

 1 **pound eggplant, peeled and cut into ¼-inch cubes**
 1 **teaspoon salt**
 1 **cup minced celery**
½ **cup minced onion**
 2 **cloves garlic, peeled and minced**
 3 **tablespoons olive oil, divided**
 1 **16-ounce can plum tomatoes, drained and coarsely chopped**
¼ **cup red-wine vinegar**
 2 **tablespoons coarsely chopped capers (optional)**
 2 **teaspoons anchovy paste**
 2 **teaspoons tomato paste**
¼ **teaspoon dried thyme**
 3 **tablespoons coarsely chopped black olives**
Freshly ground black pepper to taste
 1 **pound fresh ripe plum tomatoes**
Minced fresh parsley for garnish

1. Place the eggplant in a colander, sprinkle it with the salt, and let it drain for 30 minutes. Rinse the eggplant, pat it dry, place it in a bowl, and set it aside.
2. In a large skillet, cook the celery, onion, and garlic in 1 tablespoon of the olive oil over moderate heat, stirring the vegetables, for 10 minutes or until they are soft. Transfer the vegetables to a bowl.
3. Add the remaining 2 tablespoons of olive oil to the skillet. Then add the reserved eggplant, sautéing it over moderately high heat for 5 minutes or until it is lightly browned.
4. Add the celery mixture, the canned tomatoes, vinegar, capers (if desired), anchovy paste, tomato paste, and thyme, and bring the mixture to a boil. Reduce the heat, and simmer the mixture, stirring it occasionally, for 15 minutes.

5. Stir in the olives, and season the mixture with the pepper. Let the mixture cool, and then cover it and chill it overnight.
6. Halve the fresh tomatoes lengthwise, scoop out the seeds, and sprinkle the cut sides with pepper. Mound the eggplant mixture into the tomato halves, and sprinkle each half with some of the parsley.

EGGPLANT AND APRICOTS

8 servings

This unusual combination is simply elegant.

Preparation tips: The long purple Chinese eggplants work best in this recipe. The dish can be set up in advance and served hot, or it can be baked ahead and served at room temperature.

 4 long purple Chinese eggplants,
    halved lengthwise
Salt to taste
Freshly ground black pepper to taste
½ teaspoon cumin
 1 teaspoon sesame oil
½ pound dried apricots
 1 tablespoon vegetable oil
¼ cup chicken stock
Juice 1 lemon
 1 tablespoon minced fresh parsley

1. Preheat the oven to 325° F.
2. Place the eggplant halves, cut sides up, in a baking pan. Sprinkle the cut sides of the eggplants with the salt, pepper, cumin, and sesame oil. Arrange the apricots on the surface of the eggplants.
3. In a small bowl, combine the vegetable oil, chicken stock, and lemon juice. Pour this over the eggplants, and bake them for about 50 minutes. Remove the eggplants from the oven, and sprinkle them with the parsley.
4. If using the eggplants as an hors d'oeuvre, cut them into bite-sized pieces, and include 1 apricot on each piece.

HERBED QUESADILLAS

24 hors d'oeuvres

Ellen Brown, creator of tasty yet healthful takeout food for the Gourmet Gazelle in New York City, is one of the best cooks on the health-conscious scene. These layered cheese-topped tortillas were included in her book *The Gourmet Gazelle Cookbook.* They were devoured by tasters of all ages. My sons, not noted for their adventurous palates, pronounced it the best of 15 recipes I prepared for a Hispanic lunch.

Preparation tips: The quesadillas can be prepared in advance for baking. Stack them, separating each with some plastic wrap. Bake them just before serving the dish. Dried herbs work well (I did not have fresh ones when I tried out the recipe). I cut each quesadilla into 6 triangles to produce easy-to-handle finger food, but you can quarter them, if you choose. See page 8 for instructions on how to roast peppers.

½ large red onion, peeled, halved lengthwise, and
　　cut into ½-inch slices
Vegetable-oil spray
　8 8-inch flour tortillas
½ pound part-skim mozzarella, grated
　2 cloves garlic, peeled and minced
　2 tablespoons minced fresh marjoram *or* 1
　　teaspoon dried marjoram
　2 tablespoons minced fresh oregano *or* 1 teaspoon dried oregano
⅛ teaspoon freshly ground black pepper
　1 red bell pepper, roasted, peeled, cored, seeded,
　　and cut into ¼-inch strips

1. Spray the onion slices with vegetable oil, and grill or broil them 6 inches from the heat for about 4 minutes per side. Separate the rings, and set them aside.
2. Preheat the oven to 400° F.
3. Soften 4 of the tortillas, 1 at a time, in a heated skillet for 30 seconds per side. Arrange the tortillas on an oiled baking sheet so that they do not overlap.
4. In a bowl, combine the mozzarella with the garlic, marjoram, oregano, and black pepper. Divide mixture among the four softened tortillas, spreading the mixture evenly to within ½ inch of the edge of each tortilla.
5. Distribute the reserved onion rings and the pepper strips on top of the cheese, lightly pressing the vegetables into the cheese mixture.
6. Soften the remaining four tortillas (see step 3, above), and place them on top of the prepared ones, pressing them gently to assure good contact. Spray the tops of the quesadillas with vegetable oil.
7. Bake the quesadillas for 5 minutes or until the cheese has melted. Cut them into sixths, and serve them immediately.

SHRIMP AND CITRUS COCKTAIL

6 servings

The Sunkist Kitchens came up with this delicious combination that pleases the eye as much as the palate. I enhanced the shrimp by poaching them in beer, but they can be cooked any way you please. Although my tasters were skeptical at first about the grapefruit and shrimp combination, one taste erased all doubts, and the platter was consumed posthaste.

Preparation tips: You can start with cooked shrimp; just skip the poaching step. The cocktail sauce can be prepared several days ahead and kept chilled.

2 to 3 grapefruits	**COCKTAIL SAUCE**
	¼ cup chili sauce
12 ounces beer	¼ cup ketchup
1 tablespoon lemon juice	Grated peel ½ lemon
1 clove garlic, peeled	1 to 2 tablespoons lemon juice,
½ teaspoon salt	to taste
½ teaspoon celery seeds	
¼ teaspoon cayenne	
¼ teaspoon thyme leaves	
1 bay leaf	
1 pound medium-large shrimp, peeled and deveined	

1. Peel, section, and chill the grapefruits.
2. In a medium-sized saucepan, combine the beer, lemon juice, garlic, salt, celery seeds, cayenne, thyme, and bay leaf, and bring the mixture to a boil.
3. Add the shrimp, and return the liquid to a boil. Reduce the heat, and simmer the ingredients for 2 to 3 minutes or until the shrimp just turn pink. Drain the shrimp immediately, cool them down, and refrigerate them.
4. To make the cocktail sauce, combine the chili sauce, ketchup, lemon peel, and lemon juice in a small serving bowl. Set the sauce aside.
5. When the shrimp are cold, remove them from the refrigerator. Alternate the shrimp and the reserved grapefruit sections along the periphery of a serving platter, placing the bowl of cocktail sauce in the center.

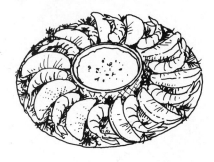

SAUCY SHRIMP

4 to 5 first-course servings

All my tasters loved these versatile spicy winners.

Preparation tips: The sauce can be prepared in advance and the shrimp cooked in the reheated sauce just before serving time. If using the dish as an entrée, start cooking the rice or pasta, and, as it cooks, heat the sauce to boiling, add the shrimp, and simmer the sauce until the shrimp are done.

Serving suggestion: The shrimp can be used as a first course to serve 4 or 5, or as an entrée to serve 2 or 3, accompanied by rice or a simple pasta.

  1 pound medium-large shrimp, peeled and deveined
     but with the last section of the shell and the tail left on
  1 teaspoon olive oil
½ cup chopped onion
1½ slices Canadian bacon, cut into small dice
  1 teaspoon flour
¼ cup canned tomato sauce
  2 teaspoons hot chili powder
  1 teaspoon sugar
  2 teaspoons minced garlic (2 large cloves)
½ teaspoon Worcestershire sauce
¼ teaspoon Angostura Bitters
  1 tablespoon lemon juice, or to taste
  2 cups hot water

1. Cut down the back of each shrimp with a sharp knife to butterfly it. Set the shrimp aside.

2. In a large nonstick skillet, heat the olive oil briefly, and sauté the onion until it is softened. Add the bacon and flour, and cook the mixture a moment longer.

3. Stir in the remaining ingredients. Bring the mixture to a boil, stirring it, reduce the heat, and simmer the sauce for 8 to 10 minutes or until it is reduced to about 1½ cups.

4. Stir in the shrimp, and simmer them for 3 minutes or until they are just firm. Serve the shrimp in the sauce.

MARINATED SHRIMP

4 to 6 servings

This is a special treat from my special friend and swimming companion Jane Quinn, fully deserving of top-quality shrimp.

- 2 pounds medium-large shrimp, peeled, deveined, and cooked
- 1 large clove garlic, peeled and minced
- ⅓ cup finely chopped celery
- 1 scallion, minced
- 1 tablespoon snipped chives
- 2 tablespoons olive oil
- ¼ teaspoon paprika
- ½ teaspoon salt (optional)
- 3 tablespoons lemon juice
- ¼ teaspoon hot pepper sauce
- 2 tablespoons chili sauce
- 2 tablespoons ketchup
- 2 tablespoons drained prepared horseradish
- 1 tablespoon prepared mustard

1. Place the shrimp in a glass or ceramic bowl.

2. Combine all the remaining ingredients in a bowl or jar, and pour the mixture over the shrimp. Toss the shrimp so that they are thoroughly coated with the mixture.

3. Cover the bowl, and chill the shrimp for 6 to 12 hours, tossing them in the marinade occasionally.

4. At serving time, remove the shrimp from the marinade, and arrange them on a plate with toothpicks.

MARINATED SCALLOPS

6 first-course servings

This deliciously aromatic treat is served at the Ord Street Café in Perth, Scotland. Although the recipe seems long, it really is not difficult and is definitely worth the effort, my tasters insisted.

MARINADE
- ⅔ cup white-wine vinegar
- ¼ cup raspberry vinegar
- ⅔ cup dry white wine
- Zest 1 orange, julienned
- ⅓ cup orange juice
- 1 tablespoon snipped fresh chives
- 2 teaspoons coriander seeds
- 1 teaspoon dried thyme
- 1 teaspoon mustard seeds
- 1 teaspoon black peppercorns
- 1 teaspoon juniper berries
- 1 teaspoon fennel seeds
- 1 teaspoon sugar
- ¼ teaspoon salt (optional)

- 1½ pounds sea scallops, halved horizontally if they are large

DIPPING SAUCE
- 1 cup fresh orange juice
- 2 teaspoons grated gingerroot
- 1½ cups dry white wine
- 1 tablespoon sugar
- ¼ teaspoon salt
- ⅛ teaspoon freshly ground black pepper
- Zest 1 orange, julienned
- 1 cup boiling water

Leaf lettuce for platter

1. In a saucepan, combine the marinade ingredients, bringing them to a simmer and stirring them occasionally. Remove the pan from the heat, and let the marinade cool.
2. In a large bowl, combine the scallops and the marinade. Cover the bowl, and refrigerate the scallops for 1 to 2 days.
3. To make the dipping sauce, in a saucepan combine all the sauce ingredients *except* the orange zest and water. Bring the ingredients to a simmer, and cook the mixture until the liquid is reduced by half. Strain the sauce into a bowl.
4. In a small saucepan, blanch the orange zest in the boiling water for 1 minute. Drain the zest, and add it to the strained sauce. Cover the sauce, and chill it for 1 hour or longer.
5. At serving time, remove the scallops from the marinade with a slotted spoon, leaving the seeds behind. Arrange the scallops around the dipping sauce on a bed of leaf lettuce.

STEAMED MARINATED MUSSELS   *8 first-course servings*

These tasty, simple mussels can be served as an appetizer or as part of a cold lunch.

48 large mussels (about 2 pounds), scrubbed and debearded
1½ cups water

MARINADE
2 tablespoons reserved strained mussel cooking liquid
2 tablespoons white wine
2 tablespoons rice vinegar
2 teaspoons Worcestershire sauce
2 teaspoons soy sauce
2 teaspoons lemon juice
½ teaspoon grated gingerroot
½ teaspoon finely minced garlic
½ teaspoon honey

1. Place the mussels in a large kettle, add the water, bring the liquid to a boil, cover the kettle tightly, and steam the mussels for 5 minutes or until the shells open. Discard any mussels that have not opened, and remove the rest of the mussels from their shells, saving 2 tablespoons of the cooking liquid for the marinade and half a dozen shells to decorate the platter. Debeard the mussels if necessary, rinse them, and drain them.

2. To make the marinade, combine the marinade ingredients in a small bowl.
3. Place the mussels in a bowl, and add the marinade. Toss the mussels in the marinade, cover the bowl, and refrigerate the mussels for about 4 hours, tossing them occasionally.
4. At serving time, remove the mussels from the marinade with a slotted spoon, and place them on a platter. Decorate the platter with the reserved shells.

MEXICAN MUSSELS

about 8 hors d'oeuvres

Yummy and pretty, too. Craig Claiborne and Pierre Franey have lived up to their reputations with this recipe. My tasters gobbled the mollusks up, even those who said, "I don't even like mussels!"

Preparation tips: If desired, strain some of the mussel cooking liquid, and add a few drops to each shell. The vinaigrette can be made a day ahead, and the entire dish can be fully prepared hours before serving time.

32 large mussels (about 1⅓ pounds)
¾ cup water

2 tablespoons finely chopped
   cilantro *or* Italian parsley
Wedges lime for garnish

VINAIGRETTE
   2 tablespoons lime juice
   2 tablespoons olive oil
   1 tablespoon seeded and finely
      chopped jalapeño
   2 teaspoons finely chopped cilantro
      or ¼ cup chopped fresh parsley
¼ cup finely chopped tomato
½ cup finely chopped red onion
¼ teaspoon salt (optional)
Freshly ground black pepper to taste

1. Remove the beards from the mussels, and scrub each mussel. Rinse the mussels, and drain them.
2. Place the mussels in a kettle, and add the water. Cover the kettle, and bring the water to a boil. Cook the mussels for 5 minutes or until the shells open. Drain the mussels, reserving some of the cooking liquid, which should be strained.
3. Remove mussels from their shells, saving half the shells. Separate the halves of the shells, and arrange them on a platter. Place one mussel in each half shell with a few drops of the reserved cooking liquid, if desired.
4. In a small bowl, combine the vinaigrette ingredients. Spoon the vinaigrette over the mussels. Sprinkle the mussels with cilantro or parsley, and garnish the platter with the wedges of lime.

FABIAN'S FLOUNDER CEVICHE

6 first-course servings

This marvelous recipe from Cheryl Jamesson of Fort Lauderdale, Florida, is one reason why I still eat ceviche, despite warnings about possible health risks from seaborne microorganisms (not a problem thus far in flounder). Given the number and amount of hot ingredients, this dish is not for the faint of taste bud, although the hotness can be tempered by using less of the peppery ingredients.

Preparation tip: The onions, scallions, garlic, and cilantro can be minced in the food processor, if you take care not to pulverize them.

     1 pound flounder fillets, cut into 1-inch pieces
 1¼ cups fresh lime juice
     1 cup minced yellow onion
     1 cup minced red onion
     3 scallions, minced
     5 cloves garlic, peeled and minced
     2 tablespoons cilantro, minced
   ½ jalapeño, seeded and minced
     1 tablespoon hot pepper sauce, or to taste
     1 teaspoon white-wine vinegar
   ¾ teaspoon Dijon-style mustard
   ½ teaspoon salt (optional)
Freshly ground black pepper to taste

1. In a shallow glass bowl, combine the flounder pieces with the lime juice. Stir in the remaining ingredients, mixing them thoroughly.
2. Cover the bowl with plastic wrap, and refrigerate the fish for at least 4 hours or up to 12 hours.

CHICKEN SATAY

40 to 48 pieces

I don't think I've ever seen an hors d'oeuvre that was attacked and devoured as quickly as this one. The marinade makes the chicken exceptionally tender and flavorful.

Preparation tip: For the sake of logistics, the chicken can be grilled in advance and reheated in the oven or microwave at serving time.

MARINADE
- ¼ cup smooth peanut butter, preferably natural
- 2 tablespoons minced onion
- 2 tablespoons lemon juice
- 1½ teaspoons soy sauce
- 1 teaspoon minced garlic (1 large clove)
- ½ teaspoon coriander
- ⅛ teaspoon cayenne, or to taste
- 2 tablespoons minced fresh parsley

- 1 pound boneless, skinless chicken breasts, cut into 1-inch pieces

1. In a medium-sized bowl, combine all the marinade ingredients thoroughly. Add the chicken pieces, and toss them to coat them well. Cover the bowl, and chill the chicken for 4 to 8 hours.
2. Remove the chicken pieces, and thread them on thin skewers. Grill or broil them for 10 to 15 minutes or until they are just cooked. Do not overcook them.

MUSTARDY MELON ROLL-UPS

4 to 6 servings

Instead of salty prosciutto, try wrapping melon with slices of smoked or roasted turkey breast (available at most good delis) for an attractive, tasty, low-calorie hors d'oeuvre.

Preparation tip: You can use any number of mustards—from Honey Mustard (see page 549) or Doubly Hot Horseradish Mustard (see page 548) to a simple coarse-grained deli mustard.

- 6 slices roasted or smoked turkey breast
- 2 tablespoons mustard
- 6 slices cantaloupe or honeydew cut 1 inch wide × ⅓ inch thick into lengths the size of the turkey slices

1. Smear each turkey slice on one side with the mustard.
2. Wrap the turkey around the melon pieces. Secure the roll-ups with tooth-picks at bite-sized intervals, and cut the roll-ups crosswise between the toothpicks.

PÂTÉ-STUFFED SHELLS

about 50 hors d'oeuvres

Here's a very tasty hors d'oeuvre with all the rich flavor of a pâté but almost none of the fat.

Preparation tips: Pasta shells break easily; be sure to stir them gently while they cook. If possible, buy American-made shells that come in a box rather than in a cellophane bag; that way you'll be less likely to end up with lots of broken shells. Also, add some oil to the cooking water, and as soon as the shells are cooked, drain them, and separate them on a platter to keep them from sticking together. This dish can be prepared ahead through step 5, then baked at party time.

   1 teaspoon butter *or* margarine *or* oil
   1 pound chicken livers, cut into 1-inch pieces
⅓ cup minced onion
   2 cloves garlic, peeled and minced
   2 tablespoons dry red wine
½ teaspoon oregano
½ teaspoon basil
¼ teaspoon salt (optional)
Dash nutmeg
   8 ounces tomato sauce (canned or homemade)
½ pound large macaroni shells, cooked for 5
     minutes or until they are very *al dente*
Chopped fresh parsley for garnish (optional)

1. Melt the butter, margarine, or oil in a large nonstick skillet, and add the livers, onion, and garlic. Cook the ingredients over high heat for 5 minutes or until the livers are just cooked through. Transfer the liver mixture to a wooden chopping bowl.
2. Chop the livers well, but do not purée them. Stir in the wine, oregano, basil, salt (if desired), and nutmeg.
3. Preheat the oven to 350° F.
4. Spread half the tomato sauce on the bottom of a shallow baking dish (ap-proximately 12 × 8 × 2 inches), or divide it between two pie plates.
5. Stuff each shell with 1 teaspoon or so of the liver mixture, and place it on top of the sauce in the baking dish. When all the stuffing is used up, spoon the remaining sauce over the shells.
6. Bake the shells for 20 minutes. Just before serving time, sprinkle the dish with the parsley, if desired.

TINY SHELLS WITH DILLED SMOKED SALMON

8 first-course servings

This is an appetizer to be eaten on a plate rather than a stand-up party food. Be forewarned: if you're cooking for a crowd, this is not for limited budgets. A mere ¼ pound of smoked salmon (I use Nova Scotia salmon since it has the least salt) costs more than $4! But it would make an elegant first course at a dinner party, served on a crisp lettuce leaf.

    5 tablespoons plain nonfat or low-fat yogurt
    3 tablespoons light mayonnaise
    ⅓ cup snipped fresh dill
    3 tablespoons finely chopped shallots
    Freshly ground black pepper to taste
    ¼ pound smoked salmon (preferably Nova
        Scotia), cut into small slivers
    ½ pound tiny macaroni shells, cooked *al dente*

1. In a medium-sized bowl, combine the yogurt, mayonnaise, dill, shallots, and pepper. Add the salmon slivers, and mix the ingredients well.
2. Add the macaroni shells to the salmon mixture, stirring the ingredients gently to combine them. Refrigerate the pasta-salmon mixture for several hours before serving it.

SOUPS

There is no better stage setter for a gourmet meal than a simple but elegant soup. By the same token, a good, hearty soup can be a great meal in itself—yes, even for company. Appetizer, soup, salad, and homemade bread form the menu for many dinner parties in the Brody household. When it comes to entertaining, the beauty of soup is that it can be prepared in advance and simply reheated at serving time.

Stocks

I repeat the stock recipes from *Jane Brody's Good Food Book* since the best soups start with homemade stock, although commercial broths can be used successfully as long as you make appropriate adjustments for salt and skim off any fat. Still, the best way to control salt and fat content—and to get that true homemade flavor—is to make your own soup stocks. They are simple to prepare and can help you use up limp vegetables and leftovers that might otherwise go to waste. The following recipes, then, should not be considered ironclad but merely guidelines. Many other ingredients and seasonings can be used. Your imagination is the limit.

Since stocks freeze well (just be sure to leave room at the top of the container for expansion), they can be prepared whenever you happen to have the ingredients on hand. Or they can be made in large batches and frozen in meal-size containers for future use. Don't forget to label and date the containers.

CHICKEN STOCK

4 to 6 cups

For easy identification, I keep a colored plastic bag in my freezer into which I put all chicken scraps: skin, fat, wing tips, gizzards (except liver), bones, sinew, tail bone, and, if I'm lucky enough to get some, feet. Sometimes they are all I need to make a stock; other times I buy some chicken backs to flesh out the pot.

Preparation tips: Frozen chicken scraps can be dumped into the pot along with the remaining ingredients. Most cookbooks suggest enclosing the herbs in a bag of cheesecloth (a tea strainer will also do); but since you are going to strain the broth anyway, I don't see the need for this. Once prepared, I freeze chicken stock in several types of containers: ice-cube trays (for 1- and 2-tablespoon cubes), 1- and 2-cup plastic tubs, and 1-quart containers. I try to use wide-mouthed containers so that I don't have to worry about defrosting the liquid before using it.

  2 pounds (approximately) chicken scraps
Cold water to cover (at least 2 quarts)
  1 large onion, peeled and stuck with 3 to 4 cloves
  1 large clove garlic, peeled
  1 to 2 ribs celery, halved crosswise
  1 to 2 carrots, peeled and cut into chunks
  1 bay leaf
  2 or more sprigs parsley *or* 1 tablespoon dried
     parsley flakes
  1 teaspoon tarragon
½ teaspoon thyme
½ teaspoon dillweed
Salt to taste (optional)
12 peppercorns *or* ½ teaspoon freshly ground
     black pepper

1. Place all the ingredients in a large pot. Bring the liquid to a boil, reduce the heat, partially cover the pot, and simmer the stock for at least 1 hour. The longer the stock cooks, the richer it will become; but don't cook it so long that the broth boils away.
2. If time permits, let the stock cool before pouring it through a fine strainer or sieve into a fat-skimming measuring cup, a bowl, or other suitable container. Press on the solids to extract as much liquid as possible.
3. If using the fat skimmer, decant the fat-free broth into containers for storage; otherwise, refrigerate the broth until the fat hardens on the broth's surface for easy removal. (Depending on the amount of gelatinous protein in the chicken scraps, the broth may gel at refrigerator temperatures.)

FISH STOCK

about 6 cups

Ask the fishmonger for the bones of a nonoily fish (any white fish) for this broth.
Or use the carcass of a white fish that you had filleted.

- 2 **pounds bones and trimmings (excluding gills)**
  of any white fish
- 1 **cup sliced onion**
- 1 **cup sliced celery**
- 1 **bay leaf**
- 6 **sprigs parsley**
- ½ **teaspoon thyme**
- 2 **tablespoons lemon juice**
- 3 **whole cloves**
- ½ **teaspoon salt (optional)**
- 10 **peppercorns** *or* **¼ teaspoon freshly ground**
   black pepper
- 6 **cups cold water**
- 1 **cup dry white wine**

1. In a heavy saucepan, combine the bones and trimmings, onion, celery, bay
   leaf, parsley, thyme, lemon juice, cloves, salt (if desired), and pepper.
   Cover the pan tightly, and let the ingredients steam in their own moisture
   over moderately low heat for 5 minutes.
2. Add the water and wine. Bring the stock to a boil, reduce the heat, skim off
   any froth, and simmer the stock for 20 minutes.
3. Pour the stock through a fine strainer or sieve, pressing all the liquid from
   the solids.

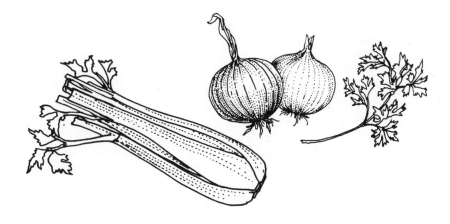

BEEF STOCK

about 8 cups

Beef bones used to be available for the asking from the butcher. But nowadays you will probably have to pay for them.

Preparation tip: Roasting the bones is optional, although it will give the stock a richer flavor.

> 4 pounds raw meaty beef *and/or* veal bones
> 1 to 3 large onions, peeled and chopped
> 2 to 4 carrots, coarsely chopped
> 2 to 4 ribs celery with leaves, chopped
> 2 cloves garlic, peeled
> 4 to 6 sprigs parsley
> 1 bay leaf
> 4 whole cloves
> 10 peppercorns
> Salt to taste (optional)
> 3½ quarts (14 cups) cold water, divided
> 2 tablespoons red-wine vinegar (optional)

1. Preheat the oven to 450° F.
2. Place the bones in a large pan, and put the pan in the hot oven for 30 minutes, turning the bones once during the roasting process.
3. Meanwhile, in a large heavy stock pot, combine the onions, carrots, celery, garlic, parsley, bay leaf, cloves, peppercorns, salt (if desired), and all but 2 cups of the water. Bring the liquid to a boil, reduce the heat, and add the roasted bones.
4. Pour off the fat from the roasting pan, and add the remaining 2 cups of water to the pan, scraping the sides of the pan with a wooden spoon. Pour this liquid into the stock pot, and return the stock to a boil. Reduce the heat, partially cover the pot, and let the stock simmer for 3 hours. Skim off the froth as needed.
5. Stir in the vinegar (if desired), and continue simmering the stock, partially covering the pot, for another 2 hours.
6. Pour the broth through a fine strainer or sieve.

VEGETABLE STOCK

about 4 to 6 cups

Here's where you can clean out the refrigerator without wasting anything (as long as it's not rotten!). All kinds of bits and pieces of raw and leftover cooked vegetables and vegetable peelings can go into a stock, as well as the liquid used for cooking vegetables. But if you want to follow a "standard" recipe, use this one.

 1 tablespoon butter *or* margarine
½ cup chopped onion
½ cup diced carrot
½ cups diced turnip
½ cup diced parsnip
 1 cup diced celery plus some inner leaves
 1 cup shredded salad greens (optional)
Vegetable scraps as available, such as tomato skins,
   potato peelings, mushroom bits, onion skins (optional)
 3 sprigs parsley
 2 whole cloves
 1 bay leaf
½ teaspoon thyme
½ teaspoon salt, or to taste (optional)
⅛ teaspoon white pepper, or to taste
Dash cayenne, or to taste
Cold water *and/or* vegetable cooking liquid to cover

1. In a large, heavy saucepan, melt the butter or margarine over moderate heat, and sauté the onion in the fat until it browns.
2. Add the remaining ingredients to the pan, bring the stock to a boil, reduce the heat, and simmer the stock, partially covering the pan, for 30 minutes to 1½ hours (the longer, the better).
3. Strain the broth through a fine sieve, pressing the solids to extract the liquid.

Hot First-Course Soups

MUSHROOM-BARLEY SOUP

6 servings

Kim Wolf, a faithful reader from Waukesha, Wisconsin, offers this swift and delicious soup. You can have all the ingredients in the pot in 15 minutes.

Preparation tip: You can substitute broth for some of the water, but you may want to reduce the salt if the broth used is salted.

```
 1  pound mushrooms, sliced
 2  medium carrots, peeled and shredded
 1  small tomato, peeled and quartered
 1  medium onion, peeled and chopped
 2  ribs celery, chopped
½  cup barley
 4  sprigs parsley, minced
¾  teaspoon salt, or to taste (optional)
Freshly ground black pepper to taste
5½  cups water
```

In a large saucepan, combine the ingredients, and bring them to a boil. Reduce the heat, cover the pan, and simmer the soup for 1 hour.

DILLY OF A MUSHROOM SOUP

4 to 6 servings

An old culinary pal, Suzanne Oakley (now Taylor) of Sweet Sue's in Phoenicia, New York, contributed this lovely Hungarian-style soup. Sue had already substituted skim milk for whole and yogurt for sour cream. I cut the fat even further with no sacrifice in flavor.

Preparation tips: This soup tastes better if you use stock instead of water. Take care *not* to boil the soup when you reheat it or the yogurt will curdle. An alternative is to leave the yogurt out of the hot soup and to add it at serving time as a dollop, mixed with additional fresh dill, if desired.

```
 2  tablespoons butter or margarine, divided
2½  cups chopped onions
 1  pound mushrooms, sliced
 3  tablespoons snipped fresh dill or 2 to 3
     teaspoons dried dillweed
 4  teaspoons paprika (use half hot paprika, if desired)
```

 4 teaspoons tamari *or* low-sodium soy sauce
2½ cups stock *or* water, divided
 2 tablespoons flour
1¼ cups skim milk
 ¾ cup plain nonfat or low-fat yogurt
2½ teaspoons lemon juice

1. In a kettle, melt 2 teaspoons of the butter or margarine, and sauté the onions in the fat until the onions are soft.
2. Add the mushrooms, dill, paprika, tamari or soy sauce, and ¾ cup of the stock or water. Bring the soup to a boil, reduce the heat, cover the kettle, and simmer the soup for 15 minutes.
3. Meanwhile, in a small saucepan, melt the remaining butter or margarine. Add the flour, cooking it over low heat and whisking it constantly for 1 minute. Then gradually add the milk, whisking the mixture continuously. Cook the mixture over a low heat, whisking it often, until the mixture thickens.
4. Gradually add several ladlesful of soup to the milk mixture, stirring the mixture until it is smooth. Gradually stir the milk mixture into the remainder of the soup along with the remaining stock or water. Cover the kettle, and simmer the soup for 15 minutes.
5. Before serving the soup, stir in the yogurt and lemon juice.

MUSHROOM SOUP MARSALA

6 servings

This aromatic soup, great for lunch or dinner, was adapted from a creation by Jeffree Brooks of Alameda, California, published in *Bon Appétit* magazine.

    1 tablespoon butter *or* margarine
    1 teaspoon olive oil
    1 pound mushrooms, chopped
    1 cup sliced scallions, white part only
    1 tablespoon flour
    ½ cup Marsala
    3 cups beef broth
    1 teaspoon thyme
    ¾ teaspoon mustard powder
    ¼ teaspoon freshly ground black pepper
    Salt to taste (optional—omit if using canned broth)
    1 cup skim milk
    2 tablespoons minced fresh parsley for garnish

1. In a medium-sized saucepan, preferably one with a nonstick surface, heat the butter or margarine and the olive oil over medium heat, add the mushrooms and scallions, and sauté the vegetables for 5 to 7 minutes or until they are just tender.
2. Sprinkle the flour over the mixture, stirring the ingredients to mix them well. Blend in the Marsala, and cook the mixture for 1 minute.
3. Transfer the mushroom mixture to a blender, and purée it.
4. Pour the broth into a measuring cup, add the thyme, mustard, pepper, and salt (if desired) to the broth, and, with the blender running, add the broth to the mushroom purée.
5. Return the soup to the saucepan, and, over medium heat, stir in the milk. Warm the soup thoroughly, but *do not bring it to a boil.* Serve the soup garnished with the parsley.

AUTUMN VEGETABLE SOUP

6 servings

Marcia Flammonde of Snydersville, Pennsylvania, created this simple, delicious soup in honor of fall produce and a friend, Richard Leland, who inspires culinary creativity. It's a wonderful recipe—you just place the ingredients in a pot and cook them until they are done.

Preparation tip: When I tested the recipe, I inadvertently omitted the water. Since I prefer a thick soup, it came out just to my liking.

⅓ cup chopped green beans
1 onion, peeled and sliced
2 carrots, peeled and sliced
2 parsnips, peeled and sliced
6 ounces rutabaga, peeled and cut into ¾-inch cubes
½ cup chopped fennel bulb
2 Granny Smith apples, peeled, cored, and chopped
3 cups chicken broth (preferably homemade or unsalted)
½ teaspoon cinnamon
¼ teaspoon ground cloves
¼ teaspoon freshly grated nutmeg
2 to 3 cups water, as needed (optional)
Salt to taste (optional)
Freshly ground black pepper to taste

1. In a kettle, combine the green beans, onion, carrots, parsnips, rutabaga, fennel, apples, broth, cinnamon, cloves, and nutmeg. Bring the ingredients to a boil over moderate heat, and cover the kettle. Reduce the heat, and simmer the ingredients for 35 to 45 minutes or until all the vegetables are tender.
2. Purée the mixture in batches in a blender or food processor. Pour purée back into kettle, and stir in enough of the water to achieve the desired consistency. Season the soup with salt (if desired) and pepper, and heat the soup thoroughly.

FENNEL SOUP

The Culloden House Hotel in Inverness, Scotland, prepares a higher-fat version of this simple, elegant soup for its lucky guests.

Preparation tip: If a thinner consistency is desired, add some skim or low-fat milk to the soup before serving time.

  1 tablespoon butter *or* margarine
  4 bulbs fennel (about 4 pounds total), tops
     trimmed and bulbs sliced crosswise
Vegetable-oil spray
  5 cups chicken broth
  2 pounds tomatoes, peeled, seeded, and chopped
  ¼ cup dry vermouth
Cheesecloth bag containing 3 sprigs parsley,
     ¾ teaspoon thyme, and 1 bay leaf
  1 clove garlic, peeled and minced
  1 teaspoon Worcestershire sauce
Salt to taste (optional)
Freshly ground black pepper to taste
Skim or low-fat milk for thinning (optional)

1. In a kettle, preferably one with a nonstick surface, melt the butter or margarine over moderately low heat, and add the fennel. Cover the fennel with a round of wax paper that has been sprayed with the vegetable oil, then cover the pot tightly. Sweat the fennel for 10 minutes.
2. Discard the wax paper, and add to the kettle the broth, tomatoes, vermouth, bag of herbs, and garlic, and bring the soup to a boil. Reduce the heat, cover the pot, and simmer the soup for 30 minutes.
3. Discard the herb bag, and purée the soup in batches in a blender or food processor. Return the soup to the kettle, and add the Worcestershire sauce, salt (if desired), and pepper. Heat the soup to near boiling, and thin it with milk, if you wish.

YELLOW PEPPER SOUP

In the fall, when domestically grown yellow peppers are available, try this wonderful soup.

Serving suggestion: Serve the soup with freshly grated Parmesan and toasted croutons.

¾ cup chopped carrot
½ cup chopped onion
½ cup chopped celery
1½ tablespoons olive oil
 4 yellow bell peppers, cored, seeded, and cut into
    large pieces
 1 pound boiling potatoes, peeled and cut into
    ¼-inch slices
 1 cup broth (any type)
 4 cups water
½ teaspoon salt (optional)
¼ teaspoon freshly ground white pepper *or* black pepper

1. In a large saucepan, preferably one with a nonstick surface, sauté the carrot, onion, and celery in the olive oil over moderately high heat for 5 minutes, stirring the vegetables until they soften.
2. Add the yellow peppers, potatoes, broth, and water, and bring the soup to a boil. Reduce the heat, and simmer the soup for 40 minutes or until the vegetables are very soft.
3. Purée the mixture in a blender or food processor, and strain it through a sieve into a bowl. Add the salt (if desired) and pepper.

GARLIC SOUP
4 servings

This easy, elegant recipe from *Medical Self-Care* magazine is amenable to variations. The lengthy cooking sweetens the garlic.

Serving suggestion: Serve the soup with toasted croutons or sliced wild mushrooms that have been sautéed in broth, sherry, or 2 teaspoons of olive oil.

 4 cups chicken broth
½ cup white wine
12 cloves garlic, peeled
 2 onions, peeled and quartered
 1 rib celery, quartered
Water (optional)
¼ cup dry sherry (optional)

1. Combine all the ingredients *except* the water and sherry in a saucepan, and, over high heat, bring the soup to a boil. Reduce the heat, cover the pan, and simmer the soup for 2 hours. Check the pan from time to time, adding water to the soup, if needed.
2. Purée the soup in a blender or food processor, return it to the pan, and add the sherry, if desired. Reheat the soup before serving it.

SPICY CARROT SOUP

4 to 6 servings

Liz Serrili of Yonkers, New York, makes this luscious soup, which withstood a significant reduction in fat.

Preparation tips: If you prefer a nonpeppery version, omit the cayenne. The soup can be made ahead and reheated before serving.

  1 pound carrots, peeled and cut into ¼-inch slices
1¼ cups boiling water
  1 large onion, peeled and finely chopped (1 cup)
  2 teaspoons unsalted butter *or* margarine
  1 teaspoon olive oil
  3 cloves garlic, peeled and minced
  3 cups chicken broth
  1 teaspoon curry powder
  ½ teaspoon freshly grated nutmeg
  ¼ teaspoon aniseed
  ⅛ to ¼ teaspoon cayenne, to taste

1. In a medium-sized saucepan, steam the carrots over the boiling water for 10 minutes or until the carrots are tender. Reserve the cooking liquid.
2. In a small skillet, sauté the onion in the butter or margarine and the olive oil until the vegetable is softened. Add the garlic, and cook the vegetables, stirring them, 2 minutes longer.
3. In a blender in batches, purée the carrots, their reserved cooking liquid, the onion mixture, and the broth.
4. Transfer the purée to a saucepan, and add the curry powder, nutmeg, aniseed, and cayenne. Place the saucepan over medium heat, and warm the soup thoroughly, stirring it often.

CREAMY ORANGE-CARROT SOUP

6 servings

Here's a carrot soup with a difference: the zip of orange and tang of yogurt. It can also be served cold.

  1 tablespoon butter *or* margarine
  1 pound carrots, scraped and thinly sliced
  1 medium onion, peeled and chopped (about ⅔ cup)
  2 cups water
Salt to taste (optional)
  ⅛ teaspoon freshly ground black pepper
Dash ground cloves
  ¾ cup orange juice
  ½ cup plain nonfat or low-fat yogurt

1. In a large saucepan, melt the butter or margarine, add the carrots and onions, and sauté the vegetables for about 5 minutes.
2. Add the water, salt (if desired), and pepper to the pan. Bring the ingredients to a boil, reduce the heat, cover the pan, and simmer the mixture for 25 minutes or until the carrots are tender.
3. With a slotted spoon, transfer just the vegetables to a blender or food processor, add 1 cup of the cooking liquid, and purée the vegetables. Return the purée to the remaining broth.
4. Add the cloves and orange juice to the pan. Heat the soup until it begins to boil. In a bowl, combine the yogurt with ½ cup of the hot soup. Mix the ingredients well, and add the yogurt mixture to the pan, stirring the ingredients well. (Do *not* boil the soup after the yogurt has been added.)

POTATO-CRESS SOUP   *6 servings*

Watercress adds zip and vitamin A to this easy-to-make soup. The evaporated milk gives the soup added richness and flavor without many calories.

Preparation tip: The soup can be prepared ahead through step 4 and frozen.

3½ cups chicken broth, divided
  1 bunch watercress, washed and coarsely chopped
  2 teaspoons vegetable oil
  1 medium onion, peeled and chopped (about ⅔ cup)
  3 medium potatoes, peeled and sliced (about ¾ pound)
  1 cup skim milk
Salt to taste (optional)
Freshly ground pepper to taste
Dash nutmeg
  ¼ cup evaporated skim milk (optional)

1. In a small skillet or saucepan, heat ½ cup of the chicken broth, and add the watercress. Cook the watercress for a few minutes until it has wilted, and set the pan aside.
2. In a large saucepan, heat the oil, add the onion, and sauté the vegetable until it is translucent.
3. Add the potatoes and the remaining 3 cups of broth to the onion. Bring the mixture to a boil, reduce the heat, cover the pan, and simmer the mixture for 10 minutes or until the potatoes are tender.
4. Add the reserved watercress mixture to the potato mixture, and purée the new mixture in a blender or food processor, in batches if necessary. (The mixture can also be puréed in a food mill.)
5. Return the purée to the large saucepan, and add the skim milk, salt (if desired), pepper, and nutmeg. Heat the soup gently to just below the boiling point. Just before serving the soup, stir in the evaporated milk, if you wish.

THREE-P SOUP *(Peanut, Pumpkin, and Potato)*   *8 to 12 servings*

This is one great pumpkin soup—rich enough to be a main dish, elegant and different enough to grace any dinner party. I served it at Thanksgiving dinner, and all my guests who cook requested the recipe, which I adapted from a favorite of Marlene and Jack Gilboy of Forest City, Pennsylvania. The original recipe was published in *Bon Appétit* magazine.

Preparation tips: Use only "natural" or "old-fashioned" peanut butter, the kind that contains no salt, sweeteners, or hydrogenated oils. This soup can be made days ahead and refrigerated or weeks ahead and frozen. Use a heavy or nonstick saucepan to reheat the soup over a low flame, stirring it often.

1½ pounds yams *or* sweet potatoes
  1 tablespoon butter *or* margarine
  2 tablespoons minced shallots *or* onion
  2 cups thick pumpkin purée, canned or homemade
  8 cups chicken broth, canned or homemade
  1 cup pure, unsalted, smooth peanut butter
  2 teaspoons coarse-grained mustard
  ½ teaspoon nutmeg (preferably freshly grated)
Salt to taste (optional)
Freshly ground white pepper *or* black pepper to taste
Snipped fresh chives for garnish (optional)

1. Preheat the oven to 350° F.
2. When the oven is hot, bake the yams or sweet potatoes on a baking sheet for 1 hour or until they are soft. Let them cool, peel them, and process them in a food mill or food processor. Measure out 2 cups of the processed potatoes (use leftovers for another purpose), and set them aside.
3. In a large, heavy pot, preferably one with a nonstick surface, melt the butter or margarine over medium heat, add the shallots or onion, and sauté the vegetable for 2 minutes.
4. Add to the pot the reserved processed potatoes and the pumpkin purée. Then alternately add the broth and peanut butter, stirring the mixture after each addition until the soup is smooth. Over medium heat, bring the soup almost to a boil, stirring it often. Reduce the heat, and simmer the soup for about 25 minutes, stirring it occasionally.
5. Stir in the mustard, nutmeg, salt (if desired), and pepper. Before serving the soup, garnish it with chives, if they are available.

POTATO AND CORN CHOWDER   *6 or more servings*

This is hearty enough to be a main-course soup. With bread and a salad, it could be a fine light meal.

¼ pound lean smoked pork, diced
1 large onion, peeled and finely chopped (1 cup)
2 pounds boiling or all-purpose potatoes, peeled and diced into ½-inch cubes
1 rib celery, finely chopped (about ½ cup)
⅛ teaspoon thyme
2½ cups water
Freshly ground black pepper to taste
Salt to taste (optional)
1 16-ounce can cream-style corn
1 cup skim milk
¼ cup minced fresh parsley

1. In a heavy saucepan or Dutch oven, preferably one with a nonstick surface, cook the pork briefly.
2. Add the onion (if you are not using a nonstick pan, you may first need to add 1 teaspoon of oil), and cook it, stirring it often, until it is soft.
3. Add the potatoes, celery, and thyme, and stir-fry the mixture for 30 seconds.
4. Add the water, pepper, and salt (if desired). Bring the mixture to a boil, reduce the heat, cover the pot, and simmer the mixture for 10 minutes or until the potatoes are just tender.
5. Stir in the corn, and simmer the soup 5 minutes longer.
6. Add the milk and parsley, and heat the soup until it is hot but not boiling.

CAULIFLOWER AND POTATO SOUP   *4 to 6 servings*

I adapted a recipe that Alison Watt devised for *National Gardening* magazine, often a source of inventive ways to use homegrown produce and always a source of useful and fascinating information about all things that can grow in a garden.

Serving suggestion: Serve this soup with garlic croutons (see the "Serving suggestion" on page 102) or biscuits (see pages 432 to 435).

```
1 head cauliflower, cut into flowerets and stems sliced
2 medium potatoes, peeled and cubed
1 tablespoon butter or margarine
1 clove garlic, peeled and minced
1 cup coarsely chopped onion (1 large)
½ cup minced fresh parsley
2 teaspoons tamari or imported soy sauce
¼ teaspoon cardamom
¾ teaspoon salt, or to taste (optional)
Freshly ground black pepper to taste
Dash or more cayenne
1 cup skim or low-fat milk
Chopped scallions for garnish
```

1. Steam the cauliflower for 5 minutes or until the flowerets are just tender. Set the cauliflower aside, and *save the cooking water.*
2. Parboil the potatoes for 10 minutes or until they are tender. Set the potatoes aside, and *save the cooking water.*
3. In a skillet, preferably one with a nonstick surface, melt the butter or margarine, add the garlic and onion, and sauté the vegetables until they are soft.
4. Combine the reserved cauliflower, reserved potatoes, garlic-and-onion mixture, and the parsley, and purée the mixture in batches in a blender or food processor, adding the reserved cooking liquids as needed.
5. Transfer the purée to a large saucepan, and add additional cooking liquid to achieve a consistency somewhat thicker than what is ultimately desired. Stir in the tamari or soy sauce, cardamom, salt (if desired), pepper, and cayenne. Add the milk, stirring the soup to blend the ingredients thoroughly. Reheat the soup, but *do not boil it.* Or chill the soup, and serve it cold, garnished with scallions.

CURRIED SQUASH SOUP

6 to 8 servings

This tasty, low-fat soup can be prepared with either Hubbard or butternut squash.

    2 pounds winter squash
    1 tablespoon butter *or* margarine
1½ cups chopped onion
 ½ cup chopped celery
    1 large sweet apple (preferably McIntosh),
       peeled, cored, and chopped
Salt to taste (optional)
Freshly ground black pepper to taste
    1 tablespoon curry powder, or to taste
    4 cups chicken broth (homemade or canned)
    1 bay leaf
    1 cup buttermilk
    2 teaspoons lemon juice

1. Preheat the oven to 375° F, and bake the squash for 30 minutes or until it is tender.
2. While the squash is baking, melt the butter or margarine in a medium-sized saucepan, and add the onion, celery, apple, salt (if desired), and pepper. Cover the pan, and cook the mixture for 5 minutes over moderately low heat, stirring the ingredients occasionally.
3. Add the curry powder, broth, and bay leaf, raise the heat, and bring the mixture to a boil. Reduce the heat, cover the pan, and simmer the mixture for 30 minutes. Discard the bay leaf.
4. When the squash is cool enough to handle, discard the seeds, peel it, and cut its flesh into chunks.
5. In batches in a blender or food processor, purée the broth mixture with the squash. Return the soup to the saucepan, and add the buttermilk and lemon juice. Adjust the seasonings, and heat the soup through but *do not boil it.*

CREAMED ACORN SQUASH SOUP   *8 servings*

My manuscript editor, Carol Flechner, offers this low-fat yet luscious soup that can be prepared with virtually any kind of winter squash, including pumpkin.

    2 tablespoons unsalted butter *or* margarine
    2 medium onions, peeled and thinly sliced
    2 pounds acorn squash, peeled, seeded, and cut
      into small cubes
    1 or 2 McIntosh apples, peeled, cored, and diced
    3 cups chicken broth
    1 cup unsweetened apple cider *or* apple juice
    1 tablespoon finely minced gingerroot, divided
    1 cup skim milk
    Freshly grated nutmeg for garnish (optional)

1. In a stockpot, melt the butter or margarine over medium heat. Add the onions, and cook them, stirring them occasionally, for 5 minutes or until they are lightly browned.
2. Add the squash, apple(s), broth, and cider or juice. Bring the mixture to a boil, reduce the heat, cover the pot, and simmer the mixture for 20 minutes or until the squash is tender.
3. Purée the mixture in three batches in a blender or food processor, adding a third of the gingerroot to each batch.
4. Transfer the purée to a large saucepan, stir in the milk, and heat the soup through, but *do not boil it.* Adjust the seasonings, and serve the soup garnished with the nutmeg, if desired.

PUMPKIN SOUP   *6 servings*

Nutmeg, especially if freshly grated, gives this simple pumpkin soup a different but delicious flavor.

Preparation tip: The soup can be prepared in advance and refrigerated or frozen after step 2.

    1 pound pumpkin, peeled, seeded, and cut into
      1-inch cubes (4 cups)
    3 cups chicken broth
    1 medium potato, peeled and diced (1 cup)
    1 medium onion, peeled and chopped
    ¼ teaspoon nutmeg (preferably freshly grated)
    ⅛ teaspoon white pepper
    Salt to taste (optional)
    ⅔ cup skim or low-fat milk

1. In a large saucepan, combine the pumpkin, broth, potato, and onion. Bring the ingredients to a boil, reduce the heat, cover the pan, and simmer the vegetables for 20 minutes or until they are soft.
2. Purée the mixture in batches in a blender or food processor.
3. Transfer the purée back to the saucepan, and heat the purée just to the boiling point. Add the nutmeg, pepper, and salt (if desired). Turn off the heat, and add the milk.

PUMPKIN SOUP PARMESAN

8 servings

I was foresighted enough to have frozen several portions of this soup, which provided some lovely luncheon accompaniments months later. The recipe comes from the Ridgewood, New Jersey, home of Arlene and Lou Sarappo via *Bon Appétit* magazine.

Preparation tip: The soup can be prepared a day ahead, and, obviously, it freezes well.

Serving suggestion: Garnish each serving with a few slivers of prosciutto and some minced fresh parsley.

2 pounds pumpkin, peeled, seeded, and cut into
$\frac{1}{2}$-inch pieces
1½ pounds baking potatoes (e.g., Idaho), peeled
and cut into ½-inch pieces
1 medium onion, peeled and coarsely chopped
(⅔ cup)
3 cups chicken broth
1 cup water
1 sprig rosemary *or* ¼ teaspoon crumbled dried
rosemary
Salt to taste (optional)
⅓ cup Parmesan (preferably freshly grated)
3 tablespoons dry Marsala
¼ teaspoon freshly ground white pepper
¼ teaspoon freshly grated nutmeg

1. In a large, heavy saucepan, combine the pumpkin, potatoes, onion, broth, water, rosemary, and salt (if desired). Bring the mixture to a boil, reduce the heat, cover the pan, and simmer the ingredients for 30 minutes or until the pumpkin is tender. Discard the rosemary sprig, if you used one.
2. Purée the soup in batches in a blender, and return the purée to the saucepan. Heat the soup to a simmer, and add the Parmesan, Marsala, pepper, and nutmeg. Adjust the seasonings before serving the soup.

SWEET POTATO SOUP

6 to 8 servings

A nourishing and richly colored soup inspired by a recipe in Marian Morash's *The Victory Garden Cookbook.*

Serving suggestion: Although Morash suggests serving it hot or cold, we all preferred the soup hot. Either way, it can be served with a spoonful or so of plain yogurt.

```
  2  teaspoons butter or margarine
 ½   cup sliced carrots
 ½   cup sliced celery
1½   cups peeled, seeded, and chopped tomatoes
       (about 2 large)
  6  cups beef broth
1½   pounds sweet potatoes, peeled and thinly sliced
```
Freshly ground black pepper to taste
Plain nonfat or low-fat yogurt for garnish (optional)

1. In a large saucepan, melt the butter or margarine, add the carrots and celery, and sauté the vegetables for about 5 minutes, stirring them often (do not brown them).
2. Add the tomatoes, and cook the ingredients until the liquid is somewhat reduced.
3. Add the broth and sweet potatoes, bring the mixture to a boil, reduce the heat, cover the pan, and simmer the mixture for 20 to 30 minutes or until the vegetables are very soft.
4. Purée the mixture in a blender or food processor, or put it through a food mill. Add the pepper to the soup, reheat the soup or chill it, and serve it garnished with the yogurt, if desired.

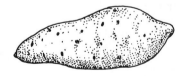

AFRICAN YAM SOUP

4 to 6 servings

This soup has a pleasant bite, a beautiful color, and is simple to prepare. It was devised by the New York City Bureau of Nutrition, which often comes up with enticing, wholesome ethnic recipes.

    1 large onion, peeled and finely chopped
    2 teaspoons vegetable oil
    2 small hot chilies (fresh, if available), seeded and
       finely chopped
    2 medium tomatoes, peeled, seeded, and chopped
    1 pound yams *or* sweet potatoes, peeled and cut
       into small cubes
    2 cups beef broth
    1 cup water
    ¼ teaspoon salt (optional)
Freshly ground white pepper to taste
    2 tablespoons finely chopped fresh parsley for garnish

1. In a large saucepan, preferably one with a nonstick surface, sauté the onion in the vegetable oil until the onion is translucent.
2. Add the chilies and tomatoes, and cook the mixture for about 5 minutes.
3. Add the yams or sweet potatoes, broth, and water. Bring the soup to a boil, reduce the heat, and simmer the soup for 20 to 30 minutes or until the yams or sweet potatoes are soft.
4. Purée the soup in a blender, or pass the mixture through a food mill. Return the purée to the pan, add the salt (if desired) and pepper, and heat the soup thoroughly. Serve the soup garnished with the parsley.

FAITH'S HOT AND SOUR SOUP

4 servings

My dear friend Faith Sullivan of Los Angeles and Minneapolis says this recipe of hers is now being duplicated by friends across the country. And with good reason. Even if it weren't so low in calories, it is marvelous.

Preparation tips: You can substitute 1 cup of cooked chicken, cut into bite-sized pieces, or cooked, slivered pork for the "sea legs." The soup can be prepared in advance through the addition of the ingredients in step 2. Then complete the cooking by heating the soup just before serving it.

    4 cups chicken broth, homemade or canned (defatted)
    2 medium carrots, peeled and thinly sliced
    2 ribs celery, thinly sliced
    1 large clove garlic, peeled and grated
    1 teaspoon grated gingerroot
    ½ teaspoon paprika
    ⅛ teaspoon red pepper flakes, or to taste
    2 fresh plum tomatoes, cored
    ½ pound "sea legs" (imitation crabmeat), cut into
        ½-inch slices
    1 cup sliced mushrooms
    1 tablespoon chopped mint leaves
    1 tablespoon chopped cilantro (optional)
    2 tablespoons or more fresh lemon juice, to taste

1. In a large saucepan, combine the broth, carrots, celery, garlic, gingerroot, paprika, and pepper flakes. Bring the ingredients to a boil, reduce the heat to medium, and cook the mixture for 5 minutes or until the carrots are tender-crisp.
2. Quarter the tomatoes lengthwise, then cut the wedges in half crosswise. Add them to the soup along with the remaining ingredients. Simmer the soup for 3 minutes or until the mushrooms and tomatoes are heated through.

THE BEST BLACK BEAN SOUP

6 to 8 main or 8 to 10 first-course servings

This one, with a distinct southwestern touch, will enliven your taste buds while preserving your health. It was derived from a recipe offered by *Gourmet* magazine. My tasters loved it. It has no added fat, it is easy to prepare, and you can make it ahead. What more can you ask for in an elegant yet hearty soup that is a definite conversation piece?

Preparation tips: You can prepare the soup up to 4 days in advance and store it, covered, in the refrigerator. Or you can freeze it. The jalapeño cream can be prepared 1 or 2 days ahead.

Serving suggestions: In addition to the jalapeño cream, try garnishing the soup with chopped red onion and/or chopped avocado. With bread and salad, this soup could be the base for a light lunch.

SOUP
- 1 pound dried black beans, picked over, rinsed, and soaked for 10 hours or longer in water to cover by at least 4 inches
- 6 cups beef broth
- 8 cups water
- 1 28-ounce or 32-ounce can tomatoes with their juice, chopped
- 2 teaspoons cumin
- Salt to taste (optional)
- Freshly ground black pepper to taste

JALAPEÑO CREAM
- ⅔ cup plain nonfat or low-fat yogurt
- 1 or 2 fresh jalapeños *or* pickled jalapeños, seeded and minced
- 3 tablespoons minced fresh parsley
- 1 tablespoon minced cilantro (optional)

GARNISHES (optional)
- ½ cup chopped red onion
- ½ avocado, peeled, seeded, and chopped

1. Drain the beans, and put them in a large, heavy pot. Add the broth and water. Bring the beans to a boil, stirring them a few times, reduce the heat, and simmer the beans in the uncovered pot for 1 hour.
2. Stir in the tomatoes with their juice and the cumin, and continue simmering the beans for 2 hours or until the beans are soft (check after 1 and 1½ hours, since the timing depends on dryness or age of the beans).
3. Transfer the mixture to a large bowl, and let the mixture cool briefly. Rinse out the pot. Then purée the mixture in batches in a blender or food processor until the mixture is smooth, returning the purée to the pot as you go.
4. Season the soup with the salt (if desired) and pepper, and bring the soup to a simmer. If the soup is too thin, simmer it in the uncovered pot, stirring it often, until the desired consistency is reached.
5. To prepare jalapeño cream, whisk together the yogurt, jalapeños, parsley, and, if you are using it, cilantro. Serve a dollop of the jalapeño cream atop each bowl of soup. If you wish, you may also garnish the soup with the chopped red onion and/or chopped avocado.

Cold First-Course Soups

WHITE GAZPACHO

8 servings

Gazpacho is a cold Spanish "salad" soup that is made with fresh, uncooked vegetables or fruits or nuts. Since there are as many versions of it as there are cooks who prepare it, I now present my twist to this summertime delight. The recipe is fat-free (unless you use low-fat instead of nonfat yogurt) and very low in calories but rich in flavor and nutrients. I keep the sodium down by adding no salt except what is in the broth.

2½ pounds cucumbers, peeled, halved lengthwise,
    and seeded, divided
2½ cups chicken broth, divided
1½ cups plain nonfat or low-fat yogurt
 ¼ cup white-wine vinegar
 2 large cloves garlic, peeled and finely minced
    but *not pressed*
Freshly ground pepper (preferably white) to taste
 1 or more dashes hot pepper sauce, to taste
 1 cup finely diced tomatoes
 ½ cup chopped scallions

1. Dice ⅔ of the cucumbers, and coarsely process them in the blender with 1 cup of the broth. Transfer the mixture to a bowl, and stir in the remaining broth, yogurt, vinegar, garlic, pepper, and pepper sauce.
2. Finely chop the remaining ⅓ of the cucumbers, and add them to the soup along with the tomatoes and scallions. Chill the soup thoroughly before serving it.

GAZPACHO

8 to 10 servings

This oil-free red gazpacho comes from a new friend, Bernice Balis, who is as concerned about health as she is about gourmet dining.

1 large cucumber, peeled, seeded, and cut into
    1-inch pieces
1 large sweet green pepper, cored, seeded, and
    cut into 1-inch pieces
1 large sweet red pepper, cored, seeded, and cut
    into 1-inch pieces
1 large rib celery, cut into 1-inch pieces
1 large carrot, peeled and cut into 1-inch pieces

1 medium onion, peeled and cut into 1-inch pieces
4 cups tomato juice
¼ cup tomato paste
¼ cup red-wine vinegar
1 teaspoon oregano
Salt to taste (optional)
Freshly ground black pepper to taste
Dash or more hot pepper sauce

1. Put the cucumber, green pepper, red pepper, celery, carrot, and onion in the bowl of a food processor, and chop them. Do not drain the liquid.
2. In a large serving bowl, combine the tomato juice with the remaining ingredients. Mix in the chopped vegetables and their juices. Chill the gazpacho for at least 1 hour before serving it.

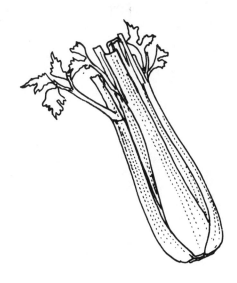

MEXICAN GAZPACHO

6 servings

One could say that it's hard to go wrong with gazpacho, as long as you use enough fresh vegetables. Still, some gazpachos are better than others, and this one, developed by Pierre Franey for his *Pierre Franey's Low-Calorie Gourmet,* is surely among the best. My tasters all asked for take-home portions.

Preparation tip: You can prepare all the chopped vegetables in a food processor, if you take care not to purée them. Since I like bigger pieces, I usually chop half the ingredients by hand and process the rest.

Serving suggestion: For those who dislike cilantro, omit it, or serve it as a topping to be added if desired. The soup is excellent with garlic croutons, which can be homemade by cutting into ½-inch dice enough slices of good white bread to make 1 cup of cubes (this will serve 6). In a nonstick skillet, heat 1½ teaspoons of olive oil with 2 cloves of peeled garlic, add the cubed bread, and over medium-low heat toss the cubes until they are toasted.

  2 **cups peeled, seeded, and chopped tomatoes**
  ½ **cup ¼-inch cubes cucumber**
  ¼ **cup chopped red onion**
  ¼ **cup chopped celery**
  ¼ **cup chopped sweet green pepper**
  ¼ **cup chopped cilantro (optional)**
  3 **tablespoons chopped scallions**
  2 **tablespoons minced green chilies** *or* **jalapeños**
  2 **tablespoons chopped Italian parsley**
  1 **tablespoon minced garlic (3 large cloves)**
  1 **cup tomato juice**
  2 **tablespoons red-wine vinegar**
  2 **tablespoons fresh lime juice**
  1 **tablespoon olive oil**
  ½ **teaspoon salt (optional)**
  Freshly ground pepper to taste (I use ¼ teaspoon)

Combine the ingredients in a large bowl. Chill the gazpacho thoroughly before serving it.

YOGURT SOUP

4 small servings

Fimi Zolas of New York City, who is described by my friend Fran Korein as a great cook, devised this wonderfully refreshing soup for a hot summer day. What could be simpler?

2 cups plain nonfat yogurt
½ cup (approximately) ice water
1 cucumber, peeled, seeded, and finely diced
2 cloves garlic, peeled and minced
1 tablespoon olive oil
2 tablespoons snipped fresh dill
¼ teaspoon salt (optional)
Freshly ground white pepper to taste
¼ cup finely chopped walnuts

1. In a bowl, combine the yogurt and ice water with the cucumber.
2. Two hours before serving the soup, stir in the garlic, olive oil, dill, salt (if desired), and pepper.
3. At serving time, stir the walnuts into the soup.

CUCUMBER-WALNUT SOUP   *6 to 8 servings*

This recipe was adapted from one in *Café Beaujolais* by Margaret S. Fox and John Bear. It is loaded with calcium and flavor.

1 cup walnuts
5 large cucumbers, peeled, seeded, and thinly sliced
2 large cloves garlic, peeled and minced
½ cup minced scallions with tops
Juice 1 lemon
4 cups (1 quart) buttermilk
1½ cups plain nonfat or low-fat yogurt
1½ tablespoons finely minced fresh dill
1 teaspoon salt (optional)
¼ teaspoon white pepper

1. Preheat the oven to 350° F.
2. Place the walnuts on a baking tray, and toast them in the oven for 15 to 20 minutes. Remove the nuts from the oven, coarsely chop them, and set them aside.
3. Combine the remaining ingredients in a large bowl. Transfer half the mixture to a blender or food processor, and purée it. Return the purée to the bowl, combining it with the unprocessed ingredients, and mix in the reserved walnuts. Cover the soup, and refrigerate it for at least 4 hours before serving it.

SPICY CORN AND TOMATO SOUP   *8 to 10 servings*

This cold soup, adapted from a recipe by Lynne Rossetto Kasper in *Bon Appétit* magazine, is not for the timid. But it is truly a *great* soup and worth the effort it takes to make it. This dish is perfect for end of summer, when fresh tomatoes and corn are plentiful and delicious.

Preparation tips: The soup and the saffron cream, both of which should be chilled for at least 6 hours, can be prepared up to 2 days before serving. If you prefer, you can peel and seed the tomatoes before adding them, quartered, to the soup. If a less hot dish is preferred, you can omit the red pepper flakes or the chilies. Anaheim chilies are large, green, and much milder than jalapeños.

Serving suggestion: The swirl of saffron cream looks best if the soup is served in a wide bowl. The cream is marvelous, by the way, with other dishes, such as cold poached fish.

SAFFRON CREAM
- 1 teaspoon butter *or* margarine
- ¾ teaspoon minced garlic
- ¾ teaspoon minced gingerroot
- ⅛ teaspoon saffron threads, crumbled and dissolved in 2 tablespoons warm water
- Pinch salt
- ¾ cup plain nonfat or low-fat yogurt

SOUP
- 2 teaspoons whole cumin seeds, toasted
- ⅓ cup water
- 5 teaspoons minced garlic (5 large cloves)
- 5 teaspoons minced gingerroot
- ½ teaspoon turmeric
- ½ teaspoon ground allspice
- ¼ teaspoon red pepper flakes
- 1 tablespoon butter *or* margarine
- 2 large onions, peeled and chopped (2 cups)
- 6 cups chicken broth
- 3½ pounds very ripe tomatoes, quartered
- Salt to taste (optional)
- Freshly ground black pepper to taste
- 2 cups corn kernels (cut from 2 large ears), steamed for 2 minutes

- 5 Anaheim chilies, roasted (see page 8), peeled, seeded, and diced, for garnish

1. First, prepare the saffron cream. In a small, heavy saucepan, melt the butter or margarine over medium-low heat. Add the garlic and gingerroot to the pan, and sauté the seasonings for about 1 minute. Stir in the saffron, and

simmer the mixture for 1 more minute. Add the salt, remove the pan from the heat, and stir in the yogurt. Refrigerate the saffron cream for at least 6 hours.

2. To prepare the soup, grind the toasted cumin seeds in a blender. Add the water, garlic, gingerroot, turmeric, allspice, and pepper flakes, and purée the mixture. Set the spices aside.

3. In a large, heavy saucepan over low heat, melt the butter or margarine, add the onions, and sauté them, stirring them occasionally, for 15 minutes or until they are very soft.

4. Add the reserved spice mixture, raise the heat to medium-low, and cook the ingredients, stirring them often, for 5 minutes or until the liquid evaporates. Add the broth, and simmer the mixture for 50 minutes or until it is reduced by one-third.

5. Add the tomatoes to the mixture, and purée the ingredients in three batches in a food processor. Then pass the mixture through a food mill to remove the tomato seeds and skin.

6. Season the soup with the salt (if desired) and pepper, and refrigerate it for at least 6 hours.

7. Before serving time, mix the steamed corn kernels into the soup, and let the soup stand at room temperature for about 20 minutes. Garnish each portion with a swirl of chilled saffron cream and a sprinkling of the chilies.

CORN SOUP WITH PESTO

6 servings

This lovely combination of flavors is good hot or cold.

Preparation tips: The soup can be made ahead. To keep the fat content low, I purée the basil in broth with just a bit of oil.

 2 onions, peeled and chopped
 1 clove garlic, peeled and minced
 1 tablespoon plus 2 teaspoons olive oil, divided
 6 ears of corn, kernels cut off the cobs and the
   cobs reserved
 4 cups chicken broth, divided
 3 cups water
 ½ cup skim or low-fat milk
 Salt to taste (optional)
 White pepper (preferably freshly ground) to taste
 1 cup packed fresh basil leaves, rinsed and spun or patted dry

1. In a large saucepan, preferably one with a nonstick surface, sauté the onions and garlic in 1 tablespoon of the olive oil over medium-low heat, stirring the vegetables frequently, until they are softened.
2. Add the corncobs, all but ¼ cup of the broth, and the water, bring the mixture to a boil, reduce the heat, and simmer the mixture for 10 minutes.
3. Add the corn kernels, and simmer the soup for another 15 minutes. Remove and discard the cobs from the soup.
4. Stir in the milk, salt (if desired), and pepper, and simmer the soup for another 5 minutes.
5. Purée the soup in batches in a blender or food processor. Transfer the soup to a bowl, cover the bowl, and chill the soup for at least 3 hours.
6. In a blender or food processor, purée the basil in two batches, adding to each batch 1 teaspoon of the remaining olive oil and 2 tablespoons of the reserved broth.
7. At serving time, ladle the soup into chilled bowls, and swirl a spoonful of the basil purée into each serving.

COLD TOMATO SOUP

6 servings

Lovely to the eye and on the palate, this no-cooking-needed soup was derived from a recipe by Freddi Greenberg in *Bon Appétit* magazine. It is a perfect end-of-summer or early fall dish, when luscious tomatoes are plentiful and the weather is still warm.

Preparation tips: The soup can be made with two 35-ounce cans of drained plum tomatoes, if fresh tomatoes are not available. For the oil, try walnut, avocado, or olive. Be sure to toast the walnuts—the flavor is marvelous.

 3 **pounds fresh tomatoes, peeled, cored, and**
    seeded (see "Preparation tips," above)
¼ **cup minced fresh basil**
 1 **tablespoon vegetable oil**
 1 **tablespoon honey**
 1 **tablespoon balsamic vinegar**
½ **teaspoon salt**
Freshly ground black pepper to taste
½ **cup toasted walnuts, chopped**

1. Purée the tomatoes in batches in a food processor or blender. Transfer the purée to a glass or ceramic bowl.
2. Add the remaining ingredients to the purée *except* the walnuts. Mix the ingredients thoroughly, and adjust the seasonings, if necessary. Cover the bowl, and refrigerate the soup for at least 3 hours.
3. Let the soup stand at room temperature for 15 minutes before serving it. Serve the soup garnished with the walnuts.

COLD SHRIMP SOUP

6 to 8 servings

A refreshing, delicate, delicious soup that is low in fat and calories regardless of how you prepare it. It can be served as the main course of a light lunch.

Preparation tip: The soup can be made either with buttermilk or with plain nonfat or low-fat yogurt thinned with some of the shrimp cooking broth.

Serving suggestion: For a special touch, at serving time add 1 tablespoon of dry vermouth to the soup.

BOILED SHRIMP
 1 pound shrimp in their shells
 Water to cover
 1 large rib celery, cut into chunks
 1 clove garlic, peeled
 1 bay leaf
 8 peppercorns
 8 cloves
 8 allspice berries *or* ¼ teaspoon ground allspice
 3 sprigs parsley
 Salt to taste

SOUP
 4 cups (1 quart) buttermilk *or* 3 cups plain nonfat or low-fat yogurt plus 1 cup reserved shrimp cooking liquid (see "Preparation tip," above, and steps 2 and 4, below)
 1 tablespoon Dijon-style mustard
 2 cups peeled (if waxed), seeded, and finely diced cucumber
 1 teaspoon sugar
 Salt to taste (optional)
 1 tablespoon or more finely snipped fresh dill, to taste
 1 tablespoon dry vermouth (optional)

1. To prepare the shrimp, place the shrimp in a saucepan with the water. Add to the pan the remaining seasonings for cooking the shrimp, bring the liquid to a boil, and cook the shrimp for 1 minute.
2. Take the pan off the heat, and remove the shrimp, reserving the broth if you will be using yogurt to make the soup. Set the shrimp aside to cool, then peel them and, if desired, devein them, saving the shells if you will be using yogurt.
3. Coarsely chop the shrimp, and set them aside.
4. If you will be using yogurt, add the reserved shrimp shells to the broth, and cook the broth 10 minutes longer. Strain 1 cup of the broth, and chill it.
5. In a large bowl, combine the soup ingredients (except the vermouth) with the reserved shrimp, and chill the soup thoroughly before serving it. Add the vermouth at the last minute, if you wish.

COLD WHITE BEAN SOUP

6 servings

A refreshing, nutritious adaptation of a recipe published years ago in *Bon Appétit* magazine. Michael McLaughlin of Brooklyn, New York, devised the original recipe.

½ pound dried Great Northern beans, picked
     over, rinsed, and soaked overnight in water to
     cover by at least 4 inches
 2 teaspoons butter *or* margarine
 2 teaspoons olive oil
 2 large carrots, peeled and quartered
 1 medium onion, peeled and finely chopped
 2 bay leaves
1½ teaspoons thyme, crumbled
 6 cups chicken broth
½ teaspoon salt (optional)
 1 cup buttermilk *or* more, if thinner soup desired
¼ cup fresh lemon juice
Thin slices lemon for garnish
Minced fresh chives for garnish

1. To cook the beans, melt the butter or margarine in a large, heavy saucepan over medium-low heat. Add the olive oil, carrots, onion, bay leaves, and thyme. Cover the pan, and cook the vegetables, stirring them occasionally, for 10 minutes or until they are golden.
2. Drain the beans, and add them to the vegetables. Stir in the broth, and bring the soup to a boil, skimming off the foam. Reduce the heat, partially cover the pan, and simmer the soup for 45 minutes or until the beans are just tender. Add the salt (if desired), and simmer the soup for another 15 to 30 minutes or until the beans are very tender. Remove the pan from the heat.
3. To prepare the soup, drain the beans, reserving the liquid. Discard the carrots and bay leaves, and in a blender purée the beans and onion with 1 cup of the reserved cooking liquid until the mixture is smooth.
4. Transfer the soup to a bowl. Stir in the 1 cup of buttermilk and lemon juice. Cover the bowl, and refrigerate the soup for at least 4 hours. Before serving the soup, thin it, if you wish, with additional buttermilk. Garnish each serving with a lemon slice and chives.

SORREL SOUP

4 servings

If you're at all familiar with sorrel, chances are it's as the main ingredient in schav, a cold soup popular with the Jews of eastern Europe. Sorrel, also known as sour grass, is rich in iron and vitamin C but also in oxalic acid, which inhibits the absorption of iron. It is cultivated widely in France for use in salads and soups.

    1 tablespoon butter *or* margarine
    ¾ cup chopped onion *or* 1 cup chopped leeks
    2 cups cubed potatoes (about 1 pound)
    4 cups chicken broth (if you use canned broth,
       use half broth and half water)
    ½ pound sorrel, rinsed and dried, with tough
       stems discarded
    ⅓ cup skim or low-fat milk
    Freshly ground black pepper to taste

1. Melt the butter or margarine in a medium-sized saucepan, add the onion or leeks, and sauté the vegetable until it is soft but not browned.
2. Add the potatoes and broth, bring the liquid to a boil, reduce the heat, partially cover the pan, and simmer the mixture for 10 to 15 minutes or until the potatoes are cooked.
3. Transfer the contents of the saucepan to a blender, and purée the mixture (you can also purée the mixture in a food mill). Transfer the purée to a serving bowl, and chill the purée.
4. Meanwhile, working in batches, stack the sorrel leaves, and cut them in half lengthwise, then cut them crosswise into thin strips. Stir the sorrel, milk, and pepper into the chilled purée, and refrigerate the soup until serving time.

RED PEPPER SOUP

4 servings

Simple, tasty, and visually magnificent, this soup is "creamed" with low-fat buttermilk.

    1 tablespoon butter *or* margarine
    2 cups chopped sweet red peppers (about 2 large)
    1 cup chopped scallions *or* leeks (white part only)
    1 cup chicken broth
    2 cups buttermilk
    Salt to taste (optional)
    White pepper to taste
    Minced fresh parsley for garnish (optional)

1. Melt the butter or margarine in a large skillet, preferably one with a non-stick surface, add the peppers and scallions or leeks, and sauté the vegetables over low heat for 15 minutes or until they are very soft but not browned (you may have to cover the pan to accomplish this).
2. Add the broth, bring the mixture to a boil, reduce the heat, partially cover the skillet, and simmer the mixture for about 30 minutes.
3. Transfer the contents of the skillet to a blender or food processor, and purée the mixture. Transfer the purée to a serving bowl, and let the purée cool.
4. Add the buttermilk, mixing the ingredients well, and chill the soup thoroughly. Prior to serving the soup, season it with salt (if desired) and white pepper. Garnish the soup with the parsley, if you wish.

ZUCCHINI AND POTATO SOUP   *8 servings*

This delicately seasoned soup is a fine accompaniment for a sandwich or a main-dish salad.

    2 cups chopped onions (2 large)
    1 large clove garlic, peeled and minced
    1 tablespoon butter
    2 pounds zucchini, unpeeled and thinly sliced
    2 medium potatoes (about ¾ pound), peeled and
       sliced
    4 cups chicken broth
 1½ tablespoons white-wine vinegar
    1 teaspoon dried tarragon, crumbled
Salt to taste (optional)
Freshly ground black pepper to taste
    1 cup plain nonfat or low-fat yogurt mixed with 1
       tablespoon crumbled tarragon for garnish

1. In a large saucepan or Dutch oven, sauté the onions and garlic in the butter for 3 minutes. Add the zucchini, potatoes, broth, vinegar, the 1 teaspoon of tarragon, salt (if desired), and pepper. Bring the mixture to a boil, reduce the heat, cover the pan, and simmer the mixture for 30 minutes. Set the soup aside to cool down to warm.
2. Meanwhile, chill the yogurt and the 1 tablespoon of tarragon.
3. Transfer the warm soup to a blender or food processor, and purée the soup (in batches, if necessary). Transfer the purée to a serving bowl, cover the bowl, and chill the soup for at least 1 hour. Serve each portion garnished with a heaping spoonful of the chilled seasoned yogurt.

ZUCCHINI-PEA SOUP

6 to 8 servings

A very good cold soup that can help gardeners use up their crop of zucchinis.

Preparation tips: This soup needs no added salt if you use salted broth. If you use fresh peas, buy 2 pounds unshelled.

Serving suggestion: Try adding to each portion a dollop of yogurt seasoned, for example, with curry, horseradish, or herbs, and lemon juice.

  2 cups fresh or frozen peas
Boiling salted water to cover
  2 cups chicken broth
  1 very large onion, peeled and thinly sliced (1½
     to 2 cups)
¼ cup minced fresh parsley
¼ teaspoon oregano
¼ teaspoon chervil, if available
Salt to taste (optional)
Freshly ground black pepper to taste
  2 pounds zucchini, unpeeled and thinly sliced
  1 tablespoon sugar
  2 teaspoons drained prepared horseradish
  1 teaspoon lemon juice
  1 cup skim or low-fat milk

1. In a small saucepan, cook the peas in the boiling salted water until they are tender. Drain the peas, and set them aside.
2. In a large saucepan, combine the broth, onion, parsley, oregano, chervil, salt (if desired), and pepper. Bring the mixture to a boil, add the zucchini, and cook the ingredients over medium heat for 5 minutes or until the zucchini is tender.
3. Add the reserved peas to the zucchini mixture, and purée the soup in a blender. Add the sugar, horseradish, and lemon juice, and blend the soup until it is smooth.
4. Transfer the purée to a bowl, and stir in the milk. Cover the bowl, and refrigerate the soup for at least 5 hours.

DOUBLE-A SOUP *(Apple and Avocado)*   *6 to 8 servings*

This unusual but delicious combination of ingredients really deserves a triple-A rating.

    1   tablespoon unsalted butter *or* margarine
    1   teaspoon vegetable oil
    1   small onion, peeled and chopped
    1   carrot, peeled and chopped
    2   teaspoons curry powder, or to taste
    2   cups chicken broth (*or* half broth and half water
        if canned broth is used)
    2   Granny Smith apples, peeled, cored, and chopped
  2½   cups skim or low-fat milk
    1   avocado, peeled and pitted
Salt to taste (optional)
Freshly ground pepper to taste

1. In a medium-sized saucepan, heat the butter or margarine with the oil, add the onion and carrot, and sauté the vegetables over moderate heat, stirring them, for several minutes or until the onion is soft. Add the curry powder, and cook the vegetables for 30 seconds more.
2. Add the broth and apples, bring the soup to a boil, reduce the heat, cover the pan, and simmer the soup for 15 minutes or until the apples are tender. Let the soup cool for about 30 minutes.
3. Add the milk and avocado to the soup, and purée the mixture in batches in a blender or food processor. Season the soup with salt (if desired) and pepper. Chill the soup for 1 hour or longer.

ENTRÉES

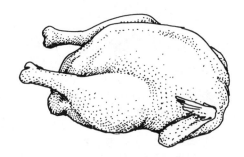

Poultry Main Dishes

Once upon a time, chicken was an economy dish. Nowadays, in fat- and cholesterol-conscious America, chicken and other poultry are widely used in meals where red meat was once king, and the price of some poultry has risen accordingly. Poultry—mainly chicken, turkey, and Cornish game hen—is now served as the main course at the most elegant affairs. You should realize that poultry is not much lower in cholesterol than the equivalent amount of red meat, but it has considerably less fat and less of its fat is the cholesterol-raising saturated kind. Of course, it is no health bargain to eat chicken or turkey with its fat-laden skin (half the fat of these birds is in the skin) or prepared in a way that adds hundreds of fat calories to each serving. Therefore, the recipes that follow were designed to take advantage of the lean, high-quality protein in poultry but still keep the fat and calorie content as low as possible. For peak flavor, try using free-range chickens and fresh (not frozen) turkeys and hens, if they are available in your area.

CHICKEN WITH YAMS

6 servings

This wonderful, unusual combination of ingredients was put together by Len Allison and Karen Hubert, the husband-and-wife team that made Hubert's in New York such a popular restaurant. I defatted it quite a bit and added more vegetables, which is my wont, but otherwise it is their recipe.

Preparation tip: This dish really sings with fresh herbs. If you must use dried rosemary (2 teaspoons) and dried thyme leaves (1 teaspoon), combine them and tie them into 2 or 3 cheesecloth bags before adding them to the casserole.

Serving suggestion: For an elegant opener, try the Mushroom Soup Marsala on page 84.

  1 tablespoon butter *or* margarine
  1 tablespoon olive oil
  6 serving-size pieces of chicken, skinned
 ½ cup cognac
 ½ cup white wine
  1 cup chicken broth
  2 tablespoons sliced garlic
  3 tablespoons sliced shallots
  3 cups very thinly sliced fennel bulbs
  1 tablespoon finely julienned gingerroot
2½ pounds yams, peeled and cut into 2-inch pieces
  1 cup dried apricots, cut into ¼-inch dice
  5 4-inch sprigs fresh rosemary
  2 4-inch sprigs fresh thyme
Salt to taste (optional)
Freshly ground black pepper to taste
 ⅓ cup toasted sunflower seeds for garnish (optional)

1. In a large skillet, preferably one with a nonstick surface, heat the butter or margarine and the oil briefly over medium-high heat, add the chicken pieces, and brown the chicken on both sides. Transfer the chicken to a large, deep (12 × 6 inch) casserole with a tight-fitting lid.

2. Pour off and reserve the remaining fat from the skillet. Add the cognac to the skillet, turn the heat up to medium, and stir up any cooked bits that have stuck to the pan's bottom and sides. Stir in the wine and broth, raise the heat to high, and boil the liquid to reduce it by about one-quarter. Pour the liquid over the chicken. Wipe out the skillet.

3. Preheat the oven to 325° F.

4. Heat 1 tablespoon of the reserved fat in the skillet, and add the garlic, shallots, and fennel. Cover the skillet, and cook the vegetables over medium-low heat for 5 minutes or until the vegetables soften. Add the vegetables to the casserole.

5. Add the gingerroot, yams, apricots, rosemary, thyme, salt (if desired), and pepper to the casserole. If possible, mix the ingredients to distribute them evenly. Cover the casserole tightly, put it in the hot oven, and bake the chicken for 2 hours or until the meat is ready to fall off the bones. Serve the dish sprinkled with the sunflower seeds, if desired.

ISLAND CHICKEN
6 to 8 servings

Norma Yovich of Ashland, Oregon, sent me this great recipe for a dish from the Seychelles. I first made it while visiting my friend Faith Sullivan in Los Angeles, who has since prepared it for countless dinner parties.

Serving suggestion: Serve the dish with plain or basmati brown or white rice or, for added zip, with the Indian Rice with Peas and Peppers on page 329.

    4 pounds cut-up, skinned chicken parts
    1 11-ounce can mandarin oranges, including juice
    ½ cup (approximately) chicken broth
    3 or more tablespoons chutney, to taste, chopped
    2 tablespoons sliced almonds
    1 tablespoon raisins
    1 teaspoon curry powder
    ½ teaspoon cinnamon
    ½ teaspoon thyme

1. Preheat the oven to 425° F.
2. Place the chicken parts, *except the breast pieces,* in a 9 × 13-inch baking pan, preferably a glass or ceramic one.
3. Drain the juice from the mandarin oranges into a measuring cup, setting aside the orange sections, and add enough broth to the juice to make 1 cup. Add the remaining ingredients to the liquid, and pour the mixture over the chicken.
4. Place the uncovered pan of chicken into the hot oven, and bake the chicken for 25 minutes.
5. Add the breast pieces and the reserved orange sections to the pan, and continue baking the chicken, basting it often, for another 25 minutes or until the thigh meat is no longer pink at the bone. Serve the chicken with its juices.

CHICKEN PROVENÇAL
4 servings

With memories of his origins as a chef in France, Pierre Franey suggests this easy and delicious way to season chicken. It is especially good if you have access to fresh herbs, but I have enjoyed it both with fresh and with dried.

Preparation tip: Be sure you have enough garlic on hand (2 bulbs) before you start to make this dish.

Serving suggestion: In keeping with the provincial theme, serve this dish with Stuffed Tomatoes Provençal on page 339.

1 3½-pound chicken, skinned and cut into
   about 10 serving pieces
⅓ cup flour
Salt to taste (optional)
Freshly ground black pepper to taste
1 tablespoon olive oil
1 teaspoon dried thyme leaves *or* 4 sprigs fresh thyme
1 teaspoon dried rosemary leaves *or* 2 teaspoons
   fresh chopped rosemary leaves
½ teaspoon dried oregano leaves *or* 2 teaspoons
   fresh chopped oregano
12 cloves garlic, *unpeeled*
1 bay leaf
⅓ cup white wine
⅔ cup chicken broth
¼ cup chopped fresh Italian parsley *or* fresh chervil

1. Dredge the chicken in the flour, which has been seasoned with the salt (if
   desired) and pepper.
2. Heat the oil in a large nonstick skillet over medium-high heat, add the
   chicken, and brown the chicken on both sides.
3. Add the thyme, rosemary, oregano, unpeeled garlic cloves, bay leaf, and
   wine, and bring the liquid to a simmer, stirring the ingredients briefly. Cook
   the chicken until the liquid is reduced by half.
4. Add the broth, and bring the liquid back to a simmer. Cover the skillet, and
   cook the chicken for about 10 minutes.
5. Before serving the dish, remove the bay leaf, and sprinkle the chicken with
   the parsley or chervil. Remind diners to squeeze the garlic cloves from the
   skins before eating the garlic.

SONIA'S COQ AU VIN

4 servings

Joanne Michaels and Mary Barile cleverly cornered more than four dozen "celebrities" who live in and around Woodstock, New York, and who like to cook. The recipes and stories that the authors gleaned were collected into a delightful spiral-bound cookbook, *Famous Woodstock Cooks.* One gem is Sonia Malkine's easy-to-prepare, nutritious, and tasty chicken casserole. Sonia is a Breton folksinger of note in the Hudson Valley.

Preparation tips: The flavor of the dish improves with age, so plan to make this a day before it will be needed, and reheat it prior to serving it. The carrots are my addition—for more flavor, color, and nutrients. Peeled pearl onions—about 1 pound of them—can also be added in step 3.

Serving suggestion: Medium egg noodles are a perfect foil.

   1 tablespoon olive oil *or* canola oil, divided
   1 medium onion, peeled and sliced
   3 large cloves garlic, peeled and minced
   4 pounds chicken parts, skinned, fat removed,
     and cut into serving-size pieces
 Salt to taste (optional)
 Freshly ground black pepper to taste
   1 pound carrots, peeled and sliced about ¼-inch
     thick (optional)
 ½ pound pitted prunes
   1 teaspoon thyme, crumbled
   1 teaspoon oregano, crumbled
   1 teaspoon basil, crumbled
   1 teaspoon rosemary
   2 cups Burgundy
  12 ounces mushrooms, sliced

1. In a large, heavy skillet or casserole, preferably one with a nonstick surface, heat 2 teaspoons of the oil briefly, add the onion and garlic to the pan, and sauté the vegetables until they are translucent. Remove the vegetables with a slotted spatula to a bowl, and set the bowl aside.
2. Sprinkle the chicken on both sides with the salt (if desired) and pepper. Add the remaining 1 teaspoon of oil to the pan, add the seasoned chicken, and brown the chicken on both sides.
3. Return the reserved onion mixture to the pan, and add all the remaining ingredients *except* the mushrooms. Bring the mixture to a boil, reduce the heat to low, cover the pan, and simmer the chicken for about 45 minutes.
4. Add the mushrooms, cover the pan, and cook the chicken for another 15 minutes or until it is very tender.

CHICKEN AND RICE WITH CURRIED YOGURT

4 servings

An easy main dish suitable for company, even for those who claim they "don't like yogurt."

Preparation tips: Note that the chicken marinates for 2 hours. If you substitute quicker-cooking white rice for the brown rice, reduce the baking time in step 3 to 15 minutes.

Serving suggestion: Okra with Onions and Apricots (page 321) would make a lovely side dish.

    1 small (2½ to 3 pounds) chicken, skinned and
         cut into serving pieces
    1 cup plain nonfat or low-fat yogurt
    2 large cloves garlic, peeled and crushed
    1 tablespoon curry powder (I use 1 teaspoon hot
         curry powder and 2 teaspoons mild)
  ½ teaspoon salt, divided (optional)
    1 cup long-grain brown rice
    2 cups boiling water
    1 medium onion, peeled and finely chopped (⅔ cup)
    1 tablespoon vegetable oil

1. Place the chicken pieces in a bowl. In a small bowl, combine the yogurt, garlic, curry powder, and ¼ teaspoon of the salt (if desired), and pour this over the chicken. Toss the chicken in the yogurt mixture to coat all the pieces. Cover the bowl with plastic wrap, and refrigerate the chicken for at least 2 hours, turning the pieces once, if possible.
2. Preheat the oven to 350° F.
3. Grease a large casserole. Add the rice, water, and remaining ¼ teaspoon salt (if desired). Tightly cover the casserole, put it in the oven, and bake the rice for 25 minutes.
4. While the rice is cooking, lightly brown the onion in the oil in a large skillet. Scrape the excess marinade from the chicken pieces, reserving it. Add the chicken to the skillet, and brown it on both sides.
5. When the rice has baked, spoon the contents of the skillet over it along with the reserved marinade. Cover the casserole, and bake the chicken for 40 minutes, uncovering the casserole for the last 10 minutes of cooking.

FRUITED CHICKEN WITH BULGUR   *6 servings*

I've yet to try a chicken-and-bulgur dish that I haven't liked. The two seem destined to get on well together, especially when accompanied by fruit.

Preparation tips: If desired, this dish can be made ahead through step 7 and then refrigerated or frozen. If you are starting with a cold casserole, bake it for 1 hour to be sure it is heated through.

Serving suggestion: Try a zippy opener like Spicy Carrot Soup on page 88 or African Yam Soup on page 97.

  1 rib celery, chopped
  1 small onion, peeled and chopped (about ½ cup)
  1 tablespoon butter *or* margarine
1½ cups bulgur
1¾ cups chicken broth
  1 chicken (about 3½ pounds), skinned and cut
     into serving pieces
  ¼ teaspoon salt (optional)
  ⅛ teaspoon freshly ground black pepper
  1 tablespoon vegetable oil
  ¼ cup honey
  ½ cup orange juice
  ¼ cup lemon juice
  ⅛ teaspoon cayenne
  8 pitted prunes, coarsely chopped

1. In a medium-sized saucepan, sauté the celery and onion in the butter or margarine for about 3 minutes. Stir in the bulgur, reduce the heat, and cook the bulgur, stirring it, until it is coated with the fat and begins to toast.
2. Stir in the broth. Bring the liquid to a boil, reduce the heat to low, cover the pan, and simmer the bulgur for 15 minutes or until the liquid is absorbed. Put the cooked bulgur into a large casserole.
3. While the bulgur is cooking, sprinkle the chicken pieces with the salt (if desired) and pepper. Heat the oil in a large skillet, add the chicken, and brown the chicken on both sides. Remove the chicken from the pan, and keep the chicken warm. Pour off any fat that may remain in the skillet.
4. Preheat the oven to 350° F.
5. In a small bowl, combine the honey, orange juice, lemon juice, and cayenne. Add the mixture to the skillet in which chicken was browned. Return the chicken to the skillet, bring the liquid to a boil, reduce the heat, cover the skillet, and simmer the ingredients for 20 minutes or until the chicken is tender.
6. Stir the prunes into the chicken mixture. With a slotted spoon, remove the chicken and prunes, and place them on top of the bulgur in the casserole.

7. Boil the remaining liquid in the skillet for several minutes to reduce it slightly, then spoon the liquid over the chicken. Cover the casserole.
8. Bake the casserole in the hot oven for about 20 minutes.

TANDOORI CHICKEN   *8 servings*

This Indian recipe, toned down a bit from the ultra-spicy version eaten in its native land, is one of the most wholesome as well as delicious ways to prepare chicken: the chicken is skinned and trimmed of fat, and the dish is made without any added fat. Since it is good both at room temperature and hot from the broiler, it is a suitable dish for a buffet table as well as for a sit-down dinner.

Preparation tip: Save the skin and wings in the freezer for preparing broth (see page 78).

Serving suggestion: This spicy chicken dish goes very well with basmati brown rice or long-grain white rice cooked with some lentils or peas. Try also the Savory Applesauce on page 307 and any of the chutneys on pages 550 to 552.

MARINADE
    1 cup plain nonfat or low-fat yogurt
    1 tablespoon finely minced or grated gingerroot
    2 large cloves garlic, peeled and minced
    1 tablespoon paprika (use some hot paprika, if desired)
1½ teaspoon coriander
1½ teaspoon cumin
    1 teaspoon salt, or to taste (optional)
    1 teaspoon freshly ground black pepper
  ¾ teaspoon cayenne, or to taste

  6 pounds chicken parts, skinned and wings removed

1. In a small bowl, combine the marinade ingredients.
2. Slash the chicken 1 inch deep at intervals. Coat the chicken pieces with the marinade, rubbing some of the marinade into the slashes. Place the chicken in a bowl, cover the bowl tightly with plastic wrap, and place the chicken in the refrigerator to marinate for at least 6 hours and up to 1 day.
3. Oil the broiler rack, and place it 6 inches from the heat. Preheat the broiler.
4. Place the chicken pieces on the rack, and broil the chicken for 20 minutes on one side. Turn the pieces over, and broil them on the other side for 15 minutes or until their juices run clear when they are pierced with a fork.

MOROCCAN CHICKEN WITH COUSCOUS

4 servings

This make-ahead dish, derived from *Bon Appétit* magazine, is tasty, simple, and attractive and is a meal in itself.

Preparation tips: Be sure to use a nonstick skillet or a well-seasoned cast-iron pan. The chicken can be reheated in a covered skillet or in a microwave oven, but it is best to prepare the couscous just before serving time (it takes only 5 minutes and will be done by the time the chicken is hot).

Serving suggestion: For geographical consistency, try the North African Carrot Salad on page 359.

CHICKEN
- 4 large chicken legs and thighs, skinned and disjointed
- Salt to taste (optional)
- Freshly ground black pepper to taste
- 1 tablespoon olive oil
- 1 large onion, peeled and chopped (1 cup)
- 1 pound carrots, peeled and cut diagonally into ½-inch slices
- 2 teaspoons paprika (use some hot paprika, if desired)
- 1 teaspoon ground ginger
- ¼ teaspoon turmeric
- ⅛ teaspoon cinnamon
- 1 lemon, cut into 8 wedges and seeded
- 1 cup chicken broth

COUSCOUS
- 2 cups chicken broth
- ⅓ cup dried currants
- ¼ teaspoon salt, or to taste (optional)
- ⅛ teaspoon allspice
- 1 cup quick-cooking couscous

TO PREPARE THE CHICKEN
1. Season the chicken with the salt (if desired) and pepper. Heat the oil in a large skillet, preferably one with a nonstick surface, and brown the chicken on both sides over medium-high heat. Remove the chicken to a platter.
2. Reduce the heat to medium-low, add the onion to the skillet, and sauté the onion for about 3 minutes.
3. Add the carrots, and sauté them for 2 minutes.
4. Add the paprika, ginger, turmeric, and cinnamon, and cook the mixture for 1 minute, stirring it.

5. Return the reserved chicken pieces with their juices to the skillet. Add the lemon wedges and broth. Bring the liquid to a boil, reduce the heat, cover the skillet, and simmer the chicken, turning it occasionally, for 30 minutes or until it is cooked through.

TO PREPARE THE COUSCOUS

6. In a medium-sized saucepan, combine the broth, currants, salt (if desired), and allspice, and bring the mixture to a boil.

7. Stir in the couscous, boil it for 2 minutes, remove the pan from the heat, cover the pan, and let the couscous stand for 5 minutes or until the liquid is absorbed.

TO ASSEMBLE THE DISH

8. Serve the chicken and carrots over the couscous, surrounded by the lemon wedges.

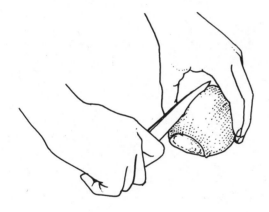

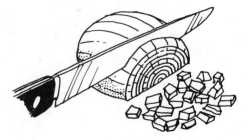

CURRIED CHICKEN WITH CHICKPEAS

8 to 10 servings

Madhur Jaffrey is a talented Indian cook, and every recipe of hers that I have tried has been delicious, even with a reduction in fat and a taming of the hot spices. The original recipe was published in *Madhur Jaffrey's Cookbook.*

Preparation tips: The dish can be prepared ahead to the last 15 to 20 minutes of cooking, or it can be completely prepared in advance and reheated at serving time. If a smaller recipe is desired, use 3 breast halves, 3 legs, and ½ can of tomatoes, and adjust the seasonings as desired. Basmati brown rice is a perfect accompaniment; start cooking it when the chicken is added to the skillet in step 4, or, if making the chicken in advance, start the rice 40 minutes before the chicken will be ready.

Serving suggestion: Try a tame, refreshing dessert like the Cranberry-Orange Sorbet on page 509 or the Citrus Delight on page 526.

- 10 large cloves garlic, or to taste, peeled
- 3 1-inch cubes of gingerroot, peeled and chopped
- 2 fresh hot green peppers (e.g., jalapeños or chilies), chopped
- 6 tablespoons plus 2 cups water, divided
- 5 pounds chicken parts, skinned and cut into serving pieces

Salt to taste (optional)
Freshly ground black pepper to taste
1½ tablespoons olive oil *or* canola oil
- 2 tablespoons coriander
- 1 tablespoon cumin
- ½ teaspoon cayenne
- 1 28-ounce can plum tomatoes, drained and chopped
- ½ teaspoon salt (optional)
- 2 to 3 cups cooked chickpeas (drained and rinsed, if canned)

1. In a blender, purée the garlic, gingerroot, hot peppers, and the 6 tablespoons of water. Set the purée aside.
2. Season the chicken parts with the salt (if desired) and pepper. Heat the oil in a large, deep skillet, add the seasoned chicken, and brown it in batches over medium-high heat. Using tongs or a slotted spoon, transfer the browned chicken to a bowl, and set the bowl aside.
3. Reduce the heat to medium, and add the garlic mixture to the skillet. Cook the mixture, stirring it, 2 minutes. Then stir in the coriander, cumin, cayenne, and tomatoes. Cook this mixture, stirring it, 2 minutes longer.

4. Return the chicken to the skillet along with the 2 cups of water and the ½ teaspoon salt (if desired). Bring the liquid to a boil, reduce the heat to low, cover the skillet, and cook the chicken for 20 minutes.
5. Add the chickpeas, cover the skillet, and cook the chicken for 10 minutes. Then uncover the skillet, raise the heat to high, and boil the mixture, stirring it occasionally, for another 5 to 10 minutes or until the liquid is reduced to a thick sauce.

CHICKEN TACOS

6 servings

This Mexican-style dish, excellent for a buffet as well as for a casual family meal, includes the salad with the "meat" and is served with salsa, a spicy tomato sauce.

Serving suggestion: Try White Gazpacho on page 100 as an opener, and serve the tacos with "Refried" Beans on page 309.

FILLINGS
- 1 pound skinless, boneless chicken breasts, cooked and shredded
- 1 small head iceberg lettuce, cut into fine shreds
- 1 large sweet green pepper *or* sweet red pepper, cut into thin strips
- ⅓ cup chopped onion *or* sliced scallions
- ½ pound zucchini, coarsely grated or cut into fine shreds
- 4 ounces Monterey Jack or Cheddar, shredded (1 cup)

SALSA
- 1 large tomato, coarsely chopped
- ¼ cup minced fresh parsley (do not substitute dried)
- 1 large clove garlic, peeled and finely minced
- 1 medium sweet green pepper, finely chopped (½ cup)
- 1 tablespoon vegetable oil (optional)
- 2 ounces canned green chilies *or* 2 fresh jalapeños, or to taste, seeded and finely chopped

12 taco shells, warmed in the oven

1. Place the individual filling ingredients in bowls of appropriate size, or place the chicken in the center of a large platter and surround it with piles of the remaining ingredients.
2. In a separate bowl, combine the salsa ingredients.
3. Serve the fillings and the salsa with the warm taco shells: each diner places the desired amount of filling ingredients in the shell and tops it with some salsa.

CINDY'S SALSA CHICKEN

6 servings

My sister-in-law, Cindy Brody, is one of those enviable people who "know" food and know how to take good care of themselves and their loved ones. Just about everything she cooks is delicious and nourishing. And she almost never consults a recipe. This is one of her creations that drew raves from my tasters.

Preparation tips: You can use commercial salsa (preferably the kind made without oil or salt), or you can make your own (see page 539). I prepared the dish without the cilantro, and it still had plenty of flavor. The dish can be made up to 2 days in advance and reheated at serving time.

Serving suggestion: While the sauciness and Mexican flavor of this dish makes rice a natural accompaniment, the chicken would also go well with pasta or mashed potatoes.

     1 tablespoon olive oil
     3 large cloves garlic, peeled and minced
  1½ cups chopped onion
     1 large sweet red pepper, cored, seeded, and cut
         into small dice (1 cup)
     1 pound boneless, skinless chicken breasts, cut
         into 1-inch chunks
     2 large tomatoes *or* 3 medium tomatoes, peeled
         and diced
     1 small head broccoli, stems sliced, flowerets cut
         into bite-sized pieces (3 to 4 cups), and steamed
         for 3 minutes
     1 16-ounce can pink beans *or* kidney beans,
         drained and rinsed (1⅔ cups)
     1 cup medium-hot salsa
   ¼ cup chopped cilantro (optional)
Salt to taste (optional)
Freshly ground black pepper to taste

1. In a large nonstick skillet or Dutch oven, heat the olive oil briefly, add the garlic and onion, and sauté the vegetables for 3 minutes or until they are softened. Add the red pepper, and sauté the vegetables for another 2 minutes.
2. Add the remaining ingredients, and bring the mixture to a boil over medium heat. Stir the mixture gently, reduce the heat, cover the pot, and simmer the chicken for 5 to 7 minutes or until the chicken is just done. Check the seasonings before serving the dish.

CHICKEN AND MUSHROOMS   *6 servings*

The secret of success of this Pierre Franey recipe is balsamic vinegar, which is partially aged in balsam wood and is now widely available in specialty food stores and from mail-order companies (see page 13).

Preparation tip: The chicken can be prepared ahead through step 3.

Serving suggestion: This dish goes well with regular pasta as well as such exotic pastas as tomato linguine or tarragon rotini (see page 11 for the source) sprinkled with grated Parmesan. Try also the Arugula and Fennel Salad on page 344.

6 boneless, skinless chicken breast halves
   (about 6 ounces each)
2 tablespoons flour
Salt to taste (optional)
Freshly ground black pepper to taste
1 tablespoon olive oil
6 cloves garlic, peeled
1 pound mushrooms, halved if large
¼ cup balsamic vinegar
1 cup chicken broth
1 bay leaf
¼ teaspoon thyme

1. Dredge the chicken pieces in the flour, which as been seasoned with the salt (if desired) and pepper, shaking off the excess flour.
2. Heat the oil over medium-high heat in a large, heavy skillet, preferably one with a nonstick surface, add the chicken, and cook the chicken for 3 minutes or until it browns on one side.
3. Add the garlic, turn the chicken pieces over, and scatter the mushrooms over the chicken. Cook the ingredients for about 3 minutes, shaking the skillet to distribute the mushrooms. Add the vinegar, broth, bay leaf, and thyme.
4. Cover the skillet tightly, and cook the chicken over medium-low heat for 10 minutes, turning the chicken once as it cooks. Uncover the skillet, transfer the chicken to a warm serving platter, and cover the platter with foil to keep the chicken warm.
5. In the uncovered skillet, cook the mushrooms over medium-high heat for about 7 minutes. Remove the bay leaf, and pour the mushrooms and the sauce over the chicken.

CBC CASSEROLE *(Chicken, Beans, and Cauliflower)* *16 servings*

Here is a good dish to serve to a large group. This whole meal in a pot has something for everyone.

Preparation tip: The dish can be prepared in advance through step 7 and reheated at serving time.

Serving suggestion: Offer rice, noodles, or mashed potatoes as a side dish.

3 cups dried pinto beans, picked over, rinsed,
    soaked for 10 hours or longer in water to cover
    by at least 4 inches, and drained
Water to cover by 2 inches
1 teaspoon salt (optional)
1 pound kielbasa (smoked Polish garlic sausage),
    quartered lengthwise, then sliced crosswise into
    ½-inch pieces
2 tablespoons olive oil, divided
4 pounds boneless, skinless chicken breasts, cut
    into 1-inch pieces
6 cups sliced Spanish onions (3 or 4 large)
1 tablespoon minced garlic (3 large cloves)
1 teaspoon oregano
5 to 6 cups (1 46-ounce can) chicken broth, divided
Freshly ground black pepper to taste
3 sweet green peppers, cored, seeded, and cut into chunks
3 sweet red peppers, cored, seeded, and cut into chunks
2 heads cauliflower, cut into flowerets
2 pounds small to medium zucchinis, cut into
    ½-inch slices
¼ cup chopped fresh parsley
½ cup grated Parmesan

1. In a large, heavy pot, cook the beans in the water for 1 to 1½ hours or until the beans are tender, adding the salt (if desired) during the last 15 minutes of cooking. Drain the beans, and set them aside.
2. Cook the kielbasa in a dry skillet over low heat or in a microwave to render some of the fat. Drain the kielbasa on paper towels, and set the sausage aside. Wipe out the skillet.
3. Heat 1 tablespoon of the oil in a large skillet, add the chicken pieces, and brown the chicken over medium-high heat. Remove the chicken from the pan, and set the chicken aside.

4. Heat the remaining 1 tablespoon of oil in the skillet, add the onions, sauté-ing them over medium-low heat until they are golden brown. Add the garlic, and sauté the vegetables 1 minute longer. Transfer the onions and garlic to an 8- to 10-quart Dutch oven or cast-iron casserole.
5. Add the reserved chicken to the pot, and sprinkle the chicken with the oregano. Add 4 cups of the broth and the ground pepper. Bring the liquid to a boil, reduce the heat, cover the pot, and simmer the chicken for 15 minutes.
6. Add the green peppers, red peppers, cauliflower, and the rest of the broth to the pot. Cover the pot, and simmer the chicken for 15 minutes.
7. Add the zucchinis and the reserved beans and kielbasa, and simmer the chicken 10 minutes longer.
8. Serve the casserole sprinkled with the parsley and Parmesan.

CHICKEN WITH NOODLES
AND GREENS

4 servings

Dorothy Hawley Bloom, a *Jane Brody's Good Food Book* fan from Oneonta, New York, has raised ordinary chicken and noodles to a high culinary and nutritional art. I made a few modifications in her recipe but used all her ingredients.

Preparation tip: The casserole can be prepared a day in advance for baking. Bring it to room temperature before putting it in the oven.

    ½ pound broad egg noodles
Water
Salt (optional)
1½ cups chicken broth, divided
    1 pound Swiss chard *or* mixed greens (e.g., chard,
       turnip, collard, and/or mustard)
    1 tablespoon olive oil
    2 cloves garlic, peeled and sliced
    4 shallots *or* 1 medium onion, peeled and sliced
    ½ pound mushrooms, sliced
    2 tablespoons flour
    ⅓ cup powdered nonfat milk
    2 tablespoons grated Cheddar
    ¼ cup grated Parmesan
    2 cups cooked, cubed boneless chicken
Freshly grated nutmeg (optional)
Freshly ground black pepper to taste

1. Preheat the oven to 350° F.
2. In a large pot, cook the noodles in plenty of boiling water (salted, if desired) until the noodles are *al dente.* Drain the noodles, and return them to the pot. Moisten them with 1 or 2 tablespoons of the chicken broth.
3. While the noodles cook, steam the Swiss chard or greens in a saucepan for 5 minutes. Then coarsely chop the chard or greens. Set them aside.
4. In a deep skillet or shallow saucepan, heat the oil, add the garlic and shallots or onion, and sauté the vegetables for a few minutes. Add the mushrooms, and cook them over medium-low heat until they begin to give up their liquid.
5. Stir in the flour, and cook the mixture, stirring it, for 1 minute. Stir in the remaining broth and the powdered milk, and cook the mixture, stirring it, until it thickens. Add the Cheddar and Parmesan, stirring the mixture until the cheeses melt. Then stir in the chicken.
6. Transfer the reserved noodles to a greased 2- or 3-quart casserole, pressing them against the sides as well as the bottom of the dish. Spoon *one-half* of the

cheese sauce over the noodles. Spread the reserved chard or greens over the sauce, and sprinkle the chard or greens with the nutmeg (if desired) and black pepper. Pour the remaining sauce over the greens.

7. Put the casserole in the hot oven, and bake the dish for 40 minutes.

CHINESE-STYLE BAKED CHICKEN *6 servings*

Here is a moist, oven-baked barbecue that will delight people of all ages and tastes.

Preparation tips: Note that the chicken should marinate for *8 hours or more.* You can save the marinade (in the refrigerator for about a week, longer in the freezer) for another use.

Serving suggestion: Rice or thin egg noodles would make a nice accompaniment. Try also the Broccoli and Baby Corn on page 313.

MARINADE
1 cup water
¼ cup dry white wine
¼ cup reduced-sodium soy sauce
¼ cup Dijon-style mustard
1 large clove garlic, peeled and minced
½ teaspoon Worcestershire sauce

3 large whole chicken breasts, skinned and halved
   (6 halves)
1 tablespoon vegetable oil

1. In a shallow dish such as a glass deep-dish pie plate, combine the marinade ingredients.
2. Add the chicken, turning each piece to coat it completely with the marinade. Cover the dish or plate, and refrigerate the chicken for 8 hours or longer, turning chicken pieces several times in the marinade.
3. Preheat the oven to 350° F.
4. Heat the oil in a large nonstick skillet. Remove the chicken pieces from the marinade (save the marinade), add them to the skillet, and brown them on both sides. Transfer the chicken to a baking dish (about 13 × 9 × 2 inches), and place the baking dish in the hot oven.
5. Bake the chicken about 30 minutes, basting it occasionally with the reserved marinade.

TERRY'S CHICKEN ROLL-UPS   *8 servings*

Along with trees, culinary delights grow in Brooklyn. Terry Quinn, Jane's husband and one of my most astute tasters, devised this delicious, attractive chicken dish, which, incidentally, can also be made with veal cutlets.

Preparation tip: If the chicken is very fresh, the roll-ups can be prepared up to 1 day in advance for baking. Keep them refrigerated, and add the vermouth just before baking them.

Serving suggestion: Broccoli Rabe on page 312 and a simple salad like Arugula Salad with Pistachios on page 344 are ideal accompaniments.

    8 large chicken breast halves, skinned and boned
      (each cutlet should weigh 5 to 6 ounces)
Olive-oil spray
    4 teaspoons olive oil, divided
    1 teaspoon butter *or* margarine
    8 shallots, peeled and chopped (about 1¼ cups)
      or 1 large onion, peeled and chopped
    1 clove garlic, peeled and minced
    2 cups diced mushrooms
    2 tablespoons fresh rosemary leaves *or* 2
      teaspoons dried rosemary, divided
    1 pound fresh spinach, washed thoroughly, tough
      stems removed, steamed, and chopped, *or* 1
      10-ounce package chopped spinach
   ½ cup pine nuts
   ½ cup fresh bread crumbs (any kind will do)
    1 egg white, lightly beaten
 2½ teaspoons oregano, divided
   ½ teaspoon salt (optional)
Freshly ground black pepper to taste
    6 ounces part-skim mozzarella, shredded
   ⅔ cup dry vermouth *or* combination of vermouth
      and dry sherry

  1. Pound the chicken breasts flat between sheets of plastic wrap, taking care not to tear the breasts. Spray the chicken cutlets with olive oil, and set them aside.
  2. Heat 2 teaspoons of the oil and the butter or margarine in a large skillet, add the shallots or onion, garlic, mushrooms, and 1 tablespoon of the fresh rosemary (1 teaspoon of the dried) to the pan, and sauté the vegetables for 3 minutes or until the shallots or onion are translucent and the mushrooms are wilted. Transfer the mushroom mixture to a large bowl.
  3. To the bowl, add the spinach, pine nuts, bread crumbs, egg white, ½ tea-

spoon of the oregano, salt (if desired), pepper, and mozzarella, combining the ingredients thoroughly.

4. Sprinkle the reserved flattened chicken breasts with the remaining 2 teaspoons of oregano. Divide the spinach mixture among the cutlets, spreading the mixture flat and leaving about 1 inch of uncovered chicken at one end. Roll the cutlets up toward the uncovered end, and secure the roll-ups with toothpicks. Place the roll-ups in an ovenproof dish, and sprinkle them with the remaining 1 tablespoon of the fresh rosemary (1 teaspoon of the dried) and the remaining olive oil. Cover the dish tightly with foil.

5. When you are ready to bake the roll-ups, preheat the oven to 400° F. Pour the vermouth or vermouth-sherry combination into the baking dish, and reseal the dish with the foil. Bake the chicken for 20 minutes (25 minutes, if you are starting out with chilled roll-ups).

DICED CHICKEN WITH PEANUTS   *4 to 6 servings*

I have included only a few stir-fried dishes in this book because many cooks, unless they are experienced in the techniques of Chinese cooking, find the last-minute preparation of a stir-fried meal too intimidating to do for company. However, it really isn't that difficult or time-consuming during a party *if* you follow the Boy Scout motto and get every ingredient pan-ready ahead of time. In fact, I use this technique now with almost everything I cook because it makes the process of putting a multicourse meal together so much easier to execute. Here, then, is a straightforward fat-reduced stir-fry I learned from Norman Weinstein, the best Jewish Chinese cook in Brooklyn!

Preparation tips: Norman's recipe calls for dark soy sauce (also called double black soy), which is sold in Chinese groceries. If this is unavailable, substitute ordinary imported or reduced-sodium imported soy sauce. Start cooking the rice for this dish before you put the chicken in the marinade. To prepare Chinese "sticky" rice that can be eaten with chopsticks, in a saucepan combine 1 cup of short-grain rice with 1¾ cups of water; bring the liquid to a boil, reduce the heat to low, cover the pan, and simmer the rice for about 15 minutes; turn off the heat, and let the rice sit on the stove, covered, while you prepare the stir-fry.

Serving suggestion: Dry Sautéed Green Beans (page 308) go well ethnically and aesthetically.

MARINADE
- 2 teaspoons cornstarch
- 1 tablespoon dark soy sauce
- 1 tablespoon dry sherry
- 1 teaspoon sesame oil
- 1 teaspoon sugar
- 1 egg white

STIR-FRY
- 2 whole chicken breasts, skinned, boned, and cut into bite-sized pieces
- 3 tablespoons oil (preferably peanut *or* canola), divided
- 1½ cups raw, shelled peanuts without skins
- 2 medium sweet red peppers, cored, seeded, and cut into bite-sized pieces
- 4 dried red chilies, or to taste
- 2 teaspoons minced gingerroot
- 5 cloves garlic, peeled and minced
- 1 cup sliced scallions
- 1 to 2 tablespoons dark soy sauce, to taste (see "Preparation tips")

1. Combine all the marinade ingredients in a medium-sized bowl. Add the chicken pieces, tossing them to coat them well with the marinade. Set the chicken aside for 15 minutes.

2. Heat 2 tablespoons of the oil in a well-seasoned wok or large nonstick frying pan. Add the peanuts, and stir-fry them for 2 to 3 minutes or until they are golden brown. With a slotted spoon, remove the peanuts to a platter, leaving as much oil as possible in the pan.

3. Add the sweet peppers to the pan, and stir-fry them for about 1 minute. Remove them with a slotted spoon to the platter.

4. Add the remaining 1 tablespoon of oil to the pan, heat the pan to hot, and add the chilies. Stir-fry the chilies for 1 minute, then add the gingerroot and garlic, and stir-fry them for a few seconds.

5. Add the reserved chicken, its marinade, and the scallions to the pan. Toss the ingredients vigorously for about 1½ minutes to cook the chicken through.

6. Add the soy sauce to the pan along with the reserved peanuts and the reserved sweet peppers. Toss the ingredients to coat everything evenly with the sauce. If possible, remove the hot chilies before serving the stir-fry, or warn diners of the presence of the chilies—*they are too hot to eat!*

CORNISH HENS STUFFED WITH FRUITED RICE

8 servings

Cornish game hens are such attractive company fare that most people forgive the indelicacies of eating them. This delicious recipe, derived from one designed for food-processor cookery, can easily be prepared with a good kitchen knife.

Preparation tips: Since Cornish hens hold so little stuffing and this stuffing is so tasty, I prefer to make extra stuffing and extra rice, which I can combine and use as a side dish. The hens can be baked in advance and reheated at serving time at 350° F for 15 minutes. If you have kitchen shears, the hens are especially easy to cut in half at serving time. Snip through the breastbone with the shears, and then use a large kitchen knife to cut through the stuffing and back.

STUFFING
- 1½ cups basmati brown rice *or* regular brown rice *or* white rice
- 3 cups chicken broth
- 1 tablespoon butter *or* margarine
- 2 large shallots (about 4 ounces), minced
- 4 ribs celery (about 6 ounces), finely chopped
- 2 Granny Smith apples, peeled, cored, and finely chopped
- 2 cups cranberries, coarsely chopped
- ⅔ cup dried currants
- 3 tablespoons honey
- ½ teaspoon salt (optional)
- 1 teaspoon ground sage
- ¼ teaspoon freshly ground black pepper, or to taste
- ¼ teaspoon freshly grated nutmeg

HENS
- 4 large Cornish game hens
- 1 to 2 teaspoons olive oil
- ½ teaspoon salt (optional)
- ¼ teaspoon freshly ground black pepper

1. In a medium-sized saucepan, cook the rice in the broth for 35 to 40 minutes (20 minutes for white rice) or until the liquid is absorbed and the rice is tender. Set the rice aside.
2. Preheat the oven to 450° F.
3. To prepare the stuffing, melt the butter or margarine in a small nonstick skillet, add the shallots and celery, and sauté the vegetables for 5 minutes or until they soften. Transfer the vegetables to a large bowl, and add the remaining stuffing ingredients and 1 cup of the reserved cooked rice, mixing the ingredients to combine them thoroughly.

4. Loosely pack the stuffing into the hens. Close the cavities of the hens with skewers or cover the cavities with pieces of foil, and tie the legs of each hen together. Combine the leftover stuffing with the remaining rice, and set the mixture aside.

5. Sprinkle the hens with the olive oil, salt (if desired), and pepper. Place the hens breast side up in a greased roasting pan, tucking the wings under the bodies.

6. Put the pan in the hot oven, and roast the hens for 30 minutes. Reduce the heat to 350° F, and roast the hens for another 30 minutes. If you are preparing this dish in advance, reduce the second roasting time to 15 to 20 minutes, and complete the cooking when you are ready to serve. At this time, heat the leftover rice-and-stuffing combination in a greased casserole, and serve this as a side dish.

7. After the roasting has been completed, cut the hens in half without removing the stuffing (see "Preparation tips," above), and serve the halves on individual plates, stuffing side down.

CORNISH HENS WITH SPICED APPLE STUFFING

4 servings

I adapted a recipe for roast chicken devised by Madhur Jaffrey, a talented Indian cook, for *Madhur Jaffrey's Cookbook.* I was so taken with the stuffing that I used the ingredients to make a "hot" applesauce (see page 536).

Preparation tips: Roast chicken can be similarly prepared. Use half again the amount of dressing ingredients to stuff 2 3½- to 4-pound chickens (you will not have any leftover stuffing). Roast the birds until the juices from the meaty part of their thighs run clear or until a meat thermometer inserted in the breast reaches 170° F. If desired, you can make extra stuffing and bake it in a covered casserole for about 30 minutes after the oven is turned down to 325° F.

HENS
- 2 Cornish game hens, about 1¾ pounds each
- 1 tablespoon olive oil
- 1 teaspoon paprika
- ¼ teaspoon thyme
- ⅛ to ¼ teaspoon cayenne, to taste
- Salt to taste (optional)
- Freshly ground black pepper to taste

STUFFING
- 1 pound tart apples (e.g., 2 large Granny Smiths), cored, peeled, and finely diced
- 2 tablespoons fresh lemon juice
- 2 tablespoons sugar
- ¼ teaspoon salt (optional)
- Scant ¼ teaspoon thyme
- Scant ¼ teaspoon cinnamon
- ⅛ teaspoon cayenne
- Freshly ground black pepper to taste

- ½ cup water (optional)

1. Preheat the oven to 450° F.
2. Rinse the hens, pat them dry, and rub them with the olive oil.
3. In a small bowl, combine the remaining seasonings for the hens, and set the mixture aside.
4. In a medium-sized bowl, thoroughly mix together all the stuffing ingredients. Divide the stuffing between the hens, closing each cavity with skewers or wooden picks or sewing it shut. Place the stuffed hens back side up in a roasting pan on a rack. Sprinkle the backs of the hens with half of the reserved seasoning mixture. Turn the hens breast side up, and sprinkle the hens with the rest of the seasonings. If desired (it helps in cleaning the pan), pour the water in the bottom of the roasting pan.
5. Place the pan in the hot oven, roast the birds for 15 minutes, then reduce the heat to 325° F, and roast the birds for another 45 minutes or until the juices run clear when the thick part of the thigh is pierced with a fork or when a meat thermometer inserted in the breast registers 170° F.
6. To serve the hens, place them on a cutting board, and, with a large, heavy

kitchen knife, cut them in half lengthwise through the stuffing. Using a large spatula to keep the stuffing from falling out, place the hen halves stuffing side down on individual platters.

ROAST STUFFED TURKEY *about 12 servings*

Roast turkey, at long last, has come far beyond Thanksgiving and other holiday meals. With or without stuffing, many people now realize its virtues for buffets and picnics, and for dinner parties during any of the cooler months of the year. Although it requires more preparation than, say, a roast beef, it goes much further *and* it offers the opportunity, via leftovers and carcass-based broth, for many a family meal as well. Since I've not found a better way to roast this noble bird than the method I offered in *Jane Brody's Good Food Book,* I repeat those instructions here and provide several new healthful and delicious stuffing ideas. You should end up with a moist and tasty bird without using a lot of fat and salt.

Preparation tips: I've found that larger birds (12 to 16 pounds) are tastier than the smaller ones and are less likely to dry out during roasting (probably because older birds have more fat and less surface area for a given amount of flesh). As for amount of stuffing, generally figure on ⅔ to ¾ cup for each pound of poultry. I prefer to make more since extra stuffing can always be baked in a covered ovenproof dish when the turkey is about 40 minutes from done.

Serving suggestion: Don't forget Cranberry-Pear Relish on page 536. Or serve the turkey with any of the chutneys on pages 550 to 552.

  1 12-pound turkey, fresh or defrosted
Salt to taste (optional)
Freshly ground black pepper to taste
12 cups stuffing (approximately, see pages 140 to 144)
  1 tablespoon vegetable oil, preferably olive oil *or* canola oil
  2 tablespoons broth *or* water
  2 large cloves garlic, peeled and mashed
  2 teaspoons sweet paprika
  1 cup water
  1 onion, peeled and sliced (optional)

1. Preheat the oven to 325° F.
2. Wash the turkey, and dry it with paper towels. Sprinkle the cavity of the bird with the salt (if desired) and pepper.
3. Spoon the stuffing into the turkey (do not pack the bird tightly), leaving some room for the stuffing to expand. If the neck skin is available, stuff that, too. Sew up the open ends (try dental floss instead of thread), or close them with skewers and cord.
4. In a small bowl, make a paste of the vegetable oil, broth or water, garlic, and paprika. Paint this mixture on the skin of the bird with a pastry brush, or

smear it on with your fingers. (Do the underside of the bird first.) Place the turkey breast side up on a rack in a roasting pan big enough to hold the turkey without squeezing it.

5. Pour the water into the bottom of the pan (you will end up with more gravy that way, and the turkey will be moister), and scatter the onion around the pan's perimeter. Cover the turkey with a tent of foil, crimping the foil around the edges of the pan to hold the foil in place. Put the turkey in the hot oven, and roast it for approximately 4½ to 5 hours or until a thermometer inserted in the bird's thigh registers 180° F to 185° F. Remove the foil from the pan, and baste the turkey with the pan juices several times during the last 30 to 60 minutes of roasting. For an unstuffed turkey, reduce roasting time by about 30 minutes.

6. To serve the turkey, remove the stuffing to a separate bowl before carving the bird. Serve the turkey without its skin, if possible.

CORN BREAD AND RICE STUFFING

about 12 cups stuffing
for 16-pound turkey

CORN BREAD FOR STUFFING
1½ cups yellow corn meal (preferably stone-ground)
1½ cups all-purpose flour
 2 tablespoons baking powder
½ teaspoon salt (optional)
1½ cups skim or low-fat milk
 2 eggs
¼ cup butter *or* margarine, melted

STUFFING
 4 cups water
Turkey giblets
¾ cup diced celery (about 1½ ribs)
 1 carrot, peeled and sliced
 1 small onion, peeled and sliced
Salt to taste (optional) *or* ½ teaspoon salt-free seasoning mix
Freshly ground black pepper to taste
 2 cups thinly sliced celery (about 4 ribs)
 2 cups chopped onion (2 large)
½ pound mushrooms, sliced
 3 tablespoons butter *or* margarine
 1 cup long-grain rice (brown *or* white)
Water
Reserved corn-bread cubes
 2 cups cubed stale whole-wheat bread
 1 cup chopped pecans
 1 teaspoon thyme leaves
 1 teaspoon sage
 1 teaspoon tarragon, crumbled
Salt to taste (optional)
Freshly ground black pepper to taste

TO PREPARE THE CORN BREAD

1. Preheat the oven to 425° F.
2. In a large bowl, combine the corn meal, flour, baking powder, and salt (if desired). Set the bowl aside.
3. In a small bowl, combine the milk, eggs, and butter or margarine. Add the ingredients of the small bowl to the flour mixture, and beat the batter with an eggbeater for about 1 minute or until the batter is smooth. Pour the batter into a greased 9 × 13-inch cake pan.
4. Put the pan in the hot oven, and bake the bread for about 25 minutes or until it turns golden brown. Take the pan out of the oven, cool the bread, cut it into ½-inch cubes, and set it aside.

TO PREPARE THE STUFFING

5. While the corn bread bakes, in a medium-sized saucepan, combine the water, giblets, the ¾ cup of diced celery, carrot, the small onion, salt (if desired) or salt-free seasoning mix, and pepper. Bring the mixture to a boil, reduce the heat, cover the pan, and simmer the giblets for 20 to 30 minutes or until they are tender. Remove the cooked giblets from the pan, strain the broth into a measuring cup, and reserve both the giblets and the broth. Remove the cooked flesh from the turkey neck, discarding the skin, chop the reserved giblets, and set them aside.
6. In a large saucepan or skillet, preferably one with a nonstick surface, sauté the 2 cups of celery, the 2 cups of onion, and the mushrooms in the butter or margarine until the onions are just soft. Stir in the rice, and brown it lightly, stirring it constantly. Add the reserved giblet broth and enough water to measure 3 cups. Bring the liquid to a boil, reduce the heat, cover the pan, and simmer the rice for 15 minutes.
7. In a large bowl, combine the rice-vegetable mixture with the reserved chopped giblets, the reserved corn bread, cubed whole-wheat bread, pecans, thyme, sage, tarragon, salt (if desired), and pepper. Mix the ingredients to combine them thoroughly.

OYSTER STUFFING

about 7 cups stuffing
for a 12-pound turkey

1 cup chopped onion (1 large)
1 cup diced celery (about 2 ribs)
1 tablespoon butter *or* margarine
2 6-ounce cans oysters, drained and chopped,
  liquid reserved
1 egg white *and* 1 egg, beaten
5 cups coarsely crumbled corn bread (see pages
  140, 143, 439, or 440) *or* white bread
1 teaspoon thyme leaves
¼ cup minced fresh parsley
Salt to taste (can be omitted since the oyster liquid
  is salty)
Freshly ground black pepper to taste
¼ cup (approximately) broth of any kind, as
  needed

1. In a large skillet over medium heat, sauté the onion and celery in the butter
   or margarine until the vegetables are soft. Remove the pan from the heat.
2. Add to the pan the chopped oysters with the reserved liquid, the beaten egg
   white and whole egg, crumbled bread, thyme, parsley, salt (if desired), and
   pepper. Add the broth, as needed, to moisten the stuffing adequately. Mix
   the ingredients well.

CRANBERRY-HAZELNUT STUFFING

about 8 cups stuffing
for a 12-pound turkey

This attractive and easy-to-prepare stuffing from *Gourmet* magazine is also based
on corn bread.

Preparation tips: The corn bread can be made ahead and frozen. The stuffing
mixture can be prepared a day ahead and refrigerated; it can also be baked
outside the bird for an almost fat-free stuffing. If you make the corn bread and
stuffing on or near the same day, start by toasting ¾ cup of hazelnuts.

CORN BREAD
- ½ cup hazelnuts, toasted
- 1 cup yellow corn meal (preferably stone-ground)
- ½ cup all-purpose flour
- ½ teaspoon salt (optional)
- 2¼ teaspoons baking powder
- 1 large egg
- ¾ cup skim or low-fat milk

STUFFING
- 1 cup thinly sliced onion (1 large)
- ¾ cup chopped sweet green pepper
- 1 cup chicken broth *plus* 1 additional cup chicken broth if you are not going to use the stuffing in the bird
- ¼ cup hazelnuts, toasted
- Reserved corn bread
- ¾ cup cranberries or more, to taste, coarsely chopped
- ⅓ cup minced fresh parsley
- Salt to taste (optional)
- Freshly ground black pepper to taste

TO PREPARE THE CORN BREAD

1. Place a rack in the center of the oven, and preheat the oven to 425° F.
2. Finely grind the hazelnuts in a spice grinder, coffee grinder, or food processor. Transfer the ground nuts to a large bowl.
3. Place an oiled 8 × 8-inch baking pan in the oven while you prepare the batter.
4. To the nuts in the bowl, add the corn meal, flour, salt (if desired), and baking powder, stirring the ingredients to combine them well.
3. In a small bowl whisk together the egg and milk, and add them to the corn-meal mixture, stirring the batter just to combine the ingredients.
4. Remove the pan from the oven, spread the batter evenly in the pan, put the pan back into the oven, and bake the bread for 8 to 10 minutes or until a tester inserted in the center of the bread comes out clean. Remove the pan from the oven. Loosen the edges of the bread with a knife, invert the bread onto a rack, and let the bread cool while you prepare the rest of the stuffing.

TO PREPARE THE STUFFING

5. In a medium-sized skillet, combine the onion, green pepper, and 1 cup of the broth. Bring the liquid to a boil, reduce the heat, cover the pan, and simmer the mixture for 5 minutes or until the vegetables are just tender. Set the pan aside.
6. Chop the hazelnuts, and place them in a large bowl. Coarsely crumble the cooled corn bread into the bowl. Add the reserved onion mixture, cranberries, parsley, salt (if desired), and pepper. Stir the ingredients to combine them well.

WILD RICE AND FENNEL STUFFING

*about 12 cups stuffing
for a 16-pound turkey*

This is a marvelous stuffing that can also serve as an elegant side dish. The recipe was adapted from one that appeared in *Gourmet* magazine.

Preparation tip: The stuffing can be prepared 2 days ahead. Cool, cover, and refrigerate it, but bring it back to room temperature before stuffing the bird.

1½ cups wild rice, rinsed well and drained
  2 teaspoons fennel seeds
  3 cups chicken broth
1½ cups water
  ½ pound sweet Italian sausage, casing discarded
  2 tablespoons butter *or* margarine
  2 cups chopped onion (2 large)
  3 small bulbs fennel, finely chopped (about 3 cups)
Salt to taste (optional)
Freshly ground black pepper to taste

1. In a medium-sized saucepan, combine the wild rice, fennel seeds, broth, and water, and bring the liquid to a boil. Reduce the heat, partially cover the pan, and simmer the rice for 45 to 55 minutes or until it is tender. Drain the rice in a fine strainer. Set the rice aside.
2. While the rice is cooking, in a nonstick or heavy skillet heated over medium heat, cook the sausage, breaking it up into small bits, until it has browned and much of the fat has been rendered out. Remove the sausage with a slotted spoon to a strainer lined with a double thickness of paper towels. With the spoon, press on the sausage to extract as much fat as possible. Transfer the sausage to a large bowl, and set it aside.
3. Wipe out the skillet, add the butter or margarine and onion, and sauté the onion over medium-low heat for 5 minutes or until it is softened. Add the fennel, cover the pan, and cook the vegetables, stirring them occasionally, for 5 to 7 minutes or until the fennel is tender-crisp. Transfer the vegetables to the bowl with the sausage.
4. When the rice is done, add it to the reserved sausage and fennel mixture along with the salt (if desired) and pepper. Toss the ingredients to combine them well.

TURKEY WITH CURRY SAUCE   *4 to 6 servings*

This is a tasty, simple dish adapted from a recipe in *Family Circle* magazine that can turn turkey leftovers into elegant as well as nutritious fare.

Preparation tip: The sauce can be prepared in advance and reheated over a low flame at serving time.

Serving suggestions: This dish goes well with basmati brown rice garnished with toasted almonds and with currants or raisins that have been soaked in cognac or dry sherry. Also, try any of the chutneys on pages 550 to 552.

```
 1  tablespoon olive oil or canola oil
 1  cup chopped onion (1 large)
½  cup chopped celery
 1  large clove garlic, peeled and minced
 1  tart apple (e.g., Granny Smith), peeled, cored,
      and finely chopped
⅛  teaspoon red pepper flakes, crushed, or cayenne
      to taste
 2  tablespoons flour
 3  tablespoons curry powder
 1  teaspoon tomato paste
 2  cups turkey broth or chicken broth
½  cup skim or low-fat milk
 1  teaspoon lime juice or lemon juice
Salt to taste (optional)
 3 to 4 cups cubed cooked turkey
```

1. Heat the oil in a large skillet, preferably one with a nonstick surface, add the onion and celery, and sauté the vegetables for 5 minutes or until they are softened. Add the garlic, and sauté the vegetables for another 30 seconds. Stir in the apple and red pepper flakes or cayenne, and cook the ingredients, stirring them, 2 minutes longer or until the apple is soft.
2. In a small bowl, combine the flour with the curry powder, and stir this mixture into the contents of the skillet.
3. In a medium-sized bowl or a measuring cup, combine the tomato paste with the broth, and add that to the skillet, stirring the ingredients to mix them well. Cook the mixture over low heat, stirring it, for 3 minutes or until it is thick and bubbly. Gradually stir in the milk, bring the mixture to a simmer, partially cover the pan, and simmer the mixture for 20 minutes. *Do not boil it.*
4. Purée the mixture in batches in a blender or food processor.
5. At serving time, transfer the purée to the skillet, add the lime or lemon juice, salt (if using), and turkey, and heat the food through over low heat.

TURKEY MEATBALL STROGANOFF   *6 servings*

Cheryl Phillips of Sonoma, California, suggests this modern, nutrition-conscious version of an old favorite. The recipe is tasty and easy, a good meal to serve to visiting relatives.

Preparation tips: The meatballs and sauce can be prepared in advance and reheated at serving time. Be sure to use a skillet with a tight-fitting lid.

Serving suggestion: Serve this dish over cooked medium-wide egg noodles (about 12 ounces dry) garnished with chopped fresh parsley.

    1 pound ground turkey
    ¼ cup finely chopped onion
    ¼ cup minced fresh parsley
    ½ teaspoon salt, or to taste (optional)
    ¼ teaspoon freshly ground black pepper
    1 teaspoon poultry seasoning *or* AHA Herb Mix
       (see page 545)
    2 slices whole-wheat bread, cubed
    ¼ cup boiling water *or* broth (any kind except fish)
    1 egg *or* 2 egg whites
Dry bread crumbs, if needed
    1 tablespoon (approximately) vegetable oil
    3 cups sliced mushrooms
    1 cup chicken broth
    1 cup plain nonfat or low-fat yogurt
    2 tablespoons flour

1. In a large bowl, thoroughly combine the turkey, onion, parsley, salt (if using), pepper, and poultry seasoning or herb mix.
2. In a small bowl, soften the bread cubes in the water or broth. Add the cubes to the turkey mixture along with the egg or egg whites. Mix the ingredients well, and shape the mixture into 24 1½-inch balls. If the mixture is too wet to form into balls, either refrigerate it for about 1 hour or add some dry bread crumbs.
3. Heat 2 teaspoons of the oil in a large nonstick skillet. Add the mushrooms to the pan, and sauté them over medium-high heat to brown them. Remove them with a slotted spoon to a large bowl. Set the bowl aside.
4. Reduce the heat to medium-low, and add the meatballs in batches of 8, browning them on all sides. Add more oil, if needed. Transfer the browned meatballs to the bowl containing the mushrooms.
5. When all the meatballs have been browned, return them and the mushrooms to the skillet, add the 1 cup of broth, bring the liquid to a simmer, cover the skillet tightly, and simmer the ingredients for about 20 minutes. With a slotted spoon, remove the solid contents of the skillet to the large

bowl, leaving the liquid in the skillet. Cover the bowl, and keep the ingredients warm.

6. In a small bowl or measuring cup, combine the yogurt and flour, stirring the ingredients until the mixture is smooth, and add the mixture to the liquid in the skillet. Bring this mixture to a near-boil, stirring it, lower the heat, and cook the mixture over low heat until the sauce thickens. Return the meatballs and mushrooms to the skillet, and combine them with the sauce.

TURKEY CHILI

10 to 12 servings

Mary Greenberg, a fan from Chicago, prepares a vat of this crowd-pleasing, nutritious chili whenever her family comes for a visit. I added some of my favorite seasonings, but the basic recipe is hers.

Preparation tips: Chili is an ideal make-ahead dish that improves with reheating. It can also be frozen with no loss of quality. If desired, you can cook the kidney beans from scratch (see page 7). Note the amount of chili powder needed to prepare this dish, then be sure you have enough on hand.

Serving suggestions: Set out a variety of garnishes: chopped onion, grated Cheddar, plain yogurt, chopped sweet green pepper, chopped tomato, diced cucumber, cold diced boiled potato, etc. Let guests serve themselves. A basket of warm flour tortillas, or corn tortillas cut into wedges and toasted (see page 44), is a nice accompaniment.

1½ tablespoons canola oil
  1 pound sweet green peppers, cored, seeded, and chopped
1½ pounds onions, peeled and finely chopped
  2 large cloves garlic, peeled and finely chopped
  2 jalapeños *or* green chilies, seeded and minced (optional)
½ cup minced fresh parsley
  3 pounds ground turkey
⅓ cup mild chili powder
  2 to 3 tablespoons hot chili powder
  2 30-ounce cans red kidney beans, drained, *or* 6 to
    7 cups cooked kidney beans
  2 28-ounce cans tomatoes with their juice
  1 to 2 tablespoons brown sugar
  1 tablespoon oregano, crumbled
  2 teaspoons cumin
1½ teaspoons freshly ground black pepper
  1 teaspoon salt, or to taste (optional)
  1 teaspoon coriander
¼ teaspoon ground cloves
¼ teaspoon allspice

1. In a very large, heavy pot or very large skillet, heat the oil, add the sweet peppers, and sauté them slowly for 5 minutes. Add the onions, and continue sautéing the vegetables for 3 minutes more. Add the garlic, jalapeños or chilies (if using), and parsley, and sauté the ingredients for 1 minute.
2. Add the turkey, stir in the mild and hot chili powders, and brown the turkey over medium heat for about 10 minutes, breaking it up and stirring it to cook it evenly. If you are not already using a very large, heavy pot, transfer the turkey mixture to one now.

3. Stir in the remaining ingredients, combining them thoroughly. Bring the chili to a boil over medium heat, reduce the heat, cover the pot, and simmer the chili for 1 hour. Then uncover the pot, and cook the chili another 30 minutes.

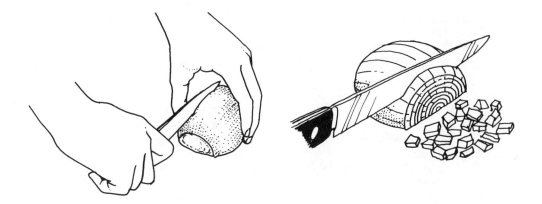

TURKEY-BEAN ENCHILADAS

8 servings

My tasters of all ages just loved these, and several asked for "people" bags.

Preparation tips: These are ideal for a party because they can be prepared for baking 1 or 2 days ahead. Or they can be baked in advance and reheated, covered with foil, before serving. There are three ways to soften the tortillas: (1) they can be dipped in the sauce, one at a time, for 10 seconds just before they are filled and rolled; (2) they can be softened, one at a time, in a nonstick skillet; (3) several can be wrapped in foil and softened in a 300° F oven. Method number 1 is the tastiest but messiest and makes the enchiladas difficult to separate at serving time.

Serving suggestions: If the enchiladas stick together, serve them in squares, lasagne-style, instead of as individual rolls. Try the Mexican Gazpacho on page 102 for an opener.

SAUCE

- 2 teaspoons canola oil
- 2 large cloves garlic, peeled and minced
- ⅔ cup finely chopped onion
- ⅓ cup finely chopped sweet green pepper
- 1 whole green chili *or* jalapeño, seeded and minced
- 2 pounds canned tomatoes, drained, juice reserved, and finely chopped
- 1 cup water (*to be added only if method number 1 is used to soften the tortillas*—see "Preparation tips," above)
- ½ teaspoon salt (optional)
- ¼ teaspoon cumin
- ¼ teaspoon freshly ground black pepper

ENCHILADAS

- 2 teaspoons canola oil
- 1 very large clove garlic, peeled and minced
- 1 pound ground turkey
- 1 tablespoon chili powder (I use 1 teaspoon hot chili powder and 2 teaspoons mild chili powder)
- ¼ teaspoon salt (optional)
- 1 16-ounce can kidney beans, *undrained*
- 16 (approximately) corn tortillas
- 1 cup shredded sharp Cheddar (about 4 ounces)

TO PREPARE THE SAUCE

1. In a large skillet, preferably one with a nonstick surface, heat the oil, add the garlic, onion, sweet pepper, and chili or jalapeño, and sauté the ingredients for 5 to 7 minutes or until the vegetables are softened.
2. Add the tomatoes with their juice, water (if necessary), salt (if desired), cumin, and pepper. Bring the sauce to a boil over medium heat, reduce the heat, and simmer the sauce for 15 minutes, stirring it occasionally. Set it aside.

TO PREPARE THE ENCHILADAS

3. In a large skillet, heat the oil briefly, add the garlic, and sauté it for about 30 seconds. Add the turkey, chili powder, and salt (if desired), and sauté the ingredients, breaking up the turkey pieces, until the turkey is browned.
4. Stir in the kidney beans and their liquid.
5. Preheat the oven to 350° F.
6. Soften 1 tortilla at a time (see "Preparation tips," above), and place ¼ cup of the turkey-bean mixture on each tortilla slightly below center. Roll each tortilla around the mixture, and set the enchiladas seam side down in a greased 13 × 9 × 2-inch baking pan.
7. Spread the sauce over the enchiladas, and top them with the shredded cheese.
8. Put the *uncovered* pan in the hot oven, and bake the enchiladas for 25 minutes. When you reheat the enchiladas, cover the pan with foil.

Fish Main Dishes

Fish, long a staple of the human diet, has become highly prized in recent years. First, it is usually low in fat and calories. Second, the oils in fish have been discovered to have myriad actual and potential health benefits: they help to lower blood cholesterol and blood pressure, stimulate the immune system, and counter arthritis, among other desirable effects. Third, the price of fish has catapulted it into the category of gourmet food, more expensive than some top-priced meats that people now shy away from. At one time it was thought that shellfish were high in cholesterol, but a recent reanalysis by government scientists of the cholesterol content of shellfish showed that this is not so for most types. Even a serving of shrimp, with 90 milligrams of cholesterol in 3½ ounces, contains less than half the cholesterol in one large egg yolk.

One problem that Americans have with fish is the amount they eat when they eat it. Most recipes call for 8 ounces of fish per person, which is more than twice the protein anyone really needs in a meal. If the meal is properly "fleshed" out with a starchy and a "green" vegetable as well as a salad, 4 ounces of fish per person is adequate—and much more affordable!

Another problem that many people have with fish is in buying it. How do you know when fish is fresh? First, find a reliable market, and stick to it. Second, fresh fish does not smell fishy. Third, try to buy fish on Monday through Friday, when the fish markets that supply them are open (Sunday's fish is at least two days old). Finally, if you should have the opportunity to see the whole fish, its eyes should be clear and bulging (not dull and sunken), its gills bright red with a clear film, and its scales brightly colored and firmly attached to the skin. Fresh fish can be frozen, if it is well wrapped to prevent dehydration; but its texture will change, and the fish may lose some of its natural delicacy and flavor, especially if it is frozen for more than a month or two.

As to the kinds of fish to buy, emphasize those that come from the ocean or that are farm-raised since these are least likely to be contaminated with industrial pollutants, as are many fish from the Great Lakes and the rivers of the United States. Also, fish from the cold seas—salmon, bluefin tuna, mackerel, bluefish, herring, halibut, sardines, eel, sablefish, and the like—contain the highest amounts of omega-3 fatty acids, the fish oils with major health benefits.

The secret of well-cooked fish is timing: overcooking toughens fish and dries it out. Your best guide is the one used by professional cooks, the so-called "10-minute rule": for each inch of thickness (measured at the thickest part of the fish), cook the fish for 10 minutes. As fish cooks, it turns from translucent white (or pink) to opaque white (like egg whites) or pink. To be certain that the fish is done, test it with a fork at the thickest point; if the fish is opaque, it is done. If it flakes easily when tested, you probably overcooked it. Fish barbecued on the grill needs but 4 to 5 minutes per side for 1-inch-thick steaks. Fish that is enclosed in foil or simmered or baked in a sauce takes longer to cook than fish that is broiled, poached, or fried in the usual way. In this case, apply a "15-minute rule" instead.

For more details on choosing and using fish, consult *The Seafood Handbook,* a 72-page volume published by Seafood Business Report. To buy a copy, send a check for $14.95 to Seafood Handbook, 21 Elm Street, Camden, ME 04843.

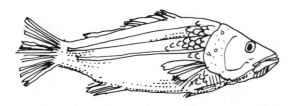

MILLER'S FISH CASSEROLE

4 servings

Mary H. Miller of Murrysville, Pennsylvania, devised this very tasty and simple-to-prepare fish-dinner-in-a-pot.

```
 2  onions, peeled and sliced crosswise
1½  pounds boiling potatoes, peeled and cut into
      ¼-inch slices
1½  teaspoons butter or margarine, cut into bits
      (optional)
 1  tablespoon olive oil, divided
 ¼  teaspoon thyme, crumbled
 3  tablespoons minced fresh parsley, divided
 ½  teaspoon salt, or to taste, divided (optional)
 ½  teaspoon freshly ground black pepper, divided
 1  cup water
 1  pound fish fillets (e.g., cod, ocean perch, flounder)
 2  cups frozen peas, thawed
 ⅓  cup minced pimiento
 2  cloves garlic, peeled and minced
```

1. Spread the onion and potato slices along the bottom of a 2½-quart flame-proof casserole. Dot them with the butter or margarine (if you wish), and sprinkle them with 1½ teaspoons of the oil, the thyme, 2 tablespoons of the parsley, ¼ teaspoon of the salt (if desired), and ¼ teaspoon of the pepper. Pour the water over the mixture, and bring the liquid to a boil over medium-high heat. Cover the pot, and simmer the vegetables for 12 to 15 minutes or until the potatoes are nearly tender.

2. Spread the fish fillets on top of the vegetables, sprinkle them with the remaining 1 tablespoon of parsley, ¼ teaspoon of salt (if desired), and ¼ teaspoon of pepper. Cover the pot, and simmer the mixture for 10 minutes.

3. Add the peas and pimiento, cover the pot, and simmer the ingredients for another 5 minutes.

4. Meanwhile, in a small skillet, heat the remaining 1½ teaspoons of oil briefly, add the garlic, and sauté it until it is lightly golden. *Do not let it burn.* Spoon the garlic over the fish, and serve the casserole.

CHINESE-STYLE SOLE

4 to 6 servings

Because fuel was always in short supply in the Far East, the people learned to conserve it through fast, high-temperature cooking in a pot that concentrated the heat where the food was—namely, a wok. Unfortunately, the cuisine is generally high in salt, although the use of reduced-sodium soy sauce helps.

Preparation tip: This dish can be prepared from start to finish in about 15 minutes, so if you're planning to serve it with rice, be sure to start the rice before you start the fish.

Serving suggestion: Broccoli and Baby Corn on page 313 would be an ideal companion.

> 2 tablespoons reduced-sodium soy sauce
> 3 to 4 slices gingerroot, minced
> 2 large cloves garlic, peeled and minced
> 1 tablespoon lemon juice
> 2 tablespoons water
> 4 teaspoons oil (preferably peanut *or* canola)
> 1½ pounds sole fillets, cut into 2-inch pieces (thaw, if frozen)
> 2 scallions (including the green tops), sliced

1. In a cup or small bowl, combine the soy sauce, gingerroot, garlic, lemon juice, and water. Set the bowl aside.
2. Heat a wok or skillet, add the oil, and heat the pan for 30 seconds. Then add the fish pieces, gently turning them to assure uniform browning and to keep them from sticking together.
3. Add the scallions and the reserved sauce. Stir the ingredients once gently, reduce the heat, and cook the fish for about 6 minutes. Serve the dish immediately.

CHINESE STEAMED FISH AND SAUTÉED VEGETABLES

4 servings

This low-fat, very colorful "bagged" fish recipe relies on Oriental seasonings.

Preparation tip: The entire recipe can be set up in advance for cooking (10 minutes' worth) at serving time. But be sure to bring the fish to room temperature before baking it.

Serving suggestion: For openers, try a cup of Asian Lentil and Brown Rice Soup on page 200 or Faith's Hot and Sour Soup on page 98.

    1 pound cod *or* similar fillets (such as turbot)
    ½ cup chicken broth *or* fish broth
    1 tablespoon soy sauce (preferably reduced-sodium)
    1 teaspoon hoisin sauce *or* sweet bean paste
    ¼ cup minced scallions (including the green tops)
    1 teaspoon grated gingerroot
    1 tablespoon vegetable oil (preferably peanut *or*
       canola *or* walnut)
    2 large carrots, peeled and cut into 1½ × ¼-inch strips
    1 large sweet red pepper, cut into 1½ × ¼-inch strips
    ½ pound snow peas, ends and strings removed,
       diagonally sliced in half lengthwise

1. Preheat the oven to 450° F.
2. Line a 9-inch square baking pan with enough foil to fold over and enclose the fish. Place the fish in the pan.
3. In a measuring cup or small bowl, combine the broth, soy sauce, hoisin sauce or sweet bean paste, scallions, and gingerroot, and pour the mixture over the fish. Fold the foil over the fish, then fold the ends together to seal the foil.
4. Put the pan in the hot oven, and bake the fish for 10 minutes or until it just turns opaque.
5. Meanwhile, in a nonstick skillet or well-seasoned wok, heat the oil, add the carrots, and stir-fry the carrots for 2 minutes. Add the red pepper, and stir-fry it for 1 minute. Add the snow peas, and stir-fry them for 1 minute more or until all the vegetables are tender-crisp.
6. When the fish is done, carefully open the foil packet (beware of steam burns). Transfer the fish to a heated serving platter or to individual plates. Top the fish with the stir-fried vegetables, and spoon the sauce over all.

BAG O' FISH

6 servings

This is an elegant Ed Giobbi suggestion. By cooking the fish in parchment, fat can be kept to a minimum while the fish stays moist. My tasters loved the individual packets of fish on their plates and the contents in their mouths.

Preparation tips: This recipe works best with a firm fillet such as monkfish, black bass, or cod. The fillets can be marinated hours ahead. The fish can be "bagged" in advance, too, but should be cooked just before serving. You can use either individual squares of parchment or one large sheet, 15 × 30 inches. Or, if parchment is not available, use aluminum foil.

Serving suggestion: I use individual pieces of parchment for each serving and let my guests do the unwrapping, cautioning them to avoid steam burns. I garnish each plate with four Memorable Mussels (see page 163) and serve green (spinach) noodles as an accompaniment.

1½ pounds skinless, boneless firm-fleshed fish fillets
    (e.g., monkfish or cod)
  2 tablespoons finely chopped Italian parsley
  1 tablespoon finely minced garlic (3 large cloves)
  1 tablespoon fresh rosemary leaves, finely
    chopped, *or* 1 teaspoon dried rosemary, crumbled
  1 to 2 tablespoons olive oil
 ⅓ cup dry white wine
Salt to taste (optional)
Freshly ground black pepper to taste
  2 small to medium-sized leeks

1. Cut the fish into individual serving pieces if the fillets are large, and place them in a large bowl. Add the parsley, garlic, rosemary, oil, wine, salt (if desired), and pepper. Toss the ingredients to combine them thoroughly. Set the bowl aside, or chill the fish for up to 4 hours.
2. Meanwhile, cut off the root ends of the leeks, and separate the layers. Wash them thoroughly, and drain them. Cut the leeks into 2½-inch lengths, then cut each length lengthwise into thin slivers, ending up with about 2 cups.

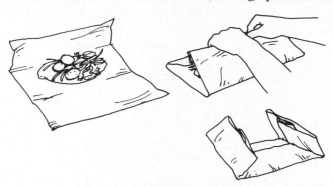

3. Preheat the oven to 400° F.
4. Lay out six 8 × 11-inch sheets of parchment paper or aluminum foil. Divide the fish pieces and their marinade among the sheets. Top the each portion with the slivers of leeks. Fold over the edges of the parchment or foil, and seal the sides as tightly as possible. Place the bags on a baking sheet.
5. Put the baking sheet in the hot oven, and bake the fish for 20 minutes or until the bags puff up. Open the bags carefully to avoid steam burns.

MELLOW CURRIED FISH
6 servings

This easy and delicious recipe, called "fish dopeyaja" or "dopiaza" (literally, "2 onions") in its native land, is adapted from one prepared by Shane Ara Kabir of the Bangladesh Institute of Research and Rehabilitation. Vilma Liacouras Chantiles published the original in her book *Diabetic Cooking from around the World.*

Preparation tip: You can modify the hotness, if you wish, by using more or less hot chili powder.

Serving suggestion: Jazz up the meal with Indian Rice with Peas and Peppers on page 329.

   1 teaspoon turmeric
   1 teaspoon mild and hot chili powders, combined
      as desired
   1 teaspoon crushed garlic
  ⅔ cup (approximately) water, divided
1½ tablespoons olive oil
   1 cup sliced onion, divided
1½ pounds fish fillets (I use Dover sole), cut into
      strips 1½ inches wide
Salt to taste (optional)
1½ cups cubed tomatoes
  ¼ cup chopped fresh parsley *or* 1 tablespoon
      minced cilantro

1. In a small bowl, combine the turmeric, chili powders, and garlic with enough water (about 2½ tablespoons) to make a paste. Set the bowl aside.
2. Heat the oil in a large skillet or flameproof casserole. Add ½ cup of the onion, sautéing it until it is lightly browned. Stir in the reserved spice paste, and cook the mixture for 30 seconds.
3. Add the fish to the pan with the remaining ½ cup of onion, the salt (if desired), and the remaining water. Shake the pan to mix the ingredients. Add the tomatoes and parsley or cilantro. Simmer the ingredients over low heat for 5 minutes or until the fish is tender.

SOLE ROLL-UPS

4 to 6 servings

This Ed Giobbi recipe (from *Eat Right, Eat Well—the Italian Way,* written with Dr. Richard Wolff) is delicious and attractive and, if you already have some pesto on hand, very easy to prepare.

Preparation tips: Since pesto freezes well, I make a lot of it during late summer, when fresh basil is plentiful and cheap (see page 541). I freeze it in various-sized containers—from 2-cup blocks to 2-tablespoon cubes (frozen in ice-cube trays). I used Dover sole for this recipe (it's the least expensive and is generally available), but gray sole or lemon sole are fine, too.

Serving suggestion: Lovely with Pasta with Broccoli Rabe on page 225.

1½ pounds sole fillets (8 pieces), rinsed and dried
Salt to taste (optional)
Freshly ground black pepper to taste
  8 teaspoons (approximately) pesto
  1 cup dry white wine
  1 tablespoon finely chopped shallots
1½ cups green peas, thawed in hot water if frozen
     or simmered in water for 4 minutes if fresh

1. Sprinkle the fish with the salt (if desired) and pepper. Spoon 1 teaspoon of pesto into the center of each fillet. Roll up the fillets, and secure each with toothpicks.
2. Place the remaining ingredients in a saucepan large enough to hold the fish rolls. Bring the liquid to a gentle boil, and add the roll-ups. Simmer the fish for 4 to 5 minutes. *Do not overcook it.* Remove the fish with a slotted spatula to a serving platter, and spoon the peas over the roll-ups.

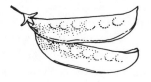

STUFFED FILLETS IN SWISS CHARD

6 servings

Rodale's Basic Natural Foods Cookbook is the source of this appealing and nutritious way to prepare fish.

Preparation tip: Next time you cook brown rice, save some to make the stuffing for this dish.

Serving suggestion: Braised Pumpkin on page 327 or Baked Acorn Squash on page 337 would make nice side dishes.

> 6 fish fillets (flounder *or* fluke *or* sole), about 6 ounces each
> White pepper to taste
> 2 scallion tops, minced
> 3 mushrooms, minced
> 1 pimiento, minced
> ⅓ cup cooked brown rice
> 3 drops hot pepper sauce
> 2 tablespoons lemon juice
> 2 tablespoons reduced-sodium soy sauce
> 1 teaspoon Oriental sesame oil
> ½ teaspoon honey
> ½ teaspoon finely minced gingerroot
> 6 large leaves Swiss chard, stems trimmed
> 1 tablespoon toasted sesame seeds

1. Preheat the oven to 400° F.
2. If the fillets are not thin and wide to start with, put them between sheets of plastic wrap, and flatten them by placing the flat side of a knife on the fillets and pounding your fist against the knife. The fillets should measure 4 inches across at their widest.
3. Sprinkle the fish with the white pepper, and set the fillets aside.
4. In a small bowl, combine the scallions, mushrooms, pimiento, and rice.
5. In another small bowl, combine the hot pepper sauce, lemon juice, soy sauce, sesame oil, honey, and gingerroot. Add this mixture to the rice mixture, and combine all the ingredients well.
6. Cut 6 pieces of aluminum foil into 12-inch squares. Place 1 chard leaf on each piece of foil. Place 1 fish fillet on each leaf, and spread 1½ tablespoons of the rice mixture over each piece of fish. Roll the chard and fish, enclosing the filling, toward one end of the foil. Starting with that end, roll the foil over the fish roll, and crimp the foil to seal the narrow ends. Place the foil-wrapped fish in a shallow, heavy baking pan.
7. Place the pan in the hot oven, and bake the fish for 15 to 20 minutes. Remove the fish from the oven, and let it rest in the foil for 5 minutes. Before serving the fish, remove the foil, and sprinkle the fish rolls with the toasted sesame seeds.

FLOUNDER WITH PUMPKIN SAUCE   *4 servings*

Those of you who have only tasted pumpkin in pie may not realize how versatile it is as a vegetable. I love the looks of this dish: white fish topped with pale orange strips of pumpkin.

Preparation tip: If you can afford it, use gray sole instead of flounder.

Serving suggestion: Try a hearty accompaniment like Rice and Bulgur Pilaf on page 330 or Wild Rice with Almonds on page 331.

    1 pound flounder fillets
    Oil for coating the aluminum foil
    ½ cup water
    ¼ cup white wine
    2 teaspoons lemon juice
    Salt to taste (optional)
    White pepper to taste
    1 tablespoon butter *or* margarine
    2 cups julienned raw pumpkin
    2 tablespoons fish broth *or* chicken broth
    4 scallions for garnish (optional)

1. Preheat the oven to "warm."
2. Make a "bed" for the flounder out of heavy-duty or double-thick foil with the edges turned up about ¼ inch. Set the foil in a skillet just big enough to hold the fish. Brush or spray the foil with the oil, and place the fish on it.
3. In a small bowl, combine the water, wine, lemon juice, salt (if desired), and pepper, and pour this mixture over the fish. Bring the liquid to a boil, reduce the heat, and simmer the fish for about 4 minutes. Lift the fish with its foil bed out of the skillet, letting the liquid drain back into the pan (reserve it), and place the fish on a platter in the oven to keep the fish warm. Cook down the liquid in the pan over high heat to reduce it to half its original volume, and pour it into a blender jar.
4. Melt the butter or margarine in the skillet, and stir in the julienned pumpkin. Add the broth, and sauté the pumpkin, stirring it occasionally, for 4 minutes or until it is soft. Remove all but ½ cup of the pumpkin to a second platter, and place the platter in the oven to keep the pumpkin warm. Add the remaining ½ cup of pumpkin to the liquid in the blender along with any juices that may have accumulated on the platter holding the fish. Purée the mixture.
5. Take the fish out of the oven. Carefully remove the fish from the foil, and place the fish on individual plates. Pour the pumpkin sauce over the fillets. Remove the reserved julienned pumpkin from the oven, and distribute the pumpkin among the plates. Garnish each plate with a scallion, if you wish. Serve the fish immediately.

FISH AND FETA CASSEROLE   *6 servings*

This recipe, from Shirley Metopoulos of West Yarmouth, Massachusetts, via *Bon Appétit* magazine, was a winner among all my tasters. And so easy to prepare! The hardest part was peeling the tiny onions.

Preparation tips: The onions peel easily if they are first placed in boiling water for about 2 minutes. The sauce can be made 1 or 2 days ahead, but be sure to bring it back to a boil before adding the fish. Many kinds of nonoily fish can be used—cod, scrod, haddock, halibut—and the shrimp can be omitted. To reduce the saltiness of the feta, soak the cheese in cold water for about 30 minutes.

Serving suggestion: Serve this dish with orzo—tiny pasta shaped like oversized rice kernels.

SAUCE

- 2 teaspoons olive oil
- 1 pound pearl onions, peeled
- 2 large cloves garlic, peeled and minced
- 1 28-ounce can stewed tomatoes, *undrained*
- ½ cup dry white wine
- 2 tablespoons chopped parsley
- ¾ teaspoon oregano, crumbled

Freshly ground black pepper to taste

FISH

- 1 pound fresh fish, boned and cut into ¾-inch pieces (you can use cod, scrod, haddock, *or* halibut)
- ¼ pound medium raw shrimp, peeled and deveined
- ½ pound feta, cut into chunks and soaked in cold water
- 1 tablespoon chopped fresh parsley for garnish

1. To prepare the sauce, heat the oil in a 3-quart saucepan over medium-high heat, add the onions, and sauté them for 5 minutes or until they brown lightly. Stir in the garlic, then add the tomatoes with their liquid, the wine, parsley, oregano, and pepper. Raise the heat to high, and bring the sauce to a boil. Reduce the heat, cover the pan, and simmer the sauce for 10 minutes, stirring it occasionally.
2. Preheat the oven to 400° F.
3. Pour the sauce into a 2½-quart casserole. Place the fish on the sauce, cover the casserole, and bake the fish for 10 minutes. Add the shrimp and feta, and continue baking the casserole for another 10 minutes. Sprinkle the parsley over the casserole before serving it.

STIR-FRIED SCALLOPS SUPREME   *4 servings*

A glorious dish to behold that becomes a complete meal when served with rice.

Preparation tips: As with all stir-fries, the secret to successful preparation is to have all the ingredients ready to cook before the pan is heated. Although this dish works best in a wok, a large nonstick skillet does a fine job. If bay scallops are unavailable, you can substitute either sea scallops that have been sliced crosswise or cleaned raw shrimp.

Serving suggestion: Although Chinese dishes are traditionally served with plain, unsalted boiled rice, basmati brown rice, perhaps cooked with green peas, would be a lovely change of pace with this dish. Start the rice before preparing the ingredients for the stir-fry.

SAUCE
- 3 tablespoons dry sherry
- 2½ tablespoons tomato sauce
- 4 teaspoons oyster sauce
- 4 teaspoons reduced-sodium soy sauce
- 2½ teaspoons Oriental sesame oil
- ½ teaspoon sugar
- ¼ teaspoon or more freshly ground white pepper, to taste
- 1 tablespoon cornstarch
- 1½ tablespoons cold water

STIR-FRY
- 2 tablespoons peanut oil *or* canola oil, divided
- 1 pound bay scallops
- 3 large cloves garlic, peeled and minced
- 2 teaspoons finely minced or grated gingerroot
- 1 large *or* 2 medium sweet red peppers, cored, seeded, and cut into ⅓-inch pieces
- 1 medium *or* 2 small zucchinis, quartered lengthwise and cut crosswise into ⅓-inch pieces
- 4 scallions (including some of the green tops), sliced diagonally

TO PREPARE THE SAUCE

1. In a measuring cup or small bowl, combine well the sherry, tomato sauce, oyster sauce, soy sauce, sesame oil, sugar, and white pepper. Set the bowl aside.
2. Place the cornstarch in a small bowl, and stir in the water until the mixture is smooth. Set the bowl aside.

TO PREPARE THE SCALLOPS

3. Heat a wok or large nonstick skillet over high heat. Add 1 tablespoon of the oil, tilting the pan to distribute the oil evenly. Add the scallops, and stir-fry them for 1 minute or until they just become opaque. Remove them with a slotted spoon to a platter.
4. Heat the remaining 1 tablespoon of oil briefly, add the garlic and ginger-root, and stir-fry them for 10 seconds. Then add the red pepper, zucchini, and scallions, and stir-fry them for 30 seconds or until tender-crisp.

5. Stir the reserved sauce (step 1), and pour it into the wok or pan along the sides. Return the scallops to the pan. Stir the cornstarch mixture, and, stirring the ingredients in the pan, add enough of it, 1 teaspoon at a time, to the pan to thicken the sauce slightly. Serve the dish immediately.

MEMORABLE MUSSELS

6 to 8 servings

These are really Great with a capital G. Thanks to Ed Giobbi for this lovely combo. I reduced the oil and hot pepper, but otherwise his recipe is intact. Remember, mussels are easy to prepare for company; they can be made ahead because nothing much changes when they are reheated.

Serving suggestions: This recipe could be used as a zippy first course or as a garnish for another dish (for example, Bag o' Fish on page 156) or over pasta as an entrée. Try a lemon linguine or fettuccine. Or, since the sauce is potent, a plain pasta would be fine.

  5 pounds mussels, scrubbed and debearded
½ cup finely chopped scallions
  1 tablespoon olive oil
¼ cup finely chopped Italian parsley
  3 tablespoons finely chopped fresh basil *or* 1½
    tablespoons dried basil
  1 tablespoon finely minced garlic (3 large cloves)
½ teaspoon or more red pepper flakes, to taste
  1 tablespoon oregano
¾ cup dry white wine
Salt to taste (optional)
Freshly ground black pepper to taste

1. Place the mussels in a large pot. Add the remaining ingredients, and cover the pot tightly.
2. Bring the liquid to a boil, and cook the mussels over high heat for 5 to 8 minutes or until the mussels open.
3. Serve the mussels in their shells. If you are serving the mussels over pasta, remove the mussels from their shells, and use the cooking liquid as the sauce.

CIOPPINO

6 servings

I should warn you: this is not a recipe for slim budgets or for delicate stomachs (although the hotness can be controlled by using less red pepper flakes). But, boy, is it good! My tasters begged me to include it despite these reservations. So here is my oil-reduced version of this wonderful recipe from *Gourmet* magazine.

Preparation tip: Note that the sauce cooks for 1½ hours. It can be made days ahead and kept chilled, but bring it gently back to a boil before completing the recipe.

Serving suggestion: This spicy stew would go well with crusty Italian or French bread (see page 406), plain capellini or thin spaghetti, or white rice.

SAUCE

- 1 tablespoon olive oil
- 1 cup chopped sweet green pepper
- 1½ cups chopped onion
- 3 14-ounce cans plum tomatoes, with their juice
- 2 tablespoons tomato paste
- 2 cups dry red wine
- 1½ teaspoons basil, crumbled
- 1½ teaspoons oregano, crumbled
- 1½ teaspoons thyme, crumbled
- 1 bay leaf
- 1 to 2 teaspoons red pepper flakes, to taste
- 1 sprig parsley

FISH

- ¾ pound (about 18) medium shrimp
- 24 small clams, cleaned
- 1½ pounds cod fillets *or* halibut fillets, cut into 1½-inch pieces
- ¾ pound sea scallops, halved crosswise if they are large
- 6 tablespoons minced fresh parsley

TO PREPARE THE SAUCE

1. Heat the oil in a large, heavy saucepan or Dutch oven, preferably one with a nonstick surface, and sauté the green pepper and onion over medium-low heat until they soften.
2. Add the remaining sauce ingredients, and bring the mixture to a boil, stirring it. Reduce the heat to low, cover the pan, and simmer the sauce, stirring it occasionally, for 1½ hours.

TO PREPARE THE FISH

3. Meanwhile, shell the shrimp. (If desired, leave the shell of the last joint and the tail in place.) With a sharp paring knife, cut down the back of each shrimp to butterfly and devein it. Set the shrimp aside.
4. When the sauce is done, remove and discard the bay leaf and parsley sprig, bring the sauce to a boil, and stir in the clams. Cover the pan, and boil the clams for 5 to 20 minutes, removing the clams with tongs to a bowl as they

open. Discard any clams that have not opened after 20 minutes in the boiling sauce.

5. Add the reserved shrimp, cod or halibut, and scallops to the sauce. Bring the stew to a simmer, stirring it gently, cover the pan, and cook the stew for 5 to 7 minutes. Adjust the seasonings. Return the clams to the pot, and sprinkle the cioppino with the parsley before serving the dish.

GRILLED TUNA
4 servings

This is simplicity itself—lightly marinated and grilled, delicious hot or cold.

Serving suggestion: To keep the meal simple, serve the tuna with rice and Dry Sautéed Green Beans on page 308.

4 small tuna steaks, about 1 inch thick (about
  1½ pounds total)
2 tablespoons white wine
2 tablespoons teriyaki sauce
2 teaspoons grated garlic
2 teaspoons grated gingerroot

1. Place the tuna steaks in a single layer in a shallow pan, preferably glass.
2. Combine the wine, teriyaki sauce, garlic, and gingerroot in a small bowl, and pour it over the tuna. Lift the steaks to be sure the marinade runs under them. Cover the tuna with plastic wrap, and chill the fish for about 1 hour, turning the steaks over after 30 minutes.
3. For rare tuna, start with chilled steaks. Otherwise, remove the fish from the refrigerator about 20 minutes before you grill the steaks. Place the steaks on an oiled rack over very hot coals, and grill the tuna for 2 to 3 minutes on each side for rare, 5 minutes on each side for well done.

SEAFOOD PAELLA

4 servings

If Spain had done nothing else for international cuisine, it would make the *What's What in Fine Cooking* with paella. Saffron is the secret, but in this version, devised by Lynne Parkhurst Ciuba of Dallas, fresh basil adds a wonderful touch. My tasters loved it, as did I. Note that the only salt in the recipe is in the broth and, if clams are used, in the clams.

Preparation tip: I use clams, when available, in addition to shrimp for a more interesting dish. Put the clams in several minutes ahead of the shrimp to be sure the clams open. This dish lends itself to doubling or tripling, if you have a large enough pot. It can be prepared ahead of time through step 3 (addition of the broth) and finished just before serving time. Be sure, though, to bring the mixture back to the boiling point before adding the shellfish and peas.

> 1 cup finely chopped onion
> 2 teaspoons butter *or* margarine
> 2 teaspoons olive oil
> 1 cup long-grain rice
> 1 small sweet green pepper, cored, seeded, and
>   finely chopped
> 1 small sweet red pepper, cored, seeded, and
>   finely chopped
> 1 tablespoon minced garlic
> ¼ cup firmly packed chopped fresh basil leaves
> ½ teaspoon (approximately) saffron threads, crumbled
> 1 to 1½ cups chicken broth
> 1 pound large shrimp, shelled and deveined, *or*
>   ½ pound cherrystone clams and ½ pound shrimp
> 1 cup peas, frozen or fresh (if fresh, parboil them
>   for 5 minutes)

1. In a large, heavy skillet, preferably cast-iron, sauté the onion in the butter or margarine and the oil over medium-low heat until the onion is softened.
2. Add the rice, and cook it, stirring it, for 3 minutes.
3. Add the green pepper, red pepper, garlic, basil, saffron, and 1 cup of the broth. Bring the mixture to a boil, stirring it. Lower the heat, cover the pan, and simmer the mixture for 10 minutes. *If you use clams,* add them to the pot after 5 minutes.
4. Add—but do not stir in—the shrimp, peas, and, if all the liquid has been absorbed, the remaining ½ cup of broth. Cover the paella, and simmer it for 8 to 10 minutes or until the shrimp are pink and just firm and the rice is tender.

SWORDFISH PRIMAVERA

4 servings

I must admit that I really splurged here, allowing half a pound of fish per person. But it was so delicious! And the dish, with only 1 tablespoon of added fat, is so low in calories. My recipe is derived from one devised by Jessica Zachs, a caterer from Avon, Connecticut, originally published in *Health* magazine.

Preparation tip: If you wish to grill the fish while the vegetables are cooking, you'll need a helper at the grill. Otherwise, the vegetables can be prepared first and covered to keep them hot while the fish is grilled.

    2   pounds swordfish steaks, about 1 inch thick
    2   tablespoons fresh lemon juice
  Salt to taste (optional)
  Freshly ground black pepper to taste
  ¾   pound young Swiss chard *or* spinach, tough
        stems trimmed
    1   tablespoon butter *or* margarine
    1   large clove garlic, peeled and minced
    1   large *or* 2 medium carrots, peeled and julienned
    1   large sweet red pepper, julienned
    1   large sweet yellow pepper, julienned
    1   leek, including the light green part, well
        washed and slivered lenthwise
  ½   pound very thin asparagus, trimmed of tough ends,
        steamed for 3 minutes, and cut into 2-inch lengths

1. One to 2 hours before serving the meal, place the fish in a shallow pan, preferably a glass one, pour the lemon juice over it, and sprinkle it on both sides with the salt (if desired) and pepper. Cover the fish with plastic wrap, and chill it. Remove the fish from the refrigerator about 30 minutes before cooking it.
2. Preheat the broiler or barbecue grill.
3. Thoroughly wash the chard or spinach, and place the wet leaves in a large, shallow nonstick saucepan or skillet. Cover the pan tightly, and steam the chard or spinach over medium heat for about 2 minutes. Keep the pan covered until serving time.
4. In a large nonstick skillet, melt the butter or margarine, and add the garlic, sautéing it for 30 seconds. Add the carrots, and sauté them for 2 minutes. Add the remaining vegetables, and sauté them for 2 to 3 minutes or until they are tender-crisp. Cover them to keep them warm until serving time.
5. Grill or broil the fish for 4 to 5 minutes on each side. *Do not overcook the fish.*
6. To serve, arrange a "bed" of chard or spinach on each of four heated dinner plates. Place one-fourth of the fish on each bed. Top the fish with the sautéed vegetables.

SALMON IN RHUBARB SAUCE

6 servings

This dish was a surprise. Although I feared I was ruining $30 worth of salmon, the result was extraordinary. The unusual combination is of Greek and Turkish derivation, where the Jews serve it instead of gefilte fish at the Passover seder.

Preparation tips: This make-ahead dish can be served hot (as it is in Greece) or chilled (as it is in Turkey). The gelatin is optional because it really does not matter whether the sauce gels—it is thick enough even not gelled. Other types of large fish steaks can be used in place of the salmon.

  1 pound rhubarb
  4 cups cold water, divided, *or* 3 cups cold water
       and 1 cup dry red wine
  2 teaspoons unflavored gelatin (optional)
  4 ounces tomato sauce (half of an 8-ounce can)
  1 teaspoon salt, or to taste (optional)
  1 tablespoon vegetable oil
  1 tablespoon sugar
  2 pounds salmon, cut into 1- to 1¼-inch steaks
  6 leaves green lettuce
Lemon wedges for garnish

1. If the rhubarb is tough, peel off the heavy filaments, and cut the rhubarb into 1-inch pieces. In a large, squat pot, cook the rhubarb over medium-low heat in 3½ cups of the water or 2½ cups of the water and 1 cup wine for about 20 minutes or until the rhubarb is very soft.
2. Meanwhile, sprinkle the gelatin (if you are using it) over the remaining ½ cup of water, and let the gelatin soften for 5 minutes.
3. When the rhubarb is done, stir in the softened gelatin mixture or the remaining ½ cup of water if you don't use the gelatin, the tomato sauce, salt (if desired), oil, and sugar. Simmer the mixture for 5 minutes.
4. Add the fish steaks, submerging them in the sauce. Cover the pot, and poach the fish for 15 minutes or until the fish is just done. Adjust the seasonings.
5. Remove the fish from the sauce with a large slotted spatula, and place the steaks on a platter with a lip. Pour the sauce over the fish, and chill the fish overnight.
6. Divide the steaks into 6 serving pieces, serving each piece on a lettuce leaf with some of the gelled sauce and the lemon wedges.

SALMON VINAIGRETTE WITH YOGURT-DILL SAUCE

3 to 4 servings

Although I cut this into bite-sized pieces and served it as an hors d'oeuvre, it would make a perfect warm-weather lunch or supper—elegant and amenable to advance preparation.

Preparation tips: Prepare the salmon steaks a day ahead, and leave them in the cooking liquid until serving time. Use only fresh dill for the sauce.

Serving suggestion: Start with a zippy cold soup like the Gazpacho on page 100 or the Spicy Corn and Tomato Soup on page 104.

SAUCE
½ cup plain nonfat or low-fat yogurt
¼ cup snipped fresh dill
½ teaspoon Dijon-style mustard
Dash hot pepper sauce
Dash Worcestershire sauce
Salt to taste (optional)

COOKING BROTH
4 cups water
2 cups white-wine vinegar
½ cup chopped onion
¼ teaspoon salt (optional)
¼ teaspoon sugar
¼ teaspoon freshly ground black pepper
1 bay leaf

1 pound salmon steaks, about ¾ inch thick

1. To prepare the sauce, combine the sauce ingredients in a small bowl, stir the ingredients to mix them well, and chill the sauce until serving time.
2. To make the cooking broth, place the cooking-broth ingredients in a medium-sized saucepan. Bring the broth to a boil, and cook it over high heat for 25 minutes.
3. Preheat the oven to 325° F.
4. Pour some of the boiling broth into a casserole large enough to hold the salmon in one layer. Place the salmon steaks into the liquid, and pour the rest of the broth over them.
5. Place the fish into the hot oven, and bake the salmon in the *uncovered* casserole for 20 minutes. Remove the casserole from the oven, cover the pot, and let the fish cool. Refrigerate the salmon until serving time. To serve, divide the steaks into individual portions, and carefully lift them with a spatula onto a serving platter. Serve the sauce over the fish or on the side.

BAKED SALMON WITH RICE STUFFING

6 or more servings

If you're lucky enough (or rich enough) to get your hands on a whole fresh salmon, this recipe for a stuffed 8-pound salmon turns it into a complete meal (with a salad, of course).

Serving suggestion: The simplest and most attractive way to serve the salmon is to cut the fish through bones and stuffing into thick slices. Garnish each serving with a sprig of fresh parsley and lemon wedges.

- 1 tablespoon butter *or* margarine
- 1 cup sliced celery
- 1 small onion, peeled and finely chopped (about ½ cup)
- ¼ teaspoon thyme
- 2 teaspoons grated lemon rind
- 2 tablespoons fresh lemon juice
- 3 cups water
- 1½ cups rice (white *or* brown *or* a combination of the two)
- ¾ teaspoon salt, or to taste (optional)
- ⅛ teaspoon freshly ground black pepper
- 2 cups sliced mushrooms
- 2 tablespoons broth (any kind *except* beef) *or*
  - 1 more tablespoon butter or margarine
- 1 8-pound salmon, cleaned

Vegetable-oil spray

1. In a medium-sized or large saucepan or a deep skillet, melt the butter or margarine, add the celery and onion, and sauté the vegetables until they soften.
2. Add the thyme, lemon rind, lemon juice, water, rice, salt (if desired), and pepper. Bring the mixture to a boil, reduce the heat, cover the pan, and simmer the mixture for 20 minutes (longer, if you are using brown rice).
3. Preheat the oven to 450° F.
4. While the rice cooks, in a small skillet sauté the mushrooms in the broth or butter or margarine. When the rice is done, add the mushrooms to the rice mixture.
5. Stuff the salmon with the rice mixture, and sew the fish up. Spray a large sheet of foil with vegetable oil, and wrap the foil around the fish. Put the fish in a baking pan.
6. Put the pan in the hot oven, and bake the salmon for 20 minutes. Open the foil, and bake the salmon 5 minutes longer or until the fish is opaque.

TOMATO-SALMON MOUSSE   *4 to 6 servings*

Here's a make-ahead dish that is delicious for lunch or supper on a warm day and looks lovely among foods on a buffet table.

Preparation tips: You can substitute tuna, canned or frozen crabmeat, or flaked lobster for the salmon. The mousse can also be gelled in individual molds. Since a number of the ingredients contain a fair amount of salt, you should not have to add any to the recipe. It is best to chill the bowl and beaters before whipping the milk.

    1 15-ounce can (or 2 small cans) salmon, drained,
          skin discarded, bones crushed
   12 ounces tomato juice
    2 tablespoons light mayonnaise *or* plain nonfat or
          low-fat yogurt
   ¼ cup chopped pimientos
    4 teaspoons fresh lemon juice
    2 teaspoons snipped fresh chives (1 teaspoon frozen)
    2 tablespoons minced scallions
   ¼ cup minced fresh parsley
   ½ cup water
    3 envelopes (3 scant tablespoons) unflavored gelatin
  Salt to taste (optional)
  Freshly ground black pepper to taste
   ¾ cup evaporated skim milk, chilled in the freezer
          for 1 hour

1. In a medium-sized bowl, flake the salmon, and add the tomato juice, mayonnaise or yogurt, pimientos, lemon juice, chives, scallions, and parsley. Combine the ingredients thoroughly, and set them aside.
2. Place the water in a small saucepan. Sprinkle the gelatin over the water, let the gelatin stand for a few minutes to soften, then heat the gelatin gently, stirring it, until it dissolves. Stir the gelatin mixture into the salmon mixture, and add the salt (if desired) and pepper.
3. Pour the evaporated milk into a chilled bowl. With an electric beater or eggbeater, beat the milk until it forms peaks. Fold the milk into the salmon mixture. Spoon the mousse into a lightly oiled mold (or into 4 to 6 individual molds). Refrigerate the mousse until it has set. Unmold the mousse to serve it.

OVEN-"FRIED" SALMON CAKES

4 servings

Mitzi Burkhart of Monroe, Ohio, whips together these tasty salmon patties in a few minutes and keeps them low in fat by baking instead of frying them. They would make a nice brunch, luncheon, or buffet offering.

Preparation tip: The patties can be prepared ahead for baking, or they can be baked ahead and reheated, covered, in the oven or in the microwave before serving.

> 1 15-ounce can salmon, drained and flaked
> 1 cup fresh bread crumbs
> 1 egg *or* 2 egg whites, lightly beaten
> ¼ cup minced scallions
> 2 tablespoons fresh lemon juice
> 1 teaspoon Worcestershire sauce
> Vegetable-oil spray

1. Preheat the oven to 400° F.
2. In a medium-sized bowl, thoroughly combine all the ingredients *except* the vegetable-oil spray, and shape them into 8 patties. Place the patties on a cookie sheet that has been sprayed with vegetable oil.
3. Put the sheet in the hot oven, and bake the patties for 5 minutes or until they are golden on both sides.

GEFILTE FISH

about 10 servings

This is a Jewish delicacy I grew up with and continue to treasure. The home-made version is far superior to any fish you can buy jarred or from a deli or appetizing store, and to me is well worth the effort. This recipe is the traditional one with a broth that gels when chilled.

Preparation tips: The 7 pounds of whole fish will become approximately 3½ pounds of fillets. Although the fish is traditionally ground with a hand-operated meat grinder (or, if you're lucky, by the fishmonger before you even get it home), the food processor makes grinding a snap. Just be sure not to process the fish into a paste; it should have the consistency of twice-ground beef.

Serving suggestion: Serve 1 or 2 fish balls (depending on their size) on a leaf of curly lettuce, garnished with some of the gelled broth and sliced carrots, if desired. Offer white and/or red horseradish.

7 pounds fish (a combination of whitefish, pike,
  and carp are best)
7 medium onions, peeled and sliced, divided
3 carrots, peeled and sliced
Water to cover
2 carrots, peeled and grated
2 egg whites
3 eggs
3 teaspoons sugar
Salt to taste (optional)
Freshly ground pepper to taste
⅓ cup water

1. Have the fishmonger fillet the fish (or do it yourself at home), and save all
   the scraps: skin, bones, heads, etc.—everything but the guts and gills. Place
   all the fish scraps, 4 of the sliced onions, and the sliced carrots in a large
   shallow pot or Dutch oven. Add water to cover, and bring the mixture to a
   boil.
2. Meanwhile, grind the fish with the remaining 3 onions and the grated carrots. Add the egg whites, whole eggs, sugar, salt (if desired), and pepper,
   mixing the ingredients thoroughly with a wooden spoon.
3. Shape the fish mixture into 10 or 20 balls or small oval loaves, using the ⅓
   cup water on your hands to assist in the shaping.
4. Place the balls in the boiling broth, reduce the heat, cover the pot, and
   simmer the fish for about 2 hours. Remove the pot from the heat, and chill
   the gefilte fish either in the broth, which will gel, or separately.

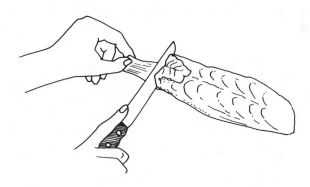

GEFILTE FISH LOAF

8 to 12 servings

This recipe, compliments of Marian Burros, *New York Times* food columnist and author of many fine cookbooks, shortens the process of making gefilte fish by eliminating the broth. The result is attractive as well as delicious.

Serving suggestion: Slice the loaf, present each slice on a leaf of curly lettuce, and garnish with a sprig of watercress and slice of tomato. Serve the gefilte fish as a first course or as the main dish of a lunch or light supper.

2 large carrots, peeled and halved lengthwise
2 pounds whitefish fillets *or* 1½ pounds whitefish
   fillets and ½ pound carp fillets or pike fillets
1 cup chopped onion (1 large)
1 medium carrot, peeled and grated (½ cup)
¼ cup matzo meal
1 tablespoon walnut oil *or* canola oil *or* olive oil
2 teaspoons sugar
¾ teaspoon salt (optional)
Freshly ground white pepper to taste
¼ teaspoon nutmeg
2 egg whites
1 egg
½ cup cold water *or* fish broth
Prepared horseradish

1. Steam the carrot halves for 7 minutes or until they are partially softened. Set the carrots aside.
2. Preheat the oven to 350° F.
3. In a food processor, coarsely grind the fish. Transfer the fish to a bowl. Add the onion to the food processor, and mince the vegetable. Transfer the onion to the bowl with the fish. Stir in the grated carrot, matzo meal, oil, sugar, salt (if desired), pepper, nutmeg, egg whites, whole egg, and cold water or fish broth. Mix the ingredients thoroughly.
4. Transfer one-third of the mixture to a nonstick 9 × 5 × 3-inch loaf pan. Place 2 of the carrot halves lengthwise on the fish. Add another third of the fish mixture, and place the remaining two carrot halves on top of that. Top with the remaining fish mixture.
5. Place the pan in the hot oven, and bake the fish for 1 hour. Remove the loaf from the oven, and cool it in the pan on a rack. When the loaf is cool, loosen the sides with a knife, and carefully turn the loaf out onto a platter. Cover the loaf, and chill it until serving time.
6. Slice the loaf, and serve it with the horseradish.

GEFILTE FISH TERRINE

12 servings

Yet another festive way to prepare gefilte fish—this one devised by Florence Fabricant, nutrition-conscious cook and author. This is decidedly the most elegant of the three recipes offered here, though less traditional. Like the Gefilte Fish Loaf, it is also easier to prepare than rolling balls of fish and cooking them in broth.

Preparation tips: This recipe is easy to do with a food processor, although a food mill can be used to prepare the vegetables and the fish can be ground in a meat grinder. To speed the preparation, cook the carrots (step 2) while the leeks are cooking (step 1). I made 2 layers of carrot purée and 1 layer of leek purée, though you could do the opposite if you prepare more leeks than carrots. Do not use a pan with a removable bottom in which to bake the fish because the water in which the pan is sitting will seep into the pan, ruining the dish. The terrine is lovely if made in a ring mold and unmolded.

Serving suggestion: Serve the fish in slices (for loaf) or wedges (for ring mold) along with horseradish.

    1 1-pound bunch leeks, white parts only, sheaths
        separated, washed, and sliced
Water to cover
    3 tablespoons chopped fresh parsley, divided
Salt to taste
Freshly ground black pepper to taste
    1 pound carrots, peeled and sliced
Water to cover
    1 tablespoon fresh lemon juice
Pinch nutmeg
Salt to taste
Freshly ground black pepper to taste
    2 tablespoons matzo meal
 ½ cup fish broth *or* chicken broth
    2 medium onions, peeled and chopped (about 1⅓ cups)
1½ pounds whitefish fillets, ground or cut into 1-inch pieces
 ½ pound pike fillets, ground or cut into 1-inch pieces
 ½ pound boneless carp, ground or cut into 1-inch pieces
    2 egg whites
    1 egg
    1 teaspoon (approximately) salt
Freshly ground black pepper to taste
Vegetable-oil spray *or* vegetable oil

1. In a small saucepan, bring the leeks with water to cover to a boil, reduce the heat, cover the pan, and simmer the leeks for 25 minutes or until they are very tender. Drain the leeks, and purée them in a food processor with 1 tablespoon of the parsley, the salt, and pepper. Transfer the leek purée to a bowl, and set the bowl aside. Do not wash out the food-processor bowl.

2. While the leeks cook, in a medium-sized saucepan, bring the carrots with water to cover to a boil, reduce the heat, cover the pan, and simmer the carrots for about 25 minutes or until they are very tender. Drain the carrots, and purée them in a food processor with the lemon juice, nutmeg, salt, and pepper. Transfer the carrot purée to a second bowl, and set the bowl aside. Do not wash out the food-processor bowl.

3. In another small bowl, combine the matzo meal and broth, and set the bowl aside.

4. Place the chopped onions in the food processor, and process them until they are finely chopped. Add the whitefish, pike, and carp, and process the fish with the onions until the mixture forms a smooth purée. Add the moistened matzo meal, egg whites, whole egg, the remaining 2 tablespoons of parsley, about 1 teaspoon of salt, and a generous amount of pepper, and process the ingredients until they are well blended.

5. Preheat the oven to 350° F. Spray or brush a 6-cup ring mold or loaf pan with vegetable oil.

6. Spread half the fish mixture in the pan, making a depression in the middle to within ½ inch of the sides. Spread half the reserved carrot mixture in the depression, spread all the reserved leek mixture over the carrots, and spread the remaining carrot mixture over the leeks. Cover the carrot mixture with the other half of the fish mixture. Rap the sides of the pan several times on the countertop to eliminate air pockets.

7. Cover the mold with wax paper or parchment paper, and set the mold in a larger pan (at least 2 inches deep). Put the pans in the hot oven, and add 1 to 1½ inches of boiling water to the outside pan. Bake the terrine for 50 minutes, then remove it from the oven, and let it cool. When the terrine is cool, turn the loaf out onto a serving dish, cover the loaf with plastic wrap, and chill it for at least 6 hours.

Meat Main Dishes

Some people express great surprise when they discover that I and my family still eat red meat. They mistakenly think that meat is the antithesis of good nutrition, when in fact it is a superb source of essential nutrients—in particular, protein, iron, and B vitamins. The trick is not to eliminate meat from the diet, but to reduce as much as possible the saturated fat and cholesterol that typically come along as unwanted baggage. Therefore, virtually all my meat-based recipes call for lean or extra-lean cuts of meat, and in most the meat is prepared to allow for even further drainage of fat. In addition, I am careful about quantities. Actually, all anyone needs in a given meal to satisfy protein requirements is 2 to 3 ounces of meat; I allow up to 4-ounce servings in my recipes. In fact, since lean and extra-lean cuts have become readily available throughout the country, I have been more generous with quantities of meat here than in the recipes in *Jane Brody's Good Food Book.*

None of this means that you should never again sit down to a big, juicy burger or steak, a half-pound slab of prime rib, or a plate full of barbecued ribs or sausages. But in a health-conscious life, these should be rare treats, if you'll pardon the pun. In most of my recipes, I use meat as a condiment—a flavoring agent (in the case of sausage)—and a means of balancing the incomplete protein in plant foods. Here, though, lean meat shines in its own right as the centerpiece of the meal. So, enjoy!

MEATBALLS AND MUSHROOMS IN YOGURT SAUCE

6 servings

Now that extra-lean ground beef is readily available (85 or 90 percent lean is what I buy), I'm less reluctant to prepare and serve "pure" meatballs on occasion. These are enhanced by a slightly tangy yogurt sauce.

Preparation tip: The meatballs can be made ahead through step 5. Or they can be completed through the preparation of the mushrooms in step 6, with the yogurt, lemon juice, and cooked meatballs added to the reheated mushrooms just before serving.

Serving suggestions: The meatballs go well with noodles, brown rice cooked in beef broth, or mashed potatoes. Garnish with minced fresh parsley. Try also the Nippy Greens on page 333.

   2 teaspoons olive oil *or* canola oil, divided
   1 medium onion, peeled and finely chopped
     (about ¾ cup)
   1 pound extra-lean ground beef
   2 slices partly stale bread, crumbled
   1 egg *or* 1 egg white, lightly beaten
2¼ cups plain nonfat or low-fat yogurt, divided
   ½ teaspoon salt, or to taste (optional)
   ¼ teaspoon marjoram
   ¼ teaspoon AHA Herb Mix (page 545) *or* other
     no-salt seasoning
Freshly ground black pepper to taste
   ½ cup wheat germ (approximately)
   2 cups sliced or chopped mushrooms
   1 tablespoon fresh lemon juice

1. Preheat the oven to 350° F.
2. Heat 1 teaspoon of the oil briefly in a small nonstick skillet, add the onion, and sauté the vegetable for 3 minutes or until it is softened. Transfer the onion to a large bowl.
3. To the bowl add the beef, bread crumbs, egg or egg white, ¼ cup of the yogurt, salt (if desired), marjoram, AHA or other no-salt seasoning, and pepper, and mix the ingredients well.
4. Shape the meat mixture into 1¼-inch balls. Roll the meatballs in the wheat germ, and place them on a baking tray such as a large cookie sheet.
5. Place the pan in the hot oven, and bake the meatballs for 20 minutes. Remove the meatballs with a slotted spoon to a colander or a bowl lined with paper towels, and cover the meatballs to keep them warm.
6. In a large nonstick skillet, heat the remaining teaspoon of oil briefly. Add the mushrooms, and sauté them until they begin to give up their liquid. Stir in the remaining 2 cups of yogurt and the lemon juice. Add the drained meatballs, and simmer but *do not boil* the meatballs for 5 to 10 minutes to heat the meat through.

BEA'S UNSTUFFED CABBAGE

6 servings

Karen Lorentz of Plainsboro, New Jersey, passed along her friend Beatrice Teitel's recipe for a simplified version of Sweet-and-Sour Stuffed Cabbage (see *Jane Brody's Good Food Book*). I had to admit that her dish was much easier to prepare—and easier to eat! I adjusted the ingredients to achieve the flavor and character of my original recipe, which I have adored since early childhood. This is a great dish to serve to a large group since the recipe can be doubled (even quadrupled, if you have big enough pots) and the prepared dish can be frozen.

Preparation tips: Note the long cooking time. This is a dish that is best prepared ahead and reheated at serving time since the flavor improves.

Serving suggestion: Mashed potatoes are an excellent accompaniment. The dish also goes well with broad egg noodles.

CABBAGE SOUP
- 1 large onion, diced (1 cup)
- 1 2-pound head green cabbage, cored and diced
- 1 cup (8-ounce can) tomato sauce
- 1 28-ounce can peeled tomatoes with their juice
- 1 cup water
- ¼ cup honey
- ¼ cup lemon juice

- ⅓ cup raisins

MEATBALLS
- 1 pound ground beef *or* veal *or* lamb
- ½ cup raw white rice
- 1 teaspoon Worcestershire sauce
- ½ teaspoon salt (optional)
- Freshly ground black pepper to taste

1. In a large, heavy pot, combine the cabbage-soup ingredients *except* the raisins, and bring them to a boil over medium-high heat while preparing the meatballs.
2. In a medium-sized bowl, combine the meatball ingredients, stirring them to mix them thoroughly. With wet hands, roll the meat mixture into 1¼-inch balls. Add the meatballs to the boiling cabbage soup, reduce the heat to medium-low, cover the pot, and simmer the meatballs for 2 hours.
3. Remove the cover, add the raisins, and cook the meatballs for another 30 minutes in the uncovered pot.

CHILI-CORN BURGERS

4 servings

These are Sloppy Joe–type burgers in which the meat is extended by combining it with nutritious vegetables. A salad makes this dish a complete meal that should appeal to children as well as adults.

Preparation tip: For the canned corn, you can substitute 1⅔ cups fresh or frozen corn kernels, cooked for 5 minutes in ⅓ cup of lightly salted water. Be sure to save the cooking liquid.

Serving suggestion: Adults would go for the Salsa on page 539 and Tortilla Chips on page 44.

½ pound extra-lean ground beef
1 cup chopped onion (1 large)
1 teaspoon minced garlic
½ cup finely diced sweet green pepper *or* sweet
  red pepper
1 15-ounce can corn kernels with liquid
1 16-ounce can tomatoes, coarsely chopped,
  liquid reserved
1 tablespoon chili powder, or to taste
¼ teaspoon freshly ground black pepper
4 or more sandwich buns, heated or toasted if desired
2 tablespoons minced fresh parsley for garnish (optional)

1. In a skillet over medium heat, brown the meat, crumbling it with a spatula. Drain off the fat, if there is any.
2. Add the onion, garlic, and sweet green or red pepper. Sauté the vegetables for 5 minutes or until the onion and pepper are soft.
3. Stir in the corn with its liquid, tomatoes and their liquid, chili powder, and black pepper. Simmer the mixture in the uncovered pan for 10 minutes or until most of the liquid has evaporated.
4. Serve the meat mixture on the buns, garnished with the minced parsley (if desired).

BEEF TAMALE PIE

6 to 8 servings

Here is a delicious tamale pie adapted from *Gourmet* magazine.

Preparation tips: The beef mixture can be prepared ahead and refrigerated until you are ready to add the topping and bake the pie. Sodium watchers may wish to eliminate the olives and use no-added-salt tomato sauce.

Serving suggestion: Yellow Pepper Soup on page 86 would be a great opener.

FILLING
- 1 pound extra-lean ground beef
- 1 cup chopped onion (1 large)
- 1 cup chopped sweet green pepper (2 medium)
- 1 tablespoon vegetable oil (preferably canola *or* olive)
- 1 8-ounce can tomato sauce
- 2 tablespoons tomato paste
- 10 ounces frozen corn kernels, thawed
- ½ cup sliced Spanish olives (pimiento-stuffed green olives)
- 1 tablespoon Worcestershire sauce
- 1 tablespoon yellow corn meal
- 2 teaspoons cumin
- 2 teaspoons unsweetened cocoa powder
- 2 teaspoons chili powder (mild or hot, as desired)
- ¾ teaspoon hot pepper sauce
- ½ teaspoon allspice
- Freshly ground black pepper to taste

TOPPING
- 1 cup whole-wheat pastry flour
- 1 cup yellow corn meal (preferably stone-ground)
- 3 tablespoons sugar
- 2 teaspoons baking powder
- 3 tablespoons unsalted butter *or* margarine, melted and cooled
- ¾ cup skim or low-fat milk
- 1 large egg, lightly beaten
- ½ cup (2 ounces) grated sharp Cheddar
- 1 4-ounce can green chilies, seeded and chopped

TO PREPARE THE FILLING

1. In a large nonstick or heavy skillet, brown the beef, stirring it and breaking up the clumps. Remove the meat with a slotted spoon to a bowl, discard the fat, and set the bowl aside. Wipe the skillet with a paper towel.
2. In the skillet over moderately low heat, sauté the onion and green pepper in the oil, stirring the ingredients often, until the vegetables have softened.
3. Return the beef to the skillet, and add the tomato sauce, tomato paste, corn kernels, olives, Worcestershire sauce, corn meal, cumin, cocoa powder, chili powder, hot pepper sauce, allspice, and pepper. Cover the skillet, and simmer the mixture, stirring it occasionally, for 30 minutes. Transfer the mixture to a shallow 2½-quart casserole.

TO PREPARE THE TOPPING

4. Preheat the oven to 400° F.
5. In a medium-sized bowl, stir together the flour, corn meal, sugar, and baking powder. Add the butter or margarine, milk, and egg, stirring the ingredients just to combine them. Stir in the Cheddar and chilies, and distribute the batter by spoonfuls around the edges of the filling mixture.
6. Place the casserole in the hot oven, and bake the pie for 10 minutes. Then reduce the oven temperature to 350° F, and bake the pie 30 minutes longer.

VEAL LOAF

6 to 8 main or 16 to 20
first-course servings

Here is a couldn't-be-simpler make-ahead dish that can be served hot as a main course or cold as a pâté-like appetizer. Oatmeal gives it the consistency of a pâté but without the fat. The recipe is one suggested years ago in a promotional booklet by the packagers of Sun-Maid raisins.

Preparation tip: The loaf can be prepared in advance and reheated, or it can be served cold.

   1 pound lean ground veal (*or* part pork, if desired)
  ½ cup raisins
   1 cup finely chopped onion (1 large)
   1 cup quick-cooking oats
   1 teaspoon salt (optional)
  ¼ teaspoon freshly ground black pepper
  ¼ teaspoon poultry seasoning
   1 egg *or* 2 egg whites, beaten
1¼ cups water

1. Preheat the oven to 350° F.
2. In a large bowl, combine the ingredients well. Pack the veal mixture into a greased 8 × 4-inch loaf pan, or shape it into a loaf and place the loaf in a baking pan.
3. Place the pan in the hot oven, and bake the loaf for 1 hour.

JAPANESE-STYLE BEEF AND VEGETABLES

4 servings

This was the first meal I cooked for Richard—on a hibachi in the dark! It ultimately got me a husband. It should at least get you a few culinary kudos.

Preparation tip: This nontraditional sukiyaki—a Japanese dish that contains lean meat, bean curd, noodles, and vegetables in a sauce—takes only 10 to 15 minutes to cook, if you set up the ingredients ahead. Start the rice that should accompany it before you start the stir-fry.

SAUCE
- ¼ cup beef broth
- 3 tablespoons reduced-sodium soy sauce
- 1 tablespoon sugar

STIR-FRY
- 1 tablespoon olive oil *or* canola oil
- 1 pound lean round steak, partially frozen and very thinly sliced across the grain
- ½ pound asparagus, tough ends trimmed, cut into 2-inch lengths
- 1 bunch scallions, cut into 2-inch lengths
- ½ Spanish onion, peeled and thinly sliced
- 12 ounces mushrooms, thinly sliced
- 1 pound spinach, well washed and drained, stems trimmed

1. To make the sauce, combine the sauce ingredients in a cup or small bowl, stirring the ingredients until the sugar is dissolved. Set the bowl aside.
2. To make the sukiyaki, in a large skillet or well-seasoned wok, heat the oil, add the steak, and brown the beef quickly, tossing it. Add the reserved sauce, cover the pan, and simmer the beef for 2 minutes.
3. Uncover the pan, toss in the asparagus, scallions, onion, and mushrooms, and mix the vegetables with the beef. Place the spinach on top of the mixture, cover the pan, and cook the sukiyaki for 10 minutes or until the spinach is tender.

MEAT TZIMMES

Tzimmes, a stew containing carrots, potatoes, and prunes, is a traditional Jewish make-ahead dish to serve to family and other visitors during winter celebrations. (See also the Vegetable Tzimmes on page 325.)

Preparation tip: If the tzimmes is prepared ahead, reheat it in a tightly covered casserole in the oven or in a microwave oven. It will stick if you attempt to reheat it on top of the stove.

Serving suggestion: Add a green vegetable and the Grapefruit and Broccoli Salad on page 365.

  3 pounds lean chuck *or* top round, cut into 1-inch cubes
Salt to taste (optional)
  1 tablespoon vegetable oil (preferably canola)
  3 large onions, peeled and thinly sliced
10 large white potatoes, peeled and cut into 1-inch cubes
10 large carrots, peeled and cut into 1-inch lengths
24 ounces pitted prunes
  1 cup dried apricots
Grated rind and juice 2 oranges
Water *or* beef broth to cover
¼ cup brown sugar
  1 teaspoon cinnamon
Several dashes freshly grated nutmeg

1. Preheat the oven to 350° F.
2. Sprinkle the meat lightly with the salt (if desired). In a large, heavy or nonstick skillet, heat the oil briefly, add the meat and onions, and brown the meat (in batches, if necessary) over high heat. Transfer the meat and onions to a large, heavy ovenproof casserole.
3. Add the remaining ingredients to the casserole, tossing them to combine them well.
4. Cover the casserole, and put it in the hot oven. Bake the tzimmes for 2½ to 3 hours, or until the vegetables are tender but not mushy.

STIR-FRIED BEEF WITH BROCCOLI   *4 servings*

Stir-fries are quick, nutritious, tasty meals that can be made with almost any combination of meat, poultry, or seafood (½ pound for four servings) and vegetables (lots!) and served with rice (white, brown, or a combination of the two), noodles, or bulgur. Their only drawback is the sodium contributed primarily by the soy sauce. I use reduced-sodium soy (Kikkoman or Angostura brand), which helps a lot since the sodium content is about half that of regular imported soy sauce (which, in turn, has less sodium than domestic brands).

Preparation tips: Since stir-fries are cooked in a few minutes, it's crucial to have all ingredients prepared and ready to toss into the pan or wok before you begin. And since the rice or alternative accompaniment takes even longer than the stir-fry to cook, start that before you even begin preparing the stir-fry ingredients. The meat is easiest to cut into thin slices if it is first partially frozen.

SAUCE
- ⅓ cup broth *or* water
- 2 tablespoons soy sauce (preferably reduced-sodium)
- 1 tablespoon dry sherry *or* rice wine
- ½ teaspoon sugar

STIR-FRY
- ½ pound extra-lean beef, well trimmed
- 1 head broccoli (about 1¼ pounds)
- 1 large *or* 2 medium carrots, scraped and diagonally sliced
- 3 cloves garlic, peeled and finely minced
- 2 teaspoons minced gingerroot
- Dash dry sherry *or* white wine
- 4 teaspoons peanut *or* canola oil, divided
- Hot pepper flakes to taste (optional)
- 1 medium onion, peeled and sliced, *or* 3 to 4 scallions, sliced

1. In a cup, combine the sauce ingredients, and set the cup aside.
2. Slice the beef paper-thin—across the grain, if possible. Set the beef aside.
3. Cut the broccoli into bite-sized flowerets. Slice the stems on the diagonal into ovals. Steam the broccoli for 3 minutes, or parboil it for 1 minute, and drain it well. Set the broccoli aside.
4. Steam the carrot slices for 5 minutes, or parboil them for 3 minutes, and drain them well. Set the carrots aside.
5. In a small dish, combine the garlic, gingerroot, and sherry or wine, and set the mixture aside.
6. Heat a wok or large skillet over high heat for 1 minute. Add 2 teaspoons of the oil, and heat the oil for 30 seconds (the oil should be very hot but not smoking). Add half the garlic mixture, stirring it with a spatula for about 5 seconds (do not let it burn). Then add the sliced beef and hot pepper flakes

(if desired), tossing the mixture constantly until the meat has just lost its pinkness. Remove the beef from the pan, and set it aside.

7. Wipe out any watery juices that may be in the pan, and heat it again for about 30 seconds. Add the remaining 2 teaspoons oil, and heat the oil until it is hot. Add the remaining garlic mixture, stirring it for 5 seconds. Then add the onion or scallions, the reserved broccoli, and the reserved carrots. Sprinkle the mixture with additional pepper flakes (if desired), toss the ingredients to combine them, and heat them through.

8. Stir the reserved sauce mixture, and add it to the pan by pouring it against the side of the pan so that it heats before it hits the vegetables. Add the reserved beef, and cook it, tossing the ingredients constantly, for 3 minutes or until the vegetables are tender-crisp. (Though not "authentic" to stir-frying, you can cover the pan or wok for a few minutes to further soften the vegetables, if you wish.)

HARVEST BEEF STEW

5 to 6 servings

Here's an all-American meal-in-a-pot that needs only bread and a green salad for accompaniments.

Preparation tip: Since the flavor of a stew improves with age, this is a perfect make-ahead dish. Or you could stop after completing step 3 and add the chopped tomatoes when you are ready to heat the stew and serve it.

    1 pound extra-lean beef, cut into small cubes
    AHA Herb Mix (see page 545) *or* another no-salt
       seasoning, divided
    ½ teaspoon salt, divided (optional)
    Freshly ground black pepper to taste, divided
    1 teaspoon oil
    1 large onion, peeled and chopped (1 cup)
    2 cloves garlic, peeled and minced
    4 large carrots (1 to 1½ pounds), peeled and
       sliced into rounds
    1 6-ounce can tomato paste mixed with 1 can water
    4 medium-large potatoes (1½ to 2 pounds),
       peeled and cut into chunks
    1 large sweet green pepper, cored, seeded, and
       cut into squares
    1 large sweet red pepper, cored, seeded, and cut
       into squares
    2 medium zucchinis (about 1 pound), sliced into
       ¼-inch pieces
    1 teaspoon oregano
    1 teaspoon Worcestershire sauce
    2 dashes hot pepper sauce
    3 tomatoes, chopped

1. Sprinkle the beef cubes with the AHA Herb Mix or another no-salt season-ing, about ⅛ teaspoon of the salt (if desired), and the pepper. To a large, deep, lightly greased skillet or 5-quart Dutch oven, add the beef, browning it on all sides. Remove the beef from the pan along with any juices that may have accumulated, and set the beef aside. Wipe out the pan.
2. Add the oil to the pan, and heat the oil briefly. Add the onion and garlic, and sauté the vegetables for about 3 minutes, stirring them. Add the car-rots, and sauté them for several minutes.
3. Stir in the tomato paste–water mixture, and return the beef and its juices to the pan. Heat the mixture until the liquid begins to boil, reduce the heat, cover the pan, and simmer the ingredients for 5 minutes. Add the potatoes, cover the pan, and simmer the vegetables for another 5 minutes. Add the green pepper, red pepper, zucchinis, oregano, Worcestershire sauce, hot pepper sauce, the remaining ⅜ teaspoon of salt (if desired),

additional AHA Herb Mix, and additional pepper. Stir the ingredients to combine them thoroughly, cover the pan, and simmer the stew for 15 minutes.

4. Add the chopped tomatoes, cover the pan, and simmer the stew for another 5 to 10 minutes or until the potatoes and carrots are just tender.

PORK MARSALA

4 servings

The pork industry promotes its product as "the other white meat." And, indeed, lean pork has less saturated fat and less cholesterol than lean beef (though more than chicken breast). Thus, I serve pork (the loin or tenderloin) from time to time when I encounter an especially good recipe, like this adaptation of one offered by the National Pork Producers Council.

Serving suggestion: This is an elegant entrée that goes well with egg noodles, rice, or wild rice—for example, the Wild Rice and Pumpkin Pilaf on page 332.

  1 **pound pork tenderloin, well trimmed**
  1 **teaspoon oil**
  1 **tablespoon minced garlic (3 large cloves)**
  1 **tablespoon tomato paste**
½ **cup dry Marsala**
½ **cup red wine**
12 **ounces or more mushroom caps (halved if large)**
  1 **tablespoon chopped fresh parsley**

1. Cut the pork diagonally into cutlets ¼-inch thick (or, if necessary, pound the cutlets to a thickness of ¼ inch). In a large nonstick skillet, add the cutlets, brown them on both sides, and remove them to a platter.
2. Heat the oil in the pan, add the garlic, and sauté the garlic for about 1 minute over medium-low heat.
3. Combine the tomato paste with the Marsala and red wine, and add the mixture to the pan. Add the mushrooms. Bring the mixture to a simmer, and cook the sauce for 3 to 5 minutes.
4. Return the reserved cutlets to the pan, and heat them through. Before serving them, sprinkle them with the parsley.

ROLLED PORK ROAST WITH FRUITED FILLING

4 servings

This is a delicious, low-calorie roast (about 250 calories per serving) that looks very festive when sliced. A friend, who had seen the recipe in a magazine, passed it along to me. Unfortunately, she did not recall its original source.

Preparation tips: If you start with a roast larger than 1 pound, be sure to increase the amounts of the stuffing ingredients. The roast is best served hot or warm, so place it in the oven 1 hour before you expect to serve it. It can also be prepared ahead and warmed in a microwave. To keep the roast from drying out, slice it just before serving it.

Serving suggestion: This dish goes very well with Savory Applesauce on page 307 or any of the chutneys on pages 550 to 552.

¼ cup dried currants
¼ cup finely chopped dried apricots
2 tablespoons bourbon
1 tablespoon water
1 pound boneless pork tenderloin
1 cup fresh pumpernickel bread crumbs
¼ teaspoon salt (optional)
¼ teaspoon rosemary, crumbled
⅛ teaspoon sage, crumbled
⅛ teaspoon freshly ground black pepper
1 egg *or* 1 egg white, lightly beaten

1. Preheat the oven to 400° F.
2. Place the currants and apricots in a medium-sized bowl, and stir in the bourbon and water. Set the bowl aside.
3. Cut the tenderloin lengthwise down the center *but not all the way through.* Spread the roast flat, and pound it between sheets of heavy plastic wrap to a thickness of ¼ inch.
4. To the soaked dried fruit, add the remaining ingredients, stirring them to mix them well. Spread the mixture across the surface of the meat, covering the meat almost to its edges on three sides but leaving 1 inch bare on the fourth side. Pat the stuffing down, and roll the roast toward the uncovered edge. Tie the pork roll in three places with kitchen cord, dental floss, or heavy-duty sewing thread.
5. Place the roast, seam side down, in a lightly greased shallow pan. Put the pan in the hot oven, and roast the pork roll for 50 to 60 minutes.

IRAQI LAMB WITH OKRA

8 servings

To think that all these years I avoided okra because it was unpleasantly gummy. What a great vegetable it can be when it is properly prepared. It is high in calcium and cholesterol-lowering fiber. And it's so cute! The simple trick to preparing it is not to cut through the flesh and not to overcook it. I served this dish, a modified version of one devised by Mrs. Daisy Iny (author of *The Best of Baghdad Cooking*), to much applause at a Passover seder.

Preparation tips: Make the dish ahead of time, if possible—the flavor improves. The recipe can be prepared several ways. The lamb can be cooked, as it is in the Middle East (where ''lamb'' is usually mutton), until it falls apart. Or it can be cooked until the cubes of meat are tender but still intact. The recipe can also be done sour (lemon juice only) or sweet-and-sour (lemon juice and 3 tablespoons of sugar). I like it best with just a small amount of sugar (1 tablespoon) to take the edge off the lemon juice.

Serving suggestion: Offer a ''bedding'' of mashed potatoes, rice, couscous, or egg noodles.

    2 pounds boneless lean lamb, cut into 1-inch
        to 1½-inch cubes
Salt to taste (optional)
Freshly ground black pepper to taste
3½ cups water
 ½ cup chopped onion
 ⅛ teaspoon turmeric
    3 large ribs celery, sliced
    3 tablespoons tomato paste
    6 tablespoons fresh lemon juice
    1 pound fresh okra, stems trimmed not quite to the flesh
    2 tablespoons minced fresh parsley
    1 tablespoon finely chopped celery leaves
 ¼ to ½ cup chopped mint leaves, to taste
    1 tablespoon sugar

1. Sprinkle the lamb with the salt (if desired) and pepper. Place the lamb in a large pot, add the water, onion, and turmeric, and bring the water to a boil. Partially cover the pot, and cook the lamb over medium heat for about 30 minutes.
2. Add the celery, and cook the lamb for another 30 minutes, adding more water, if necessary, to cover three-fourths of the meat.
3. Add the tomato paste and lemon juice, stirring the ingredients to combine them well. Bring the liquid to a boil, and add the okra, parsley, celery leaves, and mint. Lower the temperature to medium-low, and simmer the lamb for 15 minutes or until the lamb and okra are tender. Sprinkle in the sugar, gently stirring the liquid so as not to crush the okra.

BUTTERFLIED LEG OF LAMB

6 to 8 servings

As if a good leg of lamb weren't scrumptious enough, the crumb topping that crowns this roast makes the dish truly memorable. After finding a recipe for such a dish in Jean Hewitt's *The New York Times Heritage Cookbook* in the early 1970s, I've made it many times for holiday celebrations, always to great acclaim. I make extra crumb topping because it's so delicious; I consider it the equivalent of stuffing in a bird.

Preparation tips: If you butterfly the leg yourself, try to keep the flesh in one piece. If the butcher does it for you, ask him or her to keep the meat whole when butterflying it. Note that the topping is put on 15 minutes before the lamb is finished roasting.

1 5- to 6-pound leg of lamb, boned, trimmed of fat, and cut to spread open like a thick steak (you should end up with 3¾ to 4¼ pounds of boneless meat)	**TOPPING**
	1 tablespoon butter *or* margarine
	1 tablespoon olive oil
	4 large shallots *or* 1 large onion, peeled and minced (1 cup)
2 teaspoons olive oil (optional—only if the lamb is very lean)	3 to 4 cups *fresh* bread crumbs (I use half whole-wheat)
3 large cloves garlic, peeled and crushed	½ cup minced Italian parsley
½ teaspoon salt (optional)	½ to ¾ cup grated Parmesan, to taste
Freshly ground black pepper to taste	¼ to ½ cup broth (any kind)
1 teaspoon oregano	1 egg *or* 1 egg white (optional—to hold the topping together)
4 tablespoons fresh lemon juice	

1. Preheat the oven to 450° F.
2. Place the lamb in a shallow roasting pan. If the lamb is very lean, sprinkle it on both sides with the olive oil. In a small bowl, combine the garlic, salt (if desired), pepper, oregano, and lemon juice, and rub the mixture over both sides of the meat.
3. Place the lamb in the hot oven for 20 minutes. Then turn the oven down to 325° F, and continue roasting the lamb for a total of 10 to 15 minutes per pound of boned weight *minus 15 minutes* to allow time for the topping to bake. (For example, a 3¾-pound piece of boneless lamb would finish roasting in about 40 minutes; therefore, I would interrupt it in 25 minutes in order to put on the topping. Then the lamb would go back in the oven for the remaining 15 minutes.)
4. While the lamb roasts, prepare the topping. Heat the butter or margarine and the oil in a large skillet. Add the shallots or onion, sauté the vegetable until it is softened, and place it in a large bowl. To the bowl, add the bread crumbs, parsley, and Parmesan, and mix the ingredients well. Stir in the broth and the egg or egg white, if you are using it.

5. About 15 minutes before the lamb is finished roasting, remove the pan from the oven, and spread the topping over the surface of the meat. Return the pan to the oven, and continue roasting the lamb for 15 minutes or until the topping is lightly browned but still soft.

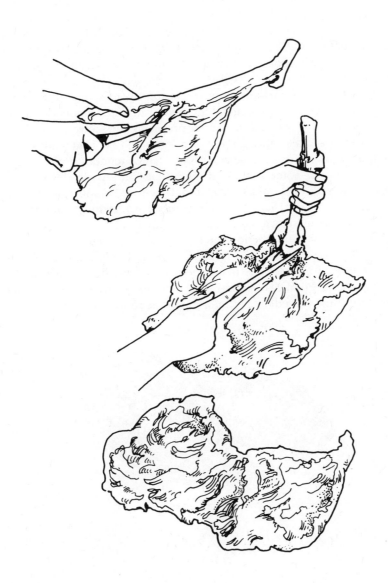

Come to a Barbecue

The usual barbecue fare—hot dogs, hamburgers, sausages, and the like, accompanied by chips and salads loaded with fat and salt—is not exactly wholesome (although far be it for me to say that you should not enjoy a meal like this once or twice a year). But I have found that there are better foods to grill, foods that require advance preparation but keep the host and hostess free to enjoy their own party. These are kebabs: skewered meat (beef, pork, or lamb), chicken, fish, and vegetables—lots and lots of vegetables—that the guests prepare for themselves and cook to their individual liking. Kebabs are colorful and perfect for parties at which people arrive at different times during an afternoon or evening.

The protein food for kebabs is marinated up to a day or even more in advance, as are some of the vegetables, and, if desired, diners can brush their other vegetables with the marinade after preparing the skewer. The skewers are grilled over hot coals—though not too close to the heat—until the meat, chicken, or fish is just done. The vegetables remain tender-crisp.

Here, then, are some suggested ingredients and marinades for your next barbecue. Vegetables should be cut into 1-inch to 1½-inch pieces. Meat and chicken can be cut into 1-inch to 1¼-inch cubes or rectangles. But fish, which is more likely to fall apart on a skewer, is better cut into 1¼-inch to 1½-inch cubes.

The marinades in this section can be used for meat, chicken, or fish that has been cut up for skewers or left in large pieces to grill. I have indicated with each recipe the foods for which the marinade is best, but you can try the marinade with other foods. Food that is marinating should be covered and refrigerated. Be sure to toss the ingredients in their marinade from time to time.

VEGETABLES FOR SKEWERS

Sweet red, green, and yellow peppers, marinated
Small to medium-sized zucchinis and yellow summer squash,
    in ¼-inch slices, marinated
Medium to large mushroom caps, marinated
Large cherry tomatoes *or* small plum tomatoes, halved crosswise
Tiny white onions, parboiled and peeled
Tiny boiling potatoes, steamed or boiled but firm
Spanish, Vidalia, and red onions, layers separated and
    cut into wedges
Artichoke hearts, frozen and thawed or marinated
Large pitted black olives

FISH AND VEGETABLE KEBABS

6 servings

Here's a simple, low-fat dish for barbecue enthusiasts.

Preparation tips: Note that the fish should marinate for several hours. Grill the kebabs only until the fish is done. The vegetables should end up hot but crunchy. For an alternative marinade, see Jeff's Fabulous Fish Marinade on page 199.

MARINADE
½ cup dry white wine
3 tablespoons reduced-sodium soy sauce
1 tablespoon oil
2 teaspoons minced gingerroot
1 teaspoon minced garlic (1 large clove)

KEBABS
1 pound swordfish *or* other firm-fleshed fish, cut into 1-inch cubes
1 medium onion, peeled, quartered lengthwise, layers separated
1 sweet green pepper, cut into 1½-inch pieces
1 sweet red pepper, cut into 1½-inch pieces
1 medium zucchini, sliced ¼ inch thick

1. In a medium-sized bowl, combine the marinade ingredients. Add the fish, tossing it in the marinade to coat it well, cover the bowl, and refrigerate the fish for 2 hours or longer.
2. About 30 minutes before serving, start the charcoal. Remove the fish from the marinade, reserving the marinade, and string the fish and vegetables on 6 long skewers. When the coals are glowing, put the kebabs on the grill, and cook the kebabs, turning them several times and basting them with the reserved marinade, for 10 to 15 minutes or until the fish is opaque.

TAMARI-ORANGE MARINADE

(For Chicken and Pork)   *about 1⅛ cups*

My good friend Jo-Ann Friedman, who strives constantly for nutritional improvements without sacrificing flavor, offered this simple marinade that works well for cubes or larger pieces of poultry or meat.

    ½ cup orange juice
    ¼ cup tamari *or* reduced-sodium soy sauce
    ¼ cup sherry *or* rice wine
    1 large clove garlic, peeled and finely minced
    2 teaspoons grated gingerroot
    1 tablespoon honey
    1 tablespoon sesame oil

Combine the ingredients in a medium-sized bowl. Add chicken or pork, tossing to coat the meat well. Cover the meat, and refrigerate it. Marinate the meat for at least 30 minutes.

INDIAN YOGURT MARINADE

(For Chicken)   *about 1½ cups*

Of half a dozen marinades I tested at one time, tasters of all ages voted this one the best. I've had it for so long, I can no longer recall where it came from.

Preparation tip: Garam masala (Hindustani for "mixed spice") can be purchased where Indian ingredients are sold, or you can prepare some yourself (see pages 247 and 546).

    1 cup plain nonfat or low-fat yogurt
    ¼ cup finely minced onion
    2 tablespoons oil (preferably canola)
    2 tablespoons fresh lime juice
    1 teaspoon salt (optional)
    2 teaspoons minced garlic (2 large cloves)
    1 teaspoon garam masala
    ½ teaspoon grated gingerroot

Combine the ingredients in a medium-sized bowl. Add cubed chicken or chicken cut into serving pieces, tossing it to coat it well. Cover the chicken, and refrigerate it. Marinate the chicken overnight.

HOISIN MARINADE

(For Lamb, Beef, and Chicken)   *about 1 cup*

This "hot" marinade is wonderful—perfect with lamb.

Preparation tips: You can minimize the hotness by reducing the amount of red pepper flakes. Any leftover marinated meat can be used to make a delicious stir-fry. Hoisin sauce can be purchased where ingredients for Chinese cooking are sold.

  6 tablespoons reduced-sodium soy sauce
  ¼ cup hoisin sauce *or* sweet bean paste
  ¼ cup rice wine *or* dry sherry
  2 tablespoons sugar
  2 tablespoons minced garlic (6 large cloves)
  2 teaspoons crushed dried red chilies *or* red
      pepper flakes
  1 tablespoon vegetable oil (preferably canola *or*
      olive)

Combine the ingredients in a medium-sized bowl. Add meat or chicken, tossing it to coat it well. Cover the bowl, and refrigerate it. Marinate the ingredients overnight.

HOT PEPPER MARINADE

(For Fish, Shellfish, and Chicken)   *about 1½ cups*

Here's another winner that can be used to "cook" scallops without heat (as in ceviche) or to prepare them for grilling.

  ¾ cup fresh lemon juice
  ¾ cup finely minced onion
  2 tablespoons minced, seeded jalapeños *or* chilies
  1 tablespoon minced cilantro
1½ teaspoons salt (optional)
  2 teaspoons minced garlic (2 large cloves)
Freshly ground black pepper to taste

Combine the ingredients in a medium-sized bowl. Add the food to be marinated, tossing the food to coat it well. Cover the bowl, and put it in the refrigerator. Marinate the ingredients overnight.

CURRY MARINADE

(For Beef and Lamb)   *about 1 cup*

This is my oldest marinade. I used it the first time I prepared shish kebab—in 1964. I have since given the recipe to many friends who love to barbecue.

½ cup dry red wine (e.g., Burgundy *or* claret)
2 tablespoons vegetable oil (preferably canola *or* olive)
2 tablespoons reduced-sodium soy sauce
2 tablespoons ketchup *or* tomato sauce
2 teaspoons minced garlic (2 large cloves)
2 teaspoons grated or minced gingerroot *or* 2 tablespoons chopped candied ginger
1½ teaspoons curry powder (mild and/or hot)
½ teaspoon freshly ground black pepper

Combine the ingredients in a medium-sized bowl. Add meat, tossing it to coat it well. Cover the meat, and refrigerate it. Marinate the meat for 12 to 36 hours.

VINAIGRETTE MARINADE

(For Vegetables)   *about ⅜ cup*

Vegetables like mushrooms, sweet peppers, and zucchinis grill better and taste better if they are first coated with a marinade (really a salad dressing) for 1 hour or longer.

¼ cup white-wine vinegar
2 tablespoons olive oil
1 teaspoon Dijon-style mustard
1 teaspoon minced garlic (1 large clove)
¼ teaspoon salt (optional)
Freshly ground black pepper to taste

Combine the ingredients in a large bowl. Add the vegetables, tossing them to coat them well. Cover the vegetables, and refrigerate them. Marinate the vegetables for 1 hour or longer.

JEFF'S FABULOUS FISH MARINADE   *about 1 cup*

My brother Jeffrey M. Brody is one of those enviable cooks who looks through the cupboard and refrigerator, and manages to throw a wonderful meal together without ever consulting a recipe. And, of course, he *never* measures anything. So getting a recipe out of him involves standing over his shoulder and recording what he does. Here, then, is my approximation of the marinade he prepares for grilling fish steaks, small whole fish, and fish kebabs. Note that it contains no oil—and the oil is never missed. Jeff explains that the marinade precooks the fish so that the fish can be grilled on the rare side. The fish, grilled no more than 4 minutes a side for a ¾- to 1-inch-thick steak, is always moist and delicious.

Preparation tips: Do not substitute dark Worcestershire sauce for the white-wine version. If you do not have the latter, use only 1 teaspoon of the dark. After combining the ingredients, taste the marinade. If it seems too sour, add more honey.

¼ cup dry white wine
¼ cup dry sherry
¼ cup rice vinegar *or* white-wine vinegar
1 to 2 tablespoons white-wine Worcestershire
  sauce, to taste
1 tablespoon soy sauce (preferably
  reduced-sodium)
1 to 3 teaspoons grated gingerroot, to taste
1 tablespoon honey, or to taste
2 tablespoons minced fresh parsley
1 tablespoon snipped fresh dill *or* 1 teaspoon
  dried dillweed

Combine the ingredients in a glass or ceramic bowl or baking dish. Add the fish, coating it well. Cover the fish, and refrigerate it. Marinate the fish for 1 hour or longer, turning it occasionally.

Main-Dish Soups

I touted soup as a main course in *Jane Brody's Good Food Book* and noted that I never hesitated to serve such a meal to guests—accompanied, of course, by a substantial salad and hearty bread. The meal typically starts with lean hors d'oeuvres or an appetizer and ends with a fruit-based dessert. My guests contin-ue to be delighted by such fare, especially since they leave the table satisfied but not stuffed. For the cook, soups are ideal entrées because virtually everything can be prepared in advance and reheated at serving time. In fact, their flavor typically improves upon reheating.

When soup is served as a main course, the trick is to provide complete protein either by balancing two or more vegetable protein sources, like beans or peas and rice or pasta, or by adding small amounts of animal protein—meat, poultry, fish, milk, cheese, or egg white—to a soup that is rich in vegetable protein. Still a third approach is not to try to complete the protein in the soup itself, but to serve the protein complement on the side. Bread, for example, is the perfect foil for a soup based on high-protein dried beans and peas.

ASIAN LENTIL AND
BROWN RICE SOUP

6 to 8 servings

Rebecca Bogert of San Francisco submitted this excellent soup recipe, which gives an Oriental twist to a favorite old combination.

```
10  cups water
 2  cups (about 12 ounces) lentils
½  cup brown rice
 1  tablespoon vegetable oil
 3  to 4 large cloves garlic, peeled and minced
 2  tablespoons grated gingerroot
 1  cup chopped scallions (including the green tops)
 1  cup chopped celery
½  cup chopped sweet green pepper
½  cup chopped fresh parsley
¼  cup reduced-sodium soy sauce
 2  tablespoons rice vinegar *or* white-wine vinegar
½  teaspoon salt (optional)
```
Hot pepper oil *or* hot pepper sauce to taste

1. In a large saucepan, bring the water to a boil. Stir in the lentils and brown rice, and boil the ingredients over moderate heat for 30 minutes.
2. Meanwhile, in a large skillet, preferably one with a nonstick surface, heat the oil briefly, and add the garlic, gingerroot, scallions, celery, green pepper, and parsley. Sauté the vegetables until they are softened.
3. When the lentils and rice are done, add the sautéed vegetables to the pan along with the soy sauce, vinegar, salt (if desired), and hot pepper oil or sauce. Mix the ingredients well.

LENTIL SOUP WITH COLLARDS   *4 to 6 servings*

I adapted this recipe for one of the most delicious and nourishing soups I've ever made from Marian Morash's *The Victory Garden Cookbook.* The small amount of meat complements the protein in the lentils. The vegetables add many vitamins and minerals, especially vitamin A from the carrots and collards and calcium from the collards.

Preparation tips: You can substitute Swiss chard or fresh spinach for the collards (with considerable loss of calcium). Instead of the smoked pork, you can use ¼ pound of ham or a firm sausage like kielbasa. Or you can omit the meat entirely and use a vegetable broth and grated Parmesan for an all-vegetarian dish. To save time, you can prepare the celery, garlic, and collards while the lentils cook in step 1.

1½ cups beef broth
2½ to 3½ cups water, as needed
  1 cup lentils, picked over and rinsed
  1 cup diced carrots
  1 cup chopped onions, divided
  ½ cup finely diced smoked pork (cut away all
     visible fat)
  1 teaspoon butter *or* margarine
  ½ cup chopped celery
  2 cloves garlic, peeled and minced
  4 cups packed, coarsely chopped collard greens
Freshly ground black pepper to taste

1. In a large saucepan, bring the broth and 2½ cups of the water to a boil. Add the lentils, carrots, ½ cup of the onions, and the pork. Return the mixture to a boil, reduce the heat to low, cover the pan, and simmer the mixture for 30 minutes.
2. Meanwhile, melt the butter or margarine in a small skillet, add the remaining ½ cup of onions and the celery, and sauté the vegetables for 5 minutes or until they turn a light gold. Add the garlic, and sauté it, stirring it, 1 minute more. Set the vegetables aside.
3. After the lentils have simmered for 30 minutes, add the reserved sautéed vegetables and the collard greens. Cover the pan, and simmer the soup for about 20 minutes, checking the liquid and adding more water, if needed. Stir in the pepper, and serve the soup hot.

ILLIRIA BEAN SOUP

8 servings

On a trip to the Antarctic aboard the Greek ship *Illiria,* I had the unexpected pleasure of being able to adhere to my nutritional goals while eating truly delicious food. The chef, Stamatis Efstratiou, was not only kind enough to give me a galley tour, but also to share his recipes for some of my favorite dishes. All I changed in this recipe was the amount of olive oil, with which the Greeks are sometimes profligate.

Serving suggestion: Serve a hearty bread to balance the bean protein.

  1 pound small white beans, picked over, rinsed,
      soaked 10 hours or longer in water to cover by
      at least 4 inches, and drained
  6 cups chicken broth
  6 cups water
1½ cups chopped onion
2½ cups sliced or diced carrots
1½ cups sliced or diced celery
  1 14-ounce can tomatoes, drained, with their
      juice reserved, and chopped
Freshly ground black pepper to taste
  2 tablespoons olive oil
¾ teaspoon salt (optional)
¼ teaspoon hot pepper sauce, or to taste

1. Place the beans, broth, and water in a large saucepan. Bring the ingredients to a boil, and cook the beans for 40 minutes or until they are half done.
2. Add the onion, carrots, celery, tomatoes with their juice, and pepper to the beans, and boil the soup gently for 40 minutes or until the beans are soft.
3. Stir in the olive oil, and season the soup with the salt (if desired) and hot pepper sauce.

MORRISON'S MINESTRONE

6 servings

Jeanne Morrison, a registered nurse from Tucson, offered this great soup, which only the cook need know is healthful. Although minestrone is basically an Italian vegetable soup, the lean meat adds flavor, body, and nutrients but little fat.

1 tablespoon olive oil
1 large onion, peeled and chopped
1 hot chili *or* jalapeño, seeded and minced (optional)
2 large ribs celery, sliced
3 carrots, peeled, halved lengthwise, and sliced crosswise
1 28-ounce can tomatoes, drained, with their
   juice reserved, and chopped
1 19-ounce can cannellini beans (white kidney
   beans), drained and rinsed
6 cups beef broth
½ pound lean ground beef, browned and fat drained
1½ teaspoons marjoram
Freshly ground black pepper to taste
1 cup uncooked small soup pasta (e.g., tiny shells *or* orzo)
¼ cup chopped fresh parsley
1 tablespoon fresh lemon juice
Hot pepper sauce to taste
Grated Parmesan or Romano for garnish

1. In a large saucepan, heat the oil briefly, add the onion, hot chili or jalapeño, celery, and carrots, and sauté the vegetables until the onion softens.
2. Add the chopped tomatoes with their juice. Bring the ingredients to a boil, reduce the heat, and simmer the mixture for 10 minutes.
3. Add the beans, broth, beef, marjoram, and pepper. Bring the soup to a boil, and add the pasta. Cook the soup for 8 to 15 minutes or until the pasta is done. Remove the soup from the heat, and stir in the parsley, lemon juice, and hot pepper sauce. Serve the soup sprinkled with the grated cheese.

SOUTHWESTERN HARVEST SOUP   *6 servings*

Kimberlie Gillis of Seattle sent me one of her favorite hearty soup recipes, which could easily become one of yours. Complete protein is provided by the combination of beans and rice.

Preparation tips: The soup "sits" well, so this is one that you can easily make ahead. If you want a completely vegetarian dish, you can substitute vegetable broth for the chicken broth.

Serving suggestion: Possible garnishes include plain nonfat or low-fat yogurt, grated Monterey Jack or queso blanco, sliced scallions, or minced cilantro.

  1 cup dried black beans, picked over, rinsed,
     soaked 10 hours or longer in water to cover by
     at least 4 inches, and drained
  6 to 7 cups chicken broth, divided
  1 28-ounce can plum tomatoes, drained, with
     their juice reserved, and finely chopped
  2 tablespoons tomato paste
  2 cups finely chopped onion (2 large), divided
  1 whole jalapeño
  1 rib celery, finely diced
  1 carrot, peeled and finely diced
  2 medium cloves garlic, peeled and minced (1½
     teaspoons), divided
  1 bay leaf
  1 teaspoon cumin
  ¾ teaspoon oregano, crumbled
  ½ teaspoon coriander
  ½ teaspoon freshly ground black pepper, or to taste
Pinch ground cloves
  1 tablespoon olive oil *or* canola oil
  ¾ cup long-grained brown rice
  1 large *or* 2 small zucchinis, diced
  ½ large *or* 1 small sweet red pepper, cored,
     seeded, and diced
  1½ tablespoons chopped fresh basil *or* 1½
     teaspoons dried, crumbled basil
Salt to taste (optional)
Freshly ground black pepper to taste
  ¼ teaspoon red pepper flakes, or to taste (optional)

1. Place the beans in a large, heavy saucepan. Add 5 cups of the broth, the tomatoes with their liquid, tomato paste, 1 cup of the onion, jalapeño, celery, carrot, 1 teaspoon of the garlic, bay leaf, cumin, oregano, coriander, the ½ teaspoon of black pepper, and cloves. Bring the ingredients to a boil, reduce the heat, cover the pan almost completely, and simmer the beans, stirring them occasionally, for 2 hours or until the beans are done.
2. Meanwhile, in a large, heavy skillet, preferably one with a nonstick surface, heat the oil briefly, add the rice with the remaining 1 cup of onion, the remaining ½ teaspoon garlic, zucchini, sweet red pepper, and basil (only if you are using dried basil), and sauté the ingredients for 5 to 7 minutes or until the onions are translucent.
3. To the cooked beans add the rice-vegetable mixture and 1 cup of broth. Bring the soup to a boil, reduce the heat to low, cover the pan, and simmer the soup for 25 to 30 minutes or until the rice is tender. Add more broth, if needed.
4. Stir in the basil (if you are using fresh basil), and season the soup with the salt (if desired), additional pepper, and red pepper flakes (if you wish). Simmer the soup 10 minutes longer. Remove the jalapeño and bay leaf from the soup before serving it.

MINESTRONE WITH PASTA VERDE   *8 or more servings*

Here's a hearty, colorful version of Italian minestrone with just a hint of pork for added flavor.

Preparation tip: Great Northern beans can be used in place of white kidney beans. Either way, be sure to soak them before you start the recipe.

2 large carrots, peeled and thinly sliced
2 stalks of celery, thinly sliced
1 large onion, peeled and chopped (1 cup)
2 large cloves garlic, peeled and minced
1 tablespoon butter *or* margarine *or* vegetable oil
1 pound white kidney beans, picked over, rinsed,
   soaked 10 hours or longer in water to cover by
   at least 4 inches, and drained
3 cups chicken broth (homemade or canned)
¼-pound piece Canadian bacon *or* ham *or* smoked pork
1 14- to 16-ounce can tomatoes, drained (reserve
   the juice) and chopped (about 1½ cups)
1 bay leaf
Freshly ground black pepper to taste
Water
⅛ teaspoon or more cayenne, to taste
½ teaspoon salt (optional)
1 cup spinach noodles or pasta, broken into
   1-inch pieces
½ cup grated Parmesan

1. In a stock pot or Dutch oven over low heat, cook the carrots, celery, onion, and garlic in the butter or margarine or vegetable oil, stirring the vegetables now and then, for about 10 minutes (do not let them burn).
2. Add the beans, broth, bacon or ham or pork, tomatoes with their juice, bay leaf, pepper, and enough water to cover the ingredients by 1 inch. Bring the soup to a boil, skim off any froth that forms, reduce the heat, partially cover the pot, and cook the soup for 1 hour 45 minutes or until the beans are tender. During the cooking process, periodically add more water to the soup to keep the solid ingredients covered by 1 inch of liquid.
3. Discard the bay leaf. Remove the bacon or ham or pork from the soup, trim off all the fat, dice the meat finely, and return it to the pot. Season the soup with the cayenne and salt (if desired). Add more water to the soup, if necessary (remember, some liquid will be absorbed by the pasta as it cooks).
4. Bring the soup to a boil, and stir in the noodles or pasta, cooking the soup for 10 minutes or until the noodles or pasta are just done.
5. Stir in the Parmesan, or sprinkle it on top of each serving.

CHICKPEA SOUP *ILLIRIA*

8 servings

This soup truly amazed me because I had not been able to eat chickpeas for years without acute gastrointestinal distress. I was determined to find out what Stamatis Efstratiou, chef aboard the ship *Illiria,* did to the chickpeas to "de-gas" them. Here in this recipe is what he told me.

Serving suggestion: Serve a hearty bread to balance the bean protein.

    1 pound dried chickpeas, picked over, rinsed, and
      soaked 10 hours or longer in water to cover by
      at least 4 inches
    2 tablespoons baking soda
Water
    6 cups broth
    2 cups water
    2 cups finely chopped carrots
 1½ cups finely chopped onions
   ¼ cup fresh lemon juice
   ½ teaspoon salt, or to taste (optional)
   ¼ teaspoon white pepper

1. Drain the chickpeas, and sprinkle them with the baking soda, tossing the chickpeas to coat them well. Put the chickpeas in a large saucepan. Let the chickpeas stand for 30 minutes.
2. Add enough water to cover the chickpeas, bring the water to a boil, and boil the chickpeas for 2 minutes. Drain and rinse the chickpeas with cold water. Add more cold water to the pan, and rub the chickpeas gently to remove their skins. Keep pouring off and adding new water until all the skins are gone. Drain the chickpeas.
3. Place the chickpeas in a large saucepan. Add the broth and the 2 cups of water, and bring the liquid to a boil. Reduce the heat, and boil the chickpeas gently for 50 minutes or until they are nearly soft.
4. Add the carrots, onions, lemon juice, salt (if desired), and pepper. Return the soup to the boil, reduce the heat, and simmer the soup 10 minutes longer or until the chickpeas and the vegetables are soft.

MUSSEL CHOWDER

6 to 8 servings

Clam chowder pales by comparison to this lovely soup, which I adapted from a recipe in *Gourmet* magazine. My tasters thoroughly enjoyed it, as did I. It would make an excellent luncheon main course.

Preparation tip: The chowder can be made ahead and reheated before serving since mussels do not get tough when cooked longer than necessary.

    5 pounds mussels, scrubbed and debearded
    1 cup plus additional water
    1 tablespoon olive oil
    4 slices Canadian bacon, finely diced
 1½ cups chopped onion
    1 bay leaf
    1 cup chopped sweet green pepper
    1 cup sliced celery
    1 pound boiling potatoes, peeled and cut into
      ½-inch cubes
    1 28-ounce can plum tomatoes, drained, with
      their juice reserved, and chopped
Salt to taste (optional)
Freshly ground black pepper to taste
Hot pepper sauce to taste (optional)

1. In a large covered kettle, steam the mussels in the 1 cup of water over moderately high heat for 5 to 7 minutes or until the shells open. Transfer the mussels with a slotted spoon to a bowl, discarding all unopened mussels and saving the cooking liquid. Remove the mussels from their shells, cutting off any remaining beards. Set the bowl aside.
2. Strain the mussel cooking liquid into a large measuring cup through a fine sieve lined with several layers of cheesecloth. Add water, if necessary, to make 4 cups. Set the cup aside.
3. Rinse and dry the kettle, and in it briefly heat the olive oil. Add the bacon, onion, and bay leaf, and sauté the ingredients until the onion is soft.
4. Add the green pepper and celery, and cook the mixture 2 minutes longer.
5. Add the potatoes, the tomatoes with their juice, the reserved mussel cooking liquid, the reserved mussels, salt (if desired), and pepper. Bring the soup to a boil, reduce the heat, cover the pot, and simmer the soup, stirring it occasionally, for 25 to 30 minutes or until the potatoes are tender. Discard the bay leaf, and season the soup with the hot pepper sauce.

NEW ENGLAND CLAM AND CORN CHOWDER

8 servings

A warming winter soup, especially lovely for a luncheon buffet.

Serving suggestion: Rather than oyster crackers, serve whole-grain rolls or a crunchy bread with this soup.

  1 tablespoon butter *or* margarine
½ cup finely chopped onion
½ cup finely chopped celery
½ cup finely minced Canadian bacon
2½ cups (approximately) clam juice (1 bottle plus
     the liquid from 3 cans of clams—see below)
  4 cups water
  6 cups (4 large) diced potatoes
  1 16-ounce can cream-style corn
  3 6½-ounce cans of clams, drained, with their
     juice reserved
  1 teaspoon thyme, crumbled
⅓ cup minced fresh parsley
Freshly ground pepper to taste
  1 cup skim, low-fat, or whole milk

1. In a large saucepan, melt the butter or margarine, add the onion, celery, and bacon, and sauté the ingredients until the vegetables soften.
2. Add the clam juice, water, and potatoes, and bring the mixture to a boil. Reduce the heat, and simmer the mixture for 10 minutes or until the potatoes are soft.
3. Add the corn, clams, thyme, parsley, and pepper, and simmer the soup for 15 minutes.
4. Stir in the milk, and heat the soup through, but *do not boil it.*

TURKEY-CABBAGE SOUP

8 servings

As a devotee of *Jane Brody's Good Food Book,* Christine Hoffman of Saginaw, Michigan, offered this low-calorie, easy-to-prepare, delicious soup.

Preparation tip: It takes just 15 minutes to get everything into the pot, and the leftovers can be frozen.

    1 pound ground turkey
    1 large onion, peeled and chopped (1 cup)
    1 46-ounce can tomato juice
1¼ pounds green cabbage, cored and chopped
    3 large carrots, peeled and chopped
    2 or 3 ribs celery, chopped
    1 bouillon cube or packet (optional)
Salt to taste (optional—omit if using the bouillon cube)
Freshly ground black pepper to taste
Water, if needed

1. In a large skillet, preferably one with a nonstick surface, brown the turkey with the onion, breaking up the meat into small bits. Drain off any fat, and transfer the mixture to a saucepan.
2. Add the tomato juice, cabbage, carrots, celery, bouillon cube or packet (if you are using one), salt (if desired), and pepper. Bring the soup to a boil, reduce the heat, cover the pan, and simmer the soup for 1½ hours. If the soup gets too thick, add a little water.

TURKEY SOUP

8 or more servings

I know what you're thinking: "Why is she trying to improve on the already perfect recipe—the one for Turkey Carcass Soup—in *Jane Brody's Good Food Book?*" Well, I thought you might like to try something different—with corn and pasta instead of barley or rice—and this recipe is both good to eat and easy to prepare.

Preparation tips: This is also delicious made with smoked turkey and bits of hot Italian sausage. You can use the Chicken Stock recipe on page 78 to prepare the broth.

   8 cups turkey broth (made from a turkey carcass)
   1 pint cherry tomatoes, halved lengthwise
   2 cups diced (½-inch cubes) *unpeeled* zucchini
   2 cups finely diced carrots
   2 cups finely diced celery
1½ cups finely chopped leeks (white part only)
  ½ cup finely chopped onion
   1 teaspoon minced garlic
  ½ cup orzo *or* other tiny pasta
   1 cup corn kernels
   3 cups cooked turkey meat, cut into ½-inch cubes
Freshly ground black pepper to taste
  ¼ cup chopped fresh parsley
  ½ cup grated Parmesan

1. In a large saucepan, bring the broth to a boil, add the tomatoes, zucchini, carrots, celery, leeks, onion, and garlic, and simmer the ingredients for 10 minutes.
2. Add the orzo or other pasta, and cook the mixture for 5 minutes.
3. Add the corn, turkey, and pepper, and cook the soup for 15 minutes. Stir in the parsley, and serve the soup with the Parmesan.

CHICKEN AND ROOT VEGETABLE SOUP

4 to 6 servings

This superb recipe is only slightly modified from one devised by Pierre Franey.

Preparation tip: The soup freezes well. If canned broth is used, no additional salt should be needed.

- 1 tablespoon butter *or* margarine
- 1 cup finely chopped onion (1 large)
- 1 pound skinless, boneless chicken breast, cut into ½-inch cubes
- 3 medium potatoes, peeled, cut into ¼-inch cubes, and placed in cold water
- 1 medium white turnip, peeled and cut into ¼-inch cubes
- ½ pound carrots, scraped and cut into ¼-inch cubes
- 1 parsnip (about ¼ pound), scraped and cut into ¼-inch cubes
- 1 large leek, washed and cut into fine dice (about 1½ cups)
- 5 cups chicken broth (preferably homemade)
- Salt to taste (optional—omit if using canned broth)
- Freshly ground black pepper to taste

1. In a heavy saucepan or Dutch oven, heat the butter or margarine, and add the onion. Cook the onion, stirring it, until it wilts.
2. Add the chicken, and stir it. Add the potatoes (drained), turnip, carrots, parsnip, and leek, and cook the mixture, stirring it, for about 2 minutes.
3. Add the broth, salt (if desired), and pepper, and bring the soup to a boil. Reduce the heat, partially cover the pot, and simmer the soup for 30 minutes.

BEEF, BARLEY, AND KALE SOUP

6 to 8 servings

An easy, hearty soup that needs only a salad and bread to make it a meal.

- 1 tablespoon vegetable oil
- ⅔ cup chopped onion
- 1 pound extra-lean boneless beef, cut into ½-inch cubes
- 6 cups beef broth
- 2 cups diced carrots
- ½ cup uncooked barley
- 1 teaspoon thyme

½ teaspoon salt, or to taste (optional)
½ pound mushrooms, sliced
1 10-ounce package frozen chopped kale *or*
1 pound fresh kale, steamed and chopped

1. In a large, heavy saucepan, heat the oil over medium heat. Add the onion and beef, and sauté the ingredients, turning them several times, until the meat is well browned.
2. Add the broth, carrots, barley, thyme, and salt (if desired). Bring the ingredients to a boil, reduce the heat, cover the pan, and simmer the soup for 1 hour or until the barley and meat are nearly tender.
3. Add the mushrooms and kale. Cover the pan, and cook the soup 5 to 10 minutes longer.

SPLIT PEA AND BARLEY SOUP

4 main-course or 6 first-course servings

I wish I knew from where this easy, delicious recipe came, but, alas, its provenance has been lost from my files.

1½ cups dried split peas
½ medium onion, peeled and chopped
1 large carrot, peeled and diced
1 rib celery, diced
1 large clove garlic, peeled and minced
7 cups chicken broth, divided
1 cup or more water (if needed)
½ cup uncooked barley
⅛ teaspoon salt-free herb seasoning
Freshly ground white pepper to taste

1. In a large, heavy saucepan, combine the split peas, onion, carrot, celery, garlic, and 6 cups of the broth, and bring the ingredients to a boil. Reduce the heat to low, and simmer the mixture in the *uncovered* pan for 1 hour, stirring it occasionally. If the liquid level gets too low, add some water to prevent scorching.
2. Meanwhile, in a small covered saucepan over low heat, cook the barley in the remaining 1 cup of broth and the 1 cup of water for 40 to 60 minutes or until the barley is tender.
3. When the vegetable mixture is done, purée it in batches in a blender or food processor. Return the purée to the saucepan, and stir in the barley, herb seasoning, and white pepper. Heat the soup over low heat, stirring it often, before serving it.

RUSSIAN BEEF BORSCHT

12 servings

Though hot borscht is typically a winter meal, I happened to test this on a chilly July night in Minnesota, where I expected few would even know what the soup was, let alone enjoy its unusual flavors. But to my delight, three generations of tasters raved about it, including a nine year old who said, "I don't like beets, but this is really delicious. Can I have more?"

Preparation tips: The flavor improves with reheating. This is a large recipe, but the leftovers can be frozen.

Serving suggestion: Offer plain yogurt as an optional topping (unless this is to be a kosher meal), and serve the soup with pumpernickel or rye bread or rolls.

      1 pound lean beef, cut into ½-inch cubes
      2 cans condensed beef broth plus enough water to make 12 cups
      1 6-ounce can tomato paste
      1 teaspoon salt
     ½ teaspoon white pepper (preferably freshly ground)
     ½ teaspoon freshly ground black pepper
      1 tablespoon vegetable oil
      1 tablespoon minced garlic (3 large cloves)
      2 large onions, peeled and sliced lengthwise (2 cups)
      4 cups coarsely shredded beets
      4 cups coarsely shredded cabbage
      2 cups coarsely shredded carrots
   1½ cups thinly sliced celery
     ¼ cup minced fresh parsley *or* 2 tablespoons dried parsley flakes
   1½ teaspoons dried dillweed
      1 teaspoon dill seed
      1 teaspoon celery seed
      2 bay leaves
   1½ teaspoons sugar
      2 to 4 tablespoons fresh lemon juice, to taste

1. In a heavy nonstick skillet, brown the beef quickly, and transfer it to a very large soup kettle.
2. Add the broth and water, tomato paste, salt, white pepper, and black pepper. Bring the ingredients to a boil, reduce the heat, cover the pot, and simmer the ingredients for 1½ hours or until the meat is tender.
3. Meanwhile, in the nonstick skillet, briefly heat the oil, add the garlic and onions, and sauté the vegetables for about 5 minutes.
4. When the meat is done, add the garlic and onions to the soup kettle along with the remaining ingredients. Bring the soup back to a boil, reduce the heat, and simmer the soup in the *uncovered* pot for 45 minutes or until the vegetables are tender. Discard the bay leaves before serving the borscht.

Pasta Main Dishes

Pasta has become increasingly popular both as everyday fare and as food fit for special occasions. And rightfully so. It is satisfying and nutritious and virtually fat-free—that is, until you add a sauce. As in *Jane Brody's Good Food Book,* my goal here has been to present attractive and delicious sauces that do not subvert pasta's nutritional advantages. Added fat and fatty ingredients like cheese and sausage have been held to a minimum, and vegetables have been used to maximum advantage. (See also the pasta salads included in the section "Main-Dish Salads," pages 249 to 271.)

In many recipes, the sauce can be prepared partly or completely in advance; in most cases, though, the pasta should not be cooked until just before serving time. However, I have been successful with the following advance-preparation trick: I cook the pasta *al dente* some hours ahead in lots of boiling water to which I add 1 tablespoon of olive oil. Then I drain and rinse the pasta under cold water and hold it at room temperature. Near serving time, I bring a large pot of water to a boil, dump in the cooked pasta, stirring the pasta long enough to heat it through, and then quickly drain it again. This trick is easiest to perform if you use a pasta pot, in which the pasta sits in a deep colander-type basket. Then you can dip the basket of pasta in the water to cook it or to heat it through, and you can lift it out without having to empty a large pot of boiling water filled with pasta.

The burgeoning popularity of pasta has prompted manufacturers—especially small, family-owned businesses—to produce an enormous variety that can help you set remarkable meals before your family and guests. There are now so many sizes, shapes, and flavors of pasta available that you could probably eat a different one every night and never repeat yourself for a year. I'm lucky enough to have one of the best family pasta businesses not 5 minutes from my home in Brooklyn, New York—Morisi's. And, lucky for you, Morisi's now has a mail-order as well as a retail and wholesale business (see page 11). However, varietal pastas are now available in many specialty-food stores around the country, and in each recipe you can substitute ordinary supermarket pasta, instead adding to the sauce or to the other ingredients in the dish a bit of the seasoning that is missing from the unflavored pasta.

SEAFOOD PASTA SUPREME

6 servings

All I can say is fabulous. My tasters asked for the recipe.

Preparation tip: I use lobster spacarelli, a comma-shaped pasta from Morisi's (see page 11). Other kinds of macaroni, like rotini or rotelle, will do, as long as they are not too dense.

Serving suggestion: For more Italian elegance, follow the pasta with the Arugula and Fennel Salad on page 344 and the Nectarine Granita on page 513.

PASTA
- 1 pound lobster spacarelli *or* plain macaroni (see "Preparation tip," above)
- Large pot boiling water
- 2 teaspoons salt (optional)
- 1 tablespoon oil

SAUCE
- 1 tablespoon olive oil
- ½ pound shrimp, shelled and deveined
- ½ pound sea scallops, sliced into ¼-inch rounds
- 1 tablespoon minced garlic (3 large cloves)
- ½ cup sliced scallions
- 2 cups peas, cooked if raw, thawed if frozen
- 2 cups fresh tomatoes, peeled (if desired) and cut into ½-inch dice
- ½ cup pasta cooking liquid
- 1 tablespoon minced fresh basil *or* 1 teaspoon dried basil
- ½ teaspoon oregano, crumbled
- Salt to taste (optional)
- Freshly ground black pepper to taste
- ¼ cup minced fresh parsley

Grated Parmesan or Romano for garnish (optional)

1. To make the pasta, place the pasta in the boiling water with the salt (if desired) and oil. Return the water quickly to a boil, and cook the pasta for 15 minutes or until it is *al dente.* Drain the pasta, and transfer it to a heated serving bowl or large platter.
2. While the pasta cooks, prepare the sauce. Heat the oil in a large skillet. Add the shrimp, and sauté them for 1 minute. Add the scallops, garlic, and scallions, and cook them for 2 minutes. Add the remaining ingredients *except* for the cheese, and heat the sauce, stirring it gently.
3. Pour the sauce over the pasta, toss the ingredients together, and serve the pasta immediately with the grated cheese (if desired).

SEAFOOD AND SPINACH NOODLES

4 main-course or 8 first-course servings

Here is a very easy dish that is a super main course for family or company or a first course at a dinner party. The recipe is adapted from one that won the *Woman's Day* Silver Spoon Award.

Preparation tips: Since the recipe calls for two canned ingredients (clams and artichokes) that usually contain a fair amount of salt, you'd be wise to refrain from adding salt until you taste the finished sauce. The sauce can be prepared while the noodles are cooking, or it can be prepared ahead and reheated at dinnertime.

NOODLES
- 12 ounces spinach noodles
- Large pot boiling water
- 2 teaspoons salt (optional)
- 1 tablespoon oil

SAUCE
- 1 tablespoon butter *or* margarine
- 2 tablespoons all-purpose flour
- 1/4 teaspoon or more grated lemon rind, to taste
- 1/8 teaspoon or more pepper (preferably white), to taste
- 1 10-ounce can baby clams, drained with 1/2 cup liquid reserved
- 1 cup skim or low-fat milk
- 1/3 cup dry white wine
- 1/2 pound cooked small shrimp
- 1 14-ounce can artichoke hearts (not marinated), drained and quartered

1. To make the noodles, place them in the boiling water with the salt (if desired) and oil. Return the water quickly to a boil, and cook the noodles, stirring them once or twice, for 8 minutes or until they are *al dente*. Drain the noodles, and transfer them to a heated serving bowl.
2. While the noodles cook, prepare the sauce. In a medium-sized saucepan, melt the butter or margarine, and whisk in the flour, lemon rind, and pepper until the ingredients form a smooth paste. Gradually whisk in the reserved clam liquid, milk, and wine, and cook the mixture, stirring it, over medium heat until it comes to a boil and starts to thicken.
3. Add the clams, shrimp, and artichoke hearts, and stir the sauce over low heat until it is heated through. Pour the sauce over the noodles, and serve the dish immediately.

LINGUINE WITH SHRIMP AND RED PEPPER SAUCE

4 servings

Lovely to look at and lovely to savor. Great for company. My personal evaluation was "Yummy!"

Preparation tips: Different pastas can be used, including plain spaghetti. The lemon linguine (see page 11) provides a subtle, tangy foil for the seafood sauce. The individual ingredients for this dish can be prepared ahead but should not be cooked until serving time, while the pasta boils.

Serving suggestion: Mango Surprise Sorbet on page 512 would make a nice palate cleanser.

PASTA
- 2 teaspoons salt (optional)
- 1 tablespoon oil
- Large pot boiling water
- 1 pound lemon linguine *or* comparable pasta

SAUCE
- 4 teaspoons olive oil
- 1 cup (1 large) chopped onion
- 2 cups (2 large) chopped sweet red pepper
- ½ cup chicken broth *or* fish broth
- 1 pound fresh shrimp, shelled, deveined, and cut into thirds
- 1 tablespoon butter *or* margarine
- ¼ cup chopped fresh parsley
- ⅛ teaspoon cayenne
- Salt to taste (optional)
- Freshly ground black pepper to taste

1. To make the pasta, add the salt (if desired) and oil to the boiling water. Add the linguine, return the water quickly to a boil, and cook the linguine for 12 minutes or until it is *al dente.* Drain the linguine, and transfer it to a heated serving bowl.
2. While the pasta cooks, prepare the sauce. In a large skillet, preferably one with a nonstick surface, heat the oil, add the onion and sweet pepper, and sauté them, stirring them often, over medium-low heat for 5 minutes or until the vegetables have softened. You may cover the pan for part of the time to facilitate the cooking.
3. Add the broth, and, when it is near boiling, add the shrimp. Cook the mixture for 1 minute or until the shrimp are just cooked through. *Do not overcook the shrimp.*
4. Remove the pan from the heat, and stir in the butter or margarine, parsley, cayenne, salt (if desired), and pepper, tossing the ingredients until they are well combined. Pour the sauce over the pasta, and serve the dish immediately.

LINGUINE WITH SQUID SAUCE

4 to 6 servings

I rarely fail when I start with a recipe of Pierre Franey's, and this one was no exception. My tasters called it wonderful.

Preparation tips: I served the sauce with lemon linguine, but other pasta flavors and shapes will also work as long as they do not compete with the seafood sauce. The sauce, incidentally, can be prepared completely in advance and reheated at serving time. Also, the hotness of the recipe can be adjusted by using more or less red pepper flakes.

SAUCE
- 2¼ pounds whole squid, cleaned, *or*
  1¾ pounds cleaned squid
- 1 tablespoon olive oil
- 1 tablespoon minced garlic (3 large cloves)
- 1 28-ounce can plum tomatoes, drained (reserve half the juice) and chopped
- ½ teaspoon oregano, crumbled
- ½ teaspoon rosemary, crumbled
- ¼ teaspoon red pepper flakes, or to taste
- Salt to taste (optional)
- Freshly ground black pepper to taste
- 1 tablespoon anise-flavored liqueur (e.g., **Pernod** *or* **Ricard**)

- ½ cup minced fresh parsley

PASTA
- 1 pound linguine
- Large pot boiling water
- 2 teaspoons salt (optional)
- 1 tablespoon oil

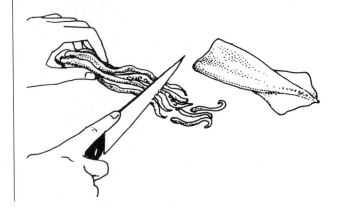

1. To make the sauce, cut the squid into bite-sized pieces by cutting the bodies crosswise into ½-inch rings and cutting the tentacles in halves or quarters. Set the squid aside.
2. Heat the oil in a large saucepan or Dutch oven, add the garlic, sautéing it briefly. Add the tomatoes and their reserved juice, oregano, rosemary, red pepper flakes, salt (if desired), and pepper. Bring the sauce to a boil.
3. Add the reserved squid, and simmer the sauce, stirring it often, for 40 minutes. Stir in the liqueur.
4. To make the pasta, about 15 minutes before the sauce is done, add the linguine to the boiling water with the salt (if desired) and oil. Return the water quickly to a boil, and cook the pasta for 12 minutes or until it is *al dente.* Drain the pasta, and transfer it to a heated serving bowl.
5. Add the sauce and the parsley to the pasta, and toss the ingredients to combine them well.

BASIL LINGUINE WITH CLAM SAUCE

4 to 6 servings

Of three wonderful pasta dishes I prepared one evening, this was my tasters' hands-down favorite. My recipe has been adapted from one devised by Carol DiGrappa of New York City.

Preparation tips: The clam sauce can be prepared completely in advance and reheated as the pasta cooks. Alternative pastas include plain or spinach linguine or almost any herb-flavored long pasta or macaroni (see page 11).

CLAMS
- 5 pounds cherrystone clams, scrubbed and soaked for several hours in cold salted water
- 1 tablespoon olive oil
- 2 cloves garlic, peeled and sliced
- ¼ cup water

SAUCE
- 1 tablespoon olive oil
- 3 large cloves garlic, peeled and minced
- 1½ cups chopped onion
- 1½ pounds fresh plum tomatoes, diced
- 15 (approximately) fresh basil leaves, minced
- 1½ teaspoons fennel seeds, crushed
- ½ teaspoon salt, or to taste (optional)

Freshly ground black pepper to taste

PASTA
- 1 pound basil linguine (see "Preparation tips," above)
- Large pot boiling water
- 2 teaspoons salt (optional)
- 1 tablespoon oil

1. To prepare the clams, thoroughly rinse the clams, and set them aside. In a pan or Dutch oven large enough to hold the clams, add the oil and garlic, and sauté the garlic briefly. Add the water and the reserved clams, cover the pot tightly, turn the heat up to high, and cook the clams for 3 to 5 minutes or until they open. Remove the clams to a bowl, strain their juice into the bowl, and set the bowl aside.
2. To prepare the sauce, heat the oil in a large skillet, preferably one with a nonstick surface, add the garlic and onion, and sauté the vegetables over medium heat until they are just softened. Add the tomatoes, basil, fennel seeds, salt (if desired), and pepper. Bring the sauce to a simmer, and cook it for 15 minutes.
3. Meanwhile, cook the pasta. Add the pasta to the boiling water along with the salt (if desired) and oil. Return the water quickly to a boil, and cook the pasta for 12 minutes or until it is *al dente.* Drain the pasta, and transfer it to a heated serving bowl.

4. While the pasta and sauce cook, shuck the clams over the bowl to catch the juice. Place the shucked clams on a cutting surface, discard the shells, and dice the meat. Add the clams along with 1 cup of the reserved clam juice to the tomato sauce, and cook the sauce 5 minutes longer. Serve the sauce over the linguine.

CAJUN LINGUINE WITH FISH SAUCE

4 to 6 servings

The mild fish sauce is a tasty complement to the spicy linguine. The colors—pale coral pasta, white fish, specks of green—make it lovely to look at, too.

Preparation tip: This is one dish you can prepare from leftover cooked fish. Or you can poach a pound of a firm-fleshed fish especially for the recipe (save 2 cups of the poaching liquid for the sauce). The sauce can be prepared while the pasta cooks.

Serving suggestion: For openers, try the Shrimp and Citrus Cocktail on page 67.

PASTA
- 1 pound Cajun linguine *or* similar spicy pasta (see page 11)
- Large pot boiling water
- 2 teaspoons salt (optional)
- 1 tablespoon oil

SAUCE
- 1 tablespoon olive oil
- 1 tablespoon minced garlic (3 large cloves)
- 2 tablespoons minced shallots *or* onion
- 1½ to 2 cups fish broth *or* fish poaching liquid
- ⅓ cup white wine
- 2 tablespoons fresh lemon juice
- ½ teaspoon thyme, crumbled
- ½ teaspoon hot paprika *or* sweet paprika, to taste
- ¼ teaspoon turmeric
- ½ teaspoon salt, or to taste (optional)
- Freshly ground black pepper to taste
- Cayenne to taste
- 3 cups cooked fish, cut into bite-sized pieces (e.g., tuna, swordfish, salmon, monkfish, *or* other firm-fleshed boneless fish)

- ½ cup chopped scallions
- ¼ cup minced fresh parsley

1. To make the pasta, place the linguine in the boiling water with the salt (if desired) and oil. Return the water quickly to a boil, and cook the linguine for 12 minutes or until it is *al dente.* Drain the pasta, and transfer it to a heated serving bowl.

2. While the pasta cooks, prepare the sauce. In a large skillet or saucepan, heat the oil briefly, add the garlic and shallots or onion, and sauté the vegetables for 1 minute. Add the broth or poaching liquid, wine, lemon juice, thyme, paprika, turmeric, salt (if desired), pepper, and cayenne. Heat the mixture until it comes to a boil. Add the fish, and cook the sauce for 1 minute to heat the fish through.

3. When the pasta is done, add the fish sauce, scallions, and parsley, tossing the ingredients to combine them well. Serve the linguine immediately.

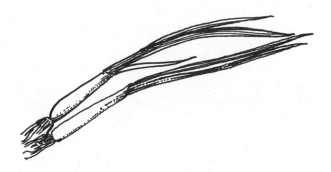

FUSILLI WITH HOT SAUSAGE

4 servings

Moderation in all things, including moderation—that's my culinary motto. Therefore, from time to time, I indulge in "no-no's" like sausage, especially when it is possible to cook out some of the fat before the meat is added to the recipe. Here is a simply prepared and simply delicious dish, derived from a *Gourmet* magazine recipe, made with corkscrew-shaped macaroni.

Serving suggestion: Tomatoes Stuffed with Eggplant on page 64 would make a lovely first course.

SAUCE

½ pound raw hot Italian sausage, casing discarded and meat crumbled
2 6½-ounce jars roasted red peppers, drained and patted dry
2 tablespoons tomato paste
1 tablespoon olive oil
1⅓ cups chopped onion
2 teaspoons minced garlic (2 large cloves)
2 cups corn kernels, raw or frozen
¼ teaspoon cayenne, or to taste
Salt to taste (optional)

½ cup thinly sliced scallions (including the green tops)

PASTA

1 pound fusilli *or* similar pasta
Large pot boiling water
2 teaspoons salt (optional)
1 tablespoon oil

1. To prepare the sauce, cook the sausage in a skillet, and drain it well, or place it on paper toweling, and cook it in a microwave. Put the sausage in a bowl, and set it aside.
2. In a food processor or food mill, purée the roasted peppers with the tomato paste. Put the mixture in a bowl, and set it aside.
3. Heat the olive oil in a large skillet, preferably one with a nonstick surface, add the onion and garlic, and sauté the vegetables over medium-low heat until they are softened. Stir in the reserved sausage, the reserved red-pepper purée, the corn, cayenne, and salt (if desired). Simmer the sauce, stirring it occasionally, for 10 minutes.
4. While the sauce is cooking, place the fusilli or other pasta in the boiling water with the salt (if desired) and oil. Return the water quickly to a boil, and cook the pasta for 10 minutes or until it is *al dente.* Drain the pasta, and transfer it to a heated serving bowl.
5. Add the sauce and the scallions to the pasta, and toss the ingredients to combine them well.

PASTA WITH BROCCOLI RABE

4 to 6 servings

This dish is easy to make, delicious, attractive, and good for you—a combination that's hard to beat. Broccoli rabe—or brocoletti di rape, as it is called in Italian—is a relative of broccoli, with slender, leafy stalks bearing clusters of tiny buds and with a slightly bitter flavor. It is rich in vitamin A, calcium, and fiber and, like other members of the cabbage family, contains natural cancer-fighting substances.

Preparation tip: You can use many kinds of pasta for this dish. My personal preference is oat-bran ricciolini or pepper-and-onion rotini from Morisi's (see page 11). Tomato linguine also makes a nice contrast with the green vegetable. If you use a long, thin pasta like spaghetti or linguine, break it into 4-inch lengths before cooking it.

PASTA
1 pound pasta (see "Preparation tip," above)
Large pot boiling water
2 teaspoons salt (optional)
1 tablespoon oil

SAUCE
1 teaspoon anchovy paste *or* 1 to 2 anchovy fillets, finely chopped
1 cup very hot water *or* chicken or vegetable broth *or* pasta cooking water
1½ tablespoons olive oil
1 tablespoon minced garlic
½ teaspoon red pepper flakes, or to taste
1½ to 2 pounds broccoli rabe, cut into 2-inch lengths, very thick stems discarded

Freshly grated Parmesan for garnish

1. To make the pasta, place the pasta in the boiling water with the salt (if desired) and oil. Return the water quickly to a boil, and cook the pasta for 10 to 15 minutes or until it is *al dente.* Drain the pasta, and transfer it to a heated serving platter.
2. While the pasta cooks, prepare the sauce. In a small bowl, stir the anchovy paste or chopped fillets into the hot water or broth. Set the bowl aside.
3. In a very large skillet or Dutch oven, preferably one with a nonstick surface, heat the olive oil, add the garlic and red pepper flakes, and sauté the ingredients for 30 seconds. Add the broccoli rabe and the reserved anchovy mixture. Toss the ingredients to combine them well, tightly cover the pan, and cook the sauce for 5 minutes, stirring it occasionally. Add the sauce to the pasta, toss the ingredients to combine them, and serve the dish with the Parmesan sprinkled on top.

STUFFED SHELLS WITH FENNEL SAUCE

4 to 6 main-course or
8 to 10 first-course servings

My tasters loved these stuffed shells, which could be served as an entrée or a first course. No one guessed that the stuffing contained tofu, which takes on a cheesy texture in this dish.

Preparation tips: The shells can be stuffed in advance and baked at the last minute, or they can be baked ahead of time and reheated (covered to prevent drying). The filling can also be used to stuff manicotti. Note that these heavier pastas take about 20 minutes to cook. To keep the shells from sticking together, after draining the cooked pasta, spread the shells out in a single layer on a greased cookie sheet.

Serving suggestion: A simple soup like Autumn Vegetable Soup on page 84 or Yellow Pepper Soup on page 86 is an ideal beginning.

PASTA
12 ounces large shells for stuffing
Large pot boiling water
 2 teaspoons salt (optional)
 1 tablespoon oil

FILLING
 1 tablespoon olive oil
 2 large cloves garlic, peeled and minced
12 ounces mushrooms, coarsely chopped
½ to 1 cup finely diced sweet red pepper
 1 teaspoon thyme
¼ teaspoon salt (optional)
⅛ to ¼ teaspoon freshly ground black pepper, to taste
 1 pound firm tofu (bean curd), drained and crumbled
 6 ounces shredded part-skim mozzarella (1½ cups)

SAUCE
 1 tablespoon olive oil
 1 cup thinly sliced scallions
 2 cups finely chopped fennel bulbs
½ teaspoon fennel seeds
¼ teaspoon freshly ground black pepper
⅛ teaspoon salt (optional)
 1 14- or 16-ounce can tomatoes, drained, with their juice reserved, and chopped
 1 tablespoon tomato paste

TO PREPARE THE PASTA

1. Place the shells in the boiling water with the salt (if desired) and oil. Return the water quickly to a boil, and cook the shells for 20 minutes or until the shells are *al dente.* Drain the shells, rinse them, and spread them out on a greased cookie sheet. Discard any broken shells, or use them for another purpose.

TO PREPARE THE FILLING

2. While the pasta cooks, in a large skillet or medium-sized saucepan, preferably one with a nonstick surface, heat the olive oil, add the garlic, and sauté the garlic briefly. Add the mushrooms, red pepper, thyme, salt (if desired), and ground pepper, and cook the mixture over high heat for 8 minutes or until the mushroom liquid evaporates. Transfer the mixture to a large bowl.

3. Add the tofu and cheese to the mushroom mixture, and toss the ingredients to combine them thoroughly. Using a small spoon or tiny spatula, press some of the filling into each of the intact cooked shells. Set the stuffed shells in a shallow baking dish that has been sprayed with vegetable oil.

4. Preheat the oven to 350° F.

TO PREPARE THE SAUCE

5. Heat the olive oil in a large skillet, preferably one with a nonstick surface, add the scallions, and sauté the scallions for 3 minutes. Add the fennel, fennel seeds, pepper, and salt (if desired), and cook the mixture, stirring it often, for another 3 minutes. Stir in the tomatoes with their juice and the tomato paste, and cook the sauce 5 minutes longer.

6. Pour the sauce over the stuffed shells, cover the shells with foil, sealing the edges, put the shells in the hot oven, and bake them for 15 minutes. Remove the foil, and continue baking the shells for another 5 to 10 minutes or until the dish is heated through.

Vegetarian Main Dishes

Meatless meals are no longer relegated to what some consider the fanatical fringe but today are enjoyed by all manner of folk, including those who still sit down to a 12-ounce steak from time to time. Vegetarian entrées are especially appreciated by luncheon guests and those who would rather not eat a "heavy" meal at night. In the dishes that follow, complete protein is derived by combining two or more complementary vegetable proteins or by the use of dairy products or eggs to complete the vegetable protein. Throughout, I was careful not to substitute one nutritional sin for another: in omitting meat, I did not go overboard with fat- and cholesterol-laden dairy products and eggs. In addition to these recipes, there are others in the sections on pasta, bean, and salad entrées that are or could readily be meatless main dishes.

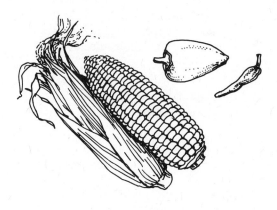

ZUCCHINI-CORN CASSEROLE

6 servings

A winning summer-vegetable recipe from Nikki and David Goldbeck's *American Wholefoods Cuisine.* This dish can be eaten lukewarm as well as straight from the oven, which makes it ideal for a buffet.

Preparation tips: While the zucchini drains, prepare the remaining ingredients. The entire casserole can be assembled in advance, to be baked at mealtime.

    3 cups (about 1 pound) sliced zucchini
    ¼ teaspoon salt
    1½ cups (12 ounces) low-fat cottage cheese
    ¾ cup dry bread crumbs (preferably whole-grain)
    ¼ cup wheat germ
    2 tablespoons minced fresh parsley
    1 tablespoon chopped fresh basil *or* ½ teaspoon
       dried basil
Kernels from 4 medium ears of corn (about 2 cups)
    3 medium tomatoes, sliced
    3 ounces cheese (e.g., Cheddar, Monterey Jack,
       muenster), cut into thin strips

1. Place the zucchini in a colander, and toss it with the salt. Set it aside to drain for at least 15 minutes. Then press the zucchini against the sides of the colander to extract more water, and pat the zucchini dry with paper towels. Set the zucchini aside.
2. Preheat the oven to 350° F.
3. In a medium-sized bowl, combine the cottage cheese, bread crumbs, wheat germ, parsley, and basil. Set the bowl aside.
4. Line the bottom of a greased 2-quart baking dish with the reserved zucchini. Using half the cottage-cheese mixture, spoon dollops on top of the zucchini, and press on the mixture with a fork or spatula to spread it around. Sprinkle the cottage-cheese layer with the corn, and distribute the remaining cottage-cheese mixture on top of the corn. Cover the casserole with the tomato slices, and arrange the cheese strips on top of the tomatoes.
5. Cover the casserole with foil, put it in the hot oven, and bake it for 15 minutes. Remove the foil, and bake the casserole for another 15 minutes. Remove the casserole from the oven, and let the casserole stand for about 10 minutes before serving it.

VEGETABLE-STUFFED PEPPERS

3 to 6 servings

This is a colorful main course that derives wholesome protein by combining beans with corn and cheese.

Preparation tip: The ingredients can be varied according to taste. For example, you could substitute green peas for all or half of the corn or replace the Cheddar with feta (which has been soaked in water for 10 minutes to reduce its salt content) and add cumin and ground coriander for a Middle Eastern flavor.

   6 medium-sized sweet green peppers
Large pot boiling water
   3 cups corn kernels (fresh, frozen, or canned)
1⅔ cups cooked pinto beans *or* small red beans
        (1 16-ounce can, drained)
  ¾ cup shredded sharp Cheddar (about 3 ounces)
   1 tablespoon oil
   1 small onion, peeled and minced
   1 large clove garlic, peeled and minced
  ¼ cup minced fresh parsley
  ⅛ teaspoon cayenne, or to taste
Freshly ground black pepper to taste
Water

1. Preheat the oven to 375° F.
2. Cut off the tops of the peppers, leaving a hole about 2 inches in diameter, and remove the seeds and inner ribs. Immerse the peppers in the boiling water, and cook them for 5 minutes. Remove the peppers carefully so as not to tear them, and place the peppers on paper towels, hole side down, to drain and cool.
3. In a medium-sized bowl, combine the corn, beans, cheese, oil, onion, garlic, parsley, cayenne, and black pepper. Divide the filling among the cooled peppers. Place the filled peppers in a baking dish cut side up, and pour a little water into the dish. Do not cover the dish.
4. Place the dish in the hot oven, and bake the peppers for about 20 minutes.

MEXICAN STUFFED PEPPERS

3 to 6 servings

This version of stuffed peppers, with green beans and nuts instead of dried beans, has a south-of-the-border flavor, especially if you add the cilantro and top the peppers with salsa (see page 539).

Preparation tips: Queso blaco is a part-skim Mexican white cheese available at most Hispanic markets. Mozzarella will work fine in its place. The peppers can be prepared for baking up to 1 day ahead but no longer. Chill the uncovered peppers until 1 hour before baking them.

Serving suggestion: Open with Herbed Quesadillas on page 66, and serve with "Refried" Beans on page 309.

    6 medium-large sweet green peppers
    2 teaspoons vegetable oil
   ⅔ cup finely chopped onion (1 medium)
    2 cups corn kernels, fresh or frozen and thawed
    1 cup diced cooked green beans, cut into ⅓-inch pieces
    2 medium tomatoes, seeded and chopped
   ⅓ cup chopped almonds
    1 tablespoon pumpkinseeds (optional)
   ¼ teaspoon salt, or to taste (optional)
   ¼ teaspoon marjoram, crumbled
   ¼ teaspoon thyme, crumbled
   ¼ teaspoon hot pepper sauce
Dash or more cayenne, to taste
    5 ounces grated queso blanco *or* part-skim mozzarella
    1 tablespoon minced cilantro (optional)

1. Preheat the oven to 350° F.
2. Cut off the tops of the peppers about ⅓ inch from the top, and scoop out the seeds and any large membranes. Stand the peppers on a steamer rack, cover them, and steam them above boiling water for 5 minutes. (If you wish, you can steam the tops and use them as decorative "hats" when you serve the dish.) Set the peppers aside to cool.
3. In a small skillet, heat the oil briefly, add the onion, and sauté the onion until it is golden brown. Transfer the onion to a large bowl, and combine the onion with the remaining ingredients. Check the seasonings, and divide the mixture among the peppers, stuffing the peppers to the top.
4. Stand the stuffed peppers in a baking dish (do not cover the dish), put the dish in the hot oven, and bake the peppers for 25 minutes.

STIR-FRIED TOFU AND "BABY TREE"   *4 servings*

When my children were babies, we told them broccoli was "baby tree," and it quickly became a lasting favorite. I've kept the name for this taste bud–stimulating stir-fry because it reminds me of dishes I've seen from time to time on Chinese menus.

Preparation tips: Be sure to prepare the sauce and have your ingredients cut up and ready to go before you start the stir-fry. If you are planning to serve rice, start cooking it about 10 minutes before you start cooking the stir-fry.

SAUCE

½ cup natural peanut butter
¾ cup hot water
¼ cup cider vinegar
 2 tablespoons reduced-sodium soy sauce
 2 tablespoons molasses
½ teaspoon crushed red pepper flakes, or to taste

STIR-FRY

 4 teaspoons canola oil, divided
 4 teaspoons finely minced garlic (4 large cloves), divided
 2 teaspoons finely minced gingerroot, divided
 1 pound firm tofu (bean curd), cut into small cubes
 2 large onions, peeled and thinly sliced (about 2 cups)
Freshly ground black pepper to taste
 1 bunch broccoli (1 to 1¼ pounds), cut into small flowerets, stems thinly sliced crosswise
 1 cup raw peanuts *or* dry-roasted peanuts, coarsely chopped
 2 tablespoons reduced-sodium soy sauce

¼ cup minced scallions

1. To make the sauce, in a small saucepan, whisk together the peanut butter and hot water. Add the remaining sauce ingredients, combining them thoroughly. Set the sauce aside.
2. To make the stir-fry, heat a wok or large skillet, preferably one with a nonstick surface, add 2 teaspoons of the oil, and a few seconds later add 2 teaspoons of the garlic and 1 teaspoon of the gingerroot. Stir-fry the ingredients for 30 seconds (do not let them burn). Add the tofu, and stir-fry it over high heat for 5 minutes.
3. Transfer the contents of the wok or skillet to the saucepan containing the peanut sauce. Mix the ingredients gently, and set the pan aside.
4. Wipe out the wok or skillet, and add the remaining 2 teaspoons of oil, the remaining 2 teaspoons of garlic, the remaining 1 teaspoon of gingerroot,

the onions, and black pepper. Stir-fry the ingredients over medium-high heat for 3 to 5 minutes or until they are soft.

5. Add the broccoli and chopped peanuts to the wok or skillet along with the soy sauce. Stir-fry the ingredients over medium-high heat for 5 minutes or until the broccoli is tender-crisp. Remove the pan from the heat.

6. Gently heat the saucepan with the tofu and peanut sauce, and pour it over the contents of the wok or skillet. Add the scallions, and toss the ingredients gently to combine them. Serve the stir-fry with cooked rice.

TOMATO-BROCCOLI QUICHE

8 servings

Despite the explosion of interest in quiche among health-food enthusiasts, it is a difficult dish to justify from a health perspective. Made in the traditional manner, it is very high in cholesterol and fat (from the eggs, cheese, cream, and crust), salt, and calories. Still, there are times when a quiche is the perfect dish to prepare and serve—perhaps for a brunch, luncheon, buffet, or picnic. With this in mind, I worked at "toning down" the negative aspects of quiches and boosting their nutritive value by using, for example, a whole-wheat crust with as little fat as possible, fewer egg yolks, milk instead of cream, relatively low-fat and low-salt cheese (such as Swiss), minimal salt, and lots of nutrient-rich vegetables. The results were more than acceptable, according to my recipe tasters.

Preparation tips: Note that the dough should stand for at least 1 hour before rolling. To save time and the need to refrigerate the prepared crust, when the dough is nearly ready to roll, prepare the filling ingredients through step 6.

Serving suggestion: Corn Soup with Pesto on page 106 would make an excellent first course.

CRUST
- ⅔ cup whole-wheat flour
- ⅔ cup all-purpose flour
- ¼ teaspoon salt (optional)
- 2 tablespoons cold butter *or* margarine, cut into small pieces
- 7 tablespoons (approximately) ice water

FILLING
- 1 tablespoon butter *or* margarine
- 3 tablespoons broth *or* water
- ½ cup chopped onion
- 4 cups chopped fresh broccoli
- 1 cup whole milk *or* ½ cup skim or low-fat milk and ½ cup evaporated skim milk
- 2 eggs
- 2 ounces Swiss cheese, shredded (½ cup)
- ½ teaspoon salt, or to taste (optional)
- ¼ teaspoon freshly ground black pepper
- ¼ teaspoon nutmeg (preferably freshly grated)
- 1 cup freshly grated Parmesan
- ½ cup dried bread crumbs (preferably whole-grain)
- 3 firm tomatoes, thinly sliced

TO PREPARE THE CRUST

1. Combine the whole-wheat flour and all-purpose flour with the salt (if desired) in a large bowl. Add the butter or margarine, coating each piece

with flour, and, with a pastry blender or your fingers, combine the ingredients until the mixture resembles small beads.

2. Using a fork to blend the ingredients, add the water 1 tablespoon at a time until the mixture forms a ball. Do not let the dough become sticky or wet. Knead the dough for 1 or 2 minutes, and form the dough into a smooth round ball. Sprinkle the dough lightly with flour, cover the dough with plastic wrap, and refrigerate the dough for 1 hour or longer or until it is firm.

3. Place the dough on a lightly floured board, knead the dough for a few seconds to form a fat rectangular pancake, and, if you are using an 11 × 8-inch quiche pan, roll the dough into a 15 × 12-inch rectangle (or, if you are using a round 10-inch round quiche pan, form the dough into a round pancake, and roll it into a 14-inch circle). Place the dough in the pan, and flute the edges. Cover the crust with plastic wrap, and refrigerate it until the filling is ready.

TO PREPARE THE FILLING

4. In a large skillet, heat the butter or margarine and broth or water, add the onion and broccoli, and cook the vegetables for 5 minutes or until they are just tender. Remove the skillet from the heat, and set it aside.

5. In a medium-sized bowl, beat the milk with the eggs, and stir in the Swiss cheese, salt (if desired), pepper, and nutmeg. Add the reserved broccoli mixture.

6. In a shallow bowl, mix the Parmesan and bread crumbs.

7. Preheat the oven to 375° F.

TO ASSEMBLE THE QUICHE

8. Remove the crust from the refrigerator. Sprinkle ⅓ of the Parmesan mixture on the bottom of the prepared crust. Dip the tomato slices into the remaining Parmesan mixture, and arrange ½ of the slices on the bottom of the crust. Pour the broccoli mixture over the tomatoes, and arrange the remaining tomatoes on top of the broccoli so that the slices overlap one another. Sprinkle any leftover Parmesan mixture on the top of the quiche.

9. Place the quiche in the hot oven, and bake it for 1 hour or until a knife that has been inserted into the center of the quiche comes out clean. Let the quiche stand for 20 minutes before serving it.

Bean Main Dishes

At long last, Americans seem to be finding their way back to the basics: those wholesome, versatile foods relied upon for millennia to sustain life. Beans are surely among the most prized, given their richness in protein and relatively low fat content. Their primary culinary drawback—how long it takes to cook them—turns out to be unfounded. Once started on the stove, they require little or no attention and really take no more time to prepare than roasting prime ribs or baking a ham. Their primary social drawback—the gaseous legacy they often leave—can also be overcome, I've discovered, by soaking them in lots of water for 10 or more hours and then cooking them thoroughly in fresh water. The short soak (boil for 2 minutes, let stand for 1 hour), I'm afraid, just does not clear away the indigestible carbohydrates that become gas in so many human digestive tracts. All this means is that you should start thinking about preparing bean dishes a day ahead. Now that's not so difficult, is it? For those willing to make the extra effort, then, here are some dishes that I and my tasters have really enjoyed and that I would not hesitate to serve to company.

BLACK BEAN BURRITOS

4 to 8 servings

I adapted a recipe from *Gourmet* magazine to prepare these scrumptious tortilla rolls topped by a simple and zippy tomato sauce. These are so substantial that I and my fellow diners found that a single burrito was sufficient for a main dish.

Preparation tips: I used beans cooked from scratch, but canned black beans will do as well. The burritos can be prepared in advance through step 4 and baked for 15 to 20 minutes before serving.

Serving suggestion: In keeping with a Mexican theme, try White Gazpacho on page 100 to start, and follow with the Orange-Jícama Salad on page 368.

SAUCE
- 1 14- or 16-ounce can whole tomatoes, drained
- ¼ cup minced onion
- 1 tablespoon minced jalapeños, fresh or canned, seeded

BURRITOS
- 8 10-inch flour tortillas
- 2 cups cooked and drained black beans
- ½ cup finely chopped red onion
- 1 cup (about 4 ounces) grated Monterey Jack, divided

- 1 avocado, diced, for garnish (optional)
- 2 to 4 tablespoons minced cilantro for garnish (optional)

1. Preheat the oven to 350° F.
2. To make the sauce, in a blender, purée the tomatoes with the onion and jalapeños. Set the sauce aside.
3. To make the burritos, in a heated skillet, soften a tortilla by heating it for about 10 seconds on each side. Spread ¼ cup of the beans across the middle of the tortilla. Top the beans with 1 tablespoon of the red onion and 1½ tablespoons of the cheese. Wrap the tortilla around the filling, and place the burrito seam side down in a greased baking pan. Repeat the procedure with the remaining tortillas, placing them side by side in the pan.
4. Spoon the reserved tomato sauce over the burritos, and sprinkle them with the remaining cheese.
5. Place the pan in the hot oven, and bake the burritos for 15 minutes or until the cheese has melted and the burritos are hot.
6. Serve the burritos topped with the diced avocado and a sprinkling of the cilantro, if desired.

BLACK-EYED PEAS AND BROWN RICE   *4 servings*

Medical Self-Care magazine offered this marvelous bean recipe in which the "hotness" of the beans is offset by the sweetness of caramelized onions. I added the brown rice to produce a dish with complete protein.

Serving suggestion: With the rice and a green salad such as the Orange-Jícama Salad on page 368, this dish becomes a full meal.

> 1 cup dried black-eyed peas, picked over, rinsed, soaked 10 hours or longer in water to cover by at least 4 inches, and drained
> 5 cups water, divided
> ¾ teaspoon salt, divided (optional)
> 1 cup basmati rice *or* long-grain brown rice
> 1½ tablespoons canola oil *or* olive oil
> 1½ cups finely chopped onions
> 2 large cloves garlic, peeled and minced
> 1 tablespoon grated or minced gingerroot
> 1 tablespoon diced green chili *or* jalapeño, fresh or canned, seeded
> 1 teaspoon molasses

1. In a medium-sized saucepan, cook the peas in 3 cups of the water for 40 minutes. Add ½ teaspoon of the salt (if desired), and cook the peas for another 20 minutes or until they are tender. Drain the peas, saving ¼ cup of the cooking liquid. Set the peas and the reserved cooking liquid aside.
2. After the peas have cooked for 40 minutes, in a medium-sized saucepan, combine the rice and the remaining 2 cups of water. Bring the rice to a boil, reduce the heat to low, cover the saucepan, and simmer the rice for 35 to 40 minutes. When the water is fully absorbed and the rice tender, turn off the heat, letting the pan sit, covered, on the stove.
3. In a large, heavy skillet, preferably one with a nonstick surface, heat the oil, add the onions, garlic, gingerroot, and chili or jalapeño, and sauté the vegetables over medium-high heat for 5 minutes.
4. Reduce the heat to medium-low, add the peas, the remaining ¼ teaspoon of salt (if desired), the molasses, and, if needed, the reserved pea cooking liquid. Cook the mixture, stirring it, for 20 minutes. Serve the peas with the cooked rice.

BLACK BEANS WITH TURKEY AND RICE

6 servings

An economical, filling, nutritious, and tasty dish to serve as a weekend lunch or on a buffet table.

Preparation tip: Note that the recipe calls for *cooked* black beans and *cooked* brown rice. See pages 7 and 238.

    1 tablespoon vegetable oil
    ½ pound ground turkey
    1 cup chopped onion (1 large)
    1 cup chopped sweet green pepper (2 small)
    2 cloves garlic, peeled and minced
    1 tablespoon fresh lemon juice
    1 tablespoon Dijon-style mustard
    1 teaspoon chili powder
    2 tablespoons soy sauce (preferably
       reduced-sodium)
    1 cup (8-ounce can) tomato sauce
    2 to 3 cups cooked black beans
    3 cups hot cooked brown rice

1. In a large skillet, preferably one with a nonstick surface, heat the oil over medium heat, add the turkey, and cook the turkey for about 5 minutes, breaking up the clumps of meat into small pieces.
2. Add the onion, green pepper, and garlic, and sauté the vegetables for 5 minutes or until they are softened.
3. In a small bowl, whisk together the lemon juice, mustard, chili powder, soy sauce, and tomato sauce, stirring the ingredients until they are smooth. Add this to the turkey mixture, combining the ingredients well.
4. Stir in the beans, and cook the mixture over medium-low heat for 20 minutes. Serve the black beans and turkey over the hot cooked rice.

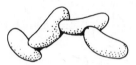

BLACK BEAN CHILI

This is one delicious souplike chili, derived from a recipe devised by Margaret Fox in *Bon Appétit* magazine, which in turn was inspired by a dish enjoyed at the restaurant Greens in San Francisco.

Preparation tips: If you prefer a thicker chili, use 5 to 6 cups of water, but be sure to check from time to time in case more water is needed to prevent the ingredients from sticking to the pot. Note the long, slow cooking time—3½ hours—to soften the beans. The chili can be prepared through step 4 up to 2 days ahead. Reheat the chili before continuing the recipe. Do not add more water until the mixture is hot and you can see if the liquid is needed.

Serving suggestions: Try the Corn Pone on page 439 or Tim's Corn Bread on page 440, and end with a fruit dessert like Minted Melons on page 522.

    2 tablespoons olive oil
 1½ cups chopped onion
    2 tablespoons chopped and seeded green chilies *or*
        jalapeños, divided
    2 teaspoons minced garlic (2 large cloves), divided
    2 teaspoons cumin
    1 teaspoon coriander
    1 teaspoon chili powder
  ½ teaspoon red pepper flakes
    7 cups water
    1 28-ounce can tomatoes, drained, with their
        juice reserved, and chopped
    1 pound dried black beans, picked over, rinsed,
        soaked 10 hours or longer in water to cover by
        at least 4 inches, and drained
  ¾ teaspoon salt, or to taste (optional)
    1 tablespoon tequila (optional)
    1 tablespoon red-wine vinegar
Plain nonfat or low-fat yogurt for garnish
Minced cilantro *or* fresh parsley for garnish

1. In a Dutch oven or large, heavy saucepan, heat the oil over medium-high heat, add the onion, 1½ tablespoons of the chilies or jalapeños, and 1½ teaspoons of the garlic, and sauté the ingredients for 1 minute.
2. Stir in the cumin, coriander, chili powder, and red pepper flakes, and sauté the ingredients for 30 seconds.
3. Stir in the water, tomatoes with their juice, and beans. Bring the mixture to a boil, reduce the heat, cover the pan, and simmer the beans, stirring them

occasionally, for 3½ hours or until the beans are very soft. Stir in the salt (if desired).

4. Purée *half* the bean mixture in a food processor or blender or food mill. Return the purée to the pot.

5. Stir in the remaining ½ tablespoon of the chilies or jalapeños and the remaining ½ teaspoon of the garlic. Simmer the mixture for 15 minutes.

6. Just before serving, stir in the tequila (if you are using it), and vinegar. Adjust the seasonings. Serve the chili with a bowl of yogurt and a dish of cilantro or parsley for diners to add to their own portions, if they wish.

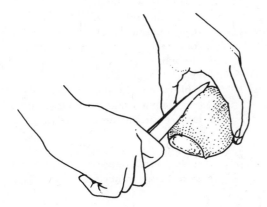

VEGETABLE CHILI PIE

6 servings

Here is a nice luncheon dish, a complete meal when accompanied by a salad.

Preparation tips: To maintain the vegetarian quality of this dish, use either water and a little salt or vegetable broth to make the chili. The chili filling can be prepared up to 3 days ahead—just be sure to cover and refrigerate it. Bring it to room temperature before completing the recipe. The dry and wet ingredients of the crust can also be prepared ahead and stored separately until baking time.

CHILI

- 2 cups coarsely chopped onion
- 4 teaspoons olive oil *or* canola oil
- 2 teaspoons minced garlic (2 large cloves)
- 2 tablespoons chili powder (you can use some "warm" or hot chili)
- 2 teaspoons cumin
- 1 teaspoon oregano, crumbled
- 1 teaspoon thyme, crumbled
- 1 teaspoon paprika
- ⅛ teaspoon cayenne, or to taste
- 4 cups chicken broth *or* vegetable broth *or* lightly salted water
- 1 bay leaf
- 2 cups water
- 2 cups lentils
- 1 14-ounce can plum tomatoes, drained, with their juice reserved, and coarsely chopped
- 1 jalapeño *or* green chili, seeded and minced
- 2 large sweet green peppers, cored, seeded, and coarsely chopped
- 3 ribs celery, coarsely chopped
- Salt to taste (optional)
- Freshly ground black pepper to taste

CRUST

- ¾ cup yellow corn meal (preferably stone-ground)
- ¾ cup all-purpose flour
- 2 teaspoons baking powder
- ¼ teaspoon baking soda
- ¾ teaspoon salt, or to taste (optional)
- 1 egg white
- 1 egg
- 6 tablespoons skim or low-fat milk
- ¼ cup plain nonfat or low-fat yogurt
- 1 tablespoon butter *or* margarine, melted
- 2 teaspoons honey
- 2 tablespoons chopped pimiento *or* 2 teaspoons minced jalapeño

TO PREPARE THE CHILI

1. In a large, heavy saucepan, sauté the onion in the oil over medium-low heat until the onion is softened. Add the garlic, chili powder, cumin, oregano, thyme, paprika, and cayenne, and cook the mixture, stirring it, for 3 minutes.

2. Stir in the broth or the water and salt, bay leaf, and the 2 cups of water, and bring the mixture to a boil. Add the lentils, partially cover the pan, and simmer the mixture, stirring it occasionally, for 40 minutes.

3. Add the tomatoes with their juice, jalapeño or chili, green peppers, celery, salt (if desired), and pepper, and simmer the chili in the *uncovered* pan for 15 to 20 minutes or until the chili is thickened. Discard the bay leaf, and transfer the chili to a 3-quart casserole.

4. Preheat the oven to 400° F.

TO PREPARE THE CRUST

5. In a large bowl, combine the corn meal, flour, baking powder, baking soda, and salt (if desired), stirring the ingredients to mix them well.

6. In a small bowl, lightly beat the egg white and whole egg, and add the milk, yogurt, butter or margarine, and honey. Stir the ingredients to combine them well. Stir in the pimiento or jalapeño.

7. Add the liquid mixture to the corn-meal mixture, and stir the batter until it is just combined.

TO ASSEMBLE THE PIE

8. Drop the batter by the tablespoonful onto the chili.

9. Place the casserole in the hot oven, and bake the pie for 30 minutes or until a tester inserted into the center of the corn bread comes out clean.

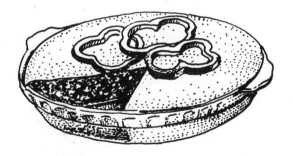

LENTILS OLÉ

This is one of the best-tasting lentil dishes I've ever prepared. I found it in the *Minnesota Heritage Cookbook,* produced in a state not noted for haute cuisine but one that harbors quite a number of wonderful cooks.

Preparation tip: Make enough of this dish to freeze some. It holds up well, and the flavor improves upon reheating.

Serving suggestions: These lentils go well with rice, plain pasta, or corn bread. Or serve them as a taco filling with chopped fresh vegetables (tomato, lettuce, cucumber, peppers, onion) and grated cheese for garnish or as the base for tostadas (prepared on softened corn tortillas) with toppings that might include shredded carrots and zucchini, chopped fresh spinach or lettuce, mashed avocado, plain yogurt, salsa, and sunflower seeds.

3 cups water
1 cup lentils
1 tablespoon olive oil
4 cloves garlic, peeled and minced
½ cup chopped scallions (including the green tops)
½ cup chopped sweet green pepper
½ teaspoon cumin seeds, crushed, *or* ⅜ teaspoon
    ground cumin
1 tablespoon chili powder (mild and/or hot)
1 8-ounce can tomato sauce
1 tablespoon red-wine vinegar
1 tablespoon molasses

1. In a large saucepan, bring the water and the lentils to a boil. Reduce the heat to medium-low, cover the pan, and simmer the lentils for 25 to 30 minutes or until the lentils are tender but not mushy. *Do not overcook the lentils.*
2. While the lentils cook, in a medium-sized skillet, preferably one with a nonstick surface, heat the oil, add the garlic, scallions, green pepper, cumin, and chili powder, and sauté the ingredients for 2 minutes or until the vegetables are tender-crisp.
3. Stir in the tomato sauce, vinegar, and molasses, and simmer the mixture for 1 minute.
4. When the lentils are cooked, add the vegetable mixture to the lentils, and heat the mixture through before serving it.

HERBED LENTIL CASSEROLE

4 servings

Helen Steinlein of Jackson Heights, New York, says she got this very easy, delicious, and nearly fat-free recipe from *The New American Diet,* an excellent cookbook developed at the Oregon Health Sciences University by Sonja L. Connor and Dr. William E. Connor. I added the sweet peppers for color and flavor, and made a few adjustments in the seasonings.

2⅔ cups water
 ¾ cup lentils
 ½ cup brown rice
 ⅔ cup chopped onion
 ½ sweet green pepper, cored, seeded, and
     finely diced
 ½ sweet red pepper, cored, seeded, and
     finely diced
1¼ cups white wine
  1 teaspoon minced garlic (1 large clove)
 ½ teaspoon basil
 ¼ to ½ teaspoon salt, to taste (optional)
 ¼ teaspoon oregano
 ¼ teaspoon thyme
Freshly ground black pepper to taste
  1 ounce grated Cheddar or reduced-fat
     cheese (optional)

1. Preheat the oven to 350° F.
2. In a 1½-quart *ungreased* casserole, combine all the ingredients *except* the cheese. Place the *uncovered* casserole in the hot oven, and bake it for 1½ to 2 hours. The casserole should be moist but not runny.
3. Sprinkle the grated cheese on top of the casserole (if desired), and bake the casserole 5 minutes longer.

LENTIL STEW MAGYAR

6 servings

This Hungarian-style stew has been updated to our modern fat-conscious tastes, with no loss in taste bud–stimulating flavor.

Serving suggestions: This dish goes best with egg noodles, but rice or mashed potatoes would also be a fine accompaniment. Try also the Red Cabbage Salad on page 354.

    1 tablespoon canola oil *or* olive oil
    2 cups coarsely chopped onion (2 large)
    1 pound mushrooms, quartered
    3 tablespoons sweet paprika
    1 tablespoon caraway seeds
  ¼ teaspoon cayenne, or to taste
    2 cups chicken broth
2½ cups water
1½ cups lentils
    1 sweet green pepper, cored, seeded, and
       coarsely chopped
    1 14-ounce can plum tomatoes, drained, with
       their juice reserved, and chopped
  ½ cup plain nonfat or low-fat yogurt
    1 tablespoon fresh lemon juice
Salt to taste (optional)
Freshly ground black pepper to taste

1. In a large skillet, preferably one with a nonstick surface, heat the oil briefly, add the onions, and sauté them until they are softened.
2. Add the mushrooms, and sauté them until their liquid evaporates.
3. Transfer the onion-mushroom mixture to a large saucepan, and add the paprika, caraway seeds, cayenne, broth, water, and lentils. Bring the mixture to a boil, reduce the heat, cover the pan, and simmer the mixture for 15 minutes.
4. Add the green pepper, and simmer the stew in the *uncovered* pan for 10 minutes or until the lentils are barely tender.
5. Add the tomatoes and their juice, and simmer the stew, uncovered, stirring it occasionally, 10 minutes longer.
6. Remove 1 cup of the lentil mixture, and purée it with the yogurt, lemon juice, salt (if desired), and pepper in a blender or food processor. Stir the purée back into the stew. Heat the stew through before serving it.

LENTIL AND POTATO STEW   *6 servings*

This is good-tasting and nutritious vegetarian dish from India.

Preparation tips: To reduce the risk of having the stew stick to the pan or scorch, the dish can be prepared ahead through step 3 and the cooking completed shortly before serving. Or it can be fully cooked in advance and reheated in the oven or microwave. You can prepare a reasonable garam masala by combining equal amounts of cardamom, cumin, cinnamon, and coriander, and smaller amounts of ground cloves and black pepper, or by using the recipe on page 546.

Serving suggestion: Serve the stew with Cucumber Raita (see page 363) or a mixed green salad and brown or white rice or with Indian Rice with Peas and Peppers on page 329.

 1 cup lentils
 4 cups water
 1 teaspoon salt (optional)
 1 bay leaf
 1 tablespoon butter *or* margarine
 1 tablespoon olive oil
 2 to 3 large potatoes, peeled and cut into ½-inch cubes
 1 teaspoon turmeric
¼ teaspoon cayenne, or to taste
Salt to taste (optional)
Freshly ground black pepper to taste
 2 large ripe tomatoes, peeled and chopped, *or* 2
  cups chopped canned tomatoes
 2 teaspoons garam masala (see "Preparation tips," above)
 1 teaspoon sugar *or* honey
Water, if necessary

1. In a medium-sized saucepan, combine the lentils, water, salt (if desired), and bay leaf. Bring the ingredients to a boil, reduce the heat to medium-low, and simmer the lentils for 30 minutes or until they are just soft. *Do not drain the lentils.* Discard the bay leaf, and set the lentils aside.
2. In a Dutch oven or large saucepan with a nonstick surface, heat the butter or margarine and oil briefly, and add the potatoes. Sprinkle them with the turmeric, cayenne, salt (if desired), and pepper. Cook the potatoes, tossing them, over medium heat for about 5 minutes.
3. Add the tomatoes, the reserved lentils and their cooking liquid, the garam masala, and the sugar or honey to the potatoes.
4. Cook the stew over medium-low heat for 10 to 15 minutes or until the potatoes are tender, stirring the mixture from time to time and adding water if the stew seems too dry.

BRETON BEANS

I cut the fat but otherwise did not monkey with Pierre Franey's wonderful bean recipe.

Preparation tips: Various beans would work here: navy, white kidney, or flageolets, among others. The exact cooking time is determined by the type of bean. (For example, if you use flageolets, they will probably require 1½ hours of cooking time.)

Serving suggestion: To use as a main course, serve the beans with mashed potatoes or brown rice to form a complete protein.

BEANS
- 1 pound dried white navy beans, picked over, rinsed, soaked 10 hours in water to cover by at least 4 inches, and drained
- 8 cups water
- Salt to taste (optional)
- Freshly ground black pepper to taste
- 1 carrot
- 1 onion, peeled and studded with 2 whole cloves
- 1 bay leaf
- 1 clove garlic, peeled
- 2 sprigs parsley

- ¼ cup chopped fresh parsley for garnish

TOMATO SAUCE
- 1 tablespoon butter *or* margarine *or* olive oil
- 1 cup finely chopped onion (1 large)
- 1 tablespoon minced garlic (3 large cloves)
- 2 cups crushed canned tomatoes
- 2 sprigs fresh thyme, chopped, *or* ½ teaspoon dried thyme
- Salt to taste (optional)
- Freshly ground black pepper to taste

1. To cook the beans, place the beans in a large saucepan, and add the water, salt (if desired), pepper, carrot, clove-studded onion, bay leaf, garlic, and parsley sprigs. Bring the mixture to a boil, reduce the heat, and simmer the beans for 1 hour or until they are tender but not mushy. *Do not overcook them.*
2. While the beans are cooking, prepare the sauce. Heat the butter or margarine or oil in a large skillet, add the onion and garlic, and sauté the vegetables until the onion is translucent. Add the tomatoes, thyme, salt (if desired), and pepper. Bring the sauce to a simmer, and cook it for 15 minutes.
3. When the beans are done, drain them, reserving 1 cup of the cooking liquid and discarding the carrot, onion, bay leaf, garlic, and parsley sprigs. Add the beans and the reserved cooking liquid to the tomato sauce. Adjust the seasonings. Bring the mixture to a boil, reduce the heat, and simmer the beans for 15 minutes. Serve the beans sprinkled with the chopped parsley.

Main-Dish Salads

Salads as entrées are becoming increasingly popular in our weight- and health-conscious society. And their welcome as the centerpiece of company meals is long overdue. In addition to being good for you, they are among the most attractive and convenient foods to serve to company. You needn't be an artist to turn a salad into a work of art—nature does it for you. And since salads can be made in advance, that means no last-minute cooking for the chef. Your guests will be grateful for being able to feast without stuffing themselves, and you will have more time to enjoy their company.

By adding one or more high-protein ingredients, you can turn a salad into a satisfying and nutritious main course. Most Americans are familiar with chef's salad, in which the protein usually comes from fatty meats and cheese. However, in most of the salad entrées offered here, the protein source is a low-fat food like turkey, chicken, shellfish, or beans. Since the dressings, too, are low in fat, you end up with a lot of nutrient-packed food in your stomach at a relatively low caloric and economic cost.

PEPPER 'N' ONION PASTA AND CHICKEN SALAD

6 to 8 servings

I made this salad to use up bits and pieces in the refrigerator, but the result was such a hit that I decided to record the recipe for posterity.

Preparation tips: I used pepper-and-onion ricciolini (see page 11), but any comparable pasta will do, especially if it has a distinctive vegetable or herb flavor. If desired, the chicken, before it is cooked, can be marinated in an extra half recipe of the dressing.

Serving suggestion: Open the meal with Cold Tomato Soup on page 107.

DRESSING
2 tablespoons balsamic vinegar
2 tablespoons red-wine vinegar
2 tablespoons olive oil
2 tablespoons white wine (optional)
½ cup plain nonfat or low-fat yogurt
2 teaspoons Dijon-style mustard
2 teaspoons minced garlic (2 large cloves)
1 teaspoon Worcestershire sauce
1 teaspoon sugar
Salt to taste (optional)
Freshly ground black pepper to taste

SALAD
1 pound pepper-and-onion ricciolini *or* comparable pasta
Large pot boiling water
1 teaspoon salt (optional)
1 tablespoon oil
1 pound boneless, skinless chicken breasts, grilled or broiled, then shredded or cut into ½-inch cubes
2 carrots, peeled and coarsely shredded
2 cups finely shredded red cabbage
½ pound green peas, cooked if fresh, thawed if frozen
1 cup diced red onion (1 large)
1 sweet green pepper, cored, seeded, and sliced into matchsticks 1½ inches long
¼ cup chopped fresh basil

1. In a small bowl, whisk together the dressing ingredients. Cover the bowl, and chill the dressing.
2. To make the pasta, place the pasta in the boiling water with the salt (if desired) and oil. Return the water quickly to a boil, and cook the pasta for 10 to 15 minutes or until it is *al dente.* Drain the pasta, rinse it, and transfer it to a large bowl. Add about ⅓ of the dressing, and toss the ingredients gently. Set the pasta aside to cool.
3. When the pasta has cooled, add the remaining salad ingredients *except* the basil. Chill the salad until 1 hour before serving.
4. Shortly before serving the salad, add the remaining dressing and the basil, and toss the salad gently to distribute the ingredients evenly.

MOROCCAN CHICKEN AND COUSCOUS SALAD

4 to 6 servings

This lovely salad, a relative of the hot dish on page 122, is based on a recipe offered by Elizabeth M. Casparian of Princeton, New Jersey, who says it's a hit on hot summer evenings, for lunches any time, and at party buffets.

Serving suggestion: Start with Cold White Bean Soup on page 109 and end with Oranges Casablanca on page 526.

 3 cups chicken broth
1½ cups couscous (whole-wheat, if available)
 1 tablespoon chopped fresh parsley
 ½ teaspoon thyme
 2 to 3 cups snow peas *or* sugar snaps *or* 1 cup
  frozen green peas
 4 to 5 scallions (including some green tops),
  thinly sliced
 ½ sweet green pepper, cored, seeded, and diced
1½ cups diced *cooked* chicken (see page 256,
  "Preparation tips")
 2 tablespoons raisins *or* currants
 2 tablespoons fresh lemon juice
 2 tablespoons olive oil
 1 teaspoon curry powder
Freshly ground black pepper to taste
Pinch red pepper flakes
 ¼ cup coarsely chopped nuts (e.g., pecans)

1. In a medium-sized saucepan, bring the broth to a boil, add the couscous, parsley, and thyme, and cook the mixture for 30 seconds. Remove the pan from the heat, cover it, and let the couscous stand for 5 minutes.
2. If the peas are fresh, steam them until they are tender-crisp (1 minute for snow peas, 2 minutes for sugar snaps). Place the peas (frozen ones need not be thawed or cooked) in a large bowl, and add the scallions, green pepper, chicken, and raisins or currants. Pour the hot couscous over the chicken mixture, and toss the ingredients to combine them well.
3. In a small bowl, combine the lemon juice, oil, curry powder, black pepper, and red pepper flakes. Pour this mixture over the couscous mixture, and chill the salad for 1 hour. Sprinkle the salad with the nuts before serving it.

INDIAN-STYLE CHICKEN AND RICE SALAD

4 to 6 servings

This delicious, attractive salad was inspired by a turkey-salad recipe devised by Richard Sax and Marie Simmons for *Bon Appétit* magazine. The dish is ideal for early summer, when succulent, nonstringy Mexican mangoes are available. It is low in salt and fat.

Preparation tips: A number of substitutions are possible: turkey breast instead of chicken, papaya (though not as sweet) in place of mango, regular brown rice (though not as aromatic) in place of basmati brown rice. If you use mango, be sure to choose one that is ripe but firm.

Serving suggestion: Start with Yogurt Soup on page 102 or Double-A Soup on page 113.

1 cup plain nonfat or low-fat yogurt
1 tablespoon minced jalapeños
1 teaspoon cumin
⅛ teaspoon cayenne
1 pound boneless, skinless chicken breasts
1 cup basmati brown rice
3 cups chicken broth *or* salted water
1 cup peeled and diced mango
¼ cup minced red onion
2 tablespoons chopped fresh parsley
2 tablespoons fresh lemon juice
1 tablespoon olive oil
¼ teaspoon salt (optional)
¼ teaspoon freshly ground black pepper

1. In a small bowl, combine the yogurt, jalapeños, cumin, and cayenne. Place the chicken breasts on a platter, and smear them on both sides with the yogurt mixture. Cover the chicken with plastic wrap, and refrigerate the breasts for at least 2 hours or up to 1 day.
2. In a medium-sized saucepan, cook the rice in the broth or water for 35 to 40 minutes or until the rice is tender. Drain the rice (do not cook it until all the liquid is absorbed, or the rice will be sticky), or you may use the method for Steamed Rice on page 5. Transfer the rice to a bowl, and let it cool.
3. While the rice cooks, broil or grill the reserved chicken breasts for about 4 minutes per side. When they are cool enough to handle, slice the breasts thinly on the diagonal, and set the chicken aside to cool.
4. Combine the cooled rice with the mango, onion, parsley, lemon juice, olive oil, salt (if desired), and pepper. Place the rice mixture in a shallow serving bowl, and top the rice with the sliced chicken.

CHICKEN AND GREEN BEAN SALAD   *4 servings*

This dish is great for a sit-down lunch or light supper, accompanied, perhaps, by a cold soup. I modified a recipe devised by Sheryl Julian of the *Boston Globe* and offered in *Walking Magazine.*

Preparation tip: If red-leaf lettuce or radicchio is unavailable, you can still prepare this salad—just make a reasonable substitution.

      4 boneless, skinless, well-trimmed chicken breast halves
      2 teaspoons olive oil
Salt to taste (optional)
Freshly ground black pepper to taste
   ¼ cup balsamic vinegar
      4 teaspoons olive oil
      2 teaspoons grainy mustard
      1 large clove garlic, peeled and minced
      1 shallot *or* 1 small white onion, peeled and finely minced
Freshly ground black pepper to taste
   12 red-leaf lettuce leaves
      8 to 12 radicchio leaves
      2 heads Belgian endive
      1 pound green beans, trimmed and steamed for 5 minutes
   ½ large sweet red pepper, slivered lengthwise

1. Rub the chicken on both sides with the 2 teaspoons olive oil, and sprinkle the breasts with the salt (if desired) and pepper. Place the chicken breasts on a broiler tray as close to the heating element as possible, and broil them for 4 to 5 minutes. Turn the breasts over, and broil them for another 4 minutes. Remove the chicken from the pan, and let the chicken cool.
2. While the chicken is cooking, prepare the dressing by combining the vinegar, the 4 teaspoons of oil, mustard, garlic, shallot or onion, and pepper in a small bowl. Set the dressing aside.
3. Cut the lettuce, radicchio, and endive into bite-sized pieces, and arrange them on 4 plates.
4. Slice each chicken breast half on the diagonal, keeping the shape of the breast, and place the slices on the lettuce beds. Divide the green beans and red pepper among the 4 plates, and pour ¼ of the reserved dressing over each salad.

CHICKEN SALAD WITH MANGO   *6 servings*

This grand salad idea from *Gourmet* magazine nobly withstood a reduction of fat in the dressing.

Preparation tip: The salad can be prepared 1 day ahead, but *do not* add the cashews or cilantro until serving time.

SALAD

1½ pounds boneless, skinless chicken breasts
Water to cover and ¾ teaspoon salt
  2 tablespoons fresh lemon juice
  2 medium-sized firm but ripe mangoes, peeled and cut into bite-sized pieces
  1 cup chopped celery
  4 scallions (including the green tops), minced

½ cup roasted unsalted cashews, coarsely chopped
  1 to 2 tablespoons minced cilantro (optional)

DRESSING

¼ cup plain nonfat or low-fat yogurt
1 tablespoon mayonnaise (*or* add another tablespoon yogurt)
1 teaspoon curry powder or more, to taste
¼ teaspoon cumin
Salt to taste (optional)
Freshly ground black pepper to taste

1. In a saucepan or deep skillet, bring the chicken breasts and salted water to a boil. Remove the pan from the heat, and let the chicken stand for 10 minutes. Remove the chicken from the pan, and cut the chicken into bite-sized pieces. Place the chicken in a large bowl.
2. Sprinkle the chicken with the lemon juice, and toss the ingredients. Add the mangoes, celery, and scallions, and toss the ingredients again.
3. In a small bowl, whisk together the dressing ingredients, add them to the chicken mixture, and toss the ingredients to combine them well.
4. Before serving the salad, toss it with the cashews and cilantro (if desired). Serve the salad chilled or at room temperature.

CHICKEN AND PEAR SALAD

4 servings

Did this go over big on a hot night in late summer! And to think it is almost fat-free.

    1 pound boneless, skinless chicken breasts
 1½ cups water
   ½ teaspoon salt
    1 tablespoon raspberry vinegar *or* rice vinegar *or*
      white-wine vinegar
    1 teaspoon tarragon, crumbled
   ¼ teaspoon freshly ground black pepper
   ⅓ cup rice vinegar *or* white-wine vinegar
 1½ teaspoons sugar
   ¼ teaspoon salt
    3 to 4 large Anjou pears
Lettuce for lining platter (preferably red-leaf)
    3 tablespoons chopped mint leaves

1. In a medium-sized saucepan or deep skillet, combine the chicken with the water, the ½ teaspoon of salt, 1 tablespoon of vinegar, tarragon, and pepper (the liquid should completely cover the chicken). Bring the chicken to a boil, remove the pan from the heat, cover the pan, and let the chicken stand for 10 minutes. Remove the chicken from the liquid, and let it cool. Then slice the chicken thinly on the diagonal. Set the chicken aside.
2. In a small jar or measuring cup, combine the ⅓ cup of vinegar, sugar, and the ¼ teaspoon of salt, mixing the ingredients to dissolve them. Set this dressing aside until serving time.
3. Just before serving, peel the pears, and, if you have a corer, core them. Then slice them thinly lengthwise, *or* slice them crosswise through the cores, if you have not already cored the pears. Arrange the pears and the reserved chicken on a lettuce-lined platter. Stir the reserved dressing, and drizzle it over the pears and chicken. Sprinkle the salad with the mint.

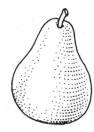

JO-ANN'S CHINESE CHICKEN SALAD   *4 servings*

My dear friend and founder of the Jane Brody Fan Club, Jo-Ann Friedman, devised this simple, delicious, and colorful salad, perfect for a luncheon or a supper or even a picnic on a hot summer day.

Preparation tips: Prepare the salad ingredients and the dressing ahead, but combine them just before serving the salad. If you are starting with raw chicken cutlets, place them in a medium-sized saucepan, and add 1½ cups of water, 1 tablespoon of vinegar, ½ teaspoon of salt, and ¼ teaspoon of hot red pepper flakes. Bring the ingredients to a boil, remove the pan from the heat, cover the pan, and let the chicken stand for 10 minutes. Remove the chicken from the liquid, and let the chicken cool.

SALAD
- 1 pound boneless, skinless chicken breasts, cooked (see "Preparation tips," above) and cut into strips about 1½ × ¼ inches
- ½ pound snow peas *or* sugar snaps, trimmed and steamed for 2 minutes
- ½ pound broccoli flowerets, steamed for 5 minutes
- 1 small zucchini, *unpeeled* and julienned
- ½ sweet red pepper, cored, seeded, and julienned
- ½ sweet yellow pepper *or* the rest of the red pepper, cored, seeded, and julienned
- 2 scallions, slivered lengthwise

- 2 teaspoons toasted sesame seeds

DRESSING
- ¼ cup rice vinegar
- 4 teaspoons Oriental sesame oil
- 1 tablespoon soy sauce (preferably reduced-sodium)
- 1 teaspoon grated gingerroot
- Several dashes cayenne to taste

1. In a serving bowl, combine the salad ingredients *except* the sesame seeds.
2. In a small bowl or jar, whisk together the dressing ingredients.
3. Just before serving, stir the dressing, and pour it over the salad. Sprinkle the sesame seeds on the salad, and toss the salad gently.

CHICKEN, SCALLOPS, AND ASPARAGUS SALAD
4 servings

This superb recipe is as good hot as it is cold. Either way, it's somewhat "hot," thanks to the jalapeños.

Preparation tip: Suitable substitutes for jalapeños include fresh serranos, hot cherry peppers, or hot Hungarian peppers.

Serving suggestions: If the dish is eaten hot, serve it with rice. As a cold salad, a crusty bread like Whole Wheat French Bread on page 406 is a suitable accompaniment.

¾ pound asparagus, tough ends trimmed
3 cloves garlic, peeled and minced
1 1½-inch piece gingerroot, grated
2 to 4 fresh jalapeños, seeded and minced
1 pound boneless, skinless chicken breasts, sliced
   diagonally into ½-inch pieces
Salt to taste (optional)
Freshly ground black pepper to taste
1 teaspoon butter *or* margarine
1 tablespoon peanut oil
½ pound bay scallops *or* sea scallops (if the
   scallops are large, cut into ¼-inch slices)
¼ cup dry white wine
¼ cup chicken broth
2 tablespoons minced fresh parsley
Greens for lining platter

1. Steam the asparagus for 1½ minutes, and refresh them under cold water. Cut the asparagus diagonally into ½-inch pieces. Set the asparagus aside.
2. In a small bowl, combine the garlic, gingerroot, and jalapeños. Set the bowl aside.
3. Pat the chicken pieces dry with paper towels, and season the chicken with the salt (if desired) and pepper. In a wok or large skillet, heat the butter or margarine and the oil, add the chicken, and sauté the chicken for 2 minutes or until the chicken is no longer pink. Stir in the reserved garlic mixture, the scallops, and the reserved asparagus, and sauté the ingredients, stirring them, for 1 minute.
4. Add the wine, broth, and parsley, and cook the ingredients over high heat, stirring them, for 1 minute.
5. Transfer the solids with a slotted spoon to a serving platter lined with the greens. Cook the liquid remaining in the pan 1 minute longer, and pour the liquid over the chicken mixture. Let the salad cool to room temperature before serving it.

TURKEY SALAD

4 to 6 servings

This colorful salad can be served on a plate or stuffed in a pita. The idea comes from Nancy Cooper, dietitian at the International Diabetes Center in Minneapolis, via *Diabetes Self-Management* magazine.

Serving suggestion: Either Potato-Broccoli Salad on page 377 or Basmati Rice Salad with Peas on page 380 would be a nice companion.

SALAD
- 1 tablespoon olive oil *or* canola oil
- 1 sweet red pepper, cored, seeded, and diced
- 1 cup sliced mushrooms
- 2 cups smoked turkey *or* plain cooked turkey, cut into ½-inch cubes
- 3 plum tomatoes, seeded and diced
- 1 medium cucumber, peeled and diced
- 1 bunch scallions, thinly sliced

DRESSING
- ¼ cup plain nonfat or low-fat yogurt
- ¼ cup buttermilk
- 1 tablespoon lemon juice
- 1 teaspoon Dijon-style mustard
- 1 large clove garlic, peeled and minced
- ¼ teaspoon salt (optional)
- Freshly ground black pepper to taste

1. To make the salad, in a skillet, heat the oil briefly, add the red pepper and mushrooms, and sauté them for a few minutes or until they are barely soft.
2. In a medium-sized bowl, combine the sautéed vegetables with the turkey, tomatoes, cucumber, and scallions.
3. To make the dressing, in a small bowl, combine the dressing ingredients.
4. Add the dressing to the turkey mixture, toss the ingredients gently, and chill the salad for about 1 hour before serving it.

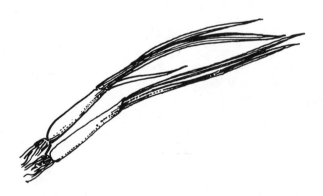

WALNUT SHELL AND TURKEY WALDORF SALAD

4 to 6 servings

When I told my guests what we were having for lunch, they appeared skeptical and hesitant. They were greatly relieved to see that they weren't going to have to crunch on real walnut shells but would be eating a delicate walnut-flavored pasta (see page 11).

Serving suggestion: A green salad like Minted Sugar Snap Salad on page 375 or Snow Pea Salad on page 374 would make a great addition.

DRESSING
- ⅓ cup plain nonfat or low-fat yogurt
- 3 tablespoons raspberry vinegar *or* cider vinegar
- 2 tablespoons light mayonnaise
- 1 to 2 tablespoons sherry
- 4 teaspoons honey
- ½ teaspoon curry powder
- ½ teaspoon salt (optional)

SALAD
- ½ pound walnut-flavored shell-shaped pasta *or* plain shell-shaped pasta
- Large pot boiling water
- 1 tablespoon vegetable oil
- 2 cups diced cooked turkey
- 1½ cups diced celery
- 2 large Red Delicious apples, unpeeled, cored, and diced
- 3 to 4 scallions, sliced, *or* ½ red onion, peeled and diced

- ½ to ⅔ cup chopped walnuts

1. To prepare the dressing, whisk together the dressing ingredients in a small bowl. Set the dressing aside.
2. To prepare the salad, place the pasta in the boiling water with the oil. Return the water quickly to a boil, and cook the pasta for 10 minutes or until it is *al dente.* Drain the pasta, and rinse it immediately under cold water until it is cool.
3. In a large bowl, combine the pasta with the remaining salad ingredients *except* the walnuts. Add the reserved dressing, and toss the salad gently. Chill the salad, but bring it almost to room temperature before serving it. Sprinkle the walnuts over the salad.

ROQUEFORT PASTA SALAD

6 to 8 servings

Roquefort-flavored pasta (see page 11 for the source) is a wonderful base for a pasta salad, which otherwise is hard to flavor without drowning it in dressing.

Preparation tips: This can be prepared without the "protein" ingredient (the beef, chicken, or beans) and used as a side-dish salad. Be sure to rinse the steamed vegetables under cold water immediately after cooking them.

DRESSING
- ⅔ cup plain nonfat or low-fat yogurt
- 2 tablespoons light mayonnaise
- 1 tablespoon balsamic vinegar
- 1 tablespoon cider vinegar
- 1½ teaspoons dillweed
- 1½ teaspoons sugar
- 1 teaspoon Dijon-style mustard
- ½ teaspoon minced garlic
- ½ teaspoon salt (optional)
- ¼ teaspoon Worcestershire sauce
- Freshly ground black pepper to taste

SALAD
- 1 pound Roquefort cavatelli
- Large pot boiling water
- 1 tablespoon oil
- 2 cups cooked lean beef, julienned, *or* cooked chicken, cubed, *or* cooked kidney beans or pink beans
- 3 cups broccoli flowerets and sliced stems, steamed for 5 minutes
- 4 medium carrots, peeled, sliced, and steamed for 10 minutes
- 4 radishes, thinly sliced
- 4 scallions (including some green tops), sliced

1. To prepare the dressing, in a small bowl, whisk together the dressing ingredients. Set the bowl aside.
2. To cook the pasta, place the pasta in the boiling water, and add the oil. Return the water quickly to a boil, and cook the pasta for 10 minutes or until it is *al dente.* Drain the pasta, and rinse it immediately under cold water until it is cool.
3. In a large bowl, combine the pasta with the meat or chicken or beans, the broccoli, carrots, radishes, and scallions. Chill the salad for at least 1 hour.
4. At serving time, remove the salad from the refrigerator, add the dressing to the salad, and toss the salad gently.

SEAFOOD TABBOULEH

6 servings

I know what you're thinking: What will she do next to tabbouleh? Well, folks, I didn't dream this one up. Joyce A. Nettleton, author of *Seafood and Health,* devised it to promote the consumption of health-promoting creatures from the sea. I substituted baby clams for sardines and quadrupled the parsley; the result was wonderful. It turns tabbouleh into a meal that needs only a green salad or cold soup to make it complete.

Preparation tips: Since the fish is salty, you probably won't need to add salt when you prepare the dish. The tabbouleh can be made a day ahead and kept chilled.

Serving suggestion: A cold make-ahead soup like the Cucumber-Walnut Soup on page 103 would make a nice opener.

  1 cup coarsely ground bulgur
  1 cup boiling water
  1 quart mussels, steamed in ½ cup white wine, *or*
      1 cup cooked shelled mussels
  1 6- to 7-ounce can shrimp, drained, *or* 1 cup
      chopped imitation crab ("sea legs")
  1 can baby clams, drained
 ¼ cup chopped fresh mint leaves *or* 2 tablespoons
      dried mint
  1 cup chopped fresh parsley
  1 bunch scallions (including the green tops),
      thinly sliced
  1 large clove garlic, peeled and minced
 ½ pint cherry tomatoes, halved
 ¼ cup fresh lemon juice *or* lime juice
Rind ½ lemon, finely chopped
  2 tablespoons olive oil
 ½ teaspoon freshly ground black pepper

1. Place the bulgur in a large bowl. Add the boiling water, and let the bulgur stand for 15 to 30 minutes or until the water is absorbed. Let the bulgur cool.
2. Add the remaining ingredients to the bulgur, tossing them to combine them thoroughly. Cover the tabbouleh, and refrigerate it for 1 hour or longer before serving it.

BASMATI RICE AND BEEF SALAD

6 servings

This salad can be adapted to taste and ingredient availability.

Preparation tips: Although I use the highly aromatic and nutritious basmati brown rice, available from health-food and specialty-food stores, you could make this salad with long-grain white rice (reduce cooking and steaming times by 5 minutes each) or regular long-grain brown rice. The "hotness" of the dish can be adjusted to taste by using more or less hot curry powder (or none at all). The salad can be served warm or at room temperature, although I have also enjoyed it straight from the frig. My husband, however, prefers it hot. If you share his preference, cook the rice for about 30 minutes before serving the dish. The beef and vegetables can be prepared in advance through step 4; complete the recipe when the rice is nearly ready.

Serving suggestion: Serve with Cucumber Raita on page 363 or Cucumber-Yogurt Salad on page 364.

> 5 quarts boiling water
> 1 tablespoon salt (optional)
> 2 cups basmati long-grain brown rice *or* an
>   alternative (see "Preparation tips," above)
> 1 pound lean boneless beefsteak, ½-inch thick,
>   well trimmed, and sliced into ¼-inch strips
> Salt to taste (optional)
> Freshly ground black pepper to taste
> 1½ tablespoons vegetable oil (preferably canola), divided
> 1 tablespoon cornstarch
> 1 teaspoon sugar
> 1½ cups water
> 3 tablespoons reduced-sodium soy sauce
> 4 teaspoons white-wine vinegar
> 1 pound carrots, scraped and thinly sliced on the diagonal
> 1½ cups chopped onion
> 1 tablespoon minced gingerroot
> 2 teaspoons minced garlic (2 large cloves)
> 1½ teaspoons hot curry powder
> 1½ to 2 cups frozen peas
> 1 bunch scallions (including the green tops), thinly sliced

1. In a large kettle, combine the 5 quarts of boiling water with the 1 table-spoon of salt (if you are using it) and the rice. Stir the ingredients, bring the water back to a boil, stir the ingredients again, and boil the rice for 15 minutes (10 minutes if you are using white rice). Drain the rice in a large strainer, rinse the rice, and drain it again. Bring about 2 inches of water to a boil in a large saucepan. Place the strainer of rice over the boiling water,

cover the rice with a dishtowel (be sure to fold the towel in so that it will not burn), and tightly cover the pan with a lid. Steam the rice for 20 minutes or until it is dry and fluffy. Transfer the rice to a large bowl.

2. While the rice cooks, sprinkle the beef with the salt (if desired) and pepper. Heat ½ tablespoon of the oil in a large nonstick skillet, and brown the beef quickly. Transfer the beef and any juices to a medium-sized bowl, and set the bowl aside.

3. Prepare the sauce in a small bowl by mixing the cornstarch with the sugar, the 1½ cups of water, soy sauce, vinegar, and any juices from the cooked beef. Stir the ingredients to combine them thoroughly. Set the sauce aside.

4. Heat the remaining 1 tablespoon oil in the skillet, add the carrots and onion, and cook the vegetables, tossing them often, until they are tender-crisp. Stir in the gingerroot, garlic, and curry powder, and stir-fry the ingredients for 30 seconds. Add the peas.

5. Stir the sauce mixture once again, and add it to the pan. Bring the mixture to a boil, and cook the ingredients, tossing them occasionally, over medium heat for 2 minutes or until the sauce is slightly thickened. Stir in the reserved beef.

6. Add the vegetable-and-beef mixture to the reserved rice. Add the scallions. Toss the mixture to combine the ingredients well, and serve the salad warm or at room temperature.

WILD RICE SALAD WITH CRABMEAT   *8 servings*

This lovely salad is based on a recipe devised by Joan M. King of Milwaukee. To create a more substantial main dish, I increased the amount of vegetables and (gasp!) crabmeat, but otherwise followed her low-fat suggestions.

Preparation tip: You can use fresh lump crabmeat (the best-tasting, but so expensive), frozen or canned crabmeat, or, for a slim budget or for large quantities, "sea legs" (imitation crabmeat).

Serving suggestions: The salad is most attractive served on a lettuce leaf and garnished with watercress and tomato slices. Let the diners add their own pepper, if desired. Try a cold soup like Sorrel (page 110), Cold Tomato (page 107), or Cucumber-Walnut (page 103) for openers.

DRESSING
- ⅓ cup minced onion
- 2 tablespoons white-wine vinegar
- 2 tablespoons olive oil
- ¾ teaspoon oregano, crumbled
- ½ teaspoon basil, crumbled
- ½ teaspoon sugar
- ¼ teaspoon salt (optional)
- 2 teaspoons snipped fresh chives *or* freeze-dried chives

SALAD
- 1 cup raw wild rice, cooked in broth, placed in a bowl, and cooled
- ⅔ cup thinly sliced carrot
- ⅔ cup finely diced sweet green *and/or* red pepper
- 1 cup diced *unpeeled* zucchini
- 12 ounces crabmeat

1. In a small bowl, whisk together the dressing ingredients.
2. Pour the dressing over the cooked rice, and toss the rice to coat it well with the dressing. Set the rice aside.
3. In a large bowl, combine the carrot, pepper, zucchini, and crabmeat. Fold in the reserved rice mixture, cover the bowl, and chill the salad for 1 to 12 hours.

MUSSEL AND POTATO SALAD

6 servings

All I and my tasters could say about this dish, devised by *Gourmet* magazine, was "Great!" Not only is the taste fabulous, but the salad is a glorious sight. My modification was a reduction in oil from ¾ cup to 3 tablespoons, which we all considered ample.

Serving suggestion: In keeping with a seafood theme, try Marinated Shrimp on page 69 or Marinated Scallops on page 70 for a first course.

DRESSING

- 4 tablespoons fresh lemon juice
- 2 teaspoons Dijon-style mustard
- Salt to taste (optional)
- Freshly ground black pepper to taste
- 3 tablespoons olive oil
- 1 tablespoon minced fresh basil leaves *or* 1 teaspoon dried basil
- ½ teaspoon tarragon, crumbled
- 3 tablespoons minced fresh parsley

SALAD

- 2 pounds boiling potatoes, peeled, quartered lengthwise, and cut crosswise into ¾-inch pieces
- 5 pounds mussels, scrubbed and debearded
- 1 cup water
- 1½ cups thinly sliced celery
- 1 cup cooked peas (1 pound unshelled) *or* frozen peas, thawed
- 2 cups (1 pint) cherry tomatoes, halved
- 6 tablespoons chopped scallion *greens,* divided
- 8 mussel shells

1. Prepare the dressing in a small bowl by whisking the lemon juice, mustard, salt (if desired), pepper, and oil together. Then whisk in the basil, tarragon, and parsley. Set the dressing aside.
2. To make the salad, steam the potatoes over boiling water in a covered pot for 8 to 10 minutes or until the potatoes are just tender, and transfer them to a large bowl. Toss the potatoes with ½ cup of the dressing, and set the potatoes aside to cool.
3. Rinse the mussels, put them in a large pot with the water, cover the pot, and steam the mussels over moderately high heat for 5 to 7 minutes or until the mussels open. Using a slotted spoon, transfer the opened mussels to a bowl. Discard any mussels that have not opened. Remove the mussels from their shells, saving 8 shells for garnishing the platter.
4. Add the mussels to the reserved potatoes along with the celery, peas, tomatoes, 4 tablespoons of the scallion greens, and the remaining dressing. Toss the ingredients well. Adjust the seasonings, adding more salt and pepper, if desired.
5. Serve the salad on a large platter, garnish the salad with the remaining 2 tablespoons of the scallion greens, and decorate it with the reserved mussel shells.

BLACK OLIVE PASTA AND
TUNA SALAD

6 servings

Black olive pasta (see page 11 for the source) has a distinctive flavor and color that gives this salad character. The salad is further enhanced by the grilled vegetables.

Preparation tips: You could substitute another olive-sized macaroni. The red peppers, zucchini, and red onion can be broiled or "grilled" on the stovetop in a nonstick pan as well as roasted on a grill.

Serving suggestion: An Italianate opener like Fennel Soup on page 86 would be lovely, plus Italian Pepper 'n' Cheese Bread on page 418.

SALAD
1 ounce dried porcini
Boiling water to cover
1 pound black olive cavatelli *or* other olive-sized pasta
Large pot boiling water
1 teaspoon salt
1 tablespoon oil
2 6- or 7-ounce cans water-packed chunk tuna, drained
2 roasted red peppers (see page 8), cored, skinned, seeded, and cut into ½-inch dice
Vegetable oil *or* olive-oil spray
½ pound zucchini, *unpeeled,* cut lengthwise into ½-inch slices
1 large red onion, peeled and sliced crosswise into ⅓-inch rounds

¼ cup minced Italian parsley
1½ cups small pitted black olives *or* medium-sized olives, halved

DRESSING
¼ cup soaking liquid from the mushrooms *or* chicken broth
2 tablespoons balsamic vinegar
2 tablespoons red-wine vinegar
2 tablespoons olive oil
2 teaspoons minced garlic (2 large cloves)
1 teaspoon white-wine Worcestershire sauce (do not substitute dark Worcestershire sauce)
½ teaspoon freshly ground black pepper
½ teaspoon sugar
¼ teaspoon salt (optional)
¼ teaspoon hot pepper sauce
6 tablespoons grated Parmesan

1. Place the mushrooms in a heat-proof bowl, and cover them with boiling water. Let the mushrooms stand for about 20 minutes to soften. Then drain them, *reserving the liquid,* and cut them into slivers.
2. Meanwhile, place the pasta in the boiling water with the salt and oil. Return the water quickly to a boil, and cook the cavatelli for 10 minutes or until it is *al dente.* To keep the pasta from breaking, avoid vigorous stirring, and do not overcook the pasta. Drain the pasta, rinse it under cold water, and transfer it to a large bowl, removing the badly broken pieces.
3. Break the tuna into bite-sized pieces, and add the tuna to the pasta along with the reserved mushrooms and the roasted peppers.

4. Brush with oil or spray the zucchini slices and red-onion rounds, and grill or broil them for a few minutes or until they are lightly golden and tender-crisp. When they are cool enough to handle, cut the vegetables into ½-inch dice, and add them to the pasta mixture.
5. In a medium-sized bowl, whisk together the dressing ingredients.
6. Before serving the salad, add the parsley, olives, and the dressing. Toss the salad gently.

HOT CHILI PASTA AND TUNA SALAD   *4 servings*

Spicy bumbola pasta (see page 11 for a source) gives this salad a terrific zing. Bumbola is a shell-like macaroni about 1½ inches long.

Preparation tip: If a spicy pasta is unavailable, add some red pepper flakes to the dressing.

DRESSING
- 2 tablespoons balsamic vinegar
- 2 tablespoons olive oil
- 1 large clove garlic, peeled and minced
- ¼ teaspoon dillweed *or* 1 teaspoon snipped fresh dill
- 2 tablespoons grated Parmesan *or* Romano

Salt to taste (optional)
Freshly ground black pepper to taste

SALAD
- ½ pound hot chili bumbola *or* other pasta, cooked *al dente,* drained, rinsed, and cooled
- 1 7-ounce can water-packed tuna, well drained
- ⅓ cup diced red onion
- 1 cup sliced steamed carrots
- 1 sweet red pepper, cored, seeded, and diced
- 1 cup cooked green peas
- ¼ cup diced celery
- ⅓ cup minced fresh parsley

Cherry tomatoes, halved, for garnish

1. In a small bowl, combine the dressing ingredients. Set the dressing aside.
2. Place the cooled pasta in a large bowl, and toss the pasta with the remaining salad ingredients *except* the cherry tomatoes. Add the dressing to the salad, and toss the ingredients again.
3. Serve the salad garnished with the tomato halves.

SIMPLE TUNA SALAD

2 to 3 servings

There is hardly anything easier or more nutritious than the mayo-free way Patricia Hogan of Westport, Connecticut, prepares tuna salad. Personally, since I've been eating tuna mixed with low-fat cottage cheese for years, I was pleased that someone else had discovered my secret. Try it as part of a luncheon buffet.

Serving suggestions: Serve this as you would any tuna salad: in a sandwich (pita bread works best), stuffed in a tomato, or as part of a salad plate. The Green Bean and Red Onion Salad on page 345 would be a good companion.

1   6½-ounce can water-packed tuna, drained
1   cup low-fat creamed cottage cheese
1   rib celery, finely chopped
1   or 2 scallions, chopped

Place the tuna in a medium-sized bowl, and flake it with a fork. Add the remaining ingredients to the tuna, and combine them well.

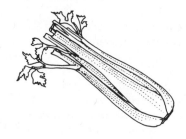

PASTA PRIMAVERA SALAD

8 servings

In this colorful salad, the cheese and yogurt in the dressing provide complementary protein for the pasta.

Preparation tips: As in all primaveras, you can substitute or add vegetables according to taste and availability. For the pasta, I used chive-flavored linguine (see page 11 for the source), but you can use any comparable pasta, such as lemon or spinach, or plain linguine. As with all pasta salads, it is best to add the dressing shortly before serving the dish.

Serving suggestion: An opener like the Cold Shrimp Soup on page 108 or the Cold White Bean Soup on page 109 would provide added protein.

DRESSING

1 cup coarsely grated Parmesan
½ cup plain nonfat or low-fat yogurt
2 tablespoons olive oil
2 tablespoons lemon juice
2 teaspoons minced garlic (2 large cloves)
1 teaspoon Dijon-style mustard
¼ to ½ teaspoon red pepper flakes, to taste
½ teaspoon oregano (optional—use if the pasta is not flavored)
½ teaspoon basil (optional—use if the pasta is not flavored)
Salt to taste (optional)
Freshly ground black pepper to taste
½ cup or more reserved pasta cooking liquid, as needed

SALAD

1 pound chive linguine, broken into 4-inch lengths
Large pot boiling water
1 teaspoon salt
1 tablespoon oil
½ pound snow peas *or* sugar snaps, trimmed and steamed for 2 minutes
1 bunch broccoli flowerets, steamed for 5 minutes
4 carrots, peeled, julienned, and steamed for 5 to 6 minutes
1 sweet red pepper, cored, seeded, and julienned
1 sweet yellow pepper, cored, seeded, and julienned
½ sweet green pepper, cored, seeded, and julienned
3 small zucchinis (about ¾ pound), *unpeeled,* julienned, and steamed for 1 minute
4 scallions, slivered lengthwise

Grated Parmesan (optional)

1. To make the dressing, in a small bowl, whisk together the dressing ingredients. Set the dressing aside.
2. To make the salad, place the pasta in the boiling water with the salt and oil. Return the water quickly to a boil, and cook the linguine for 10 minutes or until it is *al dente.* Drain the pasta, reserving about 1 cup of the cooking liquid. Rinse the pasta, and transfer it to a large bowl.
3. Add the remaining salad ingredients *except* the grated Parmesan to the linguine, tossing the ingredients gently to distribute them evenly. Cover the bowl, and chill the salad.
4. Add enough of the reserved pasta cooking liquid to the dressing to achieve a desirable consistency. Whisk the ingredients, and chill the dressing.
5. About 1 hour before serving, add the dressing to the salad, and toss the salad gently. If desired, serve the salad with the grated Parmesan.

TRICOLOR ROTINI AND BEAN SALAD   *6 servings*

This garlicky pasta salad has a fresh tomato sauce. The salad can be used as a main dish if you add the beans or as a vegetable side dish without beans.

TOMATO SAUCE
- 1 tablespoon olive oil
- 2 tablespoons minced garlic (6 large cloves), divided
- 12 ripe but firm plum tomatoes, peeled and diced

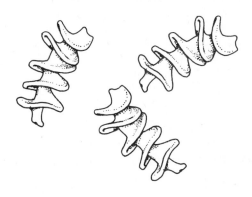

SALAD
- 1 pound tricolor rotini
- Large pot boiling water
- 1 teaspoon salt
- 2 tablespoons olive oil, divided
- 2 tablespoons minced garlic
- ½ pound fresh imported mushrooms *or* 1 ounce dried shiitake or porcini, soaked in warm water, drained, and slivered
- 1 ounce sun-dried tomatoes, slivered (optional; if they have not been packed in oil, steam them first)
- Freshly ground black pepper to taste
- 1 bunch arugula, tough stems removed and large leaves halved
- 2 cups cooked kidney beans *or* 1 19-ounce can kidney beans, drained and rinsed
- ¼ cup grated Romano
- ¼ cup pine nuts

1. To prepare the tomato sauce, in a medium-sized skillet, heat the oil for a few seconds, add the garlic, and sauté the garlic over low heat until it is lightly browned. Take care not to burn it. Stir in the tomatoes, and cook the sauce over moderately low heat for 15 minutes. Set the sauce aside.
2. While the sauce simmers, prepare the salad. Place the pasta in the boiling water with the salt and 1 tablespoon of the oil. Return the water quickly to a boil, and cook the pasta for 12 minutes or until it is *al dente.* Drain the pasta, and rinse it.
3. Meanwhile, heat the remaining 1 tablespoon of olive oil briefly in a very large skillet. Add the garlic, reduce the heat to low, and sauté the garlic, stirring it constantly, until it is lightly browned. Be careful not to burn it.
4. Add the mushrooms, sun-dried tomatoes, and pepper. Sauté the mixture briefly until the mushrooms (if they are fresh) wilt. Turn off the heat.
5. Add the drained pasta to the skillet along with the arugula, beans, and the reserved tomato sauce. Toss the ingredients to combine them well.
6. Add the Romano and pine nuts, and toss the salad again. Let the salad cool in the pan, transfer it to a large bowl, and then chill the salad until serving time.

CHICKPEA AND CHEESE SALAD   *6 servings*

Once the chickpeas are cooked, preparing this adaptable salad could hardly be simpler.

Preparation tips: Substitutions are possible for the cheese—for example, you could use 1 cup of slivered smoked turkey or ham. If the chickpeas are gently simmered and not vigorously stirred or overcooked, their skins will remain on. The chickpeas can be prepared 1 day in advance. Of course, you could also use 2 cups of canned chickpeas, well rinsed. The dressing can also be prepared ahead, but the basil should be added just before serving the salad.

Serving suggestion: Eggplant Spread on page 58 and pita bread or Sesame Biscuits on page 433 would go well with this dish.

SALAD
- ½ pound (1 cup) dried chickpeas, picked over, rinsed, and soaked 10 hours or longer in water to cover by at least 4 inches
- 8 cups water
- ½ teaspoon salt
- 2 ounces slivered tangy cheese (e.g., hot pepper cheese)
- 1 red onion, peeled and diced (about ¾ cup)
- 1 sweet green pepper, cored, seeded, and diced
- 1 large tomato, cored and diced

DRESSING
- ¼ cup minced fresh parsley
- ¼ cup shredded fresh basil leaves
- 3 tablespoons balsamic vinegar
- 2 tablespoons fresh lemon juice
- 1 tablespoon olive oil
- 1 teaspoon Dijon-style mustard
- 2 cloves garlic, peeled and minced
- ¼ teaspoon oregano, crumbled
- ¼ teaspoon tarragon, crumbled
- ¼ teaspoon salt, or to taste (optional)
- ¼ teaspoon freshly ground black pepper

1. To prepare the salad, drain the chickpeas, and place them in a large saucepan with the water. Bring the water to a boil, reduce the heat, cover the pan, and simmer the chickpeas *very gently* for about 1 hour or until they are nearly tender. Add the salt, and simmer the chickpeas 15 minutes longer or until the chickpeas are just done. Drain the chickpeas, and set them aside to cool.
2. In a large bowl, combine the cooled chickpeas with the remaining salad ingredients.
3. To prepare the dressing, in a small bowl, whisk together the dressing ingredients. (*Note:* if you prepare the dressing well in advance, shred and add the basil shortly before serving the salad.)
4. Add the dressing to the salad, and toss the salad gently. Chill the salad for at least 1 hour before serving it.

Pizzas

Too many pizza lovers feel guilty about indulging in this popular food. However, pizza need not be a high-fat, high-salt, high-calorie meal—if you prepare your own. The traditional ungarnished Italian-style pizza consisting of crust, tomato sauce, and melted cheese has in recent years undergone radical transformations that are decidedly American. There are now broccoli, spinach, bean, zucchini, onion, mushroom, eggplant, potato, shrimp, and tuna pizzas. In other words, almost anything but sweets will do as the topping for a pizza crust, if it can withstand baking at temperatures in excess of 400° F.

The crust, too, can be varied. Many potential pizza cooks are intimidated by the need to prepare a yeast dough, knead it, roll it, and fit it into the pan. For those of you willing to try it, I offer a few excellent crust recipes. I can tell you that making a pizza is similar to, but easier than, baking a yeast bread (only one rising is needed, and the dough can be prepared in advance and refrigerated or frozen), and the dough is much easier to roll than a pie crust because pizza dough is not crumbly. But you do have a choice: you can buy a prepared bread dough and roll it out to form a crust; you can use pitas of varying sizes as the pizzas' base, if the tops do not require long baking; you can use tortillas, a crumb crust, or a vegetable-based or grain-based crust. While to some pizza aficionados, a doughless pizza is not a "real pizza" but more like a deep-dish pie, I see no point in such culinary rigidity: if it is prepared and eaten like a pizza, why not call it a pizza?

PIZZA BIANCA
4 to 6 servings

Tomatoless pizza may seem inconceivable to some, but to me and my tasters it was a rare treat. This pizza is also gorgeous to look at. The prebaked crust is crispy, and the dish could easily be served at a party buffet. In keeping with the "white" theme, this one has a crust made from all-purpose flour.

Preparation tips: The crust recipe makes enough for 2 12-inch pizzas; you can freeze half the dough for future use. Note that the crust is partially baked before the topping is added. You can prepare the topping while the dough is standing (step 5) or baking (step 7) and be ready to add it as soon as the crust comes out of the oven.

CRUST

1 cup warm water (105° F to 115° F)
1 package (1 scant tablespoon) active dry yeast
Pinch sugar
3 cups (approximately) all-purpose flour
½ teaspoon salt (optional)
3 tablespoons olive oil

TOPPING

1 15-ounce container light or part-skim ricotta (2 cups)
1 cup shredded part-skim mozzarella (4 ounces)
½ cup grated Romano
1 tablespoon fresh lemon juice
½ teaspoon oregano, crumbled
½ teaspoon freshly ground black pepper
Several dashes cayenne, or to taste
¾ cup thinly sliced scallions (including the green tops)
1 sweet red pepper, cut lengthwise into strips ¼ inch wide

TO PREPARE THE CRUST

1. Place the water in a small bowl, and sprinkle the yeast and sugar into the bowl, stirring the ingredients to dissolve them. Let the mixture stand for 5 to 10 minutes or until it is bubbly.
2. In a large bowl, combine the flour and salt (if desired). Stir in the yeast mixture and the oil, adding more flour, if needed, to form a ball of dough. Turn the dough out onto a floured surface, and knead the dough for 5 minutes or until it is smooth and elastic.
3. Place the ball of dough in an oiled bowl, turning the dough to coat it with the oil. Cover the bowl, and let the dough rise in a warm, draft-free place for 45 minutes or until the dough has doubled in bulk.
4. Punch down the dough, and divide it in half, saving half for another use. Form the remaining dough into a ball or circle, and roll it out on a lightly floured surface into a 13-inch circle. Transfer the dough to a 12-inch pan, and form a thick rim by doubling the dough around the edge.
5. Cover the crust lightly, and let it stand for 15 minutes.
6. Meanwhile, place a rack on the lowest rung in the oven, and preheat the oven to 450° F.
7. Place the crust in the hot oven, and bake it for 10 minutes. Remove the crust, and set it aside until the topping is ready. *Do not turn the oven off.*

TO ASSEMBLE THE PIZZA

8. In a medium-sized bowl, combine the ricotta, mozzarella, Romano, lemon juice, oregano, black pepper, and cayenne.
9. Spread the cheese mixture over the prebaked crust, leaving a border of about ½ inch. Sprinkle the cheese with the scallions. Arrange the pepper strips, wagon-wheel fashion, around the outer edge of the pizza (that is, pointing toward the center).
10. Place the pizza in the hot oven, and bake it for 15 minutes or until the top of the cheese begins to turn golden. Remove the pizza from the oven, and let it cool for about 5 minutes before slicing it.

BROCCOLI PIZZA WITH POTATO CRUST

6 servings

I am very fond of this crust, which resembles a potato pancake but is not fried.

Preparation tip: You can try the crust with other toppings that are slightly moist, such as sautéed onions and cabbage (lots) with sliced kielbasa (Polish garlic sausage) and grated Cheddar.

CRUST

1½ pounds potatoes, peeled and coarsely shredded
½ teaspoon salt (optional)
1 egg white
1 egg
1 medium onion, peeled and grated (about ⅓ cup)
Vegetable oil for brushing or spraying

TOPPING

1 head broccoli, cut into flowerets with short stems (about 4 cups)
2 teaspoons olive oil
1 large onion, peeled, halved, and thinly sliced (about 1 cup)
1 tablespoon chopped garlic (3 large cloves)
¼ teaspoon red pepper flakes, or to taste
2 cups sliced mushrooms (6 ounces)
1 teaspoon Worcestershire sauce
1 cup light or part-skim ricotta
1½ cups (about 6 ounces) grated extra-sharp Cheddar, divided
½ teaspoon oregano, crumbled
Paprika for garnish

TO PREPARE THE CRUST

1. Place the grated potatoes in a colander, sprinkle them with the salt (if desired), tossing them to coat them with the salt, and let them drain for 15 minutes. Then press out as much water as you can.
2. Preheat the oven to 400° F.
3. In a medium-sized bowl, lightly beat the egg white and whole egg, and stir in the drained potatoes and the onion. Press the potato mixture into an oiled 11-inch quiche pan (or similar-sized rectangular pan).
4. Place the crust in the hot oven, and bake it for 30 minutes. Remove the crust from the oven, and brush or spray the crust's surface lightly with oil. Return the crust to the oven, and bake it for another 10 to 15 minutes or until it is golden and crisp.

TO PREPARE THE TOPPING

5. Blanch the broccoli in boiling water for 2 to 3 minutes, or steam the flowerets for 5 to 6 minutes. Drain the broccoli in a colander, and immediately rinse the broccoli under cold water. Transfer the broccoli to a bowl, and set the bowl aside.

6. In a small skillet, heat the oil, and add the onion and garlic, sautéing the vegetables for 2 minutes. Add the red pepper flakes, mushrooms, and Worcestershire sauce. Continue cooking the mixture, stirring it often, for 5 minutes or until the mushrooms give off their liquid and become dry. Add the mushroom mixture to the reserved broccoli.

7. In a small bowl, combine the ricotta, 1 cup of the Cheddar, and the oregano.

TO ASSEMBLE THE PIZZA

8. Preheat the oven to 375° F.

9. Spread the ricotta mixture on the bottom of the baked crust. Arrange the broccoli mixture on top of the cheese, setting the flowerets with stems downward. Sprinkle the broccoli with the remaining ½ cup of Cheddar and the paprika.

10. Place the pizza in the hot oven, and bake the pizza for 20 minutes or until the filling is hot and the cheese begins to turn golden.

BROCCOLI PIZZA WITH WHOLE WHEAT CRUST

2 to 4 servings

This recipe, from *Gourmet* magazine, makes a great pizza despite my drastic reduction of its fat content. The crust is very simple to handle and would be a good starting point for anyone unfamiliar with yeast-raised dough.

Preparation tips: The crust is deliciously crispy when baked on a pizza stone—a round, flat ceramic "pan" about 14 inches in diameter. The pizza can be set up about 30 minutes in advance of baking.

CRUST

- ⅔ cup warm water (105° F to 115° F), divided
- 1 packet (1 scant tablespoon) active dry yeast
- ½ teaspoon sugar
- 2 tablespoons olive oil
- ¼ cup whole-wheat flour
- ¼ cup unprocessed bran
- 1⅔ to 2 cups all-purpose flour
- ½ teaspoon salt (optional)

Corn meal for sprinkling the pan

TOPPING

- 1 tablespoon olive oil
- 1 bunch broccoli, cut into ¾-inch flowerets (3 to 4 cups)
- ¼ cup water
- ⅔ cup light or part-skim ricotta
- 1 large egg
- 2 large cloves garlic, peeled and minced
- ¼ teaspoon salt (optional)
- ⅔ cup freshly grated Parmesan, divided

Freshly ground black pepper to taste

Olive-oil spray

TO PREPARE THE CRUST

1. Place ⅓ cup of the warm water in a small bowl, and sprinkle the yeast and sugar into the bowl, stirring the ingredients to dissolve them. Let the mixture stand for 5 to 10 minutes or until it is bubbly.

2. Transfer the yeast mixture to a large bowl (or to the bowl of a food processor—see step 3). Add the remaining ⅓ cup warm water, the olive oil, whole-wheat flour, bran, 1⅔ cups of the all-purpose flour, and the salt (if desired). Stir the mixture until a ball of dough is formed.

3. Turn the dough out onto a floured surface, and knead the dough for 5 minutes, adding as much of the remaining all-purpose flour as needed to form a nonsticky dough. (Or process the dough in a food processor, adding flour 1 tablespoon at a time if the dough is too wet or adding water 1 teaspoon at a time if the dough is too dry, until the dough forms a ball. Then process the dough for an additional 15 seconds.)

4. Place the ball of dough in an oiled bowl, turning the dough to coat it with the oil. Cover the bowl with plastic wrap, and let the dough rise in a warm, draft-free place for 1 hour or until the dough has doubled in bulk. If the dough is made in advance, it can be refrigerated at this point.

TO PREPARE THE TOPPING
5. In a large, heavy skillet, preferably one with a nonstick surface, heat the oil until it is hot, add the broccoli, and sauté the vegetable, stirring it often, for 1 minute or until the broccoli is bright green. Add the water, cover the pan, and cook the broccoli over low heat for 3 minutes or until it is tender-crisp. Set the broccoli aside.
6. In a small bowl, whisk together the ricotta and egg. Mash the garlic with the salt (if desired) to form a paste (if you are not using salt, crush the garlic in a press), and stir the garlic into the cheese mixture. Add 1/3 cup of the Parmesan and the black pepper, and mix the ingredients well.

TO ASSEMBLE THE PIZZA
7. If your oven is an electric one, place the rack on the lowest rung. If your oven is a gas one, remove the rack. Preheat the oven to 500° F.
8. Punch down the dough, form it into a ball, and roll it out on a lightly floured surface to a diameter of 14 inches. Place the dough on an oiled pizza stone or in a black-steel pizza pan that has been sprinkled with the corn meal.
9. Spread the ricotta mixture evenly across the surface of the crust to within 1/2 inch of the edge. Place the broccoli flowerets on top of the cheese in concentric circles with stems facing the center. Sprinkle the broccoli with the remaining 1/3 cup of Parmesan and, if desired, more pepper. Spray the top of the pizza with a light coating of olive oil.
10. Place the pizza in the hot oven (on the lowest shelf of an electric oven or on the floor of a gas oven), and bake the pizza for 10 to 15 minutes or until the crust is golden brown. If you used a pan for baking the pizza, transfer the pizza to a cutting board before slicing it into wedges.

PEPPER AND PEPPERONI PIZZA   *2 to 4 servings*

Are you surprised? Well, the amount of pepperoni in this pizza isn't worth worrying about, although it adds beauty and flavor to the finished product.

Preparation tip: I use the whole-wheat crust on page 276 for this pizza, but you can use any kind of crust you like, including pitas.

    1 recipe pizza dough (see "Preparation tip," above)
    1 large clove garlic, peeled and minced
 1½ tablespoons olive oil, divided
    1 28-ounce can Italian plum tomatoes, drained
    1 cup thinly sliced onion
    1 tablespoon chopped fresh basil
 ¼ teaspoon red pepper flakes
 ¼ teaspoon oregano, crumbled
 ¼ teaspoon sugar
 ¼ teaspoon salt (optional)
    1 large sweet green pepper, cored, seeded, and
        sliced crosswise into thin rings
Corn meal for sprinkling the pan
    4 ounces part-skim mozzarella, thinly sliced
 10 thin slices pepperoni

1. While the pizza dough is rising, sauté the garlic in ½ tablespoon of the oil in a medium-sized saucepan—preferably one with a nonstick surface—over medium-low heat until the garlic is just golden (do not let it burn). Add the tomatoes, chopping them into small pieces with a spatula or wooden spoon. Stir in the onion, basil, red pepper flakes, oregano, sugar, and salt (if desired). Bring the mixture to a boil, reduce the heat, and simmer the mixture, stirring it occasionally, for 45 minutes or until the liquid has almost evaporated.
2. In a large skillet, briefly heat the remaining 1 tablespoon of oil. Add the green-pepper rings, and sauté them over high heat, turning them once, for 1 to 2 minutes or until they are tender-crisp. Transfer the rings to paper towels, drain the rings, and pat them dry.
3. Place the rack of an electric oven on the bottom rung, or remove the rack from a gas oven. Preheat the oven to 500° F.
4. Punch down the dough, form it into a ball, and roll it out on a lightly floured surface to a diameter of 14 inches. Place the dough on an oiled pizza stone or in a black-steel pizza pan that has been sprinkled with the corn meal.
5. Spread the sauce evenly over the crust to within ½ inch of the edge. Arrange the green pepper slices in decorative, overlapping fashion on top of the sauce. Place the mozzarella and the pepperoni slices decoratively and evenly on top of the pizza.

6. Place the pizza in the hot oven, and bake it on the lowest shelf of an electric oven or on the floor of a gas oven for 10 to 15 minutes or until the crust is golden brown. If you baked the pizza in a pan, transfer the pizza to a cutting board before slicing it into wedges.

SHRIMP AND LEEK PIZZA

4 servings

I adapted a recipe offered by Abby Mandel in *Bon Appétit* magazine for a scrumptious and beautiful pizza.

Preparation tip: You can prepare the dough, shrimp, sauce, and leeks in advance. About 25 minutes before serving, turn on the oven, and start to assemble the pizza.

CRUST

- 1 cup plus 3 tablespoons warm water (105° F to 115° F)
- 1 package (1 scant tablespoon) active dry yeast
- 1 teaspoon honey
- 1¼ cups (or more) bread flour *or* all-purpose flour
- 1¼ cups whole-wheat flour (preferably stone-ground)
- 1 teaspoon salt
- 1½ tablespoons olive oil

Vegetable-oil spray

TOPPING

- 2½ tablespoons olive oil, divided
- 1¼ pounds plum tomatoes, seeded and chopped
- 2 tablespoons tomato paste
- ¼ teaspoon salt
- ¼ teaspoon red pepper flakes
- ⅛ teaspoon sugar
- 1 tablespoon minced fresh basil *or* ¾ teaspoon dried basil, crumbled
- 1 pound medium shrimp, peeled and deveined
- 2 cups sliced well-rinsed leeks (white and light green parts)
- ⅛ teaspoon salt (optional)

Freshly ground black pepper to taste

- ½ cup freshly grated Parmesan

TO PREPARE THE CRUST

1. Place the water in a small bowl, and add the yeast and honey, stirring the ingredients to dissolve them. Let the mixture stand for 10 minutes or until it is bubbly.
2. In a large bowl, combine the bread flour or all-purpose flour, whole-wheat flour, and salt. Add the yeast mixture and the olive oil, stirring the ingredients to form a ball of dough. Turn the dough out onto a floured surface, and knead the dough for 5 minutes or until it is smooth, adding bread flour or all-purpose flour 1 tablespoon at a time, if needed, to prevent sticking.
3. Place the ball of dough in an oiled bowl, turning the dough to coat it with the oil. Cover the bowl with oiled plastic wrap, and let the dough rise in a warm, draft-free place for 1 hour or until the dough has doubled in bulk. If prepared in advance, the dough can be refrigerated at this point. But be sure to bring it back to room temperature (this takes at least 1 hour) before assembling the pizza.

TO PREPARE THE TOPPING

4. In a medium-sized saucepan, heat ½ tablespoon of the oil, and add the tomatoes, tomato paste, salt, red pepper flakes, and sugar. Cook the mixture, stirring it often, over medium-low heat for 35 minutes or until the sauce is reduced to about 1½ cups. Stir in the basil just before assembling the pizza.

5. In a medium-sized nonstick skillet, heat 1 tablespoon of the oil, add the shrimp, and sauté them for 1½ minutes or until they just turn opaque. With a slotted spoon, remove the shrimp to a plate, and set them aside to cool. When the shrimp are cool, slice them in half lengthwise.

6. In the same skillet, briefly heat the remaining 1 tablespoon of oil, and add the leeks, salt (if desired), and pepper. Sauté the leeks, stirring them often for 5 minutes or until they are very tender.

TO ASSEMBLE THE PIZZA

7. Place the oven rack on the lowest rung, and preheat the oven to 475° F.

8. Punch down the dough, form it into a ball, and turn it out onto a lightly floured surface. If you have a 15-inch pizza stone or pan, roll out the dough into a circle 13 inches in diameter. Or, if you are using two smaller pans, divide the dough in half, and roll each piece into a round 2 inches in diameter smaller than the pans. Place the circle of dough on a pizza pan sprayed with vegetable oil, and, with the heel of your hand, stretch it to the edges of the pan, forming a slight lip around the pan's perimeter.

9. Spray the surface of the dough with vegetable oil, and spread the tomato sauce evenly over the crust to within ½ inch of the edge. Sprinkle the leeks over the sauce, and arrange the shrimp halves in concentric circles on top of the leeks. Sprinkle the Parmesan over the pizza.

10. Place the pizza in the hot oven, and bake the pizza for 12 minutes or until the crust is crisp and lightly browned.

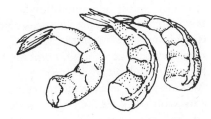

TURKISH MEAT PIZZA

12 mini-pizzas
(6 servings)

This dish makes a tasty lunch or supper. Or smaller pizzas can be prepared and served as hors d'oeuvres.

Preparation tips: If time is limited, use a 1-pound loaf of frozen bread dough (defrosted) to make the crust, or make extra dough the next time you bake a white or part-whole-wheat bread; after the first rising, divide the dough into 12 balls of dough, and freeze them for future use as pizza crust. Also, the pizza can be prepared in advance, baked, and frozen for future reheating.

Serving suggestion: Serve these pizzas topped with nonfat or low-fat yogurt, either plain or mixed with blanched, minced garlic or minced fresh parsley.

CRUST

- ¾ cup warm (105° F to 115° F) water
- 1 package (1 scant tablespoon) active dry yeast
- ½ teaspoon sugar
- 1 cup (approximately) all-purpose flour
- 1 cup whole-wheat flour
- 1 teaspoon salt (optional)
- 1 tablespoon oil
- Water, if needed

TOPPING

- ¾ pound extra-lean ground beef
- 1 cup finely chopped onion
- ¼ cup finely chopped sweet green pepper
- 1 16-ounce can tomatoes, drained and finely chopped
- ¼ cup minced fresh parsley
- 1 large clove garlic, peeled and minced
- ¼ teaspoon cumin
- ¼ teaspoon coriander
- ⅛ teaspoon allspice
- ⅛ teaspoon freshly ground black pepper
- Several dashes cayenne, to taste
- Salt to taste (optional)

TO PREPARE THE CRUST

1. Place the water in a small bowl, and sprinkle the yeast and sugar into the bowl, stirring the ingredients to dissolve them. Let the mixture stand for 5 to 10 minutes or until it is bubbly.
2. In a medium-sized bowl, combine the all-purpose flour and whole-wheat flour with the salt (if desired).
3. Add the yeast mixture and the oil to the flour mixture, blending the ingredients with your hands or a wooden spoon. Add more flour or water, if needed, to form a soft but not sticky dough.
4. Turn the dough out onto a lightly floured surface, and knead the dough for 8 minutes or until it is smooth and elastic. Place the dough in an oiled bowl, turning the dough to coat it with the oil. Cover the bowl, and let the dough rise in a warm, draft-free place for 1 hour or until the dough has doubled in

bulk. Punch the dough down, divide it into 12 pieces, and shape each piece into a ball. Place the balls of dough on a lightly floured surface, cover them, and let them rest for 30 minutes.

TO ASSEMBLE THE PIZZA

5. While the dough is resting, prepare the topping. In a medium-sized bowl, combine the topping ingredients, mixing them thoroughly.
6. Place the oven rack near the top of the oven, and preheat the oven to 450° F.
7. When the dough is ready, on a lightly floured surface, roll each ball into a 6-inch circle. Place about 3 tablespoonfuls of the meat mixture on each circle, and spread the topping to within ¼ inch of the edges.
8. Line baking sheets with foil, place the pizzas on the sheets, put the sheets in the hot oven, and bake the meat pies for 10 minutes or until the dough is crisp and golden around the edges.

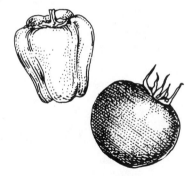

PITA-BEAN PIZZAS

4 servings

Simple and delicious, these nourishing little pizzas, based on a recipe in *Gourmet* magazine, make a lovely luncheon dish.

Preparation tips: These pizzas can also be cut into wedges or prepared on mini-pitas and used as hors d'oeuvres. If full-size pitas are to be cut into wedges, it would be best to use plum tomatoes, placing a tomato slice in each quarter for easy cutting.

 4 5-inch to 6-inch pitas (preferably whole-wheat)
Olive-oil spray
 1 tablespoon olive oil
 1 cup chopped onion (1 large)
 1 tablespoon minced garlic (3 large cloves)
 2 cups cooked white beans *or* canned white
    beans, rinsed and drained
⅔ cup dry white wine
Salt to taste (optional)
Freshly ground black pepper to taste
 2 tablespoons finely chopped fresh basil
 4 medium tomatoes *or* 8 plum tomatoes, sliced crosswise
 4 ounces part-skim mozzarella, grated

1. Place the oven rack in the middle of the oven, and preheat the oven to 350° F.
2. With a sharp knife, cut the pitas in half horizontally. Spray the rough side of each half with olive oil. Place the pita halves on a baking sheet, put the sheet in the oven, and bake the pitas for 8 minutes or until they are lightly toasted and crisp.
3. While the pitas are baking, in a large skillet, preferably one with a nonstick surface, heat the 1 tablespoon of olive oil, add the onion and garlic, and sauté the vegetables over medium-low heat until the onion is very soft.
4. Stir in the beans, wine, salt (if desired), and pepper, and simmer the mixture, stirring it occasionally, for 5 minutes or until about half the liquid has evaporated. Transfer the mixture to a blender or food processor, and purée the mixture.
5. Preheat the broiler.
6. Divide the bean mixture evenly among the pita toasts, spreading the mixture almost to the edge of each pita. Sprinkle each toast with basil, and top the toast with the sliced tomatoes and the grated mozzarella.
7. Place the pita pizzas in the hot broiler about 4 inches from the heat for 3 to 4 minutes or until the cheese melts and turns golden.

Pancakes and Crêpes

Many health-conscious people shy away from pancakes. They think that pancakes have too many calories, too much fat and cholesterol, and too little nutritional compensation. But, as you may have already discovered in *Jane Brody's Good Food Book,* both of these reservations can easily be overcome if you make your own batter from scratch. The fat and cholesterol content is easily controlled, as are the sugar and calories. And the ingredients you use can vastly increase a pancake's "nutrient density"—that is, the amount of essential nutrients for a given number of calories.

And pancakes are such a lovely way to entertain family or houseguests on a weekend morning. The batter can be prepared the night before in some cases; or, at the least, the dry ingredients can be mixed in one bowl and the wet ingredients in another, to be combined just before "frying" the pancakes on a nonstick griddle. The table can look so inviting, adorned with various kinds of fruit and fruit butters and plain yogurt for toppings.

As for crêpes, they are perfect for a light lunch, informal supper, or elegant afterdinner dessert. They can be set up in advance and briefly baked to heat them through before serving them.

NORWEGIAN PANCAKES

about 16 4-inch pancakes
(4 servings)

These delicate pancakes are delicious and almost fat-free, quite unlike the Swedish pancakes I used to make (before I saw "the light") that contained 1 stick of butter in pancakes for 4! Contrary to the impression created by its name, buttermilk is a low-fat (1 or 1½ percent butterfat) liquid. It is so named because it is the liquid left behind when the cream is skimmed from the milk to make butter.

DRY INGREDIENTS
- 1 cup whole-wheat flour
- 1 cup all-purpose flour
- 1 tablespoon sugar
- 2 teaspoons baking soda
- ⅛ teaspoon salt (optional)

WET INGREDIENTS
- 1 egg
- 3 cups buttermilk
- ¼ teaspoon vanilla extract

POSSIBLE TOPPINGS
- ½ cup fruit butter (e.g., apple, pear, peach)
- 2 cups plain nonfat or low-fat yogurt
- 3 cups berries, sliced if large

1. In a large bowl, combine the dry ingredients, mixing them well.
2. In a medium-sized bowl, beat the egg lightly, and add the buttermilk and vanilla, mixing the ingredients well.
3. When you are ready to cook the pancakes, lightly oil a nonstick griddle (for example, spray it with vegetable oil), and heat it over medium heat. Make a well in the dry ingredients, and pour in the wet ingredients, mixing the two just enough to moisten the dry ingredients.
4. On the heated griddle, pour sufficient batter to make 4-inch pancakes—4 of them at a time on an 11-inch square griddle. Cook the pancakes until they begin to bubble on the surface, then flip them over, and lightly brown them on the other side. Repeat the procedure until all the batter is used up, re-oiling the griddle only to prevent the pancakes from sticking to it.
5. Serve the pancakes with the desired toppings.

GINGERBREAD PANCAKES

These low-fat, high-nutrient pancakes are served at Fess Parker's (aka "Davy Crockett") Red Lion Inn in Santa Barbara. They are great-tasting and very light for a batter made only with whole-wheat flour.

Serving suggestion: Serve the pancakes with apple or other fruit butter or with apples that have been pared, cored, thinly sliced, sautéed just until soft in 1 tablespoon butter or margarine, and sprinkled with cinnamon-sugar.

DRY INGREDIENTS
1 cup whole-wheat flour
¾ teaspoon baking soda
½ teaspoon ground ginger
½ teaspoon cinnamon
¼ teaspoon ground cloves
¼ teaspoon salt (optional)

WET INGREDIENTS
2 teaspoons instant decaffeinated coffee
¼ cup boiling water
¾ cup thawed apple-juice concentrate
1 egg
2 tablespoons margarine, melted, *or* 2 tablespoons canola oil

1. In a large bowl, combine the dry ingredients, mixing them well.
2. In a small bowl, dissolve the instant coffee in the boiling water, stirring the coffee, and add the apple-juice concentrate. Mix the ingredients well, and set the bowl aside.
3. In a medium-sized bowl, lightly beat the egg, and stir in the melted margarine or oil. Add the reserved coffee mixture, stirring the ingredients to combine them well.
4. When you are ready to cook the pancakes, make a well in the center of the dry ingredients, and pour in the liquid ingredients, stirring them just enough to moisten the dry ingredients. The batter will be lumpy.
5. Spray a nonstick griddle with vegetable oil or grease it lightly, and heat it until it is hot. For each pancake, spoon 2 tablespoons of batter (if available, use a ⅛-cup measure for your "spoon") onto the hot griddle. Cook the pancakes until they brown lightly on the bottom, and flip them over to brown them on the other side.

BERRY PANCAKES

about 24 3-inch pancakes
(4 servings)

Pancakes with fruit—both within and atop—have long been my favorite. Here is a simple way to prepare them. The results are light and nutritious.

⅔ cup whole-wheat flour
⅔ cup all-purpose flour
2 tablespoons sugar
1½ teaspoons baking powder
1 teaspoon baking soda
1 egg white
1 egg
⅔ cup plain nonfat or low-fat yogurt
1 cup skim or low-fat milk
1 tablespoon butter *or* margarine, melted and cooled
2 cups fresh berries (e.g., raspberries, blueberries, sliced strawberries)

1. In a large bowl, combine the whole-wheat flour, all-purpose flour, sugar, baking powder, and baking soda.
2. In a medium-sized bowl, lightly beat the egg white and whole egg. Whisk in the yogurt, milk, and melted butter or margarine. Stir the liquid mixture into the flour mixture until the two are just combined. Gently fold in the berries.
3. Heat a griddle, preferably one with a nonstick surface (if it is not a nonstick griddle, spray it with vegetable oil before heating it), and pour on a scant ¼ cup of batter for each pancake. Cook the pancakes over medium-low heat until the bottoms are golden brown. Then flip them over, and cook them on the other side.

CHIVE PANCAKES

4 servings

I found the original recipe on which mine is based tucked in my "Pancake" file and attributed to Kathy Casey. Unfortunately, I failed to note who she is and from where the recipe came. But thanks anyway, Kathy.

Preparation tips: These are prepared from a make-ahead batter that should stand for at least 30 minutes and up to 12 hours in the refrigerator. If you prefer thinner pancakes or crêpes, add more beer to the batter.

Serving suggestion: My tasters enjoyed these tasty cakes as an hors d'oeuvre with a dollop of seasoned yogurt (for example, yogurt with mustard and dill, yogurt with horseradish, yogurt with lemon juice and basil) or plain nonfat or low-fat yogurt. These pancakes can also be served as a vegetable side dish, a first course, or the main course of a light luncheon or supper, with soup and salad.

DRY INGREDIENTS
½ cup whole-wheat flour
½ cup all-purpose flour
¼ cup corn meal
¼ teaspoon salt (optional)
¼ teaspoon freshly ground white pepper

WET INGREDIENTS
2 egg whites
1 egg
⅓ cup or more beer, as needed
¼ cup dry sherry
2 tablespoons melted butter *or* margarine
¼ cup finely diced sweet red pepper *and/or* sweet yellow pepper
2 tablespoons finely minced fresh chives
1 teaspoon grated lemon rind
½ teaspoon hot pepper sauce
½ teaspoon finely minced garlic
½ teaspoon dillweed *or* 1 teaspoon chopped fresh dill

1. In a medium-sized bowl, combine the dry ingredients, stirring the ingredients to mix them thoroughly. Make a well in the center of the mixture.
2. In a second medium-sized bowl, lightly beat the egg whites and whole egg. Stir in the remaining wet ingredients, mixing the ingredients to combine them well. Pour the wet ingredients into the well of the dry ingredients, and stir the mixture just until the ingredients are well blended. Cover the batter, and chill it for at least 30 minutes or up to 12 hours. If possible, bring the batter back to room temperature before making the pancakes.
3. Using a nonstick or lightly oiled (I use vegetable-oil spray) griddle or crêpe pan, heat the pan over medium-high heat. For small, thick pancakes, drop 2 tablespoons of batter on the griddle for each pancake, browning the pancakes lightly on one side before flipping them over and browning them on the other side. For thinner, crêpe-sized pancakes, thin the batter with additional beer so that the batter has the consistency of buttermilk, and pour a scant ¼ cup of the batter into an oiled, heated crêpe pan, tipping the pan to distribute the batter evenly over the bottom of the pan. Brown the crêpe lightly, flip it, and brown it on the other side. Arrange the finished pancakes on a heat-proof serving dish, and keep them covered with foil and warm (in a low oven) until all the pancakes are cooked.

CORN-OFF-THE-COB CAKES

about 24 small pancakes
(4 to 6 servings)

These work best as a main-dish accompaniment with a dab of butter or margarine, or as a brunch or luncheon dish with plain or herb-seasoned yogurt.

½ cup yellow corn meal (preferably stone-ground)
1 cup skim or low-fat milk
2 cups *uncooked* corn kernels (2 to 3 large ears)
2 egg whites
1 egg
2 tablespoons melted butter *or* margarine
½ cup all-purpose flour
1 teaspoon baking powder
1 to 2 teaspoons sugar
¼ teaspoon salt (optional)

1. In a small bowl, combine the corn meal and milk, and set the mixture aside.
2. Process the corn kernels in a blender or food processor. Add the egg
   whites, whole egg, and butter or margarine, and blend the ingredients until
   they are combined. Transfer the mixture to a medium-sized bowl.
3. Add the reserved corn-meal mixture to the corn-egg mixture, and set this
   aside.
4. In a small bowl, combine the flour, baking powder, sugar, and salt (if
   desired). When you are ready to make the pancakes, add the flour mixture
   to the corn mixture, stirring the ingredients until they are just blended.
5. Heat a griddle that has been lightly oiled if it does not have a nonstick
   surface. Using a scant ¼ cup of batter for each pancake, cook the pancakes
   until they are golden brown on the bottom. Then flip them over, and cook
   them until the undersides are golden brown.

POTATO PANCAKES

about 18 pancakes
(6 servings)

Better known by their Yiddish name, *latkes* (LOT-kis), these pancakes are traditionally served during Hanukkah, the Festival of Lights. But they are good
almost any time of the year. There are as many different versions of potato
pancakes as there are cooks who make them. This one, from *Jane Brody's Good
Food Book,* is as good as any I've tried.

Preparation tips: Potato pancakes are fried in oil and can be very greasy if not
done properly. Be sure the oil is hot before you add the batter. Also, drain the
oil from the cooked pancakes by placing the latkes on paper toweling. The
amount of milk and flour you'll need depends on how moist the potatoes are.

Serving suggestions: Potato pancakes are usually served with applesauce and sour cream; however, I've found nonfat or low-fat yogurt to be an acceptable substitute for its fatty cousin. Try the Cranberry Applesauce on page 517 or the Savory Applesauce on page 307.

2 pounds (6 medium) potatoes, peeled and
  coarsely grated
1 large onion, peeled and coarsely grated
½ cup (approximately) milk
1 carrot, peeled and finely grated (optional)
1 egg white *and* 1 egg, lightly beaten
½ cup flour *or* ¼ cup matzo meal (approximately)
1 teaspoon salt, or to taste (optional)
Freshly ground black pepper to taste
Oil for frying (preferably canola)

1. Place the grated potatoes and onion in a colander set over a large bowl, and press the solids to squeeze out the excess liquid. Let the vegetables stand for about 5 minutes, and press them again. Transfer the liquid to a measuring cup, but leave in the bowl any starch that may have collected.
2. Add the potato mixture to the bowl. Note how much liquid is in the measuring cup, and discard it; then add the same amount of milk to the potato mixture along with the carrot, beaten egg white and whole egg, flour or matzo meal, salt (if desired), and pepper. Stir the ingredients to combine them thoroughly.
3. Preheat the oven to very low.
4. In a large, heavy skillet or nonstick pan, heat enough oil to cover the pan's bottom with ¼ inch of oil. Using about ¼ cup of batter for each pancake, add the batter to the pan, and fry the pancakes a few at a time, turning them when they are golden brown on the bottom. When each batch of pancakes has finished cooking, set the pancakes on paper towels, preferably laid over a rack, and keep the pancakes warm in the oven.

ZUCCHINI PANCAKES

2 to 3 main-course or
4 side-dish servings

The late Bert Greene, author of *Greene on Greens,* proposed a version of these pancakes as one way to "dispose of" those "Jolly Green Giant"-sized zucchinis that home gardeners (and their friends) so often wind up with.

Preparation tip: If you wish to avoid adding salt, place the grated zucchini in a clean dishcloth or in several layers of cheesecloth, and squeeze out some of the liquid.

¾ pound zucchini (remove the seeds if they are
   very large)
Salt to taste, divided (optional)
 1 egg, lightly beaten
¼ cup skim or low-fat milk
¼ cup grated Parmesan
¼ teaspoon hot pepper sauce, or to taste
Freshly ground black pepper to taste
½ cup all-purpose flour
1½ teaspoons baking powder
Vegetable-oil spray for the pan

1. Grate the unpeeled zucchini—you should have about 3 cups. Place the zucchini in a colander, and lightly sprinkle the zucchini with the salt (if desired). Let the zucchini stand for 20 minutes. Then with your hands, gently press on the zucchini to remove the excess liquid.
2. In a large bowl, combine the zucchini, egg, milk, Parmesan, hot pepper sauce, additional salt (if desired), and pepper.
3. Sift or stir the flour with the baking powder, and add this to the zucchini mixture, combining the ingredients well.
4. Preheat the oven to very low.
5. Over medium heat, heat a nonstick griddle or a heavy skillet that has been sprayed with vegetable oil until the pan is hot. Place about 3 tablespoons of the batter on the griddle for each pancake, and cook the pancakes for 3 minutes or until they are lightly browned on the bottom. Then flip them over, and brown them on the other side for 1 minute or so. Transfer the cooked pancakes to the warm oven while you cook the rest of the pancakes.

BASIC CRÊPES

about 8 crêpes

Crêpes can be stuffed with a number of fillings for a make-ahead main course, a dessert, or an appetizer. This recipe first appeared in *Jane Brody's Good Food Book.*

Preparation tips: Crêpe batter is best made ahead and refrigerated for at least 1 hour before cooking. Leftover batter will keep in the refrigerator for several days, or it can be frozen for longer periods. In cooking crêpes, it is important to start with a hot pan. *Unfilled* crêpes can be stacked with pieces of wax paper placed between them, wrapped airtight in heavy foil, and frozen for up to 3 months. Crêpes will also keep in the refrigerator for about 3 days (be sure the crêpes are well wrapped to keep them from drying out). For larger batches, this recipe can be increased fourfold (to make 32 to 36 crêpes), but do not use more than ¼ teaspoon salt and ¼ cup melted butter in the batter.

  1 egg
Pinch salt (optional—omit for dessert crêpes)
½ cup all-purpose flour
⅝ cup (½ cup plus 2 tablespoons) milk
  1 teaspoon sugar (for dessert crêpes only)
¼ teaspoon vanilla extract (for dessert crêpes only)
  2 tablespoons (approximately) melted butter *or*
    margarine, divided

1. In a mixing bowl, combine the egg and salt (if desired). While beating the egg with a whisk or an electric mixer, gradually add the flour alternately with the milk. *For dessert crepes only,* add the sugar and vanilla. Add 1 tablespoon of the melted butter or margarine. Mix the ingredients well to eliminate lumps. Or combine all the ingredients in a blender jar, and blend them in a blender for about 1 minute. Scrape the batter off the sides of the jar, and blend the batter for another 15 seconds.
2. Heat a 7- or 8-inch crêpe pan or nonstick skillet with sloping sides. (If the pan does not have a nonstick surface, melt about 1 teaspoon of butter in the pan, tipping the pan to distribute the butter over the pan's bottom. *Do not burn the butter.*) Add 2 tablespoons of the batter to the hot pan, and swirl the batter around by tipping the pan gently so that the batter completely covers the pan's bottom. Cook the crêpe over moderately high heat for 30 to 40 seconds or until the bottom of the crêpe is lightly browned. Flip the crêpe over, and cook the other side for 15 seconds. Turn the crêpe out onto wax paper.
3. Repeat the cooking procedure with the remaining batter, brushing the pan very lightly with butter or margarine, if needed, to keep the crêpes from sticking to the pan's surface. (With a nonstick pan, little, if any, butter or margarine will be needed.)

POTATO CRÊPES

about 16 crêpes

These tender, delicious crêpes are ideal for a vegetarian filling such as broccoli or beans and cheese. But I have used them, to great acclaim, for the Broccoli and Chicken Crêpes on page 295.

> 3 egg whites
> 2 eggs
> 1 cup skim milk
> ¾ cup mashed potatoes
> ¼ to ½ teaspoon salt, to taste (optional)
> ⅛ teaspoon white pepper
> Dash nutmeg
> ½ cup all-purpose flour
> 2 tablespoons melted butter *or* margarine
> Vegetable-oil spray for the pan (optional)

1. In a blender or bowl, combine the egg whites, whole eggs, milk, potatoes, salt (if desired), pepper, and nutmeg. Blend or beat the ingredients until they are well combined.
2. Gradually add the flour, blending or beating the mixture after each addition until it is smooth. Add the butter or margarine, and mix the batter thoroughly. Let the batter stand in the refrigerator for at least 1 hour. Before cooking the crêpes, stir the batter thoroughly.
3. Heat a crêpe pan or 7-inch nonstick skillet over medium heat. Spray the pan with the vegetable oil, if needed, and add about 3 tablespoons of the batter, tipping the pan to coat the bottom evenly with the batter.
4. Cook the crêpe for 1 minute or until the top of the crêpe is no longer wet and its bottom is lightly browned. Using a wide spatula, carefully flip the crêpe over to lightly brown its other side. Turn the cooked crêpe out onto a clean cotton or linen (but *not* terry) kitchen towel.
5. Repeat the cooking procedure with the remaining batter until the batter is used up. If you are using a nonstick pan, it should not be necessary to oil it before cooking the remaining crêpes. If you are preparing the crêpes long before stuffing them, let them cool on the cloth. Then stack them, separating each with a sheet of wax paper, and refrigerate or freeze them.

BROCCOLI AND CHICKEN CRÊPES   *8 servings*

These are like a stir-fry in a pancake and so flavorful that they don't need a sauce.

Preparation tip: The crêpes can be assembled in advance and heated in the oven at serving time.

  1 tablespoon olive oil
  1 pound boneless, skinless chicken breasts, slivered
  3 cups thinly sliced broccoli flowerets and stems
 ¾ cup (about 5) thinly sliced scallions
  2 cups sliced mushrooms
1½ cups chicken broth
Freshly ground white pepper *or* black pepper to taste
1½ tablespoons cornstarch
  3 tablespoons reduced-sodium soy sauce
 ¾ cup coarsely chopped roasted unsalted cashews
16 crêpes (see page 293 or 294)

1. In a large skillet, heat the olive oil, add the chicken, and stir-fry the chicken over medium-high heat until it just loses its pink color. Add the broccoli, scallions, and mushrooms, and stir-fry the ingredients 1 minute longer.
2. Add the broth and the pepper, cover the pan, reduce the heat to medium-low, and cook the mixture for about 5 minutes.
3. In a small bowl, combine the cornstarch and soy sauce, stirring the mixture until it is smooth. Add the mixture to the pan, and cook the ingredients, stirring them, until the sauce thickens. Stir in the cashews.
4. Fill the crêpes with the chicken mixture, and place the crêpes, seam side down, on a lightly greased baking pan.
5. At serving time, preheat the oven to 300° F. Place the baking pan in the hot oven, and warm the crêpes for about 15 minutes.

PEAR CRÊPES

about 12 crêpes
(6 servings)

I served these wonderful crêpes with plain yogurt at a Sunday brunch. They would also make a lovely dessert. The recipe was originally published in *Cooking Light* magazine.

Preparation tips: Note that the crêpe batter must be chilled for 1 hour before cooking. It is easiest to use a ⅛-cup measure to pour the batter and fill the crêpes. The crêpes can be assembled in advance. Lightly cover them with foil to prevent them from drying out, and heat them in the oven just before serving.

CRÊPES
- ⅔ cup all-purpose flour
- ⅛ teaspoon cinnamon
- ⅔ cup skim or low-fat milk
- 1 tablespoon vegetable oil (preferably canola)
- 3 egg whites
- Vegetable-oil spray for the pan (optional)

FILLING
- 1 tablespoon butter *or* margarine
- 1 tablespoon brown sugar
- ¼ teaspoon cinnamon
- ⅛ teaspoon salt (optional)
- 4 cups (about 4) peeled, chopped firm but ripe pears
- 1 tablespoon light maple-flavored syrup
- 1 tablespoon fresh lemon juice
- ½ teaspoon vanilla extract

TO PREPARE THE CRÊPES

1. In a small bowl, combine the flour and cinnamon, and whisk in the milk, oil, and egg whites. Cover the bowl, and chill the batter for at least 1 hour and up to 24 hours.

2. Heat a 7-inch nonstick skillet or crêpe pan over medium-low heat until the pan is very hot (if the pan does not have a nonstick surface, spray it with vegetable oil before heating it). Holding the pan in one hand off the heat, use the other hand to add 2 tablespoons (⅛ cup) of batter to the pan, quickly tilting the pan to distribute the batter evenly across the pan's bottom. Place the pan back on the burner, and cook the crêpe for 1 minute or until it is lightly browned on the bottom. When the edge of the crêpe can be lifted with a spatula, flip the crêpe over, and cook the other side for 30 seconds. Place the cooked crêpe on a cotton or linen dishtowel to cool. If they are prepared in advance, the crêpes can be stacked, each separated by a sheet of wax paper.

TO PREPARE THE FILLING

3. In a large skillet, melt the butter or margarine over medium heat. Add the brown sugar, cinnamon, and salt (if desired), and stir the ingredients well.

4. Add the pears, tossing them to coat them with the seasonings, and cook the mixture, stirring it occasionally, for 10 minutes. Add the syrup, and cook the mixture, stirring it, for another 2 minutes. Remove the pan from the heat, and stir in the lemon juice and vanilla.

TO ASSEMBLE THE CRÊPES

5. Spoon 2 tablespoons (⅛ cup) of the pear mixture into the center of a crêpe. Roll the crêpe around the filling, and place it, seam side down, on a serving plate or in a shallow baking pan. Repeat the filling process with the remaining crêpes.

BRODY'S BLINTZES

These do indeed take me back to my childhood. As far back as I can remember, blintzes—crêpes stuffed with pot cheese and/or fruit—were a favorite special-event meal. In fact, years after I left home, I threw a "blintz party" for all my non-Jewish friends and prepared 150 blintzes of various kinds. I made so many, I had to store them in the attic (it was winter in Minnesota) until the party. But not one blintz was left by the party's end. In those days, my blintzes were a high-cholesterol affair, fried in butter and topped with sour cream. Today, I use a different technique, but the results are still wonderful.

Preparation tips: The blintzes can be readied for baking in advance and kept covered and refrigerated. But bring them to room temperature before heating them. The apple filling can also be used to prepare dessert crêpes (see page 293). If you plan to make both cheese and apple blintzes (24 total), be sure to double the recipe for the crêpes, below.

Serving suggestion: Serve these blintzes with plain or fruit-flavored nonfat or low-fat yogurt, fresh berries, or a lightly sweetened fruit sauce. Sautéed apples (see "Serving suggestion" on page 287) also are delicious with cheese blintzes.

CRÊPES
- ½ cup whole-wheat flour
- ½ cup all-purpose flour
- 1 teaspoon sugar
- ½ teaspoon salt (optional)
- 1 egg white
- 1 egg
- 1½ cups buttermilk
- ¼ cup skim or low-fat milk
- 1 tablespoon melted butter *or* margarine *or* canola oil
- Vegetable-oil spray for the pan (optional)

CHEESE FILLING
- 1 pound (2 cups) pot cheese *or* dry-curd cottage cheese
- ½ pound (1 cup) low-fat creamed cottage cheese
- ¼ cup dark raisins
- ¼ cup golden raisins *or* another ¼ cup dark raisins
- 1 egg yolk
- 2 tablespoons sugar
- 1 teaspoon vanilla extract
- ½ teaspoon cinnamon

APPLE FILLING
- 1 tablespoon butter *or* margarine
- 6 cups (about 3 large or 4 medium) peeled, thinly sliced apples
- ¼ cup fresh bread crumbs *or* cracker crumbs
- ¼ cup raisins (optional)
- ¼ cup brown sugar
- ½ teaspoon cinnamon

TO PREPARE THE CRÊPES

1. In a medium-sized bowl, combine the whole-wheat flour and all-purpose flour with the sugar and salt (if desired).

2. In a second bowl, lightly beat the egg white and whole egg. Add the buttermilk, skim or low-fat milk, and butter or margarine or oil. Stir the ingredients to combine them well.

3. Stir the wet ingredients into the dry ingredients, whisking them until they make a smooth batter.

4. Heat a 7-inch skillet with sloping sides over medium-high heat until the pan is hot. (You do not have to oil the pan if it has a good nonstick surface. Otherwise, spray the pan with vegetable oil—at least for the first crêpe.) Pour a scant ¼-cup of batter into the hot pan, tipping the pan to distribute the batter evenly over the bottom of the pan. After about 1 minute, when the crêpe is no longer runny on top and is lightly browned on the bottom, flip the crêpe over, and cook the other side for 30 to 60 seconds. Turn the cooked crêpes out onto a linen or cotton dishtowel or wax paper. Continue cooking the crêpes until all the batter has been used up.

TO PREPARE THE FILLINGS

5. To prepare the cheese filling, in a medium-sized bowl combine the filling ingredients, stirring the ingredients to mix them well.

6. To prepare the apple filling, in a nonstick saucepan or skillet, melt the butter or margarine, and stir in the remaining ingredients. Tightly cover the pan, and cook the mixture over low heat, stirring it often but gently, for 15 minutes or until the apples are soft.

TO PREPARE THE BLINTZES

7. Place about 3 rounded tablespoons of the filling of your choice in the center of each crêpe, spreading the filling into an oblong to within 1½ inches of the right and left sides of the crêpe. Fold the crêpe up egg-roll style by first folding over the shorter sides of the crêpe toward the middle and then folding the longer bottom and top of the crêpe toward the middle. Place blintzes seam side down on a lightly oiled baking tray, leaving about ½ inch of space between them. Cover the tray with plastic wrap, and chill the blintzes until 1 hour before baking them.

8. When you are ready to bake the blintzes, preheat the oven to 350° F. Place the tray in the hot oven, and bake the blintzes for 20 minutes or until they are heated through.

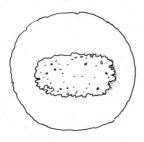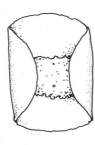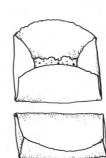

Egg-based Main Dishes

Unless you are dealing with a serious cholesterol problem or have coronary artery disease, there is no reason to eliminate eggs totally from your diet. They are extremely versatile and useful, an inexpensive source of protein, vitamins, and minerals. Their primary drawback—the extremely high cholesterol content of the yolk (the yolk of a single large egg contains about three-fourths of the cholesterol an adult should consume in an entire day)—can be partly overcome by using fewer yolks, instead substituting 2 egg whites (and perhaps 1 teaspoon of oil) for each whole egg eliminated. When using eggs as a minor ingredient, you could use a cholesterol-free egg substitute. But when eggs are the basis for the dish, I prefer to use the real thing.

The recipes that follow contain no more than 1 egg yolk per serving and usually less. On a day that you eat eggs, it would be wise to avoid other high-cholesterol fare such as fatty meats and organ meats (like liver) as well as other foods made with egg yolks.

APPLE-MUSHROOM OMELET

4 servings

I prepared this one morning for my brother and sister-in-law, and, after the two of them consumed servings for three, they said, "Is there any more?" I got the idea for this omelet from a recipe published in *Family Circle* magazine.

Serving suggestion: Try the Tropical Breakfast Treat on page 42 or the Indian Breakfast Drink on page 42.

- 2 egg whites
- 3 eggs
- ¾ cup skim milk
- ¼ teaspoon salt (optional)
- ¼ teaspoon freshly ground black pepper
- 2 teaspoons butter *or* margarine
- 1 small onion, peeled and thinly sliced
- 2 cups sliced mushrooms
- 3 medium Golden Delicious apples, peeled, cored, and thinly sliced
- 3 ounces shredded Cheddar (¾ cup)
- 2 tablespoons minced Italian parsley for garnish

1. Preheat the oven to 400° F. Wrap the handle of a large nonstick skillet with aluminum foil (unless the skillet has a metal or ovenproof handle).
2. In a small bowl, beat together the egg whites, whole eggs, milk, salt (if desired), and pepper. Set the bowl aside.
3. In the skillet, melt the butter or margarine over medium heat. Add the onion, mushrooms, and apples, and sauté them for 3 to 5 minutes or until they are tender-crisp. Spread them out evenly in the skillet, and sprinkle them with the cheese.
4. Reduce the heat to medium-low, stir the reserved egg mixture, and add it to the skillet, tilting the pan or using a spatula so that the eggs run under the apple mixture. Cook the omelet until it is nearly set and its bottom is lightly browned.
5. Place the skillet in the hot oven, and bake the omelet for 5 minutes or until it sets on top. Cut the omelet into quarters, and serve the portions garnished with the parsley.

ZUCCHINI-CORN SOUFFLÉ

6 servings

This is a lovely luncheon or brunch dish that even children enjoy. It is not spicy and has no "disagreeable" or hard-to-chew pieces. I based my recipe on one devised by the New Jersey Department of Agriculture.

Serving suggestion: Serve the soufflé with rolls such as the Herbed Whole Wheat Rolls on page 425.

> 1 cup corn kernels (fresh or frozen)
> 2 cups (1 pound) grated zucchini
> ½ cup finely chopped sweet red pepper
> 2 teaspoons plus 2 tablespoons butter *or* margarine, divided
> ¼ cup finely chopped scallions
> 3 tablespoons all-purpose flour
> ½ teaspoon salt (optional)
> ¼ teaspoon freshly grated nutmeg
> ⅛ teaspoon freshly ground black pepper
> 1 cup skim or low-fat milk
> 2 egg yolks, lightly beaten
> ½ cup (2 ounces) shredded Swiss cheese
> Vegetable-oil spray
> Flour for dusting soufflé dish
> 6 egg whites
> ½ teaspoon cream of tartar

1. In a medium-sized skillet, sauté the corn, zucchini, and sweet red pepper in the 2 teaspoons of butter or margarine for 5 minutes. Add the scallions, and set the skillet aside.
2. In a large saucepan, heat the remaining 2 tablespoons of butter or margarine. Whisk in the flour, salt (if desired), nutmeg, and pepper, and cook the ingredients, stirring them, for 1 minute. Gradually whisk in the milk, and cook the mixture, stirring it, over medium-low heat until the mixture thickens. Cook the mixture 1 minute longer, and remove the pan from the heat.
3. Slowly add the egg yolks to the hot milk mixture, stirring the mixture constantly. Then add the corn mixture, and stir in the cheese. Set the pan aside.
4. Preheat the oven to 350° F. Fit a 2-quart soufflé dish or casserole with a foil collar that rises 2 inches above the top of the dish. Spray the dish and collar with the vegetable oil, and dust them with the flour.
5. With a mixer, beat the egg whites on high speed until they are foamy. Add the cream of tartar, and continue beating the egg whites until they form stiff peaks. Blend ⅓ of the beaten egg whites into the corn mixture. Then care-

fully fold in the remaining ⅔ of the egg whites just until the white streaks disappear. *Do not overblend the mixture.*

6. Pour the mixture into the prepared soufflé dish or casserole, put the dish into the hot oven, and bake the soufflé for 50 to 60 minutes or until it is puffy and golden brown on top. Serve the soufflé immediately.

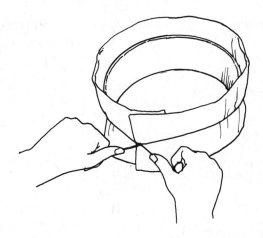

ASPARAGUS SOUFFLÉ

4 servings

Lovely to look at and a delight to devour, this soufflé, based on a recipe from Janet Ballantyne, author of the *Joy of Gardening Cookbook,* is surrounded by a fence of asparagus tips that cook while the soufflé bakes. It's a great dish to make in the spring, when asparagus are plentiful and inexpensive.

Serving suggestion: Dilled Bran Muffin Rolls on page 431 would go well with this soufflé.

    2 pounds asparagus
Vegetable-oil spray
    1 tablespoon butter *or* margarine
    1 tablespoon canola oil
    3 tablespoons snipped fresh chives
    3 tablespoons flour
    1 cup skim or low-fat milk
    1 egg yolk, lightly beaten
    ½ teaspoon salt (optional)
Freshly ground black pepper to taste
    3 egg whites
    ½ teaspoon cream of tartar

1. Cut the asparagus tips into lengths equal to the depth of a 1-quart soufflé dish plus ½ inch. If there are not enough tips to completely line the dish, cut some of the remaining stems to the same length. Remove the asparagus pieces from the dish, and set them aside.
2. Dice enough of the remaining asparagus to make 1 cup of pieces. Steam the pieces for 5 minutes, and purée them in a food mill or food processor. Set the asparagus purée aside.
3. Preheat the oven to 350° F. Spray the soufflé dish with vegetable oil.
4. In a large saucepan, heat the butter or margarine and the oil, add the chives, and sauté the chives for 1 minute. Stir in the flour, and cook the mixture, stirring it, for 1 minute. Gradually add the milk, stirring the mixture constantly to form a smooth liquid. When the mixture thickens slightly, stir in the reserved *puréed* asparagus, egg yolk, salt (if desired), and pepper.
5. In a mixing bowl, beat the egg whites on high speed until they are foamy. Add the cream of tartar, and continue beating the egg whites until they form stiff peaks. Blend ⅓ of the beaten egg whites into the asparagus mixture. Then carefully fold in the remaining ⅔ of the egg whites just until the white streaks disappear. *Do not overmix the soufflé.*
6. Pour the mixture into the prepared soufflé dish. Stand the reserved asparagus spears, tips pointing up, around the edge of the dish to form a fence. Put the soufflé in the hot oven, and bake it for 40 minutes or until its top is puffy and golden brown. Serve the soufflé immediately.

TRIPLE CORN PUDDING

6 servings

The cornier the better may not be an apt adage for comedians, but it sure works for corn pudding. This one has three corn sources: grits, meal, and kernels. The resulting dish is lovely for brunch, lunch, or a light supper.

Preparation tip: The pudding can be prepared through step 4, refrigerated, and baked 1½ hours before serving time.

Serving suggestion: Serve the pudding with sliced tomatoes and a salad such as the Three-Pepper Salad on page 373.

  2 cups water
½ cup hominy grits
Salt to taste, divided (optional)
  1 tablespoon butter *or* margarine
  1 17-ounce can cream-style corn
½ cup yellow corn meal (preferably stone-ground)
  2 egg whites *and* 2 eggs, lightly beaten
¼ cup skim or low-fat milk
  4 ounces Monterey Jack, grated (1 cup)
  1 4-ounce can green chilies, drained and minced
Several dashes cayenne, to taste

1. In a medium-sized saucepan, bring the water to a boil, and gradually add the grits, stirring them constantly, and salt (if desired). Reduce the heat, cover the pan, and simmer the grits, stirring them occasionally, for 25 minutes or until all the water has been absorbed.
2. Stir in the butter or margarine, cover the pan, and let the grits stand for 10 minutes.
3. Preheat the oven to 350° F.
4. Transfer the grits to a large bowl, and stir in the cream-style corn, corn meal, beaten egg whites and whole eggs, milk, cheese, chilies, cayenne, and additional salt (if desired). Transfer the mixture to a greased 1½-quart casserole.
5. Place the casserole in the hot oven, and bake the pudding for 1¼ hours or until a knife or skewer inserted in the center of the pudding comes out clean. Let the pudding stand for 10 minutes before serving it.

SIDE DISHES

Vegetables and Grains

I wish my mother were alive to hear me say this: I *love* vegetables. All kinds and colors of vegetables. Even vegetables that I thought I disliked only a few years ago. Now I can't think of one vegetable I wouldn't enjoy (except, perhaps, those I have yet to taste). Vegetables allow a cook to prepare nutritious and creative meals that stimulate both the eye and the palate. Most vegetables are simple to cook and lend themselves to health- and calorie-conscious dining. Grains and starchy vegetables like potatoes add stick-to-the-ribs substance to meals but little or no fat and absolutely no cholesterol. And all vegetables and grains provide much-needed gut-stimulating fiber. After sampling some of the recipes that follow, you may find yourself wondering why you don't simply serve "just vegetables" for dinner.

SAVORY APPLESAUCE

3 cups (about 8 servings)

If I hadn't already been an ardent fan of *Gourmet* magazine, this recipe would have made me a friend for life. Every taster begged for the recipe, which turns applesauce into a "vegetable" side dish. I reduced the fat and salt, which I found unnecessary—the latter especially if canned broth is used.

Preparation tips: The sauce can be made ahead and even put up in sealed canning jars or frozen. Although the original recipe calls for McIntosh apples, which give the dish more color, I like it better with Golden Delicious.

Serving suggestion: Try the applesauce with meat and poultry dishes, sandwiches, or potato pancakes.

   5 large cloves garlic, peeled and left whole
   6 McIntosh apples *or* Golden Delicious apples,
      unpeeled, cored and cut into eighths
½ cup chicken broth
   2 tablespoons white-wine vinegar
   1 red onion, peeled and chopped
   1 teaspoon butter *or* margarine

1. In a large saucepan, combine the garlic, apples, broth, and vinegar. Bring the ingredients to a boil, reduce the heat, cover the pan, and simmer the mixture, stirring it occasionally, for 15 to 18 minutes or until the apples are tender.
2. Meanwhile, in a small skillet, preferably one with a nonstick surface, cook the onion in the butter or margarine over medium-low heat, stirring the onion, until it is very soft. Add the onion to the apple mixture.
3. Process the apple mixture in a food mill (*not* a food processor), and serve the purée at room temperature.

GARLIC GREEN BEANS

4 to 6 servings

My notes on this say simply, "Easy. Great!"

Preparation tips: These can be made ahead and served at room temperature or heated very briefly in a microwave at serving time. Parboiling the garlic reduces its sharpness and sweetens it. You can, if you prefer a more pungent garlic flavor, skip that step and instead mince the raw cloves.

        1 pound green beans, ends trimmed
    Boiling water (1 inch deep)
        1 cup water
        2 cloves garlic, *unpeeled*
        1 tablespoon red-wine vinegar
        1 tablespoon walnut oil *or* olive oil
      ⅛ teaspoon salt (optional)
      ⅛ teaspoon freshly ground black pepper

1. Place the beans on a steamer rack over the boiling water, cover the pot, and steam the beans for 5 to 7 minutes or until the beans are tender-crisp. Rinse the beans briefly under cold water to preserve their color, but do not chill them. Cover the beans to keep them warm.
2. While the beans steam, in a small saucepan, bring the 1 cup of water to a boil, add the garlic, and simmer the garlic for 5 minutes. Drain, peel, and mince the garlic.
3. In a large bowl, combine the garlic with the remaining ingredients. Add the warm green beans, and toss the green beans in the dressing until they are well coated. If desired, heat the beans in a microwave before serving them.

DRY SAUTÉED GREEN BEANS

4 to 6 servings

When served in a Chinese restaurant, this dish is nearly always loaded with oil. At home, however, you can make it just as tasty while reducing the fat—especially if you use a wok.

Preparation tip: The beans are supposed to be tender-crisp and shriveled or even charred a bit on the outside. If you like tenderer beans, cover the pan after adding the sesame oil and salt, and continue cooking the beans for a few minutes over moderately low heat.

        5 teaspoons peanut oil *or* canola oil
        1 clove garlic, peeled and finely minced
        1 teaspoon finely minced gingerroot
        1 pound green beans, trimmed and cut into 2-inch lengths
        1 teaspoon Oriental sesame oil
      ½ teaspoon salt (optional)

1. Heat the oil in a wok or skillet. Add the garlic and ginger, and stir-fry the ingredients for 30 seconds.
2. Add the green beans, and stir-fry them over high heat for 2 to 4 minutes.
3. Add the sesame oil and salt (if desired), toss the ingredients to coat them, and serve the beans.

"REFRIED" BEANS

6 to 8 servings

The word "refried" is in quotes because I don't really fry them in the traditional way. The recipe is nearly fat-free, save for the oil that is naturally in the beans. Rather than from bacon fat, the beans get their smoky flavor from bits of Canadian bacon, which is very lean. Still, the refried-bean aficionados among my tasters said, "Best I ever had." When asked for improvements, one suggested, "Offer a takeout service."

Preparation tip: This dish can be made ahead and reheated in the oven or microwave at serving time.

1 pound dried pinto beans, picked over, rinsed,
   and soaked 10 hours or longer in water to cover
   by at least 4 inches
Water to cover by 2 inches
2 large cloves garlic, peeled, divided
1 medium onion, peeled
1 teaspoon salt, divided
2 teaspoons olive oil *or* canola oil
½ cup minced onion (1 small)
2 tablespoons minced Canadian bacon
2 dashes hot pepper sauce *or* cayenne, or to taste

1. Drain the beans, rinse them, and place them in a large saucepan with water to cover by at least 2 inches. Add 1 of the garlic cloves and the peeled onion. Bring the liquid to a boil, reduce the heat, partially cover the pan, and simmer the beans for 40 minutes. Add ½ teaspoon of the salt, and cook the beans 20 minutes longer or until the beans are tender. Drain the beans, *reserving the cooking liquid.* Discard the garlic and onion.
2. Transfer the beans to a bowl with a flat bottom, and mash them lightly, leaving lots of whole or partially mashed beans.
3. Mince the remaining clove of garlic. In a small skillet, heat the oil briefly, add the minced garlic, minced onion, and Canadian bacon, and sauté the ingredients for several minutes or until the onion turns golden. Add the onion mixture to the beans along with the hot pepper sauce or cayenne and the remaining ½ teaspoon of the salt. Stir the mixture to combine the ingredients well.

BLACK-EYED PEAS ITALIAN STYLE   *6 to 8 servings*

Delicious and versatile.

Preparation tip: If Italian-seasoned tomato paste is not available, add ½ teaspoon of oregano, ½ teaspoon of basil, and 1 to 2 dashes of cayenne or hot pepper sauce to the recipe.

Serving suggestions: Serve the black-eyed peas as a side dish with chicken or fish, or as part of a vegetarian platter with rice or pasta and a green vegetable.

   1 pound dried black-eyed peas, picked over,
      rinsed, soaked 10 hours or longer in water to
      cover by at least 4 inches, and drained
Water to cover
 ¼ pound Canadian bacon, chopped
   2 medium onions, peeled and chopped (about 1⅓ cups)
   2 ribs celery, chopped
   1 bay leaf
   2 large cloves garlic, peeled and minced
   1 dried hot red pepper *or* fresh hot red pepper
   1 6-ounce can tomato paste, preferably
      Italian-seasoned
 ½ teaspoon salt (optional)
 ¼ teaspoon freshly ground black pepper

Place the peas in a large saucepan with water to cover. Add the remaining ingredients. Bring the ingredients to a boil, reduce the heat to low, cover the pan, and simmer the mixture for 1 hour or until the peas are tender. Adjust the seasonings, and remove the red pepper before serving the peas.

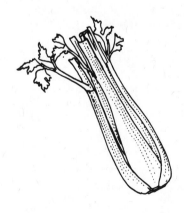

LIMA BEANS *ILLIRIA*

6 to 8 servings

Once again, Chef Stamatis Efstratiou of the Greek ship *Illiria* offers a bean recipe I adore. I have enjoyed this version of plaki at home for lunch topped with a slice of muenster and heated in the microwave, toaster oven, or a covered skillet.

Preparation tip: Steps 3 and 4 can be skipped if you are serving the beans immediately after preparing them. However, the baking does meld the flavors.

1 pound dried large lima beans, picked over,
    rinsed, and soaked 10 hours or longer in water
    to cover by at least 4 inches
Water to cover
½ teaspoon salt
2 tablespoons olive oil
1 large onion, peeled, halved lengthwise, then
    thinly sliced crosswise
2 cups thinly sliced carrots
1 cup thinly sliced celery
1 16-ounce can tomatoes, drained, with their
    juice reserved, and chopped
Salt to taste (optional)
Freshly ground black pepper to taste
⅓ cup minced fresh parsley

1. Drain the beans, rinse them, and place them in a large saucepan with water to cover by 2 inches. Bring the water to a boil, reduce the heat, cover the pan, and cook the beans for 1¼ hours or until they are almost done. Add the ½ teaspoon salt, and continue cooking the beans until they are very tender. Drain the beans, and put them back in the pan.
2. While the beans cook, in a large skillet, heat the oil, add the onion, and sauté the onion for a few minutes. Add the carrots, celery, and tomatoes with their juice, and cook the vegetables until they are tender-crisp. Add the vegetables to the beans along with additional salt (if desired), the pepper, and parsley.
3. Preheat the oven to 350° F.
4. Transfer the bean mixture to a casserole, cover the casserole, put the casserole in the hot oven, and bake the beans for 15 to 20 minutes.

BROCCOLI RABE

4 servings

This nutritious and good-tasting Italian green vegetable (called brocoletti di rape in its native land) is not used nearly enough in this country. If you've never seen it, it looks like a poorly developed head of broccoli—more leaves and stems than flowerets. With broccoli rabe, all green parts of the plant—leaves, tender stalks, and flowers—are eaten. It makes a lovely topping for pasta as well as a nice side dish for almost any entrée. Ed Giobbi, a fine Italian cook, suggests this combination of ingredients and preparation technique.

Preparation tip: In step 2, the broccoli rabe can be steamed for 4 minutes instead of parboiled, and, in step 3, you can use ⅓ cup of the steaming liquid.

1½ pounds broccoli rabe
Water to cover
Salt to taste (optional)
  1 tablespoon olive oil
  1 large clove garlic, peeled and minced
¼ to ½ teaspoon red pepper flakes, to taste
  1 teaspoon anchovy paste *or* 1 anchovy, finely minced

1. Peel or cut off and discard any tough stems from the broccoli rabe.
2. In a large pot, boil enough water to cover the vegetable when it is added. Add salt to taste (if desired). Add the broccoli rabe, and cook the vegetable for 1 minute. Drain the broccoli rabe, reserving ⅓ cup of the cooking water.
3. In a large skillet, preferably one with a nonstick surface, heat the oil briefly, and stir in the garlic. Within 30 seconds, stir in the red pepper flakes, anchovy paste or minced anchovy, and the reserved cooking liquid. Immediately add the parboiled broccoli rabe. Cook the ingredients, tossing them continuously, for about 2 minutes.

BROCCOLI AND BABY CORN

4 to 6 servings

Since this dish is as good at room temperature as it is hot, you can make it ahead of time if you are serving something for dinner that requires last-minute preparation. My sons suggest that I say, "The corn is optional."

Preparation tip: You can omit the corn or replace it with 2 cups of carrots thinly sliced on the diagonal or julienned and then steamed for 5 to 7 minutes.

SAUCE

- 2 teaspoons cornstarch
- 1 tablespoon sherry
- 1 teaspoon vegetable oil
- 2 teaspoons minced or grated gingerroot
- 1 large clove garlic, peeled and minced
- 2 scallions (including the green tops), sliced crosswise
- 1 tablespoon oyster sauce
- 2 teaspoons soy sauce *or* 1 tablespoon reduced-sodium soy sauce
- ⅓ cup chicken broth

VEGETABLES

- 2 teaspoons vegetable oil (preferably canola *or* peanut)
- 1 large clove garlic, peeled and minced
- ¼ cup sliced scallions (including the green tops)
- 4 cups broccoli flowerets, steamed for 5 minutes
- 1 cup canned baby corn *or* 2 cups carrot slices or sticks, steamed tender-crisp

1. To prepare the sauce, place the cornstarch in a small bowl, and stir in the sherry until the mixture is smooth. Add the remaining sauce ingredients, stirring the ingredients to combine them well. Set the sauce aside.
2. To prepare the vegetables, in a large skillet, preferably one with a nonstick surface, or in a well-seasoned wok, heat the oil briefly, add the garlic and scallions, and stir-fry the vegetables for 30 seconds. Then add the broccoli and corn or carrots, and stir-fry the vegetables for 1 minute.
3. Stir the reserved sauce, and add it to the vegetables, bring the ingredients to a boil, and cook the vegetables, tossing them continuously, for 1 minute or less. Serve the dish hot or at room temperature.

BRUSSELS SPROUTS AND
TINY ONIONS

6 servings

This recipe, adapted from *Cooking Light* magazine, combines two nutritious, low-calorie vegetables in a flavorful, festive way. I increased the amount of onions and caraway seeds in the original recipe, developed by Elizabeth Schneider, author of *Uncommon Fruits and Vegetables.*

Large pot water
  1 pound tiny (sprout-size) pearl onions, unpeeled
1½ pounds (about 2 pints) Brussels sprouts
  1 cup chicken broth
¼ teaspoon sugar
½ teaspoon dried thyme leaves *or* 1½ teaspoons
    fresh thyme
  1 bay leaf
  1 teaspoon caraway seeds
  1 to 2 teaspoons butter *or* margarine, to taste

1. Bring the water to a boil, and drop in the unpeeled onions. Return the water to a boil, and cook the onions for about 2 minutes. Drain and rinse them under cold water. When they are cool enough to handle, peel them, and place them in a large skillet.
2. Remove any discolored outer leaves from the Brussels sprouts, trim the ends, and cut a shallow "X" on the bottom of each sprout. Add the sprouts to the skillet along with the broth, sugar, thyme, and bay leaf. Bring the liquid to a boil, cover the skillet, reduce the heat, and simmer the mixture for 7 minutes or until the sprouts are tender-crisp.
3. Uncover the pan, raise the heat to medium-high, and cook the mixture for 3 to 5 minutes or until the liquid is nearly evaporated. Discard the bay leaf, stir in the caraway seeds, and cook the vegetables for 1 minute. Remove the pan from the heat, add the butter or margarine, and stir the ingredients so that the vegetables are coated with the butter or margarine.

BULGUR WITH LEMON AND CHIVES

4 servings

I've yet to find a bulgur dish I don't like—as long as the grain does not get mushy. This one gives me a chance to use some of the chives that grow prolifically in my garden.

Preparation tips: Do not skip toasting the bulgur in step 2—it gives the grain texture. Use a medium-ground or coarsely ground bulgur.

1 tablespoon butter *or* margarine
¼ cup thinly sliced scallions (including some
   green tops)
1 cup bulgur
1 tablespoon grated lemon rind
1½ cups chicken broth
¼ cup snipped chives
Salt to taste (optional)
Freshly ground black pepper to taste

1. In a medium-sized saucepan, melt the butter or margarine over medium heat, add the scallions, and sauté the scallions until they soften.
2. Add the bulgur and lemon rind, and cook the ingredients, stirring them, for 1 minute.
3. Add the broth, bring the mixture to a boil, reduce the heat, cover the pan, and simmer the bulgur for 10 minutes or until the liquid is absorbed. Stir in the chives, and season the bulgur with the salt (if desired) and pepper.

COUSCOUS WITH PEPPERS

6 servings

Here is another grain-based side dish that is colorful as well as tasty and simple.

1 tablespoon butter *or* margarine
1 large onion, peeled and finely chopped (1 cup)
2 teaspoons curry powder
⅔ cup finely chopped sweet green pepper
⅔ cup finely chopped sweet red pepper
1 cup chicken broth
1 cup couscous
Salt to taste (optional)
Freshly ground black pepper to taste

1. In a medium-sized saucepan, heat the butter or margarine, add the onion, and sauté the onion over medium-low heat until it is softened.
2. Stir in the curry powder, and cook the ingredients, stirring them, for less than 1 minute. Add the green and red peppers, and stir-fry them for 1 to 2 minutes.
3. Add the broth, and bring it to a boil. Stir in the couscous, cover the pan, and remove the pan from the heat. Let the couscous stand for 5 minutes or until the liquid is absorbed. Season the couscous with the salt (if desired) and ground pepper.

QUICK EGGPLANT CASSEROLE

4 to 6 servings

This is a kissing cousin of ratatouille but easier to prepare and more elegant to serve.

1½ tablespoons olive oil *or* canola oil
  2 cloves garlic, peeled and finely minced
  2 medium onions, peeled and thinly sliced
¾ pound eggplant, peeled and diced
½ pound zucchini, unpeeled and sliced
  1 sweet green pepper, cored, seeded, and
    sliced into rings
  1 teaspoon oregano, crumbled
  1 teaspoon sugar
Salt to taste (optional)
Freshly ground black pepper to taste
  4 medium tomatoes (fresh *or* canned), peeled and
    sliced crosswise

1. Preheat the oven to 375° F.
2. In a large iron or nonstick skillet (with an ovenproof handle) or flameproof casserole, heat the oil, add the garlic, onions, eggplant, zucchini, and green pepper, and sauté the vegetables until they are barely tender.
3. Add the oregano, sugar, salt (if desired), and ground pepper, mixing the ingredients to combine them well. Arrange the tomato slices on top of the mixture, place the skillet or casserole in the hot oven, and bake the casserole for 10 to 15 minutes or until the tomatoes are cooked.

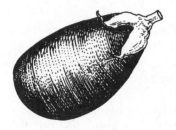

MIDDLE EASTERN RATATOUILLE   *4 servings*

This may seem like a contradiction in terms (at the very least, languages), but the seasonings in this recipe are a wonderful change of pace. You may even prefer it to the French version, as does my dear friend Margaret Shryer of Minneapolis, who gave me the idea.

  1 pound eggplant, unpeeled, cut into 1-inch cubes
Salt for draining the eggplant
  4 teaspoons olive oil
  1 cup chopped onion (1 large)
  1 tablespoon minced garlic (3 large cloves)
  1 large sweet green pepper, cored, seeded, and
     cut into 1-inch pieces
½ pound zucchini, unpeeled, cut into 1-inch cubes
  3 medium tomatoes (about 1¼ pounds), cored
     and cut into 1-inch cubes
½ teaspoon salt (optional)
½ teaspoon ground cumin
½ teaspoon turmeric
¼ teaspoon coriander
Freshly ground black pepper to taste
  2 tablespoons minced fresh parsley

1. Place the eggplant in a colander, and sprinkle the eggplant with the salt, tossing the cubes to coat them with the salt. Weight the eggplant with a plate or bowl, and let the eggplant stand for 30 minutes to drain. Rinse the eggplant, drain it, and pat it dry with paper towels. Set the eggplant aside.

2. In a deep skillet or Dutch oven, preferably one with a nonstick surface, heat the oil, add the onion and garlic, and sauté the vegetables until the onion is translucent. Add the reserved eggplant and the green pepper, and sauté the mixture, stirring it often, for about 10 minutes. Add the zucchini, tomatoes, salt (if desired), cumin, turmeric, coriander, ground pepper, and parsley, and cook the ratatouille, stirring it, for 5 minutes or until the zucchini is tender.

FENNEL AND MUSHROOMS

6 to 8 servings

This wonderful side dish was devised by a Brooklyn friend, Beatrice Jacoby, who has never put anything but a great meal on the table. My tasters begged for the recipe. Fennel (called anise in some markets) is an anise-flavored herb, the bulb of which is delicious cooked or raw. It has long been used in Mediterranean cooking and is now reaching a widening market in the United States.

Preparation tip: This recipe can be prepared in advance through the addition of the last ingredients in step 3. Do the final simmer just before serving the dish.

    1 tablespoon olive oil
    1 tablespoon butter *or* margarine
    2 cloves garlic, peeled and sliced
    1 large tomato, peeled, seeded, and chopped
    2 large bulbs fennel (1 or more pounds each),
        cored, trimmed of tops and stems, and thinly
        sliced lengthwise
    1 pound mushrooms, sliced
    ¼ cup hot chicken broth
    ½ teaspoon dried basil *or* ¼ teaspoon thyme
    ½ teaspoon or more salt, to taste (optional)
    ¼ to ½ teaspoon freshly ground black pepper, to taste

1. In a large skillet, preferably one with a nonstick surface, heat the oil and butter or margarine briefly. Add the garlic, and cook it until it browns. Then remove and discard it.
2. Add the tomato and fennel, cover the pan, and simmer the ingredients for 5 minutes, stirring them often, or until the fennel is half-cooked.
3. Add the mushrooms, broth, basil or thyme, salt (if desired), and pepper. Cover the pan, and simmer the mixture 5 to 10 minutes longer or until the vegetables are tender but firm.

BAKED FENNEL

4 servings

This simple dish was devised by Richard Hill, chef at the Grand Hotel in Washington, D.C. My only modification was to halve the butter.

Preparation tip: This make-ahead dish can be reheated at serving time or served at room temperature.

2 medium bulbs fennel (about ¾ pound each),
　　tops trimmed to 1 inch of bulbs
Boiling water to cover
1 tablespoon butter *or* margarine
1 cup chicken broth
4 teaspoons fresh lemon juice
1 teaspoon sugar
Dash salt (optional)
Freshly ground black pepper to taste
1 to 2 tablespoons minced fresh parsley
1 to 2 tablespoons grated Parmesan (optional)

1. Preheat the oven to 350° F.
2. In a large saucepan, plunge the fennel bulbs into the boiling water, and parboil them for 8 to 10 minutes. Drain the fennel bulbs, and cool them. Cut the bulbs lengthwise into quarters.
3. In a large ovenproof skillet or shallow pot, preferably one with a nonstick surface, melt the butter or margarine, and add the fennel. Sauté the fennel for a few minutes, then add the broth, lemon juice, sugar, salt (if desired), and pepper.
4. Place the pot in the hot oven, and bake the fennel for 20 minutes. Remove the fennel from the oven, cool the fennel down, and chill it until 1 hour before serving it.
5. Reheat the fennel at serving time, or serve the fennel at room temperature topped with the parsley and sprinkled with the Parmesan (if desired).

MEDITERRANEAN MUSHROOMS

6 servings

These are good warm or cold, as a vegetable side dish, hors d'oeuvre, or "salad." The original recipe, of Spanish derivation, was devised by Martha Rose Shulman for her excellent cookbook *Mediterranean Light.*

1 tablespoon olive oil
1 to 2 shallots, peeled and minced, *or*
   2 tablespoons minced onion
4 to 6 cloves garlic, peeled and minced, divided
2 pounds mushrooms, halved or, if large, quartered
1 cup dry white wine
½ teaspoon thyme
½ teaspoon rosemary
Salt to taste (optional)
Freshly ground black pepper to taste
½ cup chopped fresh parsley, divided

1. In a large, heavy skillet, preferably one with a nonstick surface, heat the oil over medium-low heat, and add the shallots or onion and ½ of the garlic. Sauté the vegetables, stirring them, until the shallots or onion are tender.
2. Add the mushrooms and the remaining garlic, and sauté the mixture over medium-high heat until the mushrooms start to release their liquid.
3. Add the wine, thyme, rosemary, salt (if desired), pepper, and ½ of the parsley. Cook the mixture, stirring it often, over medium heat for 20 minutes or until the mushrooms are tender. Adjust the seasonings, and sprinkle the mushrooms with the remaining parsley before serving the dish.

OKRA WITH ONIONS AND APRICOTS   *6 servings*

Okra's nutritional virtues are finally moving this underappreciated vegetable into the limelight. Rich in calcium and cholesterol-lowering soluble fiber, it is also very low in calories. I am grateful to the late Bert Greene, author of *Greene on Greens,* for this interesting and tasty Armenian recipe.

Preparation tips: To prevent the okra from becoming gummy, trim the stems not quite down to the flesh, and do not stir the vegetable while cooking it. The apricots are easiest to slice if they are first chilled or partially frozen. The dish can be prepared in advance and reheated at serving time.

    1 tablespoon butter *or* margarine
    1 large onion, peeled, quartered, and sliced
 1½ cups beef broth
  ¼ cup tomato paste
  ¼ cup fresh lemon juice
  ½ teaspoon ground allspice
    1 pound okra, stems trimmed not quite down to
       the flesh
  ¼ pound (about 16) dried apricots, halved crosswise
Salt to taste (optional)
Freshly ground black pepper to taste
    2 tablespoons chopped fresh parsley

1. In a large saucepan, melt the butter or margarine, add the onion, and sauté the onion for about 4 minutes.
2. Add the broth, tomato paste, lemon juice, and allspice, and mix the ingredients well. Stir in the okra, and top the mixture with the halved apricots.
3. Bring the mixture to a boil, reduce the heat to a simmer, cover the pan, and cook the okra for about 40 minutes.
4. Sprinkle the okra with the salt (if desired) and pepper. Add the parsley just before serving the dish.

PEARLS AND RUBIES

(Onions and Cranberries)   *6 to 8 servings*

This attractive and unusual dish will enhance your winter holiday table without adding many calories to the meal.

Preparation tips: The dish should be baked just before serving it. It will look and taste best if it is prepared for baking not more than 8 hours ahead of time. If you use an ovenproof skillet, it will save washing another pan.

1½ pounds pearl onions
Boiling water to cover
  1 tablespoon butter *or* margarine
  ¼ cup sugar
  ¼ teaspoon salt (optional)
  ¼ teaspoon freshly ground black pepper
  1 cup cranberries
  ½ cup chicken broth

1. Drop the onions into a pot of boiling water for about 2 minutes. Drain and rinse the onions under cold water. When they are cool enough to handle, slice off the root ends of the onions, and slip off their outer skins.
2. Preheat the oven to 400° F.
3. Heat the butter or margarine in a large skillet, preferably one with a non-stick surface, add the onions, and cook them in a single layer until they are lightly browned, turning them occasionally to prevent sticking and to brown them evenly.
4. Sprinkle in the sugar, salt (if desired), and pepper, and add the cranberries, tossing the ingredients to combine them. Add the broth.
5. Transfer the mixture to a glass or ceramic baking dish, place the dish in the hot oven, and bake the onions and cranberries in the *uncovered* dish for about 30 minutes.

TIBETAN POTATO CURRY

6 servings

This unusual and easy-to-prepare dish is tasty without being really "hot" (at least not by my relatively tame standards). It is flavored by fenugreek seeds, used to produce artificial maple flavoring and frequently found in Middle Eastern and Indian cooking.

Preparation tip: The dish can be prepared in advance and served at room temperature. If fenugreek is unavailable, don't worry—the curry is still tasty without it.

  4 pounds boiling potatoes, *unpeeled* and cooked
     until just tender
½ cup chopped tomato
  1 teaspoon hot chili powder
  2 large cloves garlic, peeled and minced
½ teaspoon minced gingerroot
¼ teaspoon turmeric
¾ teaspoon salt, or to taste (optional)
  1 medium shallot *or* ¼ medium onion, peeled
     and chopped
  1 tablespoon olive oil
½ teaspoon fenugreek seeds
½ cup thinly sliced sweet green pepper for garnish

1. When the potatoes are cool enough to handle, peel them, and cut them into ½-inch dice. Transfer the potatoes to a serving bowl.
2. In a blender, combine the tomato, chili powder, garlic, gingerroot, turmeric, salt (if desired), and shallot or onion, and process the ingredients until the mixture is nearly smooth.
3. In a small skillet, heat the oil, and brown the fenugreek seeds. Add them to the blender mixture, and pour the mixture over the potatoes, tossing the ingredients gently to coat the potatoes evenly. Serve the curry garnished with the green pepper.

POTATO PUDDING

8 to 10 servings

Potato pudding—or *kugel* as it is called in Yiddish—is another traditional holiday dish that I modified to simplify preparation and to reduce its nutritionally questionable ingredients without sacrificing its special flavor and texture. As prepared below, it is kosher for Passover.

Preparation tips: If you have no food processor, the ingredients can be grated by hand. But the machine is decidedly faster and saves fingertips. The potatoes will start to darken right after shredding. But don't worry—it won't affect the final product as long as you don't let them sit around raw for too long. Since I like a thin, crisp pudding, I often bake it in a cookie pan.

3½ pounds potatoes, peeled
  2 large carrots, peeled
  1 large onion, peeled
  2 egg whites
  1 egg
  2 tablespoons vegetable oil (preferably canola)
  5 tablespoons potato starch *or* ½ cup matzo meal
1½ teaspoons salt (*not optional*)
¼ to ½ teaspoon freshly ground black pepper
¼ teaspoon cinnamon

1. Grate by hand or shred with the fine shredder of a food processor the potatoes, carrots, and onion. Combine the vegetables in a large bowl.
2. Preheat the oven to 400° F.
3. In a small bowl, whisk the egg whites and whole egg until they are fluffy, and add them with the remaining ingredients to the potato mixture. Stir the ingredients to combine them well. Pour the mixture into an oiled shallow pan that holds about 1½ quarts (test its capacity first with water).
4. Place the pan in the hot oven, and bake the pudding for 1 hour or until the top of the pudding is crisp and brown.

VEGETABLE TZIMMES

6 to 8 servings

As a traditional hearty winter holiday dish, tzimmes is a nostalgic favorite among many Jews of all ages. The word *tzimmes,* which in Yiddish means "a big deal" or "fuss," belies the simplicity of the basic recipe.

  1 pound carrots, peeled and cut into 1-inch pieces
Water to cover
  6 sweet potatoes, peeled and cut into 1-inch pieces
½ cup pitted prunes
Vegetable-oil spray
  1 cup orange juice
½ cup honey
½ teaspoon salt (optional)
½ teaspoon cinnamon
  1 tablespoon margarine *or* vegetable oil

1. Put the carrots in a large pot with water to cover, bring the water to a boil, and cook the carrots over medium heat for 5 minutes. Add the potatoes, and cook the vegetables 10 minutes longer or until the vegetables are tender but firm.
2. Drain the cooked vegetables, and transfer them, along with the prunes, to a baking dish lined with foil that has been sprayed with vegetable oil.
3. Preheat the oven to 350° F.
4. In a measuring cup or bowl, combine the orange juice, honey, salt (if desired), and cinnamon, and pour the mixture over the vegetables. Dot the vegetables with the margarine, or drizzle them with the oil. Cover the tzimmes with foil, place it in the hot oven, and bake it for 30 minutes. Uncover the tzimmes, stir it gently, and bake it 10 minutes longer.

SWEET POTATO SPECIAL

10 servings

Even my sons, who have never liked sweet potatoes, went for this. It can be made without any added fat, sugar, or salt.

Preparation tips: This can be prepared two days ahead for baking (through step 4). Cover the dish and refrigerate it, but bring it to room temperature before baking it. Although canned pineapple can be used, the flavor is not as good as when fresh fruit is used.

  5 pounds sweet potatoes
Water to cover
  1 12-ounce package pitted prunes
  1 cup water
  2 cups (½ large) fresh pineapple, slivered
¼ cup dark brown sugar (optional)
  1 tablespoon butter *or* margarine (optional)

1. Cook the potatoes, whole and *unpeeled,* in water to cover until they are very soft. Drain the potatoes, pierce them one at a time with a fork, peel them, place them in a large bowl, and mash them.
2. Preheat the oven to 350° F.
3. In a small saucepan, cook the prunes in the 1 cup of water for 5 minutes. Add the prunes, their cooking liquid, and the pineapple to the potatoes, mixing the ingredients to combine them well.
4. Place the potato mixture in a large ovenproof casserole. Sprinkle the potatoes with brown sugar (if desired), and dot the top with the butter or margarine (if you wish).
5. Place the uncovered casserole in the hot oven, and bake the potatoes for 20 minutes or until the potatoes are heated through.

BRAISED PUMPKIN

4 servings

Here's yet another role for the versatile pumpkin, a vegetable rich in the vitamin A precursor and cancer-fighting nutrient beta-carotene.

½ cup chicken broth
 1 teaspoon reduced-sodium soy sauce
 1 teaspoon sugar
 1 tablespoon vegetable oil (preferably peanut *or* canola)
 2 cups peeled, seeded, and coarsely shredded pumpkin
 1 scallion, minced, *or* 1 teaspoon minced onion
Salt to taste (optional)
Freshly ground black pepper *or* white pepper to taste

1. In a small bowl, combine the broth, soy sauce, and sugar. Set the bowl aside.
2. Heat a wok or nonstick skillet over medium-high heat for 30 seconds. Add the oil, and heat the pan for another 30 seconds. Add the pumpkin and scallion or onion, and stir-fry the vegetables for 3 minutes.
3. Reduce the heat to low, add the reserved broth mixture, and mix the ingredients well. Cover the pan, and simmer the pumpkin for 8 to 10 minutes. Season the pumpkin with the salt (if desired) and pepper.

STUFFED MINI-PUMPKINS

6 servings

I must admit that until *Cooking Light* magazine offered a recipe for vegetable-filled mini-pumpkins in its Thanksgiving 1989 issue, I thought these pumpkins, called Jack-Be-Littles, were simply decorative, not edible. They are not only sweet, but attractive when hollowed out, stuffed, and topped with their caps. I tried an adaptation of the magazine's already low-fat recipe, using fresh peppers and more seasonings. Then I experimented with other fillings and flavorings, such as a curried combination of onion, zucchini, mushrooms, peppers, and peas, all with similar success.

Preparation tips: The pumpkins should be baked in advance and allowed to cool before stuffing them. They can also be prepared ahead through step 4 and refrigerated until 1 hour before reheating (steps 5 and 6).

   6 miniature (about 8 ounces each) pumpkins
   1 teaspoon olive oil *or* vegetable-oil spray
   ½ cup finely chopped onion
   ½ cup finely diced green pepper
   1 fresh seeded jalapeño *or* 3 tablespoons canned
      green chilies, minced
   1½ cups green beans, steamed tender-crisp and cut
      into ¾-inch lengths
   1½ cups corn kernels
   1 teaspoon chili powder
   ½ teaspoon cumin
   ¼ teaspoon sugar
Salt to taste (optional)
   ⅛ teaspoon or more freshly ground black pepper,
      to taste

1. Preheat the oven to 375° F.
2. Make two 1-inch-long slits on either side of the stem of each pumpkin to allow steam to escape. Place the pumpkins in one layer in a shallow baking dish, put the dish in the hot oven, and bake the pumpkins for 50 minutes or until the pumpkins are tender but not mushy. Remove the dish from the oven, and let the pumpkins cool.
3. Meanwhile, prepare the filling. Oil a large nonstick skillet, and heat it over medium-high heat. Add the onion, green pepper, and jalapeño or chilies, and sauté the vegetables, stirring them often, for about 3 minutes. Add the remaining ingredients, stirring them to combine them well. Cover the pan, reduce the heat to low, and simmer the mixture for about 5 minutes.
4. When the pumpkins are cool enough to handle, cut a circle about 1½ inches in diameter around the stem of each pumpkin, and remove the lid. With a small spoon (a grapefruit spoon is ideal), remove the seeds and strings from

the center of each pumpkin and from the lid, leaving the flesh intact. Spoon the vegetable filling into the pumpkins, and cover the pumpkins with their lids. Return the pumpkins to the baking dish, and cover the dish with foil.

5. Preheat the oven to 375° F.
6. Place the pumpkins, still covered, in the hot oven, and bake them for 15 minutes or until they are heated through.

INDIAN RICE WITH PEAS AND PEPPERS *8 servings*

Basmati rice, when cooked, gives off an aroma even more delicious than it tastes—which is pretty good. It is available as white or brown rice. Though traditionally from India, it is now being grown in the southern United States. If you buy it at a health-food store that sells it in bulk, you'll pay about a third of the cost of the commercially packaged varieties sold in specialty-food stores.

Preparation tips: You can control the "hotness" of the dish by varying the kinds of curry used. I use ½ teaspoon of hot curry powder for every 1 teaspoon of mild. The dish can be prepared in advance through step 2 and completed in a microwave with the peas and peppers.

```
  1  teaspoon olive oil
  1  teaspoon butter or margarine
  2  cloves garlic, peeled and minced
  1  medium onion, peeled and finely chopped (⅔ cup)
1½  teaspoons curry powder
  4  cups water
  ¾  teaspoon salt (optional)
  2  cups basmati brown rice
  1  cup cooked green peas (if you use frozen peas,
       thaw them)
  1  cup diced sweet red pepper
```

1. In a large saucepan or Dutch oven, heat the oil and butter or margarine briefly, add the garlic and onion, and sauté the vegetables for a few minutes.
2. Stir in the curry powder, and sauté the vegetables 1 minute longer. Then add the water and salt (if desired), and bring the ingredients to a boil. Stir in the rice, reduce the heat to low, cover the pan, and simmer the rice for 40 minutes or until the water is almost completely absorbed.
3. Add the peas and red pepper, and cook the rice 5 minutes longer.

RICE AND BULGUR PILAF

8 side-dish or
4 main-course servings

This can be used as a main dish or side dish. Either way, it's delicious and refreshing. It's also nice for a buffet.

```
  1 tablespoon butter or margarine
 ½ cup finely chopped onion (1 small)
  1 cup uncooked brown rice or white rice
 ½ cup uncooked bulgur
2¼ cups chicken broth
 ¼ cup dried currants
 ½ teaspoon allspice
Freshly ground black pepper to taste
Salt to taste (optional)
  2 cups plain nonfat or low-fat yogurt
 ½ cup pine nuts or almond halves, lightly toasted
```

1. In a heavy saucepan, melt the butter or margarine, and add the onion, sautéing it until it is translucent.
2. Add the rice and bulgur, stirring them to coat them with the butter or margarine. Then add the broth, currants, allspice, pepper, and salt (if desired). Stir the ingredients to combine them well, bring the mixture to a boil, reduce the heat, cover the pan, and cook the grains for 20 minutes (25 to 35 minutes, if you use brown rice) or until the broth is absorbed.
3. Serve each portion topped with a generous dollop of the yogurt (½ cup for a main dish) and 2 tablespoons of the nuts.

WILD RICE WITH ALMONDS

4 to 6 servings

Although wild rice is traditionally eaten as a vegetable or stuffing ingredient (few could afford to do otherwise!), I enjoy making this "stir-fry" combination the centerpiece of a lunch or light supper. The nuts and rice create a complete protein, and the vegetables do the rest.

Preparation tip: The snow peas, mushrooms, water chestnuts, and almonds can be prepared while the rice cooks.

  2 teaspoons butter *or* margarine
  4 scallions, white parts minced, green stems cut
      diagonally into 1-inch pieces
  1 cup wild rice, rinsed several times and drained
  2 cups (approximately) chicken broth
Salt to taste, divided (optional)
  1 tablespoon peanut oil *or* canola oil
  ½ pound snow peas *or* sugar snap peas, trimmed
  8 large mushrooms, sliced
  1 6-ounce can water chestnuts, drained and sliced
  ¼ teaspoon freshly ground black pepper
  ½ cup slivered almonds, lightly toasted

1. Heat the butter or margarine in a medium-sized saucepan, add the minced (white part) scallions, and sauté the scallions for a few minutes or until they are tender.
2. Add the rice, broth, and salt (if desired). Bring the mixture to a boil, reduce the heat, cover the pan, and simmer the rice for 35 minutes, checking after 25 minutes to see if more broth is needed.
3. When the rice is nearly done, heat the oil in a wok or large skillet. Add the reserved scallion stems, peas, mushrooms, water chestnuts, pepper, and salt (if desired). Sauté the ingredients for 3 minutes or until the vegetables are hot and the mushrooms tender. Remove the pan from the heat, and toss in the slivered almonds.
4. Combine the cooked rice and the vegetables in a large heatproof serving bowl. Keep the rice warm in the oven until serving time.

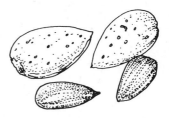

WILD RICE AND PUMPKIN PILAF

6 servings

Carol Atwater of Knoxville sent me this delicious recipe. It has a blend of textures and flavors my tasters really enjoyed. My sole change was to use only wild rice instead of a mixture of wild and brown.

Preparation tips: The recipe can be prepared in advance through step 2 and then cooked in the broth 1 hour before serving. Or it can be completely finished a day ahead and reheated in a microwave or regular oven in a covered casserole.

Serving suggestion: I served this with grilled fish steaks, but it would also go well with poultry.

  1 cup wild rice *or* ¾ cup brown rice and ¼ cup wild rice
  2 tablespoons olive oil
  2 medium onions, peeled and finely chopped (1⅓ cups)
  3 cloves garlic, peeled and minced
  ½ cup chopped sweet green pepper *or* sweet red pepper
  ⅓ pound mushrooms, sliced
2¼ cups chicken broth
1¼ cups (½ pound) peeled, diced pumpkin *or*
    winter squash
  ½ teaspoon savory *or* thyme
  ¼ to ½ teaspoon rosemary, to taste
  1 tablespoon soy sauce
  2 tablespoons dry sherry (optional)
  ¼ cup sliced almonds, lightly toasted

1. In a large ungreased skillet, toast the rice over medium heat, stirring it frequently, for 3 to 5 minutes. Do not let the rice burn. Set the rice aside.
2. In a Dutch oven or large saucepan, heat the olive oil briefly, add the onions, garlic, pepper, and mushrooms, and sauté the vegetables until they are just softened.
3. Add the toasted rice to the vegetable mixture along with the broth, pumpkin or squash, savory or thyme, rosemary, soy sauce, and sherry (if desired). Bring the mixture to a boil, reduce the heat, cover the pan, and simmer the rice for 40 to 60 minutes or until the liquid is absorbed and the rice is tender. Toss the rice with the toasted almonds before serving the pilaf.

NIPPY GREENS

4 to 6 servings

Here is a simple but tasty way to prepare "pedestrian" greens like spinach, Swiss chard, beet greens, or kale, compliments of Martha Rose Shulman, author of *Mediterranean Light,* who learned it at the source—in southern Italy.

Preparation tips: For tender results when using Swiss chard, choose young leaves. While the vegetable is best if it is cooked just before serving, all the ingredients can be pan-readied in advance. Or the dish can be prepared through the addition of the ingredients in step 3 and the cooking finished just before serving. *Be forewarned:* the dish is very "hot" if the full ½ teaspoon of red pepper flakes is used.

Serving suggestion: If the greens are cut into 3-inch pieces before cooking, the vegetable would make a nice topping for pasta.

    2 pounds greens (e.g., spinach or
      Swiss chard), stems removed
    2 teaspoons olive oil
    2 large cloves garlic, peeled and minced
    ¼ cup finely chopped feathery fennel tops (use
      either wild fennel *or* the bulbous fennel)
    ¼ to ½ teaspoon red pepper flakes, to taste
    Salt to taste (optional)
    Freshly ground black pepper to taste
    2 tablespoons lemon juice

1. Thoroughly wash the greens to remove any sand. Do not dry the greens.
2. In a very large nonstick skillet or Dutch oven, heat the oil briefly. Add the garlic, and sauté it over medium-low heat for about 45 seconds. Add the greens, raise the heat to medium-high, cover the pan, and cook the greens for 1 minute or until the greens wilt.
3. Stir in the chopped fennel, red pepper flakes, salt (if desired), and pepper. Cook the greens, stirring them, for about 4 minutes.
4. Remove the pan from the heat, and toss the greens with the lemon juice.

STUFFED PATTYPAN SQUASH

4 servings

Pattypan squash, for those who've never seen it, is a summer squash that looks like a flying saucer, and it makes for a most attractive edible "serving dish."

Preparation tips: These squash can be stuffed and baked in advance and served at room temperature. Or, if you prefer them hot, stuff them ahead and bake them just before serving time. If you must avoid salt, rather than sprinkle the inside of the squash, let them drain for an hour, and wipe them out with a paper towel before stuffing them.

Serving suggestions: The squash can be the main course of a light meal or a side dish with a hearty salad. The baked squash can also be quartered (leaving the pieces together to maintain the original squash shape) and served as hors d'oeuvres or as a buffet offering.

      4 large pattypan squash (about 8 to 10 ounces each)
Salt for sprinkling and seasoning, to taste (optional)
      1 pound fresh spinach *or* Swiss chard (*or* 1 10-ounce
         package of chopped frozen spinach *or* Swiss chard)
      2 teaspoons butter *or* margarine
    ½ cup thinly sliced scallions *or* ⅓ cup finely
         chopped onion
    ⅔ cup light or part-skim ricotta *or* low-fat cottage cheese
    ⅛ teaspoon nutmeg (preferably freshly grated)
    ⅛ teaspoon cayenne, or to taste
Salt to taste (optional)
    ⅛ teaspoon freshly ground black pepper, or to taste
      3 tablespoons grated Parmesan
  1½ tablespoons dried bread crumbs

1. Steam the squash over boiling water for 10 minutes. Rinse them under cold water, and pat them dry. Slice off a broad but thin cap at the stem end of each squash. With a grapefruit spoon or melon baller, scoop out and save the pulp from each squash, leaving a ¼-inch-thick shell. Sprinkle the insides of the squash shells with salt (if desired), and place the squash upside down on a rack to drain for 30 minutes. Chop the reserved pulp, and set it aside.
2. If you are using fresh spinach or chard, place the greens in a saucepan, cover the pan, and steam the washed leaves in the water that clings to them until the greens are just wilted. Drain the greens, squeeze them dry, and chop them. If you are using frozen greens, defrost them, let them drain, and squeeze them dry. Set the greens aside.
3. In a large skillet, heat the butter or margarine briefly, add the scallions or onion, and sauté the vegetable, stirring it, for 1 to 2 minutes or until the

vegetable is soft. Add the reserved squash pulp, and cook the ingredients until the liquid has evaporated. Stir in the reserved spinach or chard, and cook the mixture, stirring it, for another minute. Add the ricotta or cottage cheese, nutmeg, cayenne, salt (if desired), and pepper, and cook the ingredients, stirring them, for 1 minute. Remove the pan from the heat, and stir in the Parmesan.

4. Preheat the oven to 350° F, setting the oven rack in the center of the oven.
5. When the squash shells have finished draining, sprinkle their insides with the bread crumbs. Divide the spinach-cheese stuffing among the shells, and set the squash on a lightly greased baking sheet.
6. Place the baking sheet in the hot oven, and bake the squash for 10 minutes.

STUFFED SUMMER SQUASH WITH TOMATO SAUCE

4 servings

My tasters loved this dish, based on a recipe devised by Elizabeth Riely for *Bon Appétit* magazine. They said it was easily a whole meal if served with pasta such as rotini or shells. The simple-to-prepare sauce is lovely on pasta or rice as well as under the squash.

Preparation tips: The stuffed squash (unbaked) and the sauce can be prepared 1 day ahead and the squash baked 30 minutes before serving time. Any summer squash—zucchini, yellow squash, or pattypan—would work equally well. Choose squash large enough (for example, 4-ounce pattypans or ½-pound zucchinis) to be easily stuffed. This recipe is best made with fresh basil.

SAUCE
- 1 tablespoon olive oil
- ⅓ cup minced onion
- 2 pounds firm, ripe tomatoes (preferably plum tomatoes), peeled, seeded, and finely chopped
- ¼ cup minced fresh basil *or* 1 teaspoon dried basil
- Salt to taste (optional)
- Freshly ground black pepper to taste

VEGETABLE
- 1 pound summer squash, parboiled for about 5 minutes
- 1 tablespoon olive oil
- ¼ cup chopped onion
- 1 large clove garlic, peeled and minced
- ¼ cup (1 ounce) diced Canadian bacon *or* prosciutto
- ¼ cup grated Parmesan
- 3 tablespoons minced fresh basil *or* 1 teaspoon dried basil
- 2 tablespoons fresh bread crumbs
- Freshly ground black pepper to taste

TO PREPARE THE SAUCE

1. In a medium-sized saucepan, heat the oil briefly, add the onion, and sauté the onion for 2 minutes or until it softens.
2. Add the tomatoes, and cook the vegetables, stirring them, for about 5 minutes. Stir in the remaining sauce ingredients. If the sauce is prepared ahead, reheat it before serving the dish.

TO PREPARE THE VEGETABLE

3. When the squash are cool enough to handle, slice them in half lengthwise (if you are using zucchini or yellow squash) or slice off a cap (if you are using pattypans), and, using a grapefruit spoon or melon baller, scoop out and reserve the centers of each squash, leaving a ½-inch-thick shell. Dice the pulp finely.

4. In a medium-sized skillet, preferably one with a nonstick surface, heat the oil briefly. Add the onion and garlic, and sauté them for 2 minutes or until they are just softened.
5. Add the squash pulp, and cook the mixture, stirring it often, until the liquid evaporates. Remove the mixture from the heat, and stir in the remaining ingredients.
6. Divide the stuffing among the squash shells, and place the shells in a baking dish. For advance preparation, cover the dish, and chill the shells until 1 hour before proceeding with the recipe.
7. Preheat the oven to 350° F.
8. At baking time, pour ¼ inch of water into the dish around the squash. Cover the dish tightly with foil, place the dish in the hot oven, and bake the squash for 15 minutes. Remove the foil, and bake the squash for another 15 minutes. Serve the squash over the heated tomato sauce.

BAKED ACORN SQUASH *6 servings*

Orange wonderfully enhances winter squash, one my favorite vegetables.

Preparation tip: The entire recipe can be prepared in a microwave (cover the dish with plastic wrap). Or the dish can be baked in advance in traditional fashion and reheated in the microwave at serving time.

 3 small acorn squash, halved lengthwise and seeded
¾ cup chicken broth
¼ cup orange juice
¼ cup orange-flavored liqueur
 2 teaspoons grated orange rind
Salt to taste (optional)
Freshly ground pepper to taste

1. Preheat the oven to 400° F.
2. Place the squash, cut side up, in a baking pan. If they do not sit straight, cut a thin slice from their bottoms, taking care not to cut through to the cavities.
3. In a bowl or measuring cup, combine the remaining ingredients, and divide the mixture among the cavities of the squash. Cover the pan tightly with foil, place the pan in the hot oven, and bake the squash for 40 minutes or until the squash are soft. Serve the squash with their liquid.

CRANBERRY-STUFFED SQUASH BOWLS   *6 servings*

This is not only delicious and simple to prepare, it's beautiful as well—a magnificent addition to a holiday meal.

  ⅓ cup water
  ⅓ cup sugar
  2 cups cranberries
  3 tablespoons port
  3 small acorn squash, halved lengthwise and seeded
Salt to taste (optional)
Freshly ground black pepper to taste

1. In a medium-sized saucepan, combine the water and sugar, and bring the mixture to a boil, stirring it. Reduce the heat, and simmer the mixture for about 10 minutes. Stir in the cranberries and port, and cook the ingredients, stirring them, 2 minutes longer or until the cranberries just start to pop.
2. While the syrup simmers, prepare the squash. Set the squash halves, cut side up, on a steamer rack over boiling water. (If the halves do not sit straight, cut a very thin slice from their bottoms, taking care not to cut through to the cavity.) Cover the pot, and steam the squash for 10 minutes or until they are tender. Remove them from the heat, and sprinkle them with the salt (if desired) and pepper.
3. To serve the squash, spoon some of the cranberry sauce into the cavity of each squash. If you have sauce left over, serve it as a condiment.

SPAGHETTI SQUASH À L'ORANGE   *4 to 6 servings*

Charlie Foster of Memphis suggests this simple means of turning the humble spaghetti squash into a memorable side dish. To keep down unwanted fat and calories, I omitted the 2 tablespoons of butter he had added in step 3.

  1 spaghetti squash (3 to 3½ pounds)
Salt to taste (optional)
Freshly ground black pepper to taste
  ½ cup orange juice (fresh, if available)
  ½ cup minced fresh parsley for garnish
  1 tablespoon finely julienned orange rind for garnish

1. Submerge the squash in a large pot of boiling water. Cook the squash, turning it occasionally, for 1 hour. Drain the squash, and let it cool for 10 minutes. Cut the squash in half, and remove the seeds.

2. Using the tines of a fork, scrape out the stringy flesh from the squash. Place the spaghetti-like strands in a heated serving dish.

3. Season the squash with the salt (if desired) and pepper. Drizzle the orange juice over it, and garnish the squash with the parsley and orange rind.

STUFFED TOMATOES PROVENÇAL   *6 servings*

Stuffed tomatoes are an ideal party dish because they look so festive and can be set up in advance for baking near serving time.

6 medium tomatoes
Salt to taste (optional)
1½ cups *fresh* bread crumbs (you can use whole-wheat, if you wish)
1 tablespoon olive oil
¼ cup minced shallots
1 teaspoon minced garlic (1 large clove)
⅔ cup minced fresh parsley
1 teaspoon basil
½ teaspoon thyme
Freshly ground black pepper to taste

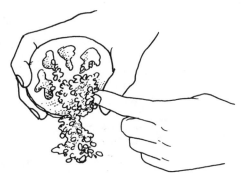

1. Slice a "cap" from each tomato, scoop out and discard the seeds from the tomato and the "cap," then gently remove the pulp from the tomato (a grapefruit spoon works well), and reserve it. Chop the reserved pulp and the seeded "caps," and set them aside. Sprinkle the cavities of the tomatoes lightly with the salt (if desired), and set the tomatoes aside.

2. Preheat the oven to 400° F.

3. In a medium-sized bowl, combine the remaining ingredients. Add the reserved tomato pulp.

4. Set the hollowed-out tomatoes in an oiled baking pan, and divide the crumb mixture among them.

5. Place the pan in the hot oven, and bake the tomatoes for 20 minutes or until the tops are golden brown.

HARVEST VEGETABLE AND CHEESE CASSEROLE

6 to 8 servings

This dish is easy to prepare and very tasty with or without the hot pepper. It could easily be the main dish of a luncheon or light supper on a late summer or fall day. It is best when made from fresh ingredients—for example, when you've prepared more corn on the cob than anyone could eat.

  1 tablespoon olive oil *or* canola oil
  1 large onion, peeled and chopped (1 cup)
  1 large clove garlic, peeled and minced
  1 small jalapeño, minced (optional)
  2 large tomatoes, chopped
  2 pounds zucchini *or* yellow summer squash, cut
     into ½-inch pieces
1½ to 2 cups corn kernels (from 2 to 3 large ears *or*
     thawed frozen kernels)
  6 ounces Monterey Jack, grated
Salt to taste (optional)
Freshly ground black pepper to taste

1. In a large skillet, preferably one with a nonstick surface, heat the oil briefly, add the onion, and sauté the onion over medium-low heat until it is softened.
2. Add the garlic, jalapeño, tomatoes, squash, and corn, and cook the mixture, stirring it, for 8 to 10 minutes or until the squash is tender.
3. Reduce the heat to low, stir in the cheese, salt (if desired), and pepper, cover the pan, and simmer the casserole for 30 seconds to melt the cheese.

VEGETABLE MEDLEY

8 servings

This colorful dish is nutrient-rich and flavorful, too. A touch of vinegar brings out the natural flavors without adding calories.

Preparation tips: If your skillet does not have a nonstick surface, you may need to use more oil. The dish can be prepared in advance through the addition of the last ingredients. Do the final sautéing just before serving.

4 teaspoons olive oil
1 pound zucchini, halved lengthwise and thinly
   sliced crosswise
2 large sweet red peppers, cored, seeded, and cut
   into ½-inch dice

2 large sweet green peppers, cored, seeded, and
  cut into ½-inch dice
2 large carrots, peeled and thinly sliced on the
  diagonal (2 cups)
2 cups thinly sliced red cabbage
4 teaspoons white-wine vinegar
Salt to taste (optional)
Freshly ground black pepper to taste

1. In a large skillet, preferably one with a nonstick surface, heat the oil until it
   is hot, add the zucchini, red and green peppers, and carrots, and sauté the
   vegetables, stirring them, for 5 minutes.
2. Add the cabbage, vinegar, salt (if desired), and ground pepper, and sauté
   the mixture 5 minutes longer or until the vegetables are tender-crisp.

ZUCCHINI WITH PINE NUTS   *4 servings*

Here is an unusual method for serving zucchini (cold) that would be a welcome
addition to a summer buffet.

Preparation tip: It can marinate for up to 1 day before serving.

 1 pound zucchini, cut into 1-inch-thick rounds
⅓ cup pine nuts, lightly toasted
¾ cup buttermilk
 1 teaspoon coarse-ground mustard
 2 tablespoons fresh lemon juice
Salt to taste (optional)
Freshly ground black pepper to taste

1. Steam or parboil the zucchini until it is tender-crisp. Drain the zucchini well,
   and stand the rounds, cut side up, on a serving dish with a small lip. Sprinkle
   the zucchini with the pine nuts.
2. In a bowl combine the buttermilk, mustard, lemon juice, salt (if desired),
   and pepper. Spoon the mixture over the zucchini and pine nuts. Refrigerate
   the zucchini for at least 2 hours before serving it.

ZUCCHINI CROQUETTES

4 to 6 servings

Bert Greene's Turkish Gozmele (sautéed zucchini cakes) in *Greene on Greens* inspired me to try these well-seasoned pancakes, which can serve as a side dish or as an hors d'oeuvre. (See also Zucchini Pancakes on page 292.)

Preparation tips: To use as little fat as I indicate, the croquettes should be cooked in a nonstick skillet or griddle. If sodium is of concern, don't salt the zucchini; simply squeeze the zucchini gently in cheesecloth or a cotton dish-towel to remove some of the water.

    2 cups (½ pound) unpeeled, grated zucchini
  Salt (optional)
    1 teaspoon chopped jalapeño (fresh *or* canned)
    2 teaspoons finely minced onion
    1 large clove garlic, peeled and finely minced
  ½ teaspoon curry powder (mild *or* hot)
    2 teaspoons olive oil
  ½ teaspoon baking powder
  ⅔ cup whole-wheat flour (preferably stone-ground)
    1 tablespoon vegetable oil (preferably canola)

1. Sprinkle the zucchini lightly with the salt (if desired), and place the vegetable in a colander to drain for about 20 minutes. Press gently on the zucchini to extract excess water, then transfer the vegetable to a medium-sized bowl.
2. Mix in the jalapeño, onion, garlic, curry powder, and olive oil. Then stir in the baking powder and flour.
3. Flour your hands, scoop up some of the zucchini mixture, shape it into a small round, and flatten it slightly to about 2 inches in diameter. Place the croquette on a dish. Repeat the procedure until the zucchini mixture has been used up. You should have about 16 croquettes.
4. Heat the vegetable oil in a large nonstick skillet or griddle, add the croquettes, and fry the cakes over medium heat for about 1 minute on each side. Reduce the heat to medium-low, cover the pan, and cook the croquettes 15 minutes longer, turning them once.

Salads

To me, a meal is not complete without a salad. And I don't mean a simple salad of iceberg lettuce and a few slices of tomato, cucumber, and radish. I mean a salad with interesting, taste-bud–stimulating ingredients, which are now widely available in markets throughout the country. I have found that since the salad is often the most memorable part of the meals I serve (perhaps because I love them so and take extra pains with them), I now make twice as much as I think I'll need because so many diners clamor for seconds.

Even if you live in the hinterlands with a limited selection of fresh ingredients, you can still make interesting salads using frozen, dried, and canned vegetables like frozen corn and peas, dried tomatoes and mushrooms, and bottled artichokes and roasted peppers. And nearly everyone can get potatoes, onions, sweet green peppers, cabbage, carrots, and celery year round.

Furthermore, almost no one has to rely on commercial dressings to enhance these creations, although there is now a broad selection of bottled dressings that are made with less or no oil and contain fewer calories than traditional salad dressings. And you'll note that I use far less dressing than you may be accustomed to. I want to enjoy the taste and texture of the vegetables, not have everything obscured by an overabundance of oily dressing. More and more, I'm finding that others share my sentiments. After all, you can always place cruets of oil and vinegar on the table for those who prefer more dressing on their salads.

ARUGULA AND FENNEL SALAD

4 servings

I discovered the glories of arugula years before it became, as my husband calls it, "a yuppie green." In fact, I used to grow it from seed under the name rocket grass. It is also known as roquette and rugola. But by any name, it is a now-popular nippy green that, if not carried locally, could be grown in a window box from early spring until the first frost (see page 15 for seed sources). It's worth the effort. And once you try this salad, you'll know why.

DRESSING
- 2 tablespoons red-wine vinegar
- 2 tablespoons olive oil
- 1 teaspoon Dijon-style mustard
- ½ teaspoon salt (optional)
- ¼ teaspoon freshly ground black pepper

SALAD
- 2 bunches arugula, tough stems removed and leaves torn in half
- 1 bulb fennel, cored and cut crosswise into ⅛-inch slices
- ⅓ cup lightly toasted pine nuts

1. In a salad bowl, whisk together the dressing ingredients.
2. Add the arugula, fennel, and pine nuts. Toss the salad lightly, and serve it immediately.

ARUGULA SALAD WITH PISTACHIOS

6 servings

See the recipe above for the virtues of arugula. This simple salad, by Larry Jacobs for *Bon Appétit,* shows arugula to similar advantage.

DRESSING
- 4 teaspoons balsamic vinegar (see page 13 for sources)
- 2 tablespoons olive oil
- ¼ teaspoon salt (optional)
- ¼ teaspoon freshly ground black pepper

SALAD
- 3 bunches arugula, tough stems removed and leaves torn into bite-sized pieces (about 8 cups)
- ⅓ cup coarsely chopped unsalted pistachios

1. In a salad bowl, whisk together the dressing ingredients.
2. Add the arugula, and toss the salad gently. Serve the salad sprinkled with the pistachios.

GREEN BEAN AND RED ONION SALAD   *4 servings*

For simplicity and color, this nifty salad from Pierre Franey is hard to beat.

SALAD

1 pound green beans, ends trimmed
1 red onion (about ¼ pound),
    peeled, sliced, and separated
    into rings

¼ cup minced fresh parsley

DRESSING

2 tablespoons red-wine vinegar
2 tablespoons olive oil
¼ teaspoon cumin
Salt to taste (optional)
Freshly ground black pepper to taste

1. Steam the beans over boiling water in a covered pot for 5 to 6 minutes or until the beans are tender-crisp. Rinse the beans immediately under cold water to preserve their color, drain them, and let them cool.
2. Transfer the beans to a bowl, and add the onion rings.
3. In a small bowl or jar, combine the dressing ingredients. Add the dressing to the green beans and onion, and toss the salad gently.
4. At serving time, add the parsley, and toss the salad again. The salad is best served at room temperature.

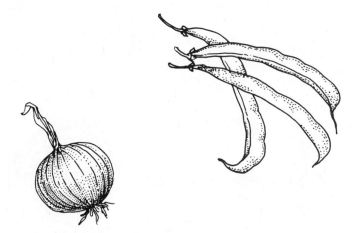

GRAND GREEN BEAN SALAD

6 to 8 servings

Horseradish in the dressing gives this salad a tasty twist.

Preparation tips: Drained bottled horseradish works fine. But be sure to make the dressing 1 hour or more ahead to give the flavors a chance to blend. You can, of course, omit the meat and perhaps substitute toasted sunflower seeds.

SALAD

- 1 pound young green beans, trimmed and halved
- 2 ounces Canadian bacon *or* baked ham *or* lean smoked pork (see "Preparation tips," above)

DRESSING

- ¼ cup plain nonfat or low-fat yogurt
- 1 tablespoon olive oil *or* canola oil
- 1 tablespoon or more grated horseradish, to taste (fresh or drained bottled)
- ½ teaspoon Dijon-style mustard
- ¼ teaspoon freshly ground black pepper, or to taste
- ⅛ teaspoon salt (optional)

1. In a covered pot, steam the beans over boiling water for 5 to 7 minutes or until the beans are tender-crisp. Rinse them immediately under cold water, then chill them.
2. Finely dice the meat, and cook it over low heat in a nonstick pan until the meat is lightly browned. Drain the meat on a paper towel.
3. In a small bowl, combine the dressing ingredients, and refrigerate the dressing for 1 hour or longer. Just before serving time, place the beans and meat in a salad bowl, and toss them with the dressing.

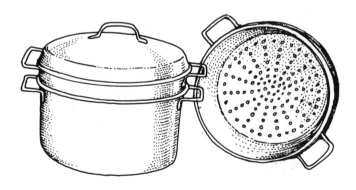

DILLY BEANS

8 servings

Dilled green beans are a country favorite wherever beans and dill grow prolifi-cally in home gardens. But there's no reason why city folk can't also enjoy them since beans and fresh dill are now available in many markets. They are a lovely accompaniment to a summer barbecue or picnic.

Preparation tip: Save the marinade after the beans are consumed. It can be reused to make another batch.

SALAD
- 1 pound green beans, ends trimmed
- 2 large cloves garlic, peeled and mashed
- 10 or more sprigs fresh dill
- 1 teaspoon red pepper flakes
- ½ teaspoon dill seeds
- ½ teaspoon mustard seeds

MARINADE
- 1 cup cider vinegar
- 1 cup water
- 3 tablespoons sugar
- ½ teaspoon salt

1. In a covered pot, steam the beans over boiling water for 5 to 7 minutes or until they are tender-crisp. Rinse them immediately under cold water, and drain them.
2. Place beans in a glass or ceramic bowl. Add the garlic, dill, red pepper flakes, dill seeds, and mustard seeds.
3. In a glass, enamel, or stainless-steel saucepan, combine the marinade in-gredients, and bring them to a boil. Pour the hot marinade over the beans, and let the mixture cool. Cover the bowl, and refrigerate the beans for 10 hours or longer.
4. To serve, remove the beans from the marinade, which can be used again either to store the leftovers or to make a new batch of beans.

NAVY AND GREEN BEAN SALAD

4 servings

I've long been fond of three-bean salad and its variations. This one, made from red onions, white navy beans, and fresh green beans, is especially good-tasting and attractive.

Preparation tips: The uniquely flavored balsamic vinegar is sold in most specialty-food stores and by some mail-order companies (see page 13). If it is unavailable, substitute red-wine vinegar. Note that the soaked navy beans need at least 1 hour of preparation time and another hour to marinate.

DRESSING
- 2 teaspoons Dijon-style mustard
- 3 tablespoons balsamic vinegar
- 1 teaspoon Worcestershire sauce
- ¼ cup chicken broth
- 2 tablespoons olive oil

SALAD
- ½ pound navy beans, picked over, rinsed, soaked 10 hours or longer in water to cover by at least 4 inches, and drained
- Water to cover
- Salt to taste (optional)

- ½ pound green beans, trimmed and steamed tender-crisp
- ⅔ cup chopped red onion

1. In a small bowl, whisk together the dressing ingredients. Set the dressing aside.
2. In a medium-sized saucepan over moderate heat, cook the drained navy beans in water to cover by 3 inches for 30 minutes or until the beans are just tender. Let them stand in their liquid 10 minutes longer, add salt (if desired), and let the beans cool until they are just warm.
3. Drain the navy beans, transfer them to a bowl, and toss them with ½ of the dressing. Let the navy beans marinate in the refrigerator for at least 1 hour or overnight.
4. Near serving time, toss the green beans with the remaining dressing.
5. To serve the salad, place the green beans in the center of a serving dish, arrange the navy beans around the green beans, and sprinkle the entire salad with the onion. The salad should be served at room temperature.

LENTIL WALDORF SALAD

6 to 8 servings

A great variation on a standard theme, this salad provides taste and nutrition without a fatty mayonnaise dressing.

Preparation tips: I soak the lentils not because they need it for speedy cooking, but to reduce their gaseous components. You can skip the soak, if you wish; however, you may have to cook the lentils a bit longer. Be sure, though, that the lentils are firm, not mushy. I suggest using canola oil. Like olive oil, it is monounsaturated and kind to your arteries. You could also use walnut or avocado oil, both of which are also monounsaturated.

Serving suggestions: Lentils look best when surrounded by curly leaf lettuce. This makes an excellent luncheon or buffet salad.

SALAD

- 1½ cups lentils, soaked overnight and drained
- 6 cups water

- 2 large sweet apples (e.g., McIntosh), unpeeled
- 1 cup diced celery
- ½ cup chopped walnuts, lightly toasted
- ⅓ cup minced fresh parsley

DRESSING

- 3 tablespoons cider vinegar
- 3 tablespoons vegetable oil (preferably canola)
- 1 tablespoon Dijon-style mustard
- 1 teaspoon salt (optional)
- Freshly ground black pepper to taste

1. In a medium-sized saucepan, bring the lentils and water to a boil, reduce the heat, partially cover the pan, and simmer the lentils for 20 minutes or until the lentils are barely tender. *Do not overcook the lentils.* Transfer them to a colander, rinse them under cold water, and let them drain and cool.

2. While the lentils drain, in a large bowl, whisk together the dressing ingredients. Add the drained lentils, toss the ingredients to combine them thoroughly, and set the lentils aside to cool further.

3. While the lentils cool, core and dice the apples into ⅓-inch cubes. Add the apples to the cooled lentils along with the celery, walnuts, and parsley, and toss the ingredients to mix them well. Adjust the seasonings, and serve the salad at or near room temperature.

MINTED LIMA BEAN SALAD

6 to 8 servings

This unusual Spanish salad, based on a recipe used in New York's Alcala Restaurant, is easy to prepare as well as delicious and nourishing.

Preparation tips: If you don't have fresh mint, don't make this salad. The salad can be prepared in advance, but the lettuce should not be shredded and added until just before serving time.

SALAD
- 2 10-ounce packages frozen baby lima beans
- 1 cup water
- 2 sprigs fresh mint

- 2 ounces prosciutto *or* serrano-style ham, cut into very small dice
- ½ head Boston lettuce (about ¼ pound), shredded

Mint leaves for garnish (optional)

DRESSING
- 1 teaspoon Dijon-style mustard
- 1 tablespoon rice vinegar
- 1 tablespoon olive oil
- ¼ teaspoon salt, or to taste (optional)
- ¼ teaspoon or more freshly ground black pepper, to taste
- 2 teaspoons finely chopped fresh mint leaves

1. In a medium-sized saucepan, cook the lima beans in the water with the mint sprigs according to package directions. *Do not overcook the limas:* the beans should be firm. Drain the beans, rinse them under cold water, and place them in a bowl. Discard the mint sprigs.
2. In a small bowl, whisk together the dressing ingredients.
3. Add the dressing and the prosciutto or ham to the lima beans, and toss the ingredients gently. Chill the beans, if you are making the salad in advance.
4. An hour before serving time, bring the beans to room temperature, and toss them with the lettuce. Serve the salad garnished with the mint leaves (if desired).

BULGUR SALAD PRIMAVERA

6 to 8 servings

I modified a version of tabbouleh devised by Marc S. Collins, a former caterer, to produce this colorful, crunchy salad.

SALAD
- 1 cup bulgur
- 2 cups boiling water
- 2 cups (2 large) chopped tomatoes
- 1 cup shredded carrot
- ½ cup dried currants
- ½ cup toasted sunflower seeds
- ½ cup finely chopped scallions
- 2 tablespoons finely chopped fresh mint

DRESSING
- ¼ cup red-wine vinegar
- 3 tablespoons tamari *or* reduced-sodium soy sauce
- 2 tablespoons olive oil
- 1 clove garlic, peeled and minced
- 1 tablespoon finely chopped fresh basil *or* 1 teaspoon dried basil
- ¼ teaspoon oregano

1. Place the bulgur in a large bowl. Add the boiling water, and let the bulgur stand for 30 minutes to 1 hour or until the bulgur is just tender. Transfer the bulgur to a strainer, and press out any excess moisture.
2. Return the bulgur to the bowl, and add the remaining salad ingredients.
3. In a small bowl or jar, combine the dressing ingredients, and pour them over the bulgur mixture, tossing the ingredients to combine them well. Cover the bowl, and chill the salad until 1 hour before serving it.

LEMON BULGUR SALAD

4 to 6 servings

Although this salad contains currants and nuts, the lemon and scallions give it a pleasant tartness and zip.

SALAD
- ¾ cup boiling water
- ¾ cup boiling chicken broth
- 1 cup bulgur
- 3 tablespoons currants
- ¼ cup chopped scallions

- ¼ cup chopped pistachios

DRESSING
- 3 tablespoons fresh lemon juice
- 1 tablespoon olive oil
- ⅛ teaspoon cinnamon
- Salt to taste (optional)
- ¼ to ½ teaspoon freshly ground black pepper, to taste

1. In a large bowl, combine the boiling water and broth with the bulgur. Let the bulgur stand for 40 minutes or until the liquid is absorbed.
2. Combine the bulgur with the currants and scallions.
3. In a small bowl, whisk together the dressing ingredients, and add them to the bulgur mixture. Chill the bulgur salad until 1 hour before serving it.
4. Just before serving the salad, stir in the chopped pistachios. Serve the salad at room temperature.

FRAN'S SWEET WHEAT SALAD

4 to 6 servings

This salad, based on a recipe devised by my friend Fran Korein, has a lovely bittersweet flavor.

Serving suggestion: Garnish the salad with orange sections and parsley sprigs.

SALAD
- 2 cups boiling water
- 1 cup coarse bulgur (preferably whole-grain)
- ½ cup currants
- ¼ cup minced Italian parsley

- ½ cup chopped pecans

DRESSING
- 2 teaspoons grated orange rind
- 1½ teaspoons olive oil
- ½ teaspoon salt (optional)
- ¼ teaspoon freshly ground black pepper

1. In a medium-sized bowl, combine the boiling water and bulgur, and let the bulgur stand for 45 minutes or until it is tender but crunchy. Drain any remaining liquid.
2. Combine the bulgur with the currants and parsley.
3. In a small bowl, combine the dressing ingredients, and add them to the bulgur mixture. Chill the bulgur until 1 hour before serving it.
4. Before serving the salad, stir in the pecans. Serve the salad at room temperature (see "Serving suggestion," above).

MEXICAN TABBOULEH

6 to 8 salad servings or
10 to 12 hors-d'oeuvre servings

This is my south-of-the-border version of a dish that's a perennial hit at parties. Perhaps it will inspire you to devise your own version of the traditional bulgur salad.

Preparation tip: For the best consistency, prepare the bulgur, the cut-up vegetables, and the dressing separately in advance, and combine them about 1 hour before serving the tabbouleh.

Serving suggestion: Instead of (or in addition to) tortilla chips, you could serve this with scoops made out of firm fresh vegetables: wedges of red, green, and yellow peppers, chunks of celery, leaves of Belgian endive, or diagonally cut slices of a large carrot. For maximum flavor, bring the tabbouleh to room temperature before serving it.

SALAD

- 1 cup bulgur, medium- or fine-grind
- 1 6-ounce can spicy hot V8 juice *or* Snappy Tom *or* tomato juice spiked with Worcestershire sauce and hot pepper sauce
- 10 ounces (1⅛ cups) beef broth
- 1 medium cucumber, peeled, seeded, and diced (1 cup)
- 2 to 3 firm plum tomatoes *or* 1 large firm tomato, chopped
- ½ cup diced sweet green pepper
- ½ cup chopped fresh parsley
- ¼ cup sliced scallions (including the green tops)
- 1 to 2 tablespoons chopped cilantro
- 1 minced jalapeño (1 tablespoon), or to taste

DRESSING

- ¼ cup fresh lime juice
- 1 tablespoon olive oil
- 1 teaspoon thyme, crumbled
- 1 teaspoon minced garlic (1 large clove)
- Cayenne *or* freshly ground black pepper to taste

1. Place the bulgur in a medium-sized heat-proof bowl.
2. In a small saucepan, heat the juice and the broth just to boiling, and pour the liquid over the bulgur, stirring the mixture once. Let the bulgur stand for about 1 hour. Then drain off any remaining liquid, pressing lightly on the bulgur to extract any excess moisture. Let the bulgur cool, then chill it until 1 hour before serving time.
3. In another bowl, combine the remaining salad ingredients. Cover the bowl, and refrigerator it until 1 hour before serving time.
4. In a small jar or bowl, combine the dressing ingredients. One hour before serving the salad, add the vegetable mixture to the bulgur, pour on the dressing, and toss the ingredients to combine them well. Let the tabbouleh come to room temperature.

RAISIN TABBOULEH

6 to 8 servings

A kind reader, Trina Lewin, sent this simple version of bulgur salad. I doubled the parsley and added a bit of salt but otherwise used her recipe.

SALAD
- 1 cup bulgur
- 2 cups boiling water
- 1 cup chopped fresh parsley
- ½ cup raisins
- ½ cup chopped scallions

DRESSING
- ¼ cup fresh lime juice
- 3 tablespoons light olive oil *or* canola oil
- ¼ teaspoon salt (optional)
- Freshly ground black pepper to taste

1. Put the bulgur in a bowl. Add the boiling water, and let the bulgur stand for 30 minutes to 1 hour or until it is just tender. Place the bulgur in a strainer, and press out any excess moisture.
2. Return the bulgur to the bowl, and add the remaining salad ingredients, tossing the ingredients to combine them well.
3. In a small bowl or jar, combine the dressing ingredients. Add them to the bulgur mixture about 1 hour or less before serving the tabbouleh. The salad is best when it is served near room temperature.

RED CABBAGE SALAD

6 servings

Sweet and simple and nourishing.

SALAD
- 1¾ pounds red cabbage, cored and shredded
- 2 Red Delicious apples, *unpeeled*, cored, and julienned
- 1 medium onion, peeled, halved lengthwise, and thinly sliced crosswise

DRESSING
- 1 cup plain nonfat or low-fat yogurt
- ⅓ cup cider vinegar
- ¼ cup vegetable oil (preferably canola)
- 2 tablespoons sugar
- 1½ teaspoons celery seeds, ground, if possible, in a mortar with a pestle
- ½ teaspoon salt, or to taste (optional)
- ¼ teaspoon freshly ground black pepper

1. In a salad bowl, combine the salad ingredients.
2. In a small bowl, whisk together the dressing ingredients. Pour the dressing over the salad, and toss the ingredients to combine them well. Cover the bowl, and chill the salad until serving time. Toss the salad again before serving it.

RED AND WHITE COLE SLAW

4 to 6 servings

Lovely and delicious. Need I say more?

SALAD
- ¾ pound red cabbage, cored and coarsely shredded
- ½ pound green cabbage, cored and coarsely shredded
- 1 large (¼ pound) carrot, peeled and coarsely shredded
- ⅓ cup finely chopped scallions

DRESSING
- 2 tablespoons white-wine vinegar
- 2 tablespoons vegetable oil (preferably canola)
- 1 teaspoon Dijon-style mustard
- ½ teaspoon cumin
- ¼ teaspoon salt (optional)
- Freshly ground black pepper to taste

1. In a bowl, combine the salad ingredients.
2. In a small bowl or jar, combine the dressing ingredients. Add the dressing to the salad, and toss the ingredients to combine them thoroughly.

APPLE AND CHEESE SLAW

4 servings

The promoters of Granny Smith apples came up with this interesting cole slaw.

Preparation tips: If you use imported Swiss rather than domestic, it has less salt and more flavor. Let the salad stand for 1 hour before serving it so that the flavors blend.

DRESSING
- 2 tablespoons salad oil
- 2 tablespoons lemon juice
- 2 tablespoons red-wine vinegar
- ¼ cup chopped onion
- 2 tablespoons minced fresh parsley
- ½ teaspoon caraway seeds
- ¼ teaspoon salt (optional)
- ⅛ teaspoon freshly ground black pepper
- ⅛ teaspoon allspice

SALAD
- 2 cups chopped, unpeeled Granny Smith apples
- 2 cups (about ½ pound) shredded cabbage
- 1 cup (about 6 ounces) diced Swiss cheese

1. In a small bowl, whisk together the dressing ingredients.
2. In a medium-sized bowl, combine the salad ingredients. Pour the dressing over the salad, and toss the ingredients to mix them thoroughly. Cover the bowl, and chill the salad for at least 1 hour before serving it.

SWEET AND SOUR SLAW

6 servings

This is one great salad, only slightly changed from Mollie Katzen's recipe for Cabbage Salad with Peanuts in her *Still Life with Menu Cookbook.* I made a huge batch for a barbecue, and it was devoured ahead of the shish kebabs and burgers. A dozen guests requested the recipe. I even caught one guest using his fingers to pick out the last shreds of cabbage.

Preparation tips: Since at the barbecue I was serving children as well as adults, I made the salad without the hot pepper flakes, which would enhance it even further. The dressing can be premixed and combined with the cabbage and pepper flakes several hours before serving, but add the peanuts at serving time.

DRESSING	SALAD
⅓ cup rice vinegar *or* cider vinegar	7 to 8 cups (about 1¼ pounds)
¼ cup natural peanut butter	shredded green cabbage
(smooth or crunchy)	Red pepper flakes to taste (optional)
3 tablespoons brown sugar	½ cup dry-roasted unsalted
½ teaspoon salt, or to taste (optional)	peanuts, coarsely chopped
1 tablespoon soy sauce	
1 teaspoon Oriental sesame oil	

1. Place the dressing ingredients in a blender, and process them on low until they are well mixed.
2. About 1 hour before serving, place the dressing in a large bowl, and add the cabbage, 2 cups at a time, tossing the ingredients after each addition. Then stir in the pepper flakes (if you are using them). Cover the bowl, and chill the salad for 1 hour, tossing it every now and then.
3. At serving time, add the peanuts, and toss the salad once more. Use a slotted spoon to serve the slaw.

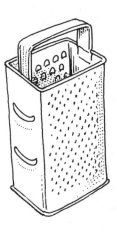

HOT DIGGITY SLAW

8 to 10 servings

We're talking major delicious here. My tasters threw caution to the wind (it is cabbage, after all) and downed three helpings apiece.

Preparation tips: You can prepare the salad ingredients and the dressing separately ahead of time and combine them 1 to 4 hours before serving the slaw. The vegetables can be cut into ½-inch pieces or slivered.

DRESSING
- ¼ cup natural peanut butter (preferably chunky)
- 1 tablespoon fresh lime juice
- 1 tablespoon grated gingerroot
- 2 teaspoons grated garlic
- 2 teaspoons sugar
- 1 teaspoon soy sauce
- ¼ cup (approximately) water

SALAD
- 1½ to 2 pounds green cabbage, cored
- 1 sweet green pepper, cored and seeded
- 1 sweet red pepper, cored and seeded
- 1 large onion (I use Vidalia, when they are available), peeled
- 1 to 3 jalapeños, seeded and minced, to taste
- ½ teaspoon salt (optional)
- ⅓ cup coarsely chopped dry-roasted unsalted peanuts

1. To prepare the dressing, in a small bowl, combine the dressing ingredients *except* the water. Add the water 1 tablespoon at a time, whisking the ingredients after each addition, until the dressing has the consistency of mayonnaise. Set the dressing aside. Do not refrigerate it.
2. To prepare the salad, cut the cabbage, green and red peppers, and onion into ½-inch pieces, or shred the cabbage, then cut the peppers and onion into thin slivers. Combine the vegetables in a large bowl with the jalapeños. Chill the salad until 1 hour before serving it.
3. Remove the salad ingredients from the refrigerator, sprinkle the salad with the salt (if desired), and toss it with the dressing. Just before serving the slaw, add the chopped peanuts, and toss the salad again.

CARROT-APPLE SALAD SUPREME   *8 to 10 servings*

Mrs. Alberta Hummell of Brewster, Massachusetts, sent me this fat-free, attractive, nutritious, tasty, easy make-ahead salad recipe.

Preparation tips: Shredding is very speedy in a food processor but can also be done with a hand grater. If golden raisins are unavailable, use another ½ cup of dark raisins. Add the peanuts at serving time to preserve their crunch.

- 1 6-ounce can frozen concentrated orange juice, defrosted
- 1 6-ounce can of cold water
- 2 pounds carrots, scraped and shredded
- 3 tart apples (e.g., Granny Smiths), peeled, cored, and shredded
- ½ cup dark raisins
- ½ cup golden raisins
- ½ cup coarsely chopped dry-roasted unsalted peanuts

Place the juice and water in a glass or stainless-steel bowl. Add in and combine well the remaining ingredients *except* the peanuts, which should be tossed in at serving time.

UP-'N'-CUMIN CARROT SALAD   *6 servings*

As an hors d'oeuvre or salad, this is delicious, fat-free, and low in calories.

Serving suggestion: Place the salad in a bowl or on individual plates surrounded by leaves of Belgian endive or radicchio, which may be used as scoops. Add a spoon or small fork for neatness.

- 4 cups shredded carrots
- 1 cup chopped fresh parsley
- ½ cup currants
- ½ cup slivered almonds, lightly toasted
- ½ cup fresh lemon juice
- 1 teaspoon cumin

Put the ingredients in a bowl, and mix them well. Serve the salad at room temperature.

NORTH AFRICAN CARROT SALAD   *10 to 12 servings*

This nippy salad is not easily forgotten. It is not too hot for most tastes. I first had it at a party and noticed that lots of people returned for seconds and even thirds.

Preparation tips: You can temper the bite by reducing the amount of cayenne. The carrots can be cut in a food processor or by hand.

SALAD
- 1 pound carrots, peeled and julienned into ⅛-inch strips
- ¼ cup dried currants (optional)

DRESSING
- 3 tablespoons fresh lemon juice
- 2 tablespoons olive oil
- 1 large clove garlic, peeled and finely minced
- ½ teaspoon or more sugar, to taste
- ½ teaspoon cumin
- ¼ teaspoon cayenne, or to taste
- ¼ teaspoon dried mint leaves, crushed
- Freshly ground black pepper to taste
- Salt to taste (optional)

1. Place the carrots in a bowl with the currants (if desired).
2. In a jar or small bowl, combine the dressing ingredients.
3. About 1 hour or less before serving time, add the dressing to the carrots. Toss the ingredients to mix them well.

JULIENNE JUBILEE SALAD

8 servings

Good-looking and good-tasting, whether it is served as a salad course, on a buffet table, or with appetizers.

Preparation tip: While you are cutting up the vegetables and preparing the dressing, bring a large pot of water to a boil. And set up a bowl of ice water near the boiling water.

Serving suggestion: This is most attractive when served on an oblong dish with the vegetables more or less lined up lengthwise.

SALAD

- 4 carrots, peeled and julienned into ¼-inch strips (2 to 3 cups)
- ½ pound snow peas, trimmed and cut into ¼-inch strips
- 1 large bulb fennel, halved lengthwise, cored, and thinly sliced lengthwise

Red lettuce for lining the serving dish
- 1 tablespoon sesame seeds for garnish

DRESSING

- 3 tablespoons fresh lemon juice
- 2 tablespoons canola oil *or* olive oil
- 2 tablespoons reduced-sodium soy sauce
- 1 tablespoon honey
- 1 teaspoon Oriental sesame oil
- 1 teaspoon minced garlic
- 1 teaspoon grated gingerroot
- ⅛ teaspoon cayenne

1. Bring a large pot of water to a boil. Place the carrots in a strainer basket, and immerse them in the boiling water for 1 to 2 minutes or until the carrots are tender-crisp. Plunge the basket immediately into a dish of ice water. Drain the carrots, transfer them to a bowl or plastic bag, and chill them.
2. Place the snow peas in the strainer basket, and plunge them into the boiling water for 5 to 10 seconds and then into the ice water. Drain the peas, transfer them to a bowl or plastic bag, and chill them. Refrigerate the fennel strips as well.
3. In a bowl or small jar, combine the dressing ingredients, and let the dressing stand for about 30 minutes.
4. At serving time, arrange the leaves of red lettuce on a platter. Toss the carrots, peas, and fennel *individually* with the dressing (or combine all three vegetables, if desired), and arrange them on top of the lettuce. Sprinkle the salad with the sesame seeds.

CORN AND BARLEY SALAD   *4 to 6 servings*

All tasters agreed that this easily prepared salad was a winner. It's a nice salad to make when you've got some leftover ears of cooked corn.

Preparation tips: Cooking the garlic takes the bitter edge off of it, but you can skip this step if you wish. You can make the salad 1 day ahead, adding the cilantro or parsley just before serving time.

SALAD

- 3 cups water
- ½ teaspoon salt (optional)
- 1 cup barley
- 2 cups cooked corn kernels, fresh if available *or* frozen and thawed
- ½ cup thinly sliced scallions
- 1 large tomato, seeded and finely chopped
- 1 to 2 4-inch fresh hot green chilies *or* jalapeños, seeded and minced, to taste

¼ cup minced cilantro *or* fresh parsley, or to taste

DRESSING

- 2 cloves garlic, cooked 10 minutes in boiling water and peeled
- 3 tablespoons white-wine vinegar
- 2 tablespoons olive oil *or* canola oil
- ½ teaspoon cumin
- ½ teaspoon salt (optional)
- ¼ teaspoon freshly ground black pepper

1. To prepare the salad, in a large saucepan, bring the water and salt (if desired) to a boil, and add the barley. Cook the barley, stirring it often, until it is just tender—about 30 minutes for pearled barley, 40 minutes for unpearled. *Do not overcook the barley.* Drain the barley in a colander, rinse it under cold water, and let it drain until it is cool.

2. Transfer the cooled barley to a large bowl. Add the corn, scallions, tomato, and chilies or jalapeños, and toss the ingredients well.

3. To make the dressing, in a blender or food processor, add the dressing ingredients, and process them. Pour the dressing over the salad, and toss the salad well to combine the ingredients thoroughly. Cover the bowl, and chill the salad.

4. One hour before serving time, stir the cilantro or parsley into the salad, and allow the salad to come to room temperature.

CORN AND KIDNEY BEAN SALAD   *6 to 8 servings*

Colorful and nutritious, this salad is one of the few that works well without any oil. It is an especially good dish at a buffet or barbecue.

Preparation tip: Flavors meld best and the garlic is tamed somewhat if the salad is prepared 1 day ahead.

Serving suggestion: For individual servings, place the salad on lettuce leaves.

SALAD
- 1 16-ounce can (1⅔ cups) red kidney beans, drained and rinsed
- 2 cups corn kernels, fresh if available *or* frozen and thawed
- 1 sweet green pepper, cored, seeded, and diced
- 1 sweet red pepper, cored, seeded, and diced
- 1 rib celery, diced
- ½ cup chopped scallions (including the green tops)

DRESSING
- ¼ cup red-wine vinegar
- 1 teaspoon lemon juice
- 2 cloves garlic, peeled and minced
- ½ teaspoon sugar
- Salt to taste (optional)
- Freshly ground black pepper to taste

1. In a large glass or stainless-steel bowl, combine the salad ingredients.
2. In a small bowl or jar, combine the dressing ingredients. Pour the dressing over the salad, and mix the ingredients well. Cover the bowl, and chill the salad until serving time.

CORN, PEPPER, AND TOMATO SALAD   *6 to 8 servings*

This delicious make-ahead salad is ideal for late summer, when you can get the main ingredients fresh. I adapted a recipe from *Gourmet* magazine.

Preparation tip: I dice all the vegetables by hand to approximately the size of corn kernels. But if you are not concerned about uniformity of size, the task can be done in a food processor.

- 2 tablespoons olive oil
- 2 large cloves garlic, peeled and minced
- ¼ cup fresh lemon juice
- ¼ cup dry white wine
- ¼ teaspoon thyme, crumbled
- Salt to taste (optional)
- Freshly ground black pepper to taste

4 cups cooked corn kernels (preferably fresh), cut
   from about 6 ears
1 sweet green pepper, cored, seeded, and finely diced
1 small red onion, peeled and finely diced
2 medium tomatoes, finely diced
4 scallions (including the green tops), thinly sliced
¼ cup finely chopped fresh parsley
2 teaspoons finely chopped fresh basil

1. In a medium-sized saucepan, heat the oil over medium heat, add the garlic, lemon juice, wine, thyme, salt (if desired), and ground pepper, and cook the ingredients for 5 minutes.
2. Stir in the corn, and simmer the mixture for 3 minutes. Transfer the contents of the pan to a large bowl.
3. Add the green pepper, onion, tomatoes, scallions, parsley, and basil to the corn mixture. Adjust the seasonings.

CUCUMBER RAITA

6 servings

This is an Indian specialty, refreshing, tasty, and especially nice as an accompaniment to a spicy main course.

Preparation tips: Garam masala is a combination of spices available at markets that sell Indian ingredients. A reasonable facsimile can be made by combining ½ teaspoon of cumin, ½ teaspoon of chili powder, and a pinch of black pepper. Or see the recipe on pages 247 and 546. The peanuts can be ground in a blender. You can whip the yogurt and add the seasonings and peanuts in advance, but do not add the cucumbers until about 1 hour before serving time.

2 cups plain nonfat or low-fat yogurt
1 teaspoon garam masala (see "Preparation tips," above)
½ teaspoon salt (optional)
Pinch cayenne
¼ cup dry-roasted ground peanuts
3 small cucumbers *or* 1 large cucumber, seeded,
   peeled if it is waxed, and thinly sliced crosswise

1. In a medium-sized bowl, whisk the yogurt until it is smooth and fluffy.
2. Stir in the garam masala, salt (if desired), cayenne, and peanuts. Cover the bowl, and chill the dressing.
3. One hour or less before serving time, add the sliced cucumbers.

CUCUMBER-YOGURT SALAD

6 servings

This refreshing salad goes especially well with fish entrées and many kinds of sandwiches.

Preparation tips: If the cucumber is waxed, peel it before slicing it. However, the cucumber skin enhances the salad's appearance and texture, so try to prepare this dish with unwaxed cucumbers such as kirbies, garden-fresh regular cucumbers, or plastic-wrapped English ("burbless") cucumbers. Don't bother making this salad unless you have fresh herbs; dried dill and mint don't do the trick here.

SALAD
- 4 medium cucumbers
- ½ teaspoon salt (*not* optional)

DRESSING
- 1 cup plain nonfat or low-fat yogurt
- 2 tablespoons snipped fresh dill
- 1 tablespoon minced fresh mint leaves
- 2 teaspoons finely minced garlic
- 2 tablespoons fresh lemon juice

1. Score the skin of each cucumber by running the tines of a fork down its length all around the vegetable. Slice the cucumbers paper-thin, and place them in a colander. Sprinkle the cucumbers with the salt, and toss the slices to coat them. Let the cucumbers drain for about 30 minutes. Press the slices to squeeze out any additional moisture, and pat them dry. Transfer the cucumbers to a bowl.
2. In a small bowl, combine the dressing ingredients. Pour the dressing over the drained cucumbers, and toss the ingredients to combine them.

CREAMY EGGPLANT SALAD

6 to 8 servings

This low-fat treat for eggplant lovers could also be prepared with raw cucumber.

Preparation tip: Note that the yogurt must be drained for 2 hours.

SALAD
- 2 pounds eggplant, peeled and cut into 1-inch cubes
- Salted water to cover
- Juice 1 lemon

DRESSING
- 2 cups plain nonfat or low-fat yogurt
- ½ cup snipped fresh dill
- ½ cup chopped scallions
- 2 tablespoons olive oil
- ¼ cup fresh lemon juice
- Salt to taste (optional)
- Freshly ground black pepper to taste

1. Cook the eggplant in the salted water mixed with the juice of 1 lemon for 10 minutes or until the vegetable is barely tender. Drain the eggplant, and set it aside.
2. Put the yogurt in a yogurt strainer or in a colander lined with 2 or more layers of cheesecloth. Let the yogurt drain for 2 hours.
3. In a small bowl, combine the drained yogurt with the remaining dressing ingredients, and toss the dressing with the reserved eggplant.

GRAPEFRUIT AND BROCCOLI SALAD   *6 servings*

I made a few adjustments to a recipe from the Sunkist Kitchens. The result is delicious and attractive.

Serving suggestions: Serve this salad on a bed of arugula or lettuce leaves, and garnish it with strips of sweet red pepper. Or serve the salad on radicchio without the red pepper.

SALAD
- 2 grapefruits, peeled
- 1 pound broccoli, cut into flowerets, steamed 5 minutes, and cooled
- ½ pound mushrooms, sliced
- ¼ cup sliced scallions

DRESSING
- ¼ cup grapefruit juice
- 3 tablespoons olive oil
- 1 tablespoon Dijon-style mustard
- ½ teaspoon dillweed *or* 2 teaspoons snipped fresh dill
- ¼ teaspoon salt (optional)

1. Working over a bowl to catch the juice, carefully separate the grapefruits into sections, and cut the sections into halves or thirds, depending on their size. Reserve ¼ cup of the grapefruit juice for the dressing (or, if needed, use prepared grapefruit juice).
2. Place the grapefruit pieces, broccoli, mushrooms, and scallions in a shallow serving bowl.
3. In a small bowl or jar, combine the dressing ingredients. Pour the dressing over the salad, cover the serving bowl, and chill the salad for 30 minutes, tossing it occasionally.

KOHLRABI AND CARROT SALAD   *about 6 servings*

The late Bert Greene, author of *Greene on Greens,* first kindled my interest in kohlrabi, a crunchy member of the cabbage family that is chock full of fiber and cancer-blocking chemicals. To maximize nutrient value without sacrificing flavor, I gave his salad a new low-fat dressing.

SALAD

1¼ pounds kohlrabi globes, peeled and coarsely shredded

2 large carrots, peeled and coarsely shredded

½ sweet red pepper, seeded and diced

½ cup chopped scallions (including the green tops)

DRESSING

2 tablespoons oil (preferably olive)

2 tablespoons cider vinegar

2 teaspoons or more snipped fresh dill, to taste

1 teaspoon sugar

½ teaspoon cumin

½ teaspoon mustard powder

¼ teaspoon crumbled tarragon

¼ teaspoon salt (optional)

¼ teaspoon freshly ground black pepper

⅓ cup plain nonfat or low-fat yogurt

1. In a large bowl, combine the salad ingredients.
2. In a small bowl or jar, combine the oil, vinegar, dill, sugar, cumin, mustard, tarragon, salt (if desired), and pepper. Stir in the yogurt, and whisk or shake the ingredients to blend them well. Pour the dressing on the salad, toss the ingredients well, cover the bowl, and refrigerate the salad for about 2 hours before serving it.

MANGO AND PEAR SALAD

4 servings

Julie Sahni, an inventive Indian cook and author, is the source for this delicious, colorful, and unusual first-course or side-dish salad, which contains no fat except for what occurs naturally in the nuts.

Serving suggestion: Serve the salad on a lettuce leaf or with sprigs of watercress or leaves of arugula.

1 medium firm, slightly underripe mango, peeled, pitted, and julienned
2 medium Anjou pears, peeled, cored, and julienned
1 small carrot, peeled and shredded (about 1 cup)
1 teaspoon or more minced fresh hot chili *or* jalapeño, to taste
¼ teaspoon salt (optional)
¼ cup toasted pine nuts *or* chopped peanuts
1 tablespoon minced cilantro (optional)

1. In a salad bowl, combine all the ingredients *except* the nuts and cilantro. Chill the salad until serving time.
2. Add the nuts and the cilantro (if you are using it) just before serving the salad.

MUSHROOM, ENDIVE, AND WATERCRESS SALAD

2 to 4 servings

Here is a light, crisp, refreshing salad that is an elegant addition to any dinner.

SALAD
½ pound fresh mushrooms, thinly sliced
2 heads Belgian endive, sliced in 1-inch-long segments
½ bunch watercress, tough stems removed
2 scallions (including the green tops), coarsely chopped

DRESSING
2 tablespoons fresh lemon juice
1 tablespoon olive oil
⅛ teaspoon salt (optional)
Freshly ground black pepper to taste

1. In a serving bowl, combine the salad ingredients.
2. In a jar or cup, combine the dressing ingredients. Pour the dressing over the salad just before serving time.

ORANGE-JÍCAMA SALAD

8 servings

Jícama (pronounced HEE-ka-ma) is a Mexican vegetable that looks something like a potato and has the mild flavor and crunchy texture of a fresh water chestnut. It is very low in calories. A salt-free version of this make-ahead salad was devised by Sara Branscum of Oklahoma City. My tasters said it was delicious—especially refreshing when the main course was spicy or heavy. The pine nuts (I use more than the original recipe) add a nice crunch, but they could be omitted.

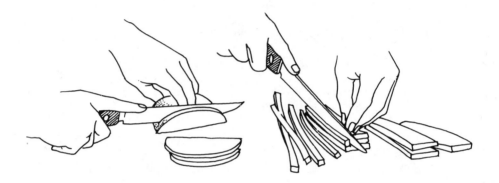

SALAD

  2 cups fresh orange sections (from about 4 oranges)
  1 pound jícama, peeled and thinly sliced into 2 × ¼-inch pieces
  1 medium red onion, peeled, thinly sliced crosswise, and separated into rings

  8 cups torn lettuce leaves (preferably romaine and red-leaf)
  ⅓ cup pine nuts, toasted (optional)

DRESSING

  ⅓ cup orange juice (preferably fresh)
  ¼ cup fresh lime juice
  2 tablespoons red-wine vinegar
  1 tablespoon olive oil
  ½ teaspoon salt (optional)
  ¼ teaspoon freshly ground black pepper

1. In a large bowl, combine the orange sections, jícama, and onion.
2. In a small bowl, whisk together the dressing ingredients. Add the dressing to the orange mixture, toss the ingredients gently, cover the bowl, and chill the salad until serving time.
3. At serving time, add the lettuce and the pine nuts (if desired), and toss the salad once more.

ORANGE, ROOT, AND FENNEL SALAD

4 servings

I love composed salads. They are fun to prepare and lovely to look at. This one is colorful, wholesome, and delicious. It is based on a suggestion from the producers of Grand Marnier.

Preparation tip: The salad can be prepared about 1 hour ahead of serving.

Serving suggestion: The dressing can be used on orange slices for dessert.

DRESSING
- 1 teaspoon grated orange rind
- ½ navel orange, peeled and sectioned
- 1½ tablespoons white-wine vinegar *or* rice vinegar
- 1 teaspoon fresh lemon juice
- 2 tablespoons orange liqueur
- 2 tablespoons olive oil

Salt to taste (optional)
Freshly ground black pepper to taste

SALAD
- ½ pound beets *or* carrots, peeled and coarsely grated
- 1½ navel oranges, peeled, halved lengthwise, and cut crosswise into ¼-inch slices
- 1 medium bulb fennel, halved lengthwise and thinly sliced crosswise
- 2 tablespoons finely chopped red onion

Greens (e.g., red- or green-leaf lettuce *or* arugula) for lining the serving platter

1. Add the dressing ingredients to a blender jar, and process them until they are smooth.
2. In 3 separate bowls, toss the beets or carrots with 2 tablespoons of the dressing; toss the oranges with 2 tablespoons of the dressing; combine the fennel and onion, and toss them with 2 tablespoons of the dressing.
3. Line a serving platter with the greens, and arrange the individual salad ingredients over them. Drizzle the salad with any remaining dressing.

ORZO SALAD

I first had this salad at an office Christmas party. The colors could not have been more appropriate, and the flavor made bells ring. However, since the dressing is a type of pesto, making it between November and June could be a problem—unless you have access to fresh basil.

  1 pound orzo (pasta that resembles
     oversized grains of rice)
Boiling salted water
1¼ cups fresh basil leaves, minced
 ⅓ cup minced fresh parsley
  4 cloves garlic, peeled and crushed
 ¼ teaspoon salt (optional)
 ¼ cup olive oil
  1 large sweet red pepper, cored, seeded, and chopped

1. Cook the orzo in the boiling salted water for 8 minutes or until the pasta is *al dente.* Drain the orzo.
2. While the orzo cooks, combine the basil, parsley, garlic, salt (if desired), and oil in a large bowl. Add the drained orzo while it is still warm, mix the ingredients well, and refrigerate the salad.
3. Just before serving time, add the red pepper, and toss the salad.

CHINESE PASTA SALAD

Although the name of this recipe may sound like cultural schizophrenia, in fact, noodles probably originated in China, where evidence for their consumption dates back to 5000 B.C. With the peanuts and peanut butter complementing the protein in the pasta, this could almost be a main course.

Preparation tips: Although I use oat-bran ricciolini (see page 11 for the source), you can prepare this salad with other sizes and shapes of pasta, including spaghetti (broken into 4-inch lengths). The vegetables can be eaten raw or, for better texture and digestibility, blanched tender-crisp. When blanching the vegetables, you can use the same boiling water for all of them, but they are best done separately since their cooking times differ: about 30 seconds for snow peas, 1 minute for sugar snaps and broccoli, and 1½ minutes for carrots. After removing the vegetables from the water, rinse them immediately under cold water. The salad and the dressing can be prepared in advance, but do not combine the two until shortly before serving time.

DRESSING

½ cup rice vinegar

¼ cup soy sauce (preferably reduced-sodium)

¼ cup natural peanut butter (smooth or chunky)

2 tablespoons vegetable oil (preferably canola)

2 tablespoons sugar

2 teaspoons mustard powder

2 teaspoons Oriental sesame oil

2 teaspoon grated or minced gingerroot

2 teaspoons minced garlic

¼ teaspoon or more hot red pepper flakes, to taste

SALAD

12 to 16 ounces oat-bran ricciolini *or* other pasta

Large pot boiling water

1 teaspoon salt

1 tablespoon oil

1 pound snow peas *or* sugar snaps, trimmed and blanched if desired and cut into bite-sized pieces

3 carrots, peeled, thinly sliced on the diagonal, and blanched if desired

1 sweet red pepper, cored, seeded, and cut into bite-sized pieces

1 sweet yellow pepper, cored, seeded, and cut into bite-sized pieces

2 cups broccoli flowerets, blanched if desired

1 bunch scallions (including the green tops), thinly sliced on the diagonal

1 cup dry-roasted unsalted peanuts

1. Prepare the dressing by adding the dressing ingredients to a blender, and processing them until they are smooth.

2. Place the pasta in the boiling water with the salt and oil. Return the water quickly to a boil, and cook the pasta for 10 to 15 minutes or until it is *al dente.* Drain the pasta, rinse it, transfer it to a large bowl, and toss it with about ⅓ of the dressing.

3. When the pasta has cooled, toss it gently with the remaining salad ingredients *except* the scallions and peanuts. Chill the salad until serving time.

4. At serving time, add the remaining dressing, the scallions, and peanuts, and toss the salad gently.

CURRIED MACARONI-BEAN SALAD   *6 to 8 servings*

This attractive, tangy salad, compliments of pasta manufacturer San Giorgio–Skinner, Inc., provides main-course protein. It was a favorite of the raisin lovers among my recipe testers. Since it is made without ingredients that spoil readily, it is a particularly good salad to take on a picnic or serve at a summer buffet.

   4 ounces (1 cup) uncooked elbow macaroni
   ½ cup grated Parmesan
   1 16-ounce can kidney beans (1⅔ cups cooked
       beans), drained and liquid reserved (if you are
       using home-cooked beans, save about ½ cup of
       the cooking water)
   ½ cup chopped onion
   ½ cup chopped celery
   Water
   1 teaspoon curry powder
   1 tablespoon honey
   ¼ cup apple-cider vinegar
   ¾ cup raisins

1. Cook the macaroni *al dente* according to package directions. Drain the pasta, transfer it to a medium-sized bowl, and immediately toss it with the cheese.
2. Add the beans, onion, and celery to the macaroni and cheese.
3. Pour the reserved bean liquid into a measuring cup, and add enough water to measure 1 cup. Transfer the liquid to a small saucepan, and add the curry powder, honey, vinegar, and raisins. Bring the mixture to a boil, lower the heat, and simmer the ingredients for 6 minutes or until the raisins are plump.
4. Pour the hot dressing over the macaroni-and-bean mixture, and toss the salad well. Chill the salad for at least 1 hour before serving it.

THREE-PEPPER SALAD

6 servings

This is one of the many wonderful creations by Ellen Brown, author of *The Gourmet Gazelle Cookbook.* I didn't change a thing.

Preparation tips: I tried the recipe with cilantro and with parsley, and although I'm not a cilantro fan, I had to admit it was better that way. However, even with parsley, it's delicious and beautiful. The salad can be made a day ahead to produce a more marinated effect. For crisper vegetables, however, add the dressing about 1 hour before serving the salad.

SALAD
- 2 sweet red peppers
- 2 sweet yellow peppers
- 1 sweet green pepper
- 2 ribs celery
- 2 medium cucumbers
- ⅓ cup chopped red onion
- 1 pint cherry tomatoes, halved

DRESSING
- 3 tablespoons fresh lime juice
- 2 tablespoons white-wine vinegar
- 1 tablespoon olive oil
- 2 cloves garlic, peeled and minced
- ¼ teaspoon salt (optional)
- Dash or more cayenne, to taste
- ¼ cup chopped cilantro *or* fresh parsley

1. Core and seed the red, yellow, and green peppers, and finely julienne them. Finely julienne the celery. Place the vegetables in a glass or stainless-steel bowl.
2. Peel the cucumbers, halve them lengthwise, remove the seeds, and finely julienne the flesh. Add the cucumbers to the bowl. Add the onion and tomatoes.
3. In a small bowl or jar, combine the dressing ingredients. Pour the dressing over the vegetables, and toss the ingredients to combine them. Cover the salad, and chill it for 1 hour, tossing it occasionally. Serve it well chilled.

SNOW PEA SALAD

4 servings

This salad takes a little more effort and money (snow peas can cost $3 to $4 a pound and good mushrooms nearly the same) than most, but to me and my tasters, it was worth it, especially since it can be used as a prepare-ahead vegetable side dish.

Preparation tips: If you don't wish to roast your own peppers, you can substitute commercially prepared ones, although the flavor will not be quite as good. Both the vegetables and the dressing can be prepared ahead, but the salad is best served at room temperature.

SALAD
- 2 large sweet red peppers, roasted (see page 8)
- ¾ pound snow peas, ends trimmed
- 1 small red onion, peeled, halved lengthwise, and thinly sliced crosswise
- ¼ pound medium to large mushrooms, sliced

Lettuce leaves for serving (optional)

DRESSING
- 1 tablespoon Dijon-style mustard
- 2 tablespoons red-wine vinegar
- Freshly ground black pepper to taste
- Pinch salt (optional)
- 2 tablespoons olive oil
- ¼ cup finely minced fresh parsley

1. When the peppers are cool enough to handle, remove their skins, cores, and seeds. Thinly slice the peppers, and place them in a salad bowl.
2. Boil enough water to cover the snow peas. Boil the peas for 2 minutes. Then drain the peas, and immediately rinse them under cold water. Drain the peas again, and add them to the salad bowl along with the sliced onion and mushrooms. If you are making the vegetables in advance, chill them until 1 hour before serving.
3. In a small bowl, combine the mustard, vinegar, pepper, and salt (if desired). Whisk in the oil, and stir in the parsley.
4. At serving time, pour the dressing over the room-temperature vegetables, and toss the salad gently. Serve the salad on the lettuce leaves (if you wish).

MINTED SUGAR SNAP SALAD

4 to 6 servings

You may think—and I may agree with you—that sugar snaps need no adornment. These succulent peas, which are eaten pods and all, were created by a persistent plant breeder in the 1970s and are now prized by home gardeners. I find it hard to get them into the house uneaten. But if you can resist temptation long enough, this is a nice way to prepare them.

SALAD
- 1 pound sugar snap peas, trimmed
- ¼ cup finely chopped red onion
- 2 tablespoons finely chopped fresh mint leaves

DRESSING
- 2 tablespoons raspberry vinegar
- 1 tablespoon olive oil
- ¼ teaspoon salt (optional)
- ¼ teaspoon freshly ground black pepper
- ⅛ teaspoon sugar

1. Parboil the peas for 2 minutes or until they turn bright green. Rinse the peas immediately under cold water, drain them, and set them aside to cool.
2. Place the cooled peas in a salad bowl, and add the onion and mint, tossing the ingredients to combine them well.
3. To prepare the dressing, combine the dressing ingredients in a small bowl or jar, and drizzle the dressing over the peas. Toss the salad again. Serve the salad chilled or at room temperature.

NEW POTATO SALAD

4 servings

Here's a salad that can be whipped together in the blink of an eye.

SALAD
- 1½ pounds new potatoes, cubed and steamed until they are just tender
- 1 small onion, peeled and shredded
- 1 large carrot, peeled and shredded
- ¼ sweet green pepper, shredded

DRESSING
- ½ cup or more plain nonfat or low-fat yogurt, to taste
- 2 tablespoons light mayonnaise
- ½ teaspoon sugar
- ½ teaspoon tarragon, crumbled
- 1 teaspoon caraway seeds
- ¼ teaspoon paprika
- ¼ teaspoon salt (optional)
- Freshly ground black pepper to taste
- Cayenne to taste

1. In a medium-sized bowl, combine the salad ingredients.
2. In a small bowl, combine the dressing ingredients. Add the dressing to the potato mixture, and toss the ingredients to mix them well.

POTATO SALAD WITH SAUSAGE   *6 to 8 servings*

Before you say "What is Jane Brody doing using sausages?" please note the amount and method of preparation. Frankly, I think life is too short to miss this fabulous potato salad, derived from a *Gourmet* magazine recipe.

SALAD
- ¼ pound cooked garlic sausage *or* smoked garlic sausage, thinly sliced
- 2½ pounds small boiling potatoes
- 6 cups beef broth *or* 3 cups beef broth and 3 cups water
- ½ cup minced onion
- 2 scallions (including the green tops), thinly sliced

DRESSING
- 2 tablespoons dry white wine
- 2 tablespoons white-wine vinegar
- 2 tablespoons olive oil
- 1 tablespoon minced fresh parsley
- 2 large cloves garlic, peeled and minced
- ¼ teaspoon salt, or to taste (optional)
- ¼ teaspoon freshly ground black pepper

1. Place the sausage in a dry skillet over low heat or in a toaster oven on low or in a microwave, and cook the sausage until most of the fat is rendered out. Drain the sausage on paper towels. Set the sausage aside.
2. Place the whole, *unpeeled* potatoes in a large saucepan or Dutch oven. Add the broth or the broth-water combination, and bring the liquid to a boil. Reduce the heat to low, cover the pan, and simmer the potatoes for 10 to 20 minutes (depending on the size of the potatoes) or until the potatoes are just tender when they are pierced with a fork.
3. Using a slotted spoon, remove the potatoes from the broth (the broth can be frozen and reused), and let the potatoes cool. When they are cool enough to handle, peel them, and cut them into ½-inch dice. Place the potatoes in a salad bowl.
4. Add to the potatoes the reserved sausage, onion, and scallions.
5. To prepare the dressing, combine the dressing ingredients in a small bowl or jar. Pour the dressing over the potato mixture, and toss the salad gently.

POTATO-BROCCOLI SALAD

4 to 6 servings

You can serve this attractive potato salad any time of year.

SALAD
- 1½ pounds small new potatoes, steamed until they are just tender
- 2 to 3 cups broccoli flowerets, steamed for 5 minutes
- ½ small red onion, peeled and sliced crosswise into rings
- ½ small sweet red pepper, cored, seeded, and sliced crosswise into rings

DRESSING
- 3 tablespoons fresh lemon juice
- 2 tablespoons olive oil
- 1 teaspoon Dijon-style mustard
- 1 large clove garlic, peeled and minced
- ¼ teaspoon paprika
- ¼ teaspoon salt (optional)
- ¼ teaspoon freshly ground black pepper

1. Halve or quarter the potatoes, depending on their size, and arrange them on a serving plate with the broccoli. Chill the vegetables until serving time.
2. At serving time, arrange the onion and red pepper over the potatoes and broccoli.
3. In a small bowl or jar, combine the dressing ingredients. Pour the dressing over the salad.

HARVEST POTATO SALAD

4 servings

A great salad to make toward the end of summer, when you can get everything fresh: corn, green peppers, and new potatoes.

Preparation tip: You can make this any time of year using frozen corn.

SALAD
- 1½ pounds new potatoes, cut into ¾-inch cubes
- 1½ cups cooked corn kernels (cut from about 2 large ears)
- 2 sweet green peppers, cut into ½-inch pieces
- 3 scallions, finely sliced
- 2 to 3 tablespoons minced jalapeños *or* green chilies

DRESSING
- ⅓ cup plain nonfat or low-fat yogurt
- 1 tablespoon salad oil
- 1 tablespoon fresh lemon juice
- ¾ teaspoon cumin
- ¼ teaspoon salt (optional)
- Freshly ground black pepper to taste

1. Steam the potato cubes for 10 minutes—maybe less—or until they are just tender. Place the potatoes in a medium-sized bowl, and add the corn, green peppers, scallions, and jalapeños or chilies. Toss the ingredients.
2. In a small bowl, combine the dressing ingredients. Add the dressing to the salad, and toss the ingredients to mix them thoroughly.

POTATO AND PEA POD SALAD

4 servings

I sometimes have to buy twice the amount of snow peas I really need because I eat half of them on the way home. As long as they are not overcooked (the inherent flaw in frozen snow peas), they are a delicacy almost without parallel. Here is a new way to eat them.

Preparation tips: The potatoes may be steamed and seasoned up to 8 hours ahead of serving them and kept covered and chilled. But the snow peas and the dressing should be added just before serving time.

1½ **pounds red boiling potatoes,** *unpeeled*
  3 **tablespoons fresh lemon juice, divided**
Salt to taste (optional)
  ½ **pound snow peas, strings removed and pods**
     halved crosswise on the diagonal
  1 **tablespoon coarse-grain mustard (I prefer**
     country-style Dijon)
  2 **tablespoons olive oil**

1. Quarter the potatoes lengthwise, then cut them crosswise into ½-inch pieces. Steam them over boiling water for 8 to 12 minutes or until they are just tender. Transfer them to a large bowl.
2. Toss the potatoes with 1 tablespoon of the lemon juice and the salt (if desired), and let them cool for 15 minutes.
3. Meanwhile, boil water in a saucepan, and blanch the snow peas for *5 seconds.* Drain the peas in a colander, and refresh them under cold water. Add them to the potatoes.
4. In a small bowl, whisk together the remaining 2 tablespoons of lemon juice, the mustard, and oil. Pour the dressing over the vegetables, and toss the ingredients gently. Serve the salad at room temperature.

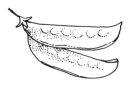

SWEET POTATO SALAD

6 servings

"Yum" is what I and my tasters said about this vitamin-packed salad. The nuts, which are optional, add a crunchy touch.

Preparation tips: Take care not to overcook the potatoes. And be sure to chill them before dicing.

SALAD
6 *unpeeled* sweet potatoes (about
　　2½ pounds)
Water to cover by 2 inches
1 small onion, peeled and minced
1 rib celery, minced
½ cup chopped fresh parsley

½ cup roasted unsalted cashews for
　garnish

DRESSING
2 tablespoons olive oil
2 tablespoons fresh lemon juice
2 teaspoons soy sauce (preferably
　tamari *or* reduced-sodium)
1 teaspoon marjoram, crumbled
Freshly ground black pepper to taste

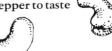

1. Put the potatoes into a large pot, add the water, and bring it to a boil. Reduce the heat, partially cover the pot, and simmer the potatoes for 30 to 40 minutes or until the potatoes are just tender. Remove the potatoes from the water, and, when they are cool enough to handle, peel them. Chill them, then cut them into ⅓-inch dice.
2. Place the diced potatoes in a bowl along with the onion, celery, and parsley.
3. In a small bowl or jar, combine the dressing ingredients, and pour the dressing over the potato mixture, tossing the salad gently.
4. Before serving the salad, garnish it with the cashews.

JAPANESE RADISH SALAD

6 to 8 servings

So low in calories it could be considered a free food.

Preparation tip: Allow 1 hour for the salad to marinate.

DRESSING
2 tablespoons rice vinegar
1 tablespoon sake (Japanese rice
　wine) *or* dry sherry
1 tablespoon reduced-sodium soy
　sauce
1 tablespoon sugar

SALAD
1 small daikon (Japanese white
　radish) *or* ½ large daikon *or* 9
　ounces red radishes, julienned
　(about 1½ cups)
1 large carrot, peeled and
　julienned (about 1½ cups)

1. Combine the dressing ingredients in a medium-sized bowl.
2. Add the radish and carrot, and toss the ingredients to combine them. Cover the bowl, and refrigerate the salad for at least 1 hour, tossing it occasionally.

CURRIED RICE AND WALNUT SALAD   *6 servings*

The nuts in this offering from the Walnut Marketing Board of Sacramento, California, give the dish a delightful crunch. Try using leftover rice.

Serving suggestion: Serve the salad on a bed of red-leaf lettuce, and garnish it with thin half slices of lemon and walnut halves.

  1 tablespoon curry powder (I use ⅓ hot curry powder)
  1 tablespoon olive oil *or* canola oil
  1 large cucumber, peeled, seeded, and thinly
     sliced crosswise
  3 cups *cooked* long-grain white rice *or* basmati brown rice
  ⅓ cup sliced scallions
  ⅓ cup golden raisins
  3 tablespoons fresh lemon juice
Salt to taste (optional)
  ½ cup coarsely chopped walnuts
Paprika for garnish

1. In a large *dry* skillet, preferably one with a nonstick surface, toast the curry powder over low heat for 2 to 3 minutes, stirring it constantly and taking care not to burn it.
2. Stir in the oil, increase the heat to medium, and add the cucumber slices. Sauté the cucumber, tossing it, for 3 minutes or until it is tender.
3. Transfer the cucumber to a large bowl. Add the rice, scallions, raisins, lemon juice, and salt (if you are using it). Toss the ingredients to combine them well, cover the bowl, and chill the salad for 1 hour and up to 2 days.
4. At serving time, stir in the walnuts, and sprinkle the salad with the paprika.

BASMATI RICE SALAD WITH PEAS   *6 servings*

Aromatic basmati rice makes a tasty and colorful rice salad.

SALAD
  2 cups water
  ½ teaspoon salt
  1 cup basmati brown rice *or*
     long-grain parboiled rice

  1 cup cooked fresh peas *or* thawed
     frozen peas
  ⅓ cup minced fresh parsley
  ¼ cup minced scallions

DRESSING
  ¼ cup plain nonfat or low-fat yogurt
  2 tablespoons fresh lemon juice
  2 tablespoons olive oil
  ½ teaspoon Dijon-style mustard
Salt to taste (optional)
White pepper to taste (preferably
     freshly ground)

1. In a medium-sized saucepan, bring the water and salt to a boil, add the rice, and stir the mixture until it returns to a boil. Reduce the heat, cover the pan, and simmer the rice over low heat for 35 minutes (15 to 20 minutes if you are using parboiled rice) or until the rice is barely done. Transfer the rice to a bowl, fluff it with a fork, and let it cool for about 10 minutes.
2. While the rice is cooking, in a small bowl, whisk together the dressing ingredients. Add the dressing to the rice along with the peas, parsley, and scallions, and toss the salad gently.

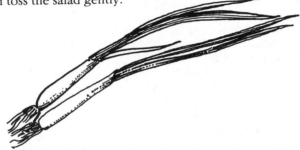

SPINACH WALDORF SALAD

6 to 8 servings

The curried yogurt dressing for this nutritious salad tastes rich without adding many calories.

Preparation tip: The dressing can be made ahead and refrigerated until serving time.

SALAD
- 1 pound fresh spinach, stems trimmed, well washed and dried, and torn into bite-sized pieces
- 3 red-skinned apples, *unpeeled,* cored, thinly sliced, and tossed with 2 tablespoons fresh lemon juice *or* a mixture of lemon juice and water
- 1 to 1½ cups diced celery
- ½ cup coarsely chopped walnuts
- ½ cup raisins

DRESSING
- ¾ cup plain nonfat or low-fat yogurt
- 2 tablespoons fresh lemon juice
- 2 tablespoons minced scallions
- 2 to 4 teaspoons chopped fresh mint *or* ¾ teaspoon dried mint
- 1 teaspoon minced garlic (1 large clove)
- 1 teaspoon sugar
- ½ teaspoon curry powder, or to taste (you can use part hot and part mild curry powder *or* all hot curry powder)
- ¼ teaspoon salt (optional)

Freshly ground black pepper to taste

1. In a large salad bowl, combine the salad ingredients.
2. In a glass jar, add the dressing ingredients, cover the jar, and shake it to mix the ingredients thoroughly. At serving time, add the dressing to the salad, tossing the salad to coat the ingredients evenly with the dressing.

SUMMER SQUASH SALAD

6 servings

Here's a dish that's easy, fat-free, inexpensive, and tasty.

Preparation tips: This salad can (and should) be made ahead. The salt in the salad ingredients is *not* optional—it is needed to wilt the squash; much of it then gets rinsed away.

SALAD
¾ pound zucchini, sliced paper-thin
¾ pound yellow summer squash, sliced paper-thin
1½ teaspoons salt (*not* optional)

1 tablespoon snipped dill

DRESSING
⅓ cup distilled white vinegar
¾ teaspoon sugar

1. Toss the zucchini and squash with the salt, place the slices in a colander over a bowl or the sink, and let the vegetables drain for 1 hour. Rinse the slices under cold running water, and drain them well.
2. In a large glass or ceramic bowl, combine the dressing ingredients, stirring them to dissolve the sugar. Add the drained squash and the dill, and toss the ingredients to combine them well. Cover the bowl, and chill the salad for 2 hours or longer. Toss the salad again before serving it.

TOMATO AND ONION SALAD

6 servings

You may think you don't need a recipe for so simple a salad. But I found this particular version so delicious (a note to myself said, "I could eat it all day") that I decided to state the obvious.

SALAD
3 large ripe tomatoes, cut crosswise into about 6 slices each
1 large red onion, peeled and thinly sliced crosswise
Salt to taste (optional)
Freshly black ground pepper to taste

3 tablespoons chopped fresh basil leaves

DRESSING
2 tablespoons red-wine vinegar
2 tablespoons olive oil
2 tablespoons grated Parmesan

1. Arrange the tomato and onion slices on a serving platter, placing 1 onion slice between every 2 tomato slices. Sprinkle the slices with the salt (if desired) and pepper.
2. In a small bowl or jar, combine the dressing ingredients, and pour the dressing over the tomatoes and onion. Sprinkle the salad with the basil.

WINTER SQUASH AND PEPPER SALAD

4 to 6 servings

Here is a stunning, oil-free salad devised by Indian cook and author Julie Sahni. It is sure to bring you compliments.

Preparation tips: If you do not have access to cumin seeds, substitute 1 teaspoon ground cumin, toasted by stirring it constantly for about 30 seconds over medium-low heat in a dry skillet. The dressed salad can be prepared up to 4 hours ahead and refrigerated, but for best flavor, bring it to room temperature before serving it.

SALAD
- 1 small (about 1 pound) butternut squash
- 1 large sweet green pepper, cored, seeded, and cut lengthwise into ¼-inch strips
- 1 large sweet red pepper, cored, seeded, and cut lengthwise into ¼-inch strips
- 3 tablespoons chopped roasted unsalted peanuts for garnish

DRESSING
- 5 tablespoons orange juice
- ¼ cup fresh lemon juice
- 2 tablespoons minced onion
- ¼ cup loosely packed fresh mint leaves, minced and mashed to a paste in a mortar with a pestle
- 1½ teaspoons cumin seeds, toasted in a dry skillet for several minutes and ground in a mortar with a pestle, divided
- 1 tablespoon sugar
- Salt to taste (optional)
- Freshly ground black pepper to taste

1. Peel the squash, cut it in half lengthwise, remove the seeds and strings, and cut the flesh crosswise into ⅛-inch slices. Steam the squash over boiling water for 4 minutes or until the squash is barely tender. Set the squash aside to cool.
2. Transfer the cooled squash to a large bowl, and add the green and red peppers.
3. In a small bowl, combine the orange juice, lemon juice, onion, mint, ½ of the ground cumin seeds, the sugar, salt (if desired), and pepper. Pour the dressing over the vegetables, and toss the ingredients gently, taking care not to tear the squash.
4. Transfer the salad to a platter, and sprinkle it with the peanuts and the remaining ground cumin or to taste. Serve the salad at room temperature.

SWISS CHARD SALAD

4 servings

Simple and delicious, this make-ahead salad is based on a nutritious yet underused green.

Preparation tips: Note that the salad should be chilled overnight before serving it. To hard-cook egg whites, hard-boil the whole eggs, and then remove the yolks, which can be fed to your dog.

SALAD

1½ pounds Swiss chard, tough stems removed

¼ cup finely chopped scallions

Red-leaf lettuce *or* radicchio for lining the plates (optional)
2 hard-cooked egg whites, chopped (optional)

DRESSING

3 tablespoon white-wine vinegar
2 tablespoons olive oil *or* canola oil
2 teaspoons Dijon-style mustard
1 large clove garlic, peeled and minced
1 teaspoon soy sauce
¼ teaspoon cumin
Salt to taste (optional)
Freshly ground black pepper to taste

1. Slice the Swiss chard crosswise into ½-inch shreds, and steam the chard over boiling water, in a covered saucepan, for about 7 minutes. Rinse the chard under cold water, drain the chard, and set it aside to cool.
2. While the chard steams, in a small bowl or jar, add the dressing ingredients, and whisk or shake them until they are well mixed.
3. In a medium-sized bowl, combine the cooled chard with the scallions. Add the dressing, and toss the ingredients to combine them. Cover the bowl with plastic wrap, and chill the chard overnight.
4. At serving time, divide the salad among 4 salad plates lined (if desired) with red-leaf lettuce or radicchio. Sprinkle each serving with some of the chopped egg whites, if you wish.

WATERCRESS AND ENDIVE SALAD

4 servings

Here, the nippy mustard vinaigrette and watercress are offset by the relatively bland Belgian endive and cucumber.

Preparation tip: Since you will not be peeling the cucumber, you should start with unwaxed ones such as kirbies or English (hothouse) cucumbers.

Serving suggestion: This dish looks especially lovely as a composed salad. Make a bed of watercress around the outer part of the salad bowl. Fill the middle with the endive leaves, using some tips as a border outside the watercress. Place cucumber slices around the endive in the center.

SALAD

1½ large *or* 2 small bunches
    watercress
2 small heads Belgian endive
1 cup thinly sliced cucumber,
    unpeeled and scored with a fork

DRESSING

2 tablespoons olive oil *or* walnut oil
1 tablespoon fresh lemon juice
2 teaspoons Dijon-style mustard
Salt to taste (optional)
Freshly ground black pepper to taste

1. Remove the tough stems from the watercress. Rinse the cress, spin it dry, and place the leaves in a salad bowl. (See "Serving suggestion," above.)
2. Discard the tough end of the endives, and slice the leaves into bite-sized pieces. Add these to the watercress along with the cucumber slices.
3. In a small bowl or jar, combine the dressing ingredients. Pour the dressing over the salad ingredients, and toss the ingredients before serving the salad. However, if you are preparing a composed salad, simply drizzle the dressing over the ingredients in the bowl without tossing them.

"WOO" SALAD *(Watercress, Onion, and Orange)*   *4 servings*

Actually, I should call this "wow" salad—attractive and with a nice bite that is enhanced by the zippy vinaigrette.

SALAD

2 large bunches watercress, tough
    stems removed
2 medium navel oranges, peeled,
    cut lengthwise into 8 wedges,
    then halved crosswise (16 pieces)
1 small red onion, peeled and
    thinly sliced into rings

DRESSING

2 tablespoons red-wine vinegar
1 tablespoon olive oil
2 teaspoons Dijon-style mustard
¼ teaspoon cumin
⅛ teaspoon salt (optional)
Freshly ground black pepper to taste

1. Wash and spin-dry the watercress, and place it in a salad bowl.
2. Add the orange wedges and onion rings.
3. In a small bowl or jar, combine the dressing ingredients. Pour the dressing over the salad just before serving it, and toss the salad well.

Salad Dressings

Too often, the most nutritious and low-calorie salad is "spoiled" by a fatty, high-calorie dressing. Just 2 tablespoons of an ordinary oil- or mayonnaise-based dressing can increase a salad's caloric value by 150 calories and make fat by far the largest source of calories in the dish. And many people use a lot more dressing than 2 tablespoons! In recent years, a number of low-fat and no-fat commercial dressings have been marketed, some of them good (although most have a large amount of salt). I offer a few of my own for you to try on your favorite salads.

JANE'S EVERYDAY VINAIGRETTE   *about ⅓ cup*

This is the dressing—more or less—that I whip together when I make an "ordinary" salad (the kind prepared with whatever ingredients are in the house). I say "more or less" because I usually don't bother to measure the ingredients (except the oil, to be sure I don't use too much) and I sometimes add herbs or other seasonings. But whatever I do, this vinaigrette always seems to work and to prompt one or more guests to ask, "What's in the dressing? It's delicious."

Preparation tips: Crushing the garlic with salt produces a pungent flavor without the bitterness that often results when garlic is mashed through a press. If desired, add ½ teaspoon of crumbled tarragon to the dressing.

    1 large clove garlic, peeled and chopped
    ⅛ teaspoon salt
    1 to 2 tablespoons balsamic vinegar, to taste
    2 tablespoons other vinegar *or* fresh lemon juice
    1 teaspoon Dijon-style mustard
    2 dashes Worcestershire sauce
    2 tablespoons olive oil
    Freshly ground black pepper to taste

In a mortar with a pestle (wooden or ceramic), mash the garlic with the salt until the ingredients form a paste. Or mash the garlic in a garlic press. Transfer the garlic paste to a small bowl or jar, and add the remaining ingredients, whisking or shaking them until the dressing is well combined.

LEMON VINAIGRETTE   *about 1¼ cups*

½ cup fresh lemon juice
½ cup water
¼ cup salad oil (preferably olive *or* canola)
2½ teaspoons Dijon-style mustard
1 teaspoon sugar
1 teaspoon freshly ground black pepper, or to taste
2 cloves garlic, peeled and crushed
½ teaspoon salt, or to taste (optional)

Add the ingredients to a blender or bowl, and blend or whisk them to mix them thoroughly.

PEAR VINAIGRETTE   *about 2 cups*

This versatile sweet-and-sour dressing, derived from a recipe in Ellen Brown's *The Gourmet Gazelle Cookbook,* would go well on fruit or poultry as well as salad greens. It is salt-free and will keep in the refrigerator, tightly covered, for a week or longer.

2 ripe pears, peeled, cored, and diced
5 tablespoons raspberry vinegar
1 tablespoon Dijon-style mustard
¼ cup roasted unsalted cashews
2 tablespoons canola oil
2 tablespoons walnut oil *or* 2 more tablespoons
   canola oil
½ teaspoon marjoram
½ teaspoon oregano
¼ teaspoon thyme
¼ teaspoon freshly ground white pepper

Add the ingredients to a blender or food processor, and process them.

QUINNS' VINAIGRETTE

about ⅔ cup

My friends Jane and Terry Quinn included this pungent dressing in their Christmas package one year, and I begged them for the recipe. I defatted it quite a bit, but it is still delicious. *Caution:* use the dressing sparingly.

- 4 tablespoons olive oil
- 4 tablespoons red-wine vinegar
- 2 teaspoons fresh lemon juice
- 2 teaspoons Dijon-style mustard
- 1 large clove garlic, peeled and cut up
- 1 teaspoon mustard powder
- 1 teaspoon freshly ground black pepper
- ½ teaspoon salt (optional)
- ½ teaspoon tarragon
- ½ teaspoon basil
- ½ teaspoon dillweed

Add the ingredients to a blender, and process them until the vinaigrette is smooth and creamy.

RASPBERRY VINAIGRETTE

about 1 cup

This dressing is based on an offering in *Spa Food* by Edward J. Safdie, also author of *New Spa Food.*

- 5 tablespoons raspberry vinegar
- ¼ cup canola oil
- ¼ cup water
- 2 tablespoons raspberries (fresh *or* frozen and thawed), if available
- 1 tablespoon fresh lime juice
- 1 tablespoon minced shallot
- 1½ teaspoons sesame oil
- ¼ teaspoon salt (optional)
- ¼ teaspoon freshly ground black pepper
- Dash hot pepper sauce

Add the ingredients to a jar, cover the jar, and shake it to combine the ingredients thoroughly. Chill the dressing for at least 1 hour before using it.

HORSERADISH VINAIGRETTE   *about ¼ cup*

    2 tablespoons olive oil
    ¼ teaspoon Oriental sesame oil
    1 tablespoon balsamic vinegar
    1 tablespoon drained prepared horseradish
    ¼ teaspoon salt (optional)
    ⅛ teaspoon freshly ground black pepper

Add the ingredients to a small jar or bowl, and mix them thoroughly.

CREAMY HORSERADISH DRESSING   *about ½ cup*

    3 tablespoons plain nonfat or low-fat yogurt
    3 tablespoons canola oil
1½ tablespoons drained prepared horseradish
    1 tablespoon white vinegar
    1 teaspoon Dijon-style mustard
Salt to taste (optional)
Freshly ground black pepper to taste

Place all the ingredients in a jar with a tight-fitting lid, and shake them until they are well combined and creamy.

BAKED GOODS

Yeast Breads

HOW TO BAKE BREAD

For the sake of those who may have missed it in *Jane Brody's Good Food Book,* I am repeating the bread-baking guidelines published there—with addenda.

Like any new skill, bread baking is a learning experience. But it's not rocket science. With a few basic principles and helpful hints, you, too, can become a master baker. I *would* recommend, however, that the first breads be made for family or close friends (they'll love them no matter how the breads turn out) and that you make them when you are not hurried or otherwise under pressure.

YEAST My husband insists that yeast knows when you're afraid of it. If you think of yeast as a bunch of mindless microorganisms (which, of course, is what yeast is), you'll have an easier time establishing your superiority. Yeast *is* a living organism that demands some care and respect. It is sold in two forms: compressed in cakes (sometimes called fresh yeast) or active dry in packages (either individual packets each containing 1 scant tablespoon of yeast or in bulk packages from which you measure out each scant tablespoon). Active dry yeast is easier to buy and easier to work with. (If you use compressed yeast, ½ ounce equals 1 packet of active dry yeast.) Active dry yeast can also be purchased in rapid-rising form, which, as its name implies, significantly speeds up the needed risings.

Active dry yeast must be dissolved in warm liquid and given a chance to start growing and producing the carbon-dioxide gas that allows bread to rise. The temperature of the liquid is very important: too cold and the yeast will sit there doing nothing; too hot and the yeast will be scalded to death; lukewarm (the temperature to which baby bottles used to be heated) is just right—to be exact, *between 105° and 115° F.* (Compressed yeast should be dissolved in liquid no hotter than 95° F.) I find it best to use a thermometer, since what feels lukewarm to me can vary greatly with the seasons and my mood. If you have no kitchen thermometer, you can reach the proper temperature by mixing equal parts of boiling water and ice water.

It is a good idea to "proof" your yeast (establish its viability) before you combine it with the rest of the more expensive ingredients. Simply mix the yeast with the warm liquid and a generous pinch of sugar for the yeast to feed on. If you add a pinch of powdered ginger, it will improve the action of the yeast. In 5 to 15 minutes, you should see the yeast start to foam. (Every recipe in this book instructs you to proof the yeast first, and you can adapt other recipes accordingly.) Then you'll be sure that you're starting with live yeast; as long as you don't overheat it before baking time, it will remain viable and produce a well-leavened loaf. It is best to store yeast in the refrigerator and to use it before its expiration date.

If you double a yeast-bread recipe, don't double the yeast—add only about 1 extra teaspoon.

FLOUR You'll notice that most bread recipes are not precise about the amount of flour needed to produce a dough that can be handled. This is because the amount varies: with the type of flour, how it was ground, how long it has been stored, the temperature and humidity of the air, and, I've come to think, a certain arbitrary independence that likes to keep bread bakers guessing. It is a good idea, when you come to the last cup of flour, to add it slowly, mixing it in as you go and stopping when you think the dough can be kneaded without becoming glued to your hands. I often find it easiest to flour my hands and work in the last cup of flour with my hands; additional flour can be worked in during kneading if the dough is still too sticky. If too much flour is added, you may end up with a dry bread. Most recipes indicate the ideal moisture content of the dough—that is, whether the dough should feel stiff or soft (after some experience, you'll know the difference) and whether you can expect it to feel sticky at first. Sticky dough usually firms up during the first rising.

Unless otherwise specified, these are my preferences in flour:

- Whole-wheat flour—stone-ground regular or graham flour (this is a coarser grind). Even though stone-ground flours cost more, the flavor and nutritive value are decidedly superior. If you're going to the trouble of making your own bread, it pays to invest in the best ingredients.
- All-purpose flour—unbleached white flour.
- Rye flour—whole-grain rye (but the refined supermarket variety called medium rye will do, if you can't get whole-grain).
- Corn meal—whole-grain meal, usually available in supermarkets.

For a bread dough to rise, it must contain an elastic protein called gluten that traps the bubbles of carbon dioxide given off by the yeast. Of all the flours used in bread baking, only wheat flour contains substantial amounts of gluten-making protein (the gluten is developed during the kneading of the dough). Therefore, virtually every yeast-bread recipe contains wheat flour. If not, gluten flour (an extract of wheat flour) may be added. So-called bread flour contains extra gluten and is often used in breads made in food processors, which aren't kneaded very long.

SALT Many people who are trying to—or who must—cut down on salt want to know if good yeast bread can be made without salt. The answer is a qualified yes. Salt-free doughs rise quickly—sometimes too quickly, resulting in air holes and incomplete development of flavor. There is also less time for the flours to absorb liquid, so the dough may be quite moist. If you omit the salt in a recipe, use less yeast to compensate for the shorter rising time, and watch the risings carefully (they will go faster than the recipe indicates). If the dough is too wet after the first rising, knead in some extra flour. You might also try simply reducing the amount of salt, rather than eliminating it entirely. I never use more than 1 teaspoon of salt per loaf (if the loaf is sliced into 16 pieces, this would equal 134 milligrams of sodium per slice), and for many recipes—especially those on the sweet side—I use only ½ teaspoon of salt per loaf.

SWEETENERS These make for a tender, flavorful bread. They also create a dark crust and prolong freshness. Honey and molasses are my favorites from a flavor standpoint. In the case of molasses, the sweetener also adds some nutrients besides calories. If you substitute honey or molasses for sugar in a recipe, you will probably need to increase the flour a bit to balance out the added liquid.

FAT Fat helps to keep breads from drying out quickly because it hangs on to moisture (that's why the fatless French bread gets stale in a day). Fat also retards the development of gluten, keeping the bread from rising too fast. Oils can be used in place of hard fats like butter or margarine, both of which can add color to a pale loaf. Omitting fat is likely to result in a chewy bread that has a lot of air holes in it.

LIQUIDS Many different liquids can be used in bread baking, each one helping to produce an excellent loaf. Water is the most common of the liquids and should always be used to dissolve the yeast. Milk or buttermilk adds protein and calcium, and produces a delicate texture and dark crust; fruit juices add sweetness and color; vegetable cooking water adds nutrients and flavor; tomato juice adds color, flavor, and salt; potato water adds starch that helps to condition the dough; beer provides food for the yeast and results in a hearty flavor. Other "liquids" can also be used, such as fruit purées like applesauce and cooked cereals.

KNEADING Some would-be bread bakers are put off by the necessity of kneading bread dough. They think of it as endless hard work. Actually, it's great fun and very therapeutic. You can think of every push on the dough as an acceptable expression of aggression, a tension-reliever, an upper-body strengthener, or a calorie-burning activity (it is all of these). It certainly gets my blood going on cold winter mornings. Breads rarely need more than 8 to 10 minutes of kneading (my husband says he never kneads dough longer than 5 minutes, and his breads always turn out great). As far as I'm concerned, all the fun goes out of the project if the dough is prepared in an electric mixer or food processor or in the new bread-baking machines into which you add the ingredients and the gadget does all the work. Besides, it's harder to tell if you've added the right amount of flour unless you use your hands. But if using a motorized device gets you to make your own healthful, delicious breads, far be it from me to say don't use it. Homemade bread from a food processor is still bound to be better than what usually comes out of a package.

Kneading is necessary to develop the gluten in the dough; the gluten allows the dough to rise properly. Dough is best kneaded on a firm surface that has been lightly floured. You can add flour as needed to keep the dough from sticking. Knead by repeatedly pressing the heels of your hands into the dough, then folding the dough over. Lean into the job, using the weight of your upper body to put pressure on the dough. The dough has been adequately kneaded when it appears smooth and bounces back after you press it in with a fingertip' (this indicates that the elastic gluten has been well developed).

RISING Yeast works best when the dough is allowed to rise in a warm (about 85° F), draft-free place. A gas oven with a lit pilot light is ideal for a rising. In an electric oven or a gas oven without a pilot light, you can heat the oven to low (about 120° F), then turn it off and wait 10 minutes before you put the dough in. Or try the top of your refrigerator, if it's warm up there. To prevent excessive drying, the dough should be covered with plastic wrap or with a cloth (usually a damp one) such as a linen or cotton dishtowel. Dough should rise until it has doubled in bulk; when pressed with a fingertip, the indentation should remain. The amount of time needed for risings will vary with the temperature and with the contents and consistency of the dough. Regardless of the times indicated in recipes, check on your dough about ½ hour before it's supposed to be finished rising. If the dough rises too much, punch it down, and let it rise again until it has doubled in bulk. Dough is punched down by pushing your fist into its center.

Dough that has been prepared to the point of rising (or even after the first rising) can be stored in the refrigerator for 1 to 2 days (be careful, though, because some aggressive doughs will rise even at refrigerator temperatures and may need an occasional punching down). Before baking a refrigerated dough, allow it to come to room temperature, and let it rise once or twice.

PANS Most breads are baked in aluminum or glass loaf pans that measure approximately 9 × 5 × 3 inches. The baking temperatures given here are usually geared toward aluminum pans; if you use glass pans, reduce the oven temperature by 25° F to prevent the crust from scorching before the middle is done. Breads can also be baked free-form on baking sheets or tiles. My favorite pans are unglazed ceramic loaf pans; when properly tempered, these require no washing and produce a superior product because they distribute the temperature more evenly than other pans.

Most pans should be greased before the dough is placed in them. You can use oil, butter, or margarine. I prefer vegetable-oil spray (sold in spray-top cans in the supermarket), which evenly distributes a thin, nonstick coating of oil. Sometimes you will be told to flour the pan or sprinkle it with corn meal after greasing it.

CRUST TYPES For a soft crust, brush melted fat on the top of the bread just before or while it's baking. For a crisp crust, brush the loaf with cold water just before or while it's baking. For a hard crust on rolls, put a pan of boiling water on the oven bottom during the baking. For a shiny crust, brush the bread with 1 egg beaten with 1 tablespoon of water. For a softer glaze, use just the beaten egg white alone or beaten with 1 tablespoon of water.

BAKING Most breads bake best in the middle of the oven; if you bake bread near the top, you may have to place a piece of foil loosely over the loaf toward the end of the baking to prevent excessive browning of the top before the inside is done. The oven should always be preheated to the proper temperature before you put the bread in. A bread is done when it begins to pull away from the sides of the pan and sounds hollow when you rap it on the bottom with your knuckles (obviously, the bread must be removed from the pan before you can do this). Overbaking produces a dry loaf.

COOLING AND STORING As soon as they're done (unless otherwise specified), breads should be removed from the pan and placed on a wire rack to cool. If you don't have a cooling rack, improvise, perhaps using a cool oven rack or the rack of a toaster oven, roasting pan, or pressure cooker.

Cooled bread should be wrapped in plastic wrap or placed inside a plastic bag and closed with a wire twist. The bread is best stored at room temperature, as long as it will be eaten within a week (or within 4 or 5 days in hot, humid weather). Breads get stale fastest in the refrigerator, although refrigeration delays spoilage. However, breads freeze very well; tightly wrapped in plastic, they keep for months. Thaw the loaves at room temperature or in the oven (wrap the loaves in foil, and place them in a 350° F oven for about 30 minutes). If you use a microwave, follow the instructions that came with the appliance.

WHEAT BERRY–OAT BREAD   *2 loaves*

This recipe makes a crunchy, great-tasting, wholesome bread.

Preparation tips: Advance preparation is required, since the wheat berries must be cooked before grinding them. A food processor works best for grinding, although the cooked berries can be chopped by hand. I recommend preparing the berries the night before you plan to bake. You can also cook a double or triple batch of wheat berries, grind them, and store them in a plastic bag in the freezer for fast future use.

    ¾ cup wheat berries
3½ cups water
    1 cup rolled oats
    ⅓ cup powdered nonfat milk

½ cup honey
¼ cup vegetable oil (preferably canola)
2 teaspoons salt (optional)
1 cup boiling water
2 packages (2 scant tablespoons) active dry yeast
1 teaspoon sugar
½ cup warm water (105° F to 115° F)
¼ cup wheat germ
4 cups whole-wheat flour (preferably
  stone-ground)
2½ cups (approximately) all-purpose flour
1 egg, beaten (optional)

1. In a heavy saucepan, combine the wheat berries and the 3½ cups of water. Bring the water to a boil, reduce the heat, cover the pan, and simmer the wheat berries, stirring them occasionally, for 3 hours. In a food processor fitted with the steel blade, coarsely grind the cooked wheat berries and water. Set the wheat berries aside to cool to lukewarm.

2. In a large heatproof bowl, combine the oats, powdered milk, honey, oil, and salt (if desired) with the 1 cup of boiling water. Stir the ingredients to combine them, and set them aside to cool to lukewarm.

3. When the oat mixture is nearly cool, in a small bowl, dissolve the yeast and sugar in the ½ cup of warm water. Let the mixture stand for 10 minutes or until the yeast starts to foam.

4. Stir the proofed yeast into the cooled oat mixture, add the ground wheat berries and the wheat germ, and combine the ingredients well. Stir in the whole-wheat flour and 1 cup of the all-purpose flour, or enough to make a dough that can be kneaded.

5. Turn the dough out onto a floured board, and knead the dough, working in as much of the remaining all-purpose flour as needed to make a soft but not sticky dough. Knead the dough for 6 minutes or until the dough is smooth and elastic.

6. Form the dough into a ball, and place it in a large oiled bowl, turning the dough to coat it with oil on all sides. Cover the bowl, and let the dough rise in a warm, draft-free place for 1 hour or until the dough has doubled in bulk.

7. Punch down the dough, divide it in half, and form each half into a loaf. Put each loaf into an oiled 9 × 5-inch loaf pan. Cover the pans, and let the loaves rise again for 30 to 45 minutes or until the loaves have doubled in bulk.

8. Preheat the oven to 375° F.

9. Brush the tops of the loaves with the beaten egg, if you wish. Place the pans in the hot oven, and bake the loaves for about 45 to 55 minutes. Let the loaves cool in the pans for about 10 minutes before turning them out onto a rack to cool completely.

WHEAT GERM BREAD

A tasty, nutritious, relatively light bread that is slightly sweet and requires very little kneading.

1¼ cups water
  3 tablespoons sugar *or* honey
  2 teaspoons salt (optional)
⅓ cup butter *or* margarine
⅓ cup light molasses
  1 cup wheat germ
¾ cup skim or low-fat milk, scalded
¼ cup warm water (105° F to 115° F)
  2 packages (2 scant tablespoons) active dry yeast
  1 teaspoon sugar
  4 cups whole-wheat flour (preferably
    stone-ground)
  2 cups all-purpose flour

1. In a saucepan, combine the 1¼ cups of water, the 3 tablespoons of sugar or honey, salt (if desired), butter or margarine, and molasses. Heat the ingredients until the butter or margarine melts. Let the mixture cool to lukewarm.
2. Meanwhile, place the wheat germ in a small bowl, and pour in the scalded milk. Let the mixture cool to lukewarm.
3. When the above mixtures are nearly cool enough, combine the ¼ cup of warm water, the yeast, and the 1 teaspoon of sugar in a large bowl. Let the yeast mixture stand for 10 minutes or until it is bubbly.
4. Add the butter mixture and the wheat-germ mixture to the proofed yeast. Add 2 cups of the whole-wheat flour and 1 cup of the all-purpose flour, beating the ingredients until they are smooth. Add the remaining 2 cups of whole-wheat flour and 1 cup of all-purpose flour.
5. Turn the dough out onto a lightly floured surface, and knead the dough for a few minutes. Place the dough in a greased bowl, cover the bowl with plastic wrap, and let the dough rise in a warm, draft-free place for 1½ hours or until the dough has doubled in bulk.
6. Punch down the dough, divide it in half, and form each half into a loaf. Put each loaf into a 9 × 5-inch oiled bread pan, cover the pans lightly, and let the loaves rise in a warm, draft-free place for 1¼ hours or until the loaves have doubled in bulk.
7. Preheat the oven to 400° F.
8. Place the pans in the hot oven, and bake the loaves for about 50 minutes. Let the loaves cool in the pans for about 10 minutes before turning them out onto a rack to cool completely.

COTTAGE CHEESE AND HERB BREAD   *1 loaf*

Try this protein-enriched seasoned white bread for a change of pace. It is a batter bread that requires no kneading and has only one rising, and so takes less time to prepare than most breads.

Preparation tip: You might consider making two loaves at once but seasoning the second one differently—say, with tarragon instead of dill.

- ¼ cup warm water (105° F to 115° F)
- 1 package (1 scant tablespoon) active dry yeast
- ½ teaspoon sugar
- 1 egg
- 1 tablespoon melted butter *or* margarine
- 1 teaspoon salt (optional)
- 1 cup low-fat cottage cheese (preferably small-curd)
- ¼ teaspoon baking powder
- ¼ cup minced scallions
- ¼ cup snipped fresh dill *or* 2 teaspoons dried dillweed
- ¼ cup soy flour *or* any other type flour
- 2¼ cups (approximately) all-purpose flour

1. Place the water in a small bowl, and slowly add the yeast and sugar to the water, stirring the ingredients to dissolve them. Let the yeast stand for 10 minutes or until it is bubbly.
2. In a large bowl, lightly beat the egg. Add the butter or margarine, salt (if desired), cottage cheese, baking powder, scallions, and fresh or dried dill, and mix the ingredients thoroughly. Stir in the proofed yeast, the soy or another flour, and enough of the all-purpose flour to make a soft dough.
3. Place the dough in a greased 1-quart baking dish. Cover the dish with greased wax paper and a dishtowel. Set the dough in a warm, draft-free place for 1 hour or until the dough has doubled in bulk.
4. Preheat the oven to 350° F.
5. Place the dish in the hot oven, and bake the loaf for 1 hour or until the loaf sounds hollow when it is tapped. Turn the loaf out onto a rack to cool completely.

PUMPKIN-WHEAT BREAD

3 loaves

Here's a divine use for puréed pumpkin.

¼ cup warm water (105° F to 115° F)
2 packages (2 scant tablespoons) active dry yeast
¼ cup sugar, divided
1¾ cups skim or low-fat milk
2 teaspoons salt (optional)
¼ cup (½ stick) butter *or* margarine
4½ to 5½ cups all-purpose flour, divided
2 cups puréed cooked pumpkin
4 cups whole-wheat flour (preferably stone-ground)
½ cup raisins

1. Place the water in a small bowl, stir in the yeast and 1 teaspoon of the sugar, and let the yeast stand in a warm place for 10 minutes or until it is bubbly.
2. Meanwhile, in a small saucepan, combine the milk, the remaining sugar, salt (if desired), and butter or margarine. Heat the ingredients until the butter or margarine melts and the sugar dissolves. Transfer the mixture to a large bowl, let the mixture cool to lukewarm, then stir in the proofed yeast.
3. Add 2½ cups of the all-purpose flour, mixing the ingredients until they are smooth, then stir in the pumpkin. Add the whole-wheat flour and enough of the remaining all-purpose flour to form a dough (it will be somewhat wet).
4. Spread some of the remaining all-purpose flour on a work surface, turn the dough out onto it, and knead the dough for about 10 minutes, working in additional flour as needed to keep the dough from sticking.
5. Form the dough into a ball, place it in an oiled bowl, turning the dough to coat it with the oil, cover the bowl with oiled plastic wrap, set the bowl in a warm, draft-free place, and let the dough rise for 1 hour or until the dough has doubled in bulk.
6. Punch the dough down, let it rest for 5 minutes, then return it to the work surface, and knead in the raisins. Divide the dough into thirds, and shape each third into a loaf. Place each loaf in a greased 9 × 5-inch or 8 × 4-inch loaf pan, and let the loaves rise for 45 minutes or until they have doubled in bulk.
7. Preheat the oven to 400° F.
8. Place the pans in the hot oven, and bake the loaves for 35 to 40 minutes. Turn the loaves out onto a rack to cool completely.

WHEAT AND BARLEY BREAD   *2 loaves*

This crunchy loaf is made with coarsely ground barley. The bread is faster to make than the wheat-berry bread because the barley does not have to be cooked.

½ cup warm water (105° F to 115° F)
1 package (1 scant tablespoon) active dry yeast
1 teaspoon sugar
1½ cups barley (unpearled *or* pearled)
1½ cups whole-wheat flour (preferably stone-ground)
2 teaspoons salt (optional)
1½ cups warm water
¼ cup honey
2 tablespoons vegetable oil (preferably canola)
3 cups or more all-purpose flour
1 egg, beaten with 1 teaspoon water

1. Place the ½ cup of warm water in a small bowl, and stir in the yeast and sugar. Let the mixture stand for 10 minutes or until the yeast starts to foam.
2. Meanwhile, in a blender (in batches) or food processor, grind the barley into a coarse flour. Transfer the barley to a large bowl, and combine it well with the whole-wheat flour and salt (if desired).
3. Add the 1½ cups of warm water, honey, oil, and the proofed yeast, and combine the ingredients well.
4. Add about 2½ cups of the all-purpose flour or enough to make a soft dough. Turn the dough out onto a floured board, and knead it for about 8 minutes, adding more all-purpose flour as needed to produce a dough that is not sticky.
5. Form the dough into a ball, and place it in an oiled bowl, turning the dough to coat it with the oil. Cover the bowl, and let the dough rise in a warm, draft-free place for 1 hour or until the dough has doubled in bulk.
6. Punch down the dough, knead it a few times, and divide it in half. Form each half into a round loaf about 6 to 7 inches in diameter. Place the loaves 2 or more inches apart on a greased baking sheet.
7. Cover the loaves with a damp dishtowel or with oiled plastic wrap, and let them rise for 45 to 60 minutes or until they have doubled in bulk.
8. Preheat the oven to 400° F.
9. Brush the loaves with the beaten egg. Place the baking sheet in the hot oven, and bake the breads for 10 minutes. Reduce the heat to 350° F, and bake the breads for another 30 minutes or until the loaves are golden brown and sound hollow when they are tapped. Place the loaves on a rack to cool completely.

WHEAT 'N' HONEY BREAD

2 loaves

The texture and flavor of this bread makes it a family favorite.

Preparation tip: The dough is easy to handle, and raisins or herbs can be added, if desired, before the loaves are formed for the second rising.

½ cup warm water (105° F to 115° F)
1 teaspoon sugar
Pinch ground ginger (optional)
2 packages (2 scant tablespoons) active dry yeast
⅓ cup honey
2 teaspoons salt (optional)
¼ cup vegetable oil (preferably canola)
1¾ cups warm water
3 cups whole-wheat flour (preferably stone-ground)
3 to 4 cups all-purpose flour
Raisins *or* currants *or* herbs (optional)
Butter *or* margarine, softened (optional)

1. Place the ½ cup of water, sugar, and ginger (if desired) in a large bowl. Sprinkle in the yeast, and stir the mixture to dissolve the ingredients. Let the mixture stand for 10 minutes or until the yeast starts to foam.
2. Stir in the honey, salt (if desired), oil, the 1¾ cups of water, and whole-wheat flour. Beat the ingredients until they are smooth. Stir in enough of the all-purpose flour to make a dough that is easy to handle.
3. Turn the dough out onto a lightly floured board, and knead the dough for 6 to 10 minutes or until it is smooth and elastic. Form the dough into a ball, and place the dough in an oiled bowl, turning the dough to coat it on all sides with the oil. Cover the bowl, and let the dough rise in a warm, draft-free place for 1 hour or until the dough has doubled in bulk.
4. Punch down the dough, and divide it in half. Flatten each half into a rectangle about 9 × 18 inches. At this point, if desired, you can sprinkle the surface of the dough with raisins or currants or herbs. Fold one of the rectangles over in thirds to make a rectangle that is 9 × 6 inches. Starting from the longer side with the unsealed end, roll the dough into a 9-inch-long cylinder, taking care not to trap air bubbles in the roll. Seal the seam by pressing the dough between your fingers. Repeat the procedure with the remaining dough. Place each loaf in a greased 9 × 5-inch loaf pan. Brush the loaves lightly with the butter or margarine (if desired). Cover the pans, and let the loaves rise for 1 hour or until they have doubled in bulk.
5. Preheat the oven to 375° F.
6. Place the pans in the hot oven, and bake the loaves for 40 to 45 minutes or until the loaves are a deep brown and sound hollow when they are tapped. Turn the loaves out onto a rack to cool completely.

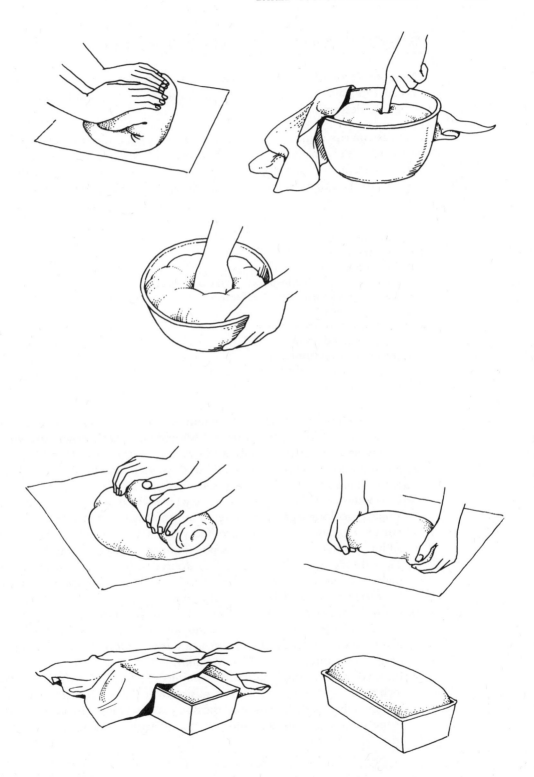

WHOLE WHEAT–RAISIN BREAD

1 large loaf

Daniel V. Edson of Rowley, Massachusetts, devised this as a frosted bread jam-packed with raisins. I make it without the sugary glaze, and it is quickly consumed for dessert and snacks.

Preparation tips: Since it disappears so fast, it's a good idea to prepare a double recipe. One loaf can always be frozen. If you wish to glaze it, combine ¾ cup of sifted confectioners' sugar with 2 to 3 teaspoons of water and ⅛ teaspoon of vanilla; stir the mixture until it is smooth. Spread the frosting over the cooled bread.

1½ cups water
1½ cups raisins
  1 tablespoon sugar
  1 package (1 scant tablespoon) active dry yeast
  2 cups whole-wheat flour (preferably
     stone-ground)
1½ to 2 cups all-purpose flour
  ½ cup powdered nonfat milk
  1 teaspoon salt (optional)
  1 egg
1½ tablespoons vegetable oil

1. In a medium-sized saucepan, combine the water, raisins, and sugar, and bring the mixture to a boil. Strain the liquid into a large bowl, reserving the raisins, and let the liquid cool until it is warm (105° F to 115° F).
2. Stir the yeast into the warm liquid to dissolve it, and let the mixture stand for 10 minutes or until the yeast starts to foam.
3. In a medium-sized bowl, combine the whole-wheat flour and 1½ cups of the all-purpose flour with the powdered milk and salt (if desired).
4. Stir the egg and oil into the proofed yeast. Then stir in the flour mixture, adding enough additional all-purpose flour to form a soft dough.
5. Turn the dough out onto a lightly floured surface, and knead it for 10 minutes or until it is smooth and elastic, adding only enough all-purpose flour to prevent the dough from sticking.
6. Form the dough into a ball, and place it in an oiled bowl, turning the dough to coat the top with the oil. Cover the bowl with a damp dishtowel or with plastic wrap, and let the dough rise in a warm, draft-free place for 1½ hours or until the dough has doubled in bulk.
7. Punch down the dough, and roll it out into a rectangle 9 inches wide and ¾ inch thick. Sprinkle the reserved raisins over the surface of the dough to within ½ inch of the edges. Roll the dough up, starting with a 9-inch end, to shape the dough into a cylindrical loaf. Place the loaf in a greased 9 ×

5-inch loaf pan. Cover the pan, and let the loaf rise for 1 hour or until the loaf has doubled in bulk.

8. Preheat the oven to 325° F.

9. Place the pan in the hot oven, and bake the bread for 50 minutes or until the top of the bread browns and the loaf sounds hollow when it is tapped. Let the loaf cool in the pan for about 10 minutes before turning it out onto a rack to cool completely.

WHEAT AND WALNUT BREAD

3 small loaves

Try this recipe from Beatrice Ojakangas's *Great Whole Grain Breads* for a whole-wheat bread that is light-textured as well as great-tasting.

Preparation tips: The dough is soft and sticky; do not make it too dry by adding excess flour. The 30-minute rest in step 2 is very important; do not omit it. It gives the whole-wheat flour a chance to absorb moisture.

- 2 cups warm water (105° F to 115° F)
- 2 packages (2 scant tablespoons) active dry yeast
- 1 tablespoon molasses (light *or* dark)
- ½ cup powdered nonfat milk
- 2 tablespoons butter *or* margarine, at room temperature
- 2 teaspoons salt
- 1 cup unprocessed bran
- 3½ to 4 cups whole-wheat flour (preferably stone-ground)
- 2½ cups coarsely chopped walnuts
- 1 egg mixed with 1 tablespoon milk

1. In a large bowl, combine the warm water with the yeast and molasses, stirring the ingredients to dissolve them. Let the mixture stand for 10 minutes or until the yeast starts to foam.
2. Stir in the powdered milk, butter or margarine, salt, and bran. Then beat in 3½ cups of the whole-wheat flour, ½ cup at a time, until a stiff dough is formed. Let the dough rest for 30 minutes before proceeding.
3. Turn the dough out onto a lightly floured board, and knead the dough, adding as little flour as possible, for 10 minutes or until it is smooth and elastic. Form the dough into a ball, and put it in an oiled bowl, turning the dough to coat the top with the oil. Place the chopped walnuts on the dough, cover the bowl with plastic wrap, and let the dough rise in a warm, draft-free place for 1 to 1½ hours or until the dough has doubled in bulk.
4. Punch down the dough, and turn it out onto an oiled work surface. Knead the walnuts into the dough until they are evenly distributed. Add only enough flour to keep the dough from being sticky. Divide the dough into thirds, and shape each piece into a ball. Flatten each ball of dough slightly, and place it on an oiled baking sheet. Brush the loaves with the egg-milk mixture, and make 4 parallel slashes about ½ inch deep across the top of each loaf.
5. Cover the loaves with a damp dishtowel, place the loaves in a warm, draft-free place, and let them rise again for 45 to 60 minutes or until the loaves have doubled in bulk and the slashes have split open.
6. Preheat the oven to 375° F.
7. Place the baking sheet in the hot oven, and bake the loaves for 35 minutes or until the loaves are evenly browned and sound hollow when they are tapped. Turn the loaves out onto a rack to cool completely.

LEMON-WHEAT BREAD

2 loaves

This delicious, slightly tart bread, based on a recipe in *The Laurel's Kitchen Bread Book,* goes especially well with fish dishes.

Preparation tips: Note that the buttermilk is at room temperature and that the dough undergoes 3 risings. The fennel seeds can be omitted.

- ½ **cup warm water (105° F to 115° F)**
- 1 **package (1 scant tablespoon) active dry yeast**
- 1 **teaspoon sugar**
- 3½ **cups whole-wheat flour (preferably stone-ground)**
- 2 **to 2½ cups all-purpose flour**
- 1½ **teaspoons fennel seeds (optional)**
- 2 **teaspoons salt**
- 1 **tablespoon grated lemon peel**
- 1 **cup buttermilk, at room temperature**
- ¼ **cup honey**
- ¼ **cup fresh lemon juice (juice from 1 large lemon)**
- 1 **cup water**
- 2 **tablespoons very cold butter *or* margarine, cut into bits**

1. In a small bowl, combine the ½ cup of warm water, yeast, and sugar, stirring the ingredients until they dissolve. Let the mixture stand for 10 minutes or until the yeast starts to foam.
2. In a large bowl, combine the whole-wheat flour, 2 cups of the all-purpose flour, fennel seeds (if desired), salt, and lemon peel.
3. In another bowl or a measuring cup, combine the buttermilk and honey, and add them to the flour mixture. Then combine the lemon juice and the 1 cup of water, and add that to the flour mixture. Stir in the proofed yeast.
4. Turn the dough out onto a floured surface, and knead the dough, using additional all-purpose flour if needed, until it becomes elastic. Then knead in the bits of butter or margarine, fully working them into the dough.
5. Form the dough into a ball, and place it in an oiled bowl, turning the dough to coat the top with the oil. Cover the bowl, and let the dough rise in a warm, draft-free place for 1½ hours or until a gentle ½-inch-deep poke in the center of the dough fails to spring back.
6. Punch down the dough, and form it into a smooth round. Then return it to the bowl to rise again, as in step 5, for about 45 minutes.
7. Punch down the dough again, and divide it in half, shaping each half into a loaf large enough to fit a greased 8 × 4-inch pan. Place the loaves in a warm, draft-free place to rise just until the dough slowly recovers from gentle finger pressure.
8. Preheat the oven to 350° F.
9. Place the pans in the hot oven, and bake the loaves for 50 minutes or until the breads sound hollow when they are tapped. Turn the loaves out onto a rack to cool completely.

WHOLE WHEAT FRENCH BREAD   *2 long loaves*

French bread is really easy to prepare: it's nothing but flour, water, yeast, and salt; and it takes but a few minutes of actual work time. The result is quite professional—crisp and delicious and more nutritious than store-bought white-flour loaves. I adapted a recipe and adopted the technique recommended by the potter who made my favorite bread pans, including my two-part French bread pan and rising couches: Margi Beyers, 7159 Beach Drive S.W., Seattle, Washington 98136. If you make such loaves often, it pays to invest in a French bread "kit." But the breads can also be made free-form and baked on baking sheets.

Preparation tips: There are two tricks that will assure high-quality results: three slow risings at relatively cool temperatures and a burst of steam when the bread hits the hot oven. Therefore, don't try this recipe during hot weather if you don't have air-conditioning. Before preparing to bake the risen loaves, you should have on hand two items: a sprayer filled with water (the kind used to spray plants is ideal, but be sure you wash it thoroughly and fill it with clean water) and a very sharp slender knife or a razor blade for slashing the dough. This recipe makes two loaves. As soon as they cool, you can wrap them in plastic and freeze them for future use. When they have thawed, refresh them in a moderate oven for about 10 to 15 minutes before serving them.

⅓ cup warm water (105° F to 115° F)
1 package (1 scant tablespoon) active dry yeast
Pinch sugar
Pinch ginger
2 cups whole-wheat flour
1½ to 2 cups bread flour *or* all-purpose flour, as needed
1 teaspoon salt
1⅓ cups warm water (about 80° F)
Corn meal for sprinkling the pans

1. Place the ⅓ cup of water in a small bowl. Add the yeast, sugar, and ginger, stirring the ingredients to dissolve them. Let the mixture stand for 10 minutes or until the yeast starts to foam.
2. In a large bowl, combine the whole-wheat flour, 1½ cups of the bread or all-purpose flour, and the salt. Add the proofed yeast to the flour mixture along with the 1⅓ cups of water. Stir the mixture with a large wooden spoon to combine it well, and gather it into a ball.
3. With floured hands, lift the ball of dough out of the bowl and onto a floured work surface. Knead the dough for 5 to 10 minutes or until it is smooth, adding flour by the tablespoon as needed to keep the dough from sticking. The dough should be soft and on the moist side. Place the dough in a clean *ungreased* bowl. Cover the bowl lightly with plastic wrap and a cloth towel,

and let the dough rise in a draft-free place, preferably no warmer than 70° F, for 2 to 3 hours or until the dough has more than doubled in bulk (the doubling time will depend on the temperature—about 5 hours at 60° F, 2 hours at 80° F).

4. With floured hands, return the dough to a lightly floured work surface, and flatten the dough into a square by pressing on it with the palm of your hand. Fold the far side to the near side, the right to the left, the left to the right, and finally the near side to the far side, forming a pillow. Return the dough to the bowl, cover the dough with plastic wrap and a cloth, and let it rise again for 2 to 3 hours or until it has more than doubled in bulk.

5. Again with floured hands, turn the dough out onto a lightly floured work surface, and cut the dough in half. Working with one piece at a time, flatten the dough into an oval about ½-inch thick. Fold the dough in half lengthwise, pinching the seam together. Then fold the dough in half again, and stretch it, if necessary, to form a slender roll about 16 inches long. Place the loaves in a lightly floured rising couch or in a French bread pan or on a baking sheet that has been sprinkled with the corn meal. Cover the loaves with a cloth, and set them in a draft-free place to rise until they have doubled in bulk.

6. Place the oven rack on the lowest rung, and preheat the oven to 450° F. If the breads are rising in couches, place the pans in which they will bake in the oven to heat. When the pans are hot, remove them and sprinkle them with the corn meal. Invert the dough into the pans. If the dough is already in its baking pan, you will not be able to heat the pan before doing the next step.

7. Make 3 diagonal slashes—each *1 inch deep* (do not skimp on the cut)—on the tops of the loaves. Place the pan in the lowest part of the hot oven, and immediately spray the oven bottom and sides and the top of the loaves with water to create a burst of steam. Shut the oven door, and repeat the spraying every 3 minutes for a total of 4 times. Bake the breads for a total of 20 to 25 minutes or until they sound hollow when they are rapped on the bottom. If desired, for a very crisp crust, spray the tops of the breads again after you take the loaves from the oven. Remove the breads to a rack to cool.

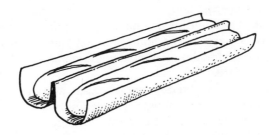

SUNFLOWER-MILLET BREAD

2 loaves

Mollie Katzen, my favorite vegetarian cook and cookbook author (*Moosewood Cookbook, The Enchanted Broccoli Forest,* and *Still Life with Menu Cookbook*), devised this crunchy loaf using millet, a grain little known to Americans except as birdseed. Katzen has an unusual technique for preparing bread dough that involves 3 risings, though the total time is not longer than that for other breads.

Preparation tip: Since this dough is stiff and difficult to knead, I suggest you cut your bread-baking teeth (and develop those kneading muscles some) on other breads before you try it.

THE SPONGE
- 2 packages (2 scant tablespoons) active dry yeast
- Drop honey
- 1 cup warm water (105° F to 115° F)
- 2 cups all-purpose flour

THE MIX
- 1½ cups water
- 1 cup raw millet
- 2½ teaspoons salt (optional)
- ¼ cup (½ stick) butter
- 3 tablespoons honey

ADDITIONS
- 1 cup hulled sunflower seeds
- 1 cup all-purpose flour
- 3 cups (approximately) whole-wheat flour (preferably stone-ground)

- 2 teaspoons melted butter

1. Prepare the sponge in a large mixing bowl. Dissolve the yeast and honey in the 1 cup of warm water. Let the mixture stand for about 5 minutes, then add the 2 cups of all-purpose flour, beating the mixture well with a whisk. Cover the bowl with a damp cloth, and set it in a warm place to rise for 30 to 60 minutes.
2. While the sponge is rising, prepare the mix. Boil the 1½ cups of water in a medium-sized saucepan, add the millet, cover the pan, reduce the heat to low, and cook the millet for 15 minutes or until the water has been absorbed. Uncover the pan, and fluff the millet with a fork. Add the salt (if desired), butter, and honey, and mix the ingredients well. Let the mix cool to room temperature.
3. When the mix is cool and the sponge has risen, add the mix to the sponge. Stir in the additions—the sunflower seeds, all-purpose flour, and as much of the whole-wheat flour as needed to form a manageable dough.
4. Turn the dough out onto a floured surface, and knead the dough for 10 minutes or longer, adding additional whole-wheat flour as needed. Form the dough into a ball, place it in an oiled bowl, turning the dough to coat it

with the oil. Cover the bowl with the damp cloth, and let the dough rise in a warm, draft-free place for 1 hour or until the dough has doubled in bulk.

5. Punch down the dough, and return it to the floured surface. Shape the dough into 2 loaves, and place each in a greased 9 × 5-inch bread pan. Cover the pans, and let the loaves rise until they have doubled in bulk (this rising is usually faster than the others).

6. Preheat the oven to 375° F.

7. Brush the loaves with the melted butter. Place the pans in the hot oven, and bake the loaves for 30 to 40 minutes or until the breads sound hollow when they are tapped. Turn the loaves out onto a rack to cool completely.

MULTIGRAIN AND SEED BREAD

2 loaves

This is a crunchy, flavorful, and nutritious bread—one of my perennial favorites—and I thank Mrs. J. W. Webb of Chattanooga, Tennessee, for contributing the recipe. You bread-baking novices should know that the heavy dough is not ideal for cutting your kneading teeth on. But for those with well-developed kneading muscles, this dough will give you a great workout and will result in hearty loaves.

Preparation tip: Note the long rising times.

    2 cups boiling water
    ½ cup bulgur
    ½ cup millet
    ½ cup warm water (105° F to 115° F)
    2 packages (2 scant tablespoons) active dry yeast
    1 teaspoon sugar
    ¼ cup sunflower seeds
    3 tablespoons sesame seeds
    ¼ cup honey
    2 tablespoons oil (preferably canola)
    2 teaspoons salt
    2 cups rolled oats (quick *or* regular)
    2 to 3 cups whole-wheat flour (preferably
       stone-ground)
    2 cups all-purpose flour
    1 egg white, lightly beaten (optional)

1. In a large bowl, combine the 2 cups of boiling water, bulgur, and millet, and let the ingredients cool until they are lukewarm.
2. When the bulgur and millet are nearly lukewarm, place the ½ cup of warm water in a small bowl, and add the yeast and sugar, stirring the ingredients to dissolve them. Let the mixture stand for 10 minutes or until the yeast starts to foam.
3. To the softened grains in the large bowl, add the sunflower seeds, sesame seeds, honey, oil, and salt. Then add the proofed yeast. Stir in the oats, 2 cups of the whole-wheat flour, and all of the all-purpose flour, forming the mixture into a ball.
4. Lift the ball of dough out onto a surface floured with some of the remaining whole-wheat flour, and knead the dough for 5 to 10 minutes, adding more flour as needed to keep the dough from sticking.
5. Place the dough in an oiled bowl, turning the dough to coat it with the oil, cover the bowl lightly, and let the dough rise in a warm, draft-free place for 2 hours or until the dough has doubled in bulk.

6. Punch down the dough, return it to the work surface, and form it into two loaves. Place the loaves, well separated, on a baking sheet, cover them lightly, and let them rise in a warm, draft-free place for 1 hour or until they have doubled in bulk.
7. Preheat the oven to 350° F.
8. If desired, brush the tops of the loaves with the beaten egg white. Place the baking sheet in the hot oven, and bake the loaves for 45 minutes or until the breads sound hollow when they are tapped. Turn the loaves out onto a rack to cool completely.

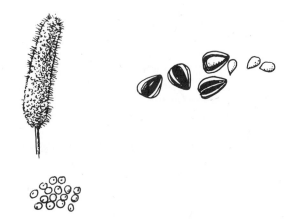

POLISH PUMPERNICKEL

1 large loaf

This recipe produces a very dark rye bread of distinction. It's especially delicious with a winter vegetable soup or chowder. The dough is easy to handle and yields a professional-looking loaf.

2 packages (2 scant tablespoons) active dry yeast
1 teaspoon sugar
½ cup warm water (105° F to 115° F)
½ cup light molasses
2 tablespoons butter *or* margarine
1 teaspoon salt (optional)
2 tablespoons caraway seeds
1 cup skim or low-fat milk, heated to lukewarm
2 cups rye flour (preferably whole-grain)
½ cup unsweetened cocoa powder
1 cup whole-wheat flour (preferably stone-ground)
1½ cups (approximately) all-purpose flour
Corn meal for sprinkling the pan
1 tablespoon melted butter (optional)

1. In a small bowl, dissolve the yeast and sugar in the warm water. Let the mixture stand for 10 minutes or until the yeast starts to foam.
2. In a large mixing bowl, combine the molasses, butter or margarine, salt (if desired), caraway seeds, and lukewarm milk. Stir the ingredients to combine them, and add the proofed yeast.
3. In another bowl, combine the rye flour and cocoa powder. Add this to the milk mixture, stirring the ingredients to combine them well, and beat the mixture with a wooden spoon about 100 times.
4. Add the whole-wheat flour and enough of the all-purpose flour to form a stiff dough.
5. Turn the dough out onto a floured board, and knead the dough for about 10 minutes, adding more flour as needed to prevent the dough from sticking. Form the dough into a ball, and put it into a large oiled bowl, turning the dough to coat the top with the oil.
6. Cover the bowl, and let the dough rise in a warm, draft-free place for 2 hours or until the dough has doubled in bulk.
7. Punch down the dough, and shape it into a round loaf. Place the loaf on a greased baking sheet that has been sprinkled with the corn meal. Cover the loaf lightly, and let it rise in a warm, draft-free place for about 45 minutes.

8. Preheat the oven to 375° F.
9. Place the baking sheet in the hot oven, and bake the loaf for 35 to 40 minutes or until it sounds hollow when rapped. Brush the bread with the melted butter (if you want a tender crust), and turn the bread out onto a rack to cool.

DELI BLACK BREAD

2 loaves

Black bread is deceiving. As a rule, the color comes from molasses and chocolate, not whole grain. This recipe gives you all three.

Preparation tip: The bread can be made either with conventional yeast, as below, or with quick-rising yeast. If you use the latter, omit step 1, mix 2 packages of the quick-rising dry yeast in with the flours, and add ½ cup water along with the milk.

Serving suggestion: Great with soups and sandwiches.

  ½ cup warm water (105° F to 115° F)
  2 packages (2 scant tablespoons) active dry yeast
  1 teaspoon sugar
2½ cups plus additional all-purpose flour, divided
  2 cups whole-grain rye flour, divided
  ½ cup whole-wheat flour
  2 cups whole-bran cereal (e.g., All-Bran *or*
     100% Bran *or* Bran Buds)
  1 tablespoon caraway seeds
  2 teaspoons salt
  2 teaspoons onion powder
1½ cups skim or low-fat milk
  ¼ cup dark molasses
  ¼ cup vegetable oil (preferably canola)
  1 1-ounce square unsweetened chocolate
  ¼ cup water
  ½ teaspoon cornstarch
Caraway seeds, regular *or* black (optional)

1. In a small bowl, combine the ½ cup of warm water with the yeast and sugar, stirring the ingredients to dissolve them. Let the mixture stand for 10 minutes or until the yeast starts to foam.
2. While the yeast is proofing, in a large mixing bowl, combine the all-purpose flour, 1 cup of the rye flour, the whole-wheat flour, bran cereal, the 1 tablespoon of caraway seeds, salt, and onion powder, mixing the ingredients thoroughly.
3. In a medium-sized saucepan over medium-low heat, warm the milk, molasses, oil, and chocolate until the mixture is very warm—120° F (the chocolate does *not* have to melt).
4. Stir the proofed yeast into the flour mixture. Then stir in the milk mixture (*make sure it is not too hot!*). Beat the dough on low speed with an electric mixer until the ingredients are well combined, then beat the dough on medium speed for 3 minutes. With a wooden spoon, mix in the remaining 1 cup of rye flour and enough all-purpose flour to form a stiff dough.

5. Turn the dough out onto a lightly floured surface, and knead the dough for 5 to 10 minutes or until it is smooth and elastic. Form the dough into a ball, and place it in an oiled bowl, turning the dough to coat the top with the oil. Cover the bowl, and let the dough rise in a warm, draft-free place for 1 hour or until the dough has doubled in bulk.

6. Punch down the dough, and divide it in half. On a lightly floured surface, form each half into a round loaf. Place each loaf in a greased 8-inch cake pan. Cover the pans, and let the loaves rise for 30 minutes or until the loaves have almost doubled in bulk.

7. Preheat the oven to 375° F.

8. Place the pans in the hot oven, and bake the loaves for 40 to 45 minutes. While the loaves are baking, combine the ¼ cup of water with the cornstarch. When the breads are just about done, remove them from the oven briefly, and brush them with the cornstarch glaze. Sprinkle the loaves with the caraway seeds (if desired). Return the pans to the oven, and bake the breads 5 minutes longer or until the glaze is glossy and the loaves sound hollow when they are tapped. Turn the loaves out onto a rack to cool completely.

PUMPKIN-RYE BREAD

3 loaves

This bread has a lovely color and flavor imparted by the pumpkin and molasses. It's a great way to dispose of your Halloween pumpkin.

Preparation tip: You can use either canned or home-cooked pumpkin purée. But be sure to let homemade purée drain through a fine strainer or cheesecloth for at least 30 minutes before measuring it.

1½ cups skim or low-fat milk
½ cup light molasses
¼ cup (½ stick) butter *or* margarine, at room
    temperature
1 tablespoon salt
2 packages (2 scant tablespoons) active dry yeast
¼ cup warm water (105° F to 115° F)
½ teaspoon sugar
3 cups whole-grain rye flour
2 cups drained pumpkin purée (drained, if
    homemade)
6½ cups (approximately) all-purpose flour
    (preferably unbleached)
1 teaspoon molasses mixed with 1 tablespoon
    water for glaze (optional)

1. In a small saucepan, scald the milk over high heat. Remove the pan from the heat, and add the molasses, butter or margarine, and salt, stirring the ingredients to dissolve them. Pour the mixture into a large bowl, and set the bowl aside until the mixture has cooled down to warm (105° F to 115° F).

2. When the milk mixture is almost at the right temperature, in a small bowl, combine the yeast with the warm water and sugar, stirring the ingredients to dissolve them. Let the mixture stand for 10 minutes or until the yeast begins to foam. Then add this to the warm milk mixture.

3. Add the rye flour, stirring the mixture until it is smooth. Then stir in the pumpkin purée.

4. Add 5½ cups of the all-purpose flour 1 cup at a time, stirring the mixture well after each addition. Cover the dough with plastic wrap, and let the dough rest for 10 minutes.

5. Turn the dough out onto a floured surface, and knead the dough for 10 minutes, adding more all-purpose flour as needed, until the dough is smooth and elastic (it will be soft). Place the dough in a very large oiled bowl, turning the dough to oil the top, cover the bowl with a dishtowel or cover it lightly with plastic wrap, and let the dough rise in a warm, draft-free place for 1½ hours or until the dough has doubled in bulk.

6. Punch down the dough, and let it rest for 5 minutes. Then divide the dough in thirds, and shape each third into a loaf. Place each loaf in a greased 8 × 4-inch or 9 × 5-inch loaf pan, cover the pans lightly, and let the loaves rise for 40 minutes or until they have doubled in bulk.
7. Preheat the oven to 400° F.
8. Place the pans in the hot oven, and bake the loaves for 30 minutes. Remove the pans from the oven, brush the loaves with the molasses glaze (if desired), return them to the oven, then bake them 10 minutes longer or until they sound hollow when they are tapped. Remove the loaves from the pans, and turn them out onto a rack to cool completely.

ITALIAN PEPPER 'N' CHEESE BREAD   *2 long loaves*

Bert Greene's passing in 1988 was a great loss to the culinary world. Fortunately, he left a wonderful legacy in his cookbooks, including this marvelous spicy bread from *Greene on Greens.*

Preparation tip: You can start with a fresh red pepper that you roast and peel (see page 8) or use a roasted pepper from a jar.

1¼ cups warm water (105° F to 115° F)
  1 package (1 scant tablespoon) active dry yeast
  1 teaspoon light brown sugar
  2 teaspoons salt
  ⅛ teaspoon cayenne
  1 teaspoon hot red pepper flakes
  1 teaspoon sesame seeds
  1 teaspoon fennel seeds
  1 teaspoon aniseeds
  1 large sweet red pepper, roasted, peeled, seeded,
     and finely chopped
  ½ cup warm skim or low-fat milk
1½ cups whole-wheat flour (preferably
     stone-ground)
  1 cup (4 ounces) grated Monterey Jack
  3 cups (approximately) all-purpose flour
     (preferably unbleached), divided
  1 tablespoon butter *or* margarine, melted

1. In a large bowl, combine the warm water with the yeast and brown sugar, and stir the mixture to dissolve the ingredients. Let the mixture stand for 10 minutes or until the yeast starts to foam.
2. Add the salt, cayenne, red pepper flakes, sesame seeds, fennel seeds, aniseeds, chopped red pepper, and milk, stirring the mixture to combine the the ingredients well.
3. Stir in the whole-wheat flour and the cheese. With a wooden spoon, gradually beat in 2 cups of the all-purpose flour to form a dough.
4. Turn the dough out onto a lightly floured board, and knead the dough for 10 minutes, working in the remaining 1 cup of all-purpose flour (or more, if needed), until the dough is elastic. Let the dough rest for 5 minutes.
5. Divide the dough in half, and roll each half into a long French-style loaf. Place the cylinders in French-bread pans or on a long, lightly greased baking sheet. Cover the loaves with a dishtowel that has been rubbed lightly with flour, and let the dough rise in a warm, draft-free place for 1½ to 2 hours or until the dough has doubled in bulk.

6. Preheat the oven to 400° F, placing the oven rack in the top third of the oven.

7. With a sharp knife or razor blade, cut one lengthwise slash in the top of each loaf. Brush the top of each loaf with the melted butter or margarine. Place a roasting pan half-filled with water in the bottom of the oven.

8. Place the breads in the hot oven, and bake them for 12 minutes. Then reduce the heat to 325° F, and bake the loaves 35 minutes longer. Turn the loaves out onto a rack to cool before slicing them.

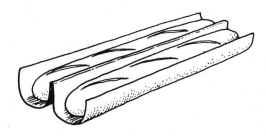

LIMPA *(Swedish Rye)*   *3 large loaves*

This bread, traditionally served at Christmas but wonderful all winter long, is my undoing. There was a time when I could sit down with a loaf of limpa, a knife, and butter, and devour half of the bread. While I now practice more restraint with this flavorful bread (and almost never butter it), I can still eat six slices at a clip. I must have tested half a dozen recipes before concluding that this one, from *Gourmet* magazine, was the best.

Preparation tip: This is a very large recipe, so unless you are making it for a crowd, be prepared to give some away or stash a loaf or two in the freezer. The loaves are somewhat flat, but, with a decent bread knife, they can be cut very easily into thin slices.

  ½ cup warm water (105° F to 115° F)
  3 packages (3 scant tablespoons) active dry yeast
  1 teaspoon sugar
  ¼ cup (½ stick) butter *or* butter-margarine blend
  3 cups dark beer
  1 cup dark corn syrup
  6 cups rye flour (preferably whole-grain), divided
4½ cups all-purpose flour (preferably unbleached), divided
  ½ to ¾ cup grated orange rind (from about 4 oranges)
  2 tablespoons aniseed, crushed
  1 tablespoon salt
  2 tablespoons molasses mixed with ¼ cup water for glaze

1. In a small bowl, combine the water with the yeast and sugar, stirring the ingredients to dissolve them. Let the mixture stand for 10 minutes or until the yeast starts to foam.

2. In a medium-sized saucepan, melt the butter or butter-margarine blend, and add the beer, heating the mixture until it is lukewarm (105° F to 115° F). Transfer the mixture to a large bowl, and stir in the corn syrup and the proofed yeast.

3. Stir in 3 cups of the rye flour and 1½ cups of the all-purpose flour, beating the mixture for 1 minute. Add the orange rind, aniseed, and salt. Then stir in the remaining 3 cups of rye flour. Add 2 more cups of the all-purpose flour, ½ cup at a time, until a soft dough is formed.

4. Let the dough rise, covered with a dishtowel, in a warm, draft-free place for 1 hour or until the dough has almost doubled in bulk. Turn the dough out onto a work surface that has been sprinkled with the remaining 1 cup of all-purpose flour. Knead the dough, incorporating the flour, for 10 minutes or until the dough is smooth and satiny.

5. Divide the dough into thirds, and shape each third into an oblong loaf about 15 inches long. Place the loaves, well separated, on greased baking sheets,

cover them with dishtowels, and let them rise in a warm, draft-free place for 1 hour or until the loaves have doubled in bulk.

6. Preheat the oven to 375° F.

7. Prick the loaves with a wooden pick, place them in the hot oven, and bake them for 15 minutes. Remove the loaves from the oven, brush them with some of the molasses glaze, return them to the oven, and bake them 15 to 20 minutes longer or until they sound hollow when they are tapped on the bottom. Remove the loaves from the oven, brush them again with the glaze, and turn them out onto racks to cool.

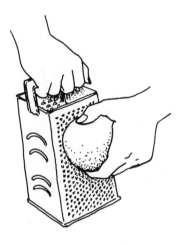

COLONIAL CURRANT TEA BREAD   *1 large loaf*

This is a long-rising but easy "dessert" bread, slightly sweet and spicy.

Serving suggestion: It is good as a coffee or tea or breakfast bread, perhaps toasted and buttered.

   1 package (1 scant tablespoon) active dry yeast
   1 teaspoon sugar
 ½ cup warm water (105° F to 115° F)
 ¾ cup skim or low-fat milk
 ¼ cup (½ stick) light butter-margarine blend
 ½ cup sugar
 ½ teaspoon salt (optional)
1½ teaspoons cinnamon
 ¾ teaspoon mace
 ½ teaspoon crushed aniseed
 ¼ teaspoon ground cloves
   2 egg whites
   1 egg
   2 cups whole-wheat flour
   3 cups all-purpose flour (preferably unbleached)
   1 cup dried currants *or* raisins

1. In a large bowl, sprinkle the yeast and the 1 teaspoon of sugar over the warm water, stirring the ingredients to dissolve them. Let the mixture stand for 10 minutes or until the yeast starts to foam.
2. In a small saucepan, combine the milk, butter-margarine blend, the ½ cup of sugar, and the salt (if desired). Heat the mixture until the butter-margarine blend melts, but *do not let the mixture boil.* Set the mixture aside to cool.
3. When the milk mixture is lukewarm, add it to the yeast mixture, and stir in the cinnamon, mace, aniseed, and cloves. Beat in the egg whites and whole egg.
4. Mix in the whole-wheat flour and 1 cup of the all-purpose flour. Stir in the currants or raisins, then stir in the last 2 cups of all-purpose flour (the dough will be sticky and heavy, and you may prefer to mix in the last of the flour with floured hands). Place the dough in a large oiled bowl, turn the dough to coat it on all sides with the oil, cover the bowl with plastic wrap or a dry cloth, and put the bowl in a warm, draft-free place for 2 hours or until the dough has doubled in bulk.
5. Punch down the dough, and turn it out onto a floured board. Knead the dough lightly, rolling the dough into a "bologna" about 15 inches long. Arrange the roll around the bottom of a well-greased 9-inch tube pan (9-cup capacity), even out the top, and pinch the ends together to hide the

seam. Cover the pan with plastic wrap or a cloth, and let the dough rise in a warm, draft-free place for 1 hour or until the dough has doubled in bulk.

6. Preheat the oven to 350° F.

7. Place the pan in the hot oven, and bake the loaf for 45 to 50 minutes or until it is brown on top and sounds hollow when it is tapped. Turn the loaf out onto a wire rack to cool to room temperature before cutting it.

Rolls and Biscuits

Rolls and biscuits are often easier to handle and more elegant to serve than sliced bread—in particular, at buffets, barbecues, and picnics (for rolls and buns), and with hors d'oeuvres, soups, appetizers, and salads (for biscuits). Most biscuits are made without yeast and need little or no kneading. Although best when freshly made, they can be prepared hours ahead or, if necessary, the day before and refreshed, covered, in a warm conventional oven or for about 10 to 15 seconds in a microwave.

WHEAT GERM BUNS

about 24 buns

These slightly sweet dinner and snack buns are easy to make because the dough needs almost no kneading. Although the recipe calls for all-purpose flour, the wheat germ returns to the buns most of the nutritional components that had been lost in refining.

Preparation tip: The buns can also be made with a combination of flours—for example, 2 cups of all-purpose flour and 1 cup of whole-wheat flour, resulting in somewhat heavier rolls.

    1 teaspoon sugar
    1 package (1 scant tablespoon) active dry yeast
    1 cup warm water (105° F to 115° F)
    1 egg
    3 tablespoons vegetable oil (preferably canola)
    ¼ cup lightly packed brown sugar
    ¾ teaspoon salt (optional)
    ⅔ cup wheat germ
    3 cups (approximately) all-purpose flour

1. In a large bowl, sprinkle the 1 teaspoon of sugar and the yeast over the warm water, stirring the ingredients to dissolve them. Let the mixture stand for 10 minutes or until the yeast starts to foam.
2. Stir in the egg, oil, brown sugar, salt (if desired), wheat germ, and 1¾ cups of the flour. Beat the mixture until it is smooth, then add enough of the remaining flour to make a dough that is easy to handle.
3. Turn the dough out onto a lightly floured board, and knead the dough for about 2 minutes.
4. Form the dough into a ball, and place the dough in an oiled bowl, turning the dough to coat it on all sides with the oil. Cover the bowl, and let the dough rise in a warm, draft-free place for 1½ hours or until the dough has doubled in bulk.
5. Punch down the dough, and shape it into balls about 1¾ inches in diameter. (You may have to grease your hands since the dough tends to be slightly sticky.) Place the dough balls in greased cake pans, leaving enough space between the balls for a rising that will double the bulk of the dough. Cover the pans, and let the buns rise in a warm, draft-free place for 45 minutes or until the buns have doubled in bulk.
6. Preheat the oven to 375° F.
7. Place the pans in the hot oven, and bake the buns for 20 to 25 minutes or until the buns are browned.

HERBED WHOLE WHEAT ROLLS

16 rolls

These dinner rolls are great-tasting and easy to prepare. They gave me a long-awaited opportunity to make use of my "antique" poultry seasoning.

1 package (1 scant tablespoon) active dry yeast
1½ cups warm water (105° F to 115° F)
3 tablespoons honey, divided
2 tablespoons butter *or* margarine, melted
1 egg
1 teaspoon salt (optional)
4 cups (approximately) whole-wheat flour
   (preferably stone-ground)
1 teaspoon poultry seasoning
1 tablespoon minced onion
1 egg white, lightly beaten

1. In a large bowl, combine the yeast and warm water, stirring the yeast to dissolve it. Stir in 1 teaspoon of the honey. Let the mixture stand for 10 minutes or until the yeast begins to foam.
2. Stir in the rest of the honey, the melted butter or margarine, egg, and salt (if desired). Add 2 cups of the flour, the poultry seasoning, and the onion. Beat the mixture well—about 100 strokes. Then stir in enough of the remaining flour to form a light dough.
3. Turn the dough out onto a floured surface, and knead the dough for 7 minutes or until the dough is light and elastic. Let the dough rest for 15 minutes.
4. Cut the dough into quarters, then cut each quarter into quarters for a total of 16 pieces. Shape each piece into a round or oval bun about 1 to 1½ inches high. Place the rolls on greased baking sheets, cover them lightly, and let them rise in a warm, draft-free place for 1 hour or until they have doubled in bulk.
5. Preheat the oven to 350° F.
6. Brush the tops of the rolls with the egg white. Place the rolls in the hot oven, and bake them for 20 minutes. If possible, serve them while they are still warm.

MARVELOUS MUFFIN ROLLS

12 rolls

These tasty dinner rolls are especially simple to make: they require no kneading or shaping and only about 1 hour to rise.

Preparation tips: The rolls freeze well, so you may want to make a double batch. You can start them 1½ to 2 hours before mealtime.

 1 **cup warm water (105° F to 115° F)**
 1 **package (1 scant tablespoon) active dry yeast**
 2 **tablespoons brown sugar *or* white sugar**
 ½ **teaspoon salt (optional)**
 1 **egg**
 2 **tablespoons butter *or* margarine**
1¼ **cups whole-wheat flour**
 1 **cup all-purpose flour**

1. Place the warm water in a large bowl, stir in the yeast and sugar until they are dissolved, and let the mixture stand for 10 minutes or until the yeast starts to foam.
2. Add the salt (if desired), egg, butter or margarine, and whole-wheat flour, beating the mixture until it is smooth. Add the all-purpose flour, stirring the batter until it is smooth.
3. Cover the bowl, and let the batter rise in a warm, draft-free place, for 30 minutes or until the batter has doubled in bulk.
4. Stir down the batter, and spoon it into 12 *greased* muffin cups, filling each about half full.
5. Let the rolls rise in the *uncovered* muffin tin for 25 minutes or until the batter reaches the top of the cups.
6. Preheat the oven to 400° F.
7. Place the tin in the hot oven, and bake the rolls for 15 minutes.

WINTER SQUASH ROLLS

24 rolls

These lightly seasoned, slightly sweet rolls are lovely with tea as well as dinner. Once you've puréed the squash, the rolls are not difficult to prepare.

Preparation tips: If you prefer a dessert roll, double the quantities of brown sugar, cinnamon, ginger, and mace. You can also use commercially prepared frozen squash.

2 packages (2 scant tablespoons) active dry yeast
1 teaspoon sugar
¼ cup warm water (105° F to 115° F)
1 cup raisins
1 cup skim or low-fat milk, scalded
1 cup puréed winter squash
⅓ cup light brown sugar, firmly packed
¼ cup (½ stick) butter *or* margarine, melted and cooled
1 egg white *and* 1 egg, lightly beaten
1 tablespoon grated lemon rind
2 teaspoons salt (optional)
¼ teaspoon cinnamon
¼ teaspoon ground ginger
⅛ teaspoon mace
2 cups whole-wheat flour
4 cups (approximately) all-purpose flour
1 egg, lightly beaten, for glaze

1. In a large bowl, dissolve the yeast and the 1 teaspoon of sugar in the warm water. Let the mixture stand for 10 minutes or until the yeast starts to foam.
2. Meanwhile, add the raisins to the scalded milk, and let the mixture cool to lukewarm.
3. In a medium-sized bowl, combine the milk and raisins with the squash, brown sugar, butter or margarine, beaten egg white and whole egg, lemon rind, salt (if desired), cinnamon, ginger, and mace. Add this mixture to the yeast mixture.
4. Stir in the whole-wheat flour and enough of the all-purpose flour to form a soft dough.
5. Turn the dough out onto a floured board, and knead the dough for about 8 minutes, adding more all-purpose flour as needed to prevent sticking.
6. Form the dough into a ball, and place the dough in an oiled bowl, turning the dough to coat it with the oil. Cover the bowl loosely, and let the dough rise in a warm, draft-free place for 1½ hours or until the dough has doubled in bulk.
7. Punch down the dough, and divide it in half. Roll each half into a log 24 inches long. Cut each log crosswise into 12 2-inch-thick pieces. Form each piece into a ball, and place the balls on greased baking sheets.
8. Cover the rolls loosely, and let them rise in a warm, draft-free place for 45 to 60 minutes or until the rolls have doubled in bulk.
9. Preheat the oven to 375° F.
10. Brush the rolls with the beaten egg, place the baking sheets in the hot oven, and bake the rolls for 15 minutes or until the rolls sound hollow when they are tapped on the bottom. Turn the rolls out onto a rack to cool.

WHOLE WHEAT PRETZELS

12 pretzels

These are so easy to make, delicious, and cute, you won't want to wait for a party to prepare them. The recipe is from *Great Whole Grain Breads* by Beatrice Ojakangas, a master of nutritious and delicious breads.

Preparation tips: Caraway seeds are exquisite, but the pretzels can also be made with sesame seeds. And they can be shaped any way you wish: into animal forms or initials or what have you.

Serving suggestions: Delicious as is with soups or salads, or smear them with mustard. Although best when used the day they are baked, they can be refreshed in 10 seconds in a microwave.

```
1 package (1 scant tablespoon) active dry yeast
1 tablespoon sugar
1 cup warm water (105° F to 115° F)
1 teaspoon salt
2½ cups (approximately) whole-wheat flour
   (preferably stone-ground)
6 cups water
2 tablespoons baking soda
1 egg white, lightly beaten
```
Caraway seeds

1. In a large bowl, dissolve the yeast and sugar in the warm water. Let the mixture stand for 10 minutes or until the yeast begins to foam.
2. Add the salt and 2 cups of the flour to the yeast mixture, and beat the mixture well with a wooden spoon. Beat in enough additional flour to form a stiff dough. Let the dough rest for 15 minutes.
3. Turn the dough out onto a lightly floured surface, and knead the dough for 5 minutes or until it is very smooth and satiny. Wash and dry the bowl, and oil it. Place the dough in the bowl, turning the dough to coat it lightly with the oil. Cover the bowl with a dishtowel or with plastic wrap, and let the dough stand for 10 minutes.
4. Divide the dough into 12 equal pieces. Working with 1 piece at a time, roll the dough on a work surface with your hands, shaping it into a rounded strand about 20 inches long; form the strand into a pretzel by turning first one end and then the other toward the middle, letting the ends cross about 2 inches before the tips (see the illustration). Repeat the procedure with the remaining dough. Place the pretzels on a baking sheet covered with wax paper or kitchen parchment.
5. Let the pretzels rise in a warm, draft-free place for 50 minutes or until the pretzels have almost doubled in bulk.
6. Preheat the oven to 400° F.

7. In a large, shallow nonaluminum saucepan, bring the 6 cups of water to a boil, and add the baking soda. Working with 1 pretzel at a time, carefully lift the pretzel off the baking sheet with a large spatula, and lower it into the boiling water. Cook the pretzel for 15 seconds or until the pretzel looks puffy, and remove it from the water with a slotted spatula or spoon, placing it on a greased nonstick baking sheet. Repeat the procedure with the remaining pretzels, placing them on greased nonstick baking sheets about ½ inch apart from one another.

8. Brush the pretzels with the beaten egg white, and sprinkle them with the caraway seeds.

9. Place the baking sheets in the hot oven, and bake the pretzels for 20 minutes or until they are golden.

CARAWAY-RYE ROLLS

Delicious and with a pleasing crunch.

Preparation tip: Note that the dough has three long risings.

Serving suggestion: Great with soup or for making sandwiches.

¼ cup warm water (105° F to 115° F)
2 teaspoons active dry yeast
1 tablespoon sugar
3 cups whole-grain rye flour
3 tablespoons caraway seeds
1 teaspoon salt (optional)
¼ cup (½ stick) melted butter *or* margarine
1¾ cups buttermilk, at room temperature
2½ cups (approximately) bread flour *or* all-purpose flour
1 egg white, lightly beaten
Black caraway seeds (nigella) for garnish (optional)

1. In a small bowl, combine the water, yeast, and sugar, stirring the ingredients to dissolve them. Let the mixture stand for 10 minutes or until the yeast starts to foam.
2. In a large bowl, combine the rye flour, caraway seeds, and salt (if desired). Stir in the melted butter or margarine, buttermilk, and the proofed yeast.
3. Add the bread flour or all-purpose flour 1 cup at a time, stirring the mixture after each addition, until a dough can be formed.
4. Turn the dough out onto a lightly floured board, and knead the dough for about 8 to 10 minutes. Form the dough into a ball, and place the dough in an oiled bowl, turning the dough to coat it with the oil. Cover the bowl with oiled plastic wrap, and let the dough rise in a warm, draft-free place for 1½ hours or until the dough has doubled in bulk.
5. Punch down the dough, cover the bowl, and let the dough rise again in a warm, draft-free place for 1 hour or until the dough has doubled in bulk.
6. Punch down the dough a second time, turn it out onto a lightly floured surface, and divide the dough into quarters. Then divide each quarter into quarters. Shape each of the 16 pieces into oval rolls, and place them about 3 inches apart on oiled baking sheets. With a sharp knife, make a lengthwise slit on the top of each roll. Cover the rolls, and let them rise in a warm, draft-free place for 1 hour or until the rolls have doubled in bulk.
7. Preheat the oven to 375° F.
8. Brush the rolls with the beaten egg white, and sprinkle them (if desired) with the black caraway seeds.
9. Place the baking sheets in the center of the hot oven, and bake the rolls for 25 minutes or until the rolls are golden brown.

DILLED BRAN MUFFIN ROLLS

12 rolls

These make excellent dinner rolls, the dill seeds providing an unusual flavor.

1½ cups all-purpose flour
  1 cup whole-wheat flour
  ½ cup unprocessed bran flakes (*not* cereal)
  1 tablespoon dill seeds
  1 teaspoon baking soda
  ½ teaspoon baking powder
  ½ teaspoon salt (optional)
1½ cups buttermilk
  3 tablespoons butter *or* margarine, melted
  2 tablespoons honey *or* light molasses

1. Preheat the oven to 375° F.
2. In a large bowl, combine the all-purpose flour, whole-wheat flour, bran, dill seeds, baking soda, baking powder, and salt (if desired).
3. Stir in the buttermilk, butter or margarine, and honey or molasses, and blend the ingredients well.
4. Spoon the batter into 12 greased muffin cups.
5. Place the muffin tin in the hot oven, and bake the rolls for 20 to 25 minutes or until the tops of the rolls are lightly browned.

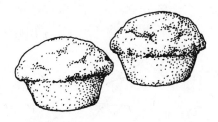

SQUASH BISCUITS

Simple and impressive.

Preparation tip: These biscuits can also be made with sweet potatoes instead of squash. If sweet potatoes are used, reduce the sugar to 1 tablespoon.

    2 cups cooked, mashed winter squash
    6 tablespoons (¾ stick) butter *or* margarine,
      melted, divided
    2 tablespoons sugar
 1½ cups all-purpose flour
  ½ cup whole-wheat flour
    4 teaspoons baking powder
  ½ teaspoon salt (optional)

1. In a large bowl, combine the squash, 3 tablespoons of the butter or margarine, and the sugar.
2. In a small bowl, combine the all-purpose flour, whole-wheat flour, baking powder, and salt (if desired). Add the flour mixture to the squash mixture, stirring the ingredients until they are just combined into a dough.
3. Preheat the oven to 375° F.
4. Roll the dough out ½ inch thick on a floured board. Using a floured biscuit cutter or thin-rimmed glass 2 inches in diameter, cut out the biscuits, and place them on a greased baking sheet. Brush the biscuits with the remaining butter or margarine.
5. Place the baking sheet in the hot oven, and bake the biscuits for 20 minutes or until the tops are lightly browned.

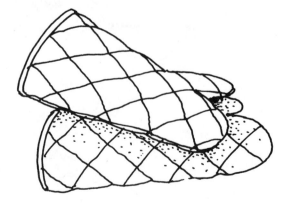

SESAME BISCUITS

about 20 biscuits

These slim biscuits, with a hint of herb, are very low in fat yet tender and flavorful. They are best eaten when they are freshly made.

Preparation tips: The dough can be prepared in advance, refrigerated, and brought back to room temperature before rolling it out on the day you plan to serve the biscuits. Though not ideal, the finished biscuits can also be frozen and refreshed briefly in a warm oven.

Serving suggestions: Great with soups, appetizers, and main-dish salads.

½ cup whole-wheat flour
½ cup all-purpose flour
1 teaspoon baking powder
¼ teaspoon baking soda
¼ teaspoon salt (optional)
½ teaspoon dried dillweed *or* other herb, to taste
3 tablespoons sesame seeds, lightly toasted
2 tablespoons cold butter *or* margarine, cut into bits
8 to 10 tablespoons plain nonfat or low-fat yogurt

1. In a medium-sized bowl, sift together the whole-wheat flour, all-purpose flour, baking powder, baking soda, and salt (if desired). Stir in the dillweed or other herb and the sesame seeds.
2. With a pastry blender or fork, blend in the butter or margarine until the mixture resembles coarse meal.
3. Form a well in the center of the flour mixture, and, combining the ingredients with a fork, add as much of the yogurt as needed to form a moist but not sticky dough (it will be soft). Turn the dough out onto a lightly floured surface, knead the dough for about 30 seconds, then roll it out ⅛ inch thick.
4. Preheat the oven to 450° F.
5. Using a floured biscuit cutter or thin-rimmed glass 2 inches in diameter, cut out rounds, rerolling and cutting the scraps. Place the rounds on a greased baking sheet.
6. Place the baking sheet in the hot oven, and bake the biscuits for 8 to 10 minutes or until the biscuits are golden.

SCALLION BISCUITS

about 20 biscuits

These nutritious biscuits are simple to prepare and simply delicious.

Serving suggestions: Great with soup, for making mini-sandwiches, or halved as a base for hors d'oeuvres.

¾ cup whole-wheat flour
¾ cup all-purpose flour
2 teaspoons baking powder
½ teaspoon baking soda
½ teaspoon salt (optional)
½ teaspoon sugar
¼ teaspoon white pepper
2 tablespoons cold butter *or* margarine, cut into bits
½ cup minced scallions (including the green tops)
½ cup low-fat, small-curd cottage cheese, drained
¼ cup skim or low-fat milk

1. In a large bowl, combine the whole-wheat flour, all-purpose flour, baking powder, baking soda, salt (if desired), sugar, and white pepper.
2. With a pastry blender or fork, blend in the butter or margarine until the mixture resembles coarse meal.
3. Stir in the scallions and cottage cheese. Then add the milk, combining the mixture until it just forms a soft, sticky dough. Turn the dough out onto a floured surface, and knead the dough gently about 5 times. Pat or roll it out into an 8 × 10-inch rectangle.
4. Preheat the oven to 425° F.
5. Using a floured biscuit cutter or thin-rimmed glass 2 inches in diameter, cut out rounds, rerolling and cutting the scraps. Place the biscuits on a greased baking sheet.
6. Place the baking sheet in the hot oven, and bake the biscuits for 12 to 15 minutes or until the biscuits are golden.

WHEAT GERM BISCUITS

about 20 biscuits

These crisp hors d'oeuvre biscuits are based on a recipe by Beatrice Ojakangas in *Great Whole Grain Breads.*

½ cup toasted wheat germ
½ cup all-purpose flour
2 teaspoons baking powder
1 teaspoon sugar
½ teaspoon salt (optional)
2 tablespoons cold butter *or* margarine, cut into bits
¼ cup ice water

1. In a medium-sized bowl, combine the wheat germ, flour, baking powder, sugar, and salt (if desired). With a pastry blender or fork, blend in the butter or margarine until the mixture resembles coarse meal. Add the water 1 tablespoon at a time, stirring the ingredients with a fork after each addition, until the mixture can be formed into a firm ball.
2. Preheat the oven to 350° F.
3. Turn the dough out onto a lightly floured surface, and roll out the dough ¼ inch thick. Using a floured biscuit cutter or thin-rimmed glass 2 inches in diameter, cut out rounds, and place them on a greased baking sheet.
4. Place the baking sheet in the hot oven, and bake the biscuits for 10 to 12 minutes.

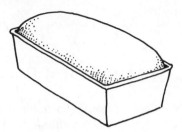

Quick Breads

Instead of yeast, quick breads are leavened with baking powder or baking soda or both. They do not require kneading or hours to rise. As a result, they are just about the simplest baked goods to prepare—even easier than muffins or cookies, which rise the same way but take a little more time and effort to get into the oven. Some quick breads closely resemble yeast breads in texture and flavor, but most are heavier than yeast breads and sweet enough to be a snack or dessert bread. Quick breads freeze well if they are wrapped tightly (they will keep in the freezer for months). I nearly always have some frozen loaves on hand for expected (and unexpected) guests and for instant treats for the family. They make precious gifts, too—at holiday time or when visiting friends and relatives. They can be made in pans of various shapes and sizes—rounds or rectangles ranging from tiny 4 × 2-inch pans to full-size 9 × 5-inch pans (the baking time must be reduced when smaller pans are used).

BETTY'S SODA BREAD   *16 servings*

Although this bread, from Betty Marks's *The High-Calcium Low-Calorie Cookbook,* is minimally sweet, it goes well with coffee or tea and would make a good breakfast or brunch bread. It is very low in fat and cholesterol.

  1 cup whole-wheat flour
  1 cup all-purpose flour plus flour for dusting the pan
¼ cup wheat germ
  3 tablespoons sugar
  2 teaspoons baking soda
  2 teaspoons baking powder
½ teaspoon salt (optional)
  2 cups buttermilk
1½ tablespoons vegetable oil (preferably canola)
  2 tablespoons lightly toasted sunflower seeds
  2 tablespoons chopped dried figs

1. Preheat the oven to 375° F.
2. In a large bowl, combine the whole-wheat flour, all-purpose flour, wheat germ, sugar, baking soda, baking powder, and salt (if desired).
3. Stir in the buttermilk and oil, mixing the ingredients until the batter is just blended but still lumpy. Stir in the sunflower seeds and figs. Pour the batter into a greased and floured 9-inch round pan.

4. Place the pan in the hot oven, and bake the bread for 50 to 60 minutes or until a tester inserted into the center of the bread comes out clean. Let the bread cool in the pan for about 10 minutes before turning it out on a wire rack to cool completely.

SIMPLE SODA BREAD   *1 loaf (about 18 servings)*

When this streamlined soda bread is made without raisins or caraway seeds, it is a suitable substitute for a yeast bread.

Preparation tip: You could take the culinary advice of my dear friend Faith Sullivan and give the bread your own distinctive signature by adding one or more of the following in step 2: wheat germ, rolled oats, cinnamon, nutmeg, sunflower seeds, raisins, currants, nuts, applesauce, chopped fresh or dried apples, or chopped dried apricots.

  2 cups whole-wheat flour
  1 cup all-purpose flour
  1 teaspoon baking powder
  1 teaspoon baking soda
  1 teaspoon salt (optional)
1½ cups buttermilk (or more, if wheat germ or oats
     are added in step 2)
  1 tablespoon butter *or* margarine, melted

1. Preheat the oven to 375° F.
2. In a large bowl, stir together the whole-wheat flour, all-purpose flour, baking powder, baking soda, and salt (if desired). (See "Preparation tip," above.)
3. Stir in the buttermilk, mixing the ingredients until the dry ingredients are just moistened.
4. Turn the dough out onto a floured board, and knead the dough for 1 to 2 minutes or until the dough is smooth. Then shape it into a ball.
5. Place the dough on a greased baking sheet, and flatten it into a 7-inch round about 1½ inches thick. With a floured knife, cut a ½-inch "X" across the top of the loaf.
6. Place the baking sheet in the hot oven, and bake the loaf for 40 minutes or until the loaf sounds hollow when it is tapped on the bottom. Turn the bread out onto a rack to cool, and brush the loaf with the melted butter or margarine.

HIGH-CALCIUM CABBAGE BREAD   *10 servings*

This little bread would rate tops in taste even if it weren't so good for you. Isn't it nice to have a double benefit? I made a few tiny adjustments and added some salt to Betty Marks's recipe from *The High-Calcium Low-Calorie Cookbook.*

Preparation tip: The bread can be made with 1 cup of only one type of cabbage at no nutritional loss. For the sake of color I would choose red cabbage.

Serving suggestion: This is a great bread to serve with a soup or salad meal. After the first day, it is wonderful toasted. Try it, too, as a sandwich bread.

½ cup finely shredded red cabbage
½ cup finely shredded green cabbage
1 teaspoon lemon juice
½ cup plain nonfat or low-fat yogurt
¼ cup orange-juice concentrate *or* ¼ cup orange
   juice and 1 tablespoon sugar
¼ cup vegetable oil (preferably canola)
¼ cup powdered nonfat milk
1 egg
1 cup whole-wheat flour
¾ cup all-purpose flour
¼ cup toasted sesame seeds
2 teaspoons baking powder
½ teaspoon baking soda
½ teaspoon salt (optional)
⅛ teaspoon mace
⅛ teaspoon ground ginger

1. Preheat the oven to 350° F.
2. Place the red cabbage and green cabbage in a small bowl, and toss it with the lemon juice. Set the bowl aside.
3. In a large measuring cup or a medium-sized bowl, combine the yogurt, orange-juice concentrate or orange juice and sugar, oil, powdered milk, and egg, blending the ingredients well. Stir in the reserved cabbage.
4. In a large bowl, combine the whole-wheat flour, all-purpose flour, sesame seeds, baking powder, baking soda, salt (if desired), mace, and ginger, mixing them well.
5. Gradually add the cabbage mixture to the flour mixture, and mix the ingredients until they are just combined. Pour the batter into a greased 8 × 4-inch loaf pan.
6. Place the pan in the hot oven, and bake the bread for 35 to 45 minutes or until a tester inserted into the center of the bread comes out clean. Turn the bread out onto a rack to cool completely before slicing it.

CORN PONE

8 servings

It's hard to beat the simplicity and flavor of this corn bread, adapted from a recipe in the *Minnesota Heritage Cookbook.*

   3 tablespoons butter *or* margarine
   1 cup yellow corn meal (preferably whole-grain)
½ cup all-purpose flour
   1 tablespoon sugar
   2 teaspoons baking powder
½ teaspoon salt (optional)
   1 egg white
   1 egg
   1 cup skim or low-fat milk
   1 jalapeño, seeded and minced

1. Preheat the oven to 350° F.
2. In a 9-inch or 10-inch iron skillet or a 9 × 9-inch pan, melt the butter or margarine in the oven, then remove the skillet or pan but leave the oven on.
3. In a large bowl, combine the corn meal, flour, sugar, baking powder, and salt (if desired).
4. In a medium-sized bowl, beat the egg white and whole egg until they are foamy. Then beat in the milk, 2 tablespoons of the melted butter or margarine, and the jalapeño. Stir the egg mixture into the corn-meal mixture until the ingredients are just combined, and pour the batter into the hot buttered skillet or pan.
5. Place the skillet or pan into the hot oven, and bake the bread for 20 to 25 minutes. Serve the corn pone warm, cut into 8 wedges.

TIM'S CORN BREAD

8 servings

Tim Wright of St. Davids, Pennsylvania, says this is his favorite corn bread.

   1 cup yellow corn meal (preferably whole-grain)
   1 cup whole-wheat flour
   2 teaspoons baking powder
   ½ teaspoon baking soda
   ½ teaspoon salt (optional)
   3 tablespoons vegetable oil (preferably canola)
   ¼ cup honey
   1 cup buttermilk
   1 egg

1. Preheat the oven to 425° F.
2. In a large bowl, combine the corn meal, flour, baking powder, baking soda, and salt (if desired).
3. In a small bowl or large measuring cup, combine the oil, honey, buttermilk, and egg, beating the ingredients until they are thoroughly mixed. Add the buttermilk mixture to the corn-meal mixture, stirring the ingredients until they are just combined. Pour the batter into a greased 8-inch square pan.
4. Place the pan in the hot oven, and bake the bread for about 20 minutes or until the top is golden and a tester inserted into the center of the bread comes out clean.

APPLESAUCE-NUT BREAD

1 loaf

Here's a moist quick bread that is low in fat.

1⅓ cups all-purpose flour
   ¾ cup whole-wheat flour
   ¼ cup soy flour *or* other flour
   ½ cup sugar
   1 tablespoon baking powder
   ½ teaspoon salt (optional)
   ½ teaspoon cinnamon
   ½ teaspoon nutmeg
   ½ cup chopped walnuts
   1 egg white
   1 egg
   2 cups (*or* 1 15-ounce jar) unsweetened applesauce
   ¼ cup butter *or* margarine, melted

1. Preheat the oven to 350° F.
2. In a large bowl, stir together the all-purpose flour, whole-wheat flour, soy flour or other flour, sugar, baking powder, salt (if desired), cinnamon, and nutmeg. Stir in the walnuts.
3. In a medium-sized bowl, beat the egg white and whole egg, and stir in the applesauce and melted butter or margarine. Add this mixture to the flour mixture, stirring the ingredients until they are just moistened. Pour the batter into a greased 9 × 5 × 3-inch loaf pan.
4. Place the pan in the hot oven, and bake the bread for 60 to 70 minutes or until a tester inserted into the center of the bread comes out clean. Let the bread cool in the pan for 10 minutes, then turn it out onto a rack to cool completely before slicing it.

APPLESAUCE-RAISIN BREAD   *1 loaf*

This bread has a lovely texture and flavor. Though dense, it is not heavy for a low-fat, low-cholesterol quick bread.

  1 cup all-purpose flour
  ½ cup whole-wheat flour
  1 teaspoon baking powder
  1 teaspoon baking soda
  1 teaspoon cinnamon
  ½ teaspoon nutmeg
  ¼ teaspoon salt (optional)
  ⅓ cup firmly packed brown sugar
  ½ cup dark raisins
  ½ cup golden raisins
  1 cup rolled oats (quick *or* regular)
  1 egg white
  1 egg
  ¼ cup vegetable oil (preferably canola)
  1 cup plus 2 tablespoons applesauce

1. Preheat the oven to 350° F.
2. In a large bowl, combine the all-purpose flour, whole-wheat flour, baking powder, baking soda, cinnamon, nutmeg, and salt (if desired).
3. Stir in the sugar, dark raisins, golden raisins, and oats.
4. In a small bowl, beat the egg white and whole egg until they are foamy, and whisk in the oil and applesauce. Add the applesauce mixture to the flour mixture, stirring the ingredients until they are just moistened. Pour the batter into a greased 9 × 5-inch loaf pan.
5. Place the pan in the hot oven, and bake the bread for 1 hour or until a tester inserted into the center of the bread comes out clean. Turn the bread out onto a rack to cool completely before slicing it.

BLUEBERRY-NUT BREAD

1 large loaf

I made a few changes in this tasty recipe developed by Minneapolis nutrition consultant Lois Lynch and published in *Dietitian's Food Favorites.*

       1 cup whole-wheat flour
       1 cup all-purpose flour
       1 cup sugar
    1½ teaspoons baking powder
       ½ teaspoon baking soda
       ¼ teaspoon salt (optional)
       2 tablespoons butter *or* margarine, melted
       1 egg, beaten
       1 tablespoon grated orange rind
       ¼ cup orange juice
       ¾ cup boiling water
       1 cup blueberries (preferably fresh)
       ¾ cup chopped pecans

1. Preheat the oven to 350° F.
2. In a large bowl, combine the whole-wheat flour, all-purpose flour, sugar, baking powder, baking soda, and salt (if desired).
3. Add the butter or margarine and the beaten egg to the flour mixture, stirring the ingredients to combine them.
4. In a small bowl or measuring cup, combine the orange rind, orange juice, and water. Add the juice mixture to the flour mixture, stirring the ingredients until they are just combined. Stir in the blueberries and pecans, and transfer the batter to a greased 9 × 5-inch loaf pan.
5. Place the pan in the hot oven, and bake the bread for 50 to 60 minutes or until a tester inserted into the center of the bread comes out clean.

CARROT-PECAN BREAD

1 large loaf

I made some healthful changes in a recipe from the Dannon yogurt people, which yielded a low-fat but moist carrot bread that is high is fiber and flavor.

    1 cup plain nonfat or low-fat yogurt
   ⅔ cup sugar
   ½ cup applesauce (preferably unsweetened)
   ¼ cup vegetable oil (preferably canola)
    1 egg white
    1 egg
 1½ cups whole-wheat flour
    1 cup all-purpose flour
    1 teaspoon baking powder
    1 teaspoon baking soda
    1 teaspoon cinnamon
   ¼ to ½ teaspoon nutmeg, to taste
   ¼ teaspoon salt (optional)
 1½ cups packed grated carrots
   ¾ cup chopped pecans
   ½ cup raisins (optional)

1. Preheat the oven to 350° F.
2. In a large bowl, combine the yogurt, sugar, applesauce, oil, egg white, and whole egg, mixing them thoroughly.
3. In a medium-sized bowl, combine the whole-wheat flour, all-purpose flour, baking powder, baking soda, cinnamon, nutmeg, and salt (if desired). Add the flour mixture to the yogurt mixture, stirring the ingredients until they are just combined. Stir in the carrots, pecans, and raisins (if desired), and pour the batter into a greased 9 × 5-inch loaf pan.
4. Place the pan in the hot oven, and bake the loaf for about 75 minutes. (After about 65 minutes, check on the doneness of the bread by inserting a tester into the center of the loaf; if the tester comes out clean, the bread is done.) Let the loaf cool in the pan for about 15 minutes. Then remove the bread, and wrap it tightly while it is still warm. If possible, let the loaf stand for a day before slicing it.

FOUR-FRUIT BREAD

5 small loaves

These loaves make nice gifts—if you can bear to part with them.

```
  2  cups whole-wheat flour
  2  cups all-purpose flour
 ¾  cup Grape-Nuts cereal
  1  cup sugar
  1  tablespoon baking powder
  1  teaspoon baking soda
 ½  teaspoon salt (optional)
  1  large banana, mashed
1½  cups orange juice
  2  eggs, beaten
  2  to 3 tablespoons grated orange peel
  2  cups cranberries, cut in half
  1  large apple, cored, peeled, and chopped
 ½  cup dried currants
```

1. Preheat the oven to 350° F.
2. In a large mixing bowl, stir together the whole-wheat flour, all-purpose flour, Grape-Nuts, sugar, baking powder, baking soda, and salt (if desired).
3. In a small bowl, combine the mashed banana, orange juice, eggs, and orange peel. Add this mixture to the flour mixture, stirring the ingredients until they are just moistened.
4. Fold in the cranberries, apple, and currants. Distribute the batter among 5 greased small loaf pans (about 6 × 3½ inches).
5. Place the pans in the hot oven, and bake the breads for 50 minutes (check for doneness after 40 minutes) or until the tops are golden brown and a tester inserted into the center of the breads comes out clean.

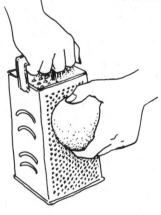

FRUIT AND NUT BREAD

2 loaves

This bread is good enough to make in mini-loaves to give as gifts.

 1 cup dried apricots, coarsely chopped
 1 cup dates, pitted and coarsely chopped
 ½ cup boiling water
 1 orange
 ⅓ cup sugar
 1 egg
 1 teaspoon vanilla extract
 2 tablespoons vegetable oil (preferably canola)
 1 cup whole-wheat flour
 1 cup all-purpose flour
 1 teaspoon baking soda
 ¼ teaspoon salt (optional)
 1 cup chopped pecans

1. Place the apricots and dates in a large bowl with the boiling water, and set the bowl aside.
2. Grate the rind from the orange, and reserve it. Remove the remaining skin and pull apart the sections. Cut the sections in pieces, discarding any seeds, and process the pieces in a blender until the mixture is smooth. Add the reserved grated rind and puréed orange to the apricots and dates. Stir in the sugar, egg, vanilla, and oil, mixing the ingredients well.
3. Preheat the oven to 325° F.
4. In a medium-sized bowl, stir together the whole-wheat flour, all-purpose flour, baking soda, and salt (if desired). Add the flour mixture to the fruit mixture, stirring the ingredients until they are just combined. Fold in the pecans.
5. Divide the batter between 2 greased 8 × 4-inch loaf pans. Place the pans in the hot oven, and bake the loaves for 35 minutes or until a tester inserted into the center of the loaves comes out clean.

PEAR-CRANBERRY BREAD

2 large or 5 small loaves

After being honored with a loaf of this lovely bread one Christmas, I begged my friend Jane Quinn for her recipe. I made a few changes for nutrition's sake, at no loss of flavor and texture.

    ¾ cup (1½ sticks) margarine *or* butter-margarine blend
    1½ cups sugar
     2 egg whites
     2 eggs
    ¾ cup buttermilk *or* plain nonfat or low-fat yogurt
     2 teaspoons vanilla
     3 cups all-purpose flour
     1 cup whole-wheat flour
     2 teaspoons baking powder
     1 teaspoon baking soda
     1 teaspoon salt (optional)
     2 teaspoons cinnamon
    ½ teaspoon ground ginger
    ¼ teaspoon nutmeg
    ¼ teaspoon allspice
     2 cups (2 large) peeled, cored, and coarsely
        chopped pears
     2 cups (8 ounces) cranberries, steamed for 2 minutes

1. With an electric mixer, in a large bowl cream the margarine or butter-margarine blend, and gradually beat in the sugar. Beat in the egg whites and whole eggs. Stir in the buttermilk or yogurt and the vanilla.
2. Preheat the oven to 350° F.
3. In a small bowl, combine the all-purpose flour, whole-wheat flour, baking powder, baking soda, salt (if desired), cinnamon, ginger, nutmeg, and allspice, mixing the ingredients thoroughly. Add the flour mixture to the wet ingredients, stirring the ingredients until they are just combined.
4. Stir in the pears and cranberries, and transfer the batter to 2 greased 9 × 5-inch loaf pans or 5 greased 6 × 3½-inch loaf pans.
5. Place the pans in the hot oven, and bake the loaves for 1 hour (50 to 55 minutes for small loaves) or until a tester inserted into the center of the loaves comes out clean.

MONTE'S PRUNE BREAD

1 large loaf

Some might say life and nutrition are not worth much if you must sacrifice all sweet treats. But thanks to my friend Monte Rogers and a few changes I made in her fabulous low-cholesterol recipe, you can still give nutrition a nod while feasting on home-baked goodies like this one.

1 12-ounce package pitted prunes, coarsely chopped
⅔ cup sugar
⅓ cup butter *or* margarine, softened
1⅓ cups water
1 teaspoon vanilla extract
1½ cups all-purpose flour
½ cup whole-wheat flour
1 teaspoon baking soda
¾ teaspoon cinnamon
¼ teaspoon ground cloves
1 cup chopped walnuts

1. In a large saucepan, combine the prunes, sugar, butter or margarine, water, and vanilla. Bring the mixture to a boil, remove the pan from the heat, and let it stand for 30 minutes. Transfer the mixture to a large bowl.
2. Preheat the oven to 350° F.
3. In a medium-sized bowl, combine the all-purpose flour, whole-wheat flour, baking soda, cinnamon, and cloves. Stir the flour mixture into the cooled prune mixture. Add the walnuts, mixing the ingredients until they are well combined. Transfer the batter to a greased and floured 9 × 5-inch loaf pan.
4. Place the pan in the hot oven, and bake the bread for 1 hour 20 minutes.

SHERRIED PRUNE AND PECAN LOAF   *1 large loaf*

Here is another delicious prune bread, enhanced by sherry and orange rind.

  1 cup diced pitted prunes
  ½ cup medium-dry sherry
  1 tablespoon grated orange rind
  1 cup whole-wheat flour
  1 cup all-purpose flour
  ½ to ⅔ cup sugar, to taste
  ⅓ cup wheat germ
  2 teaspoons baking powder
  ¼ teaspoon baking soda
  1 teaspoon ground ginger
  ½ teaspoon salt (optional)
  2 egg whites
  1 egg
  ⅓ cup skim or low-fat milk
  ¼ cup vegetable oil (preferably canola)
  ¾ cup coarsely chopped pecans

1. In a small bowl, combine the prunes, sherry, and orange rind, and set the bowl aside.
2. In a second small bowl, combine the whole-wheat flour, all-purpose flour, sugar, wheat germ, baking powder, baking soda, ginger, and salt (if desired).
3. Preheat the oven to 350° F.
4. In a large bowl, beat the egg whites and whole egg until they are foamy, and whisk in the milk and oil.
5. Stir the reserved prune mixture into the egg mixture. Then stir in the flour mixture, mixing the ingredients until they are just combined. Stir in the pecans, and transfer the batter to a greased 9 × 5-inch loaf pan.
6. Place the pan in the hot oven, and bake the loaf for 45 to 50 minutes. Let the loaf cool in the pan for 10 minutes, then turn it out onto a rack to cool completely. Wrap the loaf in foil, and store it overnight before slicing it.

Muffins

Homemade muffins, loaded with nutritious as well as flavorful ingredients, are a mainstay at my house. They are quicker and easier to make than cookies, generally contain much less fat and sugar, and lend themselves to preparation with nourishing ingredients like fruits and vegetables and whole-grain flours. I serve them to company at breakfast and brunch, and offer them to friends who drop in for tea or coffee. Mini-muffins (the tins are now widely available, and there are even mini-muffin paper and foil inserts sold in many markets) are a lovely alternative to cookies when serving a fruit or frozen fruit dessert after dinner. They are also a tempting addition to a buffet table and a picnic basket. You can use any of the following recipes to make mini-muffins; they work best when added fruit is cut into very small pieces.

Unlike yeast-leavened baked goods, muffins are raised with baking powder and/or baking soda, both of which contain quite a bit of sodium. But recent evidence suggests that only the sodium in salt—not in these other products—raises blood pressure. The salt in the recipes that follow can be omitted, if necessary (I have already reduced it to the minimum I consider desirable). Nonetheless, those on strict low-sodium diets should be moderate in their consumption of muffins and other baked goods raised without yeast.

Take care not to overbake muffins or they will be dry and hard: they usually start to pull away from the sides of the cups when they are done; or use a toothpick or cake tester to determine when they are fully baked. For the sake of time and convenience, I strongly recommend using paper muffin cups inside the muffin tins: they simplify cleanup and make the muffins more portable. However, if the muffins are to be served at a buffet or fancy meal, it may be more elegant and easier on your guests if you omit the paper or at least remove it before serving. I also recommend using a vegetable-oil spray (for example, Mazola No Stick or Pam) to grease muffin tins and paper muffin cups. And if you have reason to believe that you will especially like a recipe, I urge you to prepare a double batch and to set 1 dozen aside for freezing. Muffins tend to go fast, especially if there are growing children in the house. A 15-second warm-up in the microwave will refresh the muffins.

APPLESAUCE-RAISIN MUFFINS

12 muffins

Jeannette A. Lillis of Cocoa Beach, Florida, contributed this recipe for whole-wheat muffins that can lighten your life.

1¾ cups whole-wheat flour
  2 teaspoons baking powder
  ¾ teaspoon cinnamon
  ¼ teaspoon salt (optional)
  ¼ teaspoon ground ginger
  1 egg
  1 cup applesauce (preferably unsweetened)
  ½ cup honey
  ⅓ cup canola oil
  ⅔ to 1 cup raisins, to taste

1. Preheat the oven to 350° F.
2. In a large bowl, combine the whole-wheat flour with the baking powder, cinnamon, salt (if desired), and ginger.
3. In a small bowl, beat the egg, and add the applesauce, honey, and oil, stirring the ingredients to combine them well. Add the applesauce mixture to the flour mixture, stirring the ingredients until they are just moist. Fold in the raisins.
4. Distribute the batter among 12 greased muffin cups.
5. Place the muffin tin in the hot oven, and bake the muffins for about 25 minutes. Cool the muffins on a rack.

BANANA-BRAN MUFFINS

24 muffins

Simple-to-make treats full of nutrients and flavor.

1¼ cups mashed banana (3 medium)
1½ cups buttermilk
  2 cups shredded bran cereal (e.g., 100% Bran or All-Bran)
  1 egg white *and* 1 egg, lightly beaten
  ½ cup vegetable oil (preferably canola)
  ⅔ cup raisins (optional)
1½ cups whole-wheat flour
1½ cups all-purpose flour
  ½ cup loosely packed dark brown sugar
  4 teaspoons baking powder
  1 teaspoon baking soda
  ½ teaspoon salt (optional)
  1 teaspoon cinnamon
  ¼ teaspoon ground cloves

1. Preheat the oven to 375° F.
2. In a large bowl, combine the banana, buttermilk, and bran cereal, and let the mixture stand for about 5 minutes.
3. Add the beaten egg white and whole egg, oil, and raisins (if desired).
4. In a small bowl, combine the whole-wheat flour, all-purpose flour, brown sugar, baking powder, baking soda, salt (if desired), cinnamon, and cloves. Add the flour mixture to the banana mixture, stirring the ingredients until they are just moist. Distribute the batter among 24 greased muffin cups.
5. Place the muffin tins in the hot oven, and bake the muffins for about 25 minutes.

BLUEBERRY-BRAN MUFFINS

12 muffins

This simple recipe from Susan Kimball of Cedar Falls, Iowa, makes marvelous muffins.

Preparation tip: Susan urges the use of foil—not paper—liners; otherwise the muffins may stick to the paper and be difficult to remove.

  1 cup unprocessed bran flakes (*not* cereal)
  ⅔ cup whole-wheat flour
  ⅔ cup all-purpose flour
1¼ teaspoons baking soda
  ¼ teaspoon salt (optional)
  1 large egg
  ¼ cup vegetable oil (preferably canola)
  ⅓ cup honey
1¼ cups buttermilk
1½ cups fresh blueberries *or* frozen drained
    blueberries
Vegetable-oil spray

1. Preheat the oven to 400° F.
2. In a large bowl, combine the bran flakes with the whole-wheat flour, all-purpose flour, baking soda, and salt (if desired).
3. In a small bowl, whisk together the egg, oil, and honey until the ingredients are well blended. Add the buttermilk, and whisk the ingredients again to combine them. Add the buttermilk mixture to the bran mixture, stirring the ingredients until they are just moist. Gently stir in the blueberries.
4. Line a 12-cup muffin tin with foil liners, and spray the liners with the vegetable oil. Distribute the batter among the the cups.
5. Place the muffin tin in the hot oven, and bake the muffins for 20 minutes or until the tops of the muffins spring back when they are lightly touched.

DATED BRAN MUFFINS

12 muffins

These quick-to-prepare muffins are also likely to be quickly devoured.

 1 cup buttermilk
1½ cups shredded bran cereal (e.g., 100% Bran or
    All-Bran)
 ½ cup chopped dates
 ⅓ cup butter *or* margarine, softened
 ¼ cup packed brown sugar
 1 egg
 ¾ cup whole-wheat flour
 ¼ cup all-purpose flour
 ¼ teaspoon salt (optional)
2½ teaspoons baking powder
 ½ teaspoon baking soda

1. Preheat the oven to 400° F.
2. In a large bowl, combine the buttermilk, cereal, and dates, and let the mixture stand for 5 minutes or until the cereal has softened.
3. Add the butter or margarine, sugar, and egg, and mix the ingredients well.
4. In a small bowl, combine the whole-wheat flour, all-purpose flour, salt (if desired), baking powder, and baking soda. Add the flour mixture to the cereal mixture, stirring the ingredients until they are just moist. Divide the batter among 12 greased muffin cups.
5. Place the pan in the hot oven, and bake the muffins for 18 to 20 minutes.

TEN-MINUTES-TO-THE-OVEN
BRAN MUFFINS

12 muffins

It's hard to find a more efficient recipe than this one, and no one would guess from how these muffins taste just how simple they are to prepare.

1¼ cups shredded bran cereal (e.g., 100% Bran or
    All-Bran)
 1 cup skim or low-fat milk
 1 cup all-purpose flour
 ¼ cup sugar
2½ teaspoons baking powder
 ½ teaspoon baking soda
 ½ teaspoon salt (optional)
 1 egg
 ¼ cup vegetable oil (preferably canola)
 ½ cup raisins

1. Preheat the oven to 400° F.
2. In a large bowl, stir together the cereal and milk. Let the mixture stand for 5 minutes.
3. Meanwhile, in a small bowl, combine the flour, sugar, baking powder, baking soda, and salt (if desired). Set the mixture aside.
4. Add the egg and oil to the bran mixture, beating the ingredients to blend them. Add the flour mixture, stirring the ingredients until they are just combined. Fold in the raisins. Distribute the batter among 12 greased muffin cups (2½ inches in diameter), filling each about ⅔ full.
5. Place the muffin tin in the hot oven, and bake the muffins for about 20 minutes.

CRANBERRY-CORN MUFFINS   *12 muffins*

These muffins, with a hint of corn and the beauty of cranberries, are perfect for a winter holiday breakfast or brunch.

¾ cup all-purpose flour
½ cup whole-wheat flour
1 cup yellow corn meal
⅓ to ½ cup sugar, to taste
2 teaspoons baking powder
½ teaspoon baking soda
¼ teaspoon salt (optional)
⅔ cup buttermilk
⅓ cup orange juice
⅓ cup vegetable oil (preferably canola)
2 egg whites *or* 1 egg
4 teaspoons grated orange rind
1 cup fresh cranberries, coarsely chopped

1. Preheat the oven to 400° F.
2. In a large bowl, combine the all-purpose flour, whole-wheat flour, corn meal, sugar, baking powder, baking soda, and salt (if desired).
3. In a 2-cup measuring cup or small bowl, combine the buttermilk, orange juice, oil, egg whites or whole egg, and orange rind. Add the buttermilk mixture to the flour mixture, stirring the ingredients until they are just moist. Stir in the cranberries. Distribute the batter among 12 greased muffin cups.
4. Place the muffin tin in the hot oven, and bake the muffins for 20 to 25 minutes.

CREAMED CORN MUFFINS

12 muffins

These are easy to prepare and yield a muffin that is wonderful for breakfast, brunch, or lunch.

Preparation tip: The batter can also be used to prepare a zingy corn bread by reducing the sugar to 1 tablespoon, increasing the salt to 1 teaspoon, and adding a minced jalapeño. Bake the bread in an 8-inch or 9-inch square pan.

> 1 cup *sifted* all-purpose flour
> 1 cup yellow corn meal (preferably stone-ground)
> 2 tablespoons sugar
> 1½ teaspoons baking powder
> ½ teaspoon salt (optional)
> ¼ teaspoon baking soda
> 2 tablespoons very cold butter *or* margarine
> 1 egg, lightly beaten
> ¾ cup (½ can) cream-style corn
> ⅔ cup buttermilk

1. Preheat the oven to 425° F.
2. In a large bowl, combine the flour, corn meal, sugar, baking powder, salt (if desired), and baking soda, stirring the ingredients to mix them well.
3. Cut the butter or margarine into bits, and blend it into the flour mixture.
4. Add the egg, corn, and buttermilk, stirring the ingredients until they are just moist. Distribute the batter among 12 greased muffin cups.
5. Place the muffin tin in the hot oven, and bake the muffins for 20 minutes or until the tops of the muffins are toasted and a tester inserted into the center of the muffins comes out clean.

RAISIN-CORN MUFFINS

12 muffins

An easy, fast muffin recipe that derives most of its sweetness from raisins.

> ¾ cup whole-wheat flour
> ½ cup all-purpose flour
> ¾ cup yellow corn meal (preferably whole-grain)
> ¼ cup sugar
> 4 teaspoons baking powder
> ½ teaspoon salt (optional)
> 2 eggs *or* 2 egg whites and 1 egg
> 1 cup milk
> ¼ cup butter *or* margarine, softened
> ¾ cup raisins

1. Preheat the oven to 450° F.
2. In a large bowl, combine the whole-wheat flour, all-purpose flour, corn meal, sugar, baking powder, and salt (if desired).
3. Add the eggs or the egg whites and egg, milk, and butter or margarine, and beat the mixture with a wooden spoon to blend the ingredients thoroughly. Stir in the raisins. Spoon the batter into 12 greased muffin cups.
4. Place the muffin tin in the hot oven, and bake the muffins for 15 to 18 minutes or until the tops of the muffins are browned.

STRABERRY MUFFINS

24 muffins

These are so pretty and scrumptious that I had to prepare a second batch the very day I made the first one. Since the muffins freeze well, I offer you a recipe for 2 dozen.

    2 cups all-purpose flour
    1 cup whole-wheat flour
    1 cup sugar
 4½ teaspoons baking powder
 1½ teaspoons cinnamon
  ¾ teaspoon salt (optional)
    1 egg white
    2 eggs
    1 cup apple cider *or* apple juice
  ½ cup vegetable oil (preferably canola)
    2 cups sliced strawberries, divided (if you are
      using frozen berries, measure them after
      defrosting and draining them)

1. Preheat the oven to 400° F.
2. In a large bowl, combine the all-purpose flour, whole-wheat flour, sugar, baking powder, cinnamon, and salt (if desired).
3. In a medium-sized bowl, lightly beat the egg white and whole eggs. Beat in the apple cider or juice and the oil. Add the egg mixture to the flour mixture, stirring the ingredients until they are just moist.
4. Gently stir in all but 24 slices of the strawberries. Divide the batter among 24 greased muffin cups. Top each muffin with a reserved strawberry slice.
5. Place the muffin tins in the hot oven, and bake the muffins for about 25 minutes.

OAT BRAN MUFFINS

12 muffins

At last! Oat-bran muffins worth making—and eating. No longer need such muffins be a culinary sacrifice for the sake of your coronary arteries. These could even be served to breakfast or brunch guests without explaining that "they're good for you." I modified a recipe developed by Virginia L. Pollenz, a nurse at the Center for Health Education at Huntsville Hospital in Alabama.

Preparation tips: Use the oat bran that is sold to prepare cooked cereal. If you use lemon extract, also use the lemon rind; use orange rind with orange extract. The batter is very loose, but it does bake through.

2¼ cups oat bran
  1 tablespoon baking powder
  ½ teaspoon salt (optional)
  2 tablespoons vegetable oil
  ¼ cup honey
1¼ cups skim milk
  2 egg whites
  1 egg
  1 teaspoon lemon extract *or* orange extract
  1 tablespoon grated lemon rind *or* orange rind
  ¼ cup chopped nuts
  ¼ cup raisins *or* chopped dates

1. Preheat the oven to 400° F.
2. In a large bowl, combine the oat bran, baking powder, and salt (if desired).
3. In a medium-sized bowl, combine the oil, honey, milk, egg whites, and whole egg. Beat the mixture until it is frothy. Stir in the desired extract and grated rind (see "Preparation tips," above).
4. Add the milk mixture to the bran mixture, and beat the ingredients with an electric mixer at medium speed for 2 minutes to allow the batter to thicken. Fold in the nuts and raisins or dates. Distribute the batter among 12 muffin cups fitted with greased paper liners.
5. Place the muffin tin in the hot oven, and bake the muffins for 15 to 17 minutes or until a tester inserted into the center of the muffins comes out moist but not wet. Turn the muffins out onto a rack to cool. When they are cool, store them in the refrigerator or freezer.

RASPBERRY–OAT BRAN MUFFINS

12 muffins

Here's an oat-bran muffin that is attractive, nutritious, and relatively light. It is only slightly modified from the one that Jodie Draut of Arlington Heights, Illinois, devised for a relative who has diabetes and elevated serum cholesterol.

Preparation tips: Since the batter is loose, let it stand for about 15 minutes before filling the muffin cups. Cleanup will be easier if you use paper liners (spray them with vegetable oil).

  1 cup oat bran
  ¾ cup all-purpose flour
  ½ cup whole-wheat flour
  ⅓ cup sugar
  1 tablespoon baking powder
  ¼ teaspoon salt (optional)
  ¼ cup very cold margarine *or* light
     butter-margarine blend
  2 egg whites
  1 cup skim milk
  1 teaspoon vanilla extract
1½ cups raspberries, divided

1. In a large bowl, combine the oat bran, all-purpose flour, whole-wheat flour, sugar, baking powder, and salt (if desired), stirring the ingredients to mix them well.
2. Cut the margarine or butter-margarine blend into bits, and add it to the flour mixture, blending it in with a pastry blender, fork, or two knifes.
3. In a small bowl, whisk together the egg whites, milk, and vanilla, and add them to the dry ingredients, stirring the ingredients until they are just moist.
4. Reserve 12 of the best raspberries, and fold the rest of the berries gently into the batter. Let the batter stand for about 15 minutes.
5. Preheat the oven to 400° F.
6. Distribute the batter among 12 greased muffin cups. Top each muffin with a reserved berry.
7. Place the muffin tin in the hot oven, and bake the muffins for 20 to 25 minutes. When the muffins are done, turn them out on their sides onto a rack to cool.

WHEAT-OAT MUFFINS

24 muffins

Here is another muffin containing oat bran that I enjoy. It's light, thanks to the beaten egg whites, and it's nearly cholesterol-free. The orange rind imparts a lovely flavor, making it an ideal breakfast muffin. Mary Bradham of Mount Vernon, Illinois, developed the recipe, which was passed along by her admiring daughter Susan, who says "they're the best" she's ever eaten. I made minor changes in Mary's recipe to suit my tastes and available ingredients.

¾ cup raisins
⅔ cup boiling water
 2 cups shredded bran cereal (e.g., 100% Bran or
    All-Bran)
 1 cup whole-wheat flour
 1 cup oat bran
½ cup all-purpose flour
½ cup wheat germ
½ cup rolled oats (quick or regular)
⅔ cup sugar
 4 egg whites
 2 cups buttermilk
½ cup vegetable oil (preferably canola)
 2 tablespoons grated orange rind
 1 teaspoon vanilla extract

1. Preheat the oven to 400° F.
2. Place the raisins in a small heatproof bowl, and add the boiling water. Set the bowl aside.
3. In a large bowl, combine the cereal, whole-wheat flour, oat bran, all-purpose flour, wheat germ, oats, and sugar.
4. In a second large bowl, beat the egg whites until they are foamy. Stir in the buttermilk, oil, orange rind, and vanilla. Stir in the reserved raisins and their soaking liquid.
5. Add the egg mixture to the cereal mixture, stirring the ingredients until they are just moist. Distribute the batter (about ¼ cup per muffin) among 24 greased muffin cups.
6. Place the muffin tins in the hot oven, and bake the muffins for 20 to 25 minutes. Turn the muffins out onto a rack to cool.

CRANBERRY-PUMPKIN MUFFINS   *24 muffins*

As Thanksgiving approaches, cranberries and pumpkins are often in my thoughts—and in my refrigerator. Why not put the two together in some breakfast muffins? These muffins are on the heavy side, so don't expect them to rise much. But they're tasty and satisfying.

Preparation tip: Cranberries are easiest to halve when they are frozen.

　　2　cups all-purpose flour
　　1　cup whole-wheat flour
　　1　cup sugar
1½　teaspoons cinnamon
　　1　teaspoon baking powder
　　1　teaspoon baking soda
　¾　teaspoon allspice
　½　teaspoon salt (optional)
　½　cup butter *or* margarine, melted
2½　cups thick puréed pumpkin (use more pumpkin
　　　and drain it first if the pumpkin is watery)
　　2　eggs, lightly beaten
　　2　cups cranberries, cleaned and halved

1. Preheat the oven to 350° F.
2. In a large bowl, combine the all-purpose flour, whole-wheat flour, sugar, cinnamon, baking powder, baking soda, allspice, and salt (if desired). Stir the ingredients to mix them well.
3. Add the butter or margarine, pumpkin, and eggs, stirring the ingredients until they are just moist. Stir in the cranberries. Spoon the batter into 24 greased muffin cups.
4. Place the muffin tins in the hot oven, and bake the muffins for 40 minutes or until a tester inserted into the center of the muffins comes out clean.

PUMPKIN MUFFINS

Versatile pumpkin purée makes these muffins moist and light.

Preparation tip: Homemade purée is usually a lot moister than commercially canned purée. If you use homemade purée, start with ¾ cup or more, and let it drain in a sieve lined with cheesecloth.

  ⅔ **cup whole-wheat flour**
  ⅔ **cup all-purpose flour**
  ¼ **cup sugar**
  2 **teaspoons baking powder**
  ½ **teaspoon salt (optional)**
  ½ **teaspoon cinnamon**
  ½ **teaspoon nutmeg (preferably freshly grated)**
  4 **tablespoons cold butter *or* margarine, cut into bits**
  ½ **cup raisins**
  ½ **cup skim milk**
  ½ **cup pumpkin purée**
  1 **large egg, lightly beaten**

1. Preheat the oven to 400° F.
2. In a large bowl, combine the whole-wheat flour, all-purpose flour, sugar, baking powder, salt (if desired), cinnamon, and nutmeg. Blend in the butter or margarine until the mixture is crumbly.
3. Add the raisins, milk, pumpkin, and egg, stirring the ingredients until they are just moist. Spoon the batter into 12 greased and floured muffin cups.
4. Place the muffin tin in the hot oven, and bake the muffins for 18 to 20 minutes. Remove the pan from the oven, and put it on a rack to cool for about 10 minutes before removing the muffins.

ZUCCHINI MUFFINS WITH LEMON

12 muffins

Here's another wonderful repository for that abundance of summertime zucchinis. But these are tasty enough to make even in the dead of winter, so don't delay! I adapted a recipe published in *American Health* magazine.

Preparation tip: The batter will be loose, but don't worry. The muffins will bake through nicely, forming a golden-brown crust.

    1 cup whole-wheat flour
    1 cup all-purpose flour
    1 tablespoon baking powder
    ½ teaspoon baking soda
    ¼ teaspoon salt (optional)
    ¼ teaspoon nutmeg
    1 egg
    3 tablespoons vegetable oil (preferably canola)
    ⅓ cup honey
    ½ cup skim or low-fat milk
    ½ cup plain nonfat or low-fat yogurt
    1 cup firmly packed shredded zucchini
    1 tablespoon grated lemon rind

1. Preheat the oven to 375° F.
2. In a large bowl, combine the whole-wheat flour, all-purpose flour, baking powder, baking soda, salt (if desired), and nutmeg.
3. In a medium-sized bowl, beat the egg, and add the oil, honey, milk, yogurt, zucchini, and lemon rind, stirring the ingredients to combine them well.
4. Add the zucchini mixture to the flour mixture, stirring the ingredients until they are just moist. Distribute the batter among 12 greased muffin cups.
5. Place the muffin tin in the hot oven, and bake the muffins for 30 to 35 minutes or until the muffins are golden and firm. Remove the muffin tin from the oven, and put the tin on a rack for 5 minutes before turning the muffins out to cool.

MARKS'S MINI-MUFFINS

12 mini-muffins

My friend Betty Marks served these wonderful, simple, and nutritious muffins at an elegant New Year's Eve dinner. The recipe is from her *International Menu Diabetic Cookbook*, written with Lucille Haley Schechter.

Preparation tip: If you have two mini-muffin tins, I suggest doubling this recipe. The muffins disappear fast.

½ cup rye flour (preferably whole-grain)
⅓ cup all-purpose flour
¾ teaspoon baking powder
¼ teaspoon baking soda
⅛ teaspoon salt
1 teaspoon caraway seeds
1 teaspoon poppy seeds
3 tablespoons finely chopped walnuts
½ cup buttermilk
1 egg
1 tablespoon walnut oil *or* canola oil
1 tablespoon apple-juice concentrate
Vegetable-oil spray

1. Preheat the oven to 400° F.
2. In a large bowl, combine the rye flour, all-purpose flour, baking powder, baking soda, salt, caraway seeds, poppy seeds, and walnuts.
3. In a small bowl, combine the buttermilk, egg, oil, and apple-juice concentrate. Add the buttermilk mixture to the flour mixture, stirring the ingredients until they are just moist.
4. Spray a mini-muffin tin with vegetable oil. Divide the batter among the cups.
5. Place the tin in the hot oven, and bake the muffins for 15 minutes.

Cookies

Cookies are as much a part of American life as are the hamburger and shake. They show up at picnics, dinner parties, luncheons, and many other settings. Unfortunately, most commercially prepared cookies are laden with fat (usually butter for the more expensive ones and highly saturated coconut or palm-kernel oil for the supermarket varieties) and are made with so much sugar that it's hard to taste anything else. Although finding decent cookie recipes that are not loaded with fat and sweetener is no easy task, I did come up with a few that taste and feel like traditional cookies but have less of the damaging ingredients and more nutritional value for their calories.

ALMOND COOKIES   *24 to 36 cookies*

These are luscious and easy (once you get the knack of shaping them). I served these flourless cookies from Iraq at a Passover seder, but they could be a lovely sweet treat any time of year.

Preparation tips: Rose water is sold at many specialty-food stores, at stores that sell Middle Eastern foods, and in some pharmacies. The almonds can be ground in a food processor, spice grinder, or electric coffee grinder. The cookie dough is easier to shape if you first roll it with damp hands into 1¼-inch balls and then pinch out 6 points to form a Star of David. The balls of dough could also be flattened into rounds about ⅓ inch thick. Note that the formed dough rests for *3 hours* before baking.

2½ **cups ground blanched almonds**
 1 **cup sugar**
 2 **tablespoons rose water plus additional
     rose water for shaping**

1. In a medium-sized bowl, combine the almonds, sugar, and the 2 tablespoons of rose water. Mix the ingredients to form a dough.
2. Pinching off pieces of dough, roll them into 24 to 36 small balls, each about 1¼ inches in diameter. Pinch the edges of each ball to form 6 points (a Star of David), or flatten the balls into rounds. Place the shaped dough on greased cookie sheets, and let the unbaked cookies stand uncovered at room temperature for 3 hours.
3. Preheat the oven to 375° F.
4. Place the cookie sheets in the hot oven, and bake the cookies for 10 minutes or until the cookies are a pale gold.

CHOCOLATE-ALMOND MACAROONS   *32 cookies*

Here is another great flourless cookie that you can proudly serve at a Passover seder or any other time.

Preparation tips: The almonds can be ground in a food processor, spice grinder, or electric coffee grinder. The cookies can be baked 2 to 3 days in advance and stored in an airtight cookie tin or jar.

½ pound blanched almonds, ground
6 tablespoons plus ¼ cup sugar, divided
3 ounces bittersweet chocolate *or* semisweet
   chocolate, finely chopped
2 large egg whites
Pinch salt
Pinch cream of tartar
¼ teaspoon almond extract

1. Place the ground almonds in a large bowl, and stir in the 6 tablespoons of sugar and the chopped chocolate.
2. In a medium-sized bowl, beat the egg whites and salt with an electric mixer until the whites are frothy. Add the cream of tartar, and continue beating the egg whites until they hold soft peaks. Add the remaining ¼ cup sugar and almond extract, and beat the egg whites until they form stiff, shiny peaks. Stir the whites into the almond-chocolate mixture, gently folding the batter until the ingredients are well combined.
3. Line 2 cookie sheets with foil.
4. Preheat the oven to 350° F.
5. Transfer the batter to a pastry bag fitted with a small (½ inch) star tip, if available, and squeeze out mounds of batter about 1½ inches in diameter, placing the mounds 1 inch apart on the prepared cookie sheets.
6. Place the cookie sheets in the hot oven, and bake the macaroons for 18 to 20 minutes or until the edges and ridges of the cookies are a pale gold. Remove the foil with the macaroons from the cookie sheets, and let the macaroons cool for about 5 minutes. Then gently peel the macaroons from the foil, and place them on a rack to cool completely.

MANDELBROT *(Almond Bread)*

72 to 96 cookies

For those of you unfamiliar with this toasted European almond cookie, you're in for a treat. The recipe was given to me many years ago by a fine Italian cook and baker, Terry Salerno of Dallas. Although this is a big recipe, the cookies go fast and have a long shelf life. You can, however, cut the recipe in half, if you wish.

> 2 egg whites
> 2 eggs
> ½ cup vegetable oil (preferably canola)
> 1 teaspoon vanilla extract
> 1 teaspoon almond extract
> 1 cup sugar
> ½ cup coarsely chopped raw almonds
> 3 to 4½ cups all-purpose flour, divided
> 1 teaspoon baking powder
> Vegetable oil *or* vegetable-oil spray
> Cinnamon-sugar

1. In a large bowl, beat the egg whites and whole eggs until they are creamy. Add the oil, vanilla extract, almond extract, and sugar, and stir the ingredients to combine them thoroughly. Stir in the almonds.

2. In a medium-sized bowl, combine 3 cups of the flour with the baking powder, and gradually stir this into the egg mixture. Continue adding flour, a little at a time, until the dough is fairly dry and easy to handle (that is, until it has the consistency of modeling clay). The final additions are best kneaded in by hand.

3. Preheat the oven to 325° F.

4. Knead the dough for 1 to 2 minutes, divide the dough into 6 pieces, and roll each piece into a long, thin strip about 1 inch in diameter. Place the strips on greased cookie sheets. Brush or spray the tops with the vegetable oil, and sprinkle the strips with the cinnamon-sugar.

5. Place the cookie sheets in the hot oven, and bake the strips for 35 minutes. *Do not turn the oven off.*

6. Carefully remove the strips from the sheets, and slice the strips on the diagonal into cookies about ½ inch thick. Lay the cookies on their sides on the cookie sheets, and sprinkle the cookies again with the cinnamon-sugar.

7. Return the cookie sheets to the hot oven, and bake the cookies 10 minutes longer or until the cookies resemble hard toast.

APPLESAUCE COOKIES

about 54 cookies

Jean Hewitt's *The New York Times Natural Foods Cookbook* is the happy inspiration for these chewy, flour-free delights.

- ⅔ cup packed brown sugar (light *or* dark)
- ¾ cup vegetable oil (preferably canola)
- 1 teaspoon vanilla
- ¼ teaspoon salt (optional)
- 1 cup unsweetened applesauce
- ½ cup chopped pecans
- 4 cups quick-cooking oats
- ½ cup chopped dates

1. In a large bowl, beat together the brown sugar, oil, vanilla, and salt (if desired). Stir in the applesauce, pecans, oats, and dates.
2. Preheat the oven to 375° F.
3. Drop rounded teaspoonfuls of the dough about 1 inch apart onto greased cookie sheets (the cookies do not spread while they are baking).
4. Place the cookie sheets in the hot oven, and bake the cookies for 25 minutes or until the cookies are well browned. Transfer the cookies from the pans to a rack to cool.

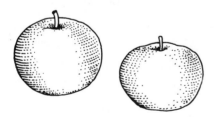

CHOCOLATE CHIP–OATMEAL COOKIES

about 36 small cookies

Many "health food" cookies use carob as a substitute for chocolate. I don't see the point: carob has more natural sugar than chocolate and doesn't taste nearly as good. When it comes to chocolate, then, go for the real thing.

½ cup butter *or* margarine, softened
3 tablespoons brown sugar
1 egg white, beaten
1 tablespoon milk
½ cup whole-wheat flour
½ cup quick-cooking oats
½ teaspoon cinnamon
¼ teaspoon baking soda
¼ cup chocolate chips

1. In a large mixing bowl, combine the butter or margarine and brown sugar. Add the egg white and milk, and blend the ingredients well.
2. In a small bowl, combine the flour, oats, cinnamon, and baking soda. Stir the flour mixture into the butter or margarine mixture. Add the chocolate chips, and mix the ingredients to distribute them well.
3. Preheat the oven to 350° F.
4. Drop rounded teaspoonfuls of the dough about 1 inch apart onto greased cookie sheets.
5. Place the cookie sheets in the hot oven, and bake the cookies for 15 minutes.

CHOCOLATE CHIP AND RAISIN COOKIES

about 60 cookies

A fan (unfortunately, I lost her name) from Fort Pierce, Florida, calls her delicious treat "Chocolate Chip Cookies (with Less Guilt)" because she substituted peanut butter for some of the margarine, cut the sugar in half, used skim milk, and added wheat germ. I made still further changes: I used even less sugar and half whole-wheat flour. Still, I ended up with a light, luscious cookie that my tasters loved.

Preparation tips: If you wish, you could add 1 cup of chopped nuts along with the chips and raisins. The cookies will keep (if they last that long) for 1 week in a tightly closed cookie tin or jar.

¼ cup margarine *or* butter-margarine blend
½ cup natural unsalted peanut butter
⅔ cup packed dark brown sugar
 1 teaspoon vanilla extract
 2 eggs *or* 2 egg whites and 1 egg
½ cup skim milk
 1 cup whole-wheat flour
 1 cup all-purpose flour
¼ cup wheat germ
 1 teaspoon baking soda
 1 teaspoon salt (optional)
 6 ounces semisweet chocolate chips
 1 cup raisins

1. In a large bowl, beat together the margarine or butter-margarine blend, peanut butter, sugar, and vanilla. Beat in the eggs or the egg whites and whole egg and the milk.
2. In a medium-sized bowl, stir together the whole-wheat flour, all-purpose flour, wheat germ, baking soda, and salt (if desired). Add the flour mixture to the large bowl, stirring the ingredients to combine them well. Then fold the chocolate chips and raisins into the batter.
3. Preheat the oven to 350° F.
4. Drop rounded teaspoonfuls of the dough about 2 inches apart onto *ungreased* cookie sheets.
5. Place the cookie sheets in the hot oven, and bake the cookies for about 10 minutes.

VIENNESE CRESCENTS

about 60 cookies

I added only a little additional sugar to Carol Cutler's recipe. These cookies are simple and delicious. All my tasters who bake requested the recipe. And at about 32 calories each, they are not even that sinful.

Preparation tips: For maximum flavor, be sure to use freshly ground almonds. The nuts can be ground in a nut grinder, food processor, or blender. The cookies can be made up to 5 days ahead and stored in a tightly closed cookie tin or jar.

¼ cup butter *or* butter-margarine blend
¼ cup sugar
2 teaspoons vanilla extract
1 teaspoon almond extract
¼ cup skim milk
1½ cups *sifted* all-purpose flour
1 cup (4 ounces) almonds, freshly ground
Sifted confectioners' sugar for dusting (optional)

1. In a medium-large bowl, beat together the butter or butter-margarine blend and sugar until the mixture is light and fluffy (this will not happen if you use margarine, but do not worry).
2. Add the vanilla extract, almond extract, and milk, and beat the mixture.
3. Resift the flour, and gradually stir it into the batter.
4. Add the almonds, form the dough into a ball, and turn the dough out onto a board. Knead the dough for a few minutes to thoroughly combine the ingredients. Form the dough into a smooth ball, place the dough on a dish, cover the dish with plastic wrap, and refrigerate the dough for at least 30 minutes.
5. When you are ready to bake the cookies, preheat the oven to 325° F.
6. Snip off a rounded teaspoon of the chilled dough, and with your hands roll it into a small oval. Using your fingers, shape the oval into a crescent about 1½ inches long, and place the cookie on an *ungreased* cookie sheet. Repeat the procedure until all the dough has been used up. You will need 2 cookie sheets.
7. Place the cookie sheets in the hot oven, and bake the cookies for 15 minutes or until the crescents just begin to turn golden. Transfer the cookies to a rack to cool, and sprinkle them with the confectioners' sugar (if desired).

YES-YES COOKIES

These high-fiber, no-cholesterol gems contain less than 50 calories each. No one need ever know they are "health food" treats that I adapted from a recipe by Nao Hauser in *American Health* magazine.

Preparation tips: If you don't mind some cholesterol in your cookies, replace the apple juice with 1 egg. If you use "light" margarine, use just 1 tablespoon of apple juice or omit the juice entirely.

    1 cup 100% bran cereal (e.g., 100% Bran or
       All-Bran)
    ½ cup all-purpose flour
    ½ cup quick-cooking oats
    ⅓ to ½ cup packed light brown sugar, to taste
    ⅓ cup margarine
    ½ teaspoon salt (optional)
    ½ teaspoon baking soda
    ½ teaspoon ground ginger
    ½ teaspoon cinnamon
    ½ teaspoon ground cloves
    ½ teaspoon grated lemon peel
    ½ teaspoon vanilla extract
    2 tablespoons apple juice

1. In a large bowl, combine all the ingredients, beating them with an electric mixer on low speed until they are well blended.
2. Preheat the oven to 375° F.
3. Drop rounded teaspoonfuls of the dough approximately 2 inches apart onto *ungreased* cookie sheets.
4. Place the cookie sheets in the hot oven, and bake the cookies for 12 minutes or until the cookies are golden.

DESSERTS

I must confess to a double standard. For ordinary family meals, I almost never serve dessert. One or more of us may have a moderately sweet snack or fruit sometime during the evening, but dessert is not a routine part of the meal. Nonetheless, when I have company—even casual company—dessert becomes the rule rather than the exception, as important a part of the meal as the hors d'oeuvres are to the predinner "cocktail" hour (almost no one drinks cocktails anymore).

I know any number of cooks and diners who believe that if dinner is healthful it's okay to go hog wild over dessert. I do not share that philosophy since I don't believe that the human body can appreciate this kind of reasoning. However, I, like most other Americans, do splurge from time to time on an outrageously rich dessert. And I have been known to clean up the ice-cream container if it is left in front of me. But my personal preference, especially after a wonderful dinner, is a light dessert—something that won't stuff me or overwhelm the flavorful memories of the meal. And with so many people now watching their cholesterol as well as their weight, I don't want to serve a dessert that others feel they have to skip or that they will eat and will then feel guilty for having done so.

The desserts that follow—especially the fruit dishes on pages 507 to 530—will not send you to the fat farm or coronary care unit. Yet they are delicious, and, I am willing to bet, your guests will be delighted with how considerate you are of their dietary needs. Chances are most diners will be surprised to discover that even those desserts that taste rich have not been prepared with many "sinful" ingredients.

APRICOT SOUFFLÉ

Too many otherwise fine cooks are unnecessarily hesitant about making soufflés, especially dessert soufflés. One inhibiting factor is the need for last-minute preparation and the near-precise timing for serving, which I'm afraid one cannot get around. However, you can simplify matters by readying everything ahead of time—the fruit mixture, the separated eggs (the whites should be at room temperature before they are beaten), the dish—and preheating the oven, leaving only the egg whites to be beaten and folded in at the last minute. If you can find a helper to serve the main course, you can finish preparing the soufflé and then slip it into the oven at that time. It should be ready just as you are about to clear the salad plates.

But the main reason cooks avoid soufflés is "fear of falling." As a novice soufflé maker, I can tell you that they are remarkably easy to make, and, if you follow the instructions, they won't collapse. But even if they do collapse, it doesn't affect the taste. They remain light and luscious. This yolkless soufflé, from *Gourmet* magazine, is especially elegant. (Cook the yolks, and feed them one at a time to the dog.)

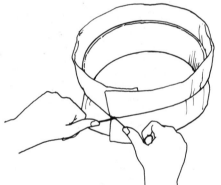

6 ounces dried apricots
1 cup apple juice
Vegetable-oil spray
Sugar
¾ cup (about 6 large) egg whites, at room
   temperature
¼ teaspoon salt
½ teaspoon cream of tartar
3 tablespoons sugar
1 teaspoon vanilla extract

1. In a small, heavy saucepan, combine the apricots and apple juice. Bring the ingredients to a boil, reduce the heat, cover the pan, and simmer the apricots for 20 minutes or until the apricots are soft. Purée the ingredients in a food processor or blender, and transfer the purée to a large bowl. Set the bowl aside.
2. Fit a 1-quart soufflé dish with a foil collar that rises 2 inches above the rim of the dish. Spray the dish and collar with the vegetable oil, and sprinkle the dish and collar with the sugar.
3. Preheat the oven to 375° F.
4. In a large bowl, beat the egg whites with the salt until they are frothy. Add the cream of tartar, and continue beating the egg whites until they hold soft peaks. Add the 3 tablespoons of sugar 1 tablespoon at a time, and beat the egg whites until they hold stiff peaks. Then beat in the vanilla.

5. Fold ¼ of the beaten whites into the reserved apricot mixture. Then fold in the remaining whites, and spoon the mixture into the prepared soufflé dish.

6. Place the dish in the hot oven, and bake the soufflé for 25 to 30 minutes or until the soufflé is puffed and golden. Remove the collar from the soufflé dish, and serve the soufflé immediately.

MATZO PUDDING   *8 to 10 servings*

Most Passover goodies are loaded with cholesterol from eggs. But not this kosher-for-Passover tart, nutritious pudding, which has only 1 egg yolk. It can be enjoyed any time of year.

Serving suggestion: Good as a dessert, snack, or breakfast treat.

    4 whole matzos (preferably egg matzos)
    Cold water
    1 egg yolk
    ¼ cup sugar
    ½ teaspoon cinnamon
    1 tablespoon grated lemon rind
    ¼ cup fresh lemon juice
    ½ cup raisins
    3 McIntosh apples, peeled, cored, and diced
    ½ cup unskinned hazelnuts (filberts) *or* almonds,
        coarsely ground
    3 egg whites

1. In a bowl or pie plate, combine the matzos (they can be broken up) with cold water to cover, and let the matzos soak for a few minutes or until they have softened. Then squeeze the matzos dry, discarding the soaking liquid.

2. In a large bowl, combine the egg yolk, sugar, cinnamon, lemon rind, and lemon juice. Stir in the raisins, apples, and nuts, mixing the ingredients thoroughly. Fold in the matzos, mixing the ingredients until they are well combined.

3. Preheat the oven to 350° F.

4. In a medium-sized bowl, beat the egg whites with an electric mixer until they form stiff peaks. Gently fold the egg whites into the matzo mixture. Transfer the mixture to a greased 8-inch or 9-inch pan (preferably a spring-form pan).

5. Place the pan in the hot oven, and bake the pudding for 1 hour or until the top of the pudding is golden. Let the pudding cool to room temperature before serving it.

PRUNE SOUFFLÉ

6 servings

There are no yolks—and no cholesterol—and only about 80 calories per serving in this soufflé, based on a recipe by Richard Sax and Marie Simmons in *Bon Appétit* magazine.

Preparation tips: If you are starting with prunes that are dry and hard, soak them briefly in hot water and drain them thoroughly, or add another 1 to 2 tablespoons of warm water to the recipe. The prune mixture can be prepared ahead through step 2. However, like all soufflés, this one should be assembled and baked so that it is done moments before you are ready to serve it. For an elegant presentation, bake the soufflé in a small soufflé dish fitted with a foil collar (see page 472); remove the foil before bringing the soufflé to the table.

½ pound *moist* pitted prunes (see "Preparation tips," above)
½ cup warm water
3 tablespoons Armagnac *or* cognac *or* brandy
1 long strip lemon peel *or* orange peel
Vegetable-oil spray
3 egg whites, at room temperature
Pinch salt
⅛ teaspoon cream of tartar
2 tablespoons sugar

1. In a small saucepan, combine the prunes, water, Armagnac or cognac or brandy, and lemon peel or orange peel, and bring the mixture to a simmer. Cover the pan, and remove it from the heat. Let the pan stand for 15 minutes or until the prunes have absorbed the liquid.
2. Transfer the mixture to a food processor, and process the mixture, using the pulse button, until the mixture forms a chunky paste. Pour the prune mixture into a large bowl, and set the bowl aside.
3. Place the rack in the bottom third of the oven, and preheat the oven to 400° F.
4. Fit a 1-quart soufflé dish with a foil collar that rises 2 inches beyond the rim of the dish. Spray the dish and collar with the vegetable oil.
5. In a medium-sized bowl, beat the egg whites with the salt until they are foamy. Add the cream of tartar, and continue beating the egg whites until they hold soft peaks. Add the sugar 1 tablespoon at a time, and beat the egg whites until they are stiff but not dry.
6. Fold ¼ cup of the beaten egg whites into the prune mixture. Then gently fold in the remaining egg whites, and pour the mixture into the prepared soufflé dish. Smooth out the top, and run your thumb around the top of the soufflé about ½ inch in from the edge.
7. Place the dish in the hot oven, and bake the soufflé for 20 minutes or until the soufflé is puffed and golden. Remove the collar from the soufflé dish, and serve the soufflé immediately.

PINEAPPLE-CHEESE NOODLE PUDDING

12 servings

Sweet noodle pudding is a delicious remnant from my childhood. It was often served with the Sabbath meal of roast chicken; and, within the guidelines of kosher cooking, which forbids the mixing of dairy and meat, the pudding was never made with milk products. Not until adulthood, then, did I discover the richness of a dairy noodle pudding.

Preparation tips: For the fruit, there are many choices—apples, pineapple (fresh or canned crushed or cubed), canned peaches or apricots, fruit cocktail, etc.—but raisins or currants are practically a must. You can prepare the pudding for baking through step 4 and refrigerate it hours in advance; or the pudding can be fully baked and reheated, covered with foil, at serving time. It is also delicious cold and at room temperature.

- ¾ pound medium-wide egg noodles
- 5 quarts boiling water
- Salt (optional)
- 2 teaspoons oil
- 12 ounces low-fat cottage cheese
- ¾ cup brown sugar
- 4 egg whites
- 2 eggs
- ½ cup plain nonfat or low-fat yogurt *or* 1 cup yogurt, drained for 30 minutes through cheesecloth to produce ½ cup yogurt cheese
- 1½ teaspoons vanilla extract
- 1½ teaspoons cinnamon
- 1½ to 2 cups diced fresh pineapple *or* canned pineapple, well drained
- ½ to ⅔ cup raisins, to taste

1. Cook the noodles in the boiling water with the salt (if desired) and oil for 6 minutes (the noodles will be firm but not hard). Drain the noodles, rinse them under cold water, and drain them again.
2. Preheat the oven to 350° F.
3. In a blender, food processor, or mixing bowl, combine the cottage cheese, brown sugar, eggs whites, whole eggs, yogurt, vanilla, and cinnamon. Blend the ingredients, or beat them well.
4. In a large bowl, combine the cheese mixture, cooked noodles, pineapple, and raisins. Pour the mixture into a greased 13 × 9-inch baking pan.
5. Place the pan in the hot oven, and bake the pudding for 1 hour or until the pudding is firm and lightly browned.

PUMPKIN CUSTARD

8 or more servings

Although this recipe is similar to the Winter Squash Custard on page 478, the sweeteners impart a different flavor.

    2 egg whites *and* 1 egg, lightly beaten
    2 cups pumpkin purée, drained if it is very moist
    ⅜ cup (6 tablespoons) packed brown sugar
    2 tablespoons molasses
    1 teaspoon cinnamon
    ½ teaspoon ground ginger
    ¼ teaspoon ground cloves
    1 13-ounce can evaporated skim milk
    2 tablespoons sherry

1. Preheat the oven to 350° F.
2. In a large bowl, combine the ingredients in the order listed, whisking or beating them by hand until they are well mixed. Pour the mixture into a greased 1½-quart baking dish.
3. Place the dish in the hot oven, and bake the custard for 50 to 60 minutes or until the custard has set and a knife inserted halfway between its center and side comes out clean.

RICOTTA PUDDING WITH STRAWBERRIES

8 servings

This winner of a pudding—rich-tasting but artery-sparing, a cross between a cheesecake and a soufflé—is based on a recipe by Richard Sax and Marie Simmons in *Bon Appétit* magazine.

Preparation tips: Note that the ricotta must be drained overnight. The pudding and sauce can be prepared ahead and chilled, but bring the pudding to room temperature before serving it.

SAUCE

12 ounces frozen unsweetened strawberries, thawed, with their juice reserved
3 tablespoons sugar
1 tablespoon fresh lemon juice

PUDDING

2 15-ounce containers light or part-skim ricotta
⅓ cup plus 1 tablespoon sugar, divided
1 egg yolk (reserve the white)
1 teaspoon vanilla extract
¼ teaspoon almond extract
¼ teaspoon cinnamon
3 tablespoons all-purpose flour
2 tablespoons finely chopped candied citron
1 teaspoon grated lemon peel
2 egg whites, at room temperature
Pinch salt
Vegetable-oil spray

1 pint fresh strawberries, sliced, for garnish

1. To make the sauce, in a food processor, blender, or food mill, purée the strawberries with the sugar and lemon juice.
2. Strain the mixture through a fine sieve into a bowl to remove the seeds, pressing on the solids to retrieve as much of the pulp as possible. Cover the bowl, and refrigerate the sauce until serving time.
3. To make the pudding, place the ricotta in a sieve set over a bowl. Cover the bowl, and refrigerate the ricotta overnight.
4. In a food processor or blender, purée the drained ricotta with the ⅓ cup of sugar, egg yolk, vanilla extract, almond extract, and cinnamon. Continue processing the ingredients for 5 minutes or until the mixture is light though grainy. Transfer the mixture to a large bowl. Fold in the flour, citron, and lemon peel.
5. Preheat the oven to 350° F.
6. In a medium-sized bowl, beat the egg whites with the salt until they form soft peaks. Gradually add the 1 tablespoon of sugar, and continue beating the egg whites until they are stiff but not dry. Gently fold the beaten egg whites into the ricotta mixture.
7. Spray a 1¾-quart baking dish with vegetable oil. Spoon the ricotta mixture into the dish. Set the dish in a larger pan, and pour enough boiling water into the larger pan so that the water reaches halfway up the sides of the smaller baking dish.
8. Place the pudding in the hot oven, and bake the pudding for 45 minutes or until the pudding is puffed and golden. Remove the pudding from the outer pan, and place it on a rack to cool to room temperature. Serve the pudding garnished with the sliced berries and topped with the sauce.

WINTER SQUASH CUSTARD

6 servings

When I asked tasters to choose between this and the Pumpkin Custard on page 476, they said, "Include them both." So here is the second of two delicious, nourishing, versatile custards.

Preparation tip: Any kind of winter squash—acorn, butternut, Hubbard, or pumpkin—can be used.

Serving suggestions: I enjoy this custard for dessert topped with whole cranberry sauce and for breakfast with low-fat cottage cheese.

    ¾ cup puréed winter squash
    ½ teaspoon cinnamon
    ¼ teaspoon ground ginger
    ⅛ teaspoon nutmeg
Generous pinch ground cloves
1¼ cups skim or low-fat milk
    ⅓ cup mild-flavored honey
    2 egg whites *and* 1 egg, beaten

1. Preheat the oven to 350° F.
2. In a large bowl, whisk together the squash, cinnamon, ginger, nutmeg, and cloves.
3. Gradually whisk in the milk, honey, and beaten egg whites and whole egg, blending the ingredients well. Pour the mixture into a 1- or 1½-quart oven-proof baking dish or soufflé dish. Place the dish in a roasting pan, and pour boiling water into the pan so that the water reaches halfway up the sides of the dish.
4. Place the custard in the hot oven, and bake the custard for 1 to 1¼ hours or until the custard has set and a knife inserted halfway between its center and side comes out clean. Serve the custard warm or chilled.

SLIGHTLY SOUSED APPLE COBBLER   *12 servings*

This is a keep-coming-back-for-more dessert loaded with nutritious fruits. Fortunately, the recipe is large.

  5 large apples (e.g., Rome Beauties or Granny
     Smiths), peeled, cored, and cut into thin slices
     (about 8 cups)
½ cup dried currants
½ cup chopped dates
½ cup golden raisins
½ cup chopped walnuts *or* pecans
½ cup applejack *or* apple juice *or* apple cider
  2 cups all-purpose flour
¾ cup sugar
  2 teaspoons baking powder
½ teaspoon salt (optional)
  1 teaspoon cinnamon
⅛ teaspoon nutmeg
⅓ cup butter *or* margarine, slightly softened
  1 cup skim or low-fat milk
  1 cup apple cider *or* apple juice, heated to boiling

1. Preheat the oven to 350° F.
2. Grease a large, shallow 4-quart baking pan.
3. Spread the apple slices on the bottom of the pan, and sprinkle the currants, dates, raisins, and walnuts or pecans over them. Pour the applejack or juice or cider over the fruit and nuts.
4. In a large bowl, combine the flour, sugar, baking powder, salt (if desired), cinnamon, and nutmeg. Cut in the butter or margarine until the mixture is uniformly grainy.
5. Stir the milk into the flour mixture, and spoon the batter over the apple mixture.
6. Gently pour the hot cider or juice over the dish.
7. Place the baking pan in the hot oven, and bake the cobbler for 1¼ hours or until most of the juice has been absorbed.

GINGERED PEAR CRISP

6 servings

"Great," "fabulous," "a scoopful of heaven" was how my tasters described this sensational crisp. It is based on a recipe from *Gourmet* magazine.

    1 cup all-purpose flour
 4½ teaspoons finely grated gingerroot
    ½ cup firmly packed dark brown sugar
    3 tablespoons butter *or* margarine, softened
    1 cup finely chopped pecans
    6 large firm but ripe pears (e.g., Bosc)

1. Place the rack in the top third of the oven, and preheat the oven to 400° F.
2. In a small bowl, thoroughly mix together the flour, gingerroot, and brown sugar. Add the butter or margarine, and work it in with a fork until the mixture is pebbly. Stir in the pecans.
3. Peel, core, and slice the pears lengthwise into sixteenths (4 slices per quarter). Spread the slices evenly in a greased 8-inch square pan.
4. Sprinkle the flour mixture over the pears.
5. Place the pan in the hot oven, and bake the crisp for 30 minutes. Serve the crisp warm or at room temperature.

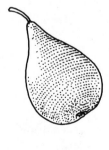

RHUBARB CRISP

6 to 8 servings

This is Delicious with a capital "D" and very easy to prepare. Although the recipe calls for a fair amount of sugar, remember that rhubarb has no natural sweetness.

FILLING

- 5 cups (about 1½ pounds) rhubarb cut into ½-inch slices
- 1 teaspoon grated orange rind
- 1 egg white *or* 1 egg, lightly beaten
- ¾ cup sugar
- ¼ cup all-purpose flour

TOPPING

- ¼ cup quick-cooking rolled oats
- ¼ cup whole-wheat flour
- ¼ cup powdered nonfat milk
- ¼ cup packed dark brown sugar
- 1¼ teaspoons cinnamon
- 2 tablespoons cold butter *or* margarine, cut into bits
- ¼ cup finely chopped nuts (optional)

1. Preheat the oven to 375° F.
2. To make the filling, in a large bowl, combine the rhubarb, grated rind, and beaten egg white or whole egg. Stir in the sugar and flour. Pour the mixture into a greased 9-inch pie plate.
3. Prepare the topping in a medium-sized bowl. Combine the oats, flour, powdered milk, brown sugar, and cinnamon, stirring the ingredients to mix them thoroughly. With a pastry blender or 2 knives, cut in the butter or margarine until the mixture looks like coarse meal. Then stir in the chopped nuts (if desired). Sprinkle the mixture evenly over the surface of the fruit.
4. Place the plate in the hot oven, and bake the crisp for 35 to 40 minutes.

PEAR PETAL TORTE WITH PECAN CRUST

8 to 10 servings

I had to corner the market on pears to keep my tasters happily supplied with this very attractive and tasty torte.

Preparation tips: The nuts are easiest to grind in a food processor. The crust may get soft, but that's okay—the flavor remains wonderful. For a sweeter torte, spread 2 to 4 ounces of apple jelly or orange marmalade on the baked, cooled crust before adding the pears. Note that the pears should soak in juice for about 1 hour.

TOPPING

- 1 tablespoon raisins
- 1 tablespoon plus ¼ cup orange liqueur, divided
- ⅞ cup (1 cup minus 2 tablespoons) orange juice
- 2 tablespoons fresh lemon juice
- 1 teaspoon grated orange rind
- 6 medium-large ripe but firm pears, peeled (I use Anjous)

- 1 envelope (1 scant tablespoon) unflavored gelatin
- 2 to 4 ounces apple jelly *or* orange marmalade (optional)

CRUST

- 8 ounces pecans, very finely ground (but *not* until they become oily)
- ¼ cup sugar
- ⅜ teaspoon cardamom *or* ¼ teaspoon coriander and ⅛ teaspoon allspice
- 4 teaspoons butter *or* margarine, melted

1. To make the topping, in a small bowl, combine the raisins and the 1 tablespoon of orange liqueur. Set the bowl aside.
2. In a large bowl, combine the ¼ cup of orange liqueur, orange juice, lemon juice, and orange rind. Core and slice the pears into wedges about ½ inch thick at the widest part. Add the slices to the orange-juice mixture as you go. Let the pears soak in the juice for about 1 hour while you prepare the crust.
3. To make the crust, preheat the oven to 400° F. In a small bowl, combine the crust ingredients. Press the mixture onto the bottom and sides of a greased 11-inch tart pan with a removable bottom. Place the pan in the hot oven, and bake the crust for 10 minutes or until the crust is firm and lightly browned on the edges. Place the crust on a rack to cool thoroughly before filling it.
4. After about 1 hour, drain the soaked pears well, catching the liquid in a small saucepan. Drain the raisins, and add their liquid to the saucepan. Sprinkle the gelatin over the liquid, and let the mixture stand for about 5 minutes to soften the gelatin. Heat the mixture, stirring it, until the gelatin

dissolves. Place the pan in a bowl of ice water, and chill the mixture, stirring it often, until the mixture has the consistency of cold egg whites.

5. If desired, brush the cooled crust with the jelly or marmalade (see "Preparation tips," above). Arrange the reserved pear slices in overlapping concentric circles on the crust, and sprinkle the raisins over them. Pour the partially gelled juice mixture over the pears, and chill the torte until it is firm.

PLUM TART

8 to 10 servings

After succumbing to a late-summer bargain on Italian prune plums (those small egg-shaped deep-purple ones), I prepared two of these beautiful tarts, which were rapidly consumed by my tasters.

Preparation tips: This tart lends itself to advance preparation. It can also be made with peaches, apples, nectarines, apricots—almost any fruit that can be sliced and baked.

DOUGH
- 1 cup plus 1 tablespoon all-purpose flour, divided
- 2 tablespoons sugar
- 1 teaspoon baking powder
- ¼ teaspoon salt (optional)
- 1½ tablespoons very cold butter *or* margarine, cut into bits
- 1 egg
- ½ teaspoon vanilla extract *or* almond extract
- ⅓ cup (approximately) skim or low-fat milk

FILLING
- 1½ pounds Italian prune plums, *unpeeled,* pitted, and quartered lengthwise
- ½ cup sugar
- 1½ teaspoons cinnamon
- ½ teaspoon nutmeg (preferably freshly grated)
- 1 tablespoon butter *or* margarine, melted

1. To make the dough, sift or stir together the 1 cup of flour, the sugar, baking powder, and salt (if desired). With a pastry blender or fork, blend in the butter or margarine until the mixture resembles coarse grain.
2. In a 1-cup measuring cup, beat together the egg, vanilla or almond extract, and enough milk to make ½ cup. Add the egg-milk mixture to the flour mixture, stirring the ingredients to form a stiff dough. Transfer the dough to a 9-inch square baking pan or a 10-inch deep-dish pie plate. Dusting some of the 1 tablespoon of flour on your palm, press the dough evenly on the bottom and partway up the sides of the pan with your hand. Sprinkle the dough with the remaining flour.
3. Preheat the oven to 425° F.
4. To make the filling, cover the dough with the plum quarters, arranging them in overlapping layers (if a round pan is used, make concentric circles with the fruit).
5. In a small bowl, combine the sugar, cinnamon, nutmeg, and melted butter or margarine. Sprinkle this mixture over the plums.
6. Place the pan or plate in the hot oven, and bake the tart for about 25 minutes.

MOCHA PUDDING PIE

8 servings

Your guests need never know that this delicious pie is a fat- and calorie-controlled dessert. And it's easy enough to prepare even when there's no special occasion. This recipe is my adaptation of one devised by Carol Cutler.

CRUST
1¼ cups chocolate-wafer crumbs
1 tablespoon sugar
2 tablespoons butter *or* margarine, softened or melted
1 egg white, lightly beaten

FILLING
¼ cup cold water
⅔ envelope (2 teaspoons) unflavored gelatin
1 tablespoon plus ½ teaspoon unsweetened cocoa, divided
1 tablespoon instant coffee
4 tablespoons plus 1 teaspoon sugar, divided
1 teaspoon amaretto *or* ½ teaspoon almond extract
1 cup boiling water
1 cup (½ pound) light or part-skim ricotta

1. To prepare the crust, preheat the oven to 425° F. In a small bowl, thoroughly combine the crumbs, sugar, and butter or margarine. Stir in the egg white, mixing the ingredients until they are well combined. Press the mixture onto the bottom and sides of a lightly greased 9-inch pie plate.

2. Place the pie plate in the hot oven, and bake the crust for 5 minutes. Cool the crust thoroughly on a rack before filling it.

3. To prepare the filling, place the cold water in a small bowl, and sprinkle in the gelatin. Let the mixture stand 5 minutes to soften the gelatin.

4. In a medium-sized bowl, combine the 1 tablespoon of cocoa, the coffee, the 4 tablespoons of sugar, and amaretto or almond extract. Add the boiling water, and stir the ingredients to dissolve them. Then add the gelatin mixture, and stir the ingredients again. Let the mixture cool.

5. When the mixture is cool, pour it into a blender. Turn the machine on low, and add the ricotta 1 tablespoon at a time. When all the cheese has been added, cover the machine, and blend the mixture for a few seconds at high speed.

6. Pour the mixture into the cooled crust, and chill the pie until the pudding sets. Then combine the remaining ½ teaspoon of cocoa and 1 teaspoon of sugar, place the sweetened cocoa in a strainer, and sprinkle the cocoa on top of the pie.

FRESH CRANBERRY CREAM PIE

8 servings

Lovely and light, this pie skirts around the fat and calories in whipped cream by using whipped evaporated skim milk.

Preparation tips: Do not prepare this pie more than a few hours before serving time because the whipped milk eventually collapses. Note that you must start with a baked crust. Although the pie works best with a firm crust, you can use the Bran-Nut Crust on page 495, which will turn out soft and moist, in which case you should serve the dessert with a spoon like a cobbler instead of slicing it like a pie. Also note that the evaporated milk must be chilled in the freezer for at least 1 hour before you whip it. If the milk still does not whip, return it to the freezer to chill some more, and try again.

¼ cup cold water
1 envelope (1 scant tablespoon) unflavored gelatin
2 cups (8 ounces) fresh cranberries
½ medium orange, peeled and sectioned
⅔ cup plus 3 tablespoons sugar, divided
½ cup evaporated skim milk, chilled in the freezer
  for 1 hour
1 teaspoon vanilla extract
¼ teaspoon salt
2 egg whites
¼ teaspoon cream of tartar
1 cold *baked* 9-inch pie shell

1. Place a medium-sized mixing bowl and the beaters of an electric mixer in the freezer or refrigerator.
2. Place the cold water in the top of a double boiler or a heatproof bowl. Sprinkle in the gelatin, and let the mixture stand for 5 minutes or until the gelatin has softened.
3. In a chopping bowl or food processor, coarsely chop the cranberries and orange. Transfer the fruit to a large bowl, and stir in the ⅔ cup of sugar.
4. Place the container with the softened gelatin over or in hot water, stirring the mixture until the gelatin has dissolved. Add the gelatin mixture to the cranberry mixture, and refrigerate the mixture until it begins to thicken.
5. In the bowl that was chilled in the freezer or refrigerator, beat the chilled evaporated skim milk and the vanilla on high until the milk has the consistency of whipped cream. Transfer the whipped milk to the bowl with the cranberries, but do not mix the ingredients. Refrigerate the bowl.
6. Wash the medium-sized bowl and the beaters, and dry them. Combine the salt and egg whites in the bowl, and beat them on high speed with an electric mixer until they have the consistency of shaving cream. Add the

cream of tartar, and continue beating the egg whites on high until they hold soft peaks. Beat in the 3 tablespoons of sugar, 1 tablespoon at a time.

7. Transfer the beaten egg whites to the bowl with the cranberries and the whipped milk, and gently fold the egg whites and the milk into the fruit mixture until all the ingredients are well combined. Pour the mixture into the prepared pie shell, swirling the top with the back of a spoon. Chill the pie until serving time.

NECTARINE-PINEAPPLE PETAL PIE   *6 to 8 servings*

Faced with a windfall of nectarines, Ann Gambrell of Torrance, California, devised this pie with just 3 tablespoons of added sugar. The nectarines are arranged in a beautiful petal-like pattern on top of the pineapple base.

Preparation tips: Either an unbaked regular flour crust or a partially baked crumb crust can be used for this pie. The original recipe calls for 3 nectarines, but I found that 2 medium-sized fruits were enough to produce the desired floral arrangement.

  1 single pie crust
  2 tablespoons cornstarch
  3 tablespoons sugar, divided
  1 20-ounce can crushed pineapple in unsweetened
    juice, drained, with the liquid reserved
  2 to 3 nectarines, unpeeled, halved, pitted, and sliced
    in wedges that measure ½ inch at their thickest part
¼ teaspoon cinnamon

1. Line a 9-inch pie plate with the crust, and flute the edge of the crust.
2. Preheat the oven to 425° F.
3. In a medium-sized saucepan, combine the cornstarch and 2 tablespoons of the sugar with the reserved pineapple juice, stirring the ingredients to blend them well.
4. Stir in the crushed pineapple, and cook the mixture over medium heat, stirring the ingredients constantly, until the mixture has thickened and is bubbly. Cook the mixture 1 minute longer, stirring it. Remove the pan from the heat, and pour the pineapple mixture into the pie crust.
5. Arrange the nectarine slices over the pineapple, skin side up, in a petal design (slices should point toward the center of the pie), starting with a circle of slices at the outer edges of the pie and working inward.
6. Combine the remaining 1 tablespoon of sugar with the cinnamon, and sprinkle the mixture over the top of the pie.
7. Place the pie plate in the hot oven, and bake the pie for 25 minutes or until the pastry is golden brown. Serve the pie chilled or at room temperature.

ORANGE-RICOTTA FRUIT PIE

8 servings

The citrus flavoring and pale orange color of the pie filling are a lovely counterpoint to such fruit as strawberries, blueberries, kiwis, green grapes, sliced oranges, or mandarin-orange segments.

Preparation tips: You can substitute cottage cheese for part or all of the ricotta. Although the optional glaze helps to secure the fruit to the pie, it also adds extra calories. In my view, the fruit looks and tastes better unadorned.

   1 envelope (1 scant tablespoon) unflavored gelatin
   ¾ cup skim or low-fat milk
   ¼ cup sugar
   2 tablespoons grated orange rind
   1 tablespoon grated lemon rind
   ¼ cup orange juice
   1 cup light or part-skim ricotta
   1 graham-cracker crust, baked and cooled (see
      page 490 or 494)
 1½ to 2 cups fruit for topping (e.g., strawberries,
      blueberries, sliced peaches, mandarin-orange
      segments), sliced if necessary
   1 tablespoon cornstarch for glaze (optional)
   ½ cup fruit nectar *or* ¼ cup apple-juice concentrate
      mixed with ¼ cup water for glaze (optional)

1. In the top of a double boiler, sprinkle the gelatin over the milk. Let the gelatin soften for 5 minutes, then add the sugar, and heat the mixture just until the gelatin and sugar dissolve. Set the mixture aside to cool to barely warm (if you are in a hurry, pour the mixture into a cold metal or glass container).

2. In a blender, combine the orange rind, lemon rind, and orange juice. Remove the center portion of the blender-jar cover, and, with the blender on low speed, gradually add the cooled milk mixture through the hole.

3. Through the same hole with the blender on low, add the ricotta by heaping spoonfuls to the milk mixture, blending the ingredients well. Pour the mixture into the prepared pie crust, and chill the pie.

4. When the filling is firm, arrange the fruit on top. If desired, prepare a glaze in a small saucepan by combining the cornstarch with the nectar or the apple-juice concentrate and water. Cook the mixture, stirring it constantly, until the glaze thickens, then clears. Spoon the glaze over the fruit.

"PAM" FRUIT PIE

8 servings

Here is a one-crust pie of fresh summer fruits—peaches, apricots, and mangoes—that is a guaranteed crowd-pleaser.

Preparation tips: Two pears can be used in place of the apricots, which are sometimes hard to obtain and may be expensive. When peeling the mango, try to avoid touching the cut skin, and wash your hands and utensils immediately afterward to avoid a poison ivy–type rash.

CRUST
- ½ cup all-purpose flour
- ½ cup whole-wheat flour
- 1 teaspoon sugar
- ¼ teaspoon salt (optional)
- ¼ cup (½ stick) very cold butter-margarine blend, cut into bits
- Ice water

FILLING
- ½ cup sugar
- 2 tablespoons all-purpose flour
- 5 peaches, peeled, pitted, and sliced
- 8 apricots, pitted and sliced
- 2 mangoes, peeled, pitted, and sliced

1. To prepare the crust, in a medium-sized bowl, combine the all-purpose flour, whole-wheat flour, sugar, and salt (if desired).
2. Blend in the butter-margarine blend with a pastry blender or two knives until the mixture resembles coarse grain.
3. Add the ice water 1 tablespoon at a time, stirring the ingredients with a fork until the mixture forms a ball of dough that holds together but is not sticky. Wrap the dough in wax paper or plastic wrap, and chill it until the filling is ready.
4. Preheat the oven to 425° F.
5. To prepare the pie, in a small bowl, combine the sugar and flour, and set the bowl aside.
6. In a deep-dish pie plate or shallow baking dish, combine the peaches, apricots, and mangoes. Sprinkle the fruit with the reserved sugar-flour mixture, tossing the ingredients gently to coat the fruit.
7. Roll out the crust on a lightly floured board so that it is 1 inch larger than the pie plate. Cut several vent holes in the crust, and place the crust over the fruit, crimping the edges of the crust so that it is sealed to the plate.
8. Place the pie in the hot oven, and bake the pie for 40 to 45 minutes or until the crust is lightly browned.

RASPBERRY-YOGURT PIE

8 to 10 servings

When the raspberries "come in" in July, I am usually lucky enough to be near a "pick your own" farm where the berries cost up to $1.50 for a heaping pint instead of the usual market price of $2.99 for a scant half pint. It is then that I become profligate with raspberries, using them for pies, muffins, pancake and cereal toppings, vinegar, sauces, and what have you. And I usually make three or four of these pies, each of which uses 4 cups (2 pints) of those precious berries. My tasters are amazed to learn that, except for the small amount of fat in the crust, this dessert is practically a health food. And it tastes wonderful—especially on a hot summer evening.

Preparation tips: Since this recipe is for a 10-inch pie, if you use a smaller plate, you may find yourself with some extra filling (what a pity!) that you can chill separately. The pie can be made 1 to 2 days ahead since the filling does not fall or weep.

CRUST
1½ cups graham-cracker crumbs
 1 tablespoon sugar (optional)
¼ cup (½ stick) butter *or* margarine (you can use "light" margarine, if you wish), melted

FILLING
 4 cups fresh raspberries, rinsed and well drained, divided
⅓ cup orange juice *or* apple juice
 2 envelopes (2 scant tablespoons) unflavored gelatin
⅓ cup sugar
 2 cups plain nonfat or low-fat yogurt
 1 tablespoon honey (optional)
 1 tablespoon raspberry vinegar *or* other mild or fruity vinegar
½ teaspoon vanilla extract

1. Preheat the oven to 350° F.
2. To make the crust, in a small bowl, thoroughly combine the crust ingredients. Press them into a large pie plate, making sure that the sides are covered up to the rim of the plate.
3. Place the pie plate in the hot oven, and bake the crust for 10 to 15 minutes or until it is a light brown. Set the crust on a rack to cool before filling it.
4. To make the filling, select enough of the best-looking raspberries to make 1 cup, and set them aside.
5. Place the orange or apple juice in a small bowl or measuring cup, and sprinkle in the gelatin. Let the mixture stand for 5 minutes or until the gelatin has softened.

6. Meanwhile, in a small saucepan, combine 1 heaping cup of the remaining berries with the sugar. Cook the berries, stirring them, over a medium-low heat for 3 to 5 minutes or until the sugar dissolves. Remove the pan from the heat, and add the softened gelatin, stirring the ingredients until the gelatin is dissolved. Set the mixture aside to cool somewhat.

7. Add to a blender or food processor the yogurt, honey, vinegar, vanilla, and the raspberry-gelatin syrup (don't worry if it is still quite warm). Process the mixture until it is smooth and well blended.

8. Place the remaining raspberries (*not* those that you reserved in step 4) along the bottom of the cooled crust (the pie looks especially beautiful when sliced if you stand each berry on its rim with the hole side down). Spoon the yogurt mixture over the berries, and place the pie in the refrigerator for about 1 hour. Then decorate the top of the pie with the reserved berries. (I arrange the berries along the perimeter and make a second circle of berries in the middle of the pie). Chill the pie for 2 hours or until it is very firm.

STRAWBERRY-YOGURT PIE

8 servings

Another winner, this one with a bran-flakes crust. My tasters scrambled to take home the leftovers.

Preparation tips: Like the Raspberry-Yogurt Pie (page 490), this can be prepared a day ahead since the filling does not collapse or weep. The pie looks lovely decorated with sliced fresh berries around the perimeter and a berry "fan" nested on mint leaves in the center. To make the fan, choose a large berry, and, using a sharp paring knife, make 4 or 5 lengthwise slits, starting from the pointed end almost, but not quite, to the fat end of the berry. If the berry does not spread out by itself, soak it in ice water until it does.

CRUST
2¼ cups bran (wheat) flakes cereal, lightly crushed
 3 tablespoons packed dark brown sugar
 3 tablespoons butter *or* margarine, melted

FILLING
 ½ cup cold water *or* berry juice (if you are using frozen berries)
 2 envelopes (2 scant tablespoons) unflavored gelatin
 3 cups fresh strawberries *or* 24 ounces frozen berries, thawed and drained, with their juice reserved, divided
 ½ cup sugar
 1 tablespoon fresh lemon juice
 1 teaspoon vanilla
1½ cups (12 ounces) plain nonfat or low-fat yogurt

1. Preheat the oven to 350° F.
2. To prepare the crust, in a medium-sized bowl, combine the crust ingredients, mixing them well. Press the mixture into the bottom of a 9-inch pie plate.
3. Place the pie plate in the hot oven, and bake the crust for 8 to 10 minutes or until the edges of the crust begin to brown. Let the crust cool on a rack before filling it.
4. To make the filling, place the water or juice in a small bowl, and sprinkle in the gelatin. Let the mixture stand for 5 minutes or until the gelatin has softened.
5. Select 8 of the best berries (if you are using fresh berries), and set them aside. Purée the rest of the berries in a blender or food processor. Transfer the purée to a medium-sized saucepan, and stir in the sugar and the softened gelatin. Heat the mixture, stirring it, until the sugar and gelatin are just dissolved.
6. Remove the pan from the heat, and stir in the lemon juice and vanilla. Set the pan in a large bowl of ice water or transfer the mixture to a bowl, and chill the mixture, stirring it often, until it thickens slightly.

7. With an electric mixer, whip the purée until it is light and fluffy (it should nearly double in volume; if not, chill it longer).

8. Whisk the yogurt, and stir it into the whipped purée. Chill the mixture further, stirring it now and then, until a spoonful of the mixture holds its shape. Then pour the purée into the cooled crust. Slice the reserved strawberries, and place them around the edge of the pie. Chill the pie for 3 to 4 hours or until it is firmly set.

LOW-CAL PEACH PIE

8 servings

It's hard to find a simpler pie to prepare or one that is lower in calories. This recipe combines unsweetened canned peaches with fresh ones.

CRUST

- 1¼ cups (1 packet or 22 squares) graham-cracker crumbs
- 2 tablespoons butter *or* margarine, melted

FILLING

- 1 16-ounce can peaches packed in juice, drained, with the juice reserved
- 2 envelopes (2 scant tablespoons) unflavored gelatin
- ¼ cup plus 1 teaspoon sugar, divided
- ½ cup evaporated skim milk
- ½ cup plain nonfat or low-fat yogurt
- 2 to 3 fresh ripe peaches, peeled, pitted, and sliced
- 1 teaspoon lemon juice
- 1 tablespoon graham-cracker crumbs for garnish (optional)

1. Preheat the oven to 375° F.
2. To make the crust, in a small bowl, combine the graham-cracker crumbs and butter or margarine. Press the mixture onto the bottom and sides of a 9-inch pie plate. Place the plate in the hot oven, and bake the crust for 10 to 12 minutes. Set the crust aside to cool, and, when it reaches room temperature, place it in the freezer.
3. To make the filling, place ½ cup of the peach juice (reserved from the canned peaches) in a small saucepan. Sprinkle the gelatin over the juice, and let the mixture stand for about 5 minutes. Stir in the ¼ cup of sugar, and heat the mixture gently, stirring it, just until the gelatin and sugar dissolve. Remove the pan from the heat.
4. In a blender or food processor, combine the canned peaches, gelatin mixture, evaporated milk, and yogurt. Purée the ingredients until they are smooth. Pour the mixture into the prepared crust.
5. Toss the fresh fruit with the lemon juice, and arrange the fruit over the purée (it will sink in). If desired, garnish the pie with the remaining 1 teaspoon of sugar combined with the 1 tablespoon of graham-cracker crumbs. Chill the pie until it is firm.

BRAN-NUT CRUST

single crust for a 9-inch pie

A fiber-filled, artery-sparing (though not exactly low-calorie) crust intended for a filling that is not baked.

> 1 cup bran cereal (e.g., All-Bran, Bran Buds, or
>   100% Bran), crushed
> 1 cup pecans, finely chopped
> 3 tablespoons confectioners' sugar
> 3 tablespoons butter *or* margarine, melted
> 3 tablespoons orange juice

1. Preheat the oven to 375° F.
2. In a medium-sized bowl, combine the ingredients, mixing them thoroughly. Press the mixture into a 9-inch pie plate, preferably a glass one.
3. Place the pie plate in the hot oven, and bake the crust for 8 minutes or until the crust is lightly browned. Let the crust cool completely before filling it.

WALNUT CRUST

single crust for a 9-inch pie

This deliciously nutty crust, derived from one of Mollie Katzen's recipes, can be the base of a fruit torte or a filling that is not baked.

> 2 cups walnuts, ground in a food processor almost
>   to a paste
> ½ cup all-purpose flour
> 3 tablespoons packed brown sugar
> ¼ teaspoon salt
> ¼ teaspoon cinnamon
> 3 tablespoons (approximately) cold water
> Vegetable-oil spray

1. Preheat the oven to 350° F, if this is to be a prebaked crust.
2. In a medium-sized bowl, combine the walnuts, flour, brown sugar, salt, and cinnamon, mixing the ingredients well with a fork.
3. Gradually add enough water to form a dough that can be pressed together. Press the mixture into a 9-inch pie plate that has been sprayed with the vegetable oil.
4. For a prebaked crust, place the pie plate in the hot oven, and bake the crust for 10 to 12 minutes or until the crust is firm.

APPLE STRUDEL

*3 17-inch rolls,
about 30 pieces*

There is nothing that tastes more like the holidays to me than apple strudel. But it wasn't until adulthood that I finally ate homemade strudel—I made it myself. Although awkward at first in manipulating the dough (these leaves of dough are very, very thin and are layered to produce a flaky crust), I soon became adept at it and will happily pass on my tips for success. Once you find a source for the dough—it is sold as strudel or phyllo in specialty stores and in stores that cater to a Middle Eastern clientele—and feel comfortable working with it, you can use it to make all sorts of goodies, hors d'oeuvres as well as desserts. The dough will keep for weeks in the refrigerator and for months in the freezer.

Preparation tips: The trick to using this dough successfully is to work fast on one sheet of dough at a time and to cover the sheets that you are not yet working on with a damp cloth or with plastic wrap. That means that *all the ingredients must be ready* before you open the package of dough. If you prefer not to use butter or margarine, you can spray each sheet of dough with vegetable oil (olive or regular); the pastry will be a little drier and flakier but still delicious and attractive. I use Golden Delicious apples, but if you prefer, you can use a tart apple like Granny Smith. The crumbs and the nuts can be prepared in a food processor, but the apples should be diced by hand to avoid chopping them too finely.

FILLING

- 2 pounds apples, peeled, cored, and finely diced
- ½ cup sugar
- ½ cup finely chopped nuts (e.g., hazelnuts)
- ½ cup raisins
- 1 teaspoon cinnamon
- 2 tablespoons grated lemon rind

CRUST

- ⅓ cup dried bread crumbs, white *or* whole-wheat
- ⅓ cup cereal crumbs (e.g., Corn Flakes or Wheaties)
- 9 sheets of phyllo dough, each about 12 × 17 inches
- 3 tablespoons melted butter *or* margarine *or* vegetable-oil spray

1. To make the filling, in a large bowl, combine the filling ingredients. Set the bowl aside.
2. In a small bowl, combine the bread crumbs and cereal crumbs.
3. Spread a large piece of plastic wrap or wax paper or a damp cloth on a large work surface. Open the box of dough, and unfold the sheets on another large piece of plastic wrap. Cover the sheets with more plastic wrap or with a damp cloth while you work. Spread 1 sheet out on the work surface with a long side nearest you. Brush the dough lightly with 1 teaspoon of the butter or margarine, or spray it with vegetable oil. Sprinkle about 2 tablespoons of the crumb mixture on the dough. Spread another sheet of dough over the first, brush it with the fat, and sprinkle it with the crumbs. Repeat the

process with a third sheet of dough. Don't forget as you remove each sheet of dough to re-cover the remaining sheets.

4. Using ⅓ of the filling, place it in a strip the long way from one side of the dough to the other, aligning the strip about 1 inch from the edge of the dough nearest you. Using the plastic wrap, wax paper, or cloth, lift the edge of the dough nearest you, and flip it over the filling. Replacing the plastic wrap, wax paper, or cloth on the work surface, finish rolling up the dough. Do not seal the ends. Place the roll on a greased baking sheet.

5. Repeat steps 3 and 4 two more times with the remaining ingredients.

6. Preheat the oven to 375° F.

7. Place the strudels in the hot oven, and bake them for 35 minutes. Slice the strudels while they are still warm.

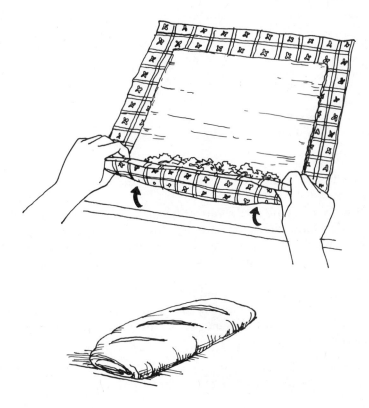

CARROT-RAISIN CAKE

8 servings

Carrot cakes are among my favorites, yet they are usually loaded with "naughty" ingredients—lots of oil, eggs, and sugar. But no one would ever guess that this moist, tasty carrot cake is low in fat and contains very little cholesterol.

1½ teaspoons baking soda
¼ cup warm water
1½ cups finely shredded carrots
½ cup plain nonfat or low-fat yogurt
¾ cup sugar
½ cup unsweetened applesauce
¼ cup vegetable oil (preferably canola)
1 egg *or* 2 egg whites
2 teaspoons cinnamon
½ teaspoon nutmeg
½ teaspoon ground cloves
½ teaspoon salt (optional)
1 cup raisins
1 cup whole-wheat flour
1 cup all-purpose flour

1. Preheat the oven to 325° F.
2. In a small bowl, combine the baking soda and warm water, and set the mixture aside.
3. In a large bowl, combine the carrots, yogurt, sugar, applesauce, oil, whole egg or egg whites, cinnamon, nutmeg, cloves, salt (if desired), and raisins.
4. Stir in the whole-wheat flour and all-purpose flour, then stir in the reserved baking-soda mixture. Pour the batter into a greased 8-inch or 9-inch square baking pan.
5. Place the pan in the hot oven, and bake the cake for 1 hour or until a tester inserted into the center of the cake comes out clean. Let the cake cool in the pan on a rack for about 10 minutes before turning the cake out onto the rack to cool completely.

FRUIT AND NUT CAKE

20 servings

You say you don't like fruit cake? Wait until you try this one, derived from an old Sun-Maid raisin recipe booklet.

Preparation tips: If citron and glazed orange and lemon peel are unavailable or not to your taste, omit them and instead reduce the sugar to ¾ cup and add about ½ cup of golden raisins or chopped dried figs and another ½ cup of chopped nuts (hazelnuts, walnuts, or pecans). If desired, after the cake is cooled, pierce the top of the cake about 12 times with a wooden skewer, and drizzle the cake with ¼ to ½ cup of rum. The cake can be frozen, wrapped in plastic wrap and then foil to keep it moist.

DRY INGREDIENTS
2½ cups sifted all-purpose flour
1½ teaspoons baking powder
½ teaspoon baking soda
½ teaspoon salt
1 teaspoon cinnamon
½ teaspoon ground cloves
½ teaspoon allspice
½ teaspoon nutmeg (preferably freshly grated)
½ teaspoon mace

"WET" INGREDIENTS
1 cup water
1 cup sugar
2 teaspoons lemon juice
½ cup (1 stick) butter-margarine blend (preferably "light"), melted
1 teaspoon vanilla extract
2 eggs, lightly beaten
1½ cups raisins
1 to 1½ cups chopped dates
⅓ cup diced citron (see "Preparation tips," above)
⅓ cup diced glazed orange peel (see "Preparation tips," above)
⅓ cup diced glazed lemon peel (see "Preparation tips," above)
½ cup coarsely chopped walnuts
½ cup coarsely chopped pecans

¼ to ½ cup rum, to taste (optional)

1. Preheat the oven to 325° F.
2. In a medium-sized bowl, sift together the dry ingredients.
3. In a large bowl, combine the "wet" ingredients (*excluding* the rum).
4. Stir the dry ingredients into the "wet" ingredients until all the ingredients are just combined. Pour the batter into a greased 9 × 3½-inch tube pan, preferably one with a removable inset.
5. Place the pan in the hot oven, and bake the cake for 1½ hours. Remove the cake with the inset, and place it on a rack to cool. When the cake is cool enough to handle, remove the inset. If desired, place the cooled cake on a platter, pierce the top of the cake in about 12 places with a wooden skewer, and sprinkle the cake with the rum. Wrap the cake well in foil. Do not slice it for at least 4 hours.

FRUITED SPONGE CAKE

8 servings

Here's a whatever-you-have-in-the-house dessert that looks and tastes like planned-for elegance.

Preparation tips: To keep the fruit from turning brown, prepare the glaze and fruit while the cake is cooling. If the glaze gels before you pour it, simply reheat it to melt it a little. To reduce "leakage" of the fruit juices into the cake and to avoid the need for refrigeration, I use a quick-setting glaze gelled by agar flakes, available in many natural-foods stores. However, unflavored gelatin should also work if the glaze is refrigerated after step 5 and the finished cake is also chilled. You can also cook the fruit, such as a combination of raspberries and sliced pears, in the glaze in step 5 to produce a delicious—albeit less elegant—topping for the cake.

CAKE
Butter for greasing
½ cup sugar, divided
¾ cup all-purpose flour, divided
3 large eggs *or* 2 eggs and 2 egg whites
Pinch salt

TOPPING
¾ cup apple juice
1½ tablespoons agar flakes (see "Preparation tips," above)
¼ cup apple-juice concentrate
3 small pears, peeled, cored, and sliced
1 pint strawberries, cleaned but left whole

1. Preheat the oven to 350° F.
2. To make the cake, butter the bottom of an 8-inch round cake pan (a square pan will also work). Cut out an 8-inch round (or square) of wax paper, place it on the bottom of the pan, and butter it. Sprinkle 2 teaspoons of the sugar around the pan, shaking the pan to coat it with the sugar, and discard any excess sugar. Then sprinkle 2 teaspoons of the flour around the pan, shaking the pan to coat it with the flour, and discard any excess flour.
3. In a medium-sized bowl, beat the eggs or the eggs and egg whites with the remaining sugar until the mixture is thick and pale yellow. Gradually stir in the remaining flour and pinch of salt. Pour the batter into the prepared pan.
4. Place the pan in the hot oven, and bake the cake for 25 to 30 minutes or until the top of the cake is golden and the cake pulls away from the sides of the pan. Let the cake cool in the pan for 5 minutes, then turn it out onto a rack to cool completely. Transfer the cake to a serving platter.
5. To prepare the topping, pour the apple juice into a medium-sized skillet, and stir in the agar flakes. (If you are using gelatin, let the mixture stand for 5 minutes before heating it.) Heat the mixture, stirring it, to dissolve the flakes. Stir in the apple-juice concentrate. Remove the glaze from the heat, and let the glaze cool until it begins to set.
6. Arrange the pear slices and strawberries on top of the cooled cake. Pour the glaze over the fruit, and allow the glaze to set.

MIXED FRUIT UPSIDE-DOWN CAKE   *10 servings*

Here is a simple cake that can be made with whatever fruit you have in the house—fresh or canned, even overripe. Hence, the seemingly odd but very tasty combination of pears, peaches, and rhubarb listed below. If you use a very sweet fruit, be sure to reduce the amount of sugar (rhubarb is mouth-puckeringly tart).

1½ tablespoons butter *or* margarine
2 large ripe pears, cored, peeled, and sliced
1 large ripe peach, peeled, pitted, and sliced
⅔ pound rhubarb, cut into ½-inch slices
⅓ cup packed brown sugar
1 cup all-purpose flour
1 cup whole-wheat flour
1 tablespoon baking powder
½ teaspoon baking soda
½ teaspoon allspice
¼ teaspoon salt (optional)
1 cup buttermilk
⅓ cup vegetable oil (preferably canola)
⅓ cup honey
2 eggs *or* 1 egg and 2 egg whites
½ teaspoon vanilla extract

1. Line a greased 13 × 9-inch baking pan or two 8-inch round pans with wax paper, and grease the wax paper, *or* generously grease a 10-inch pan that has a removable bottom.
2. In a medium-sized skillet, melt the butter or margarine, add the pears, peach, and rhubarb, sprinkle the fruit with the brown sugar, and sauté the fruit for 5 minutes or until it is soft. Spread the fruit evenly on the bottom of the prepared baking pan or pans.
3. Preheat the oven to 350° F.
4. In a medium-sized bowl, combine the all-purpose flour, whole-wheat flour, baking powder, baking soda, allspice, and salt (if desired).
5. In a separate bowl, combine the buttermilk, oil, honey, eggs or egg and egg whites, and vanilla. Pour the buttermilk mixture into the flour mixture, and stir the ingredients to combine them thoroughly. Spoon the batter evenly over the fruit layer.
6. Place the cake in the hot oven, and bake the cake for 40 minutes or until it is nicely browned. Let it cool for about 15 minutes. Then turn it upside down onto a serving platter or tray, and carefully remove the wax paper or pan bottom.

HONEY SPICE CAKE

8 servings

This moist, tender, low-fat, and easy-to-prepare cake, from Bobbie Hinman and Millie Snyder's *More Lean and Luscious,* would make an excellent tea or snack cake. It is packed with more nutrients than calories (about 120 a serving).

Preparation tips: The cake is very good even when the raisins are omitted. The batter does not fill the pan, but the cake will expand nicely during baking.

¾ cup whole-wheat flour
1 teaspoon cinnamon
½ teaspoon baking soda
½ teaspoon nutmeg
¼ teaspoon ground cloves
¼ teaspoon allspice
2 tablespoons plus 2 teaspoons very cold "light"
  margarine *or* butter-margarine blend, cut into bits
½ cup plain nonfat or low-fat yogurt
1 egg
2 tablespoons honey
2 tablespoons plus 2 teaspoons sugar
1 teaspoon vanilla extract
¼ cup raisins (optional)

1. In a medium-sized bowl, combine the flour, cinnamon, baking soda, nutmeg, cloves, and allspice, mixing them well.
2. With a pastry blender or fork, blend in the margarine or butter-margarine blend until the mixture resembles coarse grain.
3. Preheat the oven to 350° F.
4. In a large bowl, combine the yogurt, egg, honey, sugar, and vanilla. Beat the mixture, using an eggbeater or an electric mixer on low, until the ingredients are well combined and smooth. Add the flour mixture to the yogurt mixture, and beat the ingredients 1 minute longer. Stir in the raisins (if desired).
5. Pour the batter into a greased 8 × 4-inch loaf pan.
6. Place the pan in the hot oven, and bake the cake for about 25 minutes or until a tester inserted into the center of the cake comes out clean. Let the cake cool in the pan on a rack for 10 minutes. Then turn the cake out onto the rack to cool completely.

PIÑA COLADA UPSIDE-DOWN CAKE   *8 servings*

This cake has a puddinglike texture—moist and milky. The recipe, derived from one in Bobbie Hinman and Millie Snyder's *More Lean and Luscious,* yields a nutritious treat that comes in at under 200 calories a serving.

Serving suggestion: This is ideal for brunch and is best served cold.

"TOPPING"
- 2 cups chopped fresh pineapple *or* 1 20-ounce can unsweetened crushed pineapple, drained, with ¼ cup juice reserved
- ⅔ cup powdered nonfat milk
- 2 tablespoons cornstarch
- 2 teaspoons shredded coconut (preferably unsweetened)
- 1 teaspoon coconut extract
- 1 tablespoon sugar

CAKE
- ¾ cup all-purpose flour
- 1 teaspoon baking powder
- 2 tablespoons plus 2 teaspoons very cold "light" margarine *or* butter-margarine blend
- 2 egg whites
- 1 egg
- ⅔ cup low-fat cottage cheese
- 2 teaspoons vanilla extract
- 3 tablespoons sugar

1. Spray a 9-inch glass pie plate or 8-inch square baking dish with vegetable oil. Line the plate with wax paper, and then spray the plate again.
2. Preheat the oven to 350° F.
3. To make the "topping," in a medium-sized bowl, combine the topping ingredients, including the ¼ cup of reserved pineapple juice, and mix them well. Spread the mixture over the bottom of the pie plate (on the wax paper). Wash and dry the bowl.
4. To make the cake, in the dried bowl, combine the flour and baking powder. Cut the margarine or butter-margarine blend into bits, and cut it into the flour mixture with a pastry blender or fork until the mixture resembles coarse grain.
5. In another medium-sized bowl, whisk together the egg whites, whole egg, cottage cheese, vanilla, and sugar. Add the cottage-cheese mixture to the flour mixture, stirring the ingredients until they are just moistened. Spoon the batter evenly over the "topping" (don't worry if there are some holes—they will fill in as the cake bakes).
6. Place the pie plate or baking dish in the hot oven, and bake the cake for 30 minutes or until the cake is golden. Let the cake cool in the pan on a rack for about 15 minutes before loosening the sides of the cake with a knife and inverting the cake out onto a serving platter. Peel off the wax paper, and chill the cake before serving it.

RICOTTA CHEESECAKE

about 10 servings

The crust is optional for this easy, light, low-fat cheesecake, which I first tasted several years ago at a friend's house and have been making ever since.

Preparation tips: You can omit the crust entirely or substitute ½ cup of graham-cracker crumbs pressed into the bottom of a well-greased pan and chilled in the freezer before the filling is added. After baking the cake, you can top it with fruit such as strawberries, mandarin-orange slices, or sliced peaches that have been tossed with a mixture of 1 teaspoon of lemon juice and 1 teaspoon of sugar.

CRUST (OPTIONAL—SEE
"PREPARATION TIPS," ABOVE)
 1 cup all-purpose flour
 ¼ cup brown sugar
 ¼ cup ground nuts
 ¼ cup (½ stick) cold butter *or* margarine, cut into bits

FILLING
 2 pounds *or* 2 15-ounce containers light or part-skim ricotta
 3 egg whites
 2 eggs
 1 cup buttermilk
 ½ cup sugar
 ¼ teaspoon salt (optional)
 2 teaspoons vanilla extract
 Grated rind 1 lime *or* grated rind ½ lemon
 2 tablespoons fresh lime juice *or* lemon juice

1. Preheat the oven to 325° F.
2. To make the crust, combine the flour, sugar, and nuts in a medium-sized bowl. With a pastry blender or fork, cut in the butter or margarine. Press the mixture into the bottom of a well-greased 9-inch springform pan.
3. Place the pan in the hot oven, and bake the crust for 10 to 12 minutes. Let the crust cool before filling it.
4. Increase the oven temperature to 375° F.
5. In a blender or food processor, purée the filling ingredients until they are smooth and airy.
6. Pour the filling into the prepared crust or into a greased 9-inch springform pan. Put a pan of water in the bottom of the oven.
7. Place the cheesecake in the hot oven, and bake the cheesecake for 45 minutes or until it is set.

RHUBARB UPSIDE-DOWN CAKE   *9 to 12 servings*

Delicious and appropriately tart, this fruited dessert takes no longer to prepare than pancakes. Although the amount of sugar in this cake is more than that used in most of my recipes, it is needed to make the very tart fruit palatable.

Preparation tips: If you share my passion for rhubarb, you could increase the amount of fruit and sugar in the bottom layer by 50 percent (1½ pounds of rhubarb and 1 cup of sugar). This cake can also be made with fresh pineapple that has been cut into small cubes or even chopped and mixed with only ¼ cup of sugar (in addition to the ⅓ cup for the batter). If desired, substitute whole-wheat pastry flour for ½ cup of the all-purpose flour.

      1 **pound rhubarb, cut into ½-inch slices (about 3 cups)**
      1 **cup sugar, divided**
    ⅓ **cup (5⅓ tablespoons) butter *or* margarine**
   1½ **teaspoons baking powder**
      1 **egg**
      1 **teaspoon vanilla**
    ½ **cup skim or low-fat milk**
   1¼ **cups all-purpose flour**

1. Preheat the oven to 350° F.
2. In a large saucepan, combine the rhubarb and ⅔ cup of the sugar. Cook the ingredients, stirring them, over a moderately low heat until the sugar melts. Spread the fruit over the bottom of a well-greased 8-inch or 9-inch square or round baking pan lined with greased wax paper.
3. In a mixing bowl, beat the butter or margarine with the remaining ⅓ cup of sugar and the baking powder until the mixture is fluffy, then beat in the egg and vanilla. Gradually add the milk, alternating it with the flour, and blend the ingredients well. Spoon the batter over the fruit layer, spreading the batter with a plastic spatula or broad knife to cover the fruit evenly.
4. Place the pan in the hot oven, and bake the cake for about 35 minutes. Let the cake cool in the pan on a rack for about 5 minutes. Then run a knife around the edges of the cake to loosen the cake, and invert the cake onto a serving platter. Carefully remove the wax paper.

SWEET POTATO CAKE

about 9 servings

Marian Morash's *The Victory Garden Cookbook* was the happy source for this cake. I cut the sugar by a third (it is still sweet), but otherwise the recipe is much like the original—moist yet low in fat.

Preparation tips: The batter is especially easy to prepare if you have a food processor to do the grating, but an ordinary hand grater will do if you use a little elbow grease. If desired, you can substitute whole-wheat pastry flour for ¼ to ⅓ of the all-purpose flour.

- 1 cup all-purpose flour
- 1 teaspoon baking soda
- ½ teaspoon salt (optional)
- ½ teaspoon nutmeg (preferably freshly grated)
- ½ teaspoon cinnamon
- ¼ cup (½ stick) butter *or* margarine
- ⅔ cup sugar
- 1 egg
- 1 teaspoon vanilla extract
- 1 large *or* 2 medium apples, peeled and grated
- 1 (½ pound) sweet potato, peeled and grated
- ½ cup chopped nuts

1. Preheat the oven to 350° F.
2. In a small bowl, sift together the flour, baking soda, salt (if desired), nutmeg, and cinnamon. Set the bowl aside.
3. In a large bowl, beat the butter or margarine and the sugar until the mixture is creamy. Beat in the egg and vanilla. Stir in the apple and potato.
4. Add the flour mixture to the potato mixture, and stir the ingredients well. Stir in the nuts. Pour the batter into a greased 8-inch or 9-inch square baking pan.
5. Place the pan in the hot oven, and bake the cake for 35 to 40 minutes. Let the cake cool in the pan on a rack for 5 to 10 minutes before turning it out on the rack to cool completely.

Fruit Desserts

Mother Nature "did good" when she made fruit. Many feel that fruit needs no improvement; most of the time, I would agree. But there are moments when I want my fruit served other than *au naturel*—for example, as a salad or sherbet for an appetizer or dessert or as a sorbet to clear the palate between courses. (For other uses of fruit, see the main "Dessert" section, and check the index for main dishes, drinks, appetizers, muffins, quick breads, side-dish salads, etc. using fruits.)

In the recipes that follow, fruit remains the centerpiece of the dish. In each recipe, I try to preserve the essential flavor of the fruit rather than overwhelm it with added sweeteners. Wherever reasonable, I use other concentrated fruits or fruit juices to provide the needed sweetening. But since certain fruits—like cranberries and rhubarb (really a vegetable)—have almost no natural sweetening, they need more help than usual to make them palatable as a dessert.

ANY-BERRY SORBET

about 1 quart

A sorbet (it used to be called sherbet) is a lovely, refreshing, and wholesome (i.e., fat-free) dessert that can be enjoyed any time of year, using fruit in season. When berries are plentiful, try this one, which can be made with strawberries, blueberries, raspberries, or blackberries.

Preparation tips: Sorbets are easiest to prepare in an ice-cream maker. The small family-sized ones that use no salt (such as Donvier) are adequate to the task and not expensive. However, even without an ice-cream maker, you can prepare these desserts in shallow pans or ice-cube trays and whip them several times as they freeze.

    4 cups (2 pints) berries (if you are using
      strawberries, slice them before measuring them)
 1/4 cup fresh orange juice
 1/4 cup fresh lemon juice
 1/4 teaspoon vanilla extract
1 1/2 cups water
 2/3 cup sugar

1. Purée the berries in a blender or food processor. Transfer the purée to a bowl, and stir in the orange juice, lemon juice, and vanilla.
2. In a small saucepan, combine the water and sugar, and heat the mixture, stirring it, until the sugar dissolves. Then boil the syrup, without stirring it, over medium-high heat until a candy thermometer inserted into the syrup reaches 238° F (just before it boils).
3. Whisk the syrup into the berry mixture, and let the mixture cool. Transfer the mixture to an ice-cream maker, and process the ingredients according to the manufacturer's directions (or see "Preparation tips," above). Transfer the sorbet to a bowl with a tight-fitting lid, and freeze the sorbet for 1 hour or longer.

CRANBERRY-ORANGE SORBET

8 servings

Although this recipe contains no milk, the whipped egg white gives it a fluffy texture. The sugar content may seem high, but cranberries are very sour.

    2 cups cranberries (they can be frozen)
 1½ cups water, divided
    1 envelope (1 scant tablespoon) unflavored gelatin
    1 cup sugar
    1 teaspoon grated orange rind
    1 cup orange juice
   ¼ teaspoon salt (optional)
    1 large egg white

1. In a medium-sized saucepan, bring to a boil the cranberries and 1¼ cups of the water. Cover the pan, and cook the cranberries over medium heat for 6 minutes or until the berries burst.
2. While the berries cook, place the remaining ¼ cup of water in a small bowl, and sprinkle in the gelatin to soften it.
3. Press the hot cooked cranberries and their cooking liquid through a sieve. Add the sugar to the hot purée and liquid, stirring the mixture to dissolve the sugar. Add the softened gelatin, and stir the mixture to dissolve the gelatin. Stir in the orange rind, orange juice, and salt (if desired).
4. Pour the mixture into a 9-inch square metal baking pan or 2 ice-cube trays without dividers, and place the mixture in the freezer until the mixture has the consistency of slush. (If it gets too hard, let it stand at room temperature for 20 minutes or until it becomes slushy.)
5. Pour the mixture into a bowl. Add the egg white, and beat the mixture until it becomes light and fluffy. Return the sorbet to the pan or trays, and freeze the sorbet until it is firm.

FRESH CRANBERRY SORBET

about 1 quart

I love the taste of fresh (uncooked) cranberries. They make this refreshing sorbet a winner.

Preparation tips: You can use an ice-cream maker or freeze the sorbet in a shallow pan, stirring it every so often as it freezes. Be sure to remove the sorbet from the freezer about 15 minutes before serving time.

Serving suggestion: Serve this with other sorbets or frozen yogurts in compatible colors, such as Lemon Frozen Yogurt, below.

- ⅔ cup water
- ½ cup sugar
- 3 cups (1 12-ounce package) cranberries
- 2 ripe pears, peeled and cored
- 2 tablespoons kirsch
- ¼ cup minced orange rind

1. In a small saucepan, combine the water and sugar. Heat the mixture, stirring it, until the sugar dissolves. Remove the pan from the heat just before the syrup boils. Transfer the syrup to a bowl, and set the syrup aside to cool. Then cover the bowl, and put the syrup in the refrigerator to chill.
2. Purée the cranberries and pears in a food processor or food mill. Combine the purée with the chilled syrup, kirsch, and orange rind.
3. Process the mixture in an ice-cream maker according to the manufacturer's directions, or pour the mixture into a shallow metal pan and freeze it. If a food processor is available, let the sorbet thaw somewhat, and process it until it becomes smooth and fluffy. Then refreeze the sorbet, removing it from the freezer 15 minutes before serving it.

LEMON FROZEN YOGURT

8 servings

The refreshing taste of fresh lemon makes this dessert, from Anne Lindsay's *American Cancer Society Cookbook,* a delight.

Serving suggestions: Be sure to remove the yogurt from the freezer and place it in the refrigerator about 20 to 30 minutes before serving it. It is especially delicious and festive topped with fresh berries.

- 3 cups plain nonfat or low-fat yogurt
- 2 teaspoons vanilla extract
- 4 teaspoons grated lemon rind
- ¼ cup fresh lemon juice
- ½ cup sugar

1. In a large bowl, combine the ingredients, mixing them thoroughly.
2. Process the mixture in an ice-cream maker according to the manufacturer's directions, or freeze the mixture in shallow metal pans. If you use the pans, remove the yogurt when it is partially frozen, and whip it before returning it to the pans to freeze solid.

MANGO SHERBET

6 servings

This sherbet, developed by Abby Mandel for *Bon Appétit* magazine, has an especially rich texture, although it is fat-free. The delicate mango is enhanced by the orange.

Preparation tips: Since you start with frozen fruit, you can prepare this sherbet without an ice-cream maker, but it would be a challenge without a food processor. The fruit can be frozen, wrapped in plastic, weeks in advance.

Serving suggestion: For an interesting monochromatic look as well as delicious taste, serve the sherbet in the center of an overlapping ring of sliced oranges, mangoes, or both.

- 1 large (about 9 ounces) navel orange
- 2 small mangoes (1½ pounds total), peeled (see "Preparation tips" on page 489) and sliced
- ⅓ cup sugar
- ½ cup plain nonfat or low-fat yogurt
- 1 teaspoon orange liqueur

1. Using a vegetable peeler or zester, remove the outer orange-colored peel from the orange, wrap the zest in plastic wrap, and set it aside. Remove and discard the remaining skin and separate the orange into sections.
2. Place the orange sections and mango slices on a baking sheet lined with wax paper, and freeze the fruit until it is firm.
3. Remove the fruit from the freezer about 15 minutes before completing the recipe. Place the frozen fruit in a food processor along with the reserved orange peel and sugar, and process the ingredients until the fruit is minced.
4. Add the yogurt and liqueur to the minced fruit, and process the ingredients 3 minutes longer or until the mixture is smooth and fluffy.
5. Serve the sherbet immediately, or transfer it to a bowl and place it in the freezer. Remove the sherbet from the freezer 20 to 30 minutes before serving time, and let it soften slightly in the refrigerator.

MANGO SURPRISE SORBET

8 to 10 servings

Hot pepper transports the tropical sweetness of mango to a new plane. This sorbet can be used as a first course, palate cleanser, or even a dessert.

Preparation tips: Since sorbets work best if they can be frozen quickly, use shallow metal or plastic trays or individual serving dishes. Unless you know that your freezer hardens foods quickly, I recommend preparing this well in advance of serving time to be sure it freezes solidly. If the sorbet gets too hard, remove it from the freezer about 10 to 15 minutes before serving time.

    2 large mangoes (about 3 pounds total), peeled
      (see "Preparation tips" on page 489) and cut
      into chunks
1½ cups warm water
  ⅓ cup honey
    1 fresh hot pepper (e.g., jalapeño), seeded and minced
    3 tablespoons lime juice *or* lemon juice
    2 tablespoons dark rum
Thin wedges lime *and/or* slices mango for
      garnish (optional)

1. Purée the mangoes in a food processor or blender.
2. In a small bowl or large measuring cup, combine the water and honey, stirring the ingredients until the honey dissolves. Add this mixture to the mango purée, and blend the ingredients until they are smooth. Transfer all but ½ cup of the mixture to a large bowl.
3. Add the minced pepper to the mango mixture remaining in the food processor or blender, and blend the ingredients until the pepper pieces are very small. Stir the pepper mixture into the mango mixture in the bowl, and add the lime or lemon juice and rum, stirring the ingredients to combine them thoroughly.
4. Pour the mixture into 2 metal ice-cube trays (dividers removed) or shallow baking pans or bowls. Place the mixture in the freezer for 1 hour or until it is almost frozen.
5. Transfer the partially frozen mixture to the food processor or blender, and purée the mixture. Return the mixture to the trays, pans, or bowls, and place them in the freezer for another 2 hours or until the sorbet is firm but not hard. At serving time, scoop the sorbet into serving dishes, and garnish each serving with lime or mango or both (if desired).

NECTARINE GRANITA

about 8 servings

Even ice-cream lovers were delighted with this refreshing fruit ice made with very little added sweetener. Martha Rose Shulman developed the basic recipe for her book *Mediterranean Light*.

Preparation tips: The granita can be made days—even weeks—in advance as long as it is tightly covered to prevent freezer dehydration. The amount of sweetener needed will depend on how sweet the fruit is. Do not use more than ⅛ teaspoon almond extract, or it will overwhelm the flavor of the fruit.

Serving suggestion: For added elegance, place the granita in the middle of a dessert dish, and surround it with fresh berries or melon balls.

2 pounds (approximately) ripe nectarines
1 to 2 tablespoons mild-flavored honey, to taste
3 tablespoons fresh lemon juice
¼ teaspoon vanilla extract
⅛ teaspoon almond extract
1 egg white

1. Place the nectarines in a large saucepan of boiling water, and blanch them for 1 minute. Drain the nectarines, chill them immediately under cold water, then slip off their skins. Cut the flesh into quarters, and place the fruit in a food processor or blender.
2. Add the honey, lemon juice, vanilla extract, and almond extract, and purée the ingredients. Transfer the purée to a bowl.
3. Whip the egg white until it holds stiff peaks. Beat it into the nectarine purée, mixing the ingredients until they are thoroughly combined. Transfer the mixture to shallow pans, cover the pans, and place the mixture in the freezer. Every 2 or 3 hours, remove the pans from the freezer, break up the granita then return it to the freezer. Repeat the procedure until the granita freezes in very small chunks.
4. About 30 minutes before serving time, remove the granita from the freezer, and place it in the refrigerator. Break the granita up with a fork to form a frozen slush before serving it.

PEACH SORBET

8 servings

A dieter's delight at less than 50 calories per ½-cup serving, this lightly sweet-ened dessert has a secret flavor enhancer—rum.

   1 1-pound can peaches packed in water
Water
   1 teaspoon lemon juice
   2 tablespoons honey
   1 envelope (1 scant tablespoon) unflavored gelatin
   1 tablespoon dark rum
   ⅛ teaspoon almond extract
Mint sprigs for garnish (optional)

1. Drain the liquid from the can of peaches into a large measuring cup, and add enough water to measure 1½ cups.
2. In a small saucepan, combine the peach liquid and water with the lemon juice, honey, and gelatin. Let the mixture stand for 5 minutes to soften the gelatin. Then heat the mixture, stirring it, until the gelatin dissolves. Remove the mixture from the heat, add the rum and almond extract, and set the mixture aside to cool.
3. In a blender or food processor, purée the peaches. Add the peach-juice mixture, and blend the ingredients a moment longer on low speed until they are combined. Pour the mixture into a shallow metal pan or bowl (preferably one that has been chilled in the freezer), and place the mixture in the freezer for 2 hours or until the mixture is firm around the edges.
4. Transfer the partially frozen mixture to a bowl, and beat the mixture with an electric mixer until the mixture is fluffy. Return the mixture to the freezer container, and freeze the mixture for 2 more hours or until it is firm. Before serving the sorbet, garnish it with the mint (if desired).

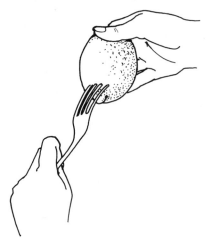

PEAR SORBET

4 servings

Simplicity itself and very refreshing.

    1 16-ounce can pear halves or slices packed in
       juice or extra-light syrup
    2 tablespoons fresh lemon juice
    Mint leaves for garnish (optional)

1. Transfer the pears and their juice to a shallow pan, and place them in the freezer for several hours, or until they are firmly frozen.
2. Break up the pear mixture, and put it into a food processor with the lemon juice. Purée the ingredients until they are smooth and creamy, stopping a few times to scrape the bowl.
3. Scoop up the purée with a small ice-cream scoop, and place the balls of purée on a tray or shallow pan. Cover the tray or pan with plastic wrap, and freeze the balls until they are firm. Place 1 ball of sorbet in each serving dish, and garnish each serving with some mint (if desired).

PIÑA COLADA SORBET

12 to 16 servings

An excellent dessert devised from a recipe in *Family Circle* magazine.

Preparation tip: If you use sweetened coconut, omit the confectioners' sugar.

    ½ large pineapple, cubed (about 2 cups)
    2 cups sliced banana
    ½ cup unsweetened coconut flakes
    1 6-ounce can pineapple-juice concentrate
    1 6-ounce can water
    ¼ cup confectioners' (powdered) sugar

1. Place the pineapple cubes and banana slices on a foil-lined tray, and put the tray in the freezer for 2 hours or until the fruit is hard.
2. Place the frozen fruit in a food processor. Add the coconut, pineapple-juice concentrate, water, and confectioners' sugar. Process the ingredients until they are smooth.
3. Serve the sorbet immediately; or put it into individual ramekins, cover the ramekins with plastic wrap, and freeze the sorbet.

DELICIOUS BAKED APPLES

4 servings

Baked apples are so "homey" that many cooks neglect them as dessert for company or holiday meals. But once you try these elegant apples, it is unlikely that you will forget them again.

½ cup dry white wine
¼ cup apple cider *or* apple juice
2 tablespoons sugar (optional)
1 tablespoon butter *or* margarine
⅛ teaspoon cinnamon
4 Golden Delicious apples, cored
⅓ cup golden raisins

1. Preheat the oven to 350° F.
2. In a small saucepan, combine the wine, apple cider or juice, sugar (if you are using it), butter or margarine, and cinnamon. Bring the mixture to a boil, stirring it occasionally, lower the temperature, and simmer it for 5 minutes.
3. Peel the top third of each apple, and place the apples, peeled side up, in a baking dish. Fill the cavities with the raisins, and pour the wine mixture over the apples.
4. Place the uncovered dish in the middle of the hot oven, and bake the apples, basting them occasionally with the wine sauce, for 1 hour 20 minutes or until the apples are tender but not mushy. Serve the apples warm, chilled, or at room temperature with the wine sauce spooned over them.

CRANBERRY APPLESAUCE

about 1 quart

This sauce is so delicious and beautiful that I canned 5 quarts of it and gave it to friends as holiday gifts, several of whom then requested the recipe.

  6 Golden Delicious apples, *unpeeled,* cored, and
    cut into eighths
  1 cup cranberries
  ½ cup apple cider
  1 2-inch stick cinnamon
  2 tablespoons packed brown sugar, or to taste
Pinch nutmeg, to taste

1. In a large saucepan, combine the apples, cranberries, cider, and cinnamon stick, and bring the mixture to a boil. Reduce the heat, cover the pan, and simmer the mixture, stirring it occasionally, for 15 minutes or until the apples are very tender.
2. Remove the cinnamon stick, put the fruit mixture in a food mill, and purée the fruit into a large bowl. Stir in the brown sugar and nutmeg.

TROPICAL FRUIT SALAD

6 servings

This is wonderfully refreshing—especially after a spicy meal.

Preparation tip: The salad can be made successfully without any alcohol, skipping step 2 or using just 2 tablespoons of lime juice mixed with 2 tablespoons of sugar.

  1 ripe pineapple, flesh removed and cut into bite-sized chunks
  2 mangoes, peeled (see "Preparation tips" on
    page 489) and cut into bite-sized chunks
  1 honeydew melon, flesh cut into bite-sized chunks
  ¼ cup fresh lime juice
  3 tablespoons tequila
  2 tablespoons triple sec
  2 tablespoons sugar, or to taste

1. Place the pineapple, mangoes, and honeydew in a serving bowl. Cover the bowl, and chill the fruit.
2. In a small bowl or 1-cup measure, combine the lime juice, tequila, triple sec, and sugar, stirring the ingredients until the sugar has dissolved. Cover the bowl or cup, and chill the mixture.
3. Before serving the salad, pour the lime-juice mixture over the fruit, and toss the ingredients gently to combine them.

CRANBERRY COMPOTE

10 servings

I had already finished this manuscript when I came across a warm version of this simple yet elegant compote in *Cooking Light* magazine. I served it to appreciative audiences at Thanksgiving and Christmas.

Preparation tip: The compote can be made a week ahead with no loss of flavor or freshness.

Serving suggestions: This is a versatile dish, delicious warm, cold, or at room temperature; with meat, poultry, pancakes, cottage cheese, or yogurt; as an appetizer, condiment, dessert, or between-meal snack.

1½ cups water
½ cup sugar
3 medium or large firm, ripe pears, peeled and
    cut into ½-inch pieces
12 dried apricots, each cut into 6 pieces
2 seedless oranges, peeled, sectioned, and cut into
    ½-inch pieces
3 cups (1 12-ounce bag) cranberries

1. In a large saucepan, bring the water and sugar to a boil, stirring the mixture occasionally.
2. Stir in the pears and apricots, reduce the heat, and simmer the fruit in the uncovered pan for 5 minutes.
3. Stir in the oranges, and continue simmering the fruit in the uncovered pan for 2 minutes.
4. Stir in the cranberries, and cook them over medium heat in the uncovered pan for 5 minutes, stirring the compote occasionally.

FABULOUS FRUIT COMPOTE

16 servings

My friend Margaret Shryer of Minneapolis, an enthusiastic and excellent cook, sent me this recipe after she had prepared it for 200 people. I adore it—for its flavor, versatility, and stability.

Preparation tips: The compote is equally delicious whether it is made with wine and honey or with white grape juice and no honey. It can be prepared a week or more ahead of time. Refrigerated, it has a long shelf life and can also be frozen with no loss of texture or flavor.

Serving suggestions: The first time I made this compote, I served it as dessert at a New Year's Eve party. I have since used it as a side dish with meat and with chicken (it is especially good with spicy entrées), and as part of a breakfast or lunch with yogurt or cottage cheese.

1½ cups (about ¾ pound) dried apricots
1½ cups (about ¾ pound) pitted prunes
　1 large *or* 2 small seedless oranges, *unpeeled,*
　　halved lengthwise, and thinly sliced crosswise
　1 large *or* 2 small lemons, *unpeeled,* halved
　　lengthwise, thinly sliced crosswise, and seeded
　2 cups red wine *or* 3 cups white grape juice
　2 cups apple juice
　5 whole cloves
　½ teaspoon nutmeg
　½ teaspoon cinnamon
　2 Red Delicious apples *or* Golden Delicious
　　apples, peeled, cored, quartered, and thinly
　　sliced crosswise
　¼ cup honey (omit if you are using grape juice)

1. In a large saucepan, combine all the ingredients *except* the apples and honey. Over medium heat, bring the mixture to a boil, reduce the heat, partially cover the pan, and simmer the mixture for about 30 minutes.
2. Remove the pan from the heat. Immediately stir in the apples and the honey (if wine was used).
3. Cool the compote, cover it, and chill it until 1 hour before serving time. Serve the compote at room temperature.

CHOCOLATE-DIPPED FRUIT

12 to 24 servings

No, Jane Brody has not flipped her nutritional lid. What good is culinary virtue without an occasional sin? And what better way to sin than with a chocolate delight?

Preparation tips: Do not prepare the dipped fruit more than 8 hours in advance. The fruit should be held in a cool place but *not* refrigerated or the chocolate will turn white; however, the fruit may become soft and leaky if it is kept too long at room temperature. When dipping the fruit, work quickly over a very low heat to keep the chocolate from changing texture before you have finished. If Swiss chocolate is unavailable, use 8 to 12 ounces of semisweet chocolate chips or baking chocolate.

2 6-ounce Swiss dark *or* semisweet chocolate bars,
  broken into small pieces
4 cups (approximately) assorted fresh fruits
  (strawberries with stems, banana chunks, fresh
  kumquats, sliced peeled kiwi, unpeeled apple
  slices, peeled pineapple wedges, etc.)

1. Line a baking sheet with wax paper.
2. In the top of a double boiler, melt the chocolate, stirring it, over boiling water. Turn the heat to low.
3. Working with one piece of fruit at a time, spear the fruit on a long thin fork, or grasp it with a small tongs. With the water in the lower portion of the double boiler simmering gently, dip the fruit into the melted chocolate until the chocolate reaches halfway up the fruit. Place the chocolate-coated fruit on the wax paper, and repeat the procedure until all the fruit has been used, leaving a small space on the wax paper between each piece of fruit.

BROILED GRAPEFRUIT

4 servings

What could be easier? This is a warming way to serve a winter fruit as an appetizer or a dessert—and at less than 60 calories per serving.

Preparation tip: If the grapefruit halves do not sit straight, cut a thin slice of skin off the bottom of each half to flatten it. If you do not have grapefruit spoons (they have tiny serrated edges), use a grapefruit knife to loosen the flesh from the rind, and cut the flesh into individual segments before starting the recipe.

    2 grapefruits, halved crosswise (through the "equator")
    8 teaspoons dark brown sugar *or* muscat *or* port
    Freshly grated nutmeg to taste (optional)

1. Preheat the broiler, positioning the broiler tray so that the grapefruit halves will be about 2 inches from the heat.
2. Set the grapefruits cut side up in a shallow baking dish. Sprinkle each half with 2 teaspoons of the brown sugar or the sweet wine. Then sprinkle the halves with the nutmeg (if desired).
3. Place the baking dish in the broiler, and broil the grapefruits for 5 minutes or until the tops of the grapefruits are bubbly. Serve the grapefruits with grapefruit spoons.

MELON SALAD WITH FIGS

4 servings

This dessert, from *Bon Appétit* magazine, is especially refreshing on a hot summer day, when melons and fresh mint are readily obtainable.

Preparation tip: If fresh figs are not available, substitute dried ones.

    1½ cups plain nonfat or low-fat yogurt
      2 tablespoons honey
      1 tablespoon fresh lime juice
      8 fresh figs, quartered (32 pieces)
      1 small honeydew melon, peeled, seeded, and
        sliced into bite-sized pieces
      4 teaspoons chopped fresh mint leaves
    ¼ cup chopped walnuts *or* pecans

1. In a small bowl, combine the yogurt, honey, and lime juice. Cover the bowl, and chill the dressing until serving time.
2. Place 8 fig quarters in a circle in the center of each of 4 individual plates. Arrange the melon pieces around the figs.
3. Before serving the salad, spoon the yogurt dressing over the fruit. Sprinkle each plate with the mint and the walnuts or pecans.

MINTED MELONS

8 to 10 servings

An abundance of mint in my garden and a recipe in *Cooking Light* magazine, which used somewhat less mint, inspired this dessert.

Preparation tips: You can prepare the sauce up to 3 days ahead and keep it in the refrigerator. Add it to the fruit about 1 hour before serving time. Melon balls are made with a melon baller (see the illustration). First, halve and seed the honeydew and cantaloupe; try to scoop out the watermelon between the heavily seeded areas. Or you can simply cut the melons into ¾-inch cubes.

Serving suggestion: If you start with a small watermelon (4 or 5 pounds), you can use half the shell as a serving bowl. Carve the edge decoratively, and scoop out any remaining flesh after you have prepared the melon balls.

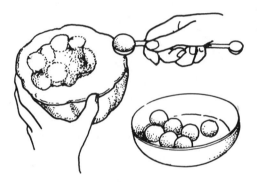

SAUCE
- 1 cup unsweetened orange juice
- ¼ cup fresh lime juice
- 2 tablespoons honey
- 2 to 3 tablespoons minced fresh mint leaves

FRUIT
- 4 cups watermelon balls
- 3 cups cantaloupe balls
- 3 cups honeydew melon balls

1. In a small saucepan, combine the sauce ingredients. Bring the mixture to a boil, stirring it often. Remove the pan from the heat, let the sauce cool, then chill it.
2. In a 2½-quart serving bowl or in a watermelon shell, combine the fruit ingredients. Lightly cover the fruit, and refrigerate it.
3. About 1 hour before serving time, pour the chilled sauce over the melon balls, and toss the ingredients gently until the fruit is coated with the sauce.

NECTARINES WITH RASPBERRY SAUCE

6 servings

I adapted this attractive dessert, devised for *Helen Nash's Kosher Kitchen.*

Preparation tips: Peaches can be used instead of nectarines. The fruit and the sauce can be prepared in advance, to be assembled before serving time.

2 teaspoons sugar
½ cup dry white wine
6 ripe nectarines, peeled, pitted, and sliced into 6 to 8 wedges each
1 10-ounce package unsweetened frozen raspberries, thawed and liquid reserved
Fresh mint for garnish (optional)

1. In a large glass or enameled saucepan or one with a nonstick surface, combine the sugar and wine, and bring the ingredients to a boil. Reduce the heat, and add the nectarines. Cover the saucepan tightly, and simmer the fruit for 2 minutes. Using a slotted spoon, transfer the fruit to a platter to cool.
2. Continue cooking the poaching liquid in the uncovered saucepan over high heat until the liquid becomes syrupy. Set the liquid aside to cool.
3. To prepare the sauce, pour off all but 2 tablespoons of the liquid from the raspberries, add the berries plus the 2 tablespoons of berry liquid to a blender, and purée the mixture until it is smooth. Strain the purée through a fine sieve, pressing on the solids to extract all their juice. Discard the seeds.
4. Spoon the sauce onto individual plates. Divide the nectarine wedges among the plates, arranging them like the spokes of a wheel, if possible. Then spoon the reserved poaching liquid over the nectarines. Serve the dessert at room temperature, garnished with the mint (if desired).

POACHED PEARS WITH ORANGE SAUCE

6 servings

Another adaptation of an elegant dessert from *Helen Nash's Kosher Kitchen.*

Juice ½ lemon
  3 cups (approximately) cold water
  6 medium firm but ripe pears with stems (e.g.,
    Anjou or Bosc)
  1 to 2 quarts orange juice, as needed
Zest (orange layer only) 2 navel oranges, julienned
½ teaspoon cinnamon
½ cup orange liqueur *or* cognac
Fresh mint for garnish (optional)

1. In a large bowl, combine the lemon juice and water.
2. Using the small end of a melon baller or a paring knife, cut the cores out from the bottom of the pears, leaving the stem ends intact. Peel the pears, placing each into the lemon juice and water to keep them from discoloring.
3. Lay the pears on their sides in a single layer in a large enamel or glass saucepan or one that has a nonstick surface. Pour in enough orange juice to cover the pears. Bring the juice to a boil over medium heat, reduce the heat, cover the pan, and simmer the pears, turning them once, for 5 minutes.
4. Remove the pan from the heat, and uncover it. Remove 1 cup of the juice from the pan, and set it aside. As the pears cool in the remaining juice, turn them over from time to time to prevent uneven coloring.
5. Place the zest in a small saucepan with the cinnamon, orange liqueur or cognac, and the 1 cup of reserved juice. Bring the mixture to a boil, reduce the heat, and simmer the mixture in the uncovered pan until the sauce is reduced by half. Remove the pan from the heat, and let the sauce cool to room temperature.
6. To serve, stand one pear on each of 6 dessert plates. Spoon the sauce over the pears, and garnish them with the mint (if desired).

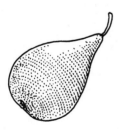

ORANGES IN CASSIS   *6 servings*

Elegant and simple, this dessert requires minimal cooking and preparation.

> 6 medium navel oranges
> Cold water
> 2/3 cup fresh orange juice *or* frozen orange juice
> 3 teaspoons cassis
> 2 teaspoons fresh lemon juice

1. Using a vegetable peeler and working from the stem end to the navel, remove the thin orange zest from 2 of the oranges. Cut the zest into long strips, about 1/8 inch wide.
2. Place the zest in a small saucepan with cold water to cover. Bring the ingredients to a boil, drain the zest, and set it aside.
3. Peel the oranges, slice them crosswise into circles 1/3 inch thick, then slice the circles in half to form half-moons. Place the oranges in a bowl.
4. Combine the orange zest with the orange juice, cassis, and lemon juice, and pour the mixture over the oranges, tossing the ingredients gently until the fruit is just coated with the mixture. Cover and chill the oranges, tossing them occasionally, for several hours or up to 2 days.

ORANGES IN MULLED WINE   *6 servings*

This recipe is a family favorite of Dorothy Rodgers, widow of songwriter Richard Rodgers, and comes to me by way of her daughter Mary Guettel.

> 6 medium to large navel oranges
> 1 cup Beaujolais
> 1/4 cup water
> 1/3 to 1/2 cup sugar, to taste
> 1 stick cinnamon
> 8 whole cloves

1. Remove three strips of zest from one of the oranges, and place them in a small saucepan. Peel all the oranges, divide them into sections, and place the sections in a glass or ceramic bowl.
2. To the saucepan, add the wine, water, sugar, cinnamon, and cloves. Bring the mixture to a boil, reduce the heat, cover the pan, and simmer the mixture for 15 minutes.
3. Strain the mulled wine into a cup or bowl, and pour the wine over the oranges. Cover the oranges, and chill them overnight or up to 2 days, tossing the fruit a few times.

ORANGES CASABLANCA

4 servings

Judy Miller from Cocoa, Florida, offered *Cooking Light* magazine this elegant make-ahead dessert that involves no cooking.

Preparation tips: The flavor imparted by orange-flower water is extraordinary, and the dessert is not the same without it. Orange-flower water is available in many specialty-food shops, especially those in Italian neighborhoods.

    4 large navel oranges
    6 tablespoons orange juice (preferably fresh)
    2 tablespoons sugar
    1 teaspoon orange-flower water
    1 tablespoon unsalted pistachios, skins removed
       and chopped

1. Peel the oranges, and cut them crosswise into ½-inch slices. Then cut the slices into quarters. Place them in a bowl, and set them aside.
2. In a small bowl, combine the orange juice, sugar, and orange-flower water. Drizzle this mixture over the cut oranges, cover the bowl, and chill the oranges for 2 hours or longer, turning the orange pieces occasionally.
3. To serve, divide the orange pieces among 4 dessert dishes, sprinkling each portion with some of the pistachios.

CITRUS DELIGHT

6 servings

An ideal winter-party treat derived from a *Gourmet* magazine recipe. My tasters requested seconds and thirds.

Preparation tip: The individual components can and should be prepared in advance—to be combined just before serving, when they are well chilled.

    ½ cup sugar, divided
    ⅔ cup water, divided
    ½ cup cranberries
    6 ounces dried apricots
    1 large grapefruit
    2 large navel oranges

1. In a small saucepan, combine ¼ cup of the sugar with ⅓ cup of the water, and bring the mixture to a boil, stirring it until the sugar has dissolved. Add the cranberries, and simmer them for 5 minutes or until the berries pop. Transfer the mixture to a small bowl, let the mixture cool, cover the bowl, and chill the mixture.

2. In the same saucepan, combine the remaining ¼ cup of sugar and the remaining ⅓ cup of water, and bring the mixture to a boil, stirring it until the sugar has dissolved. Add the apricots, cover the pan, and simmer the fruit for 5 minutes or until the apricots are tender. Transfer the mixture to another small bowl, let the mixture cool, cover the bowl, and chill the mixture.

3. Working over a bowl to catch the juice, remove the skin and pith from the grapefruit and oranges, and separate the fruit into sections. Halve the orange sections, and cut the grapefruit sections into thirds, removing and discarding any pits. Cover the bowl, and chill the fruit.

4. Before serving the dish, stir the apricots and their syrup into the citrus mixture. Then sprinkle the cranberries and their syrup on top, barely mixing them in.

CRAZY STRAWBERRIES   *8 servings*

Unless you've had the pleasure of this combination of ingredients before, you're likely to think that vinegar and pepper have no place in a fruity dessert. But don't pass judgment until you've tried this creation of Michael Chiarello's, which can be used as an appetizer (without the chocolate garnish) as well as a dessert. Mr. Chiarello is the chef/owner at Tra Vigne Restaurant in St. Helena, California.

    2 tablespoons sugar
    5 tablespoons balsamic vinegar
    1 teaspoon freshly ground black pepper
    4 cups (2 pints) ripe strawberries, stemmed and quartered
    Grated unsweetened chocolate for garnish (optional)

1. In a glass, ceramic, or stainless-steel bowl, combine the sugar, vinegar, and pepper. Stir in the strawberries, and let them stand for 10 minutes.
2. Serve the strawberries garnished with the grated chocolate (if desired).

STRAWBERRY MOUSSE

4 servings

Arthur Grosser, author of *The Cookbook Decoder* (about the chemistry of cooking), offers this dessert to demonstrate the effectiveness of gelatin mixed with beaten egg whites to form a stable structure for a mousse (in place of the more traditional high-fat, high-calorie whipped cream). The result is a light, satisfying, sin-free dessert.

  1 cup orange juice, divided
1½ envelopes (4¼ teaspoons) unflavored gelatin
  2 cups (1 pint) strawberries
 ½ cup sugar
 ½ teaspoon vanilla extract
1½ teaspoons orange-flavored liqueur (optional)
  2 egg whites
 ⅛ teaspoon cream of tartar

1. Place ¾ cup of the orange juice in a medium-sized saucepan, sprinkle in the gelatin, and let the mixture stand for 5 minutes to soften the gelatin.
2. Meanwhile, in a blender or food processor, purée the strawberries with the remaining ¼ cup juice.
3. Heat the gelatin mixture over low heat until the gelatin has dissolved. Add the purée and the sugar, and heat the mixture to a simmer.
4. Remove the pan from the heat, stir in the vanilla and liqueur (if desired), transfer the mixture to a large bowl, and refrigerate the mixture only until it begins to thicken.
5. In a medium-sized glass or ceramic bowl, beat the egg whites with the cream of tartar until the egg whites hold stiff peaks. Using a spatula or wooden spoon, fold the beaten egg whites gently into the chilled gelatin mixture. Divide the mousse among 4 individual serving dishes, or transfer it to a serving bowl, and refrigerate the mousse immediately for 1 hour or until the mousse is firmly set.

STRAWBERRY-RHUBARB CRÈME

8 servings

This treat is ideal in early summer, when fresh strawberries and rhubarb are readily available.

Preparation tips: The crème can also be made from frozen fruit—providing the fruit was measured before freezing it. Make the dessert well ahead of time to permit it to chill thoroughly. Rather than trying to unmold it, which is chancy, chill the crème in individual serving dishes, or scoop out portions from a large serving bowl.

1¼ **pounds rhubarb, cut into 1-inch slices**
 2 **cups sliced strawberries**
¾ **cup sugar**
 2 **envelopes (2 scant tablespoons) unflavored gelatin**
⅓ **cup cold water**
 2 **tablespoons kirsch**
1¼ **cups plain nonfat or low-fat yogurt**
 8 **strawberry fans (see "Preparation tips"**
   on page 492) for garnish (optional)

1. In a large saucepan, preferably one with a nonstick surface, combine the rhubarb, strawberries, and sugar. Cover the pan, and cook the ingredients over medium-low heat for 10 minutes or until the fruit has released its liquid. Uncover the pan, and cook the fruit 5 to 10 minutes longer or until the fruit is tender.
2. Meanwhile, in a small bowl, sprinkle the gelatin over the cold water, and let the gelatin stand for about 5 minutes to soften it. When the fruit is tender, add the gelatin mixture to the pan, stirring the ingredients to dissolve the gelatin.
3. Purée the fruit mixture in a blender or food processor. Pour the purée into a large bowl, and stir in the kirsch and yogurt, mixing the ingredients to combine them thoroughly. Transfer the crème to a serving bowl or to individual serving dishes, and chill the dessert for several hours. Serve the crème garnished with the strawberry fans (if desired).

SUNRISE-SUNSET SAUCE

(Apricots and Strawberries)   *about 3 cups*

This dessert topping is as beautiful as it is delicious.

Preparation tip: The sauce can be prepared up to 2 days ahead of time.

Serving suggestions: Serve this over angel-food cake (fat- and cholesterol-free) or Strawberry-Rhubarb Crème (see page 529). Or use it as a topping for frozen vanilla yogurt or sliced melons.

½ **cup sugar**
¾ **cup water**
1 **pound fresh apricots, pitted and quartered**
2 **cups (1 pint) strawberries, hulled and halved**
1 **tablespoon fresh lemon juice**

1. In a large saucepan, combine the sugar and water, and bring the mixture to a boil, stirring it. Simmer the mixture for 5 minutes.
2. Add the apricots, and cook the fruit at a slow boil, stirring the mixture occasionally, for 15 minutes or until the apricots are very soft.
3. Purée the mixture in a blender or food processor or food mill. Transfer the purée to the saucepan, and add the strawberries and lemon juice. Bring the mixture to a boil, and simmer it for 1 minute or until the strawberries are tender but still intact.
4. Transfer the sauce to a bowl, and let the sauce cool. Then cover the bowl, and chill the sauce for 2 hours or longer.

SAUCES AND SEASONINGS

Sauces and seasonings are integral to culinary success. While you can enjoy many foods with no additions—steamed fresh vegetables, vine-ripened tomatoes, and home-baked breads, for example—others are greatly improved by these enhancements. Sauces and seasonings also add variety to meals and can often turn pedestrian fare into high culinary art.

Unfortunately, too many of the traditional sauces are steeped in fat and/or salt and thus fall nutritionally short. I have found, however, that this need not be the case. If fat is an essential part of the sauce, as in mayonnaise or pesto, at the least the fat can be one that does not damage blood vessels. In addition, a little bit of the sauce should go a long way. Here are some sauces I have used successfully for various purposes. You can probably think of other uses for them. (See the index for other sauces, and see pages 386 to 389 for salad dressings.)

As for seasonings, you will find that you can greatly reduce your dependence on salt by being more liberal with herbs and spices and salt-free seasoning mixes. The possibilities are almost endless; I offer but a start.

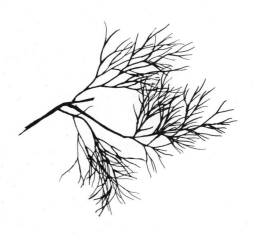

EASY MAYONNAISE

about 1 cup

I used to marvel at cooks who made their own mayonnaise. It seemed like such a risky venture. But the blender and food processor have brought homemade mayo to the masses.

    1 egg, at room temperature
    4 to 6 teaspoons fresh lemon juice, to taste
    1 teaspoon Dijon-style mustard
    ¼ teaspoon salt (optional)
    ¼ teaspoon white pepper
    ¾ cup oil (preferably a combination of olive oil
        and canola oil)

1. In a food processor or blender, combine the egg, lemon juice, mustard, salt (if desired), and pepper, and process the ingredients on high speed.
2. With the motor still running, slowly add the oil. By the time you finish, the consistency of the mixture should be thick.

BASIL MAYONNAISE

about 1¼ cups

This rich-tasting dressing requires only a thin smear to flavor a sandwich or salad.

    2 cups packed fresh basil leaves, coarsely chopped
    1 large egg, at room temperature
    4 teaspoons fresh lemon juice
Salt to taste (optional)
    ¼ teaspoon freshly ground black pepper
    1 cup canola oil

1. In a food processor or blender, combine the basil, egg, lemon juice, salt (if desired), and pepper, and process the ingredients at high speed.
2. With the motor still running, slowly add the oil, and process the ingredients until all the oil has been amalgamated and the mixture has thickened.

BASIL-GARLIC VINEGAR

2 cups

Flavored vinegars are a cinch to make. After the initial mixing, all you have to do is shake the bottle now and then for 2 to 3 weeks.

> 1 clove garlic, peeled and mashed
> ½ cup chopped fresh basil
> 2 cups white-wine vinegar

1. Place the garlic and basil in the jar of a blender.
2. In a small nonaluminum saucepan, bring 1 cup of the vinegar to a boil. Pour the hot vinegar over the garlic and basil, and process the ingredients briefly. Transfer the mixture to a clean wide-mouthed bottle, and let the mixture cool.
3. Add the remaining 1 cup of vinegar to the bottle. Cover the bottle tightly, and set it aside for 2 weeks, shaking it every few days.
4. Strain the vinegar mixture, and pour the clarified vinegar into a clean bottle suitable for kitchen or table use.

SHALLOT VINEGAR

about 3½ cups

A pleasantly flavored vinegar with a hint of onion and garlic that is nice in salads and marinades or as a seasoning for cooked vegetables.

Preparation tip: You don't have to strain the vinegar, if you don't want to.

> 3½ cups cider vinegar
> 6 shallots, peeled
> 2 sprigs parsley
> 8 whole peppercorns
> 1 bay leaf

1. In a medium-sized nonaluminum saucepan, bring the vinegar to a boil. Let the vinegar cool somewhat, and transfer it to a sterilized 1-quart bottle with a tight-fitting lid.
2. Add the shallots, parsley, peppercorns, and bay leaf. Cover the jar, and put it aside for 3 weeks, keeping it at room temperature and shaking it occasionally. After 3 weeks, strain the vinegar mixture, and pour the clarified vinegar into a scalded bottle, if you wish.

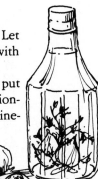

TEXAS BARBECUE SAUCE

about 1¾ cups

A good barbecue sauce can turn a simple cookout into a gourmet affair. Here is a taste-bud tickler that works equally well indoors and out.

    1 cup tomato juice
    ½ cup water
    ¼ cup vinegar
    ¼ cup ketchup
    2 tablespoons Worcestershire sauce
    2 tablespoons brown sugar
    1 tablespoon paprika (sweet or hot, as desired)
    1 teaspoon mustard powder
    ¼ teaspoon salt (optional)
    ¼ teaspoon or more chili powder, to taste
    ⅛ teaspoon cayenne

Combine the ingredients in a small nonaluminum saucepan, stirring them until they are well blended. Bring the mixture to a boil, reduce the heat, and simmer the sauce for 15 minutes or until it thickens slightly.

SAFFRON CREAM

about ¾ cup

This is so pretty and delicious and low in calories that you'll find yourself trying different ways to use it.

Preparation tips: Note that the finished sauce should be chilled for at least 6 hours. It can be made 1 to 2 days ahead of time.

Serving suggestions: Try it on hot or cold puréed soups, as a topping for fish, or as a dressing for sliced fresh tomatoes.

    ⅛ teaspoon saffron threads, crumbled
    2 tablespoons warm water
    1 teaspoon butter *or* margarine
    ¾ teaspoon minced garlic
    ¾ teaspoon minced or grated gingerroot
    Pinch salt
    ¾ cup plain nonfat or low-fat yogurt

1. In a small bowl, dissolve the saffron in the water, and set the bowl aside.
2. Melt the butter or margarine in a small saucepan, add the garlic and gingerroot, and cook the ingredients over low heat for about 1 minute.
3. Add the saffron and water to the saucepan, and simmer the ingredients for 1 minute.

4. Remove the pan from the heat, add the salt and yogurt, and stir the ingredients to combine them thoroughly. Transfer the sauce to a glass bowl or jar, cover the container, and chill the sauce for at least 6 hours.

POPPY SEED SAUCE

about 1½ cups

This is a delicious topping for fresh fruit. The recipe is a slightly modified version of one devised by my dear friend Betty Marks for *The High-Calcium Low-Calorie Cookbook.*

    1 cup plain nonfat or low-fat yogurt
    3 tablespoons poppy seeds
    2 tablespoons raspberry vinegar *or* cider vinegar
    1 tablespoon frozen concentrated orange juice,
       thawed
    1 tablespoon honey
    2 teaspoons grated orange rind
    1 teaspoon grated lemon rind

Combine the ingredients in a small bowl, stirring them until they are well blended. Cover the bowl, and chill the sauce for 1 hour or longer.

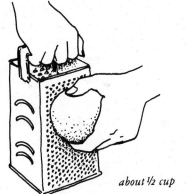

ORANGE DIPPING SAUCE

about ½ cup

A simple dip for various hors d'oeuvres such as cold chicken or turkey meatballs or seafood.

    ½ cup rice vinegar
    1 tablespoon minced scallion
    1 tablespoon orange juice
    1 teaspoon grated orange rind
    1 teaspoon grated or minced gingerroot

Combine the ingredients in a small bowl. Cover the bowl, and chill the sauce.

"HOT" APPLESAUCE

about 3 cups

This recipe started life as a "mistake." I prepared extra dressing for Cornish hens (see page 138); by the time I remembered to remove the casserole from the oven, the dressing had turned to mush. However, my tasters rated it a delicious condiment, worthy of inclusion as a real recipe.

Preparation tips: The applesauce can be prepared ahead of time. Toss it in the oven when you are baking something else. It can also be put up and as used as gifts. If you wish, you can bake the applesauce at 325° F for 40 to 45 minutes.

    3 pounds (6 large) tart apples (e.g., Granny Smiths)
    6 tablespoons (⅜ cup) fresh lemon juice
    5 tablespoons sugar
    ½ to 1 teaspoon salt, to taste (optional)
    ½ teaspoon thyme, crumbled
    ½ teaspoon cinnamon
    ¼ teaspoon cayenne, or to taste
    Freshly ground black pepper to taste

1. Preheat the oven to 350° F.
2. Peel, core, and chop or finely dice the apples. Combine them in a casserole dish with the remaining ingredients.
3. Place the tightly covered casserole in the hot oven for about 35 minutes.

CRANBERRY-PEAR RELISH

about 3 cups

The University of Oklahoma Health Sciences Center offers this scrumptious alternative to traditional cranberry sauces.

Preparation tips: This is a snap to make in a food processor. Don't worry about overprocessing: although the directions say "coarsely chopped," the relish is equally delicious as a purée. The relish lasts for 5 days or more in the refrigerator. Since it also freezes well, don't be afraid to make more than you expect to use immediately.

Serving suggestion: In addition to the usual roles for cranberry sauce, try this on bread or toast or with yogurt or cottage cheese.

    1 orange, unpeeled, washed, cut into eighths, and seeded
    ½ cup walnuts
    1 large Bosc pear, unpeeled, cored, and cut into eighths
    2½ cups (10 ounces) fresh cranberries (defrost
        them if they are frozen)
    ½ cup sugar

1. Place the orange sections and walnuts in the bowl of a food processor, and chop them coarsely, turning the machine on and off for about 30 seconds.
2. Add the pear sections and cranberries, and process them briefly until they are coarsely chopped.
3. Transfer the mixture to a bowl, and stir in the sugar. Cover the bowl, and chill the relish.

RHUBARB RELISH

about 1 cup

A simple and delicious sauce based on a recipe devised by Judith Benn Hurley, cookbook author from Pennsylvania.

Preparation tips: The relish will keep for about 2 weeks in the refrigerator. It can also be prepared in a microwave: put it in a glass pie plate, cover the plate with vented plastic, place the plate in the microwave, and cook the relish on full power for 2 minutes or until the rhubarb is tender.

Serving suggestions: Use the relish as a condiment with Indian dishes and roasted or grilled meats and poultry and as a spread on sandwiches. Or serve it as an hors d'oeuvre to spread on whole-wheat pita wedges or bland crackers.

1½ **cups (about ⅔ pound) rhubarb, cut into ½-inch pieces**
¼ **cup dried currants**
⅓ **cup minced onion**
1½ **tablespoons cider vinegar**
1 **tablespoon sugar**
½ **teaspoon grated gingerroot**

Combine the ingredients in an enamel or stainless-steel or nonstick saucepan. Cook the mixture, stirring it often, over medium heat for 5 to 10 minutes or until the rhubarb disintegrates.

CURRIED FIG CONDIMENT

about 1½ cups

This excellent make-ahead condiment takes but moments to prepare.

Preparation tips: Note that the fruit marinates for 2 days. The condiment tastes best when served at room temperature.

Serving suggestions: Try the condiment with pâtés, plain yogurt, or melons. Or use the condiment with Indian dishes, lentils, or rice.

> 1 cup finely diced dried figs (I use Calimyrna)
> ½ cup peeled, cored, and finely diced apple
> ¼ cup tawny port
> ¼ cup plain nonfat or low-fat yogurt
> ¼ teaspoon curry powder
> ⅛ teaspoon salt (optional)
> ⅛ teaspoon freshly ground black pepper

1. Place the figs and apple in a bowl, and combine them with the port. Cover the bowl, and set the mixture aside for 4 hours.
2. Add the yogurt, curry powder, salt (if desired), and pepper. Stir the ingredients well, cover the bowl, and chill the mixture for 2 days.

HEAVENLY HAROSET

about 3 cups

Haroset, a mixture of chopped fruit and nuts sweetened with wine, in the Passover seder symbolizes the mortar used by the Jews when they were slaves in Egypt. I found this Sephardic version of haroset in an advertisement years ago and liked it so much that I make it as a spread all year round.

Preparation tips: Note that the fruit should soak overnight and that the mixture is cooked for about 2 hours. The haroset seems to last indefinitely in the refrigerator. If the mixture gets too dry, stir in additional sweet wine.

Serving suggestion: Try the spread on toast, as the "jelly" in a peanut butter and jelly sandwich, or as a condiment with poultry or meat.

> ½ pound pitted dates
> 1 cup dried currants
> 1 cup raisins
> ¼ cup pitted prunes
> Water to cover
> 1 to 1¼ cups sweet red Passover or kosher wine
> ½ cup chopped walnuts *or* pecans
> 2 tablespoons ground almonds

1. Place the dates, currants, raisins, and prunes in a medium-sized bowl, add the water to cover, and soak the fruit overnight. Drain the fruit, reserving the soaking liquid.
2. Coarsely chop the drained fruit, and place it in a heavy nonreactive saucepan (stainless-steel, enamel, glass, or nonstick). Add 1 cup of the wine and 1 cup of the soaking liquid, and bring the mixture to a boil. Reduce the heat, and simmer the mixture, stirring it occasionally, for 2 hours or until all the liquid has been absorbed and the mixture is very thick.
3. Let the mixture cool. Then stir in the walnuts or pecans, almonds, and, if needed, the remaining ¼ cup of wine.

SALSA

about 3½ cups

Here is a standard salsa—with adjustable hotness—that my tasters enjoyed even without added salt.

Serving suggestions: Serve this as an hors d'oeuvre with tortilla chips, as a topping on tostadas, tacos, and other Mexican dishes (like beans and rice), or as a condiment with baked or grilled fish.

  2 cups peeled, finely chopped fresh tomatoes
  1 cup finely chopped sweet green pepper
½ cup finely chopped onion (1 small)
  1 to 2 jalapeños, to taste, seeded and minced
  1 small green chili, seeded and minced
  2 large cloves garlic, peeled and minced
  1 tablespoon olive oil *or* canola oil
  1 tablespoon minced fresh cilantro, or to taste (optional)
Salt to taste (optional)

Combine the ingredients in a glass or ceramic or stainless-steel bowl. Cover the bowl, and chill the salsa.

MELON SALSA

about 3 cups

This unusual condiment was devised by the Cafe Terra Cotta in Tucson. It is so elegant that I served it as part of a wedding feast.

Preparation tip: The salsa can be made a day ahead but does not store well much beyond that.

Serving suggestion: Although it was originally designed as a condiment for grilled swordfish, the salsa also would go well with all manner of grilled fish, cold sliced turkey, and plain yogurt or cottage cheese.

   ½ honeydew melon, peeled, seeded, and finely chopped
   ½ cantaloupe, peeled, seeded, and finely chopped
   1 or more teaspoons minced fresh jalapeño, to taste
   2 tablespoons fresh lime juice
   1 tablespoon olive oil
   2 tablespoons minced fresh mint leaves
   ¼ teaspoon salt (optional)
   ¼ teaspoon freshly ground black pepper

In a medium-sized bowl, combine the ingredients, mixing them thoroughly. Cover the bowl, and chill the salsa for 1 hour or up to 1 day.

FRESH TOMATO-GARLIC SAUCE

about 4 cups

A tangy, low-calorie sauce that is easy to whip together.

Serving suggestion: Try it hot on pasta or fish, or as a cold "salad" with canned tuna or cold sliced poultry.

   10 to 12 firm but ripe plum tomatoes
    2 tablespoons minced garlic (6 large cloves)
    1 tablespoon olive oil
   ½ teaspoon salt (optional)
   ½ teaspoon freshly ground black pepper

   1. Peel and chop the tomatoes. (The yield should be about 4 cups.)
   2. In a bowl, combine the tomatoes with the remaining ingredients.

PESTO

I am repeating the pesto I first offered in *Jane Brody's Good Food Book* because pesto has become so popular. I have used it in ravioli, soups, hors d'oeuvres, salads, and pizzas. The oil in pesto is olive, which helps to lower blood cholesterol, and I use about half of what you'll find in a traditional recipe. Keep in mind that a little of this rich, potent sauce goes a long way.

Preparation tips: Pesto is easiest to make in a food processor, although it can also be prepared—in batches—in a blender. If you want a thinner sauce or have difficulty processing the ingredients, add some chicken or vegetable broth in step 2. Pine nuts (pignoli) are traditionally used, but if they are too expensive for your budget or unavailable, substitute walnuts. Pesto can be frozen and keeps many months that way. I freeze it in ½-cup and 1-cup containers and by the tablespoon or two in ice-cube trays. Once frozen, the cubes can be removed from the trays and enclosed in tightly sealed plastic freezer bags.

  3 cloves garlic, peeled and chopped
¼ teaspoon salt (optional)
¼ cup olive oil
  2 cups firmly packed fresh basil leaves
¼ cup pine nuts *or* walnuts
½ cup grated Parmesan

1. In a food processor or blender, combine the garlic, salt (if desired), and oil. Process the ingredients until they are smooth.
2. Add the basil and pine nuts or walnuts, and process the ingredients until they are smooth. (You may have to stop the machine once or twice to scrape the bowl or jar.)
3. Transfer the mixture to a bowl, and stir in the Parmesan. Serve the pesto at room temperature.

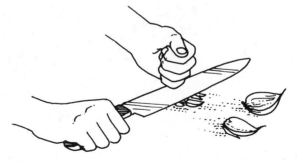

EGGPLANT PESTO

about 3 cups

This versatile sauce combines the flavor of fresh basil with low-fat, nutritious ingredients. The pesto has no cheese and very little oil; nearly all the fat comes from the walnuts. I clipped the recipe from an article by Diana Shaw in the *Los Angeles Times*. Ms. Shaw is the author of the forthcoming *Vegetarian Entertaining*.

Preparation tip: Salt is needed to extract the bitter juices from the eggplant. After the eggplant has drained, some of the salt can be washed off by rinsing the eggplant in cold water and patting it dry with paper towels.

Serving suggestions: For hors d'oeuvres, try stuffing hollowed-out cherry tomatoes or medium-sized pasta shells with the pesto. Or serve the pesto as a spread for toasted pita chips, crackers, or crisp vegetables. For a pasta entrée, thin the pesto with some of the pasta cooking water, and use the pesto as a sauce.

1¼ pounds small eggplants, peeled and sliced
   ½-inch thick
Salt for sprinkling eggplants
  2 tablespoons olive oil
  1 cup chopped onion (1 large)
  5 teaspoons minced garlic (5 large cloves)
  ¾ cup packed basil leaves, minced, divided
  2 tablespoons water
  ¾ cup chopped walnuts
  1 square (4 ounces) tofu, well drained and diced
Salt to taste (optional)
Freshly ground black pepper to taste

1. Sprinkle both sides of the eggplant slices with the salt, and place the slices on paper towels for 30 to 60 minutes to drain. Pat the eggplant dry, and dice the slices.
2. In a large skillet, preferably one with a nonstick surface, heat the oil, add the onion and garlic, and sauté the vegetables for 3 minutes or until the onion becomes translucent. Add the eggplant, and sauté it a few minutes longer or until the eggplant begins to brown. Add ¼ cup of the basil and the water, stirring the ingredients to mix them well. Tightly cover the pan, reduce the heat to medium-low, and cook the ingredients for 5 minutes or until the eggplant is tender.
3. Transfer the contents of the skillet to a food processor or blender, and purée the mixture. Add the walnuts, the remaining basil, and the tofu. Using the pulse button, process the mixture until it is grainy but not liquefied. Season the pesto with the salt (if desired) and pepper.

LILIAN'S CRIMSON SAUCE

4 servings

If you saw Dr. Lilian Chueng, a bright, beautiful, trim mother of three and a
health educator at Harvard, you'd want to eat whatever she does. For starters, I
offer her low-fat but very tasty sauce for fish.

  1 cup chicken broth
  ½ cup dry white wine
  1 small leek (white and light-green parts), sliced
  1 small carrot, peeled and sliced
  1 bay leaf
  1 teaspoon cornstarch
  2 tablespoons cold water
  1 tablespoon olive oil
  2 chopped shallots
  1 sweet red pepper, seeded and diced
  ½ cup port
Freshly ground black pepper *or* white pepper to taste

1. In a medium-sized saucepan, combine the broth, wine, leek, carrot, and bay
   leaf. Bring the ingredients to a boil, reduce the heat, and simmer the mixture in the uncovered pan for 15 minutes. Strain the liquid, and, if necessary, return it to the saucepan and boil it until it is reduced to about ¼ cup.
2. In a small bowl, combine the cornstarch and water, mixing the ingredients
   until the mixture is smooth.
3. In a nonstick skillet, heat the oil briefly, add the shallots and red pepper, and
   sauté the vegetables for about 2 minutes. Add the port, and cook the mixture for 2 to 3 minutes. Add the reduced broth and ground pepper. Stir the
   cornstarch mixture, and add it to the pan. Cook the sauce until it thickens.

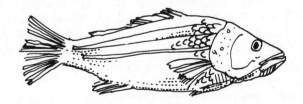

RED PEPPER SAUCE

4 servings

Another fine sauce for fish. The color and flavor are hard to beat.

 1 teaspoon butter *or* margarine
 ¼ cup finely diced onion
 2 medium sweet red peppers, cored, seeded, and
    diced (about 1½ cups)
Salt to taste (optional)
Freshly ground black pepper to taste
 ½ cup chicken broth
 1 tablespoon olive oil (optional)

1. In a medium-sized nonstick saucepan or skillet, melt the butter or margarine, add the onion, and cook the onion for 1 to 2 minutes or until the onion
   is glazed. Add the red peppers, salt (if desired), black pepper, and broth.
   Bring the ingredients to a boil, reduce the heat, and simmer the mixture in
   the uncovered pan for 15 to 20 minutes.
2. In a blender, process the red-pepper mixture with the olive oil (if you are
   using it) until the sauce is smooth.

YOGURT CHEESE

about 2 cups

Yogurt cheese can be used to prepare dips or low-fat spreads for sandwiches and
snacks. It can also be used as the base for a nutritious "cheesecake." It is made
simply by draining some of the liquid from plain yogurt. If you catch the drip-
pings in a bowl, you can use them in soup, bread, or other recipes, since this
liquid is rich in nutrients.

 1 quart (4 cups) plain nonfat or low-fat yogurt

1. Line a colander or bowl with several layers of cheesecloth or with a cotton
   kitchen towel or with a clean cloth diaper. Place the yogurt in the cloth,
   gather the ends of the cloth together, and tie them. Or use a yogurt strainer.
2. Suspend the "bag" of yogurt from a hook or knob over the sink or over a
   large bowl, and let the bag hang overnight. Do not squeeze the yogurt;
   simply allow the liquid to seep through.
3. Remove the yogurt cheese from the cloth, and proceed with your recipe, or
   refrigerate the cheese.

AHA HERB MIX

about ¼ cup

This is a repeat of a no-salt seasoning mix from the American Heart Association that I offered in *Jane Brody's Good Food Book.* It continues to be a favorite. I give this herb mix as gifts as well as use it in some of the recipes in this book.

Preparation tips: This can be made in large quantities and stored in airtight spice jars. If you start with herbs that are in leaf form, use 1½ teaspoons of basil, parsley, and sage, and 1¼ teaspoons of thyme and savory.

    1 tablespoon garlic powder
    1 teaspoon ground basil
    1 teaspoon ground thyme
    1 teaspoon ground parsley
    1 teaspoon ground savory
    1 teaspoon ground mace
    1 teaspoon ground sage
    1 teaspoon onion powder
    1 teaspoon ground black pepper
    ½ teaspoon cayenne

Combine the ingredients, and store the herb mix in a spice jar. If you are using herbs in leaf form, combine all the ingredients, and process them in a blender until they are ground.

CAJUN SPICE MIX

about 2 cups

A few years ago, I made up a batch of this and included it in my Christmas packages. It made a big hit. Although I shy away from garlic powder in general, it is fine in this kind of seasoning. The recipe was devised by Pat Zito, author of the *Supermarket Guide to Cholesterol and Saturated Fat.*

Serving suggestion: This is marvelous on fish fillets, obviating the need for any other flavoring, including fat. Try it, too, on shellfish, in pasta dishes, or on baked potatoes.

    1⅛ cups sweet paprika
    ¼ cup cayenne
    ¼ cup freshly ground black pepper
    2 tablespoons oregano
    2 tablespoons thyme leaves
    2 tablespoons onion powder
    1 tablespoon celery seed
    1½ teaspoons garlic powder

Grind the ingredients together in a blender or food processor, and store the mix in spice jars.

GARAM MASALA

An Indian spice mix.

4½ teaspoons cumin seeds
4½ teaspoons coriander seeds
 2 teaspoons black peppercorns
 1 1½-inch stick cinnamon, broken into small pieces
1½ teaspoons cardamom seeds (remove them from
    the pods)
 ½ teaspoon whole cloves

1. Heat a small heavy skillet over medium-high heat. Add the ingredients, and cook them, shaking the pan, for about 5 minutes or until the spices are brown but not burned.
2. Transfer the spices to a bowl, and let them cool. In a mortar with pestle or in an electric coffee grinder or in a spice grinder, grind the spices to a fine powder. Store the garam masala in an airtight jar.

KAY'S SALTLESS SEASONING

Kay Buttenheim of Mount Kisco, New York, is an herb enthusiast and a wonderful, health-conscious cook who prepares vats of this seasoning to use as gifts as well as at home.

Serving suggestions: Kay says she uses the seasoning on fish and chicken, in soups, curry sauces, Bloody Marys, and on vegetables like winter squash.

 1 tablespoon whole cumin seed
 5 whole cloves
 1 teaspoon cardamom seeds (remove them from
    the pods)
 1 4-inch stick cinnamon
 1 teaspoon black peppercorns
 3 bay leaves
 ½ teaspoon freshly grated nutmeg
10 to 12 allspice berries
 ¼ cup dried parsley flakes
 2 tablespoons freeze-dried minced onion
 2 tablespoons ground turmeric
 4 teaspoons ground coriander
 3 tablespoons fenugreek seeds
 1 teaspoon ground ginger
 2 tablespoons celery seeds
 3 cups powdered nonfat milk

Combine the ingredients in a bowl, and grind them in batches in a spice or coffee grinder or in a mini-jar of a blender until the seasoning is finely powdered. Store the seasoning in spice jars.

HERB MIXES

The following dry herb mixes can be prepared using equal amounts of the herbs or using more of one and less of another, to taste.

FOR MEAT	FOR FISH	FOR POULTRY
Thyme	Fennel	Tarragon
Basil	Marjoram	Rosemary
Savory	Savory	Marjoram
Fennel	Sage	Basil
Lavender	Thyme	Dill

Combine the ingredients, and store the mixes in airtight jars.

GIFTS FROM YOUR KITCHEN

There is no better present than one you make yourself. Traditional food gifts—from wine and liquor to homemade quick breads, cookies, and preserves—often lack nutritional value or virtue. I offer here some of my own make-ahead favorites that, for the various reasons noted, will be welcomed by health-conscious recipients. Don't, however, limit yourself to the choices offered in this section; there are a host of other possibilities throughout the book, especially among the sauces and seasonings, quick breads, yeast breads, cookies, and frozen-fruit desserts. You might also consider one of my most treasured gifts that requires no more than repackaging and labeling by you: specialty pastas. If not available in your area, they can be mail-ordered (see page 11).

DOUBLY HOT HORSERADISH MUSTARD

about ¾ cup

This is one helluva mustard. I make it in large batches and give it as gifts. Recipients appreciate it more than a bottle of wine or flowers and invariably ask for the recipe. So, for all the world to know, here is Brody's famous mustard—an extremely low-sodium, low-fat condiment that's sure to stimulate your taste buds. It keeps for months—even a year or more—in the refrigerator.

Preparation tip: A little of this mustard goes a long way. But since it keeps without being processed or sealed, you can prepare a double or quadruple batch by doubling or quadrupling the ingredients listed.

　¼ cup cider vinegar
　3 tablespoons white-wine vinegar
　2 tablespoons mustard seeds
　¼ cup mustard powder (mild and/or hot)
　½ teaspoon red pepper flakes
1½ tablespoons honey
　1 tablespoon drained bottled horseradish

1. Add the ingredients to a blender or food processor (if your blender has a mini-jar, use that for a single batch), and process the ingredients at high speed until the mixture is smooth.
2. Transfer the mustard to a small clean jar, cover the jar tightly, and refrigerate the mustard.

HONEY MUSTARD

about 1 cup

This takes about 2 minutes to prepare and costs a fraction of the amount paid for commercially available versions.

Preparation tip: If desired, you can make the mustard sweeter (by using more honey) or hotter (by using more pepper sauce or by adding cayenne).

   ¾ cup coarse-grain Dijon-style mustard
   2 tablespoons cider vinegar
   2 tablespoons honey
1½ teaspoons hot pepper sauce

In a small bowl, whisk together the ingredients until they are thoroughly combined. Store the mustard in the refrigerator in a tightly covered clean jar.

HOT SPICED OIL

about 1 cup

This olive oil can be used to perk up any number of foods, including pizzas, soups, stews, sautéed vegetables, and salads.

Preparation tip: The following recipe can be made in larger quantities simply by doubling or tripling the ingredients.

   1 strip orange peel, 2 × ½ inches
   2 dried long red chilies
   2 bay leaves
   6 allspice berries
 12 peppercorns
Olive oil to cover (about 8 ounces)

Place the ingredients in a decorative 10-ounce bottle (or, if you are making a large recipe, 1 large bottle). Close the bottle tightly, and let the ingredients steep for at least 2 weeks, shaking the bottle occasionally. When you are done steeping the ingredients, you can either leave all the ingredients in the bottle, or you can decant the oil into another container.

SPICY APPLE-PEAR CHUTNEY

about 3 half-pints

This chutney is based on a recipe developed by Giant Food stores in the Washington, D.C., area, one of the first supermarket chains to promote good nutrition both inside and outside the stores.

  2 cups (about 2 large) peeled, diced apple
     (preferably Granny Smith)
  1 cup (about 1 large) peeled, diced pear
  ½ cup sugar
  ½ cup cider vinegar
  ½ cup raisins *or* dried currants
  ½ cup diced onion
  1 teaspoon grated gingerroot
  ½ teaspoon red pepper flakes
  ¼ teaspoon cinnamon
  ¼ teaspoon ground cloves

1. Place the ingredients in a large nonaluminum or nonstick saucepan. Cook the mixture over low heat for about 1 hour.
2. Pack the chutney into hot sterilized canning jars, cover the jars, and process the chutney for 10 minutes in a boiling water bath.

PINEAPPLE CHUTNEY

about 4 to 6 half-pints

Jean Hewitt offers this recipe in *The New York Times Heritage Cook Book.* I made the mistake of preparing only half a recipe when I tested it; it didn't last very long. Fortunately, since the chutney is a snap to make, I did it again.

Preparation tip: Macadamia nuts are high in fat, costly, and sometimes hard to find outside of specialty-food stores. You can substitute cashews, pecans, or pine nuts, or you can omit the nuts entirely.

Serving suggestions: Serve the chutney on crackers or toast as well as with chicken, fish, roasted or grilled meats, and curries.

  4 cups finely chopped fresh pineapple
1½ cups cider vinegar
1½ cups light brown sugar
  1 15-ounce package (about 2½ cups) raisins *or* dried currants
  1 tablespoon salt
  2 tablespoons minced gingerroot
  2 tablespoons minced garlic (6 large cloves)
  3 hot peppers (e.g., jalapeños), seeded and minced
  1 cup chopped unsalted macadamia nuts (see
     "Preparation tip," above)

1. In a large nonreactive saucepan (enamel, nonstick, or stainless-steel), combine the ingredients *except* the nuts. Bring the ingredients to a boil, reduce the heat to medium-low, and simmer the mixture, stirring it often to prevent it from sticking, for 45 minutes or until the mixture is very thick. The finished chutney should have the consistency of thick preserves.
2. Stir in the nuts, and ladle the hot chutney into hot sterilized jars. Seal the jars with melted paraffin. Or cover the jars with canning lids, and process the chutney according to the manufacturer's instructions. Or, if you plan to use the chutney quickly, it can be stored, covered, in the refrigerator for weeks.

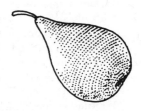

TOMATO-PEAR CHUTNEY
about 3 half-pints

A treat that can be served on crackers or toast or as a condiment with meals. I modified a recipe originally published in *Woman's Day Gifts from Your Kitchen* to make it considerably less sweet and spicier.

1 pound tomatoes, peeled and chopped
1 pound firm ripe pears, cored, peeled, and chopped
1 sweet green pepper, cored, seeded, and chopped
1 onion, peeled and chopped (about 1 cup)
2 teaspoons grated gingerroot
1 teaspoon salt
½ teaspoon mustard powder
¼ teaspoon cayenne
½ cup cider vinegar
½ cup sugar
1 small pimiento, finely chopped (optional)

1. In a medium-sized nonstick, enamel, or stainless-steel saucepan, combine the ingredients *except* the pimiento. Simmer the mixture, stirring it often, for about 1 hour.
2. Stir in the pimiento (if desired), pour the chutney into hot sterilized canning jars, cover the jars, and process the chutney for 10 minutes in a boiling water bath.

GREEN TOMATO CHUTNEY

4 to 5 half-pints

When the first frost is imminent and you (or your neighbors) still have green tomatoes on the vine, use some of them to make this condiment, originally published in *Stocking Up*, edited by Carol Hupping Stoner.

2¼ cups chopped green tomatoes
2¼ cups peeled and chopped tart apples (e.g., Granny Smiths)
1½ cups dried currants
 1 cup minced onion (1 large)
 1 lemon, quartered lengthwise, seeded, and thinly sliced crosswise
 1 clove garlic, peeled and minced
 1 teaspoon minced gingerroot
½ cup honey
½ cup cider vinegar
½ cup water
 1 tablespoon mustard seeds
¾ teaspoon salt
¼ teaspoon cayenne

1. In a large nonaluminum or nonstick saucepan, combine the ingredients. Bring the mixture to a boil, reduce the heat to medium-low, and simmer the mixture for 40 to 60 minutes or until the fruit is soft and much of the liquid has evaporated.
2. Pack the chutney into hot sterilized canning jars, leaving ¼ inch headspace. (If there is still a lot of liquid left after 1 hour of cooking, use a slotted spoon to pack the jars.) Cover the jars, and process the chutney for 10 minutes in a boiling water bath.

PICKLED GREEN CHERRY TOMATOES

about 4 half-pints

These have been hit every time I've served them. One fall, when faced with a garden full of green cherry tomatoes that were doomed to freeze, I searched for a recipe and found this treasure (accredited to Blanche Rottluff) in Jeanne Lesem's *The Pleasures of Preserving and Pickling*. The tomatoes last for a year or longer in the brine.

1 pound (approximately) green cherry tomatoes,
   stemmed, well washed, and dried
1 small clove peeled garlic per half-pint jar
3 whole peppercorns per half-pint jar
¼ cup coarse (kosher) salt *or* 3 tablespoons
   pickling salt *or* 3 tablespoons uniodized salt
2 cups water
1 cup cider vinegar

1. Pierce each tomato two or three times with a small bamboo skewer or, if this is unavailable, with a round toothpick. Pack the tomatoes into hot sterilized half-pint or pint jars to within 1 inch of the top. Add the garlic and peppercorns to each jar.
2. In an enamel or stainless-steel saucepan, combine the salt, water, and vinegar, and heat the mixture, stirring it, until it is hot. Add the hot brine to the jars to fully cover the tomatoes. Cover the jars, and store the tomatoes in a cool place for 6 weeks or longer, adding more brine, if needed, to keep the tomatoes covered.

APPLE-PEAR BUTTER

about 6 one-half pints

This simple, lovely spread is made without added sugar. The cider and fruit provide natural sweetness.

1 gallon apple cider
3 pounds ripe pears (e.g., Anjous or Bartletts)
2 pounds tart apples (e.g., Granny Smiths)

1. In a wide-mouthed kettle, boil the cider for 30 or more minutes or until the cider is reduced by half (to 2 quarts).
2. Peel, core, and dice the pears and apples, and add them to the cider. Boil the mixture for 1 hour or until the fruit is reduced to a very thick pulp.
3. Purée the mixture in a food processor or blender. If the purée is too thin for a spread, return it to a nonstick saucepan, and simmer it over low heat, stirring it often (wearing an oven mitt to avoid splash-up burns) to prevent sticking, for 20 minutes or until the purée is reduced to about 6 cups (the purée will thicken when it is chilled).
4. Pack the hot purée into hot sterilized canning jars, cover the jars, and process them for 10 minutes in a boiling water bath.

CONCORD GRAPE CONSERVE

about 10 half-pints

I hesitate to publish this recipe, for this conserve is the specialty of the house. Every fall, with the help of my husband and anyone else I can enlist, I convert 24 pounds of home-grown Concord grapes into this conserve, which I then proudly present all year long to those who entertain us. If you don't want to make this yourself, why don't you invite me for dinner? You may be in for an unforgettable treat.

Preparation tips: Pinching the grapes is a picky job best done with a companion. Wear old clothes, and protect your table. Hold a bunch of grapes over a bowl, and pull off one grape at a time, popping the pulp into the bowl and placing the skin into a second bowl. Underripe grapes can go into the bowl with the pulp with their skins on. I use undyed California oranges since the rinds go into the conserve. Do not try to make more than a triple batch (12 pounds of grapes) at one time, regardless of how big your jelly pot may be. Use mason jars and lids for putting up this conserve; do not seal the jars with paraffin unless you expect to use up the conserve within a few months.

  4 pounds Concord grapes, washed and drained
  2 large oranges (preferably seedless), washed and dried
2½ cups sugar
  1 cup raisins
Pinch salt
  1 cup chopped walnuts

1. Pinch the skins from the grapes (see "Preparation tips," above), placing the pulp into one bowl and the skins into another. Save the skins, discarding only the stems.
2. Transfer the pulp to a small saucepan, and cook it for about 6 to 8 minutes to loosen the seeds. Then pass the pulp through a food mill (or press it through a fine strainer), discarding the seeds. Transfer the pulp to a large, heavy pot.
3. Grate the rind from the oranges while the oranges are whole, and then squeeze out their juice. Or, if you are using seedless oranges, cut the

oranges into 8 wedges each, and chop them to a pulp—skin and all—in a food processor. Add the rind and juice or the pulp to the pan containing the grape pulp.

4. Stir in the sugar, raisins, and salt. Cook the mixture over low heat, stirring it often, until the sugar dissolves. Then increase the heat, and bring the mixture to a boil, cooking it somewhat vigorously, stirring it often, for 30 minutes or until it thickens.

5. Stir in the grape skins, and cook the conserve 10 minutes longer or until the conserve is thick.

6. Remove the conserve from the heat, and stir in the walnuts. Pack the conserve into hot sterilized canning jars, cover the jars, and process the conserve for 10 minutes in a boiling water bath.

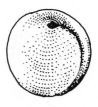

NECTARINE-PINEAPPLE PRESERVES

5 to 6 half-pints

My manuscript editor, Carol Flechner, gave me a jar of these preserves as a holiday gift. I thought it had come from heaven, even though it was made without added sweeteners. Carol adapted a recipe developed by Madelaine Bullwinkel for *Gourmet Preserves Chez Madelaine*.

4 pounds fresh ripe nectarines, pitted and
  coarsely chopped
3 6-ounce cans frozen unsweetened
  pineapple-juice concentrate
3 cinnamon sticks, each about 3 inches long

1. In a heavy nonstick or stainless-steel saucepan, combine the ingredients. Bring them to a boil, reduce the heat to medium, and simmer the mixture, stirring it constantly, for 12 to 15 minutes or until the mixture thickens and most of the liquid has evaporated.

2. Remove the pan from the heat, and remove the cinnamon sticks from the pan. Pack the preserves into hot sterilized canning jars to within ½ inch of the top, cover the jars, and process the preserves for 10 minutes in boiling water that covers the jars by 1 inch.

DRIED FRUIT BALLS

about 50 balls

This is a wholesome treat I adapted from *Woman's Day Gifts from Your Kitchen.*

Preparation tips: A food processor makes preparation a snap. The fruit balls can be prepared way in advance and frozen in layers separated by wax paper. For freezer storage, seal the fruit balls in plastic, or place them in a tightly covered container.

    1 cup dried apricots
    1 cup pitted dates
    1 cup raisins
    1 cup coconut flakes (preferably unsweetened)
    ½ cup confectioners' sugar
    2 tablespoons sherry *or* orange juice
    Coconut flakes for garnish (optional)
    Ground nuts for garnish (optional)

1. In a chopping bowl or food processor, finely chop the apricots, dates, raisins, and coconut. Stir in the sugar and sherry or juice, mixing the ingredients thoroughly.
2. Snip off enough of the mixture to shape into 1-inch balls (first dusting your hands with powdered sugar, if necessary). Roll the fruit balls in the coconut or ground nuts (if desired). Place the fruit balls in layers in a container, separating the layers with wax paper, and tightly cover the container.

CINNAMON-TOASTED NUTS

2 cups

When my friend Betty Marks gave me a jar of these, I promptly told her that I could not live without the recipe. It turned out to be so simple that it's almost embarrassing to call it a recipe.

    1 cup almonds
    1 cup hazelnuts (filberts) *or* 1 more cup almonds
    1 tablespoon ground cinnamon

1. Preheat the oven to 350° F.
2. Place the nuts in a baking pan in one layer. Sprinkle them with the cinnamon.
3. Place the pan in the hot oven for 15 minutes, stirring the nuts at 5-minute intervals.

SPICY CARAMELIZED PECANS

about 2 cups

I guarantee a warm reception for these nuts, which can be prepared in 5 to 10 minutes and may be used as an hors d'oeuvre, salad ingredient, fruit-salad garnish, or finishing finger-food touch to a fine dinner. Be sure to make extra for yourself.

  2 **cups pecan halves**
Water to cover
  2 **tablespoons butter *or* butter-margarine blend**
  3 **tablespoons sugar**
¼ **teaspoon salt (optional)**
¼ **teaspoon or more cayenne, to taste**

1. Place the pecans in a large skillet or saucepan with water to cover. Bring the ingredients just to a simmer over high heat. Drain the nuts immediately, and set them aside.
2. Melt the butter or butter-margarine blend in a large skillet, preferably one with a nonstick surface. Remove the pan from the heat, and stir in the sugar, salt (if desired), and cayenne. Then add the nuts.
3. Return the pan to medium-high heat, and cook the nuts, tossing them constantly with a spatula, until they turn a caramel color. Remove them from the pan to a platter, and let them cool in a single layer. Store the nuts in layers separated by wax paper.

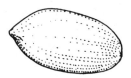

STUFFED DATES

These have been favorites of mine ever since the days when my kitchen expertise was limited to cooking oatmeal. Although they are simple enough for a child to prepare, they are an elegant and nutritious alternative to candy or cookies at the end of a meal for company or as a companion to midday tea or coffee.

Preparation tips: The dates can be stuffed in advance and frozen for future use. I do not specify quantities; you can prepare as many as you wish, providing you have an equal number of dates and nuts. If desired, the stuffed dates can be rolled in unsweetened cocoa powder or in cocoa powder sweetened with an equal amount of confectioners' sugar.

> Pitted dates
> Pecan halves

1. Starting from the end of the date with the hole (where the pit was removed), slice the date from end to end *on one side only.* Place the pecan half sideways into the cut, and squeeze the sides of the date together to hold the nut in place.
2. Arrange the stuffed dates on a plate, or, if you are preparing them in advance, place the stuffed dates in an airtight container in single layers separated by wax paper.

OTHER GIFT FOODS

Hot Nuts (page 62)
Basil-Garlic Vinegar (page 533)
Shallot Vinegar (page 533)
Garam Masala (page 546)
AHA Herb Mix (page 545)
Cajun Spice Mix (page 545)
Herb Mixes (page 547)
Cranberry Applesauce (page 517)
"Hot" Applesauce (page 536)
Chilied Chickpeas (page 62)
Quinns' Vinaigrette (page 388)
Heavenly Haroset (page 538)
Breads—both yeast and quick (pages 390 to 422 and
   436 to 448)

MENU SUGGESTIONS

There is an art to putting together meals for company and still having enough energy to enjoy them yourself. I gave you some hints on pages 3 to 4. Here I will offer some menu possibilities that involve little, if any, last-minute food preparation and provide nicely coordinated dishes that are not only nutritious, but are also attractive and tasty. My menus are just a guide; there are many alternatives in the book besides the ones I list here. And if this book doesn't give you enough options, consult *Jane Brody's Good Food Book* for still more choices.

Sunday Brunch

Twist of O.J. *or* Orange Sunrise
Apple-Mushroom Omelet *or* Zucchini-Corn Soufflé *or* Pear Crêpes
Bulgur Salad Primavera *or* Lemon Bulgur Salad
Blueberry-Bran Muffins *or* Raspberry–Oat Bran Muffins
Piña Colada Upside-Down Cake *or* Strawberry-Yogurt Pie

Easter Dinner

Garlic Soup *or* Mushroom Soup Marsala
Butterflied Leg of Lamb *or* Rolled Pork Roast with Fruited Filling
Couscous with Peppers *or* Rice and Bulgur Pilaf
Okra with Onions and Apricots *or* Stuffed Tomatoes Provençal
Arugula Salad with Pistachios *or* Watercress and Endive Salad
Herbed Whole Wheat Rolls *or* Lemon-Wheat Bread
Fruited Sponge Cake *or* Pear Petal Torte with Pecan Crust

Passover Seder

Heavenly Haroset
Salmon in Rhubarb Sauce *or* Gefilte Fish *or* Gefilte Fish Terrine
Iraqi Lamb with Okra *or* Bea's Unstuffed Cabbage
Potato Pudding *or* Vegetable Tzimmes
Savory Applesauce
Fennel and Mushrooms *or* Garlic Green Beans
Grapefruit and Broccoli Salad *or* Mushroom, Endive, and Watercress Salad
Oranges Casablanca *or* Poached Pears with Orange Sauce
Almond Cookies *or* Chocolate-Almond Macaroons

Memorial Day Buffet

Grapefruit-Pineapple Slush
Tortilla Chips
Vegetable Platter *with* Chili Dip, Guacamole Grande, *and* Salsa
Mexican Gazpacho
Chili-Corn Burgers
Chicken Tacos
Mexican Tabbouleh *or* "Refried" Beans
Orange-Jícama Salad
Mango Sherbet *or* Tropical Fruit Salad

Fourth of July Barbecue

Cucumber-Walnut Soup *or* Yogurt Soup *or* White Gazpacho
Kebabs of marinated meat *or* chicken *and/or* fish *and* vegetables
Basmati Rice Salad with Peas *or* Lentil Waldorf Salad *or* New Potato Salad
Minted Sugar Snap Salad *or* Minted Lima Bean Salad *or* Dilly Beans
Betty's Soda Bread *or* High-Calcium Cabbage Bread
Raspberry-Yogurt Pie *or* Crazy Strawberries *and* Viennese Crescents

Labor Day Picnic

Hot Nuts
Hummus
Baba Ghanoush
Pita wedges and vegetable "spoons"
Cold Tomato Soup *or* Yogurt Soup
Moroccan Chicken and Couscous Salad *or* Mussel and
    Potato Salad *or* Salmon Vinaigrette with Yogurt-Dill Sauce
Corn, Pepper, and Tomato Salad *or* Tomato and Onion Salad
Scallion Biscuits
Gingered Pear Crisp *or* Nectarine-Pineapple Petal Pie

Thanksgiving Dinner

Mulled Cider with Apple Brandy
Pumpkin Soup Parmesan *or* Three-P Soup
Roast Turkey *with* Wild Rice and Fennel Stuffing *or*
    Corn Bread and Rice Stuffing
Broccoli Rabe *or* Garlic Green Beans
Sweet Potato Special *or* Cranberry-stuffed Squash Bowls
Cranberry-Pear Relish
Arugula and Fennel Salad *or* "Woo" Salad
Pumpkin-Wheat Bread *or* Winter Squash Rolls
Fresh Cranberry Cream Pie *or* Pumpkin Custard
Chocolate-dipped Fruits

Hanukkah Supper

DAIRY-BASED MEAL
Dilly of a Mushroom Soup
Potato Pancakes (with yogurt)
Savory Applesauce *or* Cranberry Applesauce
Julienne Jubilee Salad *or* Carrot-Apple Salad Supreme
Mandelbrot (Almond Bread) *or* Honey Spice Cake *or* Apple Strudel
Dried Fruit Balls

MEAT-BASED MEAL
Autumn Vegetable Soup *or* Mushroom-Barley Soup
Meat Tzimmes
Savory Applesauce
Green Bean and Red Onion Salad *or* Red and White Cole Slaw
Wheat and Barley Bread *or* Caraway-Rye Rolls
Fabulous Fruit Compote *or* Monte's Prune Bread
Stuffed Dates

Christmas Dinner

Christmas Pâté
African Yam Soup *or* Creamed Acorn Squash Soup
Cornish Hens Stuffed with Fruited Rice *or* Baked Salmon with Rice Stuffing
Baked Fennel *or* Braised Pumpkin *or* Mediterranean Mushrooms
Pearls and Rubies (Onions and Cranberries)
Orange, Root, and Fennel Salad *or* Snow Pea Salad
Limpa (Swedish Rye) *or* Marvelous Muffin Rolls
Oranges in Mulled Wine *or* Delicious Baked Apples
Fruit and Nut Cake

Winter Party

South-of-the-Border Cider
Chilied Chickpeas
Herbed Quesadillas
Turkey-Bean Enchiladas
Black Bean Burritos
Three-Pepper Salad *or* Orange-Jícama Salad
Corn Pone
Piña Colada Sorbet *or* Citrus Delight

Post-Tennis Breakfast

Grapefruit-Pineapple Slush *or* Tropical Breakfast Treat
White Gazpacho *or* Cucumber-Walnut Soup
Corn-off-the-Cob Cakes *or* Salmon Vinaigrette with Yogurt-Dill Sauce
Strawberry Muffins *or* Blueberry-Nut Bread
Tropical Fruit Salad *or* Citrus Delight

"Instant" Dinner Party

Mustardy Melon Roll-Ups *or* Terrific Turkey Spread
Faith's Hot and Sour Soup *or* Spicy Carrot Soup
Pork Marsala *or* Island Chicken *or* Stir-fried Scallops Supreme
Indian Rice with Peas and Peppers *or* brown or white rice
Dry Sautéed Green Beans *or* Broccoli Rabe *or* Braised Pumpkin
Arugula Salad with Pistachios *or* Tomato and Onion Salad
Italian-style bread (store-bought)
Crazy Strawberries *or* Broiled Grapefruit *or* Gingered Pear Crisp

Elegant Dinner Party

Cherry tomatoes stuffed with Eggplant Pesto *and* mushroom
    caps stuffed with Sun-dried Tomato Spread
Shrimp and Citrus Cocktail *or* Marinated Scallops *or* Memorable Mussels
Fennel Soup *or* Yellow Pepper Soup *or* Cold Shrimp Soup
Terry's Chicken Roll-Ups *or* Cornish Hens with Spiced Apple Stuffing
Wild Rice with Almonds
Whole Wheat French Bread *or* Winter Squash Rolls
Arugula and Fennel Salad *or* Winter Squash and Pepper Salad
Oranges in Cassis *or* Plum Tart *or* Apricot Soufflé
Chocolate-dipped Fruits *or* Almond Cookies *or* Viennese Crescents

INDEX

PERMISSIONS

The page numbers on which the following recipes appear are listed in brackets [ ].

Tomatoes Stuffed with Eggplant [64], Cranberry-Hazelnut Stuffing [142], Wild Rice and Fennel Stuffing [144], Cioppino [164], Beef Tamale Pie [182], Mussel Chowder [208], Fusilli with Hot Sausage [224], Black Bean Burritos [237], Chicken Salad with Mango [254], Mussel and Potato Salad [265], Broccoli Pizza with Whole Wheat Crust [276], Pita-Bean Pizzas [284], Savory Applesauce [307], Corn, Pepper, and Tomato Salad [362], Potato Salad with Sausage [376], Limpa [420], Apricot Soufflé [472], Gingered Pear Crisp [480], Citrus Delight [526]. Above adapted and reprinted courtesy of *Gourmet.*

Mushroom Soup Marsala [84], Cold Tomato Soup [107], Fish and Feta Casserole [161], Black Bean Chili [240], copyright © 1985 by Bon Appétit Publishing Corp.; Arugula Salad with Pistachios [344], copyright © 1986 by Bon Appétit Publishing Corp.; Pumpkin Soup Parmesan [95], Moroccan Chicken with Couscous [122], Melon Salad with Figs [521], copyright © 1989 by Bon Appétit Publishing Corp. Above adapted and reprinted with permission of Bon Appétit.

Spicy Corn and Tomato Soup [104] by Lynne Rossetto Kasper, copyright © 1985 by Bon Appétit Publishing Corp. and Lynne Rossetto Kasper; Cold White Bean Soup [109] by Michael McLaughlin, copyright © 1985 by Bon Appétit Publishing Corp.; Shrimp and Leek Pizza [280], Mango Sherbet [511] by Abby Mandel, copyright © 1985 by Bon Appétit Publishing Corp. and Abby Mandel; Stuffed Summer Squash with Tomato Sauce [336] by Elizabeth Riely, copyright © 1985 by Bon Appétit Publishing Corp.; Indian-Style Chicken and Rice Salad [252] by Richard Sax and Marie Simmons, copyright © 1989 by Bon Appétit Publishing Corp.; Prune Soufflé [474], Ricotta Pudding with Strawberries [476] by Richard Sax and Marie Simmons, copyright © 1988 by Bon Appétit Publishing Corp. Above adapted and reprinted with permission of the authors and Bon Appétit.

Pear Crêpes [296], January/February 1989 issue; Orange-Jicama Salad [368], Minted Melons [522], July/August 1989 issue; Brussels Sprouts and Tiny Onions [314], Stuffed Mini-Pumpkins [328], Cranberry Compote [518], November/December 1989 issue; Oranges Casablanca [526], March/April 1989 issue. Above reprinted with permission of *Cooking Light.*

Sole Roll-Ups [158] from *Eat Right, Eat Well—the Italian Way* by Edward Giobbi and Richard Wolff, M.D., copyright © 1985 by Edward Giobbi and Richard Wolff, M.D.; Pickled Green Cherry Tomatoes [552] from *The Pleasures of Preserving and Pickling* by Jeanne Lesem, copyright © 1975 by Jeanne Lesem; Herbed Cauliflower [63], Sweet Potato Soup [96], Lentil Soup with Collards [201], Sweet Potato Cake [506] from *The Victory Garden Cookbook* by Marian Morash, copyright © 1982 by Marian Morash and WGBH Educational Foundation. Above reprinted by permission of Alfred A. Knopf, Inc.

Nectarines with Raspberry Sauce [523], Poached Pears with Orange Sauce [524] from *Helen Nash's Kosher Kitchen* by Helen Nash, copyright © 1988 by Helen Nash; Lemon-Wheat Bread [405] modified from *The Laurel's Kitchen Bread Book* by Laurel Robertson, Carol Flinders, and Godfrey Bronwen, copyright © 1984 by The Blue Mountain Center of Meditation, Inc. Above reprinted by permission of Random House, Inc.

Raspberry Vinaigrette [388] from *Spa Food* by Edward Safdie, copyright © 1985 by Edward Safdie. Reprinted by permission of Clarkson N. Potter, Inc.

Herbed Quesadillas [66], Three-Pepper Salad [373], Pear Vinaigrette [387] adapted from *The Gourmet Gazelle Cookbook* by Ellen Brown, copyright © 1989 by Ellen Brown; Baba Ghanoush [50], Mediterranean Mushrooms [320], Nippy Greens [333], Nectarine Granita [513] adapted from *Mediterranean Light* by Martha Rose Shulman and Anthony Russo (illustrator), copyright © 1989 by Martha Rose Shulman, illus. copyright © 1989 by Anthony Russo. Above used by permission of Bantam Books, a division of Bantam, Doubleday, Dell Publishing Group, Inc.

Cucumber-Walnut Soup [103] adapted from "Chilled Bulgarian Cucumber Soup" in *Café Beaujolais* © 1984 by Margaret Fox. Adapted with permission from Ten Speed Press, P.O. Box 7123, Berkeley, CA 94707.

Mellow Curried Fish [157] modified from *Diabetic Cooking from Around the World* by Vilma Liacouras Chantiles, copyright © 1989 by Vilma Liacouras Chantiles. Reprinted by permission of Harper & Row, Publishers, Inc.

Zucchini Pancakes [292], Okra with Onion and Apricots [321], Zucchini Croquettes [342], Kohlrabi and Carrot Salad [366], Italian Pepper 'n' Cheese Bread [418] modified from *Greene on Greens* © 1984 by Bert Greene. Used by permission of Workman Publishing Company. All rights reserved.

Stuffed Fillets in Swiss Chard [159] reprinted from *Rodale's Basic Natural Foods Cookbook* © 1984 by Rodale Press; Green Tomato Chutney [552] reprinted from *Stocking Up III* © 1986 by Rodale Press. Permission granted by Rodale Press, Inc., Emmaus, PA 18098.

Lemon Frozen Yogurt [510] adapted from Frozen Lemon Cream from *The American Cancer Society Cookbook,* copyright © 1988 by the author. Reprinted by permission of William Morrow & Co.

Nectarine-Pineapple Preserves [555] from *Gourmet Preserves Chez Madelaine* by Madelaine Bullwinkel, copyright © 1984 by Madelaine Bullwinkel. Reprinted by permission of Contemporary Books, Inc.

Blueberry-Nut Bread [442] modified and reprinted with permission of Cahner's Publishing Company from *Dietitian's Food Favorites.*

Sonia's Coq au Vin [118] modified with permission from *Famous Woodstock Cooks* by Joanne Michaels and Mary Barile, published by JMB Publications.

Lentils Olé [244], Turkey Salad [258] modified with permission of the Minnesota Division of the American Cancer Society from *The Minnesota Heritage Cookbook.*

Iraqi Lamb with Okra [191] modified and reprinted with permission from *The Best of Baghdad Cooking* by Daisy Iny, copyright © by the author.

Terrific Turkey Spread [54], Turkey Salad [258] modified with permission of Nancy Cooper from *Diabetes Self-Management,* January/February 1989 issue.

Zucchini Muffins with Lemon [461], Yes-Yes Cookies [470] modified and reprinted with permission from *American Health.*

Chicken and Green Bean Salad [253] adapted and reprinted with permission from *The Walking Magazine,* August/September 1988 issue.

Garlic Soup [87], Black-eyed Peas and Brown Rice [238] modified and reprinted with permission from *Medical Self-Care* magazine.

Cauliflower and Potato Soup [92] adapted and reprinted with permission from *National Gardening,* the monthly publication of the National Gardening Association, 180 Flynn Avenue, Burlington, VT 05401.

Cajun Spice Mix [545] reprinted with permission from *Supermarket Guide to Cholesterol and Saturated Fat.*

Seafood and Spinach Noodles [217] modified with permission from *Woman's Day.*

Curried Chicken with Chickpeas [124], Cornish Hens with Spiced Apple Stuffing [138] adapted and reprinted with permission from *Madhur Jaffrey's Cookbook* by Madhur Jaffrey, published by Harper & Row, Publishers, Inc.

Viennese Crescents [469], Mocha Pudding Pie [485] modified and reprinted with permission from *The Woman's Day Low-Calorie Dessert Cookbook* by Carol Cutler, published by Houghton Mifflin.

Asparagus Soufflé [304] modified and reprinted with permission from *Garden Way's Joy of Gardening Cookbook* by Janet Ballantyne, published by Garden Way Publishing.

Strawberry Mousse [528] modified with permission from *The Cookbook Decoder* by Arthur Grosser.

Black Bean and Salmon Spread [52], Sardine Spread [53], Betty's Soda Bread [436], High-Calcium Cabbage Bread [438], Poppy Seed Sauce [535] modified with permission from *The High-Calcium Low-Calorie Cookbook* by Betty Marks, published by Contemporary Books; Marks's Mini-Muffins [462] reprinted with permission from *The International Menu Diabetic Cookbook* by Betty Marks and Lucille H. Schechter, published by Contemporary Books.

Chicken Provençal [116], Chicken and Mushrooms [127], Chicken and Root Vegetable Soup [212], Linguine with Squid Sauce [219], Breton Beans [248], Green Beans and Red Onion Salad [345] modified with permission of Pierre Franey. Mexican Gazpacho [102] modified with permission from *Pierre Franey's Low-Calorie Gourmet* by Pierre Franey and Richard Flaste, published by Times Books.

Herbed Lentil Casserole [245] modified with permission from *The New American Diet* by Sonja L. Connor and William E. Connor, published by Simon & Schuster.

Honey Spice Cake [502], Piña Colada Upside-Down Cake [503] reprinted with permission from *More Lean and Luscious* by Bobbie E. Hinman and Millie Snyder, published by Prima Publishing & Communication.

Seafood Tabbouleh [261] adapted and reprinted with permission from *Seafood and Health* by Joyce A. Nettleton, published by Van Nostrand Reinhold/AVI.

Zucchini-Corn Casserole [229] modified and reprinted with permission from *Nikki and David Goldbeck's American Wholefoods Cuisine* by Nikki and David Goldbeck, published by New American Library.

Tahini Dip [45], Tofu-Sesame Dip [46], Sunflower-Millet Bread [408] from *The Enchanted Broccoli Forest* by Mollie Katzen, published by Ten Speed Press; Sweet and Sour Slaw [356], Walnut Crust [495] from *Still Life with Menu* by Mollie Katzen, published by Ten Speed Press. Adapted and reprinted with permission.

Wheat and Walnut Bread [404], Whole Wheat Pretzels [428], Wheat Germ Biscuits [435] modified and reprinted with permission from *Great Whole Grain Breads* by Beatrice Ojakangas, published by Pfeifer-Hamilton Publishers, Duluth, MN.

Butterflied Leg of Lamb [192], Pineapple Chutney [550] from *The New York Times Heritage Cookbook* by Jean Hewitt, published by Crown Books; Applesauce Cookies [466] from *The New York Times Natural Foods Cookbook* by Jean Hewitt, published by Times Books; Christmas Pâté [56], Turkey with Curry Sauce [145], Apple-Mushroom Omelet [301], Piña Colada Sorbet [515] by Jean Hewitt in *Family Circle* modified and reprinted with permission.

Tomato-Pear Chutney [551], Dried Fruit Balls [556] adapted and reprinted from *Woman's Day Gifts from Your Kitchen.*

Sun-dried Tomato Spread [54], Swordfish Primavera [167] modified with permission of Jessica Zachs, Jessica Zachs Food & Style, Inc. Chicken with Yams [114] adapted with permission of Maren Hubert, Huberts Restaurant, New York, New York. Diced Chicken with Peanuts [134] modified with permission of Norman Weinstein, Proprietor, The Hot Wok, Brooklyn, New York. Baked Fennel [319] modified with permission of Richard Hill, Chef de Cuisine, Grand Hotel, Washington, D.C. Minted Lima Bean Salad [350] modified with permission of Alcala Restaurant, New York, New York. Crazy Strawberries [527] used with permission of Michael Chiarello, Executive Chef/Owner, Tra Vigne Restaurant, St. Helena, California. Melon Salsa [540] adapted with permission of Cafe Terra Cotta, Tucson, Arizona.

Walnut Spread [59] adapted with permission of Gwennyth Noroian. Bag o' Fish [156], Memorable Mussels [163] modified with permission of Edward Giobbi. Gefilte Fish Loaf [174] modified with permission of Marian Burros. Gefilte Fish Terrine [176] modified with permission of Florence Fabricant. Basil Linguine with Clam Sauce [220] adapted with permission of Carol DiGrappa. Mango and Pear Salad [367], Winter Squash and Pepper Salad [383] used with permission of Julie Sahni. Eggplant Pesto [542] used with permission of Diana Shaw.